Walking in Britain
a Lonely Planet walking guide

David Else

Walking in Britain

1st edition

Published by
Lonely Planet Publications
Head Office: PO Box 617, Hawthorn, Vic 3122, Australia
Branches: 155 Filbert St, Suite 251, Oakland, CA 94607, USA
                10a Spring Place, London NW5 3BH, UK
                71 bis rue du Cardinal Lemoine, 75005 Paris, France

Printed by
Colorcraft Ltd, Hong Kong
Printed in China

Photographs by
David Else, Bryn Thomas, Tony Wheeler, Pat Yale, John Harvey, Charlotte Hindle
Front cover: Crowns Mine – a deserted tin mine near Botallack on the South West Coast Path (Pat Yale)

Published
May 1997

Although the authors and publisher have tried to make the information as accurate as possible, they accept no responsibility for any loss, injury or inconvenience sustained by any person using this book.

National Library of Australia Cataloguing in Publication Data

Else, David.
    Walking in Britain.

    Includes index.
    ISBN 0 86442 478 7.

    1. Hiking - Great Britain - Guidebooks. 2. Great Britain -
    Guidebooks. I. Title. (Series: Lonely Planet walking guide).

    914.104

text & maps © Lonely Planet 1997
photos © photographers as indicated 1997

All rights reserved. No part of this publication may be reproduced, stored in a retrieval system or transmitted in any form by any means, electronic, mechanical, photocopying, recording or otherwise, except brief extracts for the purpose of review, without the written permission of the publisher and copyright owner.

David Else

David Else was born in London and over the following 36 years slowly trekked northwards, via Wiltshire, South Wales and Derbyshire, to his present base on the edge of the Peak District in Northern England. Originally introduced to the Great British Outdoors as a cyclist, David's own walking in Britain properly started during university years when any chance to head for the hills was always taken in preference to visiting the library. His first long-distance path was the Pennine Way, done on a bicycle in the days before mountain bikes were invented, when passing ramblers used to think such illegal escapades amusing.

Now much more respectable, although still rarely seen in libraries, David is a full-time writer – dividing his time between walking in Britain and travel in Africa. David's other activities include cycling and mountain-biking, and occasional bouts of rock-climbing.

David's other books for Lonely Planet include: *Trekking in East Africa; Malawi, Mozambique & Zambia;* and *Africa – The South.* He has also contributed to the *Kenya* and *East Africa – travel survival kits,* and to *Africa on a shoestring.*

The following writers also made significant contributions to this book.

Tony Wheeler

Tony Wheeler was born in England, but grew up in Pakistan, the Bahamas and the USA. He returned to England to do a degree in engineering at Warwick University, worked as an automotive design engineer, returned to London Business School to complete an MBA, then set out on an Asian overland trip with his wife, Maureen. That trip led to Tony and Maureen founding Lonely Planet Publications in Australia in 1973, and they've been travelling, writing and publishing guidebooks ever since.

Bryn Thomas

Born in Zimbabwe, where he grew up on a farm, Bryn contracted an incurable case of wanderlust during camping holidays by the Indian Ocean in Mozambique. Since then, travel on five continents has included eight Himalayan treks, a 2500 km Andean cycling trip, and 45,000 km of rail travel in India and Siberia.

Bryn's first guide, the *Trans-Siberian Handbook*, was short-listed for the Thomas Cook Guidebook of the Year awards. He is also the author of Trailblazer's *Trekking in the Annapurna Region* and co-author of the Lonely Planet guides to *Britain* and *India.*

Rob Beckley

Having travelled extensively, usually by bicycle, in Europe, Africa, South America and Asia, research for this book was a very different type of assignment for Rob. He simply took his walking boots out of storage, walked out of his house, which is by the River Thames in London, and proceeded in a westerly direction to plod to the source.

Rod Grant

Rod lives in East Anglia in the UK. He works in the shadowy world of addictions and has developed a need to don his walking boots at every available moment. He has walked extensively in Britain, and plans increasingly outrageous holidays to various parts of Africa, although his previous publications bear little relevance to travel or the outdoors.

Chris & John Harvey

The Harveys have spent much of their married life communing with the Great Outdoors, especially mountain-walking and sailing, including sorties in North America, New Zealand and Indonesia. In recent years, after early retirement, they have run a guesthouse on the side of Loch Lomond in Scotland, from where they also organise activity breaks. They have contributed articles to various outdoor magazines, and researched and written *Walks from the West Highland Railway*.

Charlotte Hindle

Born in Caerphilly, Wales, Charlotte studied History of Art at Leicester University. She au-paired in France, worked in a Swiss ski-resort, and sold theatre tickets in London, before travelling to Australia. From 1988 she worked at Lonely Planet's head office in Melbourne before returning in 1991 to set up and run Lonely Planet's London office. She has also worked on *Australia – travel survival kit* and *Mediterranean Europe on a shoestring*.

Chris Hollis

Dragged kicking and screaming up mountains from an early age, it seemed unlikely that Chris would ever share (or even begin to understand!) his parents' love for walking. However, student life in the urban mass of Birmingham changed all that and he has been an avid walker ever since. He has a particular passion for long-distance walking, and treks to date have included the Everest region and, closer to home, the Pennine Way and Coast to Coast.

Angela Kalisch

Originally from Germany, Angela is a climber and keen walker. She has been travelling and leading adventure treks to Nepal and the Indian Himalaya and to South India since 1989. She has written articles in newspapers and magazines about her travels.

Frith Luton

Frith Luton worked as an editor with Lonely Planet for many years and was involved in the coordination of Lonely Planet's trekking guides. Frith now works as a freelance editor in Melbourne when she's not enjoying walking in the great Australian outdoors.

Ric Potter

Born with walking boots on, and with a passion for climbing mountains, Ric has been trying to work out how to make a living at it ever since. After training to be a teacher, the only cure seemed to be a few years of trek leading, travelling and climbing, which included making first ascents in the Andes and the Himalayas. Ric worked for two years as an instructor at Plas y Brenin National Mountain Centre in Wales. He now works as a freelance mountain guide and instructor in the UK.

Miles Roddis

Over 25 years Miles lived, worked and walked in eight different countries. A keen runner and walker, he celebrated his retirement by cycling 12,000 miles around the rim of the USA. Wild about wilderness, he's trekked, among other trails, the Zagros mountains in Iran, Britain's Pennine Way and the Pyrenees from Atlantic to Mediterranean. He writes for outdoor and athletic magazines and has contributed to Lonely Planet's *Africa on a shoestring*.

Roly Smith

Roly is Head of Information Services for the Peak National Park in the UK and lives in Bakewell, Derbyshire, in the UK. He is an award-winning writer on the British outdoors, with about 20 books to his name, the latest of which is *On Foot in the Yorkshire Dales*. He has written extensively on British national parks for which he has campaigned for many years. He is also chairman of the Outdoor Writers' Guild.

Pat Yale

Pat Yale spent several years selling holidays before throwing up sensible careerdom to head overland from Egypt to Zimbabwe. She then mixed teaching tourism with travel in Europe, Asia and Central and South America, before becoming a full-time writer.

She has worked on LP's guides to *Britain, Ireland, Dublin* and *Turkey*. She currently lives in Bristol in the UK.

From David Else

First, I'd like to thank my wife, Corinne; she helped with the initial research and wrote up a lot of the background material, and together we covered a great selection of British footpaths, from the southern tip of the Isle of Wight to the far north of Scotland, from West Wales to East Anglia, testing pubs and buses, ferries and hostels en route. Thanks also to various friends who joined us on our walks and 'expeditions'; without their company, humour and sandwiches we'd have never made it. I'd also like to thank various experts who gave me their thoughts and the benefit of their experience: Roly Smith; Ken Wilson of Baton Wicks; Dave Mitchell of Scarthin Books; and Roger Gook of Footloose Travel. Thanks also to Diccon, Simon and the staff at Lonely Planet's London office who helped with some of the research. And, finally, thanks to all the staff at the national park offices, walking and hostel organisations, various conservation bodies and, especially, the many tourist information centres (Britain's greatest tourism asset), for their professional knowledge and always helpful service.

About this Book

This book was compiled by David Else over an 18 month period through 1995 and 1996. Although David managed to break away from his desk occasionally and walk up the odd hill himself, this book's production was very much a team effort, with valuable input

from several researchers, contributors and route-checkers.

The introductory sections on The History of Walking in Britain, National Parks, and Walkers Rights & Responsibilities were provided by Roly Smith. Award-winning outdoor journalist Clive Tully contributed information on clothing and equipment. The sections on the Welsh language were provided and checked by Bethan Evans, Lindsay Banks, Colin Goodey and Ceiri & Ann Griffith.

The sections on the West Highland Way and the Pembrokeshire Coast Path were written by Bryn Thomas. Bryn would like to thank Anna Jacomb-Hood, Clive & Jo Evans, Muriel Carbonnet, Chris Jenney, Conny Ott, Alex Todrick and Isabel Whitely, who all provided helpful advice and entertaining companionship on these two walks. Lonely Planet author Pat Yale took time off from researching *Turkey – travel survival kit* to brave the South West Coast Path in August. Pat was helped by Sharon North and Claire McElwee. Charlotte Hindle, covered the North Downs Way, ably assisted by Simon (who didn't complain once about the terrible weather) and Ken Kelling. Offa's Dyke was covered by former LP staffer Frith Luton, who came all the way from Australia with her husband, Rainer, to do the walk. Richard Everist, another LP escapee from Australia, covered various parts of Scotland and Southern England. Tony Wheeler covered the Pennine Way, the Cotswold Way, the Tennyson Trail and the Clarendon Way.

Rob Beckley, who helped research Lonely Planet's *Trekking in East Africa* a few years ago, stayed a bit closer to home this time and covered the Thames Way and the eastern half of the Ridgeway. He was joined on the Thames by his wife, Sue, who helped record the evidence and gave much needed support. The western half of the Ridgeway was covered by John Else, who also covered the Kennet & Avon Canal. Miles Roddis (with help from Damien Roddis) covered the South Downs Way. Other walkers and world-travellers roped into service were Neil Robertson (North York Moors), Rod Grant (Peddars Way & Norfolk Coast Path), Angela Kalisch (Edale Skyline and Coast to Coast), Jill Leheup (Limestone Way), Chris Hollis (Glyndwr's Way) Robin Saxby (Dartmoor) and Harry Bitten (Epping Forest).

North Wales was covered by climber, trekker, and general all-round mountain man Ric Potter, who also covered parts of the Lake District. Additional Lakes routes came from Rachel Hollis, who also provided a contribution on An Teallach plus more background on the Yorkshire Dales, and Vicky Pearson, who also assisted with desk-bound research. Material on the Preseli Hills was provided by walker, writer and surfer Alf Alderson. Many parts of Scotland were covered by the energetic walker-writer-photographer team of Chris & John Harvey, from their base on the bonny banks of Loch Lomond.

From the Publisher

The mapping and design in this first edition of *Walking in Britain* were coordinated by Chris Klep and Andrew Smith, who were assisted by Trudi Canavan, Sally Gerdan, Paul Piaia, Jacqui Saunders and Geoff Stringer.

The editing and proofing were coordinated by Steve Womersley, who was assisted by Janet Austin, Lindsay Brown, Liz Filleul, Lyn McGaurr, Paul Smitz, and Chris Wyness. Thanks to David Kemp for the cover design, Andrew Smith and Margaret Jung for layout and David Andrew and Reita Wilson for illustrations.

Disclaimer

Although the authors and publisher have done their utmost to ensure the accuracy of all information in this guide, they cannot accept any responsibility for any loss, injury or inconvenience sustained by people using this book. They cannot guarantee that the tracks and routes described here have not become impassable for any reason in the interval between research and publication.

The fact that a trip or an area is described in this guidebook does not necessarily mean that it is a safe one for you and your walking party. You are ultimately responsible for judging your own capabilities in light of the conditions that you encounter.

Warning & Request

Things change – prices go up, schedules change, good places go bad and bad places go bankrupt – nothing stays the same. So, if you find things better or worse, recently opened or long since closed, please tell us and help make the next edition even more accurate and useful.

We value all of the feedback we receive from travellers. Julie Young coordinates a small team who read and acknowledge every letter, postcard and E-mail, and ensure that every morsel of information finds its way to the appropriate authors, editors and publishers.

Everyone who writes to us will find their name in the next edition of the appropriate guide and will also receive a free subscription to our quarterly newsletter, *Planet Talk*. The very best contributions will be rewarded with a free Lonely Planet guide.

Excerpts from your correspondence may appear in updates (which we add to the end pages of reprints); new editions of this guide; in our newsletter, *Planet Talk*; or in the Postcards section of our Web site – so please let us know if you don't want your letter published or your name acknowledged.

Contents

Asides

Map Legend

BOUNDARIES

........................International Boundary
........................County/Region Boundary
........................Disputed Boundary

ROUTES

........................Freeway
........................Motorway
........................Major Road
........................Unsealed Road or Jeep Road
........................City Road
........................City Street
........................Railway
........................Underground Railway
........................Walking Track
........................Route
........................Cable Car or Chairlift
........................Ferry Route

AREA FEATURES

........................Parks
........................Built-Up Area
........................Pedestrian Mall
........................Market
........................Building
........................Glacier, Icecap
........................Beach or Desert
........................Rocks

HYDROGRAPHIC FEATURES

........................Coastline
........................River, Creek
........................Intermittent River or Creek
........................Rapids, Waterfalls
........................Lake, Intermittent Lake
........................Canal, Swamp
........................River flow

SYMBOLS

✪ CAPITAL		National Capital
◉ Capital		County or Regional Capital
◍ CITY		Major City
● City		City
● Town		Town
● Village		Village
■ ▼		Place to Stay, Place to Eat
☕ 🍷		Cafe, Pub or Bar
✉ ☎		Post Office, Telephone
❶ ❸		Tourist Information, Bank
⬤ ⬤		Bus Station or Terminal, Bus Stop
🏛 ⌂		Museum, Youth Hostel
⚏ ◭		Caravan Park, Camping Ground
✝ ✚		Church, Cathedral
◐ ✡		Mosque, Synagogue
⬛ ✛		Temple, Hospital
★		Police Station or Check Post
◔	⚐	Embassy, Petrol Station
✈	✝	Airport, Airfield
⌦	✿	Swimming Pool, Gardens
❖	🐖	Shopping Centre, Zoo
⚘	☷	Winery or Vineyard, Picnic Site
←	A25	One Way Street, Route Number
🏛	⬣	Stately Home, Monument
◫	◨	Castle, Tomb
⌒	⌂	Cave, Hut or Chalet
▲	△	Mountain or Hill, Trig Station
)(	◎	Pass, Spring
🔲	⚲	Lookout, Beach
※	⍁	Lighthouse, Shipwreck
∴		Archaeological Site or Ruins
		Ancient or City Wall
		Cliff or Escarpment, Tunnel
		Railway Station

Note: not all symbols displayed above appear in this book

Preface

Britain's countryside is one of such immense diversity and fascination that the best – indeed the only – way to become truly familiar with it, and to savour its many riches, is to explore it on foot. Millions of people in Britain do just that, all year round. Walking is by far the most popular recreation in Britain, and its popularity is growing all the time. It is enjoyed by people of all ages, abilities and incomes. Walking can involve a short stroll on local footpaths, or a long-distance challenge spread over two or more weeks. The opportunities are endless.

Walkers in Britain are fortunate in having – in England and Wales at least – an intricate network of paths which in law are public rights of way. Many of these paths date back centuries, some even to Roman times or earlier. Public forests, which cover more than two and a half million acres (about one million hectares) of land, offer freedom to roam for the walker. And there are large areas of beautiful open countryside in the ownership of the National Trust, the National Trust for Scotland, and other benevolent landowners where people can wander at will. In Scotland, there is a long tradition of people walking with reasonable freedom over open country. All these rights and traditions have been fought for and defended over many years, and campaigns for public access to the countryside in Britain continue today as strongly as ever.

At the same time, it is important to recognise that the British countryside is home and workplace for many people. In the national parks, for example, most land is still in private ownership and is inhabited and farmed by families who may have lived there for generations. The first rule for all walkers is to respect the life of the countryside, and to treat with courtesy everyone you meet there.

This book will doubtless be of particular value to visitors from outside Britain who want to spend a walking holiday here; and to people living in Britain who want to take up walking as a recreation. Wherever you come from, may I offer you a warm welcome on behalf of the Ramblers' Association. You are about to embark upon an adventure which will bring you lasting memories of some very beautiful places. And the exercise will do you no end of good!

Have a great time.

Alan Mattingly

Alan Mattingly is Director of the 120,000-member Ramblers' Association. Formed in 1935, the association promotes walking as a recreation. It campaigns to protect rights of way in Britain, and to protect the natural beauty of the countryside. The association is at the forefront of efforts to protect and extend the rights of members of the public to wander freely through forests and over uncultivated land such as mountain and moorland. Many of the national trails now open to walkers were originally proposed and surveyed by members of the Ramblers' Association. Members also help to waymark rights of way, and install and repair footpath stiles and bridges. The association has over 400 local groups around the country, each one organising programmes of walks for its members and for the public.

Introduction

Walking in Britain is one of the best ways to see and experience the varied landscape and to meet the people. Visitors to Britain from other countries list several more reasons why walking here is so attractive: there's the extensive footpath network, and the traditional 'right to roam' in many upland areas, which lets you walk over hills and mountains, beside rivers and lakes, through valleys and across moors. And there are the traditional villages and small country towns, where two unique British institutions – the pub and the B&B – make walking so easy and so pleasurable.

Other attractions include the historical sites (from ancient stone circles to medieval castles) that many walking routes pass, good public transport, and (for many visitors) few language problems. From a practical point of view, there are plenty of maps, books and information sources available. Some visitors rave about the untamed wilderness areas of north-west Scotland, while others love the accessibility and human scale of walks through the gentle fields and farmland of Southern England.

This book describes a broad selection of walking routes in Britain, ranging from easy to hard, from a few hours to a few weeks, from Land's End to (almost) John o'Groats, with something suitable for every type of walker. The options for walking in Britain are almost limitless, so providing a complete list is impossible; there are many areas and routes which we have been unable to cover due to lack of available space. But what we have included is enough to keep you busy for a long time! Although aimed mainly at visitors from abroad, this book will be valuable for many British walkers too.

The day-walks we describe are provided as samples of what each area of Britain has to offer. Most are circular, so you start and finish in the same place, and in some areas we use the same starting point for various routes, so you can be based in one place and go out in different directions each day.

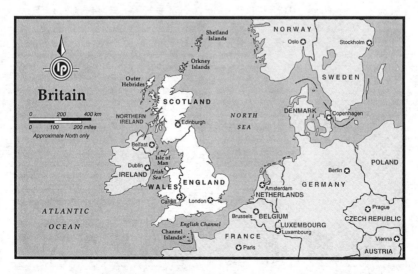

Several of the linear day-walks can be extended into two days – ideal for a weekend, or if you simply want to keep going! We also outline shorter alternatives, good if you only want to walk for a morning or afternoon. Likewise, the long-distance paths don't *have* to be followed in their entirety – you can just do a couple of days if you prefer. Some of the day-walks and long-distance paths in this book deliberately overlap, which gives you even more scope for several walks in the same area.

Many different types of accommodation are available in Britain; where you stay may depend on how much money you want to spend, or how much time you have, and this can affect the type of walking you do. On the long routes, you may want to carry all your gear and camp, or you may prefer to travel light, staying in hostels, B&Bs or hotels. More details are provided in the text. Many walkers visit two or more areas during their time in Britain, or go to other areas around the country, so we also include details on local transport: how to get to the start of a route, how to get away at the end, and how to 'escape' halfway through, should you want to.

As well as transport and places to stay and eat, we also cover many other subjects of interest to visitors walking in Britain: information centres, local guidebooks and maps, guided walks and so on. This book has just about everything you need.

We have concentrated on the national parks and other more popular areas of Britain simply because these are where the walking is best! Some of the routes we cover are long-time classics, others are personal favourites based on our own local knowledge. We have also described a few out-of-the-way routes, and provided brief outlines of many more places, which you can enjoy exploring for yourself. Have fun, and let us know how you get on, so your information can be used for the next edition.

Facts about Britain

HISTORY OF BRITAIN

Walkers come across so many historical sites and features as they follow the footpaths and trails of Britain. In a single day you could walk along a Roman road, pass a Bronze Age burial mound and visit a classic 13th-century cathedral. You might see battle sites, grand castles, humble workers' cottages or ancient Celtic crosses. Within a few miles you could walk through prehistoric stone circles and beneath the arches of a Victorian railway viaduct. There are also, of course, stretches of open countryside and even wilderness, but very few of these areas have completely escaped the effects of human activity.

The history of Britain is complex and spans several millennia, and so can be quite daunting and difficult to grasp. This very brief historical outline will help you put things in order and perspective. It is followed by a more detailed section on the history of walking in Britain.

4000 BC – Stone Age peoples arrive in Britain from mainland Europe.

3000 BC – Construction of ceremonial complexes such as Stonehenge and Avebury.

800 BC – Arrival of the Celts from central Europe, and the birth of the Bronze Age.

500 BC – The start of the Iron Age. By now there are three main Celtic tribes: the Britons in the south, the Picts and the Scots in the north.

43 AD – The Roman invasion of Britain.

122 – Emperor Hadrian orders the building of a wall to keep out the Scots, having failed to conquer them.

313 – The Romans bring Christianity to Britain, after its acceptance by Emperor Constantine in Rome

410 – End of Roman power in Britain.

5th & 6th centuries – Migration of Angles and Saxons from northern Europe to Britain. These newcomers absorb the Celts, or force them to move to the extreme northern and western parts of the British Isles.

635 – St Aiden founds monastery on Lindisfarne, which becomes a major centre of Christianity.

7th & 8th centuries – Emergence of three powerful Anglo-Saxon kingdoms: Northumbria, Mercia and Wessex.

8th century – Offa's Dyke created by King Offa of Mercia to mark the border between Anglo-Saxon Mercia and Celtic Wales.

9th century – Vikings conquer northern Britain. The Danes invade eastern England and make York their capital. Wessex remains Anglo-Saxon under King Alfred the Great.

843 – The Pictish culture disappears after a Scot, Kenneth MacAlpine, becomes the king of the north (the territory that later became known as Scotland).

Essential Definitions

Right here at the start, before you read any further, some essential definitions are required. This book covers the state of Great Britain (shortened to 'Britain' throughout) which is made up of three countries: England, Wales and Scotland. The United Kingdom (UK) consists of Great Britain, Northern Ireland and some semiautonomous off-shore islands such as the Isle of Man and the Channel Isles. The island of Ireland consists of Northern Ireland and the Republic of Ireland. The latter, also called Eire, is a completely separate country. The British Isles is a geographical term for the whole group of islands that make up the UK and the Republic of Ireland.

It is common to hear 'England' and 'Britain' used interchangeably, but you should avoid this, especially in Wales or Scotland, where it may cause slight offence. (Calling a Scot 'English' is something like calling a Canadian person 'American', or a New Zealander 'Australian'.) Visitors can plead ignorance, and get away with an occasional mix-up, but some of the worst offenders are the English themselves, many of whom seem to think that Wales and Scotland *are* parts of England. This naturally angers the Scots and Welsh, understandably fuelling nationalist sentiments in some quarters. This is usually completely misunderstood by the English, who simply think their neighbours carry ancient and unreasonable grudges. ■

9th & 10th centuries – Repeated attacks on the Welsh by Anglo-Saxon tribes.

10th century – Edward the Elder, Alfred's successor, gains control of both northern 'Danelaw' territories and southern Wessex, uniting England for the first time.

1066 – The Norman Conquest of Britain led by William the Conqueror.

1085 – The Domesday Book produced, providing a census of England's people, landowners and potential.

1215 – Signing of the Magna Carta by King John, ending the absolute authority of the monarchy.

1272-1307 – The reign of Edward I, who establishes authority over Wales, builds the castles of Conwy, Beaumaris, Caernarfon and Harlech, and removes the Scots' coronation stone, the Stone of Destiny, from Scone to England.

1314 – The English defeated by Robert the Bruce, King of Scotland, at the Battle of Bannockburn.

1337 – Start of the Hundred Years' War between England and France.

1349 – The Black Death in England kills more than 1.5 million people, one-third of the population.

1381 – Suppression of the Peasants' Revolt during Richard II's reign.

1400-06 – Owain Glyndwr leads a rebellion of the Welsh against the English, but is defeated by Henry IV.

1445-85 – The War of the Roses between the Houses of York and Lancaster. (Edward IV of York eventually emerged victorious and Henry VI of Lancaster died in the Tower of London).

1483 –12 year old Edward V and his brother murdered in the Tower of London, possibly by Richard III

1485 – Henry VII, the first Tudor king, succeeds to the throne.

1536 – The start of the Dissolution of the Monasteries by Henry VIII, famous for his six wives and the creation of the Church of England.

1536-43 – The Acts of Union between England and Wales.

1558 – Elizabeth I becomes queen. Enter William Shakespeare, Francis Bacon, Walter Raleigh and Francis Drake.

1560 – Reformation of the Church of Scotland.

1567 – Mary Queen of Scots is imprisoned in Loch Leven Castle.

1603 – James VI of Scotland also becomes James I of England.

1605 – Guy Fawkes' Gunpowder Plot to blow up the Houses of Parliament fails.

1625 – Charles I becomes king.

1644 – Start of the Civil War between the Royalists and the Parliamentarians.

1649 – Charles I executed. Establishment of the Commonwealth, ruled by Oliver Cromwell.

1660 – The Restoration of the Monarchy by parliament, and the crowning of Charles II as king.

1688 – William of Orange defeats James II at the Battle of the Boyne in Ireland to take the crown of England.

1707 – The Act of Union to join the Scottish and English parliaments.

1714 – Queen Anne, the last of the Stuart monarchs, dies. The Hanoverian kings follow.

1715 –1st Jacobite Rebellion – an attempt to restore the Stuart monarchs to the throne.

1745 – 2nd Jacobite Rebellion led by Charles Stuart (Bonnie Prince Charlie), supported by the Scottish Highlanders.

1746 – Bonnie Prince Charlie flees Britain after defeat at the Battle of Culloden.

1750s – The start of the Industrial Revolution in Britain.

1837-1901 – Reign of Queen Victoria.

1840s-1860s – 'The Clearances' of people from the land in the Highlands of Scotland.

1914-18 – WWI.

1919-21 – The Anglo-Irish War results in independence for the Republic of Ireland. (Six counties in the north became Northern Ireland and remained part of the United Kingdom).

1936 – King Edward VIII abdicates to marry a US divorcee. George VI becomes king.

1939-45 – WWII.

1952 – George VI dies.

1953 – Elizabeth II is crowned queen.

HISTORY OF WALKING IN BRITAIN
Prehistory

The current boom in walking for leisure in Britain has its roots in a tradition which goes back to prehistory. Many of the routes enjoyed by present-day walkers were first trodden by prehistoric humans, for whom walking was obviously the only means of getting from A to B.

A good example of this is the Ridgeway, dubbed the oldest road in Europe because of its continuous use for at least 5000 years, and now a waymarked national trail. It winds for 85 miles over the chalk downs of Southern England, from Wessex to the Chilterns, passing Neolithic and Bronze Age burial mounds, Iron Age hillforts, and modern power stations en route – truly a walk through history. Its chronicler, JRL Anderson, has suggested that there is something humbling in tripping over the same stone that may first have stubbed a human toe 10,000 years ago.

It used to be thought that prehistoric

Top Left: Peak District sheep
Middle Left: Foxgloves, in the New Forest
Bottom Left: Seals, on the Isle of Arran
Centre: A lonesome walker on the Pennine Way

Top Right: Highland cattle in Scotland
Middle Right: Primroses in Scotland
Bottom Right: Hermaness to Out Stack and Puffins

TONY WHEELER
TONY WHEELER
BRYN THOMAS
TONY WHEELER
BRYN THOMAS
BRYN THOMAS

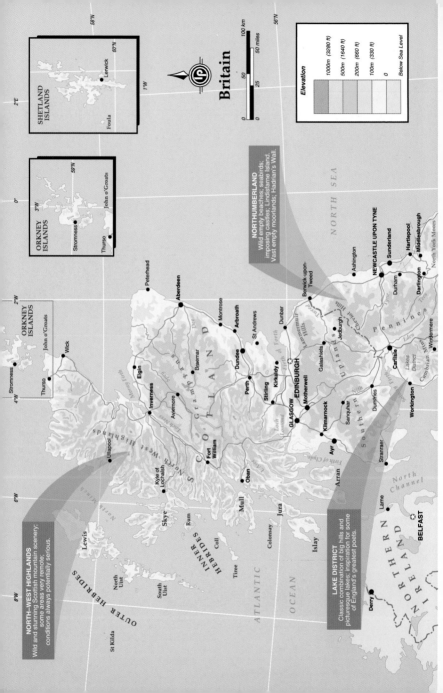

Britain

SHETLAND ISLANDS
Lerwick
Foula

ORKNEY ISLANDS
Stromness
John o'Groats
Thurso

Elevation
1000m (3280 ft)
500m (1640 ft)
200m (660 ft)
100m (330 ft)
0
Below Sea Level

100 km
50 miles

NORTHUMBERLAND
Wild empty beaches; seabirds;
imposing castles; Lindisfarne Island.
Vast empty moorlands; Hadrian's Wall.

NORTH-WEST HIGHLANDS
Wild and stunning Scottish mountain scenery;
serious area for climbers and walkers;
conditions always potentially serious.

LAKE DISTRICT
Classic combination of big hills and
picturesque lakes; inspiration for some
of England's greatest poets.

SCOTLAND

S P E Y S I D E

G r a m p i a n s

S o u t h e r n   U p l a n d s

N O R T H   S E A

ATLANTIC
OCEAN

North
Channel

NORTHERN
IRELAND

BELFAST

OUTER HEBRIDES
INNER HEBRIDES
HEBRIDES

North Minch

S   N o r t h   W e s t   H i g h l a n d s

Pennines
Cheviot Hills
Lammermuir Hills
Cumbrian Mtns
North York Moors

Stromness
Thurso
Wick
Ullapool
Peterhead
Aberdeen
Montrose
Arbroath
Dundee
St Andrews
Elgin
Inverness
Aviemore
Braemar
Perth
Stirling
Kirkcaldy
Dunbar
Berwick-upon-Tweed
EDINBURGH
GLASGOW
Motherwell
Galashiels
Jedburgh
Kilmarnock
Sanquhar
Dumfries
Carlisle
Ayr
Arran
Stranraer
Workington
Windermere
Whitehaven
Larne
Derry
Fort William
Oban
Kyle of Lochalsh
Skye
Rum
Mull
Coll
Tiree
Colonsay
Jura
Islay
Lewis
North Uist
South Uist
St Kilda
John o'Groats
Lake
District
Ashington
NEWCASTLE UPON TYNE
Sunderland
Durham
Hartlepool
Darlington
Middlesbrough

Dee
Spey
Loch Ness
Moray Firth
Loch Lomond
Firth of Forth
Forth
Tay
Firth of Clyde
Eden
Tees
Tyne
Wear

8°W
6°W
4°W
2°W
0°
2°E
1°W
3°W
56°N
58°N
59°N
60°N

YORKSHIRE DALES
Limestone country; high rolling hills; wide valleys; drystone walls. Crossed by the Settle-Carlisle Railway Line – Victorian engineering at its most impressive.

PEAK DISTRICT
Great variety of walks and scenery; Limestone valleys, high remote boggy moreland.

SNOWDONIA
Rugged Welsh mountains; stiff walking and exciting scrambling; easy access. Nearby castles to explore on rainy days.

COTSWOLD HILLS
Quintessential English countryside; honey-stone cottages and tranquil farmland.

SOUTH WEST COAST
Dramatic rocky coastline; tiny fishing villages; beaches, wildflowers and birds.

See Channel Islands Inset

CHANNEL ISLANDS

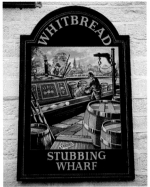
TONY WHEELER

DAVID ELSE

DAVID ELSE

TONY WHEELER

DAVID ELSE

Top Left: Pub sign, in Hebden Bridge,
  on the Pennine Way
Top Right: Cycle camping, on the Isle of Arran
Middle: Cam High Road, near Gayle Beck

Bottom Left: Bridge at Low Force Fall, Pennine Way
Bottom Right: A millstone, symbol of the Peak
  District National Park

people kept to the airy ridges and hilltops for long-distance walking, because the valleys were heavily forested and full of dangerous wild animals. But recent archaeological research in places like the Somerset Levels has shown that there was also a well-developed network of lowland tracks such as the so-called 'Sweetway', which crossed even the most inhospitable swamps and marshes.

Alfred Watkins, in his book *The Old Straight Track*, claimed prehistoric sites were linked by an unseen system of what he called 'ley lines'. This is open to dispute, and dismissed by serious archaeologists. Even so, there are still many 'ley hunters' walking in Britain.

The earliest tracks linked settlements, or settlements to hunting grounds, but there is now also a great deal of archaeological evidence that trading existed in prehistoric times. The discovery in Southern England and the Midlands of beautifully polished axeheads manufactured in stone from as far away as North Wales or the Lake District, shows that trade routes were well established across the country.

Romans & Anglo-Saxons

Some of these early routes, such as the Icknield Way and Watling Street, were later followed by the ruler-straight roads constructed by the Roman legions during their 400 year occupation of most of Britain from the 1st century AD. And in turn, many Roman roads are still faithfully followed by modern main roads; for example, the A5 from London to North Wales follows much of the Watling Street route, while the Fosse Way is largely followed by modern roads from Exeter, through the Cotswolds and across the spine of the Midlands, to Lincoln.

Many other Roman roads are followed by modern footpaths too. Long-distance paths (LDPs) which follow sections of Roman road include the Pennine Way, the Dales Way and the Peddars Way (all described in detail in this book).

After the Romans abandoned their British province, the Anglo-Saxon people (originally from northern Germany and around the Baltic) who became the foundation stock of modern England largely ignored the Roman roads and set up their villages well away from the imperial network. It was these settlers who created most of the villages which are such a typical feature of the modern British landscape. There can be little doubt that these villagers were the first to walk the parish paths which have developed into the current British rights-of-way network. Although originally purely local routes for getting to and from a place of work, they are now almost exclusively used for leisure purposes, and are jealously guarded by local people and organisations such as the Ramblers' Association (RA).

Medieval Times

The more important trade routes widened as a result of the use of horses and oxen to transport goods to and from local markets or further afield. Large herds of sheep or cattle were also driven for vast distances along these 'drove roads', which became part of the bridleway and green lane network of Britain that is still legally open to horse and wheeled traffic, such as mountain bikes.

Other important trade routes crossed the high moorlands and hill country of the north of England, where long trains of up to 50 packhorses carrying panniers of goods slung either side of their saddles were the big trucks of their day. The single-file causeways (locally called 'causeys') that they used to cross the boggy sections were often paved, or 'pitched', with large stone slabs. These causeways still make excellent walking routes today, and modern path restorers on routes such as the Pennine Way have reverted to using exactly the same construction techniques to give walkers a firm footing as they cross the high Pennine moors.

Another national trail, the Peddars Way, also follows a medieval trade route. That trade route, in turn, takes the same path as a road built by the Romans to enable them to subdue the warring tribes of Boudicca's Iceni – a road that probably utilised a prehistoric route along the low-lying north-west Norfolk ridge to the coast.

But trade was not the only reason for walking in Britain. From the Middle Ages onwards there was a well-established network of pilgrim routes leading to important religious sites such as Canterbury, Walsingham and Winchester. Geoffrey Chaucer's *The Canterbury Tales* describes the various types of people (including the well-to-do who were mainly horse-riders) who made the journey to the shrine of St Thomas à Becket at Canterbury.

The Romantics

The increase in travelling for pleasure from the later part of the 18th century was largely due to the creation of turnpike roads. Before that, travel on Britain's country roads and tracks had often been a nightmare battle against mud, water and quagmire.

The Romantic Movement, which glorified nature as a source of inspiration rather than regarding it with the horror it had previously inspired, was by now the height of fashion. And the leaders of the new movement were often great walkers, realising that the best way to appreciate the wonders of the natural world was on foot.

One of the greatest exponents of the joys of walking and nature was the Lake District poet William Wordsworth. From his homes at Grasmere and Rydal Mount, Wordsworth would walk in the surrounding hills and valleys, with his sister Dorothy taking the notes which were later to form the basis of such classic works as *The Prelude*.

As his reputation grew, Wordsworth gathered a nucleus of like-minded writers around him in Cumbria. One was opium addict Thomas de Quincey, who estimated that Wordsworth's 'certainly not ornamental' legs must have walked at least 175,000 miles during his lifetime. It was, said de Quincey, 'a mode of exertion which, to him, stood in the stead of alcohol and all other stimulants whatsoever to the animal spirits; to which, indeed, he was indebted for a life of unclouded happiness, and we for much of what is most excellent in his writings'.

Other Romantic writers who settled in the Lake District included Samuel Taylor Coleridge, who became a close friend of the Wordsworths and who is credited with one of the earliest recorded rock climbs in the district with his ascent of Broad Stand on Scafell Pike during a 100 mile walking tour in 1802.

Encouraged by the Romantic poets, or perhaps merely to escape the horrors of wheeled transport, 'pedestrian touring' suddenly became popular. In 1801, 78 year old Birmingham businessman, William Hutton, walked the whole length of Hadrian's Wall and back – a round trip of over 595 miles – in just over a month. His entertaining account of his marathon is a classic in walking literature, as is George Borrow's *Wild Wales*, published in 1862, in which this eccentric linguist colourfully recounted his adventures during a 239 mile walking tour of Wales, including an ascent of Snowdon.

The great distances travelled by these tourists were reflected in the popular Victorian sport of 'pedestrianism', in which contestants competed against the clock.

The Industrial Revolution

Most of the best known of the early walkers came from the upper or middle classes – among them, intellectuals such as Charles Dickens. But by the earliest years of the Industrial Revolution, members of the lower classes – the factory workers – were also walking in the countryside for enjoyment.

As early as 1777, there was a flourishing botanical society at Eccles in Lancashire, whose millworker members thought nothing of 'rambling' 30 or 40 miles on a Sunday afternoon searching for interesting specimens on the moors. And they were not alone. According to the British Association for the Advancement of Science, the Manchester district was 'the scene of one of the most remarkable manifestations of popular science which has ever been recorded'.

But the Enclosure Acts of the early 19th century resulted in the wholesale appropriation of large areas of moor and mountain which formerly had been 'common land' – open to all. Many of those early ramblers were forcibly excluded from walking where they wished on the hills by stick-wielding gamekeepers, charged with protecting grouse that their masters would later hunt. Many long-established rights of way were extinguished during this period.

Early Walking Organisations

As early as 1824, ramblers were organising themselves against the landowners. An Association for the Protection of Ancient Footpaths in the vicinity of York was founded in 1824, followed two years later by the Manchester Association for the Preservation of Ancient Footpaths, later to become the Peak District & Northern Footpath Preservation Society. (This organisation is still active in footpath protection on the hills of Northern England, and their metal signs are often seen where footpaths cross or meet public roads.)

The Manchester association, in the words of one of its founders, 'spread among the country gentlemen a wholesome terror of transgressing against the right of the poor to enjoy their own without anyone to make them afraid'. Despite these bold words, access to the high moors of the Pennines and Peak District was still strictly limited, and in 1877 the Hayfield and Kinder Scout Ancient Footpath Association reported that the public 'imagining that what was once their own is now their own, have not infrequently come into unpleasant collision with gamekeepers'.

Thomas Arthur Leonard, a Congregational minister from Colne, Lancashire, founded the Co-operative Holidays Association (CHA) in 1897. Its aim was to provide working-class people with walking holidays in the hills for the price of a week's wages. Leonard later formed the more spartan Holiday Fellowship (HF), because he felt that, despite its working-class origins, the CHA was becoming 'too middle-class in spirit and conservative in...ideas'.

By this time, rambling clubs were springing up all over the country. Among the earliest were the Sunday Tramps, formed among intellectuals around London in 1879 by the mountaineer and biographer Leslie Stephen. Soon to follow were the Manchester YMCA Rambling Club, formed in 1880, and the Forest Ramblers Club based on Epping Forest, formed in 1884.

One of the most active of these early rambling clubs was the Sheffield Clarion Ramblers, formed in 1900 by GHB Ward and named after the socialist newspaper the *Sheffield Clarion*. Ward personified the self-taught nature of these early northern ramblers, and his annual Clarion Handbooks reflect his spartan views.

They are filled with home-spun axioms such as 'A rambler made is a man improved' and 'The man who never was lost never went very far'. Ward, like most of the ramblers' leaders of the time, was a life-long campaigner for access to the forbidden moorlands of the Peak District.

The 1920s & 1930s

After the WWI, soldiers returning from the trenches to 'a land fit for heroes' were still faced with 'Keep Out' and 'Trespassers will be Prosecuted' signs when they went for a walk on the moors. The latter signs were known as 'wooden liars' by the rambling movement, because trespass was not a criminal offence. The situation was made worse by the strong-arm tactics of some gamekeepers, and there were many unpleasant incidents.

In the meantime, rambling clubs had formed themselves into regional federations based on the major cities of Britain. Eventually, in 1931, the National Council of Ramblers' Federations was set up, and in 1935 this became the Ramblers' Association.

From the very start, the ramblers had three main issues on their agenda: the creation of national parks, the protection of rights of way, and access to mountains and moorland. Things came to a head in the early 1930s, when a series of well-attended annual open-air rallies were held in the Peak District. Deliberate trespasses were organised, culminating in what became known as 'The Battle of Kinder Scout' – a major landmark in the history of British walking.

The Battle of Kinder Scout

In the spring of 1932, some members of the communist-based British Workers' Sports Federation (BWSF) were forced off the Peak District high moorland of Bleaklow by some abusive gamekeepers. They resolved to come back in force, and a 'mass trespass' over Kinder Scout was organised and advertised locally. Kinder Scout, at 636m (2088 ft), was the highest point of the Peak District, visible from the streets of Manchester yet uncrossed by any public path.

On 24 April 1932, a bright Sunday morning, about 400 ramblers set off from the small town of Hayfield towards the summit of Kinder, determined to exercise what they saw as their 'right to roam'. They soon outpaced their police escort, and made their way up a right of way in a small valley called William Clough, before deliberately setting off across country. They were met by a small force of gamekeepers. Some scuffles occurred and a gamekeeper fell with an injured ankle.

Five of the mass trespass ringleaders were arrested and eventually tried in Derby where they received a total of 17 months imprisonment. Ironically, it was the severity of the sentences which united the rambling establishment, which until then had been opposed to the direct action of the BWSF. Indeed, some ramblers said it had put back the access cause by 20 years. ∎

National Parks & National Trails

As well as the battle for access, the other great cause célèbre of the rambling movement was the creation of national parks, but this had to wait until after WWII, and the visionary 1945 report of architect, planner and rambler John Dower.

The postwar Labour government was committed to national parks, based on the protected wilderness areas which had been established in the USA in the late 19th and early 20th centuries (see the National Parks & Other Protected Areas section of this chapter for more details). In 1949 parliament passed the National Parks & Access to the Countryside Act, allowing for the necessary powers to create parks in England and Wales (Scotland has a separate legal system).

The first park was created in 1951 in the Peak District, scene of the great access battles of the 1930s. One of the first actions of the new Peak National Park was to negotiate access agreements with landowners on those once-forbidden moorlands. Over 81 sq miles are now covered by access agreements, allowing walkers their cherished freedom to roam, subject to a common-sense set of by-laws.

The 1949 Act also set up the National Parks Commission (now the Countryside Commission), which was charged not only with the creation of national parks and areas of outstanding natural beauty (see the National Parks & Other Protected Areas section of this chapter) but also with the creation of LDPs, now known as national trails. The first and best known of these was the Pennine Way, a 260 mile route from the Peak District to the Scottish border.

But the 1949 Act did not give the walkers all they wanted. There was still no right to roam freely on uncultivated mountains and moorland. The Ramblers' Association, now one of Britain's foremost pressure groups, with over 100,000 members, is still vigorously campaigning for that right – a right enjoyed by walkers in most other European countries.

GEOGRAPHY

Despite its small size, the geography of Britain is extremely varied, so it is easier to outline the main features by dividing the country into its constituent parts

England

Covering just over 50,000 sq miles, much of England is flat or low-lying. England can be divided into four main geographical areas. Northern England is dominated by the Pennines, a series of mountains, hills and valleys stretching for 250 miles in a central ridge from Derbyshire to the border with Scotland. Britain's first LDP, the Pennine Way, winds

Administrative Boundaries
England and Wales are administratively divided into counties or 'shires' (eg Kent, Essex, Wiltshire and Yorkshire). Some of these derive their titles from the names of ancient kingdoms (eg Cumbria and Gwynedd), while others date from the 1970s when various new counties were introduced (eg Avon and Tyne & Wear). However, you will still come across the old county names, particularly in tourist literature, even though the places haven't officially existed for more than 20 years. This is especially so in Wales (eg Pembrokeshire and Montgomeryshire). In Scotland, where the population is lightly distributed, regions (eg Highland and Borders) are more or less equivalent to English and Welsh counties, although they cover larger geographical areas (and, confusingly, are subdivided into units called counties too). ∎

through the range. To the west are the scenic Cumbrian Mountains of the Lake District, especially popular with walkers, and containing England's highest point, Scafell Pike, measuring 978m (3209 ft) above sea level (ASL).

The central part of England is known as the Midlands. It is heavily populated and has been an industrial heartland since the 19th century. At its centre is Birmingham, Britain's second-largest city after London.

The south-west peninsula, also known as the West Country, has a rugged coastline, numerous beaches and a mild climate, making it a favourite holiday destination. The South West Coast Path, Britain's longest LDP, and the wild, grass-covered moors of Dartmoor and Exmoor are popular with walkers.

The rest of the country is known geographically as the English Lowlands, which is a mixture of farmland, low hills, an industrial belt and densely populated cities

Local Landscape
Note that in different parts of Britain, geographical features have various names, according to local dialect. For example, a stream is a beck in the Lake District or a burn in Scotland; a valley can be a cwm in Wales or a coombe in Southern England; a col (pass) is a bwlch in Wales, a haus in the Lakes or a bealach in Scotland. ∎

including London, the capital. To the south are hills of chalk known as downs, including the North Downs (followed by another LDP), stretching from London to Dover, where the chalk is exposed as the famous white cliffs.

Wales

Covering just over 8000 sq miles, Wales is surrounded by sea on three sides. Its border to the east with England still runs roughly along Offa's Dyke, a giant earthwork constructed in the 8th century, and followed by an LDP today. Wales has two major mountain areas: the Black Mountains and Brecon Beacons in the south, and the mountains of Snowdonia in the north-west. At 1095m (3650 ft), Snowdon is the highest peak in Wales. The population is concentrated in the south-east, along the coast between Cardiff and Swansea and in the old mining valleys that run north into the Brecon Beacons.

Scotland

Scotland covers about 30,000 sq miles, two-thirds of which is mountain and moorland, and therefore popular with walkers. The Southern Uplands, south of Edinburgh (the capital and financial centre) and Glasgow (the industrial centre), have fertile coastal plains and ranges of hills bordering England. The Southern Upland Way (Scotland's longest LDP) runs through this area. The Central Lowlands comprise a slice from Edinburgh and Dundee in the east to Glasgow in the west, and include the industrial

ORKNEY

SHETLAND

WESTERN
ISLES

Moray Firth

HIGHLAND

GRAMPIAN

TAYSIDE

**Britain:
England & Wales Counties,
Scotland Regions**

FIFE

*ATLANTIC
OCEAN*

CENTRAL

STRATHCLYDE

LOTHIAN

BORDERS

NORTH SEA

NORTHERN
IRELAND

NORTH
CHANNEL

DUMFRIES &
GALLOWAY

NORTHUMBERLAND

1

DURHAM

2

CUMBRIA

NORTH
YORKSHIRE

1 TYNE & WEAR
2 CLEVELAND
3 MERSEYSIDE
4 GREATER MANCHESTER
5 WEST YORKSHIRE
6 SOUTH YORKSHIRE
7 WEST MIDLANDS
8 WEST GLAMORGAN
9 MID GLAMORGAN
10 SOUTH GLAMORGAN
11 BUCKINGHAMSHIRE
12 BEDFORDSHIRE
13 HERTFORDSHIRE

ISLE
OF MAN

IRISH SEA

LANCASHIRE

5

HUMBERSIDE

6

NOTTINGHAMSHIRE

LINCOLN-
SHIRE

3

4

CHESHIRE

DERBYSHIRE

GWYNEDD

CLWYD

STAFFORD-
SHIRE

LEICESTER-
SHIRE

SHROPSHIRE

7

NORFOLK

ST GEORGES CHANNEL

POWYS

HEREFORD &
WORCESTER

WARWICK-
SHIRE

NORTHAMPTON-
SHIRE

CAMBRIDGE-
SHIRE

SUFFOLK

DYFED

12

GLOUCESTER-
SHIRE

11

13

ESSEX

8

9

GWENT

OXFORD-
SHIRE

GREATER
LONDON

10

AVON

BERKSHIRE

Bristol Channel

WILTSHIRE

SURREY

KENT

SOMERSET

HAMPSHIRE

WEST
SUSSEX

EAST
SUSSEX

DEVON

DORSET

ISLE OF
WIGHT

STRAIT OF DOVER

CORNWALL

ENGLISH CHANNEL

0   100   200 km
0   50   100 miles

belt and the majority of the population. A coastal plain runs all the way up the east coast.

To the north are the Highlands, a vast, sparsely populated area where most of the major mountain ranges are found. Ben Nevis, the highest mountain in Scotland, and Britain, at 1322m (4406 ft), is near the town of Fort William. The most spectacular (and most remote) mountains are those in the far north-west.

Scotland has 790 islands, 130 of them inhabited. The Western Isles comprise the Inner Hebrides and the Outer Hebrides. To the north of Scotland are two other island groups, Orkney and Shetland, the northernmost part of the British Isles.

CLIMATE

In keeping with its geography, the climate of Britain varies widely from place to place, and from day to day, so visitors will soon sympathise with the locals' conversational obsession with the weather. The following section provides an overview. For more details see the When to Walk section in the Facts for the Walker chapter.

The winter months (November, December, January and February) are least hospitable to visitors, and least pleasant for walking. It's cold, and the days are short, although the hills are less crowded at these times. Snow and ice cover most highland areas at this time, making walking potentially dangerous or impossible, without mountaineering experience.

The variation in weather conditions around the island is quite extreme, but it's generally true to say that the further north you go, the colder it gets (although temperature is also greatly influenced by altitude). There's also a substantial difference in the number of hours of daylight from one place to another (again, see the When to Walk section in the Facts for the Walker chapter).

But it's not all doom and gloom. Through spring, summer and autumn weather conditions can often be very pleasant for walking: dry and cool, or even warm. In summer

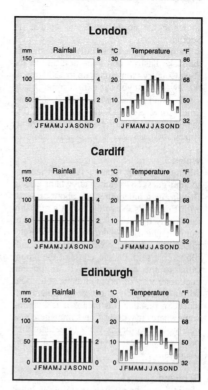

you'll need sunscreen to avoid getting burnt, even if it's windy and overcast.

Some information on weather forecasts is given in the Danger & Annoyances and Safety sections of the Facts for the Walker chapter.

England

Climatologists classify England's climate as 'temperate maritime', for which read mild and damp. Temperatures are moderated by light winds that blow off seas warmed by the Gulf Stream. In winter, this stops temperatures inland falling very far below 0°C, and keeps summer temperatures from rising much above 30°C. The average high in Southern England for June through August is 21°C, the average low 12°C. It tends to be colder in the north but not as cold as in Scotland.

Rainfall is greatest in hilly areas, such as the Lake District and Pennines, and in the West Country (sometimes up to 4500 mm of rain a year), but you can expect some cloudy weather and rain anywhere in Britain at any time. Come prepared and you needn't find the weather as depressing as the locals appear to.

Wales
Although Wales' weather is as difficult to second-guess as weather anywhere else in Britain, its temperatures are about on a par with England's. Nevertheless, it's probably fair to say that it suffers from an excess of rainfall, which can make walking here pretty miserable, especially when westerly winds blow. That said, the closeness of the mountains to the coast means that you can encounter very different climatic conditions within a relatively short geographical distance. In practice this means if it's raining somewhere, it will be fine somewhere else nearby. It also means you can get sun then rain then sun again in the space of a couple of hours.

Scotland
'Varied' may be a vague description, but it perfectly describes Scotland's climatic moods. Whenever you visit, you're likely to see both sun and rain. One good thing about the climate is that it does change quickly – a rainy day is often followed by a sunny one. There are also wide variations in climate over surprisingly short distances. While one glen broods under a cloud, the next may be enjoying full sunshine.

Considering how far north the country lies (Edinburgh is on the same latitude as Moscow), you might expect a colder climate, but the Atlantic winds are warmed by the Gulf Stream and the west coast has a relatively mild climate, with over 1500 mm of rain and average summer highs of 19°C. May and June are generally the driest months, and the best for mountain-walking, but the Highlands can have extreme weather at any time:

in the Cairngorm Mountains snow has been recorded in *every* month of the year.

FLORA & FAUNA
In a place as small as Britain, with its long history of human occupation, it is hardly surprising that the countryside you see today is largely the result of human activity. Following WWII, Britain's push for food self-sufficiency meant farming practices changed dramatically. This in turn had a similarly dramatic effect on the country's native flora and fauna. Modern farming methods included linking small fields into vast prairie-like areas by removing the thick hedgerows – a valuable wildlife habitat – that once separated them. Since 1946, tens of thousands of miles of hedgerow have been destroyed, along with the plant and animal species they contained. The destruction continues; since 1984 a further 23% of Britain's hedgerows have disappeared.

Britain's wildlife habitats have also been reduced over the last 50 years by numerous other causes, including the increased use of pesticides, blanket planting of conifers, massive house and road-building schemes and the construction of out-of-town shopping centres. Despite seemingly overwhelming odds however, Britain still boasts a great diversity of flora and fauna, and some of the best examples of the natural habitats now are protected to a greater or lesser extent, thanks to the creation of national parks and other protected (or 'designated') areas. These are discussed later in this chapter.

(For details of books about British flora and fauna, see the Books section of the Facts for the Walker chapter.)

(For details on wildlife and conservation groups in Britain see the Useful Organisations section of the Facts for the Walker chapter.)

Habitats
The variety of plants and animals in Britain is a reflection of the diverse range of natural habitats found here. This section covers the main natural habitats, giving an overview of the plants and animals that occur in each one. It is not intended to be a comprehensive

guide. Rather, it is an attempt to paint a broad picture of the sort of things that you might see.

Many of the areas mentioned as examples of habitat types are crossed by walks covered in the main route descriptions. However, in Britain many of the plants and animals are small and sometimes hidden away; the birds don't stand around posing. You will often need patience and some perseverance to get the most out of studying the wildlife here. Don't be discouraged; there is such a variety of species that your efforts will often be well rewarded, and if you appreciate the wealth of life above and below, your walking will undoubtedly be enhanced.

The thistle – as prickly as the issue of Scottish independence.

Grassland & Farmland Probably the best examples of grassland are found on the chalk downs in Southern England (notably on the South Downs) and on the limestone areas further north, such as the Peak District and the Yorkshire Dales.

Much natural grassland has now disappeared, principally because it has been ploughed up and replaced with ryegrass, or because it has been fertilised, leading to the overgrowth of a few extra-strong species. However, some grasslands and meadows are now protected, and here the summer brings a great profusion of wildflowers, such as kidney vetch, knapweed, yellow rattle and thistles, with other species such as autumn gentian appearing later. Orchids also thrive in this environment.

With the flowers come the insects, especially colourful butterflies and hidden grasshoppers. Birds here tend to be less prolific, but you will commonly see meadow pipits, skylarks, wheatears and kestrels.

With the belated realisation that farm hedgerows support a great deal of wildlife, farmers are now encouraged by bodies such as English Nature (EN) to maintain their hedges, and to 'set aside' the perimeters of fields to grow wild. These areas now serve as havens for birds like robins, wrens, blackcaps and yellowhammers. Many fields are now edged with red poppies during the summer months. With time the hedgerows will contain increasing numbers of plant species. Look for woody species such as blackthorn, dogwood and hawthorn, as well as climbing plants such as bramble, and old man's beard. Elderflower, good for wine-making, is also common.

Another place to look for flowers are road verges that have not been cut back, particularly in the summer months; you may see rosebay willowherb, cowparsley, harebells and red campion to name but a few.

Verges and hedgerows frequently support small mammals such as voles and shrews, so kestrels are often seen hovering overhead. In Scotland you may see buzzards perched by the roadside. Pheasants, originally introduced from Russia but now considered native, are commonly seen in a variety of habitats, including farmland, woodland and moorland, and now breed in the wild as well as being reared for shooting.

Woodlands Britain was once almost entirely covered with woodland, but following large-scale deforestation since the Industrial Revolution tree cover has fallen to a mere 7.3% today, the lowest figure for any country in Europe after Ireland. (Italy has

22% tree cover, France 27%.) As long ago as 1919, the Forestry Commission, a government agency, was established to halt this decline with a long-range plan to plant five million acres (two million hectares) of trees, mainly in Northern England, Scotland and Wales, by the year 2000. Substantial grants for landowners ensured that this target was achieved by the early 1980s. However, most trees planted were fast-growing conifers, and the environmental problems they cause have been recognised only in the last few decades.

In recent years, however, there has been a switch to establishing new broadleaf woodlands. This is an all-embracing term, encompassing woods of mainly deciduous trees such as oak, ash, sycamore, beech, hazel and lime. The New Forest and the Forest of Dean are classic examples of this type of habitat. The biodiversity of these woodlands is enormous, and each season seems to bring something new.

In spring, before the leaf canopy is fully developed, enough sunlight reaches the ground to encourage a carpet of woodland flowers, such as wood anemone, wood sorrel and primroses. No-one who has seen a sea of

Scots pine (*Pinus sylvestris*).

bluebells underneath these imposing trees can fail to be impressed. The plants and trees in their turn encourage numerous insects, especially butterflies, and the birds that can be spotted include willow warblers, chiffchaffs, thrushes, wrens, woodpigeons, jays and woodpeckers.

Moving towards autumn, you will see a variety of fungi, both on the ground and on tree trunks. Grey squirrels will be plentiful, as will smaller rodents – all collecting and storing fruit and seeds for the winter. You may be lucky enough to see fallow deer or roe deer in some areas, and the endangered red squirrel is a real bonus (see aside).

Most coniferous woodland has been planted, but in Scotland there are still a few areas of native Caledonian pine forest, best seen in the Cairngorms. Here, the Scots pines are not uniformly spaced. This allows light to get through to the ground which becomes covered with bushes such as juniper and holly. It is here that you may see birds such as crossbills, crested tits and ospreys. The dense canopy that the conifer plantations produce encourages little growth beneath the

The persistent drumming of the Great Spotted Woodpecker can be heard in forests and woodlands.

trees, with the end result that there is little biodiversity in this type of woodland. (Put simply, the plants don't grow, so the insects leave, and there is nothing for the birds to eat.) Before the forest is too dense you may see birds such as goldcrests, hen harriers, goshawks, and sparrowhawks, but most of these will eventually depart.

Heathland Heathland used to be widespread in southern Britain, but most has now disappeared due to land usage; agriculture, roads and property development have all taken their toll. Heathland is typified by the vivid yellow of its gorse in the spring, and the swathe of purple heathers later in the summer. Bilberry bushes, recognised by the tiny blue-black fruit they produce in the summer, may be interspersed with the heather, particularly on higher ground. Other characteristic plants are broom and, increasingly in some areas, bracken. The boggy pools often found on the heaths are a breeding ground for a variety of dragonflies and damselflies, whilst birds such as tree pipits, meadow pipits and stonechats are commonly seen. After dark you may hear the whirring song of nightjars.

Stonechat commonly perch on top of heathland gorse bushes.

Moorland This is essentially heathland on higher ground, and supports a similar collection of plants. Classic moorlands include those of Dartmoor, Exmoor, the northern Peak District (the Dark Peak), the North York Moors, the North Pennines and Scotland. As you stride across these moors you will almost inevitably scatter grouse. Other birds you may spot include curlews, golden plovers and wheatears, which nest here. Birds of prey such as merlins and hen harriers are also seen. Many of the high moors are covered extensively with peat, but these areas have declined dramatically in the last few decades due to the commercial use of peat for gardens, and the establishment of large plantations.

Mountains There are mountains in Snowdonia and the Lake District, but the vast majority of the high mountains are in Scotland, particularly in the west and north-west Highlands and in the Cairngorms. On the high peaks in Scotland you may see the grouse's northern cousin, the ptarmigan – dappled brown in the summer but white in the winter. Snow buntings are another good sighting. Golden eagles, Britain's largest birds of prey, are found principally in the mountains of Scotland, although there are a few heavily protected pairs in the Lake District.

Many hardy alpine plants are unique to the mountains. Plants such as purple saxifrage, mossy saxifrage, moss campion, rock speedwell and mountain avens are best looked for on rocky ledges or under stones, where the ubiquitous sheep can't get to them. One of the best places to see this type of vegetation is at Cwm Idwal in Snowdonia. Here, the ledges below the Devil's Kitchen are known as the Hanging Gardens, and for years have been a botanists' paradise.

Freshwater Areas Streams and rivers in lowland areas are a picture in the summer, with a profusion of flowers such as meadowsweet, great willowherb, tussock sedge and yellow irises along their banks. Mayflies, damselflies and dragonflies glide over the water. The iridescent kingfisher may be spotted perching on a low branch over the water, whilst little grebes, grey herons and moorhens are also seen.

In contrast, upland streams are often fast running and crystal clear. To witness salmon jumping in the rivers of Scotland is an unforgettable sight. The abundance of insects both in and above the water encourages the presence of birds such as dippers and grey wagtails.

In the open water of smaller ponds and lakes it is worth looking for frogs, toads and newts, especially in the early spring breeding season. Towards summer you will start to see tadpoles in the pools. Dragonflies, damselflies, and waterfowl such as great crested grebes, mallards, tufted ducks and coots are also seen. In winter they may be joined by migrant birds including teal, pintails and shovelers.

Marshes and reedbeds, such as those found in the Norfolk Broads, are an ornithological paradise. Nesting birds such as bearded tits, reed buntings, redshanks and, rarely, bitterns may be seen. Look for marsh harriers gliding low overhead. Closer inspection of the rushes and reeds themselves will reveal a number of springtime flowers, including marsh orchids, marsh bird's-foot trefoil and marsh marigold.

The Dipper inhabits freshwater streams, where it feeds by chasing insects and other small creatures underwater.

Coastal Areas The dramatic cliffs and beaches around the coast of Britain, particularly in Pembrokeshire, around Land's End and along the north-east coast, are a marvellous sight in themselves, but they are most spectacular during early summer, when they are home to breeding sea birds. Some sheltered cliffs will host literally thousands of birds; guillemots, razorbills cormorants, fulmars, kittiwakes and shags all fight for space on impossibly crowded rock ledges. Other birds such as jackdaws and rock pipits also make use of holes in the cliffs for nesting. Puffins, with their distinctive

The Golden Eagle, Britain's largest bird of prey, is mainly found in the Scottish mountains.

Threatened Coastal Areas
The coast has been subjected to more than its fair share of abuse from human activity. Damage to dunes by holiday-makers has led to erosion and consequent loss of plant life and nesting sites. More worrying still is the ever-present threat of pollution from the sea. The massive oil spillage from a beached tanker near Milford Haven on the Pembrokeshire coast in 1996 caused devastation, and once again temporarily brought the issue into sharp focus. Toxic waste continues to be dumped at sea. More insidious, but equally serious, is the persistent overfishing of the seas, and the decline of vital food stocks for birds and sea mammals. ■

The aptly named Tufted Duck is just one of many attractive species of waterfowl to be seen on lakes and estuaries.

rainbow beaks, can be seen burrowing into the ground on clifftops to make their nests. Look to the bottom of the cliffs, and you may see seals. To complete the picture, the clifftops will be adorned with wildflowers such as sea campion, thrift, gorse and heather.

Numerous migrant wading birds, such as dunlins, curlews, ringed plovers, godwits and redshanks make estuaries and mudflats their feeding grounds, on the Norfolk coast

Puffins nest on sea cliffs and off-shore stacks. The comical-looking bill is razor sharp.

for example. They feed on molluscs and crustaceans using carefully designed beaks that allow each species to feed from a different level in the mud. Ducks such as teal and wigeon, and several species of geese are also found. Plants such as glasswort and sea lavender flourish on the mudflats.

The apparently inhospitable dunes and beaches support a range of plant life, including the tough marram grass, which holds the dunes together. Other specialised plants that thrive on the dunes include marsh orchids and creeping willow. These in turn bring in a variety of butterflies and grasshoppers. Even shingle beaches can support plants such as sea holly and sea milkwort. Some birds, including oystercatchers and black-headed gulls, choose to nest on the dunes. You are unlikely to see this on the busy beaches in southern Britain, but on quiet and protected dunes you should take care not to disturb any nesting birds.

Mammals

The red deer is the largest British mammal, with herds found on Exmoor and Dartmoor, in the Lake District and in such large numbers in Scotland that culling is required (see aside). Male red deer grow a pair of large antlers between April and July, which are shed again in February. Fallow deer – smaller than red deer and distinguished by white spots on their backs – are the most common woodland deer of England and Wales, but are not truly native to Britain; they are thought to have been introduced by the Normans in about the 12th century. Roe deer are even smaller, and are native. They are most commonly found in Northern England and Scotland, where they are widespread on moorland and farmland and do considerable damage to young trees.

Britain has few other large mammals. The reindeer, beaver and auroch (wild ox) are all now extinct; and the last wolf was shot in Scotland in the 17th century. Wildcats still live in the Highlands of Scotland but are rarely seen.

The fox is prospering, despite the number of fox corpses that line Britain's roads.

The Red Squirrel – a species in decline

The red squirrel used to be commonplace in woodland areas, but it is now one of Britain's most endangered species. Populations have declined significantly over the last 50 years to about 160,000, following the importation of the larger grey squirrel from America. The problem isn't that the grey squirrels attack their red cousins, they just eat all their food. Unlike the red squirrels, the greys are able to eat fruit such as hazelnuts and acorns when they are still very green, and so devour all the food before it has ripened, depriving the reds of their food source. Once grey squirrels have arrived in an area the reds are usually gone within about 15 years.

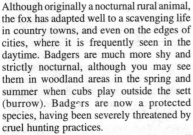

Paradoxically, the enlightened policy of replanting broadleaf woodland rather than conifers favours the greys and provides a further threat to the reds. Until recently, the one area where the reds came out on top in the feeding stakes was the coniferous woodlands, since unlike greys, reds can get the seeds out of pine cones. However, even this advantage is now threatened, because the indomitable greys are learning to utilise pine cones.

The distribution of the red squirrel is now mainly confined to Scotland, Ireland, and isolated populations in the Lake District, Norfolk and the Isle of Wight. Initiatives by environmental groups such as the WWF are now underway to try to halt its further decline. ∎

Although originally a nocturnal rural animal, the fox has adapted well to a scavenging life in country towns, and even on the edges of cities, where it is frequently seen in the daytime. Badgers are much more shy and strictly nocturnal, although you may see them in woodland areas in the spring and summer when cubs play outside the sett (burrow). Badgers are now a protected species, having been severely threatened by cruel hunting practices.

Hedgehogs are also native. They roll themselves into a spiny ball at the first sign of danger, but sadly this is no protection against the motor car, and they are more likely to be seen as a roadside casualty.

The grey squirrel, introduced from North America, is very common and has almost entirely replaced the smaller native red squirrel (see aside). The mink was introduced from abroad to stock fur farms, from where some subsequently escaped; it is now prospering, and is seen mainly on river banks. Once very rare, the pine marten is again being seen in some forested regions, especially in Scotland.

Although otters have suffered from the effects of polluted water and prey, and also from persecution by fishers, they are now protected, and their numbers are growing. They are mainly nocturnal and inhabit the banks of rivers and lakes, particularly in upland areas. In Scotland they frequently live on the coast.

The Stoat is closely related to the weasel. In far northern Europe its white-coated variety is known as ermine.

The Red Deer – a species on the increase

The red deer, the so-called 'Monarch of the Glen', is rapidly becoming a serious ecological problem in Scotland. Unlike many species, the red deer is not hurtling towards extinction, rather it's multiplying way out of control. The ecological balance was upset when the natural predator of the red deer, the wolf, was eradicated in the 17th century. More recently, milder winters over the last few decades have meant that fewer deer have died from lack of food. There are now over 300,000 of them, and huge areas of mountain, moorland and woodland vegetation are simply being eaten away.

In some parts of Scotland, no new trees have been able to grow since deer populations started to increase 300 years ago. But fencing off woodland is not the answer to the problem as it reduces the territory of the deer and leads to even heavier grazing of the moorland areas.

Culling has been proposed as a solution, but it seems that not enough deer have been culled by farmers and estate managers to stabilise the situation. Conservationists report that if nothing is done to reduce deer numbers, the last few areas of indigenous forest in Scotland may be destroyed. ■

Roe Deer – justifiably shy in the stalking season.

legs and ears, choose to stay in the open where they can see predators, so are often seen on downland. Territorial battles between males in early spring have given rise to the expression 'mad as a March hare'.

Small rodents found in a variety of habitats include harvest mice, shrews and voles. These are preyed upon by larger mammals such as weasels and stoats. Moles are rarely seen, but evidence of their digging can be found all over grasslands in the form of piles of earth or 'molehills'.

The most common aquatic mammal in Britain is the water vole, which is often seen low down on river banks. It may be confused with the brown rat, also a riverside inhabitant. Bats are widespread, and often roost in house roofs and barns. The pipistrelle is Britain's commonest species of bat.

Two species of seal frequent British coasts: these are the larger grey seal and the common seal, which is actually less common than the grey.

Snakes

Britain has only three native snakes. The grass snake is the longest and is completely harmless. It can be recognised by the pale

Rabbits are extremely common, and flourish in Britain, having recovered from the myxomatosis epidemic of the 1950s. They are not native to Britain and are thought to have been introduced by the Normans for their meat and fur. Brown hares, with longer

Fox Hunting

There can scarcely be a sport more redolent of England than fox hunting; whether it's the English countryside, the English class system or the English landed gentry. Nor, in the closing years of the 20th century, can there be a sport more ideologically unsound. Oscar Wilde summed it up 100 years ago as 'the unspeakable in pursuit of the uneatable'.

Remarkably, fox hunting does survive and, even more remarkably, foxes do too. It's estimated that Britain's 200-odd hunts kill about 20,000 foxes a year, but 40,000 are killed by vehicles and over 100,000 are trapped or shot. Strangely enough, many foxes may actually owe their existence to the hunters, since it's believed that many fieldside stretches of hedge and small woods are there due to fox-hunting farmers intent on providing more living quarters for foxes.

Fox hunting is an undeniably cruel sport. Antihunting sentiment in England runs strong and polls have revealed that two-thirds to three-quarters of the population would support a hunting ban. It's also undeniably an upper-class sport, or at least of the wealthy. Annual membership of a hunt typically costs around £400, and while the cost of a day out hunting can be as little as £10, the price for joining a classy hunt like the Quorn can be more than £100. The curious attire, starting with a 'pink' (which in fox-hunting parlance means 'red'!) jacket, can cost thousands of pounds from a London tailor. And then there are the horses; most fox hunters, a survey by the National Trust revealed, own two or more horses, in part because different hunts require different types of horse. ■

ring on its neck and is common in England and Wales. The smooth snake, also harmless, is much smaller and its distribution is limited to the heathlands of Southern England. The adder is the only poisonous snake, although its venom is rarely fatal. It is found throughout mainland Britain in dry, open country and can be easily recognised by the dark zigzag stripe down its back. It grows to about 60 cm in length.

NATIONAL PARKS & OTHER PROTECTED AREAS

National Parks

It was William Wordsworth, famous poet and great walker, who first came up with the idea in 1810 that the Lake District should be 'a sort of national property, in which every man has a right and interest who has an eye to perceive and a heart to enjoy'. But it was to take more than a century before the Lake District became a national park in Britain, and it was very different from 'the sort of national property' which Wordsworth had envisaged.

Today, there are 11 national parks of England and Wales: the Brecon Beacons, the Broads, Dartmoor, Exmoor, the Lake District, Northumberland, the North York Moors, the Peak, the Pembrokeshire Coast, Snowdonia and the Yorkshire Dales. 'National park' is the highest designation for landscape protection in Britain, but despite their title, these parks are not owned by the nation; neither are they uninhabited wilderness, as in many other countries. About 250,000 people live and work inside national park boundaries, some of them in industries which do great damage to their supposedly protected landscapes.

When the parks were originally formed, only two of them, the Lake District and the Peak, had their own independent national park authorities with special duties to protect and enhance their landscapes and to promote understanding and suitable open-air enjoyment. The remaining parks initially remained under county council control, which resulted in inevitable conflicts of interest with regards to management and

The History of Britain's National Parks

During the 19th century, there was an increased appreciation of wild, uncultivated landscape. By the early 20th century, outdoor recreational activities such as walking and cycling enjoyed ever greater popularity, particularly among the middle and working classes. These people became frustrated when vast tracts of moor and mountain were closed to the public by owners anxious to keep the land for activities such as grouse shooting.

The Peak District was a classic example of these restrictions. The area totalled around 150,000 acres (around 60,000 hectares), but only about 1,200 acres (480 hectares) were open to the public. Disputes between walkers and landowners finally culminated in the Mass Trespass on Kinder Scout in 1932. Popular demand for access to the moorlands and mountains grew, and led to the formation of a number of recreational societies, such as the Ramblers' Association, which campaigned for the rights of walkers.

The other significant development during the early 20th century was increased awareness of the need to protect Britain's open spaces from ill-conceived and unrestricted building developments. Various conservation bodies amalgamated into organisations, the most notable being the Council for the Protection of Rural England.

These societies grew in strength and in influence, and parliament finally had to start taking note. In the 1870s, the world's first national park had been created at Yellowstone in the USA, specifically to protect the land and allow its use for outdoor activities, and in 1929 the British prime minister agreed to set up an enquiry into the possibility of national parks in Britain. The subsequent report, published in 1931, recommended the establishment of a national park authority to select the areas most appropriate for designation as national parks. A change of government and the Depression of the 1930s meant that these recommendations were not put into effect.

Frustration with the lack of progress resulted in a large conference being held in London in 1935. As a direct result of this, the Standing Committee on National Parks (SCNP) was born in 1936, with the single goal of creating national parks. SCNP members were drawn from several societies, representing the interests of both the conservationists and the recreationists. They published a manifesto which stated their general objective: '(a) That a sufficient number of extensive areas, carefully selected from the unspoilt wilder country of Britain, should be strictly preserved and specifically run as National Parks; (b) that the remainder of the unspoilt wilder country should be regarded as a reserve for further National Parks in the future, any developments therein being permitted only if shown to be essential in the public interest'.

This formed the crux of their campaign over the following decade, which culminated in the National Parks & Access to the Countryside Act of 1949. The door was now open: between 1951 and 1957 there were 10 national parks created; the first was the Peak District, and the last the Brecon Beacons. In 1989 the Norfolk & Suffolk Broads Special Area achieved the same status as a national park, bringing the total to 11. ∎

developments within the parks. However, the Lake District and the Peak still had their problems – the cement factory in the heart of the Hope Valley in the Peak and the new A66 carving its way through the countryside to Keswick in the Lake District were felt by many to be wholly inappropriate constructions.

More recently, the ever-increasing pressures of tourism have been felt, with conflicts over issues such as traffic control, caravan sites and footpath erosion. The Peak National Park is now the second-most visited park in the world (Mount Fuji being the busiest), with 22 million visitors each year. The control and protection of beautiful landscapes by the national park authorities is clearly vital.

The 1995 Environment Act made all national park authorities freestanding – ie independent of county council control – but they still perform a difficult tightrope act, balancing the need for the conservation of their superb landscapes with the needs of the people who live and work in them and the huge numbers of visitors who use them for recreation. They represent a typically British compromise, and in cases of conflict they can often find themselves in a no-win situation.

The current total number of visits to the British national parks is over 100 million every year. Some conservationists – particularly those in Scotland – believe that parks are counterproductive. They point out that the designation of areas as national parks creates an increase in visitors, which in turn puts an unsustainable pressure on the land and local resources. It seems there is never an easy solution.

Areas of Outstanding Natural Beauty & Heritage Coasts

The second tier of protection covers Areas of Outstanding Natural Beauty (AONBs). There are about 40 such areas including the Cotswold Hills, the Wye Valley, the North Pennines and the Sussex Downs – all areas which have excellent walking opportunities and which are covered in this book. In AONBs, planning authorities are charged with having a special concern for the protection of the landscape, but they don't have the teeth of a national park authority.

Areas protected primarily for their landscape, such as national parks and AONBs, are 'designated' by the Countryside Commission (CC), a government body that can also designate important coastal regions as heritage coasts.

National Scenic Areas

In Scotland, for various historical reasons, there are no national parks or AONBs. Instead, National Scenic Areas (NSAs) have been set aside where the local authorities must have special concern for the landscape. Examples of these areas are Ben Nevis & Glen Coe, the Cairngorms, North Arran and Kintail. Again, all these areas are ideal for walking and are described in this book.

Other Designated Areas

As well as national parks, AONBs and heritage coasts, there is a seemingly endless variety of other 'designated', or protected, areas in Britain, and an even greater number of connected abbreviations. You will see NNRs, SSSIs, FNRs, ESAs, CSSs and SPAs, many of which overlap. Far be it from us to mock any scheme established to protect Britain's unique and fascinating variety of

landscapes and wildlife, but it is hard for visitors (and locals) to make sense of this plethora of initials and distinguish between the places they stand for.

Those who suspect a conspiracy claim that the sheer number of governmental organisations charged with environmental protection is a deliberate move to prevent any one body becoming too powerful. Whether this is true or not, there are two important points to remember: like national parks, most designated areas consist of privately owned land; and these special designations do not normally affect rights of way – where they exist, you can use them without worry.

National Nature Reserves NNRs have been established by English Nature (EN), which is a government body responsible for wildlife conservation in England, to protect the most important areas of wildlife habitat and geological formation in Britain, and as places of scientific research. Examples include such diverse places as Blakeney, which is on the Norfolk coast, and Benn Eighe in the Torridons. The largest is the Cairngorms, and the smallest is Swanscombe in Kent – the site of the oldest human bones found in Britain.

Sites of Special Scientific Interest SSSIs are also designated by English Nature. In Scotland and Wales, designated areas are the responsibility of Scottish Natural Heritage (SNH) and the Countryside Council for Wales (CCW). (For more details, see the Useful Organisations section of the Facts for the Walker chapter.)

Forest Nature Reserves FNRs are run by the Forestry Commission (a government agency renamed Forest Enterprise in some areas) and they have been selected to represent the very best forestry conservation sites, with an enormous variety of forest types and wildlife habitats. All are accessible to the public, and many have established nature trails and footpaths.

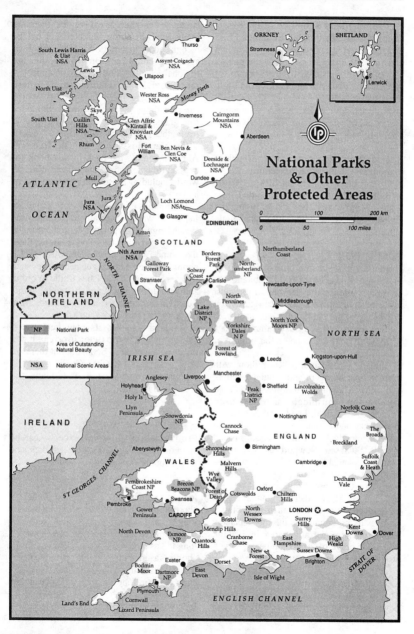

Environmentally Sensitive Areas & Countryside Stewardship Schemes ESAs and CSSs are intended to protect farmland and make it more accessible to the public. These are administered by the Ministry of Agriculture, Fisheries and Food (MAFF), in consultation with EN and the CC, although critics such as the Ramblers' Association claim such schemes are ineffective and underutilised.

Special Protection Areas One final abbreviation: SPA, for Special Protection Area. An NNR can be designated an SPA under the ECBD (European Community Birds Directive). What does this actually mean? Probably that you should leave your shotgun at home...

POPULATION

Britain has a population of over 56 million, or around an average of 600 inhabitants per sq mile, making the island one of the most crowded on the planet. To these figures you can factor in an annual influx of nearly 20 million tourists. (On a busy summer's day, many of these seem to be on the summit of Scafell Pike.)

England's population is 48 million, with most people living in and around London, and in the Midlands and northern conurbations around Birmingham, Manchester, Liverpool, Sheffield, Leeds and Newcastle. Wales has a population of around three million, mostly based in the south around Cardiff, Swansea, Newport and the industrial Valleys area. Scotland has a population of just over five million people; the largest cities are Glasgow, Edinburgh, Aberdeen and Dundee. The northern Highlands region of Scotland, containing much of Britain's finest walking country, is the most sparsely populated administrative area in Britain, with an average of 20 people per sq mile – 30 times less than the national average.

LANGUAGE

The English language is perhaps Britain's most significant contribution to the modern world. In the 'home country', though, the language continues to evolve, and there are many English words which would not be recognised or understood in other English-speaking countries. On top of this are regional accents (some verging on dialects – most notably the Geordie of Northern England), using many local words, which can sometimes be virtually impenetrable for foreigners, and often difficult for people from other parts of England too!

See the Glossary of British Terms & Abbreviations at the back of this book for explanations of some peculiarly English words, including those relating to mountains and walking.

But English is not Britain's only language. In parts of Wales (especially in the north), the Welsh language is spoken as a mother tongue by many. (So don't be surprised or insulted, like some English people are, when Welsh people use their own language in places such as pubs and shops.) Welsh is Celtic in origin and very different to English, making it difficult for foreigners (including those from England) to pronounce (see aside).

Scotland also has its own language – Gaelic – which is also Celtic in origin. It was once spoken in all of Scotland, but there are now only about 80,000 Gaelic-speakers, mainly in north-west Scotland and the Hebridean islands.

Welsh

Pronunciation All vowels except y can be short or long. A circumflex (^) lengthens the vowel sound.

long **a**	as in hard	*tad* (father)
short **a**	as in ham	*mam* (mother)
long **e**	as in sane	*hen* (old)
short **e**	as in ten	*pen* (head)
long **i**	as in geese	*mis* (month)
short **i**	as in shin	*prin* (scarce)
long **o**	as in more	*môr* (sea)
short **o**	as in fond	*ffon* (walking stick)
long **w**	as in moon	*swn* (sound)
short **w**	as in look	*gwn* (gun)

The Welsh Language

The one thing that marks Wales out so distinctly from the rest of Britain is the survival of Welsh as a living language. Welsh, with its weird-looking and seemingly unpronounceable chains of consecutive consonants, is an Indo-European language. It is part of the Celtic group of languages which also includes Scots Gaelic, Irish, Manx, Cornish and Breton.

The Welsh language was spoken in various early forms during the first millennium BC. During the Roman occupation of Britain, many parts of Wales were colonised. People in positions of authority probably spoke Latin, while the commoners spoke Welsh. Gradually, a bilingual Latin/Welsh-speaking population emerged, and the influence of Latin on Welsh is clear. The language as it is spoken today seems to have been more or less fully developed by the 6th century, making it one of Europe's oldest languages, although later influences included French (from the Norman period) and, of course, English.

From around the 13th century, English attempts to colonise Wales (and their eventual success) had a detrimental effect on the language. Following the Act of Union in 1536, it was forbidden for people to hold high office unless they spoke English as well as Welsh. Bishop Morgan's translation of the Bible in 1588 is thought to have played an important part in keeping the language alive.

During the 17th and 18th centuries, the nonconformist sects that made such headway in Wales also supported the native language. However, the 19th century Industrial Revolution brought a whole new class of industrial landlords and employers, few of whom spoke Welsh. From then on, the number of native Welsh-speakers went into steep decline. At the start of the 19th century, 80% of the population probably spoke Welsh, but by 1901 this had fallen to 50%. In 1991, only 19% of the population spoke Welsh.

Today, Welsh speakers are concentrated particularly in the north-western and western parts of the country, where up to 75% of the population of a given locality may speak the language. In contrast, only 2.4% of people living in the southern county of Gwent know more than the odd word.

Reasons for the decline in the number of people speaking Welsh are not hard to find: TV, better communications, emigration, mixed marriages and tourism are just some of those commonly cited. Perhaps more surprising is that so many people have continued to speak the language despite all these threats. Indeed, in the 1980s and 1990s there was revived interest in the language, not least among 'incomers' (people originally from elsewhere, usually England, who came to settle in Wales).

Since the 1960s, the importance of Welsh has been officially recognised, and in 1967 the Welsh Language Act ensured that Welsh-speakers could use their own language in court. Since then an increasing number of publications have been bilingual, and it's rare nowadays to see a road sign in just one language. Various government grants are available to promote and encourage the continued use of Welsh. In 1982, Channel 4 set up S4C, which broadcasts daily Welsh TV programmes. Radio Cymru also transmits in Welsh, and roughly 400 books a year are published in the language.

In 1988, a Welsh Language Board was set up to advise the Secretary of State for Wales on everything to do with the language, while in 1994, a new Welsh Language Act gave equal validity to Welsh as a language for use in public-sector businesses – it's now illegal to discriminate against Welsh-speakers, in employment for example. Some shops and food producers have developed bilingual signing and packaging.

If all this sounds almost too good to be true, there are those who would argue that the cause of the Welsh language has been mainly espoused by middle-class incomers as a way of ensuring themselves grants and jobs. There are also English visitors who get very hot under the collar when they visit Welsh-speaking areas and find themselves unable to understand what is being said. The Welsh-speakers point out that it's no different from going to any other country where, naturally, everybody speaks their own language, and the anger is just another example of English arrogance. For non-British visitors it's a fascinating subject, but one on which it's probably not wise to express strong opinions without first getting a good grip on the facts. ■

y	has three possible pronunciations:	
	as the 'ee' in geese	*dyn* (man)
	as the 'i' in tin	*cyn* (before)
	as the 'u' in run	*dynion* (men)
oe	is pronounced 'oy'	
	as in annoyed	*coed* (wood)

u	is pronounced 'i'	
	as in pimp	*pump* (five)

Welsh consonants are similar to English, but there are a few extra specialities:

c   is always hard, pronounced as in the

Llanfair PG

Wales is famous for having the longest place name in the world. On the island of Anglesea, just a short distance from Snowdonia, is a small village called Llanfairpwllgwyngyllgogerychwyrndrobwllllantysiliogogogoch. Translated, it means 'St Mary's church in the hollow of the white hazel near a rapid whirlpool and the church of St Tysilio near the red cave'. Can be tricky – those four 'L's in a row are a real stumbling block – so most people call it Llanfair PG. (Llanfair is pronounced 'Lchan-viyer'.) Local myth has it that the name is not original but was invented by the local hotel owner in Victorian times when trade was a bit slack and he wanted a gimmick to pull the crowds. It worked, and still pulls them in today. ■

English word 'cat' for example: *cwm* (valley or corrie)

ch	as in loch	*fach*	(small)
dd	as 'th' in them	*mynydd*	(mountain)
f	as in of	*fach*	(small)
ff	as in off	*ffenestr*	(window)
g	as in garden	*gwyn*	(white)
th	as in three	*byth*	(ever)
ll			

there is no exact equivalent sound in English, although it comes somewhere between an English 'l' and the Scottish 'ch' (as in 'loch'), only a bit softer, something like the 'tl' in antler *llyn* lake

Words & Phrases – English to Welsh

If you're feeling brave, here are a few expressions you might try out in the Welsh-speaking parts of the country (the accent usually falls on the second-last syllable in Welsh pronunciation):

Good morning	*bore da*
Good afternoon	*prynhawn da*
Good night	*nos da*
How are you?	*sut mae?* or *S'mae?*
Thank you	*diolch*
good	*da*
very good	*da iawn*
cheers	*hwyl*

Words & Phrases – Welsh to English

It's more likely that you'll need to translate Welsh words into English. Words you may come across include the following:

merched	women
dynion	men
allanfa	exit
ar agor	open
ar gau	closed
Cymru	Wales
am byth	forever

While walking you may see the following words on maps and signposts:

aber	river mouth
afon	river
bach/fach	small
bryn	hill
bwlch	pass
cadair	stronghold/chair
caer	fort
capel	chapel
carnedd	mountain
clogwyn	cliff
coch	red
coed	wood/forest
craig	crag
crib/grib	ridge
cromlech	burial chamber
cwm	cirque/corrie/valley
de	south
din/dinas	fort
du	black
dyffryn	valley
ffordd	road
ffynnon	spring

glan	shore	*newydd*	new
glas	blue	*ogof*	cave
glyn	valley	*pen*	headland or peak
goch/coch	red	*pistyll*	spout or well
gwyn	white	*pont*	bridge
gwyrdd	green	*pwll*	pool
llan	church	*rhaeadr*	waterfall
llwybr cyhoeddus	public footpath	*rhiw*	slope
		rhos	moor/marsh
llyn	lake	*tre*	town
mawr/fawr	big	*twr*	tower
moel	hill	*ty*	house
mynydd	mountain	*ynys*	island
nant	stream/valley	*ystwyth*	winding

      =

Facts for the Walker

This chapter is divided into several sections. Sections covering general matters for all visitors (eg passports, visas and public holidays) are fairly brief, as this information can be found in other sources (see the Books section of this chapter for some recommendations). Sections containing information specifically for walkers (eg accommodation and maps) are more comprehensive.

WHEN TO WALK
Read the Climate section of the Facts about Britain chapter and you'll see that the best seasons for walking in Britain are Spring, Summer and Autumn. This means March/April to September/October, which is, not surprisingly, the time when most Brits go on holiday too. There are more public transport options and more tourist information centres (TICs) open during this period.

July and August are school holidays and the busiest months. Public holidays (see the Business Hours & Public Holidays section later in this chapter) are also very busy. At these times the crowds on the coasts and in the national parks can affect some of the routes we describe in this book and there are some regional factors which have to be taken into account, such as midges in Scotland (see the Scotland – Short Walks chapter).

Generally speaking, the further north you go, and the higher the mountains, the shorter the walking season. This is because in the high northern areas winter conditions stretch from September to April, making walking not just unpleasant but actually dangerous if you're not properly equipped. Particularly, this bad weather means snow and ice, which make most walking routes impassable without ice-axe, crampons and specialist knowledge. 'Technical' walks of this nature are beyond scope of this book.

Once you come off the high mountains, however, you can walk in Britain at any time of year. The landscape of Southern England, and some parts of Wales and Northern England,

is such that even in winter, although the weather might be bad, it is never bad enough to make conditions 'technical'. In fact, a beautiful crisp midwinter's day is always preferable to one of the damp, misty days that can occur in high summer and at any other time of the year.

The other factor to consider is hours of daylight. In summer in Northern England it's light from around 5 am to 8 or 9 pm. In winter you get little more than half this, as it's only light between 8 am and 5 pm. As you go further north you encounter greater extremes. In Scotland in summer it only gets dark for a few hours around midnight, and your days out can be luxuriously long. Conversely, during a Scottish winter you only have about five or six hours to play with.

WHAT TO BRING
We're assuming that you've come to Britain to combine walking with 'normal' travel, but most of the clothing and equipment you need is suitable for both. Don't forget that Britain is full of markets, department stores and outdoor equipment shops, so anything you forget or don't have can easily be bought on the spot as you need it.

Equipment
Your No 1 essential item is a rucksack. Many travellers these days use 'travelpacks' – a combination of backpack and shoulder bag, where straps and harnesses can be zipped away when not needed, making it easy to handle in airports and on crowded public transport. They also look reasonably smart if you want to escape the 'backpacker' image at a high-class establishment, and can be made reasonably thief-proof with small combination locks. However, if you are going to use one of these bags for a long-distance walk (ie carrying most of your gear) be absolutely sure it's comfortable. Some travelpacks have sophisticated shoulder-strap adjustment systems and can be used

Events & Festivals

As well as taking walking seasons into account as you plan your trip to Britain, you might like to also consider some of the diverse events and festivals held around the country at various times of year. (In a few instances this brief list may even help you to decide which places to avoid.) The following is only a selection, and are mostly near walking routes or areas described in this book. There's always something going on in London, so those events are not listed here. For more details get the British Tourist Authority (BTA) publications *Forthcoming Events* and *Arts Festivals*.

Last week in March
> *Oxford/Cambridge University Boat Race* – traditional rowing race; River Thames, Putney to Mortlake, London

Mid-May
> *Royal Windsor Horse Show* – major showjumping event; Windsor

Last week in May
> *Bath International Festival* – arts festival; runs for two weeks

Mid-June
> *Appleby Horse Fair* – traditional Gypsy fair; Appleby, Cumbria

Late June
> *Henley Royal Regatta* – premier rowing and social event; River Thames, Henley-on-Thames, Oxfordshire
> *Glastonbury Festival* – huge open-air music festival and hippy happening; Glastonbury, Somerset
> *Royal Highland Show* – Scotland's national agricultural show; Edinburgh

Mid-July
> *Royal Welsh Show* – national agricultural show; Llanelwedd, Builth Wells

Late July
> *Cowes Week* – yachting extravaganza; Isle of Wight

Early August
> *Royal National Eisteddfod of Wales* – cultural festival; Wales, different venues every year

Mid-August
> *Edinburgh International & Fringe Festivals* – premier international arts festivals
> *Derbyshire Well Dressing* – decorated springs and wells in villages all over Derbyshire

Late August (August Bank Holiday)
> *Reading Festival* – outdoor rock & roll for three days; Reading, Berkshire

Early September
> *Braemar Royal Highland Gathering* – kilts and cabers; Braemar, Grampian

5 November
> *Guy Fawkes Day* – in memory of an attempted coup; bonfire and fireworks celebrations around the country

Of special interst to walkers is the Scottish Borders Festival of Walking (see the Scotland – Long-Distance Paths chapter for more details). ■

comfortably, even for long hikes, but you have to take a lot more care with your packing, otherwise they tend to sag. Try it before you depart on a long-distance route, by loading it up and walking for a day. If it's not right, consider a conventional rucksack, and a large and lightweight plastic kit bag that the whole rucksack can fit in for those times you want to look smart.

Walking in Britain does not require a tent, although you may choose to camp to save money or to give yourself independence and flexibility. Exactly what type of tent you use depends on your own preference. It does not need to be too high-tech, as you are unlikely to be camping in Himalayan hurricane conditions (although some parts of the Lakes and Scotland can get pretty blowy in Autumn), but it should be light enough to carry easily.

Next on the list are sleeping bag, mat, stove and cooking gear. If you are camping, or if you plan to use bothies and bunkhouses (see the Accommodation section of this chapter for more details) you will need these items. Open fires are generally not allowed anywhere.

Many people prefer to use hostels, which usually have kitchen facilities and bedding (see the Accommodation section of this chapter): all you need is a personal wash kit and (in some hostels) a sleeping bag sheet. You may decide to use only bed & breakfasts (B&Bs) or hotels, where everything is supplied, allowing you to travel light.

The following items are also required or recommended wherever you walk and travel in Britain and whatever your accommodation choice:

compass – essential for some walks, as is the skill to use it

pocketknife – with bottle and can opener (and strong corkscrew if you plan to live well)

padlock – to secure your bag or hostel locker

torch (flashlight)

alarm clock or watch

sunglasses

sunscreen & sunblock

lip salve

whistle (for emergency signalling)

polythene survival bag (emergency shelter for mountain or moorland walks)

water bottle or flexible carriers

medical & first aid kit

For more details on walking equipment, or emergency situations and how to avoid them,

see the Safety section of this chapter. For details of what to include in a medical & first aid kit, see the Health section of this chapter.

Clothing

A minimum packing list for general travel could include two pairs of trousers, a pair of shorts or a skirt, a few T-shirts or shirts, underwear, socks, a warm sweater or sweatshirt, a solid and comfortable pair of shoes, sandals or thongs, a weatherproof coat.

For walking, you'll need to add to this. If you're a keen walker, you may already possess much of what's required, although you must be prepared for the vagaries of the British climate. You should also be aware that the weather can change very quickly. So the best rule, if in doubt, is to go prepared for the worst! With that in mind, the advice given here is weighted towards what you should have for hill or mountain-walking; you can compromise to an extent for lowland walks.

In general, the best approach to clothing is the layering principle, using several thin layers which you can peel off or add to in order to maintain your comfort level.

British summers may have been getting warmer, but a good set of waterproofs – jacket and trousers – is advisable for lowland walks, and absolutely essential for upland areas, where wind and rain can make hypothermia a reality. Fabrics that breathe, such as Goretex or Sympatex, improve your comfort level, but design is also important. The jacket should have a storm flap over the main zip, drawcords at either waist or bottom hem (or both), and some kind of hood. A stiffened peak helps keep rain off your face, and the best modern designs are cut away at the sides to maintain peripheral vision – a useful safety feature if you're picking your way across tricky terrain. Waterproof trousers should preferably have zips, so they can be pulled on without your having to take your boots off first; and if they're going to do their job properly, the leg zips should be backed by gussets, so there's no chance of leaks.

You need something to keep you warm, and whilst a woollen pullover will do the job, a lightweight polyester fleece top integrates better with a waterproof jacket made of a fabric that breathes. You can buy fleece tops with windproof membranes, but these reduce the flexibility of your layering system. Your waterproof jacket will provide windproofing if you need it. If you want something less bulky, consider a lightweight windshirt made from a synthetic microfibre fabric.

The same principle applies to what's worn next to the skin. You can live with cotton, but for optimum comfort and performance, go for a synthetic base layer which is able to 'wick' sweat away from the skin.

Legwear for hill-walking should ideally be something with some 'give' to allow freedom of movement – when you're stepping up, for example. Tracksuit bottoms and their variants are very popular – otherwise go for lightweight windproof trousers made from polycotton or synthetic microfibre. Denim jeans are heavy, unyielding, and can be dangerous when wet, so save them for the pub in the evening.

Other essentials are a hat and gloves, which provide valuable insulation in cooler conditions. And, not forgetting Britain's varied weather, you should also have a wide-brimmed or peaked hat for sun protection in the summer.

Footwear Even if the rest of your gear is not top flight, you should never try to compromise on footwear. It is, after all, the key to an enjoyable and successful walk. Ideally, this is something you need to sort out before your holiday, as you can run into problems taking brand new boots on a long walk. Whilst walking boots are generally less painful to 'break in' these days, it's still wise to allow a little time for your feet and new boots to get to know each other before doing anything more than a short stroll, particularly if you're doing a multi-day walk with a weighty pack on your back.

Walking shoes or trainers will probably be fine for short or lowland walks, but for several routes described in this book, boots are highly recommended. These can be made of good-quality fabric or lightweight leather – as epitomised by the Brasher Hillmaster, Britain's best-selling boot of this kind, proceeds from the sale of which, incidentally, support the John Muir Trust (see the Useful Organisations section of this chapter) in its purchase and preservation of wilderness areas.

There are plenty of alternatives to choose from, but the main thing to look for in a boot for upland walking is good support underfoot and protection around the ankles. A sole with widely spaced treads and a stepped heel provides the best security on rough terrain. This latter point is important if you're more used to networks of well-maintained trails, since in many places – the Pennines, for example – what's marked as a footpath on the map may in practice be undefined rough terrain. Leather can be waxed or treated to make it waterproof for several hours, and many makes of fabric boot also have waterproof linings. Lightweight fabric boots without a waterproof lining are best suited to lowland walking, well-defined paths or hot, dry summers in the hills.

Good boots make a difference, but so do socks. Synthetic or synthetic/wool mix loop stitch socks provide the best cushioning for

feet. Quality socks will have flat seams around the toes to avoid causing discomfort. Whether you prefer to walk in two pairs of socks or one is down to personal preference and the idiosyncrasies of your feet. Thin liner socks are often useful for fine-tuning the fit of your boots.

Gaiters are a very useful piece of kit for walking in Britain, when conditions underfoot can be wet, rough, boggy or all three. They don't need to be the extreme 'yeti'-type which are fixed to your boot with a rubber seal. They just need to keep the infamous British mud from falling into the top of your boot.

TOURIST OFFICES
Local Tourist Offices

There are Tourist Information Centres (TICs) all over Britain. Every city and large town has at least one TIC, and even small places in tourist areas have TICs in the summer season (April through October) or a Village Information Point – a noticeboard or leaflet dispenser – in a post office or shop. TICs give advice on accommodation (often with a free booking service which saves you lots of chasing around) and have plenty of information about their region, including local events and festivals, and walking routes. In national parks, the Park Information Centre (PIC) and the TIC often share premises but give different sorts of information. You will find that PICs help with wildlife and conservation questions, and TICs with accommodation and transport. PICs and TICs are listed in the sections of this book describing the individual walks.

A very useful and free national telephone information service called Talking Pages (☎ 0800 600900) can give you details of all 560 TICs in Britain, telling you the nearest one to the place you want to visit, their opening times, the services they offer etc.

Tourist Offices Abroad

The British Tourist Authority (BTA), representing the tourist boards of England, Scotland and Wales, has offices in several countries around the world. It has an extensive collection of information, quite a lot of it free, including accommodation lists and a very good leaflet called *Britain for Walkers*, listing routes, maps and walking-tour companies. The BTA can also advise on public transport passes and discounts, but you should contact it before you leave home, because some items are only available outside Britain. Addresses of some BTA offices abroad are:

Australia
  8th floor, University Centre, 210 Clarence St, Sydney, NSW 2000 (☎ (02) 9267 4555; fax (02) 9267 4442; E-mail 100247.243@compuserve.com)
Canada
  Suite 450, 111 Avenue Rd, Toronto, Ontario M5R 3JD (☎ 416-925 6326; fax 416-961 2175)
Denmark
  Montergade 3, 1116 Copenhagen K (☎ 33 33 91 88)
France
  Tourisme de Grand-Bretagne, Maison de la Grande Bretagne, 19 rue des Mathurins, 75009 Paris (entrance in les rues Tronchet et Auber; ☎ 01 44 51 56 20)
Germany
  Taunusstrasse 52-60, 60329 Frankfurt (☎ 069-238 0711)
Ireland
  18-19 College Green, Dublin 2 (☎ 01-670 8000; fax 670 8244)
Italy
  Corso V, Emanuele 337, 00186 Rome (☎ 06-6880 6821)
Japan
  Tokyo Club Building, 3-2-6 Kasumigaseki, Chiyoda-ku, Tokyo 100 (☎ 03-3581 3603)
Netherlands
  Stadhouderskade 2 (5e), 1054 ES Amsterdam (☎ 020-685 50 51)
New Zealand
  3rd floor, Dilworth Building, cnr Queen & Customs Sts, Auckland 1 (☎ 09-303 1446; fax 09-377 6965)
Norway
  Postbox 1554 Vika, 0117 Oslo 1 (☎ 095-468 212444)
Singapore
  24 Raffles Place, 19-06 Clifford Centre, Singapore 048621 (☎ 535 2966)
South Africa
  Lancaster Gate, Hyde Lane, Hyde Park, Sandton 2196 (☎ 011-325 0343)
Spain
  Torre de Madrid 6/5, Plaza de Espana 18, 28008 Madrid (☎ 91-541 13 96)

Sweden
> Klara Norra Kyrkogata 29, S 111 22 Stockholm
> (☎ 08-21 24 44)

Switzerland
> Limmatquai 78, CH-8001 Zurich (☎ 01-261 42 77)

USA
> 625 N Michigan Ave, Suite 1510, Chicago IL
> 60611 (personal callers only)

There are more than 40 BTA offices worldwide. Addresses are listed on their web site (http://www.bta.org.uk).

USEFUL ORGANISATIONS

Britain has a huge number of organisations which administer and/or promote walking, outdoor activities and other countryside matters. Some are very useful to join, as they provide services such as handbooks and discounts for members. Others you might want to contact for information, or it might simply be helpful to know who they are, as you may come across their names during your walking trip.

Ramblers' Association

The RA (☎ 0171 5826878), at 1-5 Wandsworth Rd, London SW8 2XX, is Britain's largest and most active national walking organisation. (For more information, see the History of Walking in Britain section of the Facts about Britain chapter and the Walkers' Rights & Responsibilities section of this chapter.) It produces a great range of booklets and leaflets (cheap or free) covering various aspects of walking in Britain, which are ideal for visitors from abroad. Also very useful is its *Yearbook*, which is free to members, or £5 to nonmembers (see the Books section of this chapter). If you're spending a while in one place, you can hook up with one of the RA's local groups and join its walks.

Long Distance Walkers Association

This club, at 117 Higher Lane, Rainford, St Helens, Merseyside WA11 8BQ, is for those who like long day-walks – more than 20 miles (32 km) – or multi-day walks in rural or mountainous areas. It also promotes challenge walking (covering set distances

within a set time). If you're a member of a similar organisation in your own country, or based in Britain for a long time, you might like to join.

Backpackers' Club

You can write to the Backpackers' Club (☎ 01491 680684) at PO Box 381, Reading, Berkshire RG4 5YY. While these days 'backpacking' generally means budget travel with a rucksack, this organisation promotes and supports backpacking in its true and original sense: completely self-contained and self-sufficient travel on foot in rural or wilderness areas. If you're based in Britain for a long period and enjoy this kind of walking, you may want to join the club. The club produces a directory to campsites and other places that members can camp on most LDPs in Britain.

Mountaineering Council of Scotland

MCofS, as it is known (☎ 01738 638227), at 4A St Catherine's Rd, Perth PH1 5SE, represents mountaineers, climbers and hill-walkers in Scotland. If you intend doing a lot of walking in Scotland, it might be worth joining, as it can help with information, particularly on the thorny issues of access and freedom to roam. It produces a useful book called *Heading for the Scottish Hills* (available from Cordee for £5.95) and can recommend qualified mountain guides if you're not competent to go alone.

British Mountaineering Council

The BMC (☎ 0161 4454747), at 177 Burton Rd, Manchester M20 2BB, is the English and Welsh equivalent of MCofS, although it tends to have a bias towards climbing rather than walking. It produces a useful book called *Safety on Mountains*, which covers everything you need to know if you're new to walking in the higher parts of Britain. It can also recommend qualified mountain guides.

Youth Hostels Association of England & Wales

The YHA (☎ 01727 855215) is at 8 St

Stephen's Hill, St Albans, Herts AL1 2DY. To use YHA hostels (described in the Accommodation section of this chapter), citizens of England and Wales must be YHA members. Visitors from abroad must be members of their own national hostel organisation, or Hostelling International (HI; also called the International Youth Hostels Federation). Membership of YHA (or HI) costs adults £9 and allows use of YHA hostels, Scottish Youth Hostels Association (SYHA) hostels in Scotland, and YHA hostels worldwide. You can join at any hostel or by writing to the above address. You can also join at YHA Adventure Shops (ring ☎ 01784 458625 for details of your nearest branch). London's branch is at 14 Southampton St, Covent Garden. YHA members also get discounts on outdoor equipment and the invaluable *YHA Accommodation Guide* listing every hostel in England and Wales, with details of facilities, prices, opening days and times, local transport and so on. If you're already a member of YHA or another hostelling organisation, you can buy the guide for £3. If you only plan to use a few hostels, temporary membership costs an extra £1.50 per night.

The YHA also produces useful leaflets for walkers, including lists of hostels along several long-distance walks (which contains a form so you can book them all in one go) and suggested walks between hostels in places like the Lake District and Peak District.

Scottish Youth Hostels Association

Like its partner organisation south of the border, the SYHA (☎ 01786 451181), at 7 Glebe Crescent, Stirling FK8 2JA, runs a network of hostels, many in walking areas. To join costs adults £6. Citizens from abroad pay the same fee to become members of YHA. The same reciprocal agreements with other countries (including England and Wales) apply. The colourful *Budget Accommodation in Scotland* handbook (£1.50 to nonmembers) lists details of every SYHA hostel and is, once again, invaluable.

The Camping & Caravanning Club

The Camping & Caravanning Club (☎ 01203 694995), Greenfields House, Westwood Way, Coventry CV4 8JH, is Britain's leading club for users of caravans, campervans and 'big tents', but it also caters for lightweight campers. The club owns several sites around the country, where members get cheap rates, and lists and certifies several hundred more. Club sites are generally very well organised, with excellent facilities like hot showers, laundrettes and shops. Staff can also provide local information. Certified sites are all good quality, but facilities vary. If you're planning to camp a lot during your visit to Britain, membership is well worthwhile. The club handbook (free to members, £8 to nonmembers) lists every club, certified and listed site in Britain and ties in very neatly with Ordnance Survey (OS) maps' coverage of the country.

National Trust

The NT (☎ 0171 2229251), at 36 Queen Anne's Gate, London SW1H 9AS, is not a government agency (although many people think it is) and has no direct link with national parks (despite the similar title). The NT is a conservation charity, established over a century ago and now a major landowner, with various estates and large wilderness areas, plus nearly 620 miles (1000 km) of coastline, parks and woods all over England and Wales, which receive some 40 million visitors every year. The NT also owns various gardens and many historic buildings. The National Trust for Scotland (NTS; ☎ 0131 2265922) has similar objectives and responsibilities in Scotland. Membership of NT or NTS gets you free or reduced rates at their properties where an entrance fee is charged (eg at several castles passed by walks described in this book). The annual fee is £24 or £10 for those under 23. Visitors from abroad can get a Touring Ticket, which gives unlimited free entrance for one or two weeks (£9/18). Walkers on NT or NTS open land usually enjoy complete freedom of access without charge. In 1996, the NT received a major grant from Barclays Bank to support conservation and access projects, including footpath improvements and repairs.

Countryside Commission & English Nature

These are two government agencies which administer, support and advise on conservation in rural areas in England. The CC has a special interest in recreational matters, including national parks, national trails and regional routes, while EN is concerned mainly with wildlife matters, including National Nature Reserves (NNRs) and Sites of Special Scientific Interest (SSSIs). (See the National Parks & Other Protected Areas section of the Facts about Britain chapter for information about NNRs and SSSIs.) These two bodies do a lot of work for walkers and other countryside users, but critics point out that as government agencies they lack the power or resolve to combat some other government-backed schemes, such as major road-building projects in environmentally important areas. (For example, see the St Catherine's Hill & Twyford Down aside in the Southern England – Long-Distance Paths chapter.)

Scottish Natural Heritage & Countryside Council for Wales

These government agencies administer and support all rural recreation and conservation matters in Scotland and Wales, including management of NNRs and SSSIs. They are also involved with administration of national parks in Wales and National Scenic Areas (NSAs) in Scotland.

English Heritage

EH (☎ 0171 9733434), at PO Box 9019, London W1A 0JA, is a government agency with responsibility for conserving and protecting ancient and historic monuments, including castles, stately homes, stone circles and major sites like Hadrian's Wall. Admission to some sites is free, but others charge between £1 and £4. Membership of EH gets you free admission to all sites in England and reduced rates in Scotland and Wales, and costs £19 for adults (or £31 for two adults at the same address), £36 for families and £20 for one-parent families. (Incidentally, members also get free entry to many historic sites in Australia and New Zealand.) Visitors from abroad can get temporary membership (£10 for two weeks). The walks described in this book pass many EH sites, so joining is well worth considering if you are a history fan. The companion organisations are Historic Scotland (☎ 0131 6888800) and Welsh Historic Monuments (☎ 01222 500200).

Members of Australia's National Trust get free entrance to English Heritage sites.

Conservation Groups

As a walker in Britain you are likely to cross land which belongs to conservation organisations. These include: The Woodland Trust (☎ 01476 74297), Autumn Park, Dysart Rd, Grantham NG31 6LL, which buys and conserves areas of woodland all over Britain and allows walkers free access to many of them; and the John Muir Trust, Freepost, Musselburgh, Midlothian EH21 7BR, which similarly buys areas of mountain and moorland.

There are many wildlife and environmental groups in Britain. International campaigning organisations include the World Wide Fund for Nature (WWF; ☎ 01483 426444), Panda House, Weyside Park, Godalming, GU7 1XR, and Friends of the Earth (☎ 0171 490 1555), at 26 Underwood St, London N1 7JQ.

Following is a list of organisations that concentrate on British issues:

The Wildlife Trusts (☎ 01522 544400), The Green, Witham Park, Waterside South, Lincoln LN5 7JR, is made up of numerous local groups actively involved in the care of nature reserves and various conservation and education projects.

The Royal Society for the Protection of Birds (☎ 01767 680551), The Lodge, Sandy, Bedfordshire SG19 2BR, runs more than 100 bird reserves, many of which can be visited from the walks described in this book. For £20 per year you get free entry to these reserves, and a quarterly magazine.

The Wildfowl and Wetlands Trust (☎ 01453 890333), Slimbridge, Gloucestershire GL2 7BT, has a more specific agenda, as its name implies. Members get free entry to its nine reserves and a magazine twice a year.

Some of the walking-holiday companies listed in the Walking Tours section of the Getting Around chapter arrange trips with a wildlife bias. Contact them directly for more details.

DOCUMENTS
Passport

All foreign citizens entering Britain need a passport. It should be valid for the whole period of your stay, and for at least six months after. You do not need your passport to travel between England, Scotland and Wales.

Visas

A visa permits you to enter a country. Citizens of Australia, Canada, New Zealand, South Africa or the USA do not need a visa. Tourists from these countries are given 'leave to enter' Britain, which means that they are generally permitted to stay for up to six months, but are prohibited from working. Citizens of the European Union (EU) do not need a visa to enter the country. Note, however, that visa requirements can change, and you should check with your nearest British embassy or high commission (or a reputable travel agent) before travelling.

Other Documents

Apart from your passport, no special documents are required in Britain, but a number are worth considering.

International Driving Permit If you intend to buy or hire a car during your visit, your own driving licence is legal for 12 months from the date you enter Britain. An International Driving Permit (IDP), available from your national driving association, is usually inexpensive and helps officials or car rental staff make sense of your unfamiliar local licence. While you're at it, if you're a member of your home country's national driving association, ask for a letter of introduction. This may entitle you to services offered by reciprocal organisations (touring maps, information, breakdown help, technical advice etc).

Hostelling Card To use youth hostels run by the Youth Hostels Association of England & Wales (YHA) or the Scottish Youth Hostels Association (SYHA) you must be a member of a recognised youth hostelling organisation. (See the Accommodation and Useful Organisations sections of this chapter for details.)

Student & Youth Cards The most useful card for young travellers is the International Student Identity Card (ISIC). It gets you discounts on many forms of transport, and to museums and sights. If you're aged under 26 but not a student, you can apply for a Federation of International Youth Travel Organisations (FIYTO) card or a Euro26 Card, which gives much the same discounts as an ISIC. Hostelling organisations or student travel agencies should be able to advise with this.

EMBASSIES
British Embassies Abroad

British embassies and high commissions abroad include:

Australia (High Commission)
  Commonwealth Ave, Canberra, ACT 2600 (☎ (06) 270 6666)
Canada (High Commission)
  80 Elgin St, Ottawa, Ont KIP 5K7 (☎ 613-237 1530)
New Zealand (High Commission)
  44 Hill St, Wellington 1 (☎ 04-472 6049)
USA (Embassy)
  3100 Massachusetts Ave NW, Washington DC 20008 (☎ 202-462 1340)

Foreign Embassies in Britain

Foreign embassies and high commissions in Britain include:

Australian High Commission
    Australia House, Strand, London WC2
    (☎ 0171 3794334)
Canadian High Commission
    Macdonald House, Grosvenor Square, London
    W1 (☎ 0171 2586600)
New Zealand High Commission
    New Zealand House, Haymarket, London SW1Y
    4TQ (☎ 0171 9308422)
US Embassy
    24 Grosvenor Square, London W1
    (☎ 0171 4999000)

CUSTOMS

When you enter Britain at an airport or seaport, there are three customs channels: red, if you need to pay duty on something you're importing; green, if no duty is payable because the amount you are importing does not exceed the allowable limit; and blue, if no duty is payable because you bought your goods in another EU country where taxes and duties have already been paid. The blue channel is relevant because a number of products (including alcohol and tobacco) are much cheaper in mainland Europe than they are in Britain. The rules allow any amount to be imported provided it is *for individual consumption*. It is illegal to resell. Consequently, many Britons make day-trips to France solely to load up with cheap grog and cigarettes, the savings on which can more than pay for the trip.

MONEY
Costs

It is likely that you have come to Britain to combine some walking with 'normal' sightseeing. Your major essential expense will probably be accommodation. In big cities, basic dormitory accommodation alone will cost from £9 to £17 a night. In towns or country areas your cheapest option will be a youth hostel for around £8 to £10, or a bottom end (though perfectly adequate) B&B for about £12 to £15. While walking you might camp (campsites charge about £2 to £5 per person) or stay in bunkhouses for about £3 to £7. Of course, upwards from here your choice is limited only by your budget. If you are walking or touring, B&Bs and

small hotels, charging about £14 to £25 per person per night, are a pleasant and relatively inexpensive way to travel. City centre or 'country house' hotels with more facilities, however, can charge £60 to £100 a double. (For more details see the Accommodation section of this chapter.)

Food is your next essential. In towns or cities you can scrape along on under £5 per day by purchasing basics from supermarkets. When walking, camping or hostelling, you may be self-catering anyway, so £10 per day will see you through nicely. Groceries and fresh food in Britain are roughly the same price as in Australia and the USA. If you have meals at hostels or cheap restaurants, £10 per day will also be your baseline. A good bar meal in a pub will be about £5, while a mid-range restaurant meal will set you back £7 to £10. Beer may not be classed as an essential by some, but just for the record, a pint will cost you £2 in London and £1.50 or less outside the capital.

Transport is the other big expense, but its cost is harder to quantify, as it depends not on how long you stay but on how far you go and how many different areas you visit. The Coach/Bus and Train Fares tables and the outline of car rental costs in the Getting Around chapter will give you more of an idea.

To get a realistic idea of how much you will need to spend, you should also take into account the cost of souvenirs, sightseeing tours, entry to tourist attractions and odds and ends like film, shampoo, books, maps and telephone calls...

So, bottom snake-belly line: you can get away with £10 to £15 per day, but you could spend as much as £20 per day without being extravagant. Move up a few comfort notches, and drink a few more pints of beer, and you'll be on £30 to £50 per day.

VAT In Britain, most prices include value-added tax (VAT), which is currently 17.5%. This is levied on virtually all goods and services except food and books. Restaurant menu prices must, by law, include VAT.

Currency

Britain's currency is the pound (£), divided into 100 pence (p). Notes (paper money) come in £5, £10, £20 and £50 denominations and vary in colour and size, although £10s and £20s are similar and can be confused if you're in a hurry. The 1p and 2p coins are copper; 5p, 10p, 20p and 50p coins are silver; and the £1 coin is gold. (A new £2 coin is planned for 1997.) The word 'pence' is rarely used; like its written counterpart, it is abbreviated, and pronounced 'pee'. Prices are written, and pronounced, thus:

£2.75: two seventy-five
£3.50: three fifty
£0.50 or 50p: fifty pee

Scotland has its own central bank and issues its own notes and coins, including a green £1 note. Scottish notes and coins are legal tender anywhere in Britain, though shopkeepers in Southern England and Wales may be reluctant to accept them. 'English' money will be accepted anywhere in Scotland.

Currency Exchange

As a guide this is what your own hard-earned cash is worth in pounds and pence.

Australia	A$1	=	£0.48
Canada	C$1	=	£0.44
France	1FF	=	£0.11
Germany	DM1	=	£0.39
Ireland	£1	=	£1.00
Japan	¥100	=	£0.52
New Zealand	NZ$1	=	£0.42
USA	US$1	=	£0.59

Cash, Travellers' Cheques & Credit Cards

Cash Wherever you arrive in Britain, all major airports and seaports have 24 hour exchange bureaux. They will accept your foreign currency in cash or travellers' cheques and give you pounds cash at the going exchange rate. You could consider getting a supply of pounds before you leave, so that you are covered for the first week or so. In Britain, travellers' cheques are rarely

used for everyday transactions (as they are in the USA, for example) except at major hotels, so you need to change them in advance and pay for things along the way with cash. Credit and charge cards are widely accepted at large hotels and guesthouses, and for buying meals at restaurants and some pubs. You can also use credit cards for long-distance train and coach travel, or for buying petrol or other goods worth over about £10. Many YHA hostels accept credit cards, but small establishments such as local shops and B&Bs always require cash.

Many of the walking routes and areas described in this book are away from towns, so you have to plan your money carefully. Wherever you go, it's usually necessary to carry enough cash for a week. On LDPs you may need to carry cash for 10 days or longer, especially if you are likely to hit the only town with a bank or post office on a Sunday.

Travellers' Cheques You could bring all the money you need in cash, but if it's lost or stolen, that's it – next flight home. If you carry the bulk of your money as travellers' cheques, on the other hand, at least it will be replaceable. You can cash your travellers' cheques in banks and *bureaux de change*, or at some TICs and post offices, but most of these places only open Monday to Friday and Saturday morning (see the Business Hours & Public Holidays section of this chapter). Rates and commissions vary, so keep a note of what the rate should be, and ask about the commission before you change your cheques. If you've got time, and a choice, it might be worth shopping around.

Credit Cards You can also use your debit card, credit card or charge card to get cash as you travel. This is an increasingly popular way of doing things, as it's swift and secure. You can either go into banks and complete the transaction with a clerk, or use an automatic teller machine (ATM or 'cashpoint'). The latter has the advantage of being open all the time. Before leaving home, ask your bank or card company which banks or

Facts for the Walker – Post & Communications 51

machines in Britain accept your card. We found that visitors from abroad often have more choice than the Brits themselves, who often must stick with branches of their own bank. Obviously, if you're using a debit card, you need the funds in your account back home. And if you're away for a long time, you need to make arrangements to have your credit or change card bills paid off.

Tipping
When calculating your costs, you may like to take tips into account. In Britain, waiters in restaurants normally expect a tip of around 10% of the bill. But you should pay a tip only if you have been satisfied with the service. It is not automatic. Some restaurants automatically include a 'service charge' of 10% to 15% on the bill, but this should be clearly advertised. If the service was satisfactory you must pay, or explain the reasons for your dissatisfaction to the manager. You do not add a further tip.

Some restaurants have been known to quietly include the service charge in the total cost shown on a credit card voucher, but still leave a blank for a further tip/gratuity. This is a scam – you only have to tip once! ∎

POST & COMMUNICATIONS
Post
First-class mail is quicker and more expensive (26p per letter) than 2nd-class mail (20p). Air-mail letters to EU countries are 26p, to non-EU European countries 31p, and to the Americas and Australasia 42p (up to 10g).

Telephone
Most public telephones in Britain are operated by British Telecom (BT). They either take coins, plastic phonecards or credit cards.

Phone numbers in Britain are written in the following form: 01234 567890 or (01234) 567890, where the first group of figures is the area code. In April 1995 all area codes had a 1 inserted after the initial 0, but many old numbers still appear in advertisements and

books. If there is no 1 after the 0 in the code, you will need to add it (except in the instances listed in the following paragraph).

Some codes have specific meanings, and these codes do not start with 01. Numbers starting with 0800, for example, are free calls. Numbers starting with 0345 are for calls charged at a local rate from anywhere in the country and are used by some transport information lines (eg Regional Railways). Numbers starting with 0990 are similar and are used by many transport companies (eg National Express). Numbers beginning with 0891, or other numbers beginning 089x, are for service calls (eg calls to weather information lines), which are charged at a higher rate than normal phone calls (eg 39p per minute cheap rate, 49p per minute at other times). Finally, numbers starting with 086 are for mobile cell-phones.

For most calls, there are three rates, according to the destination of the call: local (when no area code is required), local area (up to about 20 miles) and long distance (anywhere in Britain). Daytime rates (Monday to Friday from 8 am to 6 pm) are more expensive, while the cheap rate applies Monday to Friday from 6 pm to 8 am and all weekend.

If you need help you can ring ☎ 100 for a BT operator. If you have a directory enquiry, ring ☎ 192 (a free call from public phones).

For international calls, direct dialling is cheaper. If you need help or want to reverse the charges (call collect) dial ☎ 155 for the international operator. It's cheaper to phone abroad Monday to Friday from 8 pm to 8 am or on weekends.

BUSINESS HOURS & PUBLIC HOLIDAYS
Business hours are traditionally Monday to Friday from 9 am to 5 pm. Shops and post offices keep roughly the same hours. All shops and large post offices are open on Saturday from 9 am to 5 pm, while larger stores also open on Sunday. In country towns, particularly in Scotland and Wales, there may be an early closing day for shops

– usually Tuesday, Wednesday or Thursday – although in tourist areas shops stay open every day during 'the season'.

Public holidays (called bank holidays) are:

- New Year's Day
- 2 January (Scotland only)
- Good Friday
- Easter Monday (not Scotland)
- first Monday in May*
- last Monday in May
- first Monday in August (Scotland only)
- last Monday in August (outside Scotland)
- Christmas Day & Boxing Day

(*There is a possibility that the first Monday in May holiday may be moved to later in the year.)

WEIGHTS & MEASURES

Britain is in a period of awkward transition when it comes to weights and measures, as it has been for about the last 20 years and probably will be for another 20. Most British people still think in terms of the imperial units of pounds (lb) and ounces (oz), even though European legislation is attempting to coax the country into metrification. Shops must sell packaged goods priced in pence per kilogram (p/kg), although other goods such as loose vegetables can still be priced in pence per pound (p/lb).

When it comes to measures, things are even worse. Most liquids are now sold in litres or half-litres, except milk and beer, which come in pints. Garages sell petrol priced in pence per litre and measure car performance in miles per gallon. Great, isn't it?

Most people still use the old units of inches, feet and yards, but on maps the heights of mountains are now given in metres only. So walkers, more than any other section of the population, have become the most familiar with the 'new' metre measure. Some are happy to talk and think in metres, while others still prefer to convert back to feet (by dividing, roughly, by three).

Despite this drift towards metres, very few British people are familiar with kilometres. All distances on road signs are given in miles, and it is more usual to see distances on footpath signs given in miles too, although a few kilometre equivalents do creep in occasionally. One annoying result of this intransigence is that on signposts 'mile' is often abbreviated to 'm', which to everybody in the world except the sign-makers means 'metre'.

In this book we have reflected this rather wacky and typically British system of mixed measurements. In the route descriptions, distances along roads and footpaths are mostly given in miles (with km equivalents given at the start of each description), while heights of hills and mountains are given in metres (with some feet equivalents). That's the way things are in Britain, and who are we to swim against the tide?

Note also that in this book short distances along roads or paths are written in metres – eg 'go through the wood for 200m then turn left'. (For conversion tables, see the back of this book.)

BOOKS

This book cannot cover every aspect of walking in Britain, nor can it cover every aspect of travel within or around the areas described. To assist in your travels, and to guide you further when you have decided which areas to visit or which routes to follow, a great number of other books are available. The following will guide you between the shelves.

It is not usual to list publishers details, as bookshops and libraries search for books under title and author. However, many of the guidebooks listed in this book are not nationally distributed, having been produced by small, sometimes obscure, publishers which bookshops may not be able to locate. For this reason a list of British publishers who specialise in books about walking is included as an appendix in this book, so that you can order direct if necessary.

Readers in North America may like to contact a company called British Footpaths (☎ 3606 711217), at 914 Mason, Bellingham WA 98225. It stocks British guidebooks and maps, and also publishes *British Footpath*

Sampler and *British Footpath Handbook*, both by Richard Hayward.

Lonely Planet

Britain is covered in *Western Europe on a shoestring*, but for comprehensive coverage of England, Wales and Scotland turn to Lonely Planet's *Britain – travel survival kit*. And keep an eye out for Lonely Planet's new *London* guide.

General Guidebooks

There are countless guidebooks covering every nook and cranny of Britain. To get an advance idea of what you will encounter, the Insight Guides to *England, Scotland* and *Wales* might be worth a look. For detailed information on history, art and architecture, the Blue Guide series also has separate guides to *England, Scotland* and *Wales*, with a wealth of scholarly information on all the important sites.

Other major publishers producing a range of books of use to anyone travelling and walking in Britain include the Automobile Association (AA) and the Ordnance Survey (OS).

Route Guidebooks

It may seem obvious, but a route guidebook is one you actually carry with you on your walk. (There are plenty of other books about walking which you wouldn't carry with you.) It seems that every bit of footpath in Britain, and most of the open mountain areas, have been covered at least once in a guidebook.

Some areas have been covered by up to 20 different books. Such a guidebook may describe one or many routes, and may include background information. They range from bland step-by-step descriptions to lovingly crafted manuals combining eloquent route descriptions with background information on local history, geology and so on. (Sometimes the route and background details are too entwined, which makes following the actual route difficult.)

There are so many guidebooks covering

Britain that the choice can be daunting and confusing for visitors, and this is one of the reasons we produced *Walking in Britain*.

Route guidebooks fall into four main groups (although there is some overlap).

Specific Route Guidebooks These books describe a single route – usually a national trail or other LDP – in great detail, often step by step. Some cover the route only, others include extra details on aspects like transport and accommodation, history or wildlife. For example, books in the National Trail Guide series published jointly by Aurum Press, the OS & the Countryside Commission include detailed descriptions, and incorporate the very useful relevant sections from OS Pathfinder (1:25,000) maps. Some circular walks are included, plus limited information about the main towns along the way.

Other LDPs are also well covered; see, for example, *The Dales Way Companion* by Paul Hannon (Hillside Publications), *The Cumbria Way* by John Trevelyan (Dalesman) or Alfred Wainwright's legendary and idiosyncratic *Pennine Way Companion* (Michael Joseph). Other titles are listed in the specific route descriptions of this book.

Area Guidebooks These cover large areas such as a county or national park. Some are all-encompassing – eg *Exploring the Far North West of Scotland* by Richard Gilbert (published by Cordee), *Walk Northumbria Guide* (published by Bartholemew) or *The Pictorial Guides to the Lakeland Fells* by Alfred Wainwright (published by Michael Joseph). Others have a specific theme within the area – eg *Mostly Downhill in the Lake District* by Alan Pears (published by Sigma), *Walking the Ridges of Lakeland* by Bob Allen (published by Michael Joseph), *Hard Walks in the Pennines, Short Walks in the Pennines* and so on.

The OS (see the Maps section of this chapter) produces a series of Pathfinder Guides to various parts of Britain. These each describe about 25 walks of varying lengths and standards, from a few hours to all day. Each walk is clearly shown on an extract from the relevant OS Pathfinder map. Pathfinder guides include *Cornwall Walks*, *Heart of England Walks* and *Yorkshire Dales Walks*. Others are listed in the route descriptions in this book.

Some publishers specialise in certain themes. If you're travelling with children, look out for the Family Walks series (published by Scarthin Books); there are about 50 books covering the country, each with a good selection of 'high interest, low mileage' walks.

Another popular theme is contained in the Pub Walks series (one set is published by Countryside Books, and another by Sigma). As the title suggests, all routes include at least one pub, suitable for a stop at lunch time, and details on the food, beer, atmosphere, facilities and so on are included. There's even a book and route called *The Donnington Way* (published by Reardon) which links several pubs owned by a small independent Cotswold brewery. Leading Edge Publications produce a Rail Trail series, including specially designed walks that use trains to reach the start/finish; these cover *Norfolk*, *Snowdonia*, *The Pennines* and several other areas.

If you have other tastes and interests, chances are they'll be catered for. Other series include Teashop Walks, Wildlife Walks, History Walks, River Walks, Canal Walks, Literary Walks and thousands of other titles, some so obscure they border on the bizarre. How about *Circular Walks to Peak District Aircraft Wrecks* (published by Footprint, £4.95)?

Area guidebooks are listed throughout this book. Most can be bought locally, or in advance from a good bookshop anywhere in the country.

Local Guidebooks These cover fairly small areas, such as the countryside around a single town, and will describe a number of walks of varying lengths (usually circular) in that area. They are often available only from local newsagents, giftshops and TICs (for a modest price). Some are listed in specific route descriptions in this book.

National Guidebooks These cover entire countries (England, Scotland or Wales, or the whole of Britain), usually with a specific angle. One of the most useful for keen walkers is *200 Challenging Walks in Britain & Ireland* by Richard Gilbert (Diadem/Cordee), combining brief route outlines and descriptions with maps and photos, covering some of the finest routes and walking areas in the British Isles.

The routes are drawn from three best-selling large-format books produced by the same publisher, *Classic Walks*, *Wild Walks* and *Big Walks* (very nice, but too big to carry!), and range from the fairly straightforward – eg 12 miles in the Chiltern Hills – to really, really hard – eg 30 miles) across the Great Wilderness – with something for everyone in between.

Several of the large-format nonportable books to the whole country are produced in condensed form as Companion Guides. These are listed in the following Walking Handbooks section, and in other appropriate sections throughout this book.

Walking Handbooks
A number of companion handbooks are produced in Britain, providing useful information to complement the detailed guidebooks which cover routes. These include:

The Ramblers' Association Yearbook The RA is Britain's leading walkers' body (see the Useful Organisations section of this chapter). Its yearbook is free to members, but can be bought by anyone in some bookshops or by post direct from the RA for £5. It contains a good summary of walkers' rights, a list of 50 popular LDPs, with details of maps, guidebooks, an equipment guide for walking in Britain and a large list of hostels, bunkhouses, B&Bs and guesthouses which welcome walkers, listed by county and region.

National Trail Companion This book, published by Stilwell (£9.99), lists every B&B and every pub providing accommodation and food on or near all Britain's national trails and 25 other LDPs. They are listed in order, as you walk along the route, which makes planning overnight stops easier. YHA and SYHA hostels and a selection of campsites are also listed. If you're doing several long routes and nothing else, this book is ideal.

Long Distance Walkers Handbook This book, published by the Long Distance Walkers Association & A&C Black (£10), is useful if you're looking for more places to go, as it lists and briefly describes about 350 long-distance walks in Britain (national trails, regional routes, waymarked or nonwaymarked LDPs), ranging from relatively minuscule 20-milers up to the super-long South West Coast Path.

Big Sites Book This is produced by the Camping & Caravanning Club (see the Useful Organisations section of this chapter for more details).

Accommodation Guides These are put out by the YHA and SYHA and are described in the Useful Organisations section of this chapter.

The Independent Hostel Guide This slim, cheap and handy book published by the Backpacker's Press (£4) covers bunkhouses and hostels in cities and country areas that are not part of the national hostelling organisations.

Campsites for Backpackers Another publication by Backpacker's Press, this book specifically covers low-tech, low-cost sites for the lightweight (ie small tent) camper. Most sites are within walking distance of a pub, so the money you save on camping you can spend on food and beer.

Other Books about Walking in Britain

These tend to be more general books, often large format, designed to inspire or inform you (or both) before you head off on your walk. For this reason they are almost as valuable as the practical guidebooks, but not a substitute for them.

Walking in Britain This book, by John Hillaby (Palladin/Collins), is not a guidebook but a collection of writings about various parts of the country by local experts, designed to enthral and inspire rather than simply inform. Chapters include 'Greatest amongst the Green Roads' (The Ridgeway), 'Bog Trotting and Other Delights' (The Peak District) and 'The Ins and Outs of Gaeldom' (The West Highland Way), plus some general ruminative sections on the spirituality of long-distance routes, the psychology of walking alone and the practicality of suitable food. John Hillaby is one of Britain's most well-known walker-writers. His other books include *Journey Through Britain*.

Exploring Britain's Long Distance Paths It may be published by the Automobile Association (AA), but it's a very nice book for walkers, although it

is aimed more at those with cars (public transport info is very brief). It gives a brief but useful historical and practical introduction to LDP walking, then describes 30 routes, either in full or by taking sample sections, from the Two Moors Way in South Devon to the Speyside Way in northern Scotland, with colour photos, wildlife and historical asides, and maps.

Land's End to John O'Groats and *Coastwalk* These are by Andrew McCloy (Hodder), and are for those walkers who really want to do long walks. The first describes three routes from one end of Britain to the other, taking in several other LDPs along the way. For many British walkers, the 'End-to-End' is a great goal, and several foreign visitors come here to do it too. This book is all you need for the initial planning. The second book is similar, but describes a single route round the entire coastline of England and Wales. You don't have to do it all in one go. Both books suggest shorter sections, ranging from a few days to a few weeks.

The Munros This book is written by Donald Bennet and published by the Scottish Mountaineering Club & Cordee (£16.95). A Munro is a mountain in Scotland which is higher than 914m. This apparently arbitrary figure is the metric equivalent of 3000 ft – the magical height at which mountains take on an extra significance for walkers. This book – the Munro-baggers bible – lovingly describes all 277 of them (although the figure is always hotly debated by Munroists), with maps, photos and route descriptions, and makes a good souvenir, even if you don't bag the set. Some of the proceeds from the sale of this book go to mountain conservation in Scotland. (For more details on the lore and tradition of Munros and the peculiar British passion for Munro-bagging, plus other details of other specific Scotland books, see the Scotland – Short Walks chapter.)

The High Mountains of Britain & Ireland This beautiful book by Irvine Butterfield (Diadem & Cordee; £18.99) lists every mountain above 914m (3000 ft). This naturally includes all Munros in Scotland (see *The Munros* above), plus 'honorary Munros' in other parts of the British Isles. Each chapter covers a single mountain or group of mountains, with maps, photos, outlines of routes to the summits and overall descriptions. The book has excellent colour photos and maps of every route. For the peak-bagger, this is all you need, but unfortunately it's too big to carry on a hike. To overcome this, the publishers have produced *The High Mountains Companion* (£4.99), with all the photos left out, and the text condensed, to produce a handy guidebook slim enough to fit in a rucksack or jacket pocket.

The Mountains of England & Wales Written by John & Ann Nuttall (Cicerone; two volumes: £11.99 and £10.99). This is another useful almanac. Divided into one volume per country, it is a definitive list of all mountains over 600m (2000 ft), providing detailed descriptions of fine circular day-walks that take them all in, with sketches and illustrations – ideal for peak-baggers south of the Scottish border.

The Relative Hills of Britain This book, by Alan Dawson (Cicerone; £8.99), is the list to end all lists. Forget Munros: these are the Marilyns, the popular name for any hill or mountain in Britain which is *relatively* high – ie 150m, or about 500 ft, above its surroundings, whatever its altitude above sea level (so you can peak-bag without necessarily going high). Anyone who thought some British walkers were obsessive could have their suspicions unequivocally confirmed by this book, although the bland statistics are balanced by some interesting facts and tongue-in-cheek observations on the art and lore of peak-bagging.

Flora & Fauna

The best all-round guide on Britain's flora and fauna is the *Nature Atlas of Great Britain* (published by Pan and Ordnance Survey), detailing 2000 places where you can watch wildlife. More portable, and ideal for visitors with a general interest, is *The Complete Guide to British Wildlife* by Arlott, Fitter & Fitter (published by Collins, £7.99); it's well illustrated and covers everything from fungi and moths to trees and birds in a neat, accessible format.

Walking and birdwatching go particularly well together. One of the best fieldguides for keen amateurs is the award-winning *Pocket Guide to Birds of Britain & Europe* by Heinzel, Fitter and Parslow (published by Collins, £9.99). Similarly handy, especially for beginners, is the *Bidwatcher's Pocket Guide*, by Peter Hayman (published by Mitchell Beazley), designed for speedy reference with clear illustrations and notes on distinctive features. If you want to choose destinations according to what you might see, *Top Birding Spots* by David Tipling is recommended, with colour maps and photos, covering 400 birdwatching sites in Britain and Ireland. Also try *The New Where to Watch Birds* by John Gooders.

If your interest in wildlife is more casual, go for the very portable and reasonably priced series of Gem Guides (published by Collins, £3.50). This includes *Birds, Insects, Trees, Fish, Wild Flowers* and many more. If you need more detail, the slightly larger Wild Guides series (also Collins, £6.99), with accessible information and colour photos, includes *Birds, Trees, Mushrooms & Toadstools, Butterflies & Moths* and *Flowers*. A similar series of Pocket Guides (published by Mitchell Beazley) includes *Butterflies, Trees* and *Wildflowers*, combining in-depth coverage with a handy format – ideal for walkers.

Several more detailed British wildlife titles are available; if you have a specific interest, a good bookshop will be able to advise. Tourist boards produce several wildlife publications. For example, The Wales Tourist Board has a leaflet called *The Great Nature Trail of Wales* covering 36 sites of particular interest to nature enthusiasts. Local Scottish and English tourist boards have similar publications.

MAGAZINES

Walking magazines can be a great source of information for visitors to Britain. Most contain news of walking events, equipment, clothing reviews etc. They also have features on day-walks or weekend routes around the country, which can be a great source of inspiration. However, as it's normally assumed that readers have cars, public transport information is light. Also useful are the advertisement sections, full of information on walking holiday companies, guides, accommodation etc.

The *Great Outdoors* has been around for years, combining a traditional pedigree and a modern look with excellent news coverage and route suggestions. *Trailwalker* and *Country Walking* are relatively new upstarts, also with plenty of route suggestions and advice for people new to walking.

MAPS

The best introductory map to Britain is published by the British Tourist Authority (BTA) and is widely available for a small fee. If you plan to catch a lot of trains, British Rail has a useful passenger map (free). If you're combining driving with walking you will need a road atlas. If you plan to drive on smaller roads (often essential to reach the start of a walk), an ideal scale is three miles to the inch. The Ordnance Survey's *Motoring Atlas of Great Britain* is good, but for walkers the AA's *Big Road Atlas – Britain* is even better, as national trails are marked on it.

Once you start walking, you need a map with more detail. Britain is covered by an excellent series of maps published by the Ordnance Survey, once part of the military – hence the name – but now a government agency. The OS produces maps to various scales but the most useful for walkers are those in the Landranger (1:50,000) series (pink covers; all priced at £4.75) or the Pathfinder (1:25,000) series (green covers; £3.95). In popular tourist areas, several Pathfinder sheets are joined to form Outdoor Leisure maps (yellow covers; £5.40) or Explorer maps (orange covers; £4.50). These have amazing detail, showing walls, fences, rock outcrops and other features, and are ideal for walkers.

Despite their popularity, OS maps do have a number of quirks. One of these is that boundaries (national, county, parliamentary constituency) are marked more clearly than paths. In fact the boundaries look like paths. Many inexperienced walkers have become lost trying to follow a row of dots on the map which turns out to be the line between two counties. OS maps also mark rights of way (see the Terms & Definitions Used in this Book section of this chapter), even when no visible path exists on the ground. The other point to watch out for is that words that aren't proper nouns have capital initial letters (eg Sheepfold, Sinkholes), sometimes making it hard for walkers (especially for foreign visitors) to distinguish between features and actual place names.

Despite these minor gripes, however, OS maps are still amongst the best in the world, and have served British walkers well for decades. Before using an OS map, familiarise yourself with the symbols on the legend.

Once you're used to the idiosyncrasies, you'll never need to be lost.

The new kid on the block is Harveys, a private mapping company beginning to penetrate the market traditionally dominated by the OS. Harveys maps are actually designed for walkers. Thus, if a path is on the ground they show it, if it isn't they don't. And there's not a boundary in sight, so although this means you may not know when you've passed from Yorkshire to Cumbria, it also means you won't try to follow the frontier.

Harveys maps are printed on waterproof paper, and with each map you get a leaflet giving a potted history of the area, suggesting some routes and detailing access restrictions (such as stalking in Scotland). Harveys covers only the most popular walking areas, mostly in Scotland, Wales and Northern England, but its range is growing. The maps are drawn to two scales: 1:40,000 (£5.75) and 1:25,000 (£6.45); maps to the latter scale are in a series called *Superwalkers*.

Maps in this Book

The maps in this book show areas of Britain, with routes of the LDPs and day-walks we describe marked on them. These maps are to show you how the route fits into the surrounding area, to help you get there and away, and to help you locate the route on proper survey maps. In the case of all the walks described in this book, the maps we provide are not enough in themselves for routefinding or navigation. You will still need a properly surveyed map, at an adequate scale, showing all important relief features. ∎

If you are doing an LDP, you often need several maps, and this can be expensive. Most specific LDP guidebooks also contain maps. Some of these are hand drawn and cover no more than a few yards either side of the route – take one wrong turn and it's a job to find your way back. So you probably need a survey map as well. More useful are the guidebooks which reproduce sections of properly surveyed maps in strip format. These cover a wider area, although if you go more than a few miles off the route, you've got the same problem again.

Full details of recommended maps are given in each route description in this book.

ON-LINE SERVICES

You can also get information on walking in Britain direct from the Internet at:

http://www.gorp.com/gorp/activity/europe/Britain.htm
   This site includes a list of holiday companies, plus details on the RA (see the Useful Organisations section of this chapter) and various LDP organisations.
http://www.gorp.com/gorp/activity/europe/ldwa.htm
   This site is the Long Distance Walkers Association page.
http://www.thebmc.co.uk
   This is the site for the British Mountaineering Council, with useful information for rock-climbers and hill-walkers.
http://www.stilwell.co.uk
   This site covers accommodation in Britain specifically for walkers, arranged by area and LDP.

HEALTH

Compared to many other countries around the world, Britain has no major health hazards. Immunisations are not normally required, unless you've arrived from an infected area (which could include stop-overs), such Asia, Africa or Latin America. Check with your travel agent and doctor. Don't leave this until the last minute, as the immunisations may have to be spread out over a period of time. Any immunisations you have should be recorded on an International Health Certificate, which is available from your physician or government health department. Although not a regulation, it is important that your tetanus immunisation be up to date.

This section concentrates on basic aspects of everyday health while walking or travelling in Britain. For details on more serious emergency situations, see the Dangers & Annoyances and Safety sections of this chapter.

Medical Services in Britain

Reciprocal arrangements allow Australians, New Zealanders and a number of other nationalities to receive free emergency medical treatment in hospitals, and subsidised dental care through the state-funded National Health Service. Nationals of EU countries are covered for emergency treatment on presentation of an E111 form. Ask your doctor or travel agent about this before departure.

To find your nearest hospital emergency department, doctor or dentist, check *Yellow Pages* phone books, or phone ☎ 100 (free call) for a telephone operator who can give you details. In a real emergency, phone ☎ 999 (free call) for an ambulance. Despite these excellent (although frequently hard-pressed) public services, travel insurance is still advisable, because it offers flexibility in where and how you're treated, as well as covering expenses for ambulance and repatriation. If you are suffering from a minor ailment, and don't need a doctor, most towns have a chemist (pharmacy) where staff can give advice, and supply the relevant pills, potions or lotions.

Predeparture Preparations

Travel Insurance A travel insurance policy to cover theft, loss and medical problems is a must. There is a wide variety of policies and your travel agent will have recommendations. The international policies handled by STA Travel or other student and youth organisations are usually good value. Some policies offer lower and higher medical-expense options – it's always worth going as high as you can afford, especially if during your trip you plan to visit other countries where medical costs can be astronomical (eg the USA, Switzerland, Germany or anywhere in Scandinavia). Check the small print: if you plan to go walking in some of the more remote areas described in this book, the policy may count this as trekking or mountaineering, and load the premium. Even if mountain-walking is considered OK, the policy may specifically exclude 'dangerous activities' such as scuba diving, motorcycling or skiing, and if you plan to do more than walk during your trip, such a policy may not be appropriate for you. You may also need to consider whether your policy covers ambulances or helicopter rescue, or an emergency flight home if required, and whether it pays doctors or hospitals directly, or expects you to pay on the spot and claim later.

Health Preparations If you wear glasses, take a spare pair and your prescription. If you require a particular medication or a specific oral contraceptive, take note of the generic name rather than the brand name, as that particular brand may not be locally available.

Medical & First Aid Kit

For walking in Britain, especially if you're doing a long-distance route or exploring a fairly remote area, it's worth carrying a small, straightforward first aid kit so that you can self-treat minor injuries or ailments. If things get serious you're rarely more than a few hours, or a day at the most, from a town with a pharmacy, doctor or hospital, but it would be a shame to spoil your walk for the lack of something simple. Items you should consider carrying include:

antidiarrhoeal preparations (eg Imodium or Lomotil), for stomach upsets (note, however, that these preparations do not cure the infection, just slow the bowel movement, so you don't have to run for the toilet every five minutes – very useful for long bus journeys)

antihistamine cream, to ease the itch from insect bites or stings

antihistamine pills, for pollen allergies or as a decongestant for colds

antiseptic cream and powder or a similar 'dry' spray, for cuts and grazes

bandages, including a large triangular bandage for slings and a crepe roll bandage or elasticised tubular bandage (eg 'tubi-grip') for sprains

pain-killers (eg paracetamol or aspirin), for fevers, headaches or other pain

scissors, tweezers and a thermometer (note, however, that mercury thermometers are prohibited on planes)

sterile wound dressings, for lacerations

sticking plasters (eg Band-aids), for minor injuries and blisters (also see Blisters, in this section)

You can make up your own kit by buying various items at a pharmacy. Alternatively, if you're really heading into the wilds, or combining walking with climbing, there are several kits put together specifically for walkers and mountaineers. The Gregson Pack is undoubtedly the most robust and user-friendly.

Basic Rules

Serious problems are unlikely in Britain, but mild stomach upsets caused by a change in water and diet are not unknown. Care in what you eat and drink and maintenance of personal hygiene are the most important health rules, wherever you travel. Many health problems can be avoided by just taking care of yourself. For example, wash your hands frequently; don't relax just because you're on holiday.

Everyday Health Body temperature or pulse can be a good indicator of health. A normal body temperature is 98.6°F or 37°C; more than 2°C higher is a 'high' fever. A normal adult pulse rate is 60 to 80 per minute (children 80 to 100, babies 100 to 140). As a general rule, the pulse increases about 20 beats per minute for each °C rise in fever. The breathing rate is also an indicator of health or illness. Count the number of breaths per minute: between 12 and 20 is normal for adults and older children (up to 30 for younger children, 40 for babies).

Water In towns and cities, water from the cold tap is always safe (water from the hot tap may have been through an unclean tank or boiler). On campsites in country areas, water may be piped straight from a spring without being filtered or chemically treated. Usually a sign will say whether or not it's safe to drink or not. In remote areas, hardened hill-walkers often drink straight from streams (and say they *love* that peaty taste). However, this is not recommended, as wherever you go in Britain you can virtually never be certain there are no people or livestock upstream.

Water Purification There are several ways of purifying water. You can boil it thoroughly (for 10 minutes), but if you're backpacking in the wilds, this means fires or a heavy use of stove fuel. It's far easier to treat water chemically, using tablets or solutions. Chlorine is the most common method (eg Puritabs, Steritabs or other brand names). Iodine is also very effective and is available in tablet form (such as Potable Aqua) or as a solution in a dropper-bottle. Note that whatever chemical you use, it will be far more effective if you filter out large matter first. There are some fancy gadgets on the market, but simple nylon filter bags are just as good.

Health Problems & Treatment

Tiredness If you're tired, you lose concentration, or start to stumble, and this can have all sorts of bad consequences. This problem can attack walkers anywhere, not just in Britain, but it's easily avoided. You should never set out on walks beyond your capability. If you feel under the weather, have a day off or get the bus halfway. Don't push on without stopping for hours on end. This is not heroic; it's daft, and could even put you in danger. Stop for rests, even if it's only a few minutes, every hour or two. And when you stop, sit down if possible to rest your legs properly. You should also eat properly, so that the energy you use up when walking is replaced. It's amazing the number of people who go out for a long day's walking with nothing more than a weedy jam sandwich. You should always take plenty of food – chocolate, dried fruit, nuts, biscuits – and eat regularly. It's better to have too much and bring some back to your tent at the end of the day, than to be on the summit of a mountain with a few hours to go and nothing for company but an empty stomach.

Blisters Once again, this is a problem which is easily avoided. Don't set out on the Pennine Way the day after you buy a new pair of boots. Go for a few shorter walks so that your feet get 'hardened' a little. Make sure your boots are not too big or too small, as both can cause blisters. The same goes for socks: make sure they fit properly. Don't use old socks – new ones provide better padding. Keep your toenails clipped, but not too short. While walking it's worth taking off your boots and socks at lunch time, to let them air a bit. This can be offensive in the pub, so you better wait until you're outside (ideal if picnicking). If the weather is too wet for airing feet, carry a spare pair of dry socks and change about halfway. If you do feel a blister coming on, treat it sooner rather than later. Either use a simple sticking plaster (Band-aid), or a 'moleskin', which is more comfortable. Outdoor gear shops sell small 'blister care packs' with a range of different shaped pads and plasters. You can also get various 'second skin' spray-on remedies, which users rate highly.

Knee Pain Like walkers anywhere else in the world, walkers in Britain suffer from knee pain, although this usually occurs in the mountainous areas, and is caused by descending more often than by ascending. The No 1 way to prevent knee pain is to descend slowly. I speak from experience here, as I used to enjoy running down scree and hill-sides, and now I'm nearing middle age, my knees often creak and groan. As I can't turn the clock back, I have found that tubular bandages go a long way towards reducing the problem. Some walkers use high-tech strap-on supports, which are designed for the job and make you look bionic. Walking poles are very effective in taking some weight off the knees on descents. These bits of kit are quite common now in the Alps and other mountain ranges, but still fairly new in conservative old Britain, so if you use them be prepared for 'going skiing?' wisecracks.

Sunburn Britain is notorious for it's changeable weather, but when the sun is out it's possible to get sunburnt surprisingly quickly – especially if you're walking on the hills or along the coast when a breeze hides the sun's heat. Even when there's a lot of cloud you can still get burnt. Use sunscreen (suncream) on arms and legs, wear a hat and cover up with a long-sleeved shirt and trousers. A sunblock (zinc cream) for nose and ears is also recommended.

Heat Exhaustion Dehydration or salt deficiency can cause heat exhaustion. If it is hot (and it can be!) and you're exerting yourself, make sure you get sufficient liquid and salt to replace what you're sweating out. A couple of beers at lunch time is fine, but it's essential to top up with nonalcoholic liquids too. Salt deficiency is characterised by fatigue, lethargy, headaches, giddiness and muscle cramps. You're unlikely to need salt tablets – just a bit extra on your food each day will probably do. If you happen to be sick, remember that vomiting or diarrhoea can rapidly deplete your liquid and salt levels, so keeping levels high at such times is even more important.

Fungal Infections When walking – especially if you're backpacking and trying to keep the weight down – it's easy to forget to wash or change clothing as often as you would normally. This can lead to fungal infections. To prevent this, wear suitable clothes, wash frequently and dry carefully. Wash your socks and underwear in hot water, and change them regularly. Always wear thongs (flip-flops) in shared bathrooms. If you do get an infection, try to expose the infected area to air or sunlight as much as possible, and consult a pharmacist.

Cold Hypothermia is a condition that occurs when you lose heat faster than you can produce it and the core temperature of the body falls. It is surprisingly easy to progress from very cold to dangerously cold due to a combination of wind, wet clothing, fatigue and hunger, even if the air temperature is above freezing. Walkers in Britain should always be prepared for difficult conditions. It is best to dress in layers, and a hat is important, as a lot of heat is lost through the head. A strong, windproof and waterproof outer layer is essential. For more details see the What to Bring section of this chapter. You should always carry food that contains simple sugars, such as chocolate or energy bars, which generate heat quickly.

Symptoms of hypothermia are exhaustion, numb skin (particularly toes and fingers), shivering, slurred speech, irrational or violent behaviour, lethargy, stumbling, dizzy spells, muscle cramps and violent bursts of energy. To treat hypothermia, first get victims out of the wind and rain. Remove their clothing if it's wet and replace it with dry, warm clothing. Give them hot liquids – not alcohol – and some high-kilojoule, easily digestible food. This should be enough for the early stages of hypothermia, but if it has gone further, it may be necessary to place victims in warm sleeping bags and get in with them. Do not rub patients, place them near a fire or remove their wet clothes in the wind. If possible, place sufferers in a warm (not hot) bath.

Diarrhoea A simple change of water, food, climate or activity can cause the runs, but the problem is usually short lived and not very serious. Diarrhoea caused by contaminated food or water is more serious. If all you're suffering is a few rushed toilet trips, with no other symptoms, then don't worry. Moderate diarrhoea, involving around half a dozen loose movements in a day, is more of a nuisance. Dehydration is the main danger, especially if you're walking and exerting yourself (this is particularly the case for children), so fluid replenishment is the No 1 treatment. Weak black tea with a little sugar (and even a sprinkle of salt) or soft drinks allowed to go flat and diluted 50% with clean water are all good. You can buy rehydration solutions at pharmacies. Stick to a bland diet as you recover. If your diarrhoea is more severe than this, you should seek medical advice.

Emergencies For information on emergencies and how to avoid them or deal with them, see the following Safety section.

SAFETY
An old adage says 'Adventure is caused by lack of planning'. In many cases the same

can be said of dangerous situations. If you plan your walking and equip yourself properly, you will have a much better chance of staying safe in the hills and mountains. (If you only plan to do lowland walks – and that would be a shame – you won't need to worry about most of this section.)

Preparation

Work out your route in advance, even if you change it on the way, and calculate how long it's going to take. We have given times required for walks described in this book, but if you go elsewhere on your own (and we hope you do) you'll need to estimate your own timings. A formula for doing this is given in the Terms & Definitions Used in this Book section of this chapter. Know your own limitations too; don't set out on a 15-miler if you haven't done any walking recently. Always be prepared to turn back or shorten the route if the weather turns bad or you don't feel up to it.

Take enough food and drink. A long walk in hot or cold conditions can use up a lot of energy. It's always better to come back with food left over than to run out halfway through your walk.

Unless you are very experienced, it is not wise to venture into wild areas alone. An ideal walking group is two to four people. In mountain areas, if possible, leave details of your route with someone (eg at the hostel or B&B where you're staying) or leave a note in your tent. And remember to tell them when you're back down safely.

Clothing

It's no good checking the weather forecast and then going up Snowdon in a T-shirt. You should carry warm and waterproof clothing, including a hat, whatever the season (if you don't use it that's fine, but it's better than needing protection and not having it). Good footwear is also important; proper walking shoes or boots are recommended. And don't forget that the British sun can be strong: a sun hat, a shirt with collar or a scarf, and sunscreen are often needed. (For more

details, see the What to Bring section of this chapter.)

Navigation

Some footpaths and trails in Britain are not well signposted, particularly in highland areas, so it is absolutely essential that you can read a map and know how to navigate with a compass. The choice of maps for walking is covered in the Maps section of this chapter. All survey maps have the 'national grid' marked on them. This is a series of vertical (north-south) and horizontal (west-east) lines which are a vital part of the map-reading process, allowing you to pinpoint exact positions and find your direction in relation to north. Grid references in Britain are usually a six-figure number, sometimes preceded by two letters for further clarification. If you are not familiar with grid references, the system is explained on all Ordnance Survey and Harveys maps. Remember that grid north (ie north on the map) and magnetic north (ie north on the compass) are not the same, and not fixed; you need to take account of magnetic variation. In 1995 magnetic north was about 5° west of grid north, and expected to decrease by 1° over the following five or 10 years. This means that when you are transferring a compass bearing between map and 'field' or vice versa you need to add or subtract 5° respectively.

Emergency Equipment

Even with good planning and navigation, things can still occasionally go wrong. Other safety essentials are:

- a whistle (blow six short blasts, repeated at intervals, if you need help)
- a polythene survival 'bivvy' bag for emergency shelter (don't slide into it like a sleeping bag – instead, pull it down over your head, and sit down on your rucksack)
- a torch (flashlight) for signalling for help if you get into trouble, or just for reading the map at the end of a longer-than-planned day (especially useful during the winter months, when it starts getting dark at 4 pm)

For details of what to include in a medical & first aid kit, see the Health section of this chapter.

Emergency Procedure

If somebody in your party is injured and can't move, leave somebody with them while another goes for help. If there are only two of you, leave the injured person with all spare clothing, food and water, the whistle and the torch, and tie something colourful such as a scarf to a tree or rock to make finding them again easier. Take a careful note of where they are (including a map reference) and go to the nearest phone. Public phones in remote areas are marked on maps, but in real emergency situations the owners of remote farms or houses will let you use theirs. Dial ☎ 999 (the national emergency number – free of charge) and ask for police and/or mountain rescue, then give them all the details (including that all-important map reference).

More Information

Much of the above may sound pretty daunting. That's good. With a bit of luck it will make you respect the mountains of Britain, and have a good time while you're amongst them. Most of the advice comes down to common sense, so with some of that and some training if required, you should be fine.

If you need to know more, many of the mountainous national parks produce leaflets such as *Safety in the Lake District* and so on. These are usually free of charge from TICs. In Scotland you can get a very handy leaflet called *Enjoy the Scottish Hills in Safety*, and another called *Learn to Read – Or Get Lost* about map-reading. If you want to know more, the British Mountaineering Council (see the Useful Organisations section of this chapter) produces a useful book called *Safety on Mountains*.

Courses If you are in Britain for a while, you can broaden you experience and skills on lower walks before heading for the high hills. If you're impatient, or lacking time, you could consider joining a course. The YHA and SYHA regularly run weekend courses at various hostels around Britain covering map and compass skills, and these are also a very good introduction to walking in Britain. Plas-y-Brenin National Mountain Centre (see the Snowdonia section of the Wales – Short Walks chapter) also runs regular courses, as do many of the guides listed in the Guided Walks sections of this book. Other places to ask about courses are outdoor gear shops, and you could also check advertisements in outdoor magazines (see the Magazines section earlier in this chapter).

DANGERS & ANNOYANCES
Dangers

You're unlikely to be mugged in the British countryside, although some LDPs (eg the Thames Path) do pass through towns and cities where the usual precautions should be taken. Generally though, walking in Britain is an easy and enjoyable way to see the country and, with correct planning, it is remarkably free of danger. However, the more remote high routes we describe in this book are not suitable for novices, so if you are new to walking, it is better to start on some of the easier lowland walks described in this book, or consider improving your skills by joining a course before heading for lofty summits.

The most potentially dangerous aspect of walking in Britain – which has bearing on all others – is the changeability of the weather, especially in highland or coastal areas. The countryside can look deceptively gentle, but sun-kissed hills can turn to arctic wastes very quickly at any time of the year. Low cloud, fog, rain and snow are the cause of walkers' troubles more often than anything else. Sometimes the problem is minor – you get lost in the mist for half an hour – but sometimes it's more serious – you get lost all night, or fall on a wet rock and injure yourself.

Before you go walking in hills and highland areas, or along the coast, always check the weather. In national parks and tourist areas such as Cornwall, Pembrokeshire,

Snowdonia and the Lake District, weather bulletins are posted at TICs and PICs. Hostels, outdoor gear shops and cafes frequented by walkers also often post information on a noticeboard. There are also several telephone information services (see aside).

Telephone Weather Services

There are several weather forecast telephone services in Britain. One is Weathercall, which divides the country into areas, with a different phone number for each. You dial ☎ 0839 500, then add 401 for the London area, 402 for South East England, and so on. More useful for walkers is Mountain call; first dial ☎ 0898, then add the following relevant numbers: Scotland West 505283, Scotland East 505284, Snowdonia 505285, Peak District 505286, Lakes 505287. Similar services are advertised in various walking magazines and at TICs. Calls cost 34p per minute at the cheap rate, 45p at all other times. ■

Other dangers to watch out for when walking through farmland are the temporary electric fences. These are designed to control cattle, but they are often placed near (or across) footpaths. They are often no more than a thin strand of wire, and can be difficult to see, but they pack a punch, so beware. It's actually illegal for farmers to put electric fences (or any barrier) across a legal right of way.

Some walks described in this book cross areas of land which are used by the army for training. When manoeuvres are happening, live ammunition may be used, so walkers are not allowed to enter. Red warning flags are raised around the area at these times. There are usually noticeboards too, which list the days and times that the area is closed to the public. When the red flags are not flying you can cross the land, but you should still keep to paths and beware of unidentifiable metal objects lying in the grass. If you do find anything suspicious, don't touch it. Make a

note of the position and report it to the police after your walk.

Annoyances

Insects in country areas can sometimes be annoying, but they are rarely anything to worry about. In summer, small bugs called ticks can bite. If left untreated the bite can become infected and *very occasionally* lead to an illness called Lyme disease. Ticks live in long grass and bracken, so if your route passes through such areas, wear long trousers. In Scotland in summer the sheer numbers of small flying insects called midges can be a real problem. (See the Scotland – Short Walks chapter for more information.)

Snake Bite

While walking in Britain, there's a very, very small chance that you might come across the island's one and only species of poisonous snake – the adder, also called the viper. (For more details, see Snakes in the Flora & Fauna section of the Facts about Britain chapter.) This shy creature will probably slither out of your way long before you even know it's there, but if you surprise or corner it, you may be bitten. The venom is rarely fatal, but there are some basic rules to follow if you are tending a victim. The first is to calm and reassure the patient. The second is to clean the wound and cover it with a dressing. (Do *not* cut the wound open and try to suck out the venom – this procedure looks good in the movies, but it is not effective and leads to infection.) The third is to get the patient to hospital as quickly as possible. If possible, the best immediate treatment is to immobilise the bitten limb and apply a bandage firmly and evenly up the whole limb. Alternatively, you could apply a tourniquet to the limb immediately above the wound, but it is absolutely vital to make sure you can still feel a pulse below the tourniquet (ie in the wrist or foot). Do not release the compression until the patient reaches hospital. ■

Other annoying things for walkers include untethered farm dogs and dangerous bulls. The RA advises you treat both with caution;

back away slowly and report the situation to the police if you consider it dangerous to the point of being unlawful.

ACCOMMODATION

The types of accommodation you can use while walking in Britain are as varied as the routes you follow. These details (listed roughly in ascending order of price) will give you a pretty good idea, but there are a lot of overlaps. You'll probably use a combination during your visit. For example, you might use a campsite for a week in the Lake District while going out on day-walks, then do the Thames Way using hostels and B&Bs, or the Dales Way using bunkhouses then finish off with a night in a luxury hotel. The range of choices is all part of the attraction.

Campsites & Wild Camping

A tent is not essential for any of the walks described in this book, although it's often a viable option, particularly if you're on a tight budget, or simply like camping for its own sake. Official campsites range from simple fields with a tap and a basic toilet where you pay £1 to £2 per person per night, to smart places with all facilities (hot showers, shop, bar, children's playground etc) charging around £5. Some sites cater for big tents and caravans on long stays and are not usually set up for walkers and lightweight campers.

If you plan to explore an area by doing several day-walks from a single base, camping is a good-value option: all national parks and other walking areas have many sites to choose from, although they can be busy in summer. Most LDPs have campsites along them, and farmers may permit your tent in their field on a one-off basis as you pass through the area. If you can't find anyone to ask, it's best to be discreet: if you camp without permission, you could be moved on rather aggressively. Use your common sense too: don't camp too close to villages or in crop fields, for example.

Before you arrive in Britain, forget the backwoods-bushwalk type of camping possible in Australasia and North America, where you can stop and pitch a tent any-

where. Except in some parts of Scotland, and the more remote areas of England and Wales, it just doesn't work like that here. Although camping may not be officially allowed where LDPs pass though open country or forest areas, it is sometimes tolerated by landowners – but you should always attempt to get permission first. In very remote areas where genuine wild camping may be required (ie more than half a day's walk from an official site or any other form of accommodation) it is similarly tolerated. Wherever you camp wild, be meticulous about cleanliness and hygiene. If you leave a mess you spoil things for the next people who come along, possibly endanger wildlife, and make landowners less likely to allow such camping in the future.

A final note: always carry a stove – open fires are not normally allowed on official sites or for wild camps. They can be dangerous and quite often there isn't enough wood anyway.

Bothies, Barns & Bunkhouses

Bothies Bothies are very simple shelters in Scotland, often in remote places. They are not locked or guarded, and are maintained on a voluntary basis by the Mountain Bothies Association (MBA). You need your own cooking equipment, sleeping bag and mat. Users should stay one night only and use the place responsibly. There's no charge, and you can't book a bothy, so to avoid overcrowding groups of more than three are discouraged. In the last few years, however, some bothies (particularly in popular areas) have been overused to the point of destruction. Consequently, the MBA is considering 'abandoning' some bothies, and prefers the location of others to remain fairly secret. Some walks in this book do pass near bothies, but those not essential to the route are not listed. Where bothies are already marked on readily available maps, they can hardly be considered secret, and are listed if relevant. Whatever, if you find a bothy and use it, that's fine, but leave it as you found it (or better).

Camping Barns A camping barn is best described as a 'bothy you pay for'. They are usually converted farm buildings, where walkers can stay for around £2 or £3 per night. There are sleeping platforms and a cooking area, in one room, with basic toilets outside. You need all the stuff you'd need for camping except a tent, which is why camping barns are sometimes called 'stone tents'. The YHA (see Hostels, in this section) also runs camping barns in various parts of the country.

Bunkhouses Bunkhouses are a grade or two up from camping barns. They have stoves for heating and cooking, and may supply utensils. Sleeping platforms may have mattresses, but you'll still need a sleeping bag. Other facilities may include showers and a drying room. Most charge around £5 per night. Some top-end bunkhouses are like hostels, and charge similar rates. In this book we outline the facilities where they may otherwise be unclear.

Hostels

There are two types of hostel in Britain: those run by the YHA and SYHA (see the Useful Organisations section of this chapter) and independent hostels. YHA and SHYA hostels all have single-sex dormitories, showers, drying room, lounge, and an equipped kitchen for members' use. YHA hostels are graded as follows (overnight charges may vary slightly between hostels):

small – fairly basic places, in remote areas, ideal for walkers, usually closed from 10 am to 5 pm (£5.50)
medium – more facilities, often in popular country areas (£8)
busy – large places with many facilities (£9)
city – in popular tourist spots like Bath or London, large, lively, open 24 hours a day (£11)

Those under 18 pay about 75% of the adult rates quoted in the above list. Prices for meals (optional) are £3 for breakfasts and packed lunches, and from £4 for evening meals (often large and very good value).

SYHA hostels are graded as follows:

simple – £4
standard L – £4.50
standard – £6
higher standard – £8 to £10.50

Those under 18 pay about 85% of the adult rates quoted in the above list. Reservations are possible, but you usually need to pay in advance, and usually by credit card. Opening times, days and seasons vary from hostel to hostel but are listed in the members' *Accommodation Guide*. Always check these before just turning up.

Independent hostels provide similar facilities to those listed above, but are privately owned. You don't have to be a member to use them. Facilities and prices vary considerably: in rural areas some independent hostels are the same as camping barns, charging £2 per night, while others (in country areas or towns) are almost up to B&B standard, charging £10 or more. (Note also that some independent hostels in London have been described as 'backpacker ghettos', crowded and with few facilities, so choose carefully.)

Where independent hostels exist near walking routes described in this book, they are listed. For addresses of hostels all over Britain, get a copy of the *Independent Hostel Guide* (see the Books section of this chapter). Also useful is the *Independent Backpackers Hostels of Scotland* leaflet available from TICs or free from Pete Thomas, Croft Bunkhouse,

Hostel Reservations

Independent hostels often accept bookings over the phone but do not require money up front. This can be very handy for travellers, but we received a very annoyed letter from a hostel owner who had lost a lot of money by holding beds for people who booked and never turned up, while turning away others who arrived on spec. If you do book ahead and your plans change, please phone and let the hostels know. Otherwise, they'll start to insist on payment in advance, or not take bookings at all. And next time you could be the one turned away to sleep in the ditch or a pricey hotel. ■

7 Portnalong, Isle of Skye IV47 8SL (enclose a stamped self-addressed envelope).

B&Bs & Guesthouses

B&Bs are a great British institution. Basically, you get a room in somebody's house, which may be a cottage, a house in the suburbs or a remote country farm. Small B&Bs may only have one room to let, in which case you will really feel like a guest of the family. (B&Bs often have no name, so you'll find them listed in this book and in other places under the name of the owner, eg *Mrs Jones*.) Breakfasts are traditionally enormous – just right to set you up for a day in the hills.

B&B prices quoted are nearly always per person (these prices are used throughout this book, unless otherwise stated), but may be based on two people sharing a room, usually with two single beds. Lone walkers may have to pay a single supplement of between 10% and 50% extra. The difference in price between one B&B and another is usually reflected in the facilities: at the bottom end (£12 to £15 per person) you get a simple bedroom and a shared bathroom. Smarter B&Bs charge about £14 to £20, and have extras like a TV or coffee-making facilities, and a private bathroom (either ensuite, or down the hall). Bathrooms are just that – ie they contain a bath. Showers are less usual.

Guesthouses are an extension of the B&B concept, tending towards a small hotel. Prices range from £15 to £30 per person per night, depending on the quality of the food and accommodation. In general, they tend to be less personal than B&Bs, although some small and friendly B&Bs call themselves a guesthouse because it sounds more up market.

A warning: in country areas B&Bs are as we describe here. In some towns and cities, however, B&Bs are set up for long-term residents – sometimes for homeless people on welfare – and are more like lodging houses. Even if they had room, they would not normally take in passing walkers or backpackers.

B&B, Guesthouse & Hotel Reservations

There are some points to bear in mind when booking accommodation. Firstly, check exactly where the accommodation is in relation to the route you are walking. In country areas, the address of the establishment includes the nearest town, but this does not mean that the place is physically close to the route itself; it may be 20 miles away! (Some accommodation guides give grid references for establishments so you can see exactly where they are.) If a place *is* some distance from your route, you may be able to arrange to get picked up by car – but check if there's a charge for this.

Secondly, if you're staying in a remote place, make sure your accommodation offers an evening meal and book one for yourself: the nearest pub or cafe may be several miles away (although, again, some B&Bs will provide a lift service).

Thirdly, in holiday times and on popular routes, book your accommodation in advance if possible. However, if your walk is a spur-of-the-moment decision, or you just prefer not to be tied down, you should still be able to find somewhere that you can book into by giving just a few days' notice; even if the place you phone is full, staff there may be able to suggest somewhere else nearby. In quieter areas you can often arrange accommodation on the morning of the day you want to arrive.

And finally, note that many B&Bs and hotels raise their rates in busy times (usually summer) and lower them at other times, so be prepared for prices which are slightly different from those indicated in this book. ∎

Inns & Pubs

As well as selling drinks and meals (see the Food section of this chapter), local pubs and inns sometimes offer B&B, particularly in country areas, and they can be good fun, since they place you at the hub of the community. Rates are normally about £14 to £25. The difference between an inn and a pub is technical and not worth worrying about, but just to confuse things some pubs are called hotels.

Hotels

The term hotel can be used to describe a wide range of accommodation, from simple local pubs with a few rooms to grand country houses. The term can also describe medium-sized places varying widely in quality and atmosphere which can charge from about £30/40 for a single/double to more than £100/150. Some are excellent value. Some overcharge.

Hotels (and some B&Bs and guesthouses) are graded by local tourist boards, with crowns instead of stars. A place with one crown has limited facilities, while a place with five will have the lot. Note, however, that crowns indicate the facilities and standard of hotels, rather than the character of the building or the attitude of the staff. Many hotels with one or two crowns are owner-managed, and here guests are made to feel especially welcome by the host. Conversely, some top-end places can feel a bit formal and impersonal.

Houses & Cottages
If you're in a group, and staying in one place for more than a few days, then consider a

Typical peakland cottage

self-catering house or cottage. Most places have two to four bedrooms, plus lounge and fully equipped kitchen. Rates for a cottage sleeping four to six people start at about £100 per week in the low season, about £175 in spring and autumn, and about £250 in high summer (which is still a bargain when divided amongst a group). We haven't listed self-catering options in this book, but if you want to stay in, say, the Lake District or Scotland for a week or two and explore the surrounding area on foot, this is a very good option. Local TICs will give you names and numbers or send you a list. Then you deal directly with the owner.

FOOD
This section deals only with the type of food you'll need or come across while walking, mostly in country areas.

Self-Catering
If you're camping or self-catering, you can buy supplies as you go along. You're rarely more than a day from a village with a shop selling bread, milk, tinned groceries and fresh veggies. Many of these are listed in the route descriptions. If your route passes a town of any size, you can enjoy takeaways: fish & chips, baked potatoes and burgers.

Cafes
For lunch while walking, your route may pass a café or cafe. In Britain, the accent is often omitted, and a British cafe (pronounced 'caffy', or often shortened to 'caff') is nothing like its stylish continental European namesake. Most are simple places serving cheap and filling food at reasonable prices (£2 to £4). Around Britain are a number of classic cafes, which have been popular with walkers and climbers for many years and become more famous than the mountain routes nearby. Many of these are listed in this book. Some cafes open early in the morning for breakfast.

Teashops
Slightly more up market than cafes are teashops, which as well as tea and coffee,

also serve snacks and light meals. Most have a menu outside or in the window, so you can check the choice and prices without going in.

Pubs

Most pubs – especially those in country areas frequented by tourists – serve bar meals or bar snacks at lunch time and in the evening. It's difficult to generalise about these: at the cheap end they don't vary significantly from cafe fare (eg toasted sandwiches for £2, sausage and chips for £3), while at the expensive end they're closer to restaurants. Many pubs actually do both, with cheaper food served in the bar and a more formal restaurant that can be twice as expensive.

The Regional Meal Divide

The term 'dinner' can be confusing. In the south of England, or at any restaurant, it's a cooked evening meal. But in common parlance in some parts of Northern England, 'dinner' is the meal eaten at midday (ie it's the meal the rest of the country calls lunch). So office or factory staff in the south have a lunch break, while those in the north have a dinner break. Depending on where you are, if somebody refers to 'after dinner', it might be worth checking if this is in the afternoon or sometime in the evening.

The term 'tea' can also have different meanings. As well as being the British national drink, in the south it's a meal – usually a light one (eg small cakes and cucumber sandwiches) – eaten at the end of the afternoon. But in the north of England, where 'dinner' is eaten only at midday, 'tea' is the cooked evening meal.

The great mystery, however, is where the border lies. Some put the line between Birmingham and Derby, but if anybody finds out exactly where 'tea' becomes 'dinner', and 'dinner' becomes 'lunch', and vice versa, we'd like them to let us know. ■

Restaurants

More expensive still, but with a wider choice, are restaurants, where meal prices usually start at about £5 or £6, and can rise to £10 or £15 at places which make an effort with interesting and good-quality menus. At the top of this category are the real high-class establishments,

---

British Beer

What the British call beer is technically 'ale' – usually brown in colour, and more often called 'bitter'. What most people from the New World know as beer (usually yellow) is called 'lager' in Britain. There are some British lagers, but imported brand names (including Fosters and Budweiser) have infiltrated in a big way. However, when in Britain you should at least try some good British beer.

If you've been raised on amber nectar, a traditional British bitter is something of a shock – a warm, flat and expensive shock. Part of this is to do with the climate (beer here doesn't need to be chilled) and the way it's often served (hand pumped, not pressurised). Pubs which serve good beer are recommended by the Campaign for Real Ale (CAMRA) organisation. Look for their endorsement sticker on pub windows. Once you've got used to British beer, you can start experimenting with some of the hundreds of different regional types, all with varying subtle flavours and strengths. Look out for 'special brews' or 'winter warmers', but beware – some are almost as strong as wine. Another popular drink is Guinness, a dark, rich, foamy 'stout'. There are many other similar brews. ■

---

where excellent food, service and surroundings are reflected in higher prices.

DRINKS

The pub is another great British institution. Stopping at a pub for lunch, or at the end of a hard day's route, is one of the great pleasures of walking in Britain. Many people plan a route around a midday beer or two, or go to a certain campsite or mountain because the nearby pub is good. There's even a whole range of 'pub-walk' guidebooks.

Pubs in Britain have restricted hours. Most are open from 11 am to 11 pm. Others open at lunch time (from 11 am to 3 pm) and in the evening (from 7 to 11 pm) only. The bell for last orders rings out at 10.45 pm. On Sunday they open from noon to 3 pm and from 7 to 10.30 pm. Beers are usually served in pints (priced from £1.50 to £2), but you can also ask for a 'half' (a half pint). You can also buy imported or boutique beers in bottles.

You can sometimes buy takeaway drinks from a pub, but it's more usual to go to a shop or 'off-licence', where it's cheaper. This is particularly the case with wine and spirits.

THE NATURE OF WALKING IN BRITAIN

This section answers the questions most visiting walkers ask: 'What is walking in Britain actually *like*?' and 'What are my options?'. Because it explains how things work for walkers, it will be useful to read this section before going on to the route descriptions themselves.

The easy answer to the first question is 'There is no easy answer', as landscapes, weather, path conditions, access rules, distances and a host of other aspects vary greatly for different routes and areas. But that's the beauty of it: with such a range of variables, Britain has something for every kind of walker. And that answers the second question: you can do anything you like, from gentle half-day rambles through farmland and picturesque villages with welcoming inns and teashops, to multi-day long-distance backpacking routes across wild moors and mountains, and anything in between.

The Brits themselves put a high value on open space and the chance to find some fresh air, and walking is one of the most popular pastimes in Britain: every weekend millions of people take to the parks and countryside, walking for half an hour or all day, usually ending up somewhere that sells tea or beer. Active holidays are becoming increasingly popular. People who a few years ago might have stayed in seaside resorts on the south coast or at the Med, now go camping or walking instead. The number of visitors from abroad is also increasing, as more people discover the delights that walking in Britain can provide.

The infrastructure for walkers makes everything easy. Maps are excellent, and hundreds of guidebooks are readily available, covering everything from strolls to expeditions (see the Books and Maps sections of this chapter). Every TIC also sells books and provides leaflets of suggested walks in the surrounding area that take in local points of interest.

Landscapes

The types of landscape you can walk through range from manicured park to cultivated farmland and rolling grassy hills to high moorland and remote mountainous areas. You may also walk through ancient woodlands or recently planted pine plantations, alongside rivers or across cliffs and beaches at the coast. Generally speaking, the lower and more cultivated the landscape, the easier the walking. The higher and wilder landscape tends to be more spectacular, but people who choose to walk in such areas need to do more in the way of preparation and normally should have map-reading skills.

Weather Conditions

Weather conditions in Britain are changeable at any time of year (see the Climate section of the Facts about Britain chapter, but generally speaking, the lower the landscape and the further south you go, the less extreme the weather, and the less serious the walking.

All the routes in this book are described in conditions that are suitable for walking. In Southern England this may be all year (it can be misty or rainy in summer, and be beautifully crisp and clear in the depths of winter), but in other parts of the country the walking seasons are more limited. For example, some routes in the Lake District and North Wales are not suitable for walkers in winter (November to March). In Scotland, many of the mountain routes are not suitable for walkers between October and April, when snow, ice and seriously bad weather turn them into mountaineering expeditions. (More details are given in the Scotland chapters.)

Path Conditions

Generally speaking, in lowland cultivated areas, paths are clear and easy to follow. In high mountain and moorland areas, if the route is popular there will be a path to follow (although sometimes this is faint on rocky ground), but if the route is rarely trodden, there may be no visible path and you'll have to use a map and compass for navigation even in clear weather.

Access

Nearly all land in Britain is privately owned, from tiny cultivated areas to vast tracts of open wilderness. Nevertheless, walkers (and some other outdoor users such as horse-riders and mountain-bikers) are often allowed access to it using rights of way (ie paths or tracks open to members of the public). The law covering this right cannot be overruled by the actual owner of the land. If there is a right of way, you can walk through fields, woodlands and even farm-house yards, as long as you keep to the correct route and do no damage. (More details are given in the Walkers' Rights & Responsibilities section of this chapter.)

In England and Wales, the countryside is crisscrossed by a network of rights of way, many used by the routes described in this book. There are also some places where walkers can move freely beyond the rights of way. These are usually areas of 'open country' (ie unenclosed and uncultivated land, such as moorland or mountain), although they are still privately owned, either by a landowner who allows the public 'freedom to roam', or by an organisation such as the National Trust (NT), which is dedicated to preserving areas of scenic value and allowing unrestricted access. In Scotland, which has a different legal system, there are fewer actual rights of way, but generally speaking there is greater access to open country.

Having said that, rights of way and the general freedom to roam are constantly under threat from landowners. Various organisations such as the Scottish Rights of Way Society (SRWS) and the Ramblers' Association maintain vigilant campaigns to keep paths and areas open for walkers.

Where access may be restricted to certain areas (for example, because hunting takes place in certain months, or because of fire danger in dry summers) notices are usually put up to inform walkers. On routes described in this book, all access restrictions, where they exist, are detailed.

Types of Route

In this book we reflect the way routes are generally defined by walking organisations and other bodies, such as the Countryside Commission.

Day-Walks In Britain, your choice of day-walks is limitless. With around 140,000 miles (225,000 km) of rights of way, plus areas of 'open country', you could spend a lifetime covering them all. Some routes have become 'classics', because they pass through spectacular scenery, because they present a challenge, or simply because people have been doing them for many years.

In this book, the day-walks we describe are all in popular walking areas, and each is an example of the walking potential that area offers. Some are classics, while some are more obscure, having been put together or recommended by local experts. Most day-walks are circular, so you can start and finish in the same place. Others are linear, but you can still get back to base by using public transport. Some of the longer day-walks can be divided in half and walked at a slower pace over two days, while others can be extended into even longer routes that will take you two full days of walking to complete.

Long-Distance Paths In Britain, LDPs are usually defined as being over about 30 miles (50 km) in length and taking two days or more to complete. They are a relatively new idea. Although, of course, walkers have enjoyed tours of many days or weeks since the time of Wordsworth, these have always been along the footpath network, with walkers deciding where to go as the fancy took them. The first set multi-day route, the Pennine Way, was established in 1965. In the following decade, other LDPs slowly emerged. These were usually inspired by local rambling clubs or guidebook writers, sometimes with help from local county

WALKS IN THIS BOOK

The Walks	Area	Duration*	Features	Page
Northern England				
The Fairfield Horseshoe	Lake District NP	5-7 hours	Wordsworth's house	93
Helvellyn & Striding Edge	Lake District NP	5-6 hours	Airy scrambling to England's second-highest peak	98
A Fairfield Circuit	Lake District NP	5-7 hours	The Dovedale Valley	102
A High Street Circuit	Lake District NP	5-7 hours	Wide open ridge walking	103
A Scafell Pike Circuit	Lake District NP	6-8 hours	England's highest peak	104
A Hadrian's Wall Walk	Northumberland NP	1-3 days	The Wall	109
Coast & Castles	Northumberland Heritage Coast and AONB	5-6½ hours	Birdlife, castles & fishing villages	118
Falling Foss & Fyling-dales	North York Moors NP	6-7 hours	Waterfall, steam-powered trains	126
The Farndale Skyline	North York Moors NP	6-7 hours	The Lion Inn	130
The Edale Skyline	Peak NP	6 hours	Sharply contrasting limestone & gritstone scenery	132
The Limestone Way	Peak NP	10-14 hours (1 or 2 days)	Steep-sided dales, well dressings	138
The Three Peaks	Yorkshire Dales NP	8-10 hours	Limestone pavements, the Pen-y-Ghent Cafe	146
Wharfedale & Littondale	Yorkshire Dales NP	5-6 hours	Scoska Wood NNR	153
The Coast to Coast Walk	Lake District, North York Moors, Yorkshire Dales NPs	12-14 days	Crossing three of England's finest national parks	157
The Cumbria Way	Lake District NP	5 days	Woodlands, fells and lakes	173
The Dales Way	Yorkshire Dales, Lake District NPs	5-7 days	Ancient villages, meandering rivers	182
The Pennine Way	Peak District, Yorkshire Dales, North Pennines & the Cheviot Hills, and Northumberland NPs	16-20 days	Bronte country, Hadrian's Wall	190
Southern England				
A Long Dartmoor Loop	Dartmoor NP	7-8 hours	Bronze Age hut circles	210
A Short Dartmoor Loop	Dartmoor NP	4-4½ hours	Ancient tumuli	214
The Centenary Walk	Epping Forest	5½-7½ hours	Ambresbury Banks	215
A Broads Walk	Broads Special Area	6-8 hours	Windmills, grazing marshes	221
The Clarendon Way	Wessex	9-11 hours (1 or 2 days)	Salisbury & Winchester cathedrals	227
The Kennet & Avon Canal	Wessex	2 days	Bath, canal-side pubs	232
The Tennyson Trail	Isle of Wight	5-6½ hours	The Needles, sea cliffs	239
The Cotswold Way	The Cotswold Hills AONB	6-8 days	Prehistoric hillforts, scenic villages	244
Peddars Way & Norfolk Coast Path	East Anglia	6-8 days	Ice Age pingos, birdwatching	257
The North Downs Way	The Surrey Hills & Kent Downs AONB	8-11 days	Hillside chalk motifs, neolithic long barrows	265
The Ridgeway	North Wessex Downs & Chilterns AONBs	6 days	Avebury stone circle, Britain's oldest road	273
The Thames Path	Chilterns AONB	10-15 days	Windsor Castle, Tower Bridge	282
The South Downs Way	East Hampshire and Sussex Downs AONB	6-8 days	Brick-and-flint villages	293
Cornwall Coast Path	Cornwall AONB	2 weeks	Secluded coves, cliff-top castles	304

The Walks

The Walks	Area	Duration*	Features	Page
Wales				
Brecon Beacons Ridge Walk	Brecon Beacons NP	6½-8 hours	Glacial corries	323
The Snowdon Horseshoe	Snowdonia	5-7 hours	Highest mountain in Wales	331
A Snowdon Traverse	Snowdonia	5-7 hours	Highest mountain in Wales	336
Tryfan & the Glyders	Snowdonia	5-6½ hours	Cwm Idwal NNR, the Cantilever Stone	338
Carneddau Three-Thousanders	Snowdonia	6-7 hours	Views of the Glyders & Snowdon	342
The Nantlle Ridge	Snowdonia	5-7 hours	Views of Irish Sea	344
Beddgelert Valley Walk	Snowdonia	3-4 hours	Industrial heritage	346
A Snowdonia Coast to Coast	Snowdonia	4 days	A traverse of North Wales' finest mountain scenery	348
A Preseli Hills Circuit	Pembrokeshire Coast NP	5½-6 hours	Neolithic monuments	350
Owain Glyndwr's Way	Central Wales	7-10 days	Powis Castle	354
Offa's Dyke Path	Welsh Marches	9-12 days	Tintern Abbey	363
Pembrokeshire Coast Path	Pembrokeshire Coast NP	13-16 days	Path-side pubs, birdlife, sea cliffs	374
Scotland				
A Goat Fell Circuit	Isle of Arran NSA	6-7½ hours	Brodick Castle	394
Glen Coe & Glen Etive Circuit	Ben Nevis & Glen Coe NSA	5 hours	Waterfalls, red deer (if you're lucky)	399
Ben Nevis	Ben Nevis & Glen Coe NSA	6-8 hours	Britain's highest peak	403
The Road to the Isles	Ben Nevis & Glen Coe NSA	8-10 hours	Ben Nevis & Glen Coe NSA	406
Cairn Gorm High Circuit	Cairngorm NNR	5-6 hours	Britain's highest cafe	411
Chalamain Gap & the Lairig Ghru	Cairngorm NSA	6-7 hours	Pools of Dee	415
Ben Lomond	Loch Lomond NSA	5-6 hours	Views along Loch Lomond	417
Glen Shiel – the Five Sisters	Kintail NSA	7-10 hours	Classic Scottish ridge walk	422
The Torridons – Beinn Alligin	Wester Ross NSA	5-6 hours	Great views of the Western Isles	425
The Great Wilderness – An Teallach	Wester Ross NSA	8-9 hours	Waterfalls, peat bogs	429
Coast & Cuillin – Elgol to Sligachan	Isle of Skye NSA	6 hours	Follow in Bonnie Prince Charlie's footsteps	434
Bruach na Frithe	Isle of Skye	6-8 hours	Views of Cuillin Ridge	438
Southern Upland Way	Dumfries & Galloway, the Borders	12-20 days	Heather-covered hills	441
West Highland Way	Scottish Highlands	6-8 days	Loch Lomond, Rannoch Moor, Ben Nevis	450

* Hours given are for walking only. These figures do not allow for time spent checking bearings, retying shoelaces or downing a pint during lunch.

AONB – Area of Outstanding Natural Beauty, **NNR** – National Nature Reserve, **NP** – National Park, **NSA** – National Scenic Area councils, national parks or tourist boards. Usually, these were not completely new routes. Rather, they linked up many stretches of existing rights of way to create the long route.

By the early 1990s LDP fever had hit Britain. Every club and writer wanted to create a long route, and the Long Distance Path Advisory Service was established to list all the routes, so that potential 'inventors' could check that their idea was new, and then 'patent' it.

There are now over 200 LDPs in Britain. Several of the well-established and most popular routes (the classics) have been turned into national trails. These are administered by the Countryside Commission (see the Useful Organisations section of this chapter). Generally their signposting (termed 'waymarking' when it refers to a specific route) and other 'facilities', such as stiles and gates, are in better condition than those of other LDPs. Footpath maintenance is also better, but then it has to be, as national trails, by their very nature, attract more walkers than other less well-known routes.

Other LDPs in Britain which do not get national trail status are sometimes termed regional routes or recreational routes, and are administered by local councils, often with the practical assistance of local rambling groups. In this book several LDPs we describe are national trails. Others may have no official status at all, having been 'invented' by a solitary guidebook writer, yet may be walked by thousands of people every year.

Walkers might choose to walk the entire length of an LDP, but many do just a section that suits their time constraints and transport. City-bound walkers often manage to walk an entire trail over a series of weekends. To show you more of Britain's long routes, some of the day-walks we describe follow sections of LDPs.

TERMS & DEFINITIONS USED IN THIS BOOK
Direction
Precise bearings have only been given where

necessary, but the *general* compass direction you need to take is often given as part of the route description (eg 'head north', 'the path goes mainly south-west' or 'keep south of east as you come off the mountain').

Distance
Most walkers can cover between about 10 and 15 miles a day, although this depends on landscape, weather and path conditions, as outlined above. In hilly conditions, this distance may be less. In easier conditions it may be more. Most routes described in this book keep to the 10 to 15 miles per day average.

As explained in the Weights & Measures section of this chapter, Britain uses both the metric and the imperial systems of measurement. We have reflected this by using both also. When converting from one to the other, we have usually rounded up or down to the nearest ½ mile or 0.5 km. This means there will be some small inconsistencies, but never enough to increase or decrease your expected distances by more than a very small fraction.

Duration
When contemplating a walk, the time required is always a more important consideration than distance alone. A calculation called Naismith's Rule uses a formula of three miles per hour (about five km per hour) plus one hour for every 450m (1500 ft) of ascent. We have adapted this rule to 2½ miles (four km) per hour, plus an hour for every 300m (1000 ft) of ascent to give walking times for each stage of a day-walk, or each day of a long-distance route. This allows for a few short stops (for map-reading, photography etc) but not for long stops (for having lunch, visiting points of interest or getting lost in the mist, for example). It also assumes good weather.

So, if conditions are kind, and you don't stop much, you'll find the timings we give about right. If you prefer to linger longer (and ideally you should – because you'll enjoy the walk more), or there's a chance of bad weather (always a possibility in mountains) then you should add extra time – about

20% for straightforward walks, up to 50% for more serious mountain routes. Thus a 12 mile route on flat, easy paths in good weather would have a walking time of around five hours, but an overall time of six. A 12 mile route through tough country, with a lot of ascents and descents, might have a theoretical walking time of seven to eight hours, but you might actually need nine to 11 hours to complete it – or even longer in bad weather.

These times also assume that you are not carrying a heavy load (unlikely on a day-walk and not always necessary even on long-distance routes). If you are backpacking, then your speed will drop even more.

Roads & Lanes

The following definitions are common in Britain and are used in this book:

motorway – major dual carriageway, linking cities (equivalent to interstate highways in the USA and Australia)

dual carriageway – main road where the traffic is divided by a central reservation

main road, or A road – as above, linking larger towns (important main roads are also called trunk roads), marked in red on OS maps

road – any tarred highway, usually wide enough for two vehicles

B road – local road, smaller than an A road, marked in orange on OS maps (in remote parts of Britain, B roads and even A roads can be just wide enough for one car)

lane – local country road, smaller than a B road, usually only wide enough for one car, or two at a squeeze (also sometimes called a C road), marked in yellow on OS maps

street – road in town or city, usually with houses and proper names including Avenue, Close, Crescent, Boulevard etc

dirt road – road that is not tarred but can still be driven on by motor vehicles

untarred lane – small, narrow dirt road (also called 'green lanes', or 'white roads' because they are marked in white on OS maps)

track – mostly used for walking, but could possibly be used by vehicles (eg a farm truck)

The last three in this list may not be public rights of way, and you should not assume that you will be allowed to use them.

You may also see the term 'metalled road'. This is a road that has been surfaced, usually with tar (bitumen) but sometimes with cobbles or stones. To avoid confusion, we have used the term 'tarred road'. (Tar is also called 'tarmac' in Britain, so in other books you may see the clumsy term 'tarmacked road'.)

Rights of Way

In England and Wales, a right of way allows you to cross private land by a certain route and with certain restrictions. The legal nature of public rights of way in Britain is covered briefly in the earlier Nature of Walking in Britain section, while more detail is provided in the following Walkers' Rights & Responsibilities section.

There are three main types of right of way:

footpath – For walkers only, shown as a line of purple dots on OS maps

bridleway – For walkers, horse-riders and cyclists, shown as a line of purple dashes on OS maps

byway open to all traffic – For walkers, riders and any kind of vehicle (abbreviated to BOAT, but usually shortened to byway), shown as a line of T-shaped dashes on OS maps

All rights of way should be signposted at their junctions with metalled roads, and the Countryside Commission (see the Useful Organisations section of this chapter) recommends that councils and other responsible bodies should use coloured arrows for waymarking where the route is unclear – yellow for footpaths, blue for bridleways and red for byways. A further category is the permissive path, where the landowner has volunteered an access route.

In this book we have used the same terms wherever possible. Note, however, that not all paths, tracks and untarred lanes that exist on the ground are necessarily rights of way. Conversely, rights of way are shown on maps, where no visible path on the ground exists. Terms such as 'green lanes' and 'white roads' generally mean untarred lanes, but this is not a legal definition.

You may also come across the term 'road used as public path' (RUPP), which is hard to define but seems to refer to an unsurfaced route used by walkers, bikes and motor vehicles. All RUPPs in England and Wales are currently being reclassified, either into bridleways or byways, but the process will take a few years.

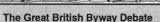

The Great British Byway Debate

Byways and RUPPs are the cause of considerable controversy. Most are old roads (sometimes thousands of years old) that fell out of use before the advent of tar and so have never had a hard surface. They have been used by walkers, cyclists or the occasional farmer's Land Rover, and have been regarded as a path or bridleway, even though any vehicle has the legal right to use them. However, in the last decade or so, 4WD (four-wheel-drive) 'leisure vehicles' have become fashionable, even though they are completely unnecessary for most British roads at any time of year, and the people who buy them have to justify their purchase by driving on byways. Off-road motorcycles also love byways, but this increase in the use of all motor vehicles on byways really annoys walkers.

The 4WD enthusiasts claim that they have a historical right to use byways, but walkers believe that byways should allow users to enjoy the peace and quiet of the country, without disturbance from cars and motorcycles, which dominate just about every other part of Britain. They also point out that off-road driving does considerable damage to the routes themselves, as vehicles often churn up a lot of mud and vegetation (especially when drivers deliberately attempt to 'do' certain stretches of byway in the most difficult conditions) making them all but impassable for those on two feet. ■

Signposts & Waymarks

Signposts are normally sited where any right of way meets a public road, and at junctions. The sign may simply say 'Public Footpath', 'Bridleway' or 'Byway', or give more detail, such as the name of the next village, bridge, lake or whatever, usually with the distance. They are sometimes called finger-posts.

Waymarks are small arrows, circles, or dots of paint that indicate you are still on the right of way. They are normally fixed to gateposts, stiles, barns, and so on. Generally, yellow waymarks are for footpaths, blue for

bridleways, and red for byways. In areas where there are a lot of footpaths there may be a lot of yellow waymarks, so don't assume they all lead the way you want to go. Keep an eye on the map too. Waymarking is better in some areas than in others, according to the diligence of the local authority, so don't worry if you can't see any. Once again, use your map.

Some walks – especially LDPs – may also have signposts and waymarks specific to that route. For example, all national trails are marked with an acorn symbol; if you keep following these you shouldn't get lost. Other routes have their own 'trademarks': a ram's head for the Limestone Way, a bishop's hat for the Clarendon Way, and so on.

Note that the spellings of place names on signposts may be slightly different to those on your map, or even those in this guidebook. This is particularly the case in Scotland and Wales, but even in England there will be slight discrepancies.

Climbing & Scrambling

The term 'climbing' has generally been avoided in this book, to avoid confusion with rock-climbing or technical mountaineering. Throughout this book, nearly every route we describe can be walked 'hands-in-pockets', even though some of the paths may be steep. Ropes and other technical bits of hardware are not required for any of the routes, as they are all described as for summer conditions. In winter (or even spring or autumn in Scotland) you might need technical gear, but such descriptions are beyond the scope of this book.

'Scrambling' comes somewhere between walking and climbing, where conditions are not serious enough to need hardware but where you do need your hands as well as your feet to follow a steep, rocky section of path. Quite often, a scramble is not technically difficult but is made more 'exciting' by sheer height or exposure. If you have no head for heights, or just like to keep your hands firmly in your pockets, most of the sections of scrambling involved in routes in this book can be avoided. Where they can't, there are often alternative routes available. These are all fully described in the relevant sections.

WALKERS' RIGHTS & RESPONSIBILITIES

Walkers' rights of access to land via rights of way are covered briefly in the earlier Terms & Definitions Used in this Book section. Under British law, these rights of way are as much a part of the 'Queen's highway' as a large main road or the M1 motorway, and the walker has exactly the same right to use them, freely and unhindered by obstructions.

You might come across 'Trespassers will be Prosecuted' signs, but as trespass is a civil wrong and you must have done damage to property to be sued, don't be too intimidated by them. The 1994 Criminal Justice Act made 'aggravated trespass' a criminal offence for anyone obstructing any lawful activity in the open air, but it was aimed at hunt saboteurs and new-age travellers, not peaceful walkers and ramblers.

Because they are highways under law, rights of way are the responsibility of the highway authorities, which in England and Wales are usually the county or metropolitan borough councils. These authorities have a duty to signpost, maintain and protect these rights of way, and any obstructions or problems encountered should be reported to them. Unfortunately for the walker, most of these councils usually have more urgent priorities than footpaths in the area of highways, but that should not stop you registering a complaint if you have one.

If a right of way is obstructed, walkers are permitted to remove enough of the obstruction to pass. If it's overgrown walkers can go legally (but carefully) through crops. Discretion is advised, however, as no farmer will appreciate damage to property, and it's usually more diplomatic to walk around the edge of the cropfield.

All rights of way are recorded on what are known as definitive maps, which have to be produced by law by the highway authorities. Usually, these routes are transferred faithfully by the Ordnance Survey onto its

excellent maps, the best of which for walkers are in the 1:25,000 Pathfinder series.

In unfenced and uncultivated mountain and moorland areas, there is often, but not always, de facto access to the hills, and in certain national park areas, you might come across signs to open country where access has been negotiated with the landowner allowing the ramblers their Holy Grail of freedom to roam wherever they wish.

Considering the size of Britain, and its complex nature of rights of way, in practice there are surprisingly few rules and regulations. Mostly it comes down to common sense (for example, if there's no stile, and you have to climb over a wall to cross a field, the chances are you shouldn't be there). Important points to remember are contained in the Country Code, promoted by the Countryside Commission, national parks and

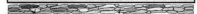

The Backpack Camping Code

- Remember that all land in Britain is privately owned, but camping may be tolerated on open mountain and moorland
- Don't camp in fields enclosed by walls without permission
- Don't camp within sight of roads or houses, or popular recreational areas
- Don't stay on a site for more than one night (occasionally two is tolerated)
- Keep groups small, and avoid pitching where another tent has recently been
- Don't light fires, and handle stoves carefully
- Deal with waste responsibly
- Avoid fouling water sources
- Take all litter out – don't bury it
- Leave the site as you found it

The Country Code

- Guard against all risk of fire
- Fasten all gates
- Keep dogs under control
- Keep to paths across farmland
- Avoid damaging fences, hedges and walls
- Leave no litter – take it home
- Safeguard water supplies
- Protect wildlife, wild plants and trees
- Go carefully on country roads
- Respect the life of the countryside

Waterway Walks

Britain has an extensive network of canals and navigable waterways. Most are used for leisure purposes, but a small percentage of Britain's commercial freight is also carried by water. Most canals were built in the days before engines were invented, and boats were pulled along by horses. Today these 'towpaths' are good for walkers – especially those who don't like hills!

Some canal-side paths have been turned into official long-distance routes called National Waterway Walks; these include the Kennet & Avon Canal, which is between Bath and Reading and is covered in detail in the Southern England – Short Walks chapter.

Other canals with good walking possibilities include: the Llangollen Canal, which is partly followed by the Offa's Dyke Path described in the Wales – Long-Distance Paths chapter; the Oxford Canal, through the heart of central England between Coventry and the River Thames at Oxford; and the big daddy of them all, the Grand Union Canal, linking London and Birmingham (which, incidentally, has its own waterway network – and more miles of canal than Venice – really). From Birmingham, the Shropshire Union continues to Ellesmere Port, making possible a cross-country journey from London to Liverpool.

If you want to know more about Britain's waterways, books on canal walks are published by Footprint Press, Cicerone and Sigma, among others, and a marvellous series of full-colour map-guides, including *The Grand Union*, *The Oxford Canal* and *The Llangollen Canal* is published by GeoProjects. (For publishers' details, see the appendix at the end of this book.) ■

other similar bodies. If you're planning to camp 'wild' (see the Accommodation section of this chapter) you should also bear in mind the Backpack Camping Code; this is based on principles produced by Dartmoor National Park, but is applicable in any area.

Getting There & Away

Information on how to reach Britain from abroad is the same for walkers as for other visitors. This subject is well covered in other guidebooks (including Lonely Planet's *Britain – travel survival kit*), so only the bare essentials are included here.

AIR

London is a global air transport hub, and severe competition between airlines means plenty of cheap flights here from just about anywhere in the world. Britain's main airports are Heathrow, Gatwick, Stansted, Luton (all on the fringes of London), Manchester, Newcastle, Edinburgh and Glasgow. Most long-haul flights arrive at Heathrow, Gatwick or Manchester. To reach other regional centres by air from here you'll have to take a separate shuttle plane (see the Getting Around chapter). If you're heading straight for Scotland from North America, there are direct flights between New York and Glasgow or Edinburgh.

If you've come in by land or on a one-way flight, and need a ticket home, London is also a major centre for discounted long-haul airfares. There are countless travel agents, most reputable, but some of dubious reliability. The best thing to do is scan through the travel-advertisement pages of a Sunday newspaper, and get on the phone to find the deal that's best for you. If you're in London, check freebie mags such as *TNT*, which carry pages of advertisements. Flights from agents registered with the Association of British Travel Agents (ABTA) are protected if the agent goes bust. Unregistered shops are riskier, but sometimes cheaper.

You may decide to pay more than the rock-bottom fare by opting for the safety of a better-known travel agent. Firms such as STA Travel, which has offices worldwide, Council Travel in the USA, Travel CUTS in Canada, Flight Centres International in Australia and New Zealand, and Campus Travel or Trailfinders in Britain offer good prices to most destinations, and are competitive and reliable.

Use the fares quoted in this book as a guide only. They are likely to have changed by the time you read this.

The USA & Canada

Newspapers like the *New York Times*, the *LA Times*, the *Chicago Tribune*, the *Toronto Star* and the *Vancouver Province* produce weekly travel sections full of travel agents' ads. You should be able to fly from New York to London return for US$350 to US$450 in the low season, or US$550 to US$650 in the high season.

Australia & New Zealand

Sydney's *Sydney Morning Herald* and Melbourne's *Age* newspapers have many advertisements offering cheap fares to London. Discounted return fares on mainstream airlines through a reputable agent like STA Travel cost between A$1600 (low season) and A$2500 (high season). Flights to/from Perth are a couple of hundred dollars cheaper. To/from New Zealand the cheapest fares to Europe are routed through the USA, and a round-the-world ticket can be cheaper than a return.

South Africa

Return fares range from R3000 to R5000 (depending on the season), but Air Namibia often has good-value offers, especially for those under 26. The South African Students' Travel Service (SASTS), on campuses around the country (in Johannesburg, ring ☎ 011-716 3045), and The Africa Travel Centre (☎ 021-235555), Cape Town, have keen prices.

LAND
Long-Distance Bus

You can travel between Britain and mainland Europe by long-distance bus (called a coach in Britain). The coach either drives onto the train and gets carried through the Channel Tunnel, or it uses a ferry (the fare for which is included in the ticket price). Eurolines, a division of National Express (☎ 0990 808080), has an enormous network of European destinations, with a main office in London and agents all over Europe. Nearly all services arrive in London's Victoria Station, from where you can get onward services to all parts of England, Scotland and Wales (see the Getting Around chapter).

Train

Britain is an island, and all overland journeys to and from mainland Europe always used to include a ferry ride. However, the Channel Rail Tunnel was opened in 1994, with two services: Le Shuttle for cars, coaches and freight vehicles, between Folkestone and Calais; and the Eurostar high-speed passenger train between London, Paris and Brussels.

In London, trains arrive at Waterloo International (the name, commemorating a certain battle, being a wonderful example of British Euro-sensitivity) with onward rail connections from other stations in London to all parts of England, Scotland and Wales.

SEA

If you're travelling overland between Britain and mainland Europe you can of course use a ferry, making your own way to/from the ports at either end. The various ferry companies all offer different prices, depending on the route, the time of day or year, the flexibility of the ticket, or vehicle size (if you're driving). It's always worth checking around.

France

France is Britain's nearest continental neighbour: on a clear day, you can see across the Channel between Dover (which is at the end of the South Downs Way, covered in this book) and Calais. It's also the cheapest link to/from Europe. Ferry companies include P&O (☎ 0990 980980), Stena Line (☎ 0990 707070) and Hoverspeed (☎ 01304 240241). Another short, cheap hop is the Sally Ferries (☎ 0990 595522) route between Ramsgate and Dunkerque. Slightly longer are the

ferries between Portsmouth and Cherbourg or Le Havre run by P&O (☎ 0990 980555).

The Rest of Continental Europe

Ferries run between Harwich or Felixstowe and the Hook of Holland (Netherlands) or Zeebrugge (Belgium). Operators include Stena Line (☎ 0990 707070) and P&O (☎ 01304 203388). Although the distance is longer, prices compare favourably with the Dover to Calais route. P&O also runs ferries and jet foils between Dover and Ostend (Belgium), and Sally Ferries (☎ 0990 595522) sails between Ramsgate and Ostend.

From Plymouth, Brittany Ferries (☎ 0990 360360) travels weekly to Santander (Spain).

Ireland

There are services from eight ports in England, Scotland and Wales (and from the Isle of Man) to six ports in Ireland. You can make booking direct, or use a travel agent. From south to north, these include:

Swansea to Cork
　　Swansea Cork Ferries (☎ 01792 456116)
Fishguard to Rosslare
　　Stena Line (☎ 01233 647047). This popular short crossing takes about four hours. A faster (99 minute) but reportedly bumpy service is available on the new catamaran (officially called the Sea Cat, but known locally as the Vomit Comet).
Holyhead to Dublin & Dun Laoghaire
　　Stena Line (☎ 01233 647047) and B&I Line (☎ 0171 7344681)
Liverpool & Heysham to Belfast
　　Norse Irish Ferries (☎ 0151 944 1010)
Stranraer to Belfast
　　Another Sea Cat service (☎ 0354 523523)
Stranraer & Cairnryan to Larne
　　Stena Line (☎ 01233 647047) and P&O (☎ 01581 200276)

LEAVING BRITAIN

People taking flights from Britain have to pay an Air Passenger Duty. Those flying to countries in the European Union (EU) will pay £5; those flying beyond it will pay £10. This is usually included in the price of your ticket. At present, there is no departure tax if you depart by sea or tunnel.

Getting Around

This chapter outlines your options for getting to or between the various walking areas and routes we describe. As with the Getting There & Away chapter, only essentials are included here, as travel information is mostly the same for walkers as for any other visitor (or for the locals, come to that) and is well covered in other guidebooks (including Lonely Planet's *Britain – travel survival kit*).

Generally speaking, your choices for getting around include: long-distance buses (called 'coaches' in Britain), which are nearly always the cheapest option for long journeys; trains, which are quicker but more expensive; and planes, which are even more expensive (and rarely necessary). For local travel (ie reaching the start of a walk from the nearest town), bus travel is normally your only option, although you may also be able to use a taxi.

Public transport in Britain is mostly of a high standard, but since the early 1980s Conservative government policy has favoured road transport, allocating billions of pounds each year to the construction of new roads, and encouraging private car ownership. (Vehicle numbers grew from 6.2 million in 1964 to 22.3 million in 1994.) The result of this is overcrowded roads and continually reduced public rail and bus services, particularly in country areas.

This may seem bad news for visitors without a car, but with determination and skilful deciphering of timetables, nearly all the routes and walking areas described in this book can be reached by public transport. In some national parks public transport is positively promoted and you can reach even quite obscure areas with remarkable ease.

For walkers, using public transport has several advantages. You can take a bus or train to get to your starting point, then do a linear walk (for as many hours or days as you like), with no worries about parking or returning to a car, and pick up a bus or train again at the other end.

Take care when asking locals for public transport information. Drivers are often blissfully unaware that their own town or village is quite well served, and will tell you there is 'one bus a week', when there are in fact three or four per day. Always contact TICs or bus/train information phone lines for details.

You can get an excellent brochure, *Getting about Britain for the Independent Traveller*, which gives details of bus, train, plane and ferry transport around Britain and into Europe, and a useful leaflet called *Scenic Britain by Bus*, from your nearest British Tourist Authority (BTA) office (see the Tourist Offices section of the Facts for the Walker chapter).

Long-term visitors may find the 1000 page *The Great British Bus Timetable* useful. It covers every service in the country (except those inside towns and cities) and is updated every four months. It's available from Southern Vectis (☎ 01983 522456), Nelson Rd, Newport, Isle of Wight PO30 1RD, for £11 (free post within Europe).

AIR

Most regional centres are linked to London, but unless you're going to the outer reaches of Britain, in particular northern Scotland, planes are only marginally quicker than trains if you include the time it takes to get to/from airports.

Prices vary enormously. For example, a return ticket from London to Edinburgh on British Airways (☎ 0345 222111) costs £240 full fare, £117 Apex, and between £99 and £109 Seat Sale. The cheapest one-way fare is £94. Air UK (☎ 0345 666777) and British Midland (☎ 0345 554554) charge £58 return on weekday departures. With most cheap tickets you must spend one Saturday night away – ie you can't return until the following week. One of the most useful flights for southern-based walkers is between London and Inverness, with British Airways Saver return fares from £100.

BUS

Public road transport in Britain is nearly all privately owned. National Express runs the largest national network of coaches, but there are often smaller competitors on the main routes. Most useful for visiting walkers who want to fly in and head straight for the hills are the National Express services that go direct from Heathrow and Gatwick airports to all parts of Britain, without going via central London. These services are more expensive, but this consideration should be weighed against the cost and hassle of going into London and out again (possibly staying overnight). One number (☎ 0990 808080) covers all National Express enquiries in Britain.

Once at your destination, each city, town or county has several small private local bus operators. Often there are two or more on the same route, each with its own timetable, which can make planning complicated. It's always best to check details with a Tourist Information Centre (TIC) or with an information phone line (numbers are given throughout this book). In towns, buses only pick up at designated bus stops. In rural areas they often stop anywhere it's safe, as long as you make it clear you want to get on or off. This system is called 'hail and ride'. In many towns there are separate terminals for buses.

Passes

National Express has several passes. The Discount Coach Card, which costs £8 per year, offers 30% off fares for full-time students in the UK, and those aged 16 to 25 or 60 plus. International Student Identity Cards (ISICs) are accepted as proof of student status, and passports are accepted as proof of date of birth. The Britexpress Card costs £12 and offers a 30% discount for all journeys taken in a 30 day period (available to visitors from abroad). The Tourist Trail Pass allows unlimited travel on all services; adults/discount card holders pay £49/39 for a three day pass, £79/65 for a five day pass in a 10 day

period, £119/95 for an eight day pass in a 16 day period, and £179/145 for a 15 day pass in a 30 day period. All passes can be bought abroad through travel agents, or at National Express agents in Britain, including agents at Heathrow or Gatwick airports.

Several smaller companies have discount cards, allowing unlimited travel for a day or a week in a certain area (such as the Lake District). These can be bought in advance or on the first bus. Sometimes an all-day ticket is cheaper than a ticket for a single long ride. Local TICs or bus information phone lines will be able to give details.

Postbus

Many rural places are served by postbuses – vans collecting or delivering mail which also carry passengers. They are ideal for walkers heading for remote locations, and are great for tours through the most beautiful areas of Britain, even if you stay in the van! Details of postbuses are given in relevant sections of this book. For the *Postbus Guide to England & Wales* contact Postbus Services (☎ 0171 490 2888), Post Office HQ, 130 Old St, London EC1V 9PQ; for Scottish timetables contact Postbus Services (☎ 01463 256273 for timetable requests – they will post one to you; ☎ 01463 256200 for postbus control enquiries), Royal Mail, 7 Strothers Lane, Inverness IV1 1AA.

Bargain Buses

Slowcoach (☎ 01249 891959), designed especially for those using YHA/SYHA hostels, runs a regular circuit from London to Windsor, Bath, Stratford-upon-Avon, the Lake District, Edinburgh, York and Cambridge, with a 'branch-line' from Bath around the West Country (including Minehead, Land's End and Exeter). You can get on and off anywhere you like (there's no compulsion to stay at a hostel) and an £89 ticket is valid for an unlimited period.

In Scotland, Go Blue Banana (☎ 0131 556 2000), 16 High St, Edinburgh, runs a similar service through Edinburgh, Perth, Pitlochry, Aviemore, Inverness, Loch Ness, Ratagan, Isle of Skye, Fort William, Glencoe, Oban,

Inverary, Loch Lomond and Glasgow for £75 with no time limit. Go Blue Banana and Slowcoach tie in their Edinburgh arrivals and departures. Also in Scotland, Haggis Backpackers (☎ 0131 5579393), 7 Blackfriars St, Edinburgh, runs a similar service for a similar price. You can book the Haggis Backpackers through Campus Travel (☎ 0171 7303402 or ☎ 0161 2731721 or ☎ 0131 6683303).

For cheap tours of Wales, the Hairy Hog Backpackers Bus (☎ 01453 872916) runs from Bath and Cardiff through the Brecon Beacons, Pembrokeshire and Snowdonia, staying at YHA hostels. The three day round trip is £65, but at the moment there's no jump-on jump-off option. There are plans to introduce this option to the service though, so it might be worth ringing to check.

TRAIN

Despite the cutbacks of the last decade, Britain has an impressive rail service, including a number of beautiful lines through sparsely populated country, which are of great use to walkers and great interest to all visitors. The main routes are served by fast InterCity express trains that whisk you from London to various regional centres. Local railways with stopping trains include the famous Settle-Carlisle Line, through the heart of the Yorkshire Dales, the Cumbria Coast Line, winding between the sea and the Lake District, and several more through the mountains of Scotland and Wales including the West Highland Railway. A combination of travel by rail and foot is one of the best ways to see Britain.

Information

One number (☎ 0345 484950) covers all rail timetable enquiries in Britain, but getting information on train travel is always a battle. The timetables are easy enough to follow, but there are about six different types of discount pass and about eight types of ticket for any journey (or more if several train companies are used), giving almost endless permutations. The secrets for successful train travel are: get a discount pass if you're using the train a lot; always buy your ticket as far in advance as possible; ask for the cheapest ticket available (always give the clerk time to check – they find the system cumbersome too); and ask what restrictions it may have. Anyone who's travelled in India will see where its system was conceived. If you do figure out the system and fully exploit it, and you're not in a rush, you can save a lot of money travelling by train. You'll also gain a lasting insight into an insane bureaucracy.

There are two classes of rail travel: 1st and

British Rail Privatisation

In the early 1990s the Conservative government announced plans to privatise the (formerly state-owned) railway network. British Rail was broken into more than 80 different businesses. The main one, Railtrack, owns the actual lines and the stations. The trains are run by various companies (eg Regional Railways, Midland Main Line, InterCity Cross-Country, North-West Railways, Network SouthEast, ScotRail, Gatwick Express and the East Coast Line) who pay Railtrack for use of the lines.

The policy of British Rail privatisation was ideologically driven, and by 1995 it had become a sacred cow for the Conservative government, determined to force the plan through at all costs, despite considerable opposition from other political parties, environmentalists, investors and trade unions (oh yes, and passengers). There are widespread misgivings. Even the government concedes that in the short term the changes will actually *cost* hundreds of millions of pounds, and that substantial parts of the system will continue to be subsidised. The general public are afraid more small country lines will close, that ticket prices will rise, that passes and various travel cards will disappear, and that planning and paying for a cross-country trip (that might involve linking a number of operators) will become a nightmare. You have been warned. ∎

Coach/Bus Fares from London

The sample fares below are for single/return travel from London on the National Express coach (bus) system. To qualify for the discount fares you must have a Discount Coach Card (£8 – see Bus in this section for details). The discount is applicable on nonadvance-purchase fares only.

If you're not eligible for a Discount Coach Card you'll need to buy your ticket at least seven days in advance and avoid travelling on a Friday (or Saturday in July and August) to avoid paying the full fares.

Fares below have been rounded up to the next pound.

| | | | Nonadvance Purchase | | | | 7-Day Advance | |
| | | | Not Fri✦ (Economy) | | Fri (Standard) | | Not Fri✦ | Fri |
miles	to	hours	Adult sgl/rtn(£)	Discount sgl/rtn(£)	Adult sgl/rtn(£)	Discount sgl/rtn(£)	Adult rtn(£)	Adult rtn(£)
51	Brighton✳	1¾	7/10	5/7	7/10	5/7	7/10	5/7
54	Cambridge	2	7/9	5/7	7/9	5/7	7/9	5/7
56	Canterbury	2	10/11	7/8	12/13	8/9	10	12
57	Oxford✳	1¾	3/6	3/5	3/6	3/5	3/6	3/6
71	Dover	2½	11/12	8/8	14/14	10/10	11	13
83	Salisbury	2¾	13/14	9/10	16/17	11/12	13	15
92	Stratford	2¾	13/14	9/10	16	11/12	12	15
106	Bath✳	3	17/19	12/13	21/22	15/16	17	20
110	Birmingham	2½	14/15	10/10	16/17	11/12	13	16
115	Bristol✳	2¼	18/19	13/14	22/23	16/17	17	21
131	Lincoln	4¾	22/23	16/17	26/28	16/17	21	25
150	Shrewsbury	4½	17/18	12/13	20/21	14/15	16	19
155	Cardiff	3¼	20/22	14/16	25/26	18/19	20	23
172	Exeter✳	3¾	23/25	17/18	28/30	20/21	22	27
184	Manchester	4	21	15	21	15	18	18
188	York✳	4	26	18	26	18	20	20
193	Liverpool	4¼	21	15	21	15	18	18
211	Aberystwyth	7¼	20/22	14/16	25/26	18/19	20	23
215	Scarborough	5¾	30	21	37	26	24	24
255	Durham	4¾	26	18	26	18	20	20
259	Windermere	7	30/33	22/23	37/39	26/28	30	35
280	Penzance	6	33/35	23/25	40/42	28/30	32	38
290	St Ives	7	33/35	23/25	40/42	28/30	32	38
299	Carlisle	5½	21/26	20/24	21/26	20/24	26	26
350	Galashiels	8	33/35	23/25	39/42	28/30	31	31
375	Edinburgh✳	8	21/26	20/24	21/26	20/24	26	26
397	Glasgow✳	7	21/26	20/24	21/26	20/24	26	26
434	Dundee	8¼	36/43	26/30	36/43	26/30	34	34
450	Perth	8¼	36/43	26/30	36/43	26/30	34	34
489	Oban	12	46/54	32/38	46/54	32/38	41	41
503	Aberdeen	10½	41/49	29/34	41/49	29/34	40	40
536	Inverness	12	41/49	29/34	41/49	29/34	40	40
590	Ullapool	14	48/60	34/42	48/60	34/42	51	51
652	Thurso	15½	40/50	33/45	40/50	33/45	50	50

✦ Not on Friday or Saturday in July and August.
✳ Other companies also operate this route and are often cheaper. National Express may have some special EarlyBird fares but they are usually only applicable for the journey into London.

Rail Fares from London

Rail travel is faster than coach travel but usually more expensive. The sample fares below are for 2nd-class single/return travel from London.

A Eurail pass cannot be used in Britain. If you're studying full-time in the UK, or are under 25, or are over 60, or are disabled, or have children, you can purchase a railcard which allows a discount (usually 34%) on all standard class fares except Apex and SuperApex.

If you don't have a BritRail pass and are not eligible for a railcard you can still save money by buying your ticket in advance, though these tickets are usually available only on journeys of more than 150 miles. Cheap tickets include Apex, which must be bought seven days in advance, SuperApex (14 days in advance) and SuperAdvance (see note below). Even cheaper promotional fares are sometimes available.

Fares below have been rounded up to the next pound. Where two routes are available between London and the station below, the fare for the cheaper route has been listed.

			Nonadvance Purchase					7/14-Day Advance	
			Peak	*Saver (Off Peak✱)*		*SuperSaver (Not Fri✦)*		*Apex*	*SuperApex*
miles	*to*	*hours*	*Adult sgl/rtn(£)*	*Adult sgl/rtn(£)*	*Railcard sgl/rtn(£)*	*Adult sgl/rtn(£)*	*Railcard sgl/rtn(£)*	*Adult sgl/rtn(£)*	*Adult sgl/rtn(£)*
23	Windsor	½	6/6	5/5	3/3	–	–	–	–
51	Brighton	¾	13/15	12/13	8/8	(Awaybreak £17)		(Stayaway £20)	
54	Cambridge	1	15/16	12/14	8/9	(Awaybreak £17)		–	–
56	Canterbury	1½	15/15	13/14	9/10	–	–	–	–
57	Oxford	¾	15/28	13/14	8/9	(Awaybreak £17)		–	–
71	Dover	1¼	19/20	17/18	11/12	(Awaybreak £20)		–	–
83	Salisbury	1¼	21/21	19/19	13/13	(Awaybreak £24)		(Stayaway £28)	
92	Stratford	2¼	15/29	15/21	10/14	(Cheap day return £18)		–	–
106	Bath	1¼	18/22	18/19	12/12	18/22	12/15	15/15	–
110	Birmingham	1½	17/34	16/23	–	17/20	–	14/14	–
115	Bristol	1½	18/22	18/32	12/22	18/19	12/12	16/17	–
131	Lincoln	1¾	33/66	33/39	22/26	31/32	20/21	–	–
150	Shrewsbury	2½	38/69	36/37	24/24	29/29	19/19	18/18	–
155	Cardiff	2	28/37	28/37	18/24	28/28	18/19	23/23	–
172	Exeter	2	39/40	34/35	22/23	34/35	22/23	24/25	–
184	Manchester	2½	53/96	44/45	29/29	34/35	22/23	26/26	19/19
188	York	2	51/102	51/56	34/37	45/46	30/30	34/35	–
193	Liverpool	2½	51/93	44/45	29/29	34/35	22/23	26/26	19/19
211	Aberystwyth	5¼	50/91	45/46	29/30	36/37	24/25	25/25	–
215	Scarborough		2¾	53/106	53/61	35/40	50/51	33/3440/41	–
255	Durham	2¾	64/128	64/70	42/46	56/57	37/38	38/39	28/28
259	Windermere	3¾	62/112	56/57	37/38	46/47	30/31	33/34	–
280	Penzance	5	50/99	50/55	33/36	46/47	30/31	30/31	–
290	St Ives	5½	50/99	50/56	33/37	47/48	31/32	31/32	–
299	Carlisle	3½	64/118	62/63	41/42	50/51	33/34	37/38	29/29
350	Galashiels	6	69/129	69/71	46/47	58/59	38/39	–	–
375	Edinburgh	4	68/72	68/72	45/48	61/62	40/41	45/46	33/34
397	Glasgow	5	68/72	68/72	45/48	61/62	40/41	45/46	33/34
434	Dundee	5¾	68/76	68/76	45/50	62/63	41/42	52/53	–
450	Perth	6	68/76	68/76	45/50	62/63	41/42	52/53	–
489	Oban	9½	79/90	79/90	52/60	75/76	50/50	59/60	–
503	Aberdeen	6½	76/83	76/83	50/55	70/71	47/47	57/58	–
536	Inverness	8¼	76/83	76/83	50/55	70/71	47/47	57/58	–
590	Ullapool		(No rail service – bus from Inverness)					–	
652	Thurso	13	84/96	84/96	55/63	83/84	55/55	70/71	–

✱ You may travel back on a peak-time train, but not on your outward journey.

✦ Not on Friday or Saturday in July and August, but you can travel on these days for this price if you buy a SuperAdvance ticket. This must be bought before 2 pm on the day before (ie Thursday for Friday travel).

'standard' (formerly, and still more often, called 2nd class). First class costs 30% to 50% more than 2nd and, except on very crowded trains, is not really worth the extra money. Unless otherwise stated, the prices quoted in this book are for 2nd-class adult single tickets. Return tickets are sometimes double the single price, but often only a few pounds more.

For very long journeys, you can use an overnight sleeper train. There's one between London and Plymouth, but the most useful for walkers and all visitors to Britain is the one between London and Scotland (see aside). These have sleeping compartments, with one berth in 1st class and two in 2nd class. It's essential to reserve in advance.

Passes

BritRail Pass This is useful for visitors, allowing unlimited travel. Prices for adults/youths in US dollars (also available in other local currencies) are: eight days $235/189, 15 days $365/289, 22 days 465/369, and 31 days 545/435. This pass is *not available in Britain* and must be bought in advance. Contact the BTA (see the Tourist Offices section of the Facts for the Walker chapter) in your country for details.

Flexipass This pass allows four days unlimited travel in a month ($199/160) or eight days in one month ($280/225).

Scottish Wayfarer If you're spending some time in Scotland, the SYHA (see the Useful Organisations section of the Facts for the Walker chapter) has a pass giving you hostel accommodation, unlimited travel by rail and Caledonian MacBrayne (CalMac) ferries, and bus discounts. Contact the association direct for information.

Railcards

Railcards available from major stations in Britain give you discounts (normally about one-third) off most tickets except Apex and SuperApex (see Tickets later in this section). They include:

Young Person's Railcard – for those aged 16 to 25, or students of any age studying in the UK (£16)

Senior Citizen's Railcard – available to anyone over 60 (£16)

Disabled Person's Railcard – for a disabled person and one person accompanying them; available through post offices or by writing to British Rail, PO Box 28, York YO1 1FB (£14)

Family Railcard – offers a 34% discount for up to four adults, while up to four children pay a flat fare of £2 each (£20)

Tickets

All prices in this book are given for adults. Children under five travel free; those aged between five and 15 pay half price for most tickets, and full fare for Apex and SuperApex tickets. Credit cards are accepted. Some tickets can be (or must be) bought in advance, either at a station or by phone. The number to ring will be found on the relevant printed timetable or through the telephone timetable enquiry line (see Information earlier in this section). You must do this five working days before travel (so they can be sent by post). Ticket types include:

Single Ticket – valid for a single journey at any time on the day specified; expensive

Day Return Ticket – valid for a return journey at any time on the day specified; relatively expensive

Cheap Day Return Ticket – valid for a return journey on the day specified on the ticket, but there may be time restrictions; often about the same price as a single

Apex – a very cheap return fare, rivalling National Express coach prices; for distances of more than 150 miles; you must book at least seven days in advance, but seats are limited

SuperApex – a very cheap return fare for journeys on certain lines between London and north-east England or Scotland; you must book at least 14 days in advance, but seats are limited

SuperSaver – a cheap return ticket with up to 50% savings; not available within Network South-East; cannot be used on a Friday or Saturday in July and August, nor in London before 9.30 am or between 4 and 6 pm

SuperAdvance – for travel on Fridays, and also Saturdays in July and August; similarly priced to the SuperSaver but must be bought before noon on the day before travel, or earlier

Saver – higher priced than the SuperSaver, but can be used any day and there are fewer time restrictions

London to Scotland by Rail – Britain's Best Kept Secret

I shall leave tonight from Euston
By the seven-thirty train,
And from Perth in the early morning
I shall see the hills again.
From the top of Ben Macdhui
I shall watch the gathering storm
And see the crisp snow lying
On the back of Cairngorm.
I shall feel the mist from Bhrotain
And pass by Lairig Glen
To look on dark Loch Einich
From the heights of Sgoran Dubh.
From the broken Barns of Bynack
I shall see the sunrise gleam
On the forehead of Ben Rinnes
And Strathspey awake from dream.
And again in the dusk of evening
I shall find once more alone
The dark water of the Green Loch
And the pass beyond Ryvoan.
For tonight I leave from Euston
And leave the world behind;
Who has the hills as a lover
Will find them wondrous kind.

Did you know that you could get on a train in London in the evening, have a meal and a good night's sleep, even breakfast in bed, and then get off next morning amongst the stunning mountains of Scotland? Late every evening (except Saturday) the *Caledonian Sleeper* train leaves London's Euston Station bound for Glasgow and Edinburgh (arriving around 7 am next day), Inverness (9 am) and Fort William (10 am).

The route to Inverness is the one described so eloquently above; it eventually leads to Kyle of Lochalsh – gateway to the Isle of Skye. Between Glasgow and Fort William the train runs on the West Highland Railway, surely the most beautiful, yet underrated, train journey in the country. As you go north the magic continues: beyond Fort William the train runs on to Mallaig, from where it's a short ferry ride to the Isle of Skye. There's also a branch line to Oban, gateway port for the Outer Hebrides.

On both lines you can leave the train at an intermediate station and head straight for the hills. For example, from Aviemore you can reach the Cairngorms, and from the West Highland Railway stations you can aim for nearby peaks as soon as you step off the platform.

With returns from Scotland leaving in the evening and arriving back in London around 8 am next day, it makes short walking breaks for mountain-starved southerners exceedingly possible, and is ideal for visitors too, especially if you've only got a few days to spare.

For a walker, this railway is a dream come true, and for any visitor to Britain a ride on the sleeper train is a thrilling way to reach Scotland and see some of the best bits of the country on the way. Until recently, the sleeper service to Fort William was under threat of closure. The train's operator, ScotRail, said this was necessary because not enough people used it, and the service didn't make a profit. ScotRail's opponents pointed out that the service was underutilised mainly because ScotRail didn't think to tell anyone that it existed. Instead of promoting the sleeper service as an alternative to driving or flying between London and Scotland, it was down-played and almost forgotten. But, ironically, the public outcry following the threat of closure created a new demand, and provided the sleeper service with a new lease of life – at least for the next five years. Now that the secret is out, there is even less excuse for thinking that you don't have the time to get into the Scottish mountains. Better get your maps out...

ScotRail currently charges £60 return for an Apex ticket between London and Fort William. On top of this you pay £27 each way for the sleeping compartment. You can make enquiries and reservations on ☎ 0345 550033.

The anonymous poem above was written on the door of a Highland walkers' shelter in the 1950s, recorded by a Mrs Pugh of East Lothian, and reprinted in 1995 in *The Great Outdoors* magazine. More details on the West Highland Railway, including nonsleeper services between Glasgow and Fort William (if you don't want to go all the way from London) are included in the Ben Nevis & Glen Coe section of the Scotland – Short Walks chapter. ■

Circular Ticket – allows you to return by indirect routes, but at a discount similar to the Saver ticket

AwayBreak Ticket – for use on Network SouthEast on journeys over 40 miles. Valid for an outward journey at any time on the day specified, with a return journey within five days. From Monday to Friday it may not be used before 9.30 am; about half the price of a straight return ticket

You might possibly be confused by this tidal wave of information. The following example may help: a standard single coach ticket from London to Edinburgh is £20.50, but with a small company you might find a return ticket for £20. A standard single rail ticket from London to Edinburgh is £61, but a Super-Apex return is £34. Easy!

TAXI

Outside London, taxis are usually reasonably priced. In the country you could expect to pay around £1.20 per mile, which means they are definitely worth considering to get to an out-of-the-way hostel or the beginning of a walk. A taxi over a short distance will not cost much more than a local bus, especially if there are three or four people to share the fare.

CAR

If you've come to Britain to combine walking with some general motorised touring, a car helps you reach remote places, and to travel quickly, independently and flexibly. For a short visit you can hire; for a longer visit you might even consider buying a car and selling it again when you leave.

Always remember that if you park your car at the start of a walk, you have to get back to it eventually. This is not usually difficult on the day-walks covered in this book, as most are circular. It can be more trouble, however, on long-distance walks, as these are usually linear. In addition, secure parking is often hard to guarantee, especially if you're away for a long time, while just *finding* a place to park can be difficult in some of the more popular areas.

The best thing to do is to find a hostel or B&B near the start of the route, explain what you're doing and leave your car there while

walking, returning by public transport afterwards (and staying another night).

For an outline of the different types of road in Britain, see the Terms & Definitions Used in this Book section of the Facts for the Walker chapter. For details on road rules, get hold of a booklet called *The Highway Code* (99p), which is often available in Tourist Information Centres (TICs) and post offices.

If you decide to rent, you might be better off making arrangements in your home country for some sort of package deal. In Britain, a small car with four seats (carrying two in reasonable comfort, three at a pinch, and four if you leave the luggage behind) can be hired for about £40 per day, dropping to about £150 for a week (with unlimited mileage). A slightly larger car is about £180 per week. Check the small advertisements in Sunday newspapers, local tourist news sheets, *Yellow Pages* phone directories and London-based free publications such as *TNT*. Big-name firms charge more, but rates are competitive and always changing, so ringing around is the best bet. If you want a car with automatic transmission you must specify this in advance.

Petrol costs between 55p and 65p per litre and diesel is only a few pence cheaper.

BICYCLE

Many visitors to Britain travel around by bike, as distances between places of interest are relatively short and the country's network of minor roads and lanes makes for excellent touring. A combination of cycling and walking is a great way to discover some of Britain's quieter, less hyped areas, although bikes are not allowed on footpaths (see the Terms & Definitions Used in this Book section of the Facts for the Walker chapter).

You can bring your own bike, or rent locally: many of the walking areas described in this book have hire centres. Of the long-distance paths described, the South Downs Way can be covered by bike as well as on foot, and half of the Ridgeway National Trail is open to cyclists. (The options for cyclists are covered in more detail in these sections.)

The BTA publishes a useful free booklet, *Cycling*, with some suggested routes, lists of cycle holiday companies and other helpful information. Many regional TICs have information on local cycling routes and places where you can hire bikes. If you're touring by bike for more than a few weeks it might be worth joining the Cyclists' Touring Club (CTC) (☎ 01483 417217), 69 Meadrow, Godalming, Surrey GU7 3HS. Members can get comprehensive information about cycling in Britain, suggested route sheets (on and off-road), lists of local cycling contacts and clubs, details of recommended accommodation and organised cycling holidays, a cycle hire directory, and a mail-order service for maps and books for cyclists. Some cycling organisations outside Britain have reciprocal membership arrangements with the CTC.

HITCHING

Hitching is never entirely safe in any country in the world, and we don't recommend it. Travellers who decide to hitch should understand that they are taking a small but potentially serious risk. However, getting around Britain by hitching is reasonably easy, except in built-up areas, where you'll need to use public transport. It's against the law to hitch on motorways; you have to use approach roads, nearby roundabouts, or service stations. In country areas, where public transport and any kind of traffic is thin on the ground, the old hitchers' rule comes into play: the fewer the cars, the better your chances. If you're just hitching 'locally' (ie from a hostel to the start of a walk, or back to camp at the end of the day), your chances are also good, especially if you *look* like a walker. In some remote parts of Scotland, hitching is so much a part of getting around that local drivers may stop and offer lifts without your even asking.

BOAT

Travelling by boat is not a common way for getting around Britain, until you get to the Highlands and Islands of Scotland, where ferries are essential. CalMac is Scotland's most important ferry operator, with services to nearly all inhabited islands, including Arran and Skye (which are covered in this book, along with their ferry services). If you plan to spend some time in the islands, CalMac's 'Island Hopscotch' travel passes are usually a good deal.

In England, the major ferry destination is the Isle of Wight, with services from Southampton and Lymington on the south coast. These are covered in the Isle of Wight section of this book.

WALKING TOURS

A number of companies run walking tours in Britain. These are either based at one or two centres with several day-walks in various directions, or are linear tours, going by foot from place to place, while baggage is carried in a van to your next destination. Some companies arrange tours led by experienced guides, which leave on certain dates for a set duration, and you will normally join a group of between six and 10 people. Other companies arrange 'self-guided' tours, where all accommodation and baggage transfer is pre-booked for you, and map and instructions provided so you can follow the route at your own pace. Of course, with self-guided holidays you can go when you like, and usually do not join a group. For more details phone the companies direct. The Ramblers' Association (see the Useful Organisations section of the Facts for the Walker chapter) produces a very good list of walking tour operators (including the smaller, often cheaper, outfits), and the BTA's *Walking in Britain* leaflet carries several advertisements. Or check the advertisements in publications mentioned in the Magazines section of the Facts for the Walker chapter.

Only national and regional companies are listed here. Smaller outfits which just cover specific areas (such as the Lake District, Brecon Beacons or North-West Scotland) are detailed in the relevant sections. Several of these organisations are well used to catering for foreign visitors and have agents and representatives in Australia, New Zealand, the USA and many other countries around the world. Contact them direct first, and you can then deal with agents if you have any questions.

The YHA and SYHA (see the Useful Organisations section of the Facts for the Walker chapter) both organise short and long walking holidays using their hostels all over Britain. For example, a weekend (two nights) of easy walking in the Peak District based at Edale or harder hill-walking in Snowdonia based at Pen-y-Pass costs from £70. Five days of winter-walking in the Lakes is about £200. Longer routes, such as the Cumbria Way (seven nights for £239) and the Coast to Coast (15 nights for £495), and less crowded routes such as the Herriot Way and the White Peak Way, include a qualified leader and full-board accommodation. Full details can be obtained from YHA Walking Holidays, PO Box 11, Matlock DE4 2XA, (☎ 01629 825850). The SYHA, 7 Glebe Crescent, Stirling FK8 2JA, (☎ 01786 451181), offers weekend walking breaks in Scotland starting from £30, and week-long trips for the fit.

Sherpa, 131A Heston Rd, Hounslow TW5 0RD, (☎ 0181 569 4101; fax 0181 572 9788), is a British-based company organising treks all over the world, including several in its own backyard, ranging from weekend breaks in the Lake District for about £200 (including accommodation and guide) to longer self-guided treks on the Cumbria Way, Dales Way, West Highland Way and several other LDPs, starting at £350 for eight days.

English Wanderer, 6 George St, Ferryhill, Co Durham DL17 0DT, (☎ 01740 653169; fax 01740 657996) offers a slick range of organised and self-guided routes in England and, despite its name, in Wales and Scotland (plus Ireland and France).

The Wayfarers, Brayton, Aspatria, Cumbria CA5 3PT, (☎ 01697 322383; fax 01697 322394), organises and leads a well-planned series of linear routes through England, Scotland and Wales (plus France and Italy), with leader, back-up vehicles and good-quality accommodation.

HF Holidays, Imperial House, Edgware Rd, London NW9 5AL, (☎ 0181 905 9556; fax 0181 205 0506), organises guided holidays on LDPs, including the Two Moors Way, the Pennine Way, Offa's Dyke and the Speyside Way in Scotland. It also runs a programme of single-base holidays in various parts of the country.

Instep Linear Walking Holidays, 35 Cokeham Rd, Lancing, West Sussex BN15 0AE, (☎ & fax 01903 766475), does a range of self-guided walking tours in England and Wales. Routes include Offa's Dyke, the South Downs Way and sections of the South West Coast Path, plus more unusual canal walks and railway walks. Prices vary according to the length of the route and the number of people in your group, but start at £169 per person for a group of six on a four day trip, rising to £458 for two weeks. Two people pay £233 each for four days, and £527 for 14.

Countrywide Holiday, Grove House, Wilmslow Rd, Manchester M20 2HU, (☎ 0161 446 2226; fax 0161 448 7113), specialises in south-west and Northern England, with a very wide range of holidays covering various lengths and standards, using experienced leaders and staying in country guesthouses.

Drystone Walking Holidays, 1A Town Head Ave, Settle BD24 9RQ, (☎ & fax 01729 825626), specialises in just two areas – popular Yorkshire and off-the-beaten-track Shropshire, with guided and self-guided holidays for groups or individuals starting throughout the year, with a range of standards and accommodations to suit taste and budget.

Northern England – Short Walks

The Lake District

If anywhere is the heart and soul of walking in England, it's the Lake District in the north-west of the country – a wonderful area of high mountains, deep valleys and, of course, lakes.

The reason for its popularity may be historical; this is where William Wordsworth and the Romantic writers first engaged in walking and enjoying the outdoors for aesthetic or spiritual reasons, rather than just to get from A to B.

Or the reason may be something to do with appearances; whereas the national parks in many other parts of England tend to be rounded dales and moors, in the Lakes you find 'proper' mountains, wild and rugged. One writer said the Lake District hills are so wonderful 'because they've got knobs on'.

Or it may be more practical; the Lake District is easy to reach from most parts of England, but at the same time it's one of few places in the country where you can get more than a couple of miles or hours from 'civilisation'. This is because the area is the remains of an old volcano, with the high ground roughly in the centre and the long lakes and valleys radiating out like the spokes of a wheel. Roads lead up to the end of several valleys, but few go right across, so the central part is still relatively remote, and can only be reached on foot.

Whatever the reason, it's true that the Lakes have an irresistible attraction to walkers. I was once on a walking tour with some friends in the Peak District, when halfway through the third day, one of the group suddenly turned round, went back to the nearest town, which happened to be Buxton, and caught the next train to Windermere, and went walking in the Lakes instead. She'd spent many other trips in the Lakes,

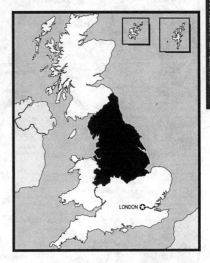

but just couldn't resist going back again for more. Although walkers always moan about the crowds and the unpredictable weather, it's still the sort of place that attracts them back year after year.

And they're not all walkers – several million visitors come here for fishing, power boating, sailing or simply driving around in cars and coaches. Various plans have been mooted to restrict the number of vehicles, such as the introduction of one-way systems and park-and-ride schemes, but in the summer you should be prepared for a crush.

Most of the area is contained within the Lake District National Park. Like all national parks in England and Wales, this is not public land but made up of many privately owned farms and estates, including many villages and even a few towns. Some people work in farming, but many more depend on tourism for their income. The park is administered by a central authority with responsibility for the conservation of the park and the promotion of its recreational virtues.

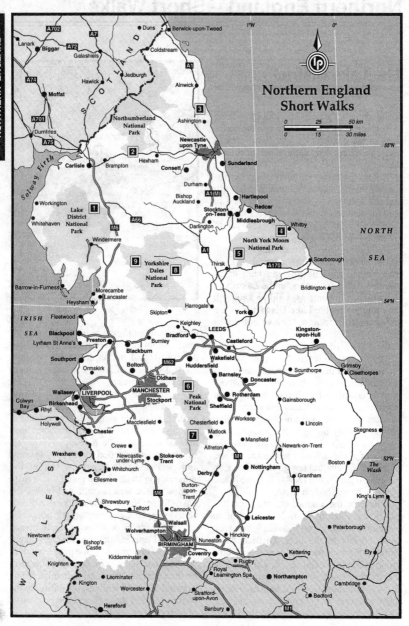

Northern England Short Walks

THE FAIRFIELD HORSESHOE

Distance 10 miles (16 km)
Duration 5 to 7 hours
Start & Finish Ambleside
Regional Centres Ambleside, Keswick, Windermere
County Cumbria
Area Lake District National Park
Summary A good-quality circular route, with paths that are easy to follow in fine weather, though boggy and eroded in places. Care and navigational skills are required in bad conditions.

NORTHERN ENGLAND

The Lake District is traditionally divided into several smaller areas: the Central Fells, the Northern Fells, the Eastern Fells and so on. (A 'fell' is a hill or mountain.) These high areas are separated by large valleys, but are also based upon the divisions used by the famous writer Alfred Wainwright in his series of classic guidebooks, which were first published in the 1950s and have inspired many walkers and influenced many guidebook writers ever since.

Of course, in a place like the Lakes the choice of walking routes is literally endless. There are hundreds of high walks, peak walks, ridge walks, valley walks and (naturally) lake walks. Even a list of 'classic' walks would run to several pages, so to pick just a few routes to represent the whole area is particularly hard.

Elsewhere in this book we have described two long-distance routes through the Lakes: the Coast to Coast Walk and the mainly lowland Cumbria Way (parts of which can be incorporated into shorter circuits).

The day-walks we describe in this section are mostly upland routes and include a batch of Lakeland's most famous mountain names. The environments these walks pass through and the nature of the walks themselves are all different. What we have attempted to do in this section is cover as broad a cross section of Lakeland walks as we can in the limited space available. Several can be done from the same base, so you won't have to 'move camp' every time you tackle another mountain.

Fairfield is the name of a large mountain in the Eastern Fells. At 873m (2863 ft), it's one of the highest in the area, along with northerly neighbours Helvellyn (950m) and the wonderfully named Dollywaggon Pike (858m), which is covered in the next route description in this section. When viewed from the south or west, the Eastern Fells appear generally more rounded than many other parts of the Lakes, and the walk we describe here provides fine open walking, relatively straightforward in good weather. (For a more serious walk from the eastern side, see later in this section.)

The route is a classic horseshoe circuit, going up one ridge and down another, on either side of the Rydal Valley, with the summit of Fairfield at the highest point of the walk, where the two ridges meet. When the weather is kind, the views are excellent. To the west you can see Scafell Pike (also described in this section) and to the east the long ridge of High Street (ditto). The view south is dominated by the vast lake of Windermere, dotted with sailing boats like scattered confetti.

Often, however, the weather is awful, with wind, rain and mist making a walk unpleasant and (even on this clear path) navigational skills necessary. As with anywhere in the Lakes, the conditions can change very quickly, so even if it looks fine, take warm waterproof clothes, plus a map and compass that you know how to use.

Ambleside is a good base for this walk; there are plenty of accommodation options, it's easy to get to and there are about a million gear shops to wander around if there's too much rain to go walking.

Direction, Distance & Duration

The route is not waymarked. We suggest going clockwise. The route we describe here is 10 miles. However, on Stage 2 you gain around 800m in height, so the walking time is five to seven hours. Allowing for lunch and photo opportunities, your overall time will probably be around six to eight hours.

Information

Ambleside's Tourist Information Centre (TIC) (☎ 015394 32582) is on Church St, open daily April to October, Friday and Saturday for the rest of the year. The nearest National Park Information Centre is at Brockholes about three miles away, on the road to Windermere. Most of the gear shops sell maps and local guidebooks, or try The Adventure Traveller bookshop on Compston Rd. Other good sources of local information are *The Visitor*, a freebie newspaper, and the *Lake District National Park Events Guide*; both are available from TICs and park information centres (PICs). The national park has a 24-hour Weatherline Service (☎ 017687 75757) for up-to-date weather forecasts and information about mountain conditions.

Books If you piled up all the books on walking in the Lake District there'd be another mountain to scale, so we can only mention a few here. Of those which cover Fairfield in some detail, including the two routes to the summit we describe in this section, foremost is the classic *Pictorial Guides to the Eastern Fells* by Alfred Wainwright, one of seven pocket-sized volumes in the series (£9.99 each). The individual 'AW' style, combining hand-drawn text and pictures, is very attractive and has influenced many subsequent outdoor writers. However, these books were written in the 1960s, and have been only slightly updated since. That's part of the charm, but you should use them alongside a detailed map for routefinding on the hill, and a more modern guidebook for route suggestions. These include *100 Lake District Hill Walks* by Gordon Brown (Sigma, £7.95) which covers every hill, fell and mountain in the area, including well-known classics and out-of-the-way rarities.

If you want a selection, the Ordnance Survey (OS) Pathfinder Guides *Lake District Walks* and *More Lake District Walks* describe routes from a few miles to all day, over high ground and along valleys, with extracts from the relevant 1:25,000 OS maps. The national park produces an inexpensive booklet called *Walks in the Countryside* and several leaflets detailing a range of circular walks all over

---

Lake District Weather

Lake District weather is notoriously bad, and notoriously unpredictable. Put simply – there's often low cloud, and it rains one hell of a lot. In fact Seathwaite village (near the start of the Scafell route we describe here) claims to be the wettest village in England. It may be true, because Sprinkling Tarn, just up the valley, gets a recorded annual average of 470 cm. Keswick, about eight miles away, only gets about a quarter of this, making it almost arid in comparison.

But Lake District walkers are notoriously hardy (or notoriously dogged). One of the contributors to this book tells a story of a two week holiday he spent one summer in the Lakes. Every day he went out alone to 'bag' a different mountain. Keen to record his exploits, he carried a camera and tripod. But every day it rained. Undeterred, our friend carried on, steadily bagging peaks and resolutely taking shots of himself standing proudly next to each summit cairn or trig point. The weather remained awful for two weeks. At the end of his trip he'd reached the top 14 major mountains, and had 14 photographs, all exactly the same, of him in a raincoat, with an indeterminable pile of stones, completely surrounded by swirling mist and raindrops.

He still had a great time (or so he says). ■

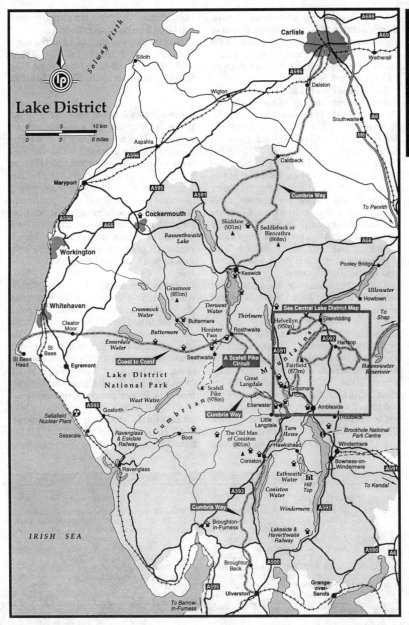

the area. If you fancy a few relaxing days, there's a choice of books covering shorter or easier routes, including *Teashop Walks in the Lake District* by Jean Patefield and *Lakeland Walking on the Level* by Norman Buckley (both published by Sigma).

The scenery of Lakeland naturally inspires a whole stack of picture books too. Once again, AW is near the top of the pile. His *Wainwright's Favourite Lakeland Mountains* (£12.99) is a homage to several large peaks, including Fairfield, Helvellyn, Scafell Pike, High Street and Glaramara (all on routes described in this section), with excellent photos by Derry Brabbs. Falling somewhere between guidebook and picture book is *Complete Lakeland Fells* by Bill Birkett. The highly acclaimed Bob Allen books *On High Lakeland Fells* and *On Lower Lakeland Fells*, with colour photos and good descriptions, also contain sketch maps.

Some other books are suggested under Other Walks in the Lake District at the end of this section.

Maps The Lake District is mostly covered by the OS Landranger (1:50,000) sheets 85, 89, 90 and 96. Ambleside and the Fairfield Horseshoe are on sheet 90. If you want greater detail, which is recommended for most walks as the landscape is often complex, the Lakes (except the far northern and southern sections) is covered also by the OS Outdoor Leisure (1:25,000) sheets 4, 5 ,6 and 7. Ambleside and most of the Fairfield

Horseshoe are on sheet 7, but a small (important) bit of the route is also on sheet 5.

Harveys maps of the Lake District cover the area in five sheets (at 1:40,000 or 1:25,000). Ambleside and the whole Fairfield Horseshoe are on the *Eastern Lakeland* sheet.

Guided Walks & Local Services

If you want to see the area, but lack the necessary skills or confidence to go it alone, consider joining a guided walk. The park wardens lead walks on set dates (details from PIC or TIC), but if these don't suit, the Lake District abounds with experienced private mountain guides who can show you around on foot or arrange more energetic activities such as rock-climbing. Ask around or look for small advertisements in the gear shops in Ambleside (most of which also rent items such as boots, tents and rucksacks).

Places to Stay & Eat

Ambleside is a compact town with most places within an easy walk from the centre. The *YHA Hostel* (☎ 015394 32304, £9.10) is one mile south of the centre, overlooking the lake, on the main A591 Windermere road. There are plenty of B&Bs in the centre of town, including *3 Cambridge Villas* (☎ 015394 32307), on Church St, charging from £14.50 per person; *Croydon House* (☎ 015394 32209), with mainly ensuite doubles for £17.50 rising to £20 at weekends; *Hillsdale Hotel* (☎ 015394 33174), from £15 to £19; and the *Norwood Hotel*

William Wordsworth

The unofficial poet laureate of the Lakes is William Wordsworth, a leading figure in the English Romantic movement. He was born in Cockermouth in 1770 and went to school at Hawkshead, near Ambleside. In 1799 (after he had begun work on his epic *The Prelude*), he and Samuel Coleridge began a tour of the Lake District. They began near Penrith and finished at Wasdale Head, but along the way Wordsworth spotted an old inn, the Dove & Olive Branch. By the end of the year he and his sister Dorothy were in residence in the old inn, which came to be known as Dove Cottage.

In 1802 Wordsworth married and, as his family and fame increased, Dove Cottage became increasingly crowded. In 1808 the family moved to Allan Bank, then to the Old Parsonage in Grasmere, and, finally, to Rydal Mount, where he lived until his death. ∎

(☎ 015394 33349, £19 for an ensuite room). Lake Rd (the one towards Windermere) is a happy hotel hunting ground, with plenty more to choose from. If you're looking for something more up market, try the luxurious *Rothay Manor Hotel* (☎ 015394 33605), with a good reputation for its food charging £114 to £120 per room.

For campers things are not so handy. The nearest site is *Low Wray* (☎ 015394 32810), three miles south of Ambleside on the western shore of Windermere (access from the B5286). This is a National Trust (NT) site. The charge is £2.50.

For food, popular places include: *Zeffirelli's Pizzeria*, under the cinema on Compston Rd, with excellent wholefood pizzas and pasta dishes (including vegetarian) from £4; the cafe above *Rock & Run* gear shop, with lots of snacks (for carnivores and veggies), plus huge all-day breakfasts for £3; and *Sheila's Cottage*, tucked away in a back street called The Slack, with meals around £5, plus fabulous cakes and toffee puddings. For more serious food, try *Stampers* (☎ 015394 32775), on Church St, where dishes cost around £8 to £12. Ambleside also has several pubs which do lunch and evening bar meals.

Getting There & Away
Bus Ambleside is easy to reach from Windermere and Keswick, which are well served by National Express coaches from all parts of the country, and by local buses from other towns around the Lake District. Most useful is the hourly No 555 Lakeslink service between Keswick and Kendal, via Windermere railway station, Troutbeck Bridge, Ambleside, Rydal and Grasmere. Three times per day this service extends at either end to Carlisle and Lancaster. There's also the No 505 Coniston Rambler service, running eight times per day (less on Sunday and in the winter) between Bowness and Coniston via Ambleside, Rydal, Grasmere and Hawkshead, and the No W1, two or three times per hour between Windermere station and Grasmere, via Ambleside. For more details of these or any service in the area,

phone the Cumbria Bus Info Line (☎ 01946 63222), or pick up the Lakeland Explorer Timetable from any TIC.

Your other option between Windermere and Ambleside, or any other town in this part of the Lakes which has a hostel, is the YHA Shuttle Bus (☎ 015394 32304).

Buses stop in Ambleside in the centre of town.

Train Frequent train services link Windermere with the rest of the country, but between there and Ambleside you'll have to take the bus.

Car The usual route into the Lake District from the south is via Windermere. Ambleside is just five miles north along the A591, although in summer traffic jams mean it can take an hour or more to do this bit. From the north, you can approach Ambleside by the A591 from Keswick, or the A592 from Penrith. This latter route goes over the Kirkstone Pass, the highest A-road in England, which is very dramatic but as it hasn't been widened much since horse and cart days, it is frequently jammed when modern buses meet head on, so is best avoided in busy times.

The Route
Stage 1: Ambleside to Rydal
1 mile (1.5 km), 30 to 45 minutes
Walk along the A591 out of Ambleside towards Grasmere, past the Charlotte Mason Collage, to reach a small bridge over a stream. Go over this then turn right, through some black gates, onto a track signposted towards Rydal Hall. Follow more footpath signs, through parkland, ignoring various tracks branching off left and right, between various buildings to meet a steep lane leading up from the main road, near Rydal Hall.

Stage 2: Rydal to Fairfield Summit
4 miles (6.5 km), 2½ to 3½ hours
Go right (north), up the steep lane, past the church and Rydal Mount (Wordsworth's

home until his death in 1850, now an NT site) on your left. Continue up the zigzags. Beyond the houses, at the top of the lane, you go through a gate. The track goes straight on, but you strike off left (north-west) on a path, steeply up over a few stiles, and then up the ridge through open moorland, on a clear path, swinging round to the north to reach the first peak of the day, Heron Pike (612m). From here the path undulates (although the ups are less steep than the first bit) over a few more peaks, including Great Rigg (766m), and then a final ascent to the top of the ridge and the broad summit plateau of Fairfield itself.

There are cairns all over the place, but the largest one, which marks the highest point, is to the north side of the plateau. The views to the north-east, down into Deepdale, are good, but this plateau is so broad that you don't get a good 360° view from just one spot. You have to walk a few hundred metres south-east to get the best view of Windermere, the same distance north-west to see Helvellyn, and so on. If the mist is down, there won't be any views, and you should take great care where you wander. Do not go too far to the north-east as the cliffs at the top of Deepdale are, as the name suggests, precipitous. If the wind is strong, sit behind one of the drystone shelter walls to stop your sandwiches blowing away.

Stage 3: Fairfield Summit to Ambleside
5 miles (8 km), 2 to 2½ hours

From the summit, retrace slightly, tending left (south-east) to reach the main ridge between the top of the Rydal Valley, to your right (south), and the top of the Deep-dale Valley, to your left (north). If the mist is down, take great care here: do not go too far left (east) towards the unforgiving cliffs at the top of Deepdale.

Once on the ridge, head east, and then south-east to go up slightly, passing just to the east of Hart Crag summit and over Dove Crag (792m), before swinging round to the south and heading straight down the ridge with Ambleside and Lake Windermere

spread out before you. A wall runs down the crest of this ridge, with paths on both sides. According to the OS map the one on the west side is the right of way, but it is important to cross to the east side of the wall at High Brock Crags. After about 1½ to two miles from Fairfield summit, the path leads you over several stiles, across Scandale Beck at Low Sweden Bridge, and past Nook End Farm, from where a lane runs down into the centre of Ambleside.

HELVELLYN & STRIDING EDGE
(from the Patterdale Valley)

Distance 7½ miles (12 km)
Duration 5 to 6 hours
Start & Finish Glenridding
Regional Centres Ambleside, Keswick, Penrith
County Cumbria
Area Lake District National Park
Summary A good-quality circular route to the summit of a Lakeland classic. The paths are generally well worn and easy to follow, but one section of steep ridge may require the use of the hands at times. Suitable for more experienced walkers.

Helvellyn (950m, 3118 ft) is the second-highest peak in England and dominates the Eastern Fells. The Thirlmere Valley forms the western border of the Eastern Fells, and they are relatively easily reached from this side. The eastern border of the Eastern Fells is the Patterdale Valley, containing the A592 road between Penrith and Windermere, via the infamous Kirkstone Pass. Helvellyn and the other peaks are harder to reach from this side, but the walking is far more rewarding.

At the northern end of the Patterdale Valley is Ullswater, with a lake steamer cruising between Pooley Bridge on the northern tip, Howtown on the east shore and the bustling village of Glenridding at the southern end. Glenridding is the area's main centre for walking and climbing, and has nearly everything you could need, from a tin of dubbin to a cream tea. A mile or so south of Glenridding is the smaller village of

Patterdale, which also makes a good base. There are other accommodation options in the Patterdale Valley at Hartsop and Brotherswater (three and four miles south of Glenridding), but where you stay depends on which of the other routes described below you want to do.

The first route we cover is a classic ascent of Helvellyn, starting and ending at Glenridding. The route goes up the Mires Beck path and includes Striding Edge, a precipitous ridge adorning countless postcards and picture books, and a favourite walkers' challenge. In contrast, the summit of

Helvellyn itself is broad and flat, part of a long spine running north to south through the area. In 1926 someone even managed to land a plane on it, and the spot is marked by a plaque. The classic route descends via the Red Tarn path.

We also describe an alternative route up Helvellyn from Patterdale village, ascending via Striding Edge and descending via Dollywaggon Pike (worth it just for the name!) and the valley of Grisedale.

Direction, Distance & Duration

It is more satisfying to reach the summit of

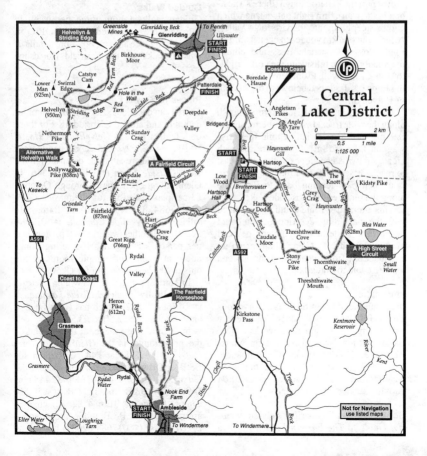

Helvellyn by an ascent of Striding Edge, so the route is described this way round. This 7½ mile route involves about 830m of ascent and requires about five to six hours walking. Allowing for stops, you should take six to seven hours.

Alternative The above description covers the ascent of Helvellyn from Glenridding. Another ascent starts and ends at Patterdale village, reached by following the A592 south from Glenridding for about one mile. This alternative route is eight miles long and will take six to eight hours walking.

Just past the Patterdale sign (there's a post-box in the wall), turn right onto a lane which climbs steeply up into the Grisedale Valley. After about one km you reach open land. The route crosses Grisedale Beck and climbs diagonally up the hillside to the north (right) to Hole-in-the-Wall. From here follow Striding Edge (as described below) to the summit of Helvellyn.

From the summit of Helvellyn go south along the wide track, first to Nethermost Pike (891m) and then for half a mile to Dollywaggon Pike (858m). From here the path zigzags down steep slopes to the south-east to reach Grisedale Tarn. From the tarn there is a good path leading back to Patterdale along the picturesque Grisedale Valley.

This alternative route could be combined with the main route description: you could go up from Patterdale village and descend via Swirral Edge to Glenridding, or go up Striding Edge from Glenridding and descend via Grisedale to Patterdale.

Information

In the middle of Glenridding is a marvellous TIC & PIC (☎ 017684 82414), open every day during the season (two weeks before Easter until 5 November) and on winter weekends, offering stacks of information, maps and guidebooks, a local mountain weather bulletin and an accommodation booking service.

Books & Maps Wainwright's classic *Pictorial Guide to The Eastern Fells* includes a good section on Helvellyn, and is worth looking at for further inspiration and to admire the detail of his work and appreciation and love for the area. (For more details on guidebooks to the Lake District see the Fairfield Horseshoe section.)

The route described here is on OS Outdoor Leisure (1:25,000) sheet 5 *The English Lakes, North Eastern Area*, and on Harveys map (1:25,000 and 1:40,000) to *Eastern Lakeland*. The national park publishes a 1:25,000 line map to Helvellyn and Fairfield which shows all major paths.

Guided Walks

Guided walks (about three per week in summer) are organised from the PIC in Glenridding (see above). For more details of guided walks see the Fairfield Horseshoe section.

Places to Stay & Eat

There is an excellent selection of accommodation in and around Glenridding. For those on a budget there is *Helvellyn YHA Hostel* (☎ 017684 82269, £7.45), about a mile from the village. There are three campsites in the area: *Gillside Farm* (☎ 017684 82346) in Glenridding, open March through October, £3 per person and £1 for a tent; *Side Farm* (☎ 017684 82337, £3.50) in Patterdale village; and *Sykeside Campsite* (☎ 017684 82239), at Brotherswater, £2.20 per tent and per person, also with self-catering bunkhouse at £7.50 and simple rooms at the on-site *Brotherswater Inn* for £8.50.

In Hartsop, near Brotherswater, there is the beautifully situated *Fellside Farmhouse* (☎ 017684 82532) which has B&B for £16 and a bunkhouse £2.50 to £3.50.

In Glenridding village, at the top end of the price range, is the *Glenridding Hotel* (☎ 017684 82228) at £44 per person for B&B or DB&B at £57 per person, and the *Ullswater Hotel* (☎ 017684 82444) at £49.50 for B&B and DB&B at £59.50. *Cherry Holme* (☎ 017684 82512) charges around £22 for B&B while the friendly *Beech House* (☎ 017684 82037) has rooms from £16 per person. There are a number of cafes, among which *Moss Crag Tea Room* (☎ 017684 82500) offers B&B for around £17. *The Travellers Rest* pub has good beer, food and a pleasant atmosphere. In the centre of the village there are two general stores and an equipment shop. There are several other places in nearby Patterdale, listed in the Coast to Coast Walk section of the Northern England – Long-Distance Paths chapter.

Getting There & Away

Bus It's easier (but not essential) to approach Glenridding and Patterdale from Penrith: there are four or five buses daily during the summer months, but fewer in the winter. If you're coming from Ambleside, go first to Windermere, from where there is a weekend bus during June and July and a more regular bus throughout August. See the Fairfield Horseshoe section for more general bus information.

Windermere and Penrith are well served by National Express coaches from all parts of the country, and by buses from other towns around the Lake District. See the Fairfield Horseshoe section above and the Cumbria Way section in the Northern England – Long-Distance Paths chapter for details.

Car Glenridding is on the A592 between Windermere and Penrith. From Ambleside you can join the A592 at the top of the Kirkstone Pass by taking the steep and narrow minor road to the west (appropriately labelled 'The Struggle' on the map, so give it a miss if you're ten-up in a campervan!). There is a large car park in Glenridding: all day costs £2.

The Route
Stage 1: Glenridding to Hole-in-the-Wall
2½ miles (4 km), 1½ to 2 hours
From Glenridding village centre, keep Glenridding Beck to your right, and follow the track signposted Helvellyn via Mires Beck. After Gillside Farm campsite (10 minutes from Glenridding), turn left up a track (still signposted). At a junction ignore signs to Greenside Mines and keep going uphill. After 100m, a path to Grisedale goes off left. You go right and further up to reach a gate in a wall marking the boundary of the open fell. On the other side of the wall, take the left fork (the right fork is where you'll come down). The clear path now climbs steadily alongside Mires Beck, to reach a ridgetop at a point east of Red Tarn, where there's a gap in the drystone wall, marked on the OS map as Hole-in-the-Wall. From here you get a great view of Helvellyn overlooking Red Tarn, with Striding Edge to the left (south) side and the pointed peak of Catstycam to the right.

Stage 2: Hole-in-the-Wall to Helvellyn Summit via Striding Edge
1 mile (1.5 km), 1½ to 2 hours
Continue following the clear path along the ridge. After about 300m the ridge narrows to about two metres in width and you're on Striding Edge proper, with steep slopes on either side. The scrambling is never difficult, and there are paths which avoid some of the most vertiginous sections, but you will need to use your hands in places and at the end of the ridge there is a short but vertical two metre rock step to descend.

The path traverses right and climbs through steep rocky ground to the summit plateau. Care is needed on this section as the passing of many boots has loosened the rocks. The summit is wide and open; there is a cross-shaped wind-shelter, but the highest point is marked by a trig point 100m further on.

Stage 3: Helvellyn Summit to Glenridding
4 miles (6.5 km), 2 hours
Walk 100m beyond the trig point and then descend to the right (east), following another narrow ridge called Swirral Edge. Care is needed here to locate the correct place. Scramble down the crest of the ridge, and after 200m or so the steepness eases; you can divert up to the dramatic summit of Catstycam or continue descending the ridge,

passing north of Red Tarn, then swinging north-east around the base of Catstycam, following the outflow stream from Red Tarn (Red Tarn Beck) across some flat grassy and boggy ground. The path is a bit vague at first but soon develops into a clear scar! Follow this down to meet Glenridding Beck, and continue along the south side. You pass the old lead mines at Greenside (to reach the YHA hostel cross the footbridge above the weir), and continue on the southern slopes of the Glenridding Valley. Keep to the path beside the wall, and to meet your outward path. Retrace the last mile or so back to Glenridding.

A FAIRFIELD CIRCUIT
(from the Patterdale Valley)

Distance 7½ miles (12 km)
Duration 5 to 7 hours
Start Cow Bridge
Finish Patterdale village
Regional Centres Ambleside, Keswick, Windermere
County Cumbria
Area Lake District National Park
Summary A good, varied circular ridge walk among some of the finest of the Eastern Fells.

Fairfield (873m, 2863 ft) is part of a long ridge system that can be followed in any direction from a number of starting points, and can also be linked with several neighbouring peaks. It can also be reached from several different starting points. The Fairfield Horseshoe route we described at the start of this section is probably the least serious approach to the summit of this mountain, but the ascent from the Patterdale Valley is a gem of a walk, through farms and woodland in the picturesque Dovedale Valley, then through craggy fellside before finally reaching the open tops. This route starts from the Cow Bridge car park at the northern end of Brotherswater (1½ miles south of Patterdale village) and ends in Patterdale village itself. The route takes in a number of other peaks, including the magnificent Dove Crag and the long ridge of St Sunday Crag.

Direction, Distance & Duration
The route can be followed in either direction but the walk up Dovedale is a very pleasant way to gain height, so we recommend following the route as described. The distance covered is about 7½ miles, but the route includes at least 700m of ascent, so will take an absolute minimum of five hours walking, probably nearer seven for most people. In reality, with stops, lunch and so on, you should allow seven or eight hours to complete the walk. Also allow time for the three km along the road between Patterdale and Cow Bridge.

Places to stay and eat, plus details on guided walks, books and maps, are listed in the Helvellyn section.

Getting There & Away
The starting point is the Cow Bridge car park (free), 1½ miles south of Patterdale village. Access to Patterdale and Glenridding is described in the Helvellyn section.

The Route
Stage 1: Cow Bridge Car Park to Fairfield Summit
4 miles (6.5 km), 3 to 4 hours
From the car park take the vehicle track along the western shore of the lake. This is flat and after a mile or so passes Hartsop Hall Farm. The farm is owned by the NT and is a working farm that dates back to the 16th century. Here the path climbs beside a wall through some old oak woodland and eventually passes alongside a stream to open hillsides beneath the imposing cliff of Dove Crag, at the head of the valley.

The path then climbs steeply to the right of the crag and then around the back to the summit. From here, follow the ridgetop north-west for half a mile to Hart Crag and then to the summit of Fairfield. For a description of the summit see the Fairfield Horseshoe section.

Stage 2: Fairfield Summit to Patterdale
3½ miles (6 km), 2 to 3 hours
From the summit of Fairfield, head north,

and descend about 200m to the col at Deepdale Hause. (From here you can descend steeply into Deepdale if the spirit is flagging.) The hardy can ascend the 150m to the top of St Sunday Crag (it's not as steep as the descent from Fairfield, you'll be glad to hear).

Follow the right of way north-east down the ridge through Thornhow End to meet the lane leading down to Patterdale church, or just before the lane turn right onto a path which takes you into the centre of Patterdale village.

A HIGH STREET CIRCUIT
(from the Patterdale Valley)

> **Distance** 8½ miles (14 km)
> **Duration** 5 to 7 hours
> **Start & Finish** Hartsop, near Patterdale
> **Regional Centres** Ambleside, Keswick, Windermere
> **County** Cumbria
> **Area** Lake District National Park
> **Summary** A fine walk along a broad, flat but high ridge, with fine views and historical interest.

High Street (828m, 2715 ft) is an unusual title for a mountain, but it gets its name from a Roman road that once ran across the long, flat summit ridge. Since the days of the legionnaires, this route has been tramped by hill-walkers and fellrunners, not to mention the odd motorcycle and a lot of sheep. The walk along High Street is very satisfying because once you gain height you can stay up and can enjoy great views all day. It's definitely hands in pockets stuff, but the wind can pick up speed over the summit plateau, so go properly prepared.

The most direct way up is from the village of Hartsop, about two miles south of Patterdale, near Brotherswater. The village is tranquil and very pretty; the 17th-century stone houses are tucked away at the entrance to the Hayeswater Valley. Hartsop means 'valley of the deer', but unfortunately you won't see any.

The route also goes over the summits of Thornthwaite Crag, Stoney Cove Pike and Hartsop Dodd, but there are a couple of alternative finishes, depending on where

you're staying, or the durability of your knees!

If you're staying in Glenridding or Patterdale village, we also describe an alternative route to High Street from there.

Direction, Distance & Duration
This circuit walk can be followed in either direction, but the clockwise way we describe is most pleasant. The total distance is 8½ miles, with at least 800m of ascent, so a minimum walking time is five hours, but allowing for stops most walkers will take between six and eight hours to do this route.

Places to stay and eat, plus information on guided walks, books and maps, are listed in the Helvellyn & Striding Edge section.

Alternative If you are staying at Glenridding or Patterdale village, you can reach High Street without following the main road to Hartsop. From Patterdale, go via Side Farm, or follow the route of the Coast to Coast from just north of the YHA hostel, to reach the open fellside and a path which leads via Boredale Hause and Angle Tarn to The Knott, where the path from Hartsop described below comes in from the right (south). Follow the route as described to High Street summit and descend to Hartsop. Follow the lane down through the village. Just before the main road a small lane (which soon turns into a track and then a path) leads past the farms of Beckstones and Crookabeck to Patterdale. If you do this route, descending via Gray Crag, it will take seven to eight hours.

Getting There & Away
From the main A592 at Horseman Bridge, two miles south of Patterdale (marked by a telephone box), go through Hartsop village to the car park at the end of the lane. For full details on reaching Patterdale see the Helvellyn & Striding Edge section.

The Route
Stage 1: Hartsop to High Street Summit
3½ miles (5.5 km), 2½ to 3½ hours
From the car park, follow the bridleway alongside Hayeswater Gill to Hayeswater

Tarn (not to be confused with the much larger lake of Haweswater, further to the east). At the small dam at the north end of the tarn, cross the stream and follow the path up steep grassy slopes to the west of The Knott (739m). You briefly join the route of the Coast to Coast Walk (described elsewhere in this book), which skirts north of The Knott's summit.

About 500m south of The Knott, the Coast to Coast Walk turns off east towards Kidsty Pike. We continue southwards, following the broad ridge path along the line of the Roman road. Note that this passes just to the west of the trig point on the summit of High Street. (In bad weather you might prefer to follow the wall which keeps to the ridge crest and leads directly to the trig point.)

Stage 2: High Street Summit to Hartsop, via Stony Cove Pike

5 miles (8 km), 2½ to 3½ hours

South of High Street the ridge broadens out and the crest swings west to Thornthwaite Crag, marked by a splendid drystone pillar. (If time is short, from here you can follow the ridge along to the north end of Gray Crag and descend to Hayeswater.)

From Thornthwaite Crag the main path descends steeply to the pass at Threshthwaite Mouth. (For another descent, you can go north from here, down into Threshthwaite Cove and along Pasture Beck to Hartsop.)

To reach Stony Cove Pike (763m) continue west from the pass, and follow the crest of the ridge north-west to the top of Hartsop Dodd, from where you descend a small path. It is very steep and requires care and strong knees! When you reach the wall, follow it to the junction with the Pasture Beck path and so to Hartsop.

Another descent from Stony Cove Pike, less steep and possibly more enjoyable, especially if you're camping at Sykeside, is via Caudale. The path is clear and follows the delightful Caudale Beck to join the main road just above the *Brotherswater Inn*, where you can reward yourself with a long cool drink, or a bowl of hot soup (weather dependent).

A SCAFELL PIKE CIRCUIT (from Borrowdale)

Distance 8½ miles (14 km)
Duration 6 to 8 hours
Start & Finish Seathwaite, near Seatoller
Regional Centre Keswick
County Cumbria
Area Lake District National Park
Summary A demanding circular route, following valleys and some high broken ground, with exposed sections. Paths are easy to follow in fine weather, although steep and eroded in places, and many side paths are encountered, so navigational skills are essential, especially as bad weather conditions are likely.

Dominating the Southern and Western Fells is Scafell Pike, at 978m (3209 ft) the highest mountain in England. It is also one of few peaks in England rising above the magical 3000 ft contour, giving it something akin to Munro status, although purists from north of the border would probably disagree. (The other English peaks above 3000 ft (914m) are all in the Lake District: Helvellyn, Skiddaw and Scafell; see aside.)

In this part of the Lakes the peaks are rugged and steep-sided. Consequently, conditions are harder, paths steeper and more circuitous, and there's far less room for error if the mist comes down and you have to rely on your map and compass to get you home. Conditions can change very quickly, so even if it looks fine, take warm waterproof clothes, plus a map and compass that you know how to use.

There are several routes up Scafell Pike, including those from Langdale, Eskdale and Wasdale. We've chosen one from Borrowdale valley simply because we think it's the nicest. However, the route we describe here should only be considered in spring, summer or autumn. In winter the days are too short to do it comfortably, while weather and ground conditions may make it dangerous for the inexperienced.

At any time of year, if the weather does turn bad while you're out, there are a number of short cuts and diversions which avoid the highest and potentially most dangerous section

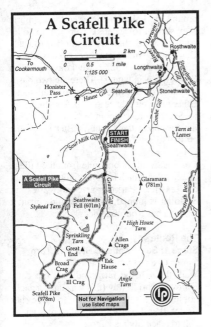

Direction, Distance & Duration
This circular route starts and finishes at the hamlet of Seathwaite. You could do it in either direction, but we have described it here anticlockwise. The route is not waymarked, and there are few signposts.

Measured on the map, to/from Seathwaite, the distance is 8½ miles. It doesn't seem far, but with all the steep ups and downs, your walking time will be five to seven hours, plus one or two extra for lunch, photos and map reading, bringing the total for the route up to seven to nine hours. On top of this, you may have to allow for getting to the start from Seatoller or Longthwaite. You can also follow the footpath (the route of the Allerdale Ramble) leaving the road at Strands Bridge, between Rosthwaite and Seatoller. (If you are staying here, an alternative finish avoids retracing this section.)

Information & Guided Walks
There's a very friendly and well-stocked TIC in Seatoller (☎ 017687 77294). It organises a whole series of guided walks, mostly in the Borrowdale valley, through the summer.

Books & Maps A selection of guidebooks is listed in the Fairfield Horseshoe section above. The Scafell Pike route described here is on OS Landranger (1:50,000) map sheet 90. If you want more detail (highly recommended for this route, as it's tricky), you need OS Outdoor

of this route. Having said that, in fair weather it's an absolutely marvellous walk, going right to the heart of the high Lakes, with dramatic scenery that seems at times to simply engulf you, and from the summit some of the finest views you could wish for.

Scafell & Scafell Pike
In the old sage of the hills' book, *Wainwright's Favourite Lakeland Mountains*, he comments: 'It is remarkable that the highest mountain in England should suffer a confusion of names'. He's right. It is not uncommon for visitors to assume that Scafell Pike and Scafell are the same thing, or to go up one instead of the other, not only reaching the top of the 'wrong mountain', but often getting into difficulties too in the complex landscape of the high ground.

Wainwright explains that the whole mountain massif was originally called Scaw Fell (this pronunciation is still used locally, and by Lakes aficionados), and early maps of the area marked three summits called the Pikes of Scawfell. Later this title was altered to Scawfell Pikes. Then two of the summits got their own names, Broad Crag and Ill Crag, leaving the highest to be singularised into Scafell Pike.

Scafell (964m) is now the name given to a separate summit on the same massif, some 800m directly south-west of Scafell Pike. Scafell is a mere 14m lower, but a much more serious mountain to tackle. (Scafell is sometimes written Sca Fell, although that seems still to be the name of the whole massif.) ∎

Leisure (1:25,000) sheets 4 and 6. Harveys *Western Lakeland* map (1:40,000 or 1:25,000) has the whole route on one sheet.

Places to Stay & Eat

At Seathwaite, the start of the walk, *Seathwaite Farm* (☎ 017687 77284) offers all you could wish for: simple camping for £1, a camping barn for £3, B&B for £16, and a very good cafe (summer only). *Thornythwaite Farm*, between Seathwaite and Seatoller, also has a campsite, camping barn and B&B. In Seatoller, B&Bs include *Seatoller Farm* (☎ 017687 77232), charging £15, or £18 including dinner, and the charming *Seatoller House* (☎ 017687 77218), where services include a drying room, charging £26 per person, with dinner for £9.

There's also *Glaramara* (☎ 017687 77222), a holiday company base, with B&B for £16, evening meals and guided walks for £6 per day. The *Yew Tree* pub does bar meals and has a smart restaurant. *Borrowdale YHA Hostel* (☎ 017687 77257, £7.45) is in Longthwaite village, one mile east of Seatoller. Two miles west of Seatoller (up a very steep hill) is *Honister Hause YHA Hostel* (☎ 017687 77267, £6.75).

There are many more accommodation choices in the nearby settlements of Stonethwaite, Longthwaite and Rosthwaite (see the Coast to Coast section of this book for details). The TIC at Seatoller has a good list. Worth a mention is the *Scafell Hotel* (☎ 017687 77208), where B&B is £36 (less in the off season) and 'Fell Break Weekends' (combining fine food and comfortable accommodation with guided walks) cost £103 all-in. At the other end of the priceband is *Dinah Hoggus Camping Barn*, £3 per person per night. Bookings are essential through the main Camping Barn Network reservations office (☎ 017687 72803). Rosthwaite also has a small general store.

For food while walking, there's no cafe on the summit, so take all you need with you.

Getting There & Away

Bus Keswick is well served by National Express coaches from all parts of the country, and by buses from other towns around the Lake District (see the Cumbria Way section for details). To reach Seatoller from Keswick, the very handy 'Borrowdale Bus' (No 79) runs eight times per day in each direction on summer weekdays (six on Sunday, less in winter). There are two buses per day from Keswick direct to Seathwaite. Otherwise you'll have to walk from Seatoller to Seathwaite (one mile). For timetable details phone the Cumbria Bus Info Line (☎ 01946 63222).

Car Seathwaite is one mile from the village of Seatoller, which is about eight miles south of Keswick. Parking at Seathwaite and Seatoller is limited, so you should consider taking a bus from Keswick.

The Route
Stage 1: Seathwaite to Styhead Tarn
2 miles (3 km), 1 to 1½ hours

Walk through the farm and past the cafe. Follow the bridleway (this was once a packhorse route into Wasdale) to Stockley Bridge, then directly up the valley of Styhead Gill to reach Styhead Tarn.

Stage 2: Styhead Tarn to Scafell Pike
2 miles (3 km), 1½ to 2 hours

From Styhead Tarn follow the path southwesterly to Styhead Pass and the Mountain Rescue First Aid Kit (a large wooden box). Take the path branching to the left (east) towards Esk Hause. (If the weather is bad, you are tired or simply want a shorter walk, continue along this path to Sprinkling Tarn and the top of Ruddy Gill from where you can get back to Seathwaite.)

For the path to Scafell Pike, a few hundred metres from the Rescue Kit a path on the right leads into the Corridor Route which heads south-west then south. The path fizzles out as you reach the rocky outcrops below the summit, so take care if the mist is down. A trig point and large cairn mark the highest point in England. You'll also find several rock shelters dotted around the summit area. The weather is often bad up here, but when it is good you'll get spectacular views over the whole Lake District: Derwent Water and

Keswick; Crinkle Crags and Bowfell, with a glimpse of Windermere; Great Gable and Buttermere; and lots more. On a clear day, you should be able to see the coast and Sellafield Nuclear Power Station!

Stage 3: Scafell Pike to Esk Hause

1½ miles (2.5 km), 1 hour

From the summit aim north-east. Take care here, especially when the weather is bad as the route is not obvious across the rocks. A path descends steeply on a rocky ridge, with cliffs and buttresses on either side of the path, to reach a small col then goes up again, passing to the right (east) of the summit of Broad Crag and north of Ill Crag. (For the peak-baggers it is possible to go on a quick detour up and down Great End for some more wonderful views. On long summer days this will be quite easy, but take care at other times of the year, as it will add about 45 minutes on to your day.) The path leads you away from Great End to Esk Hause and a meeting of paths at a windshelter (shaped like a cross) just below Allen Crags. From here there are two ways home.

Stage 4A: Esk Hause to Seathwaite, via Ruddy Gill

3 miles (5 km), 1½ to 2 hours

From the shelter take the path west towards Sprinkling Tarn. After about 500m, a path on the right (north) goes down Ruddy Gill. The stream is Grains Gill and the path leads down to Stockley Bridge where you find the bridleway described in Stage 1. Retrace your steps to Seathwaite Farm.

Stage 4B: Esk Hause to Strands Bridge, via Glaramara

3½ miles (6 km), 2½ to 3 hours

If you are staying at Seatoller or Longthwaite, you do not need to return to Seathwaite Farm. From Esk Hause, aim north-east, over the top of Allen Crags and then along the broad ridge, with several ups and downs, to reach the summit of Glaramara (781m). From here the path descends through pleasant woodland on the lower section to finally reach Strands Bridge, where the main road crosses the River Derwent between Seatoller and Longthwaite.

OTHER WALKS IN THE LAKE DISTRICT

Mountain Walks

Within the Southern, Eastern and Far Eastern Fells (as defined in Wainwright's *Pictorial Guides*) are several more major mountains, which we don't have the space here to describe in full. For example, to the north of Scafell Pike is Great Gable, with scree-ridden sides which always look so sheer, while to the east lies the impressive peak of Bowfell, at the head of the Great Langdale Valley. Bowfell can be approached from Langdale (covered in the Cumbria Way section of this book), while Great Gable can be approached from Seatoller (covered in the Scafell Pike section).

Great Gable can also be reached from Wasdale, one of Lakeland's more remote and less easy-to-reach valleys, although it makes a good gateway to the Western Fells, usually much quieter than the popular central parts of the Lakes, and worthy of a few days exploration if you have the time, skills and inclination. The Wasdale Head Inn (and nearby campsite) has been a popular base for walkers and climbers for almost a century (early photos show the leading climbers of the day limbering up on the inn's barn wall).

To the north of Fairfield and Helvellyn are the peaks of Great Dodd and Stybarrow Dodd. These can be approached from the east from Patterdale or Glenridding (described in the Helvellyn & Striding Edge section), or from the west from the settlement of Legburthwaite (near Thirlmere YHA hostel) in the Thirlmere Valley.

Probably the most pleasing way of bagging these peaks is as part of a spectacular long ridge walk, along the 'Backbone of the Eastern Fells' between Clough Head (south-east of Keswick) and Grisedale Tarn (north of Grasmere), which also includes Helvellyn and Dollywaggon Pike. You can even continue southwards and do Fairfield as well, to finish at Ambleside (where a bus can take you back to your starting point). The route can also be done south to north, but either way it's long and potentially serious: one to leave for the fine days of summer.

This route is described fully by Bob Allen

in his book *Walking the Ridges of Lakeland* (published by Michael Joseph, £16.99), which also describes three other long, linear routes and about 20 other circular routes of varying lengths in the Central, Eastern and Far Eastern Fells, linking sets of peaks in a series of spectacular ridge walks. Each route has a map and the whole book is illustrated with colour photos.

Valley & Lakeside Walks

There are many other high peaks in the Lake District to explore, but if the weather is bad or you just want to stay on flatter ground for a while, there's also a whole set of valley and lakeside walks as well. Elsewhere in this book, we describe the Cumbria Way, a long-distance route which makes its way through the Lakes from Ulverston, through Coniston, Elterwater, Great Langdale, Borrowdale, Derwent Water, Keswick, Skiddaw and Caldbeck to finish at Carlisle, skilfully keeping to low ground for much of the way. Any of the stages of this route can be followed as a day-walk, or used as part of a circular route, if you base yourself at, say, Coniston village, Elterwater village, Keswick or anywhere in the Langdale or Borrowdale valleys (places to stay and eat are listed in the Cumbria Way section of the Northern England – Long-Distance Paths chapter).

Other places for short or flat walks include the west bank of Windermere. For example, from Bowness-on-Windermere you can take the ferry across the lake, then follow the shore northwards on paths and tracks through woodland. You can either continue northwards to Ambleside (from where you can return by bus or lake steamer back to Windermere), although the last bit involves walking on roads, or you could come back through the woods on the higher ground slightly further to the west; a small hill called Letterbarrow has a splendid lookout. You could even base yourself on this side: there are B&Bs, campsites and YHA hostels in and around Hawkshead. If you did stay here, another nearby place for easy walks is Grisedale Forest, which has a good network

of waymarked walks, including a Sculpture Trail, which takes you past about 25 large and imaginative outdoor works of art. From Grisedale, Coniston and Elterwater are both within an easy day-walk.

Using the lake steamers is always an enjoyable way to travel, especially if you can tie it in with a walk. In the Cumbria Way section there's information on the Coniston and Derwent Water boats. Apart from these and the Windermere boats mentioned above, there's also a service on Ullswater between Glenridding and Pooley Bridge via Howtown. A good walk from Glenridding goes round or over Place Fell to Howtown, from where you can return on the steamer to Glenridding. This is an ideal walk if you're based at Glenridding for the Helvellyn walk or the High Street Walk described in this section.

In between the large lakes in the valleys and the high peaks of the fells lie the many tarns (small upland lakes and ponds) that are so characteristic of Lakeland. Many people include a tarn or two during their walk as it gives the satisfaction of a definite point to aim for (and is usually nice for a picnic). One outdoor magazine even suggested 'tarn-bagging' might become as popular as 'peak-bagging'.

All the Wainwright *Pictorial Guides* include coverage of tarns, and for more modern guidance you should get *The Tarns of Lakeland* by J & A Nuttall (published by Cicerone, £9.99). The same publisher also has *The Borders of Lakeland* by Robert Gambles, which describes 30 walks in the less visited fringes of the area.

Longer Walks

Apart from the Cumbria Way and the Coast to Coast Walk (also described fully in this book), there are some other long routes which are worth looking at if you're in the Lakes for a few days. On the far west side of the Lake District is the 'forgotten' Cumbria Coast, completely overshadowed by the nearby Lakeland mountains when it comes to tourist destinations – but for some, this is the attraction. The Cumbria Coastal Way

(125 miles, 201 km) follows the coast from Roa Island, near Barrow-in-Furness in the south, via quiet farmland and the River Esk estuary around Ravenglass and the slightly more dubious attraction of Sellafield Nuclear Power Station, through St Bees Head (start of the Coast to Coast Walk) and Whitehaven, around the shore of the Solway Firth to end at Carlisle, from where you can return to your starting point, or elsewhere in the Lakes, on the charming Cumbria Coast Railway. The route is described in a free leaflet published by Cumbria County Council, and available from local TICs.

Another long route is the Cumberland Way (80 miles, 128 km), which goes west to east across the Lakes, starting at Ravenglass and going mainly via valleys through Wasdale, Black Sail Pass, Buttermere, Keswick and near Penrith, to finish at Appleby-in-Westmorland. At the finish there's a very handy station on the Settle-Carlisle Railway to take you onwards to Northumberland or the Yorkshire Dales. The route is described in *The Cumberland Way* by Paul Hannon (Hillside Publications, £5.50).

Northumberland

Taking its name from the Anglo-Saxon kingdom of Northumbria (north of the River Humber), Northumberland is one of the largest, emptiest and wildest of England's counties. There are probably more castles and battlefield sites here than anywhere else, vivid reminders of long and bloody struggles between the English and the Scots. The castles all have fascinating histories; most changed hands several times as the Scottish border was pushed back and forth over the centuries. Many have now lapsed into peaceful, though still impressive, ruins. Others have been enlarged and converted into great houses, which can be visited today. Northumberland is also home to one of

Britain's most famous historical monuments – Hadrian's Wall.

For walkers, Northumberland has two main attractions: the starkly beautiful hills and valleys of Northumberland National Park (which takes up much of the west of the county and contains parts of Hadrian's Wall); and the eastern coast, between Berwick-upon-Tweed and Alnmouth, which has been declared an Area of Outstanding Natural Beauty.

In this section we describe a three day walk on Hadrian's Wall (easily reduced to just one or two day-walks if you prefer), and a day-walk along one of the finest stretches of coast, taking in two of the area's most splendid castles, again with various longer or shorter alternative routes. We also outline several other possibilities in the Northumberland National Park.

A HADRIAN'S WALL WALK

> **Distance** Minimum 7½ miles (12 km); maximum 27 miles (43.5 km)
> **Duration** Three separate day-walks, which can be joined to form a single two day or three day route
> **Regional Centres** Newcastle-upon-Tyne, Carlisle, Hexham
> **County** Northumberland
> **Area** Northumberland National Park
> **Summary** Routes are not strenuous, and daily distances are not long, but they can take some time as there are so many sights of interest along the way. Paths are mostly clear and easy to follow.

Hadrian's Wall was built by the Romans during their occupation of Britain during the early centuries of the first millennium. It strides across a neck of Northern England, virtually from coast to coast, for more than 70 miles (112 km) between the modern-day cities of Newcastle-upon-Tyne and Carlisle. An impressive feat of military engineering, the Wall marked the outer limit of the great Roman Empire, which at its zenith stretched across Europe and into North Africa. Today, only a small proportion of the Wall remains visible (and some of that is in pretty poor

NORTHERN ENGLAND

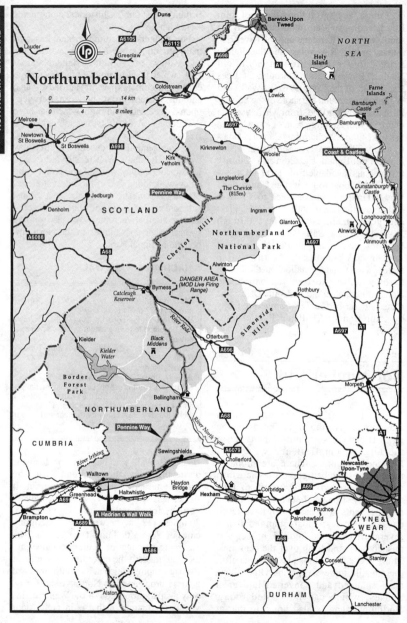

condition), but other sections have survived the ages remarkably well and are a fascinating sight.

In recognition of the area's important archaeology, culture and landscape it has been declared a World Heritage Site, with the rather ominous-sounding title of Hadrian's Wall Military Zone, under the auspices of UNESCO and English Heritage (EH). The actual borders of this zone have yet to be finally defined, and the process has proved controversial, with many local farmers and landowners resisting EH's wide-ranging plans for conservation and development.

Despite this latter-day battle between the Wall's guardians and the restless natives thereabouts, the best way to experience the Wall is to walk along it – Roman soldier-style – but this is not as straightforward as it may seem. In many places the Wall's route passes through private land and there's no public access. In other places, even if you can get close to the Wall, the walking itself (through city suburbs or along busy roads) is far from pleasant.

So in this section we describe three days of good-quality walking which take in the best preserved, most accessible and most interesting Wall remains, from Sewingshields (between Hexham and Haltwhistle) and Birdoswald (east of Brampton). As well as the Wall itself, this route takes in several Roman forts, including Housesteads and Vindolanda, various turrets and temples, some excellent museums, plus several historical sites from other ages including Thirlwall Castle and Lanercost Priory. This section also passes through Northumberland National Park, where the scenery is at its finest, and it's no surprise that a chunk of this prime central section of the Wall is also followed by the Pennine Way (described elsewhere in this book).

By marching in 'the footsteps of bygone shadows' you really enjoy the Wall, and absorb its unique atmosphere. You can look out across the austere landscape, unchanged for millennia (except for the addition of a few farmhouses and the lack of rebellious tribes), just as the centurions and legionnaires must have done all those years ago.

Direction, Distance & Duration

To avoid lugging gear as you march the Wall or explore antiquities, it's perfectly possible (and recommended) to base yourself at one place (such as in or around Haltwhistle, or at Once Brewed) and cover this route on three separate day-walks, making use of the good local public transport system. If you prefer linear walks though, there are places to stay along the route at Greenhead, Gilsland and Brampton.

This combination of day-walks can be done in any order or direction. When you're actually on the Wall, prevailing weather patterns may recommend walking east but history dictates a westbound walk. The Wall is thought to have been built from east to west, the milecastles and turrets are numbered from east to west and most guidebooks and walking guides to the Wall also proceed towards the west. We go with the flow.

The total distance of the route we describe here is 27 miles, spread over a relaxed three days. If you're a mile-eater, you could cover it in two, although your schedule may often need to be adjusted to mesh with opening and closing times of the various historical distractions.

Alternatives Each stage of the three day route we describe here could be done as a single day-walk. Each day's walk is not long, as there's so much to see along the way, but they could still be shortened further by using taxis and buses. For example, on Day 1 instead of starting at Once Brewed, take the bus on to Vindolanda and start there, or on Day 2 return to your base from Great Chesters instead of Greenhead.

Information

Haltwhistle's TIC (☎ 01434 322002) is on Main St, and there's an excellent seasonal PIC (☎ 01434 344396) at Once Brewed on the B6318 west of Housesteads. If you're coming from further afield, there are TICs at Newcastle (☎ 0191 261 0691) and Carlisle (☎ 01228 512444), both with information on the Wall and how to reach it.

The county council produces the excellent

Northumberland Public Transport Guide, available for £1.25 from local TICs.

Books There are numerous books on the Wall and its history, including Stephen Johnson's excellent illustrated *Hadrian's Wall*. Walking guides include *Exploring from Hadrian's Wall* by John Barker, describing routes on and beyond the Wall, *Hadrian's Wall: The Wall Walk*, mentioned above, plus *Walks in Hadrian's Wall Area*, a selection of walks of between three and eight miles, produced by Northumbria National Park.

Maps The OS *Historical Map & Guide – Hadrian's Wall* covers the Wall in strip-map format at scales of 1:25,000 and 1:50,000, and is adequate for finding your way, with the route of the original Wall superimposed on the modern information. If you want to get beyond the strip, OS Landranger (1:50,000) sheet 86 *Haltwhistle* covers the route we describe here.

Places to Stay & Eat

The small market town of Haltwhistle is one suggested base, as it has good transport connections, plus a selection of places to stay. B&Bs include the central and friendly *Manor House Hotel* (☎ 01434 322588) and the nearby *Grey Bull Hotel* (☎ 01434 321991), both from £15, or the quieter *Hall Meadows* (☎ 01434 321021, £15). Both hotels do evening meals, or try the *Spotted Cow* which promises 'canny food, canny ale, canny crack'. There's also a Chinese takeaway. There's a well-equipped CCC *campsite* (☎ 01434 320106) at Burnfoot, about two miles south-west of Haltwhistle.

Another possible base is the tiny settlement of Once Brewed, east of Haltwhistle, about a mile from the Wall. The *Twice Brewed Inn* (☎ 01434 344534) has B&B from £17 to £22 (plus bar meals from £2 to £5), the *Vallum Lodge Hotel* (☎ 01434 344248) charges £22 to £25. There's also the *Once Brewed YHA Hostel* (☎ 01434 344360, £8.25).

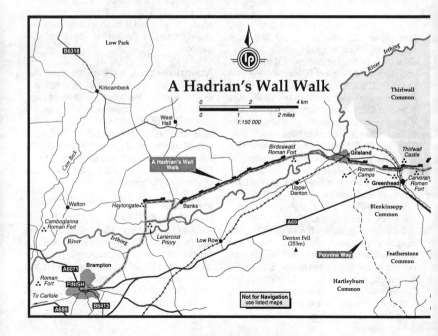

If you take the linear route option, places to stay at Greenhead include *Holmhead Farm* (☎ 016977 47402), near Thirlwall Castle, with B&B from £23 and a camping barn for £3. There are several more B&Bs around the A69/B6318 junction, plus a *YHA Hostel* (☎ 016977 47401, £6.75) in a former Methodist chapel. At Gilsland, *Alpha Mount* (☎ 016977 47070) does B&B from £15, and the *Samson Inn* and *Station Hotel* do beer and food. Brampton has *Irthing Vale Caravan & Camping Park* (☎ 016977 3600), and B&B at *Halidon* (☎ 016977 2106) and *Beechwood* (☎ 016977 2239) for around £15. The TIC (☎ 016977 3433) near the church can provide more addresses, while the *Pointer Dog Inn* and *White Lion Inn* provide food and drinks.

Getting There & Away
Bus Haltwhistle is easily reached by bus (with an hourly service during the day) from Carlisle and Newcastle, which both have good National Express links with the rest of the country. Services are run by Northumbria and Stagecoach Cumberland: their timetable contains two-for-the-price-of-one vouchers to various historical sites.

Most useful for visitors are the Hadrian's Wall Tourist Buses. There are two services: one from the east run by Waugh's Coaches (☎ 016977 47251) and one from the west run by Stagecoach (☎ 01946 63222). The services run between Carlisle and Vindolanda, and Hexham and Birdoswald, both via Greenhead, Gilsland, Haltwhistle, Once Brewed and other sites along the Wall. TICs have the timetable.

The county council produces the excellent *Northumberland Public Transport Guide*, available for £1.25 from local TICs. The principal operator is Northumbria (☎ 01912 324211).

Train There are several trains each day between Carlisle and Newcastle along the

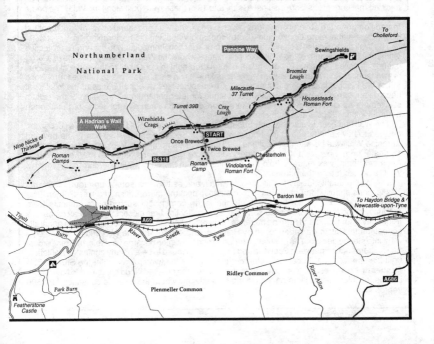

Hadrian's Wall

Despite the fact that the Romans dominated Britain for 350 years, the island colony remained a constant headache. The nub of the problem was the need to make the colony both profitable and secure. If military expenditure was reduced, the mineral-rich north, and even the lowland agricultural areas, were threatened. But the enormous military budget could not be justified on economic terms – it has been estimated that 10% of the empire's army was committed in Britain, probably the least important colony.

In 122 AD the Emperor Hadrian decided that the rebellious Picts to the north were a lost cause and rather than conquer them he'd settle for simply keeping them at bay. Accordingly he ordered a wall to be built right across the country to establish control over a clearly delineated frontier and to reduce the demand on manpower at the same time. To the south would be civilisation and the Roman Empire, to the north would be the savages. His plan became the greatest engineering project undertaken by the Roman Empire – it involved moving two million cubic yards of soil and took over six years to build.

There was already a military road, the Stanegate, running across the country and the course of the new Wall was surveyed just to the north of this road. The Wall was intended to be 10 ft wide at the base and somewhere between 12 and 20 ft high. Budgetary constraints later forced parts of the Wall to be built with a narrower eight ft width, although some parts are even narrower. There are places where you can see that the original foundations were intended for the wider section, but the narrower Wall was then built upon it. West of the Irthing River the Wall was originally constructed in turf but was later replaced with stone.

The Wall follows a standard pattern for its entire length of 80 Roman miles, about 74 modern miles (119 km). Every Roman mile there was a milecastle, in between each milecastle were two turrets. They are numbered right across the country starting with Milecastle 0 at Wallsend, now a suburb of Newcastle, and ending with Milecastle 80 at Bowness-on-Solway, west of Carlisle. The intermediate turrets are tagged A and B, so Milecastle 37 (quite a good one) will be followed by Turret 37A, Turret 37B and then Milecastle 38. At some stage after the Wall's completion it was decided that larger forts were also necessary and 16 of these were built along the Wall. The prime remaining forts are Cilurnum (at Chesters), Vercovicium (Housestead) and Banna (Birdoswald). In addition there are several other forts which predate the Wall and stand some distance behind it. The best of these are Corstopitum (Corbridge) and Vindolanda (Chesterholm).

The Wall also followed a standard pattern in cross section. Immediately to the north a protective ditch runs the full length of the Wall, except in places where the Wall runs along the tops of a large inland cliff called the Whin Sill and has a natural drop right in front of it. To the south of the Wall is a wider ditch known as the vallum with embankments on each side. This sometimes runs close to the Wall, sometimes some distance away. In many places where all traces of the Wall itself have disappeared (it made a fine source of stone for later generations), the ditch or the vallum still remain as clear as ever. Wall walkers soon develop a keen eye for signs of these often natural-looking irregularities in the landscape.

The Wall had been in place for only about 20 years when Antoninus Pius, Hadrian's successor, decided to have another go at the unruly residents of Scotland and pushed north. The new turf Antonine Wall was built across Scotland, 40 Roman miles from coast to coast, but it only lasted 15 years, from the early 140s to the late 150s, before the Romans retreated to Hadrian's Wall. Another attempt was made to hold the Antonine Wall in the early 160s but after that Hadrian's Wall remained the northern frontier.

The Wall brought stability to this area of Britain and settlements sprung up around the forts. These vicus supplied the garrisons, which steadily became more British and less Roman. The Wall continued through the third and into the fourth century but such remote outposts were gradually being forgotten by the Roman Empire, busy fighting fires closer to home. Pay came less frequently from Rome and farming began to replace soldiery as a source of income. It's generally accepted that Britain was abandoned by Rome around 410 AD and the Wall and its settlements went into steady decline. The population dropped and the region became unstable and dangerous.

The borderlands between Scotland and England continued to be a bitterly contested battlefield until the start of the 17th century, after the unification of the two crowns under the Stuarts. The clashes of the armies, vicious raids and endless vendettas ensured blood continued to flow. There can be few bloodier frontiers on the planet, certainly few where the struggle continued for 1500 years. ■

Hadrian's Wall Long-Distance Paths
If you want to walk more of Hadrian's Wall, possibly end-to-end, you're better off waiting. In the next few years, a national trail will be developed (due for completion in 2001) with path improvements, waymarks, bridges where needed and very little road-walking. Alternatively, a route devised by Mark Richards, and enthusiastically described in his detailed book *Hadrian's Wall – The Wall Walk* (Cicerone), includes the best bits and avoids the worse bits by taking pleasant detours through the surrounding countryside, via villages and other historical sites. ∎

Tyne Valley Line via Brampton, Haltwhistle and Bardon Mill.

Car Haltwhistle is on the A69 which runs between Carlisle and Newcastle, roughly parallel to the Wall. The B6318 follows the Wall more closely (sometimes it runs *over* the Wall) and is still known as the Military Road.

Taxi Hadrian's Wall Taxi Service (☎ 01434 344272) operates a service from Bardon Mill to most sites in the area. Sproul's (☎ 01434 321064) and Bainbridge's (☎ 01434 320515) in Haltwhistle have a similar service.

The Route
Day 1: Once Brewed Circuit
7½ miles (12 km), 3 to 4 hours
Today's circular outing starts and ends at Once Brewed, so if you're staying at Haltwhistle you'll need a bus or taxi ride to get here (see Getting There & Away). You might want to bring lunch, although Vindo-

landa and Housesteads both have snack bars. First stop should be the excellent Once Brewed PIC, where you can get leaflets and maps, or check with the infinitely patient staff about public transport connections. That done, head south on the tarred lane for just under half a mile, then turn left onto a track that takes you straight to Vindolanda Fort at Chesterholm. This EH site (☎ 01434 344277) is open from 10 am to 4 pm daily and later in high season. Entry is £3.25 with a discount to members. (Combined entry to Vindolanda and the Roman Army Museum at Carvoran is £5.)

This fort has reconstructions of a stone turret, and an earlier wooden turret and there's a fine museum with some extraordinary written records, the Roman equivalent of stray memos and notes which somehow avoided the office shredder. The evocative fragments include a birthday party invitation to the commander's wife, an officer's complaint that his men didn't have enough beer, a mention of the 'wretched British', a note accompanying a parent's present of warm

Wall Briefing
If you're coming from the east, before walking the wall, you may like to orientate yourself by visiting the Museum of Antiquities at Newcastle University. This museum exhibits items found along the Wall and a reconstruction of the Mithras temple at the Brocolitia Fort at Carrawburgh. One of the most interesting exhibits is a model of the Wall at a scale of 6 inches = 1 mile or 1:10,560. It neatly reduces the whole walk to 36 ft. Entry is free.

If you're coming from Carlisle, the award-winning Tullie House Museum (☎ 01228 34781), open daily, has a good Roman collection, including a reconstructed section of turf Wall. It also has exhibits and reconstructions from the 1000-year period of clan warfare and general unrest after the Romans pulled out, when Carlisle and the border country between England and Scotland became 'the Debatable Lands', the domain of warlords and 'reivers'. ∎

socks and underpants and a child's piece of schoolwork with the teacher's acidic comment: 'sloppy'.

From Vindolanda, join a lane heading north towards the B6318, forking right, then joining a footpath which leads across fields, over the B6318, to the fort of Vercovicium at Housesteads and your first meeting with the Wall itself.

Housesteads is arguably the finest fort along the Wall, and the most popular Roman site in Britain. It certainly has the most impressive location perched atop the ridge, and the long stretches of wall leading to it from either direction add to its importance. The fort's huge flushing latrine is a prime attraction but there are a host of other buildings, including the hospital and four fine gateways. The site is run by EH (☎ 01434 344363) and is open April through September, daily 10 am to 6 pm, the rest of the year 10 am to 4 pm. Entry is £2.50.

From Housesteads, you can add a mile or so to today's route by doing an out-and-back branch east along a fine section of wall and the Whin Sill escarpment, past the remains of Turrets 33B, 34A and 35A, to the impressive lookout at Sewingshields, overlooking where the Wall meets the B6318 and disappears. (This road was first constructed in the 18th century as a military highway by troops of the infamous General Wade. They flattened the wall and used the stones to provide an excellent foundation.)

From Sewingshields and Housesteads continue west along this finest section of the Wall, with superb views to the north and along the Wall in both directions. Don't forget to look back as well as forward, as the view of the Wall and Housesteads Woods from Housesteads Crags and Milecastle 37 is superb. Half a mile beyond Housesteads the Pennine Way joins the Wall and shares the route for the next eight miles.

The walk drops down to Milking Gap, then up and over the dramatic cliffs of Steel Rigg to Turret 39A, which has superb views. Before the next turret a road crosses the Wall, running south back to Once Brewed.

Day 2: Once Brewed to Greenhead
7 miles (11 km), 3 to 4 hours
From Once Brewed PIC, cross the B6318 and retrace yesterday's final stage back up to the wall near the site of Turret 39B. From here, head west over Winshields Crags, at 375m (1230 ft) the highest point along the Wall.

The Wall continues west to Cawfields Milecastle, dramatically perched on the ridge edge, past Milecastle 42, in excellent shape, and on to the remains of the Aesica Fort at Great Chesters, now occupied by a farmhouse. The Walltown Crags section is particularly fine and rollercoasters up and down the 'Nine Nicks of Thirlwall', past Turret 45A, where the Wall ends abruptly at a quarry.

Just beyond the quarry there's no sign of the Magnis Fort which once stood here, but the Carvoran Roman Army Museum

---

Some Hadrian's Wall Requests
During your visit to Hadrian's Wall, please walk beside the Wall, rather than actually *on* it. It's in poor condition in a few places, and the constant marching of 20th-century feet will just about finish it off.

All the land next to the wall and in the surrounding area is privately owned. Some of it is owned by the NT, the county council or similar bodies, and are open to the public. Other land belongs to local farmers and the public have no legal access to or over it, apart from legal rights of way. If you keep to paths, follow signs and use only stiles to cross walls and fences you should be OK. If you start climbing over things and walking across un-tracked farmland, chances are you're breaking the law, and likely to be chased by angry rangers or farmers (and their dogs). Play the game, and everybody has an easy life. Thanks. ■

(☎ 016977 47485) at the site gives an excellent impression of life on the Wall for the troops. It's open 10 am to 4, 5, 5.30 or 6 pm depending on the time of year, but closed from mid-November to mid-February. Entry is £2.50; combined tickets with Vindolanda are available.

If you've run out of time, from Carvoran it's about 2½ miles back to Haltwhistle, or you can continue from the museum down to the pretty little Pow Charney Burn, crossing the stream by a footbridge, in the shadow of the Thirlwall Castle ruins, to reach Greenhead. Or you can follow the footpath a little further, beside the remains of the Vallum, into Gilsland, and take the bus back to Haltwhistle or Once Brewed from there. If you decide to sleep at Greenhead or Gilsland, see the Places to Stay & Eat section for details.

Day 3: Greenhead to Brampton
12½ miles (20 km), 5 to 6 hours

If you stayed at Haltwhistle or Once Brewed, start the day once again with a bus or taxi ride back to last night's finishing point at Carvoran or Greenhead or Gilsland. The walk crosses the railway line and the B6318, yet again, then parts way with the Pennine Way and crosses a golf course to Gilsland where the very fine Poltross Burn Milecastle 48 is wedged up against the railway embankment.

Cross over the railway embankment beyond the milecastle and look for the stretch of Wall to the right (although it's fenced off as if it is private property). A few more steps brings you to a long stretch of Wall that leads down to Willowford Farm, where you're asked for a 40p entry charge. Beyond here another stretch of Wall leads past Turret 48B to the Willowford Bridge abutment. Time and the Irthing River have long ago swept the bridge away but the alterations the Romans had to make in order to cope with the wayward water are quite intriguing.

There's no right of way on the opposite bank, so officially you have to make a long backtrack around to get to the other side of the river.

On the other side is Milecastle 49, con-nected by a fine stretch of Wall to Banna Fort at Birdoswald. This fort has an interesting museum and a very pleasant little cafe but if the weather's fine its principal delight is the picnic area at the southern edge of the fort, with fine views over the Irthing River Valley. This EH-managed site (☎ 016977 47602) is open daily from April through October, 10 am to 5.30 pm. Entry is £1.95, free for EH members.

The Wall follows a lane westwards away from the fort. There's Turrets 49B, 51A and 51B to look at plus the Pike Hill signal tower which predated the Wall, was incorporated into it and then blithely chopped in half by more recent road builders. It still offers wonderful views. To the west of the Irthing River the Wall was at first constructed in turf with wooden turrets, probably as a cost-saving exercise, but was later replaced with stone. So, between Milecastles 49 and 51 the replacement stone Wall runs along different lines to the original turf Wall, and you can clearly see the vallum and the ditch of the turf Wall. The Banks East Turret 52A is an example of a turf Wall turret later remodelled when the stone Wall was completed. There's a short but quite high chunk of Wall on Hare Hill, just past the village of Banks.

That was the final flurry of Wall sites; nothing much remains to be seen from here to the coast, so divert from the Wall south down to Lannercost Priory. It was built in 1166 by Augustinian monks, making liberal use of building material from the Wall, including a number of Roman altars. After Henry VIII's dissolution of the monasteries in 1539-40 it fell into ruins, although many splendid arches and windows survive intact and the nave was converted to become the Parish church in 1740. The ruins (not the church) are managed by EH, entry £1.

Continue south from the priory on a lane, over the Irthing once again and along to the charming small town of Brampton. From here you can take a bus to Once Brewed, or bus or train to Haltwhistle, Carlisle or Newcastle. If you prefer to sleep here, see the Places to Stay & Eat section.

COAST & CASTLES

Distance 20 miles (32 km), with an optional extension of 7 miles (11 km)
Duration 5 to 6½ hours, 3 to 3½ hours for extension
Start Bamburgh
Finish Craster, or extension to Alnmouth
Regional Centres Alnwick, Berwick-upon-Tweed
County Northumberland
Area Northumberland Heritage Coast & Area of Outstanding Natural Beauty
Summary A mostly flat coastal walk, not too strenuous, although the cold winds which blow off the sea can make it tiring. Paths mostly good. Also possible (at low tide) to walk along the beach.

This day-walk takes in the finest section of the Northumberland coast and neatly links two of the county's most spectacular castles – Bamburgh and Dunstanburgh, near Craster. The beaches here never get very crowded, mainly because there are no large 'resort' towns anywhere nearby. And the reason for that is the weather – probably one day in three, the coast is shrouded by a sea mist, known locally as a 'fret' – so the sun and fun seekers go elsewhere, leaving the beautiful, wild and windswept coast relatively untouched for walkers and wildlife fans to enjoy.

Birdlife here is particularly impressive: you'll see cormorants, shags, kittywakes fulmars, terns, gulls and guillimots, on the beach or on the rocky islets and points that the route passes. There are several reserves on or near the route (some with hides) and the off-shore Farne Islands are world-famous for their sea-bird colonies. You are also likely to see seals.

The Farne Islands can be reached by boat from the port-resort of Seahouses, which is passed on this route, and with a full day you could combine walking with boating and birding. The route also passes the quieter fishing villages of Embleton and Beadnell.

Direction, Distance & Duration

This linear route could be done in either direction, but we have described it here from

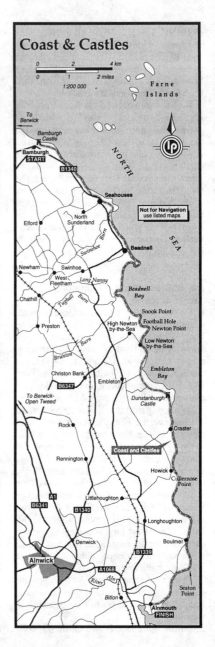

north to south. The total distance by coastal footpath between Bamburgh and Craster is 13 miles, but this can sometimes be a bit shorter if you walk on the firm sand of the beach (although this is only possible at low tide). Walking time is five to 6½ hours but you should allow extra for looking round the castles, lunch, swimming, bird spotting etc.

Alternatives Although there are no short cuts, doing only part of this route would mean missing one of the castles. However, good local transport means there are various options for reducing the route, without missing the highlights: for example, walk from Bamburgh to Seahouses, then go by bus to Embleton and walk the final stretch to Craster, reducing the route to about six miles. Or you could look round Bamburgh, catch the bus to Beadnell and walk to Craster from there (7½ miles).

There is also a possible extension from Craster to Alnmouth, lengthening the walk to 20 miles (32 km), which is possible for fit walkers on a long and fine summer's day, but would in reality be better split over two days. Places to stay overnight are listed below.

Information
The main TICs in the area are at Alnwick (☎ 01665 510665) (pronounced 'Annick'), near Alnmouth, and at Seahouses (☎ 01665 720884). The TIC in Berwick (☎ 01289 330733) is also very helpful. All TICs stock walking leaflets and maps, and also have timetables for the area's buses.

Books & Maps Books on the Northumberland Coast include an excellent, inexpensive series of homespun maps, guides and leaflets produced by local octogenarian walker Alfred Hobson. These cover all parts of the coast and several places of interest in the hinterland. Available in TICs.

The coastal walk described here is covered on OS Landranger (1:50,000) sheets 75 and 81.

Guided Walks
The NT organises walks on the Northumber-

land coast about twice a month. They're free. For details contact the NT (☎ 01670 774691) or any of their local sites.

Places to Stay & Eat
Bamburgh is a small village just inland from the beach, and dominated by the giant walls of its famous castle. Campers can head for *Waren Mill Caravan Site* (☎ 01668 214366) or *Glororum Caravan Park*, both a mile or so west. B&Bs in Bamburgh include *Greengates* (☎ 01668 214535, £19 to £25), and *Squirrel Cottage* (☎ 01668 214494, £22.50).

Craster has camping at *Proctor Steads* (☎ 01665 576613) from £7.50 per night for two people. B&Bs include *Stonecroft* (☎ 01665 576433), *Howick Scar Farm* (☎ 01665 576665) and *Mrs Lloyd* (☎ 01665 576062), all around £15.

If you decide to go for the two day option, Alnmouth has several places to stay. These include *Bilton Barns* (☎ 01665 830427) and *Copper Beach* (☎ 01665 830443), both around £22 for B&B. For sea views and tartan carpet, try *Marine House Hotel* (☎ 01665 830349) with ensuite B&B from £25 per person. For a bit more atmosphere, the friendly *Hope & Anchor* pub (☎ 01665 830363) does B&B from £22 to £26, and good bar food. There are a couple of other pubs nearby too.

Other places to stay, if you want to split the route somewhere else, include Seahouses, Beadnell and Embleton. We mention a few places here, and TICs can provide full local accommodation lists. Places in Seahouses include *Southfield House* (☎ 01665 720059) and *Leeholme* (☎ 01665 720230), both around £15. Beadnell has a CCC *campsite* (☎ 01665 720586) and *Low Dover B&B* (☎ 01665 720291), charging £24. Embleton has *The Blue Bell Inn* (☎ 01665 576573) and *The Sportsman*, overlooking the beach, both with B&B and bar food. There's also the nearby CCC *campsite* (☎ 01665 576310) at Dunstan Hill.

Getting There & Away
Bus Alnwick and Berwick can be reached

Bamburgh Castle

This impressive fortress rising from the sea dominates the coast for miles around. It stands on an outcrop of intrusive basalt, part of the great Whin Sill, which stretches across the county, also providing natural defences for Hadrian's Wall, and continuing east out to sea where it forms the Farne Islands. For obvious defensive reasons, this site has been occupied since prehistoric times. It is thought that both early Britons and Romans had forts here. Bamburgh was the capital of the Anglo-Saxon kingdom of Northumbria from the sixth to ninth centuries, but the oldest part of the castle visible today is the 12th-century Norman keep, built in the reign of Henry II with walls over three metres (10 ft) thick. Probably the most famous battle to take place here was during the War of the Roses in 1464, when Yorkist Edward IV defeated Lancastrian Henry VI.

Much later, at the end of the 19th century, the castle was bought by Lord Armstrong, a wealthy industrialist, who did a major rebuild; just about everything you see today dates from his time or later. It is still the home of Lady Armstrong, his descendant. Tours of the castle take in various halls, the armoury, and exhibitions of later weapons and machinery from Lord Armstrong's time. Views from the upper castle walls, out to the islands, and along the coast to Dunstanburgh provide inspiration for the walk to come. The castle is often floodlit at night. The castle (☎ 01668 214515) is open daily, April through October, from 11 am to 4.30 pm. Entry is £3.00. ■

from all parts of the country by National Express. An exceedingly useful local bus service (No 501) is operated by Northumbria (☎ 0191 232 4211) between Newcastle and Berwick via Alnwick, Craster, Beadnell, Seahouses and Bamburgh, five times per day in each direction. Alnmouth is about five miles south-east of Alnwick, and the two are linked by Northumbria's hourly X18 service which also goes to/from Newcastle (four services on Sunday). This means you can base yourself somewhere for two nights, do the walk on the day in between and easily get back to your start by bus. It might be best to catch the bus to the start of the route and walk back, so you've got no worries about keeping time.

Train The nearest railway station is at Alnmouth, about 1½ miles to the west of town, on the Regional Railways service between Newcastle and Berwick.

Car Bamburgh, Craster and Alnmouth are all on the coast to the east of the main A1 between Newcastle-upon-Tyne and Berwick-upon-Tweed.

The Route
Stage 1: Bamburgh to Beadnell
5½ miles (9 km), 2 to 2½ hours
After looking round the castle, descend to the

beach, turn right (south), and stride out along the beach. To your right are large sand dunes, and to your left is the sea, with Lindisfarne and the Farne Islands (see aside) clearly visible, unless you hit one of Northumberland's notoriously unpredictable frets (sea mists) which will completely spoil your view.

After an hour or so, you'll reach the outskirts of Seahouses, where it's easier to join the road for the last half a mile into town. This is a strange place; half traditional fishing village, half tacky seaside resort, it's a shoddy conglomerate of cheap modern buildings with a central roundabout hedged in by fish & chips shops. Having said that, they are right on the sea and competition is fierce, so this is probably one of the better places to try the traditional English dish. Less greasy is the *Koffee & Kream* teashop with hot drinks, snacks and meals. The harbour is interesting, and usually busy, as this is where you find boats for the Farne Islands.

Work your way out of the north-east side of town, past the caravan park, round the golf course, along some strange parallel ridges, and back onto the beach again (possibly being forced onto the road for a short distance to get over the mouth of a small river that flows in here). Continue down the beach

Dunstanburgh Castle

Dunstanburgh Castle dates from the 14th century. It was built in a strategic position, protected to the north and east by the sea and to the west by the cliffs of the Whin Sill; on the vulnerable south side a large wall was constructed. It was home to John of Gaunt and his son Henry V and, like neighbouring Bamburgh, was a Lancastrian stronghold during the War of the Roses. The castle was abandoned in the 16th century. Today, only the gateway, a tower and some of the wall survives, but these are impressive and the castle is still well worth a visit. It's an NT property, managed by EH, and entrance is £1. ∎

for another mile to reach Beadnell. Once again, it's easier to use the road through the village, past holiday homes and fishermen's shacks, all the way to the harbour, where there's some interesting old lime kilns. If you need to refuel, there's also a fish & chips shop and small grocery.

Stage 2: Beadnell to Craster

7½ miles (12 km), 3 to 4 hours

From Beadnell Harbour continue southwards round the wide sandy stretch of Beadnell Bay down to Snook Point, a spit of exposed rock sticking out into the sea. Beyond here is Newton Point and the path crosses a tar lane running down from a beacon at the end of the point. Go straight

on, to the north and east of an old coastguard station to meet a lane which goes down into the tiny fishing village of Low Newton-by-the-Sea. The village consists of three rows of houses in a square, with the fourth open to the sea, so boats could be pulled up in bad weather. One of the houses is now *The Ship* pub, which does lunch-time food, including crab sandwiches. (Incidentally, the bay between Snook Point and Newton Point is called Football Hole. It seems a modern title, but the 1850 map on the wall of the pub shows it with this name, so it can't be *that* new.)

If you want a change from the beach, a pleasant footpath runs through a NT nature reserve, round Embleton Bay, with the

Alnwick Castle

Alnwick (pronounced 'Annick') is a charming market town that has grown up in the shadow of magnificent Alnwick Castle, the second-largest inhabited castle outside Windsor. This is the ancestral home of the Percy family, who have owned the castle since 1309. The Percys, Earls and Dukes of Northumberland, are probably best known for their ancestor Harry Hotspur, born here, killed in rebellion against the king, and later immortalised by Shakespeare in *Henry IV*. The attractive old town still has a medieval feel with narrow, cobbled streets and a market square.

The castle is on the northern side of town, overlooking the River Aln. On the road up to the castle, through the entrance, you are greeted by a sculpture of a lion on the wall – the Percy symbol. Outwardly the castle has not changed much since the 14th century, but the interior has been substantially altered, most recently in the 19th century. If you enjoy castles, don't miss this one.

The six rooms open to the public – state rooms, dining room, guard chamber and library – have an incredible display of Italian paintings, including 11 Canalettos and Titian's *Ecce Homo*. There are also some fascinating curiosities, including Oliver Cromwell's camp pillow and night cap, and a hair net used by Mary Queen of Scots which is actually made from her hair.

The current owners are also very much in evidence among the treasures. The Duchess of Northumberland supervises the displays and adds many personal mementos, including pictures of her family with the royal family and an odd assortment of visitors, including a photo of a very young looking Muhammad Ali.

The castle (☎ 01665 510777) is open from April to mid-October from 11 am to 4.30 pm; £4.70. ∎

Farne Islands

The Farne Islands (owned and managed by the NT) lie three to four miles off shore from Seahouses, and despite being basically bare rock, they provide a home for 18 species of nesting sea birds, including puffins, kittiwakes, arctic terns, eider ducks, cormorants and gulls. There are also colonies of grey seals. There are few places in the world where you can get so close to nesting sea birds – so close you can almost touch them. It's an extraordinary experience. The best time to go is in the breeding season (roughly May to July), when you can see the chicks being fed by their parents.

In summer (when there's more daylight), a trip to the Farne Islands combines nicely with a walk along the Northumberland Coast. If you're going north to south, you could take a morning trip here and still get to Craster by evening.

Crossings can be rough – and may not be possible at all in bad weather. The tours take between two and three hours; inexplicably, none of the boats have proper cabins, so make sure you've got warm waterproof clothing if there's a chance of rain. You can land on Inner Farne, where there's an exhibition and shop, and one or two other islands. The rest you look at from the boat.

Various boats operate from Seahouses, including John Mackay (☎01665 721144), Billy Shiel (☎ 01665 720308) and Hanveys (☎ 01665 720258) all with ticket offices on the pier. Just choose a timetable and price which suits you. There's really nothing to separate the operators, but it is definitely worth landing on one of the islands – preferably Inner Farne. From April to August, tours start at 10 am. A three hour tour around the islands and a landing on Inner Farne will cost £4 plus £3.50 to the NT (if you're not a member). ∎

ruined tower of Dunstanburgh Castle (see aside), now large on the opposite headland like a jagged tooth waiting to be pulled. From here it's only a mile or so to Craster, another picturesque fishing village, particularly famous for its kipper factory, although the crab sandwiches in *The Jolly Fisherman* pub are pretty splendid too.

Stage 3 (Day 2): Craster to Alnmouth
7 miles (11 km), 3 to 3½ hours

From Craster, continue south over the rocky, wave-cut platform to reach Cullernose Point. From here, keep to the inland path or walk on the beach, or over the rocks, past the outcrops of Longhoughton Steel and the small fishing village of Boulmer. The route passes Seaton Point, the sandy beach of Fluke Hole, the Marsden Rocks outcrop and then a last stretch of beach which leads to Alnmouth.

The small town of Alnmouth has a dramatic location on a steep ridge overlooking the estuary of the River Aln. Once a significant grain-shipping port and smuggler's haven, it's now a sedate holiday resort, and a striking finish to this walk along the coast. You might choose to stay the night here (see Places to Stay & Eat), or catch public trans-

port back towards the north. If you want more castles, your nearest is in Alnwick, just five miles up the road.

OTHER WALKS IN NORTHUMBERLAND

Away from the coast, most of Northumberland's options for walkers are in the Northumberland National Park, often called 'the loneliest park in England', covering 398 sq miles between Hadrian's Wall in the south and the Scottish border in the north. There are few roads, and the landscape is characterised by windswept grassy hills, cut by streams, and is almost empty of human habitation. Much of the area is fine walking country, and the Pennine Way (described elsewhere in this book) traverses the whole park.

For day-walkers, the best areas of the park are the southern section, including Hadrian's Wall (described earlier), the central area around Bellingham, and the northern section, including the Cheviot Hills, which we outline briefly here. In the western area, around Kielder Water, the Forestry Commission has planted huge pine plantations, which have less appeal, and north of Otterburn is a Ministry of Defence (MOD) army training area, which is usually closed to the public.

The involvement of the army is not completely inappropriate, because this is one of the most war-torn corners of England. The Romans built Hadrian's Wall in an attempt to control rebellious tribes, and after they left the region remained a contested zone between Scotland and England, home to warring clans and families lead by ruthless warriors called 'reivers'. Few buildings from this time remain. The families lived in simple structures of turf that could be built quickly and cheaply, and be equally quickly abandoned. Peace came in the 18th century, but coincided with new farming practices, so the tenant farmers were dispossessed, leaving large estates. Unlike the rest of England, this area has no scattering of villages, no stone walls and few small farms. Scenically, it has a bleak grandeur, with wide horizons and vast skies.

Information

There are PICs at Rothbury (☎ 01669 620887) and Ingram (☎ 01665 578248), which can provide more information on walking routes, accommodation and transport in the park. You can also contact the park HQ at Hexham (☎ 01434 605555) for information.

Books & Maps Guidebooks on the area, with several route suggestions of varying lengths, include *Walks in Reiver Country*, *Walks in the Cheviot Hills* and *Walks in the High Hills Country*, all produced by Northumberland National Park (all £4), and Alfred Hobson's series of miniguides (as described in the Coast & Castles section). There's also *Pub Walks in Northumbria* by Stephen Rickerby (Sigma, £6.95). The OS Pathfinder Guide *Northumbria Walks* also has a good selection. All are available in TICs.

The park is covered by several OS Landranger sheets (mostly on 74, 75, 79, 80 and 86), so decide where you're going before buying them all. Harveys maps produce a handy twin-set of maps covering the Western & Eastern Cheviots at 1:40,000.

Central Area

Places to base yourself in the central part of the park include Bellingham, Byrness or Rothbury. Bellingham is surrounded by beautiful countryside, which you could explore by following a section of the Pennine Way, which passes through the town. You could even get here on foot by walking from Once Brewed, on Hadrian's Wall, about 18 miles south. There's a TIC (☎ 01434 220616), on Main St, and a simple *YHA Hostel* (☎ 01434 220313, £6.10). For B&B, *Lynn View* (☎ 01434 220344), opposite the tourist office, charges from £18 per person, and *Westfield House* (☎ 01434 220340) charges £18 to £25. Campers can use *Demesne Farm* (☎ 01434 220258), from £4.50. There are bus connections to Otterburn and Hexham (☎ 01434 602217), where you can connect with services to/from Carlisle and Newcastle.

Byrness also lies in splendid countryside, and is also on the Pennine Way. You could walk here along the route from Bellingham (15 miles), or use the National Express coach between Newcastle and Edinburgh which passes through three times per day. Places to stay are limited to the *YHA Hostel* (☎ 01830 520425, £6.10) and the nearby campsite.

Rothbury has a PIC (☎ 01669 620887) which provides leaflets and information on walking routes in the area. The town makes a good base for circular walks in the hills to the north and provides relatively easy access to the Simonside Hills on the eastern side of the park, where you get some of the widest views in Northumberland, from the Cheviots to the coast. Nearby is Cragside House Country Park (☎ 01669 620333), built by Lord Armstrong (who also rebuilt Bamburgh Castle – see the Coast & Castles section), which has a well-developed network of walks and trails; grounds open at 10.30 am and the house opens at 1.00 pm, daily except Monday (£5.60 for House and Grounds and £3.60 Grounds only). Places to stay include *Orchard Guesthouse* (☎ 01669 620684) and *Snitter Farm Campsite* (☎ 01669 620216) just over a mile away. In summer months you can get here by direct bus from Newcastle.

To the west of here is Alwinton, with footpaths leading north of the Otterburn Training Area up into the fells of the southern

Cheviots. You can stay at *Clemmell Hall Campsite* (☎ 01669 650341) and get here on the twice-daily postbus from Rothbury.

Northern Area

The best place to base yourself for walks in this area is the market town of Wooler, from where you can walk up the quiet and beautiful Harthorpe Valley into the Cheviot foothills. There are several circular day-walks possible in this area, between Harthorpe Valley and the road between Wooler and Kirknewton, and some longer walks become viable if you tie in with the local postbus that goes up the valley to Langleeford. Another option would be to follow the Pennine Way right over the Cheviots to Kirk Yetholm in Scotland, 14 miles away.

If you have wheels there are more valleys nearby, such as Breamish Valley and College Valley, where you can park and continue walking onto the high ground, possibly all the way to the summit of The Cheviot itself (815m, 2674 ft) the highest point in the county, and the remains of an ancient volcano. (Only consider this if you've got enough time and the right equipment – the weather can be terrible up here, and as the area is not so well frequented, paths are often faint on the ground.) College Valley is restricted to 12 cars a day and you have to get a permit; it's free and straightforward, but only available Monday to Friday, although it does ensure everyone has a peaceful day-out. The TIC (☎ 01668 281602), open summer only, will provide all the details.

The TIC also has a leaflet called *Walks by Bus from Wooler* which details several routes in the area designed for the nonmotorist. The town itself can be easily reached by bus from Newcastle, Berwick or Alnwick, ideal if you want to combine a walk in the hills with a walk on the coast (as described in the next section). There's a *YHA Hostel* (☎ 01668 281365, £7.45) in the town centre. Other places to stay include *Southgate* (☎ 01668 282004) on the high street, with B&B for £13.50, and the nearby *Anchor Inn* (☎ 01668 281412) on Cheviot St, with B&B for £16.50 (£18.50 ensuite). They also do bar meals and the town has a couple of cafes and teashops on the high street. There's also a very nice second-hand bookshop on High St, which specialises in guidebooks to the area.

North York Moors

The North York Moors stand between the North Sea coast and the Vale of York, buttressed by steep hills and escarpments, with stunning views of the coast and surrounding farmland, and cut by dales (valleys) which shelter woods, fields and small villages, plus the occasional ruined abbey or castle. The coast itself is also superb, with high cliffs, quiet bays and not too many caravan parks. The whole area is a national park, covering just over 550 sq miles.

One of the principal glories of the moors is the vast expanse of heather – the largest in

---

Heather

The North York Moors have the largest expanse of heather moorland in England. Three types can be seen: ling is the most widespread, has a pinkish-purple flower and is most spectacular in late summer; bell heather is deep purple; and cross-leaved heather (or bog heather) prefers wet ground, unlike the first two, and tends to flower earlier. Wet and boggy areas also feature cotton grass, sphagnum moss and insect-eating sundew plants.

The moors have traditionally been managed to provide an ideal habitat for the red grouse – a famous game bird. The shooting season lasts from the 'Glorious Twelfth' of August to 10 December. The heather is periodically burned, giving managed moorland a patchwork effect – the grouse nests in mature growth, but feeds on the tender shoots of new growth. ■

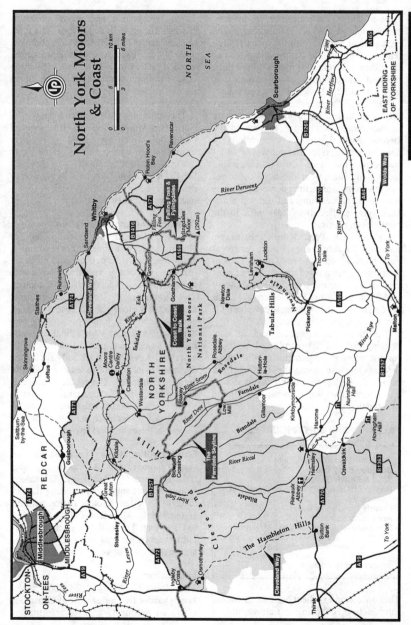

Britain. There are a number of different species, and they flower spectacularly, in an explosion of purple, from July to early September. Even outside the flowering season, their browns-tending-to-purple on the hills, in vivid contrast to the green of the dales, give the park its characteristic appearance.

Although the heather-covered moors might appear to be true wilderness, they were in fact created by human activity. In the Bronze Age, the moors were relatively densely populated and the remains of settlements and burial mounds are scattered across the region. These people cleared the forest that covered the area, their domestic animals prevented regeneration, and the soil nutrients were leached away, leaving it to the hardy heath plants.

Later North York Moors inhabitants included Captain James Cook, the great explorer, who led pioneering expeditions to far-flung places around the world, but most famously Australia. You will find many buildings in Whitby, Middlesbrough, Great Ayton and Staithes claiming to have been his birthplace, home, school, pub etc.

The moors are a popular walking area, offering exposed flat or rolling landscapes for the most part, punctuated with steep descents into lush green valleys before rising back to the high ground again. In this section we describe two walks which give a good introduction to the area.

FALLING FOSS & FYLINGDALES

> **Distance** 16½ miles (26.5 km)
> **Duration** 6 to 7 hours
> **Start & Finish** Grosmont
> **Regional Centres** Whitby, Pickering, Middlesbrough
> **County** North Yorkshire
> **Area** North York Moors National Park
> **Summary** A fairly long circular walk but not too arduous as it follows clearly defined tracks and paths with few stiles or gates. Some parts are muddy in winter. The route undulates but gradients are mostly gentle.

This walk is an excellent North York Moors introduction, covering a rich variety of scenery and terrain, and several points of interest. The route includes some fine open sections across Fylingdales Moor, complete with North Sea views, plus a stretch of wooded valley around May Beck and Falling Foss – an impressive waterfall. The moors are particularly scenic in late summer when the heather is in flower.

This route also passes through the typical North York Moors villages of Grosmont and Goathland, which are linked by lovingly restored steam-powered trains on the North Yorkshire Moors Railway, the revived Whitby & Pickering line, built by none other than George Stephenson way back in 1836 – one of the first in Britain.

Direction, Distance & Duration
The best place to start is the village of Grosmont (pronounced 'Grow-mont'); easily reached by car or train. May Beck car park then makes a good halfway point with a snack van present for much of the summer. This circular route can be done in either direction, but clockwise, as described here, gets the steep section of road walking over with early, and allows for a final train-ride back to base, if required. If you have a car, you could start at May Beck and have a more luxurious lunch in a pub or teashop at Goathland or Grosmont. The whole distance is 16½ miles with a walking time of six to seven hours, although you should allow an hour or so extra for lunch, train-spotting and, of course, the excellent views.

Shorter Alternatives The most obvious way to shorten this walk is to use the steam train between Goathland and Grosmont, cutting the last stage, and reducing the distance to 13 miles. Another option is to cut across Sleights Moor from Falling Foss back to Grosmont. This makes a 10 mile circuit, but you get only distant views of Fylingdales, and retrace some of your outward walk.

Information
The Moors Centre (☎ 01287 660654) at Danby, about five miles west of Grosmont, offers an excellent range of information.

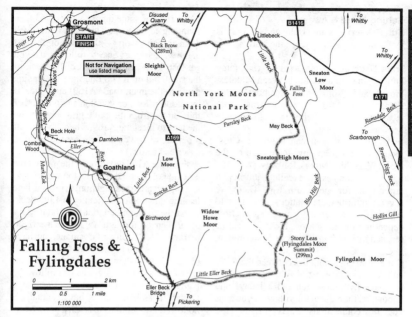

Falling Foss & Fylingdales

0   1   2 km
0   0.5   1 mile
1:100 000

This can be easily reached by car, or by train, as it's near Danby Station on the Middlesbrough to Whitby line, which also goes through Grosmont. In Whitby, the TIC (☎ 01947 602674) is in New Quay Rd. Both places have local *Where to Stay* and *Where to Eat* leaflets.

Books & Maps If the routes described here tempt you to explore further, try *Longer Walks on the North York Moors* by V Grainger (Dalesman). The whole area is covered by the OS *North York Moors Tourist Map* (1:63,360). For more detail, use OS Landranger (1:50,000) sheet 94 or OS Outdoor Leisure (1:25,000) sheet 27.

Guided Walks
The North Yorkshire Moors Railway organise guided walks in the summer, starting at one of its stations (see Getting There & Away).

Places to Stay & Eat
Grosmont has several cheapish B&B options. *Hazlewood House* (☎ 01947 895292), on Front Street, is comfortable at around £16 and has a tearoom downstairs with good home baking. Others at a similar price are *Eskdale* (☎ 01947 895385) and *Fairhead Farm* (☎ 01947 895238). Camping is possible at *Priory Farm* (☎ 01947 895324, £1), but there are no facilities. Pubs in the village serve standard bar food – the *Station Tavern* is basic but friendly. Alternatively, if you are feeling affluent, the steam train does an evening trip with a full dinner served on board. Ask at the railway station (☎ 01751 472508) for details.

On the walk, there is usually a van at May Beck car park between April and September selling tea, cake and ice-cream, but it's probably a good idea to carry some refreshments just in case. There are pubs and teashops in Goathland.

Getting There & Away

Bus Bus services are erratic and the train is by far the best way to reach the start.

Train There are five trains per day (including Sunday) in each direction between Middlesbrough and Whitby via Grosmont. Some trains run direct from Darlington which is on the main east coast line from London to Scotland.

Alternatively, you can approach Grosmont from Pickering by steam train on the North Yorkshire Moors Railway (☎ 01751 472508), which is an excellent journey at around £9 for the return trip. There are several intermediate stations, and five to eight services per day in each direction, depending on the season. Pickering can be reached by bus from Thirsk or Scarborough.

Car & Taxi Grosmont lies between the A171 and A169, south-west of Whitby. There is a car park by the station (£1 all day) and another on the edge of the village. If you miss your bus connections, Galaxy Private Hire (☎ 01947 895230) has six-seater cars running to order between Grosmont and surrounding towns.

The Route
Stage 1: Grosmont to Falling Foss

5½ miles (9 km), 2 hours

From the railway station, head east up the steep hill out of the village. At two forks go right, signposted Goathland. The lane continues steeply, across a cattle grid, to reach a point where a track and a footpath branch off left (north-east). Take the footpath, heading

to the right of some quarry works, and then swinging to the east. This path is not well defined (don't worry – the paths on the rest of the walk are very easy to follow), so if you get lost, keep just to the left of the peak of the small hill until you find the path leading down to the main road (A169) at a gate. (If the cloud is low, or you don't mind another mile on tar, from the cattle grid continue on the lane to meet the A169, where you go left – beware of fast cars – to meet the route as described below.)

From the A169, go through the gate on the east side of the road. Follow the wide track, turning left at a track junction, to join the lane leading down into the hamlet of Littlebeck. Cross the river, and continue on the lane for 30m, then go through a gate on the right, marked 'CtoC'. Since Grosmont you have been on a section of the Coast to Coast LDP (described elsewhere in this book) and there are a few more CtoC signs as you follow the path through woods, past the Hermitage (which looks like a cave, but is actually a hollowed-out boulder) to reach a point overlooking Falling Foss waterfall (impressive after rain).

Stage 2: Falling Foss to May Beck Car Park

1½ miles (2.5 km), 30 minutes

From Falling Foss take the path to the left of Midge Hall (an old house) over a footbridge, then up to meet a track near a stone bridge. Do not go over the bridge. The original Coast to Coast route goes straight on here, and that's the way most walkers go, but its legal status is unclear. The OS map shows rights

The Fylingdales Golf Balls

Before advances in technology, this structure on top of Fylingdales Moor used to include a huge white globe on top of a concrete base which made it look like a giant's golf ball placed upon a tee. There were several more in this area, and the Fylingdales Golf Balls eventually became quite a popular landmark, even though initially there had been considerable opposition to their being sited here. When the golf balls became obsolete, there was some discussion as to whether they should stay or not. Many people thought they had more character than the square monolith which blots the landscape now. ■

DAVID ELSE

DAVID ELSE

DAVID ELSE

DAVID ELSE

Top Left: Tea break in damp conditions, Lake District
Top Right: The magnificent view from Froggatt Edge, Peak District
Bottom Left: Dunstanburgh Castle, on the Northumberland coast
Bottom Right: Stake Pass, on the Cumbria Way

TONY WHEELER

TONY WHEELER

DAVID ELSE

DAVID ELSE

Top Left: Sign at the start of the Pennine Way
Right: Gordale Scar, near Malham, on the Pennine Way
Middle: Flower car at the start of the Cumbria Way
Bottom: Wharfedale, on the Dales Way

of way just to the west of here, passing through woods and past Old May Beck Farm.

Continue heading south to the car park and picnic site at May Beck. Between April and September there is usually a refreshment van at this car park where you can have a welcome cup of tea and piece of cake.

Stage 3: May Beck Car Park to Fylingdales Summit
3 miles (5 km), 1 hour

At the far end of the car park, take the track to the right rather than the tarred road which doubles back on itself to the left. Continue uphill through the Forestry Commission conifers. Keep on the main track at junctions, always going up, until suddenly the woods give way and you find that you have come out onto Fylingdales Moor – quite a contrast seeing the wide open expanse after being enclosed by trees.

At its highest point the track passes through a gate. About 50m to the left is a trig point marking the summit of Fylingdales Moor, and a mile or so to the south-west is a large incongruous building – a MOD air attack early warning station.

Stage 4: Fylingdales Summit to Goathland
3½ miles (5.5 km), 1¼ hours

Aim south on the track until you reach a junction, where you take another clear track heading off to the right. Continue on this track for a few hundred metres, but leave it on a path (marked by a cairn and a Lyke Wake Walk or LWW signpost) to the right. (Straight on is MOD property. Staying on the main track may result in a meeting with a security forces Alsatian. You have been warned!) You are now on part of the Lyke Wake Walk, another famous LDP, originally a 40 mile route along which the people from the east of the North York Moors, near Osmotherley, used to carry the coffins of their deceased to bury them at sea. People who complete this walk nowadays are presented with a small badge in the shape of a coffin.

Follow the path across the moors until it meets the main road at Eller Beck Bridge. This is a rather unwelcome intrusion after the peacefulness of the moors, so turn right across the bridge and take the first left down the minor road back to quieter climes.

As the road drops away towards the railway bridge (look out for steam trains) take the tarred lane on the right, signed to Birchwood. This skirts to the right of some houses and then joins a lane into Goathland. Cross straight over, following the footpath, and keep high above the railway line until a clear path to the left cuts down to the railway station. This is another stop on the North Yorkshire Moors Railway and is like stepping onto the set of a 1950s film. An option from here is to catch the train one stop up the line back to Grosmont – quite a good idea if your legs are starting to ache, and the short journey gives a glimpse of the golden era of steam travel (soot in your eye, hacking cough etc).

Goathland is a very typical North York Moors village. A popular TV series called *Heartbeat* was filmed here, which did wonders for the local tourist trade. At this point you could veer off into the village to have a look around or stop for a snack in a pub or teashop.

Stage 5: Goathland to Grosmont
3 miles (5 km), 1 hour

Go uphill from the station, towards the village, then take the first small road to the right (Mill Green Way), which leads on to another road. Turn left here, to see a footpath on the right, signposted Grosmont Rail Trail. This follows the route of a steep incline (downhill), which was the original route of the railway.

Keep to the line of the old railway (signposted Rail Trail deviations add extra distance), and this final stretch leads you quickly but pleasantly through woods and fields straight back to Grosmont, passing the steam railway engine sheds on the way.

To finish the walk in traditional North Yorkshire fashion, a good way to replace your energy is to take a short drive or train ride into Whitby and have a large portion of fish &

chips, out of paper, down by the harbour! Alternatively, a pie and a pint in the *Station Tavern* or tea and cakes at *Hazlewood Tea Rooms*, both in Grosmont, are good alternatives.

THE FARNDALE SKYLINE

Distance 16 miles (26 km)
Duration 6 to 7 hours
Start & Finish Low Mill
Regional Centres Pickering, Thirsk, Middlesbrough
County North Yorkshire
Area North York Moors National Park
Summary A long route of mainly easy walking on wide tracks on level ground across moors, with only one major climb and descent. Paths are well defined and easy to follow.

This route circles the high ground around Farndale, a large valley which almost cuts the North York Moors in two. The description is short, as many aspects are shared with the Fylingdales route described above, but

the Farndale Skyline is a popular classic in the heart of the moors which deserves including. The route we describe here meets a section of the Cleveland Way and the Coast to Coast Walk at Bloworth Crossing on the north edge of the moors, and also includes the Lion Inn at Blakey Ridge – a long-time walkers' favourite. This area is at its best in mid-April, when daffodils flower in the valley, or in August/September when heather blooms on the moors.

Direction, Distance & Duration
This circular route is best done clockwise, if only because the Lion Inn is better placed for refuelling. The 16 miles takes six to seven hours of walking. Add more for stops.

Alternative A nice way to shorten this route is to follow the path (popular on summer weekends) from Low Mill alongside the river to Church Houses. From here you can

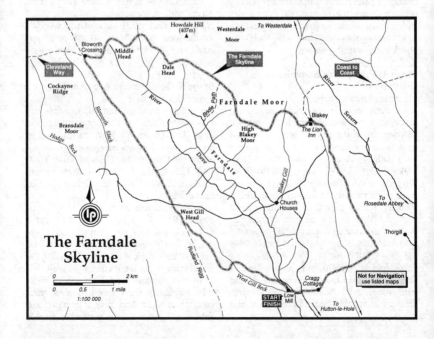

take the quiet tar lane about two miles further up the valley, until a bridleway on the right leads up to join the route between Bloworth Crossing and the Lion Inn. The total for this circuit is 10½ miles, four to five hours walking.

Information
Most of the details in the Falling Foss & Fylingdales section apply here, except that you need the OS Outdoor Leisure (1:25,000) sheet 26.

Places to Stay & Eat
In Farndale, at Oak House (about a mile north of Church Houses), there's a *YHA camping barn* (☎ 01904 621756), charging £2.75. Near Low Mill, Mrs Featherstone at *Keysbeck Farm* (☎ 01751 433221) does B&B for £11 and DB&B for £16. Your next nearest options are in the village of Gillamoor, about three miles south of Low Mill, where B&Bs include *Platters* (☎ 01751 431934), charging £17. The *Royal Oak* pub in Gillamoor does evening meals.

On the walk itself, it's best to carry refreshments. The only place doing food and drinks is the *Lion Inn* (☎ 01751 417320) at Blakey. This is about two-thirds of the way along the circuit but well worth the wait. It is a classic British pub, having cheered travellers for centuries with its cosy atmosphere, good food, good beer and a roaring log fire when the weather warrants it. It is a real oasis in a sometimes bleak setting. The pub also has B&B at around £20 and camping at £1.50.

Getting There & Away
Bus It really helps to have your own transport to do this walk, as Low Mill is not well served by public transport. The Moors Bus (which runs on Sunday, Tuesday, some Wednesday and public holidays, from late May to late September) goes to Low Mill and the Lion Inn from Kirkbyside and Pickering. Check times by phoning the Moors Centre (☎ 01287 660654) at Danby.

Car Low Mill is best reached from the main A170 Thirsk to Pickering road, via Kirkby Mills, Hutton-le-Hole and several miles of narrow lane. In the village there is a free car park.

The Route
Stage 1: Low Mill to Lion Inn
12 miles (19 km), 5 hours
From Low Mill car park, turn right to head north up the road and take the signposted footpath to the left towards Horn End. This path eventually turns left to cross a stream. Through the gate on the other side, turn back to the left briefly to go through the stile, then turn right and go up the hill to another track. Take this to the right until (about 2½ miles from Low Mill) it brings you to a broad dirt road running north-west to south-east straight across the moors. This is Rudland Rigg – an ancient road. Follow this to the right all the way to the junction of tracks at Bloworth Crossing (5½ miles from Low Mill), where this route meets the Cleveland Way and Coast to Coast LDPs.

Turn right to follow the Coast to Coast, along the route of a disused railway line which winds its way along the crest of the hills, with great views into Farndale, until a permissible path on the left takes you up to the Lion Inn for a late lunch or early-evening drink.

Stage 2: Lion Inn to Low Mill
4 miles (6.5 km), 1½ hours
Turn right from the front door of the Lion and pick up the footpath on the other side of the road, which leads to another disused railway line. Turn right. About 2½ miles from the Lion, at a junction with a fenced-off deep shaft in the ground, take the path to the right. Cross the road, pick up the path on the other side (signposted) and go across the heather and down the hill to Cragg Cottage. Follow the track back to the road junction just below Low Mill.

The Peak District

The Peak District is a broad area of moors and valleys in the northern part of central England (or the southern part of Northern England, depending on your point of view). Much of the area is contained within the Peak National Park; Britain's first – created in 1951. It is one of the largest national parks and is spread over the counties of Derbyshire, Staffordshire, South Yorkshire, Lancashire and Cheshire. Often simply called the Peak, this area is notable for its distinct lack of pointed mountain tops (the title actually derives from the name of some early inhabitants). Nevertheless, it is a very popular walking area, with a limitless choice of routes of all lengths and standards.

Geological diversity separates the area into the 'High' or 'Dark Peak' in the north, mostly peat-bog and heather-covered moor where the grey and brown shades of gritstone outcrops form an imposing backdrop for adventurous walkers, and the lower 'White Peak' in the south, characterised by the more friendly atmosphere of pale limestone and green fertile farmland.

Surrounded by large cities, such as Manchester and Sheffield, the Peak has often been compared with an island in a sea of industrial conurbations. On weekends and holidays, streams of oxygen-starved urbanites invade its quiet serenity in pursuit of every conceivable kind of outdoor activity, of which the consumption of ice-cream is only one. Except when seasons of serious drought cause fire risk or when landowners close large tracts for grouse shooting, the Peak is visited by 22 million people each year, making it the second-busiest national park in the world, after Mount Fuji.

Many visitors stay in the picturesque limestone villages, or never go more than a mile from the nearest car park, so naturally walkers have a better chance than most of escaping the crowds and discovering the Peak's less accessible attractions. However, even in more remote parts of the Peak you're rarely alone for long, especially on summer weekends.

The lowland parts of the Peak can be explored at any time of year, but walking the upland areas can be serious in winter, when sunny days turn arctic in less than an hour. Even in summer, mist and rain can quickly turn an easy day-out into an epic adventure. Warm clothes and waterproofs are necessary on any walk in the Dark Peak, and often needed for White Peak walks too.

But don't let these warnings put you off. If you are properly prepared, the Peak is a marvellous walking area, with options for every kind of walker at any time of year. In this section we describe two routes, one in the Dark Peak, the other in the White Peak, as samples of what the area has to offer. Use these as tasters, and then go on to explore for yourself. We provide some pointers for further walks in the area at the end of this section.

THE EDALE SKYLINE

Distance 11 miles (18 km)
Duration 6 hours
Start & Finish Hope village, Hope Valley
County Derbyshire
Area Peak National Park
Regional Centres Sheffield and Manchester
Summary A circular walk on ridges and across open moor, also through meadows and farmland, mostly on good paths with marvellous views. Enthusiastic walkers with average fitness will find this a satisfying day-out.

Hope and Edale valleys are among the most attractive valleys in the Dark Peak. Geologically, the ridge separating the valleys forms the boundary between the dark grit and the white limestone, between Dark and White Peak. North of Edale lies heather-covered moor, while the hills south of Hope are covered in a patchwork of fields. Another feature of Hope Valley is the billowing clouds coming from the nearby Castleton cement works, an industry established there in the 17th century, amidst a lush and tranquil scene. Aesthetically, the works are an eyesore, but economically they are a lifeline to local people and have prevented depopulation of the area. Castleton village, at the head

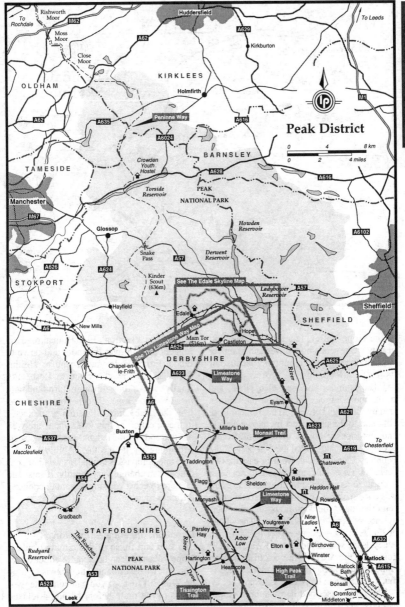

Peak District

NORTHERN ENGLAND

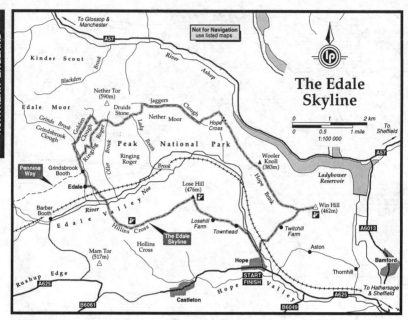

To Glossop & Manchester

Not for Navigation
use listed maps

Kinder Scout

Blackden

Nether Tor
(590m)

Edale Moor

Jaggers

Druids
Stone

Nether Moor

Grinds Brook

Golden
Clough

Grindsbrook
Clough

Ringing Roger

Clough

Lady
Booth

Oller Brook

Peak

Ringing
Roger

National

Brook

Pennine
Way

Grindsbrook
Booth

Edale

Barber
Booth

River

Edale   Valley

Noe

Hillins Cross

Mam Tor
(517m)

Hollins
Cross

Rushup   Edge

B6061

A625

Castleton

**The Edale
Skyline**

0   1   2 km
0   0.5   1 mile
1:100 000

River Ashop

Hope
Cross

Park

Wooler
Knoll
(383m)

Lose Hill
(476m)

Losehill
Farm

Townhead

The Edale
Skyline

Hope   Valley

Hope

Hope Bank

A57

To
Sheffield

Ladybower
Reservoir

Win Hill
(462m)

Twitchill
Farm

Aston

Thornhill

A6013

Bamford

To Hathersage
& Sheffield

A625

B6049

---

of the Hope Valley, is a tourist honeypot; nearby are several show-caves and Mam Tor – called 'the shivering mountain' because of its frequent landslips.

Edale is more enclosed than Hope, and seems more remote, flanked on its southern side by the ridge between Mam Tor and Lose Hill, and to the north-west by the windswept and notoriously boggy expanse of Kinder Scout, traditionally called the first peak of the Pennines. Entering Edale from the east, the two peaks of Lose Hill and Win Hill act as a gateway to its secluded farmsteads. (Lose Hill was once spelt Loose Hill: after a battle many centuries ago, the victorious and the vanquished sides retired to a hill each.) The village of Edale, at the western end of its namesake valley, is the start of the Pennine Way, an LDP going all the way to the Scottish border. Although this attracts many visitors, Edale is much quieter than Hope or Castleton.

The route described here starts in Hope, ascends steep Win Hill, then follows the

ridge along a section of the Roman road via Jaggers Clough over the moor and down to Edale. From Edale you ascend to Hollins Cross and follow the ridge to Lose Hill, finally descending through farmland and meadows to Hope. The panoramic views over the Derbyshire hills are a prime factor in the selection of this walk. Paths are well defined and signposted, but muddy in places, depending on the weather. Ability to use a map and compass is crucial, as weather conditions can change very rapidly. If mist and rain are forecast you might want to choose a different route.

Direction, Distance & Duration

The start and finish of this circular route is Hope village. It can be done in either direction, but we describe it anticlockwise, going up Win Hill first, so you can complete two-thirds of the route before having a relaxed lunch in Edale village.

The route is not specifically waymarked, but signposts to the next village, summit or other feature will guide you for most of the way, except for the northern section of the route, along the edge of the Kinder Plateau. Here you will be well advised to have your compass ready, especially if the weather is changeable.

The total distance of the described route is 11 miles. This is measured on the map and is likely to be fairly accurate as there are not many ups and downs. The average hill-walker who enjoys a steady pace and a few pauses to enjoy the views will take approximately six hours, not including lunch or other long stops.

Alternatives Alternative start/finish points include Edale or Castleton (from where you can join the route at Hollins Cross). If you prefer a shorter walk, you can follow the described route to Win Hill and along the ridge to Hope Cross, returning to Hope village along the Roman road that drops diagonally down the valley side (5½ miles). Or you can simply follow the first part of the route as far as Edale (6½ miles), and get the train back to Hope from there. Another option is the low path from Jaggers Clough to Edale, which is only slightly shorter, but worth considering if the weather on the high ground looks doubtful.

Longer options are to descend Crowden Clough or Jacob's Ladder to Barber Booth. From here Mam Tor might be an irresistible temptation via Harden Clough; alternatively, the ascent to Hollins Cross might seem more attractive.

If you are feeling strong, fit and ready for a challenge, the longest option is to keep to the skyline for the whole walk, missing Edale village and continuing round the western end of the valley from the head of Grindsbrook Clough, past the top of Jacob's Ladder, over Bown Knoll, Rushup Edge and Mam Tor to rejoin the described route at Hollins Cross. This 20 mile epic is best left for long, fine summer days.

Information
The PICs at Edale (☎ 01433 670207) and Castleton (☎ 01433 620679) are the best sources of information on all aspects of the area, including accommodation, food, transport and weather forecasts. (For walkers, Edale is the better of the two.) It is worth contacting them directly as Sheffield and Manchester TICs do not seem to hold any detailed information.

Books There are many guidebooks on walking in the Peak, and several cover the Edale and Hope valley areas. *Parkes in the Peak* by Ted Parkes (Pentland Press) describes the ridge section between Lose Hill and Rushup Edge from Castleton and a low-level walk from Castleton to Win Hill and back. It's a simple, clearly laid-out book with historic notes about some of the major sites. *Best Walks in the Peak District* by Frank Duerden (Constable) is probably the most extensive and informative guide to the Peak District, with several other walks in the Edale and Kinder area. (Some more books on the area are listed in the Other Walks in the Peak District section.)

Maps The Peak District is covered by OS Landranger (1:50,000) sheets 110 and 119, but far more useful for this route is the OS Outdoor Leisure (1:25,000) sheet 1 *The Dark Peak*. Harveys also produce Walkers' maps (1:40,000) and Superwalker maps (1:25,000) covering the Dark Peak in two sheets. The route described here is on *Dark Peak South*.

Guided Walks & Local Services
Edale PIC organises a series of walks

throughout the year, guided by a park ranger. Contact them direct for details. In the summer, Hope Valley Railway runs a programme of guided tours called 'Hope Valley Explorer' starting at various stations along the line between Sheffield and Manchester (see Getting There & Away). They often link in with local events like farm shows and sheepdog trials. TICs and PICs have details or you can phone the organisers (Sheffield ☎ 0114 2726411, Manchester ☎ 0161 832 8353).

The Peak National Park's Study Centre (☎ 01433 620373), at Lose Hill Hall, near Castleton, runs courses and special-interest holidays, as well as a booking system for camping barns in the Peak.

Places to Stay & Eat
There are at least four *campsites* in Hope, and two in Edale, mostly attached to farms, all charging about £2.50 per person. The nearest *YHA Hostels* are at Edale (☎ 01433 670302, £9.10) and Castleton (☎ 01433 620235, £8.25).

B&Bs in Hope include *Underleigh House* (☎ 01433 621372) and *Moorgate* (☎ 01433 621219), both just off Edale Rd, and both around £20. Pubs in Hope include *The Woodroffe* (☎ 01433 620351), where B&B is £24.50 per person, and *The Poachers Arms* (☎ 01433 620380), £39 a single and £52 a double. *The Cheshire Cheese* on Edale Rd has an old country pub feel and serves tasty lunches and dinners (mostly meat-based). Its B&B facilities, however, are expensive at £45 to £60 per room. *The Woodbine Cafe* on the main road is a favourite with walkers and cyclists for breakfast, lunch and afternoon tea, with a sumptuous selection of home-made cakes and a roaring open fire on cold days. This is also a hangout for roosting paragliders; the cafe has a direct radio link with a weather gauge on Rushup Edge, so the flyers can see if it's worth leaving their table.

On the walk, you may prefer a picnic on the hill. Otherwise, we suggest lunch in Edale, where *The Old Nag's Head* does meals from around £4. Vegetarians will find reasonably priced specials here, such as leek

and potato bake. With an exotic selection of desserts such as Mozart lemon brulee and choc-o-nut sundae and several good-quality ales on offer, you might have a problem remembering why you were there. If you decide to start and finish the walk at Edale, there's a selection of places to stay – see the Pennine Way section.

Getting There & Away
Bus Hope and Castleton are very well served by frequent buses from Sheffield. Operators are Mainline (☎ 0144 2567000) and Hulleys (☎ 01246 582246). There are buses between Manchester and Castleton on summer Sundays.

Train Frequent and very convenient trains run between Sheffield and Manchester, stopping at Hope and Edale stations. Very few other national parks have such handy access. Timetables are available from local TICs/PICs or direct from Regional Railways.

Car Hope is on the A625 between Sheffield and Chapel-en-le-Frith, which is linked to Manchester by the A6. There's a car park in the centre of the village, opposite The Woodbine Cafe often busy on summer weekends.

The Route
Stage 1: Hope to Win Hill Summit
1½ miles (2.2 km), 45 minutes to 1 hour
From The Woodbine Cafe head along the main road towards the church, then turn left into Edale Rd. Go along here for 300m, fork right onto a lane and follow this until you pass under a railway bridge. Ignore the sign for Killhill Bridge, leading to Aston. Turn right onto a track which leads to Twitchill Farm. (The farm buildings have been converted into holiday cottages, a clean and attractive sight but also a reflection of developments in countryside management. Farms find it increasingly difficult to survive by farming alone.)

The path leads past the cottages, and the gate on the other side takes you into steep fields. The path is well signposted (to Win Hill), although not always visible in the grass. Continue diagonally up to the ridge to a junction of paths on the ridge-crest, where you turn right and walk for about 700m to reach the summit. If you stop for a rest here, beware of greedy (and fearless) sheep, keen to snatch sandwiches from your teeth.

Stage 2: Win Hill to Edale
5 miles (8 km), 2½ to 3½ hours

Enjoy the views then retrace your steps to the junction and continue straight on (north-westerly) along the ridge-crest. A Roman road joins from the left and the path goes between a wall and the edge of a plantation. Up here, you really get the feeling of being near the sky. Panoramic views and a fresh breeze will blow away any cobwebs in mind and soul.

Follow this path to Hope Cross (an old stone marker-post – built in 1737 – showing the old roads to Hope, Edale, Glossop and Sheffield). Go through a gate here, then after about 300m, at another gate, a signpost to Edale sends you left down a track into Jaggers Clough (a small steep-sided valley). If it's been windy on the ridge, you can listen to the birds and enjoy the peace here.

Cross the stream, and join the track leading towards Edale for about 20m until it bends up sharply to the left. Don't follow this but carry straight on, along an overgrown path (not signposted and easy to miss, so take care, and see the warning below) leading up Jaggers Clough itself, aiming for the top edge of Kinder. The path winds up the valley, crossing the stream a few times. Sometimes it's so narrow you have to use the stream, climbing up the rocks or skirting along the edge. Just before the top it becomes quite steep and rocky. When the gradient eases, you meet a good path.

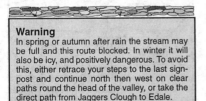

Warning
In spring or autumn after rain the stream may be full and this route blocked. In winter it will also be icy, and positively dangerous. To avoid this, either retrace your steps to the last signpost and continue north then west on clear paths round the head of the valley, or take the direct path from Jaggers Clough to Edale.

At the good path running along the southern edge of Kinder, turn left (south-west). Follow this path along the edge (past the Druid's Stone) to the top of a ridge called Ringing Roger, where a path leads down to Edale. You can take this, but it's more enjoyable to continue on the high ground a little further along the edge to Golden Clough where another path leads straight down into Grindsbrook Clough at the head of a plantation. From here, keep going downhill, a gentle, pleasant stroll through the trees, to Grindsbrook Booth. Cross the bridge and you are in Edale village.

Stage 3: Edale to Lose Hill
2½ miles (4 km), 1½ to 2 hours

Walk south through the village. Opposite the church is an old cemetery just before the PIC. Turn left at the signpost, then right to cross the meadow, continue under the railway bridge and cross the road to a good farm track. Follow this uphill, cross a stile and you are on the steep path to the ridge between Mam Tor and Lose Hill. You reach the ridge-crest at a low point called Hollins Cross. Pause to savour the view over Castleton, its castle, caves and the collapsed road below Mam Tor. If conditions are right, the sky will be full of paragliders.

From Hollins Cross head east along the ridge path, with excellent views down in both directions. It will take you about half an hour to reach Lose Hill summit.

Stage 4: Lose Hill to Hope
2 miles (3 km), 30 to 45 minutes

After admiring more views, descend to a stile, where a low path from Hollins Cross meets yours. Cross the stile and continue descending with the wall on your left to Losehill Farm. After the farm, the path divides: the left branch (straight on) goes to Hope via Townhead, Edale Rd and The Cheshire Cheese pub; the right branch goes over another stile and then through fields direct to Hope, The Woodbine Cafe and the cream tea you've been waiting for all day.

THE LIMESTONE WAY

NORTHERN ENGLAND

> **Distance** 26 miles (42 km)
> **Duration** 10 to 14 hours (one or two days)
> **Start** Matlock
> **Finish** Castleton
> **Regional Centres** Matlock, Derby, Sheffield, Manchester.
> **County** Derbyshire
> **Area** Peak National Park
> **Summary** A route for walkers of all abilities through valleys and farmland, neatly avoiding busy bits of the Peak. Most paths are well defined and easy-going.

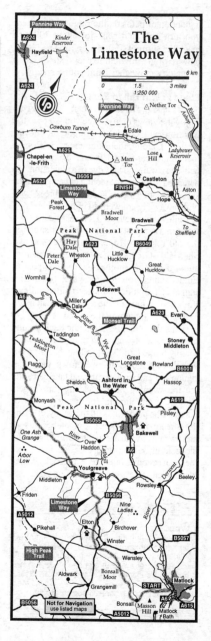

The route we describe here follows a section of the Limestone Way, winding through the White Peak, from Matlock to Castleton – where the White gives way to Dark.

The Limestone Way was originally promoted as a route from Matlock to Castleton (26 miles) by Derbyshire Dales District Council. More recently, with the help of other interested bodies, the route now covers a total distance of 46 miles from Castleton to Rocester, a village north of Uttoxeter, where it links with another route called the Staffordshire Way (see Other Walks in the Peak District, at the end of this section). This new route now passes slightly to the west of Matlock, but it can be easily reached on the short 'Matlock spur'.

Limestone country is characterised by steep-sided dales cloaked in ash woodland, fields edged with drystone walls, clear spring water and annual well dressings (see aside). Before the onslaught of modern intensive farming methods, fields were multi-coloured with some of the most flower-rich grassland in Britain. Commonplace plants mingled with rarer species and harboured a wonderful array of invertebrates that in turn attracted many birds. Although depleted, such meadows do still exist and can be appreciated on this route. Look out for orchids along the dales in spring.

Despite the natural beauty, the limestone dales also have a hard edge. The first part of the route follows tracks used by generations of lead miners. Centuries of mining have left a rash of shafts and spoil heaps which

NORTHERN ENGLAND

Well Dressing

Well dressing is a custom unique to the Peak District. It is the practice of decorating wells or springs in thanksgiving for a local supply of water. The practice may have started in pre-Christian times. It seemed to have died out by the early 17th century, but was revived by the inhabitants of Tissington as a thanks offering for their supply of pure water, which they believed protected them from the Great Plague of 1665.

Each year about 20 village wells are 'dressed' (decorated) with large, colourful pictures depicting scenes from the Bible, local history or events, or more modern conservation issues such as dolphins and rainforest protection. The pictures are produced by spreading a thin layer of clay over a wooden frame, then outlining the design with bark and filling in the colours with an intricate mosaic of flower petals and leaves. And in these conservation-minded days, the traditional practice of using slow-growing mosses and lichens as colour is beginning to decline, with seeds, acorn cups and coloured stones creating a textured background instead.

Well dressing takes place in Peak District villages from May to mid-September, with June and July being the main months. TICs will have a list of when village well dressings will be displayed. Wirksworth, Eyam and Youlgreave are three villages particularly renowned for this tradition. ■

---

pockmark the hillsides. Although many are capped, some mines are still a potential hazard, so don't leave the path in these areas.

Direction, Distance & Duration

The Limestone Way can be walked in either direction but is described here south to north from Matlock to Castleton. Walked in this direction it is a fine approach to the Pennine hills.

Some of the route is signposted as the Limestone Way and sports the Derby Ram logo, but waymarking is sporadic in places, although more new signs are planned. Confusion can arise where other footpaths cross the main route, so knowing where you are on the map is a good idea.

The route described here is 26 miles. It can be completed in a long day (10 to 14 hours), but is best split into two days. An ideal stopover is Monyash (which has B&Bs and a camping barn). If you use YHA hostels, your only choices are at Youlgreave and Miller's Dale (eight and 18 miles respectively), with a good day's walk in the middle and shorter stretches at either end.

Alternatives The Limestone Way is never far from a bus route, and there are many options for doing just part of the route before returning to your starting point. The White Peak area is covered in a network of foot-paths, so endless opportunities exist for shorter circular routes incorporating parts of the Limestone Way. Look at a map or local guidebook (see the following Books & Maps section) and design one to suit your own ambitions and form of transport.

If you want to tackle something longer, you could do the route south to north, following the Limestone Way from Castleton via Bonsall (near Matlock) all the way to Rocester.

Information

There are TICs at Matlock Bath (☎ 01629 55082) and Castleton (☎ 01433 620679). These will advise on walking, accommodation and public transport, and give details of well dressings and other events around Derbyshire.

TICs and newsagents also sell *The Peak District Bus & Train Timetable*, published by Derbyshire County Council (60p), a pocket source of tourist information, including places of interest, well dressing dates, markets, hospitals and cycle hire – especially useful if you're spending a few days in the area. It contains a map showing all bus routes and long paths and trails in the area, including the Limestone Way – invaluable for connections.

Books & Maps Derbyshire Dales District

Council (☎ 01629 580580) publishes two leaflets which describe the Limestone Way south to north. These are available from local TICs. For more detail, get a copy of *The Limestone Way* by R & E Haydock and B & D Allen, published by Scarthin Books. This covers the whole route, north to south and vice versa, including the Matlock Spur, plus several circular walks in the area based on the route, with illustrations and Wainwright-esque hand-drawn maps, showing (among other things) every stile along the way.

Most of the Limestone Way is marked on the OS Outdoor Leisure 1:25,000 sheet 24 *White Peak*. Castleton and the final 2½ miles are on the *Dark Peak* map of the same series. The whole route is also marked on the OS *Peak District Tourist Map* (1:63,360) but the scale and lack of detail make routefinding on the ground impossible. The northern half of the route is also on Harveys Map *Dark Peak South*, available at scales of 1:25,000 or 1:40,000.

Places to Stay & Eat

At the start of the route we describe, Matlock has an excellent *YHA Hostel* (☎ 01629 582983, £9.10), up the hill from the town centre. B&Bs in the town include *Edgemount* (☎ 01629 584787), near the hostel, charging from £14, and *Derwent House* (☎ 01629 584681), just off Dale Rd on level ground (a rare commodity round here!) near the town centre and railway station, charging £16 per person, with vegetarian breakfast on request. There are several other B&Bs along Dale Rd.

A mile south of Matlock (walk along the A6, or take a two minute train journey) is Matlock Bath, a landlocked village decked out somewhat bizarrely as a seaside town, complete with promenade, giftshops, ice-cream, discarded fish & chip wrappers and a cable car. Other attractions include the famous 'illuminations' which delight the crowds at weekends from August Bank Holiday to the end of October. This appeal merits many B&Bs, mostly a bit cheaper than Matlock. *1 Greenbank* (☎ 01629 583909, £15), welcomes nonsmokers.

For food, Matlock has lots of options, mostly in Dale Rd. *Queens Diner* is open every day except Wednesday. More up market is *The Strand*, which does good food, often with live music on the side. You can also get takeaway pizzas, kebabs, Chinese or Indian. Try the *Boat House* pub for bar food (they also do B&B), or go to the supermarket near the bus station. In Matlock Bath there are more takeaways. For a sit-down meal *The Balti* is justifiably popular and has a good veggie selection. For healthy picnic food go to *Beano's* wholefood shop and stock up for a few days.

At the end of the route, Castleton has a *YHA Hostel* (☎ 01433 620235, £8.25), and several B&Bs including *Cryer House* (☎ 01433 620244), near the hostel, charging £16, with big rooms and a good breakfast (it also has a good cafe), and *The Ramblers Rest* (☎ 01433 620125), on Mill Bridge, north of the main road, charging from £15. Smarter is *Ye Olde Nags Head Hotel* (☎ 01433 620248), dating from the 17th century, with four-poster beds and many facilities, from £39 per person.

Castleton also has many eating choices, as befits a major tourist spot. Try *The Peak Hotel*, on the main road opposite the bus stop – they do good food and beer, and welcome muddy boots (they also do B&B). *The George* and *The Castle* are two other pubs doing food and B&B, and cafes include *Four Seasons* near the hostel, and *Rose Cottage* on the main street (closed Friday).

If you're splitting the route in two, places to stay include Elton, Youlgreave, Monyash and Miller's Dale. Details are given in the main route description.

Getting There & Away

Bus Derby has good National Express and regional bus connections to the rest of the county. There are at least 10 local buses per day between Derby and Matlock. For timetable details phone Busline in Derby (☎ 01332 292200). Most also go to/from Bakewell.

At the end of the walk, from Castleton buses go to Bakewell (three times per day), from where you can get another bus back to

Matlock. Buses also go to Sheffield (at least 10 per day), Buxton (once daily, summer weekends) and Manchester (two per day, summer Sundays).

If you need to 'escape' along the route, buses go from Monyash to Bakewell on schooldays. Much more handy is the Transpeak Bus which you can catch where the Limestone Way crosses the A6 near Taddington. This will take you northwards to Buxton, Manchester or south to Matlock, Derby and Nottingham.

For information on local bus services phone Busline in Buxton (☎ 01298 23098, open 7 am to 8 pm) or buy the very handy *Peak District Bus & Train Timetable* (mentioned in Information earlier).

Train InterCity trains link Derby to the rest of the country. Local trains run regularly (except winter Sundays) between Derby and Matlock and Matlock Bath. From the finish at Castleton, your nearest station is at Hope village, three miles east, from where you can reach either Manchester or Sheffield and the main InterCity network.

Accessing the Limestone Way by train avoids the backtrack to Matlock and a few days worry about leaving cars unattended.

Car Matlock is on the A6 north of Derby. There are two car parks near the railway station; the long-stay car park is free. Castleton is on the A625 between Sheffield and Chapel-en-le-Frith, but parking here is expensive and limited.

The Route
Stage 1: Matlock to Bonsall
1½ miles (2.5 km), 45 minutes to 1 hour
From the car park near the railway station go up Snitterton Rd. After 100m turn left where a small board shows distances of various points along the Limestone Way. Follow the path steeply uphill, crossing many fields. As you catch your breath, glance behind to views over Matlock and the Derwent Valley, High Tor and Riber Castle. Pass to the right of Masson Lees Farm, then bear right along the edges of fields skirting Masson Hill. (This is known locally as the 'first hill of the Pennines' as it's the area's southernmost hill over 1000 ft high.) A narrow lane on the left is followed to a junction where a left turn leads down to the stone market cross at the village of Bonsall. It is probably too early for eating or drinking, but if you need refreshment the nearby *King's Head* pub can provide it.

Stage 2: Bonsall to Elton
4 miles (6.5 km), 2 to 3 hours
Climb the steps of the narrow walled path opposite the King's Head, which takes you to Upper Town, then go along the road opposite for a few hundred metres to the next road junction. Follow a field path on the right, then keep left by a small barn on the less obvious path along the wall. Go left into the

Robin Hood's Stride & Cratcliffe
Robin Hood's Stride is a prominent gritstone outcrop seven miles from Matlock. It's a good lookout, and a popular picnic site, especially for walkers with children, as the castle-like rocks make a fine scrambling playground. (Local rock-climbers find it fun too.)

In medieval times, Sherwood Forest once covered much of Derbyshire and allowed the legendary Robin Hood to perform his wealth-redistribution antics in this area as well as his traditional Nottinghamshire home. A local legend has him leaping between pinnacles on top of the rocky outcrop, although this would have been quite a feat. (Incidentally, Robin Hood's trusty lieutenant, Little John, is buried at Hathersage, about four miles east of Castleton.)

Nearby Cratcliffe is another outcrop, not especially impressive on one side, but with steep green cliffs on the other. There is a holy feel to the cave at the foot of the cliffs hidden behind ancient yew trees. It once housed a hermit, and you can see a crucifix carved on the cave's shadowy wall. ∎

un-tarred Moorlands Lane, then right through a stile and across the fields of Bonsall Moor. (Stanton Moor, on the near horizon to the north, is an important Bronze Age site. On the heather-clad top is a small stone circle.)

The Way crosses more fields and a few lanes and tracks, bypassing the village of Winster, to join a green lane leading to the main road near a junction and the Lead Ore House (the history of this old building is explained on a plaque). From here you follow an unsurfaced lane known as the Portway (the remains of a prehistoric track, originally linking Nottingham to Mam Tor, near Castleton) which leads to the eastern end of Elton village. Detour left (west) along the village main street for B&Bs or the YHA hostel (if you plan to stay here) or for the classic Elton Cafe, which serves fine food such as home-made soup, things with chips (£1.50 to £3.50) and a selection of yummy cakes, making it a mecca for cyclists and walkers. It's open weekends from Easter to late October, but only Sunday in winter. The cafe also does B&B (☎ 01629 650217), £14 to £16.50 in a four-poster bed.

Stage 3: Elton to Monyash
8 miles (13 km), 3½ to 5½ hours

If you're not stopping, and can resist the lure of cakes and cholesterol, cross the road and walk down Dudwood Lane. Just before meeting a main road, cross a stile on the left and head up a track signed to Cliff Lane. At the top of the field leave the track and go straight up, passing between the gritstone outcrops of Robin Hood's Stride (on the left) and Cratcliffe (on the right).

Beyond the rocks of Cratcliffe go through a gap in the wall and cross two fields to reach a minor road where you turn right. After 300m, go left on a path through woods, then over fields to the left of a small lake. You meet a lane on the outskirts of the village of Youlgreave (which has a YHA hostel, B&Bs, pubs and shops).

The route crosses the River Bradford, then follows its north bank (upstream), recrossing first by a flat stone bridge, then once again

over an arched bridge. Go up a zigzaging track to the road, where you go right for 500m then left over a stile by a gate, and up an unclear path to the road above. Turn left along this road for 100m then right through a squeeze gate, continuing diagonally uphill across fields to Moor Lane car park and picnic site.

Go through the picnic site, across a lane, and over a stile opposite, then through several fields to skirt Calling Low Farm and reach Cales Dale (part of Lathkill Dale National Nature Reserve). The route goes steeply down into the dale and then just as steeply up the other side, across fields to One Ash Grange.

One Ash Grange

One Ash Grange is now a camping barn administered by the Peak National Park, and makes a good cheap place to break your walk if you're doing it over two days. The very simple accommodation costs £2.80 per person. You don't need a tent, but you need everything else, and bookings are essential through the national park offices at Losehill Hall (☎ 01433 620373).

The farm and much of the surrounding area was owned in medieval times by the monks of Roche Abbey in Yorkshire and was used as a penitentiary for rebellious brethren. Some results of their toil remain in nearby Lathkill Dale, where old trout pools and a sheep-wash can still be seen. ∎

The Limestone Way follows a track with One Ash Grange on the left, and the monks' cold-store and pig sties on the right. About 100m beyond the modern barns go through a gate and immediately leave the track to follow a wall, then cross more fields, eventually to meet a lane down to Monyash.

Monyash At roughly the halfway point of this route, the quiet village of Monyash makes a good place to stay. B&Bs include *The Bull's Head* pub (☎ 01629 812372), good value at £12.50 per person. It also does lunch and evening bar food. Others include

NORTHERN ENGLAND

Sheldon House (☎ 01629 813067), from £18.50, and *Shuttle Hill Cottage* (☎ 01629 813979), from £17. Monyash also has the *Village Store & Tearoom* and the *Old Smithy Tearoom* – open every day except Monday all year. It is very friendly – it even welcomes muddy boots!

Stage 4: Monyash to Miller's Dale
5 miles (8 km), 2½ to 3½ hours

Leave Monyash heading north along the lane, past the Pinfold (where stray animals were once kept until their owner paid a fine and collected them), then left along a walled lane by Dale House Farm, which leads to fields by Knotlow Farm. Cross these, joining a track which leads to a road. Keep to the lane through Flagg, then take green lanes over Taddington Moor, down to the Waterloo Inn on the A6 near Taddington. (The bus stop opposite the pub serves the Transpeak Bus (No R1) which is your last chance of direct escape to Matlock.)

Cross the A6 and walk along the road opposite to a crossroads. Turn left, and when the road bends left carry straight on along a track. This meets a road which leads downhill to Miller's Dale village.

Miller's Dale & the Monsal Trail The village of Miller's Dale lies at the bottom of a steep-sided gorge. Overhead two viaducts straddle the gap; they carried the railway lines between Manchester and the Midlands before short-sighted closures in 1960s forced trains off the rails. Now known as the Monsal Trail, this spectacular route has been converted into a cycle and walking track between Bakewell and Chee Dale. If you've got a few more days to spare in the Peak, it's a great walk. There are information boards at the old station, just uphill from the Limestone Way route. If you need refreshment, also nearby is the small and basic *Wriggly Tin Cafe*, originally built by 'navvies' working on the viaduct, now with good-value meals and snacks, and a sign saying 'Boots, bags and bikes always welcome'. If you don't want to walk up the hill, lunches

and drinks are sold at *Milne House* (☎ 01298 871832) on the main street near the church (they also do B&B).

Stage 6: Miller's Dale to Castleton
7½ miles (12.5 km), 3 to 5 hours

Go eastwards along Miller's Dale main street, under the viaducts and past the church before taking a minor road on the left up a hill (opposite the *Angler's Rest* pub). After 100m turn sharp left on a rough track which leads through the yard of Monksdale Farm and along a walled track. To the left (west) the fields drop into Monks Dales. Follow tracks to meet a tarred lane at Monksdale House. Go left. At the bottom of the hill, turn right over a stile to follow paths northwards up Peter Dale and Hay Dale.

Peter Dale & Hay Dale Orchids
Like many dales in the White Peak, in spring and summer these two small dales are full of flowers specially adapted to living on the thin limestone soil. The show of orchids in April/May can be especially enchanting. Unfortunately, orchids have become rare due to generations of pickers, but they need their own special soil fungi to grow, and won't germinate in people's gardens: a sad outcome to a fruitless gathering. Picking rare flowers is actually against the law now, and people are marginally better informed these days. Needless to say, any orchids you see should be left in peace. ■

At the end of Hay Dale go right on a track to reach a lane, then left to reach a main road (A623). Go left, then quickly right through a gate and down a walled track to meet a section of tarred lane, past Cop Farm, then across a field to join another walled track. After a small gate follow the path left between a wall and large pond.

Cross more stiles and gates as the route leads across the upland pasture of Brad-well Moor. Follow this path downhill to where it forks by a wall. Go through a small gate down into Cave Dale where you can almost imagine yourself in the cavern system before it collapsed to form this steep-sided valley.

This dale leads you into the heart of Castleton through a narrow gap in the rocks beneath Peveril Castle (see aside). Turn left along Bargate and finish the Limestone Way in the village square by the YHA hostel. Nearby are several pubs and cafes (see Places to Stay & Eat). If you're not staying the night, go past the square to the main road, then turn right round sharp corners to reach the bus stop.

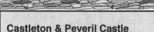

Castleton & Peveril Castle
Peveril Castle was built in 1080 by William Peveril, illegitimate son of William the Conqueror, when he was made Steward of the Royal Forest of the Peak. It was built on a rock bastion above the town which grew up beneath its protective walls. Henry II added the great keep in 1176 and used the castle as a hunting lodge. Despite these regal connections Castleton never became important. Its present honeypot status is derived from the nearby caves and caverns (source of Blue John – a semiprecious mineral) which are visited by several thousand tourists each year (seems like several million in high summer). ∎

OTHER WALKS IN THE PEAK DISTRICT
We have described just two walks in this chapter which represent the different landscapes of the Peak District, but the walking possibilities here are almost endless, and with a good infrastructure for walkers. The Peak District boasts no fewer than 16 YHA hostels within the park and has a good public transport network, except in the south.

Information
TICs for the Peak District include Bakewell (☎ 01629 813227), Buxton (☎ 01298 25106), Matlock Bath (☎ 01629 55082), Glossop (☎ 01457 855920) and Leek (☎ 01538 381000). *Losehill Hall* (☎ 01433

620373) in Castleton provides information on camping barns in the Peak.

Books & Maps A series of leaflets describing walking routes between hostels is available from local hostels, or from YHA Northern Region, PO Box 11, Matlock, Derbyshire DE4 2XA. For books on the Peak, a lot of walking guides exist which can be bought in many shops in the area. Try the specialist Scarthin Books in Cromford (☎ 01629 823272), which also publishes *Family Walks in the White Peak* by Norman Taylor, containing 16 circular 'high interest, low mileage' walks.

There's a similar guide to the Dark Peak. Also for short routes, *Walk the Peak District*, published by Bartholomews, is a fully mapped guide to 40 scenic walks, mostly short, at easy or moderate standard. For a wider range, the area is comprehensively covered in a trilogy of books, *High Peak Walks*, *White Peak Walks – north* and *White Peak Walks – south* by Mark Richards (Cicerone, £8.99 each). For more information on maps see the introductory Peak District Books & Maps section.

Central Area
Worth considering is the White Peak Way, a 90 mile circular walk linking the hostels at Bakewell, Hathersage, Castleton, Ravenstor, Hartington, Ilam and Youlgreave. Each stage is between nine and 17 miles. The walk is described in *The White Peak Way* (Cicerone Press). More information about this route can also be obtained from the relevant youth hostels.

In the centre of the park is Bakewell; it's easy to reach (as outlined in the Limestone Way section) and a good base for a number of walks. The Monsal Trail, a path following a disused railway line, will take you to Monsal Head, Miller's Dale and almost to Buxton, another possible place to stay, also with good transport connections. Alternatively, there's a host of circular walks through the lovely valleys of Monsal Dale, Miller's Dale and Chee Dale, and the dales radiating from them, combined with paths over the surrounding hills, crisscrossed with classic limestone walls. Similar routes, also utilising long-gone railway lines, are the Tissington Trail and the High Peak Trail; both provide effortless walking.

If you wanted something linear, but with a few hills thrown in, from Bakewell you could also head for Baslow and follow the gritstone 'Edges' (inland cliffs), a classic Peak District feature. This would take you north along Baslow Edge, Curbar Edge and Froggatt Edge, down to Grindleford Station (which has a classic walkers' cafe – ideal for a break), then up Padley Gorge, past the ancient hillfort of Carl Wark, over Higger Tor and across to Stanage Edge, which can then be followed all the way down to the A57 and a bus to Castleton, Manchester or Sheffield.

Alternatively, from Grindleford you could head back south along the Derwent Valley following its lovely river for most of the way to Baslow or back to Bakewell. Grindleford station is one of the stops on the railway line between Sheffield and Manchester. With other stations at Hathersage, Hope and Edale, this railway is an ideal way of getting into (or out of) the heart of the national park without clogging it up with yet more cars.

Western Area

There is some good walking to be done in the west of the park around Gradbach, along the River Dane and on the Roaches, a high gritstone outcrop popular with climbers. Another long route, the Staffordshire Way, skirts the south-western side of the Peak, on its route between Mow Cop, near Congleton, and Kinver Edge, near Sourbridge. Staffordshire County Council (☎ 01785 223121) provides a leaflet. North of here, the Goyt Valley is also well worth exploring, but difficult to reach without your own transport.

Southern Area

In the far south of the Peak District are some beautiful river walks along Dovedale and the Manifold Valley. These two can be joined to make an excellent day-walk, but are to be avoided like the plague at weekends and during the holidays, as day trippers swarm here. Public transport is thin on the ground, but a good base would be the YHA hostel at Ilam.

Northern Area

Heading north again, you are in the Dark Peak – where the moorland is high and wild, and a map and compass are absolutely essential. The walking here is 'specialised'; sinking up to your knees in peat in the middle of a featureless moor may not be your ideal day-out, but for those who think that this sounds like heaven, Kinder Scout, Bleaklow and the other moors all offer endless possibilities. Mile-eaters could try the 40 mile Derwent Watershed. This tough two day walk should only be undertaken by fit and experienced walkers. It will take you from Yorkshire Bridge near Bamford, up Win Hill, along the ridge from Lose Hill to Mam Tor ridge, round the head of the Edale Valley to Kinder Low, Kinder Downfall and Mill Hill, then across the A57 to Bleaklow Head, Bleaklow Stones, Howden Moor and back south to where you started via Back Tor, Strines Edge and Stanage Edge.

A little less daunting is a 13 mile circuit of the Kinder Plateau, which can be done from Edale. If you want to experience the high moor, but prefer the comfort of a good path across the peat hags, the first day of the Pennine Way is a rewarding walk from Edale over to Crowden Youth Hostel and campsite. From here you can find transport to Sheffield or Manchester.

Another good idea would be to head for Fairholmes, at the meeting point of the Derwent and Ladybower reservoirs. You can reach here by bus from Chesterfield, Sheffield or Castleton. The reservoirs and the enormous dam walls are worth a look. A good circular walk takes you along the east side of Derwent reservoir, up Abbey Brook onto the moors, and follows the ridge south over Back Tor and along Derwent Edge, past rocky outcrops with great names such as Cakes of Bread, the Salt Cellar and Wheel Stones, ending back down at Ladybower Reservoir.

The Yorkshire Dales

The Yorkshire Dales is an area of valleys and hills, roughly in the centre of Northern England. Some of the hills are in fact fairly mountainous, with steep sides, exposed cliff edges and several peaks over 600m (2000 ft), but most are lower, smoother and less foreboding. Overall, there are very few parts of the Dales which are not ideal for walkers, making it justifiably one of the most popular areas in England. Added to the natural landscape are human influences: remains of ancient settlements, scenic farms and villages, classic limestone walls and field-barns, and the occasional eyesore quarry. There is no great wilderness here (although some of the higher parts can get pretty wild in bad weather), but for many people that is the Yorkshire Dales' most important attraction.

The Yorkshire Dales are surrounded on three sides by other mountain areas. To the north extends the Pennine chain, to the west are the rugged fells of the Lake District, and to the east lie the rolling North York Moors. South of the Dales are the great urban conurbations of Manchester, Burnley, Bradford and Leeds. These cities look close on the map, but are surprisingly distant when you're on the open high ground or wandering through quiet valleys.

There's even a traditional connection between the Dales and these industrial cities. In the early 20th century, and particularly since the end of WWI, factory workers would come to the Dales on Sundays, as a break from the drudgery of the 'dark satanic mills'. It's still something like that today. Every summer weekend the population of the Dales probably doubles as visitors from the northern cities, and further afield, come for walking, cycling, caving, rock-climbing, fishing or just touring by car and coach.

The opportunities for walking in the Dales are almost endless. In this section we describe two walks: the Three Peaks route – a classic circuit, which is undeniably long and hard, although with several shorter options; and a less demanding circuit through Wharfedale and Littondale. We also outline a few more possibilities in other parts of the Dales.

Much of the area lies within the boundaries of the Yorkshire Dales National Park. Like all national parks in England and Wales, this is not state land but made up of many privately owned farms and estates, administered by a central park authority with responsibility for the conservation of the park and the promotion of recreational purposes. Conservationists question the authority's support for quarrying in the area but, quarries or not, this is very much a working park – with more than 60,000 people living in the Dales area, many engaged in farming, and an increasing number in tourism-related jobs. Despite, or perhaps because of, the influx of visitors, the people of Yorkshire seem to have the strongest 'national identity' of any county in England.

Curiously, some parts of the Dales lie outside the county of Yorkshire (now actually three counties – North, South and West Yorkshire), following boundary reorganisation in the 1970s. If you go to the outer edges of the Dales you may well stray into Lancashire, Cumbria or even County Durham. Passports are not required, although some Yorkshire folk may think otherwise.

THE THREE PEAKS

Alternative Name The Three Peaks of Yorkshire
Distance 21 miles (34 km)
Duration 8 to 10 hours
Start & Finish Horton-in-Ribblesdale
Regional Centres Settle and Skipton
County North Yorkshire
Area Yorkshire Dales National Park
Summary A long circular day-walk through high dale country, across open hillsides and sections of farmland. Paths are mostly clear and well defined, although some are boggy and eroded. Others have been repaired with stone slabs and boardwalks. A good challenge for fit and competent walkers.

The three highest peaks in the Yorkshire Dales are the summits of Whernside (736m,

NORTHERN ENGLAND

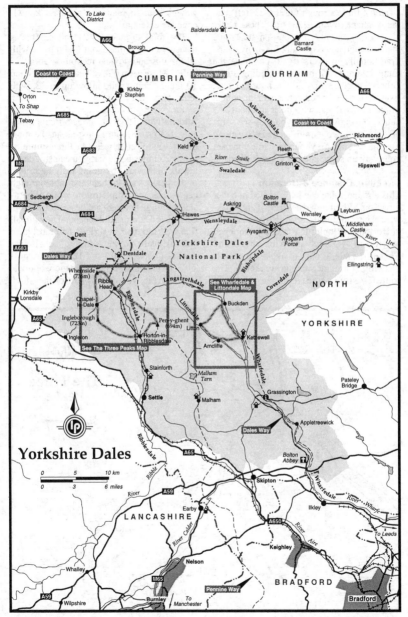

NORTHERN ENGLAND

2416 ft), Ingleborough (723m, 2376 ft) and Pen-y-ghent (694m, 2231 ft). These peaks are the main points of a long circular route that has been a classic walk for many years. Traditionally, walkers try to complete the route in under 12 hours, including stops. Others knock it off in eight hours or less. Even faster are the fell-runners in the annual Three Peaks Race, who do it in about 2½ hours. During your walk you may see some of these runners out training; bounding along like finely tuned greyhounds, while you pant your way up some endless boggy hillside...

Direction, Distance & Duration

This circular route can be followed in either direction, although we describe it anticlockwise. The traditional start/finish is the village of Horton-in-Ribblesdale (usually shortened to Horton). Others are Ribblehead and Chapel-le-Dale, if only to avoid the crowds that clog Horton at summer weekends. The route is signposted in places, but not waymarked, so map and compass knowledge are essential.

The total distance is 21 miles. This is measured on the map, so it's a bit more with all the ups and downs: reckon on about 25 miles. Most people take between eight and 10 hours. You should allow up to 12, with lunch and other stops.

Alternatives There are no short cuts available; the usual route is just about the most direct way to get between the three summits. But if 25 miles is too far, you can still enjoy a walk in this area by doing just one or two of the peaks. Pen-y-ghent and Ingleborough can be reached from Horton, while Whernside and Ingleborough are best reached from Chapel-le-Dale or Ribblehead. They are all fine walks in their own right, and most have various paths to the summit, so circular routes of between 5½ and 12 miles are possible. Using the train opens up more options. For example, you can do part of the Three

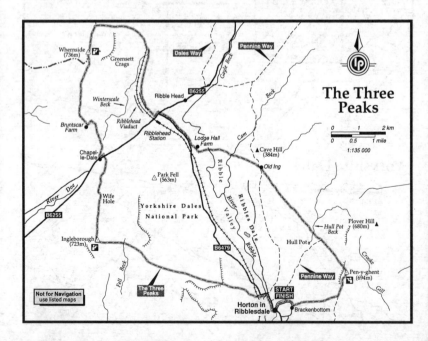

Walkers' Clock-in Service

If you start and finish in Horton, the Pen-y-ghent Cafe (see the Places to Stay & Eat section) runs a clock-in-and-out service, where you complete a card with your name and details, get the time punched onto it by the automatic clock (actually an old factory clock), and leave it in the cafe. When you get back you punch in your finish time. Less than 12 hours earns you membership of the Three Peaks Club and a certificate, which you can apply for at the cafe (they send it to you after scrutiny). The first recorded completion was in 1887. Note, however, that this is not a race. All you have to do is finish inside 12 hours – you don't get extra points for shorter times. (The service does not operate on Tuesday and Friday.)

More importantly, the clock is a useful safety scheme in case anyone gets lost or injured. Although the cafe closes at 6 pm, the staff often wait until 8 pm or later to check everybody back in. (If by any chance you clock out and don't manage to get back to Horton, it is essential that you phone the cafe to tell them you're OK. Otherwise they'll report you missing, and that wastes time for a lot of people, including the police and the mountain rescue team.) ■

Peaks walk from Horton to Ribblehead, via Pen-y-ghent or Whernside, then catch the train back to Horton.

Information

Horton's TIC is in the Pen-y-ghent Cafe (☎ 01729 860333); this is also a National Park Information Point, and they offer a local accommodation booking service. Other PICs, TICs and sources of information in the area are listed in the Dales Way section of the Northern England – Long-Distance Paths chapter. All public transport in the area is in *Dales Connections*, a free leaflet.

Books & Maps Specific Three Peaks guidebooks include *The Three Peaks of Yorkshire* by Harry Rée, which details the route with background information on aspects such as wildlife, and *The Three Peaks Map & Guide* by Arthur Gemmell (Stile Publications, £1.50), which describes the classic route and other routes in the area, plus background on geology and history.

Guidebooks on the Three Peaks area include: *Settle & the Three Peaks* by Mick North, *Rail Trail Guide to Settle & Carlisle Country* (published by Leading Edge, £5.95) and *Walks in the Three Peaks Country* by Paul Hannon (Hillside, £3.99), all with routes between three and 10 miles.

The Three Peaks route is all on the OS Landranger (1:50,000) sheet 98. For more detail, the route is also covered by the OS Outdoor Leisure (1:25,000) sheet 2.

Guided Walks

Free guided walks in this part of the Yorkshire Dales (mostly weekends, also weekdays June to August) are run by Friends of the Settle-Carlisle Line (see aside), starting and ending at stations and tying in with train times. These are listed in the Regional Railways timetable. Lancashire Rail Ramblers (☎ 01772 720865) organises similar walks linked to the Ribble Valley Line (see the following Getting There & Away section). Details are available from stations and TICs. The national park also organises guided walks in the area throughout the year.

Yorkshire Pride

A local poem reads 'Whernside, Ingleborough and Pen-y-ghent – the highest hills twixt Tweed and Trent'. The River Trent is in Nottinghamshire and the Tweed on the Scottish border, but some walkers point out that as the Lake District (which contains Scafell – England's highest mountain) is only about 40 miles away, the rhyme is a little misleading. Although Yorkshire people are known to be proud of their county, this might be just a tad too much hype. ■

Contact the Grassington PIC (☎ 01756 752774) for details. Other local guiding services include Dales Discovery (☎ 01729 830581) and Yorkshire Dales Guides (☎ 01729 860357).

Places to Stay & Eat

Horton has *Home Farm Campsite* with limited facilities for £2 per night. Another bargain is the camping barn at *Dub-Cote Farm* (☎ 01729 860238), less than half a mile outside the village, with straightforward self-catering facilities. *The Knoll Independent Hostel* (☎ 01729 860283) has accommodation from £12. B&Bs include *Studfold House* (☎ 01729 860200, £14); *Rowe House* (☎ 01729 860212, £16.95 to £20.75); and *Willows Guest House* (☎ 01729 860373) £18 to £20.

The *Crown Hotel* (☎ 01729 860209) and the *Golden Lion Hotel* (☎ 01729 860206), both on the main street, do B&B from £16. Three miles south is *Stainforth YHA Hostel* (☎ 01729 823577, £7.45) a renovated country house. The TIC (see Information) can recommend and/or reserve other places in Horton and the surrounding area.

For eating, you can't do better than the classic *Pen-y-ghent Cafe* (☎ 01729 860333), with filling meals, home-made cakes and pint mugs of tea (open from 9 am to 6 pm every day except Tuesday, from 8 am on weekends). They also sell maps, guidebooks and walking gear, and the staff are very friendly. (When we passed through last year, having started the walk at Ribblehead, the sole was falling off one of my boots. The cafe owner tried good naturedly to sell me a new pair, but when he realised that was a lost cause he gave me some tape free of charge which fixed it enough to allow me to finish the walk). For evening meals, the pubs both do bar food, for around £3 to £6. The cafe sells takeaway food, and there's a post office shop, for groceries and supplies.

At Ribblehead, you can camp for free on the common ground near the road junction. The *Station Inn* (☎ 015242 41274) does B&B for £16 to £19, and has a six person bunkhouse for £30 per night. Campers can use the pub toilets, but are asked to donate money to a local charity. The pub does bar food, £2 to £6, but it's nothing special.

At Chapel-le-Dale, the *Old Hill Inn* does B&B from £17.50, and has a campsite charging £3 per tent. The lively bar is often crowded at weekends, when local bands sometimes play. Bar food is good, in the £3 to £8 range.

Getting There & Away

Bus Pennine Motors (☎ 01756 749215) buses run hourly between Skipton and Settle during the day (five buses each way on Sunday). Between Settle and Horton there's a single bus, which only runs on schooldays. The operator is Ingfield (☎ 01729 822568). For other bus services tying in with local trains see below.

Train Most convenient are the Regional Railways trains between Leeds and Carlisle, via Skipton, Settle, Horton and Ribblehead. This is the famous Settle-Carlisle Line (see aside). From May to September there are six trains running daily between Leeds and Carlisle (three on Sunday). If you're coming from Lancashire, the Ribble Valley Line joins the Settle-Carlisle Line.

Tied in with the trains on the Settle-Carlisle Line are a series of tourist buses. For example, Settle to/from Malham and Grassington (both popular walking centres), Appleby to/from Penrith (Lake District) and Carlisle to/from Hadrian's Wall (also covered in this book). For more details phone Travel-link (☎ 01228 812812), or consult *Dales Connections*.

Car Horton is on the B6479, about six miles north of Settle, which is just off the A65 between Skipton and the M6 motorway. The car park in the village often fills at weekends. The TIC will direct you to alternative parking places. Cars left on verges or in gateways may be towed away.

The Settle-Carlisle Railway

The Settle-Carlisle Railway – also called the Leeds-Settle-Carlisle (LSC) line, because that's where most of the trains start – is one of the greatest engineering achievements of the Victorian era, and it takes passengers across some of the best countryside in England.

The line owes its existence to the competition that existed between the Midland Railway Company (MRC) and the London & North Western Railway Company (L&NWRC). The MRC was unable or unwilling to use the L&NWRC's existing line (further to the west), so it decided to build its own line. Legend has it that the MRC company chairman looked at a map of Yorkshire, saw the big gap that was the Dales and drew a line across it with a pencil, saying 'That's where I'll have my railway'. This took 5000 men more than seven years to build, and cost over £3.5 million and 100 lives (through accidents and because of the appalling conditions in the workers' camps).

It was the last major railway to be built by pick and shovel, by gangs of navvies, and involved some amazing work. The Ribblehead Viaduct has 24 arches, the tallest almost 50m high, and the viaducts at Dent Head and Arten Gill are almost as impressive. The longest tunnel is under Blea Moor and is over one mile long. Altogether there are 325 bridges, 21 viaducts and 14 tunnels.

In the 1970s British Rail decided the expense of repairing the line was unjustifiable and the line was threatened with closure, but the ensuing public outcry has ensured its survival, at least for the time being. During summer there are occasionally steam-hauled trains on the route, but normally there are simply two-carriage diesels. Nevertheless, the views from the windows are amazing.

The history of the Settle-Carlisle Railway is covered in *The Line that Refused to Die*, by Stan Abbott (published by Leading Edge, £7.99). The Friends of the Settle-Carlisle Line (FOSCL) is a campaign group dedicated to promoting the line as part of the national rail network, and as a benefit for visitors and local people. For more details contact the membership secretary, 16 Pickard Crt, Leeds LS15 9AY, enclosing a stamped self-addressed envelope. ∎

The Route
Stage 1: Horton to Pen-y-ghent Summit

2½ miles (4 km), 1½ hours

Leave Horton southwards down the main street to the church. Cross over the stream and turn left into a lane, which leads uphill to a farm at Brackenbottom. A path leads straight up the hillside, over several stiles and on boardwalks in places, to the southern shoulder of Pen-y-ghent. The cliffs look steep as you approach – and they are – but the path winds its way up between the worst bits, to flatten out near the top, just a few minutes from the summit trig point.

Stage 2: Pen-y-ghent Summit to Ribblehead

5 miles (9 km), 3 hours

Cross the ladder stile over the wall which runs across the summit plateau, and drop north-westerly downhill. Horton is over to your left. You'll also see the great hole of Hull Pot. Even more obvious is the board-walked route of the Pennine Way coming up to meet you. Do not take the Pennine Way back to Horton, but continue north-west,

dropping gradually down into the Ribble Valley, over several streams and bogs. (In wet weather, your route is likely to be blocked by Hull Pot Beck, in which case from the summit of Pen-y-ghent *do* follow the Pennine Way towards Horton to meet a track going up the west side of the beck, which leads you back onto the path described above.)

The path finally meets a dirt track near a house called Old Ing. From here you continue downhill through fields to cross the River Ribble on a metal bridge to reach Lodge Hall Farm. From here the minor road leads to the B6479, which you follow north to Ribblehead junction. Meals and liquid refreshments are available in the *Station Inn*, or at the *tea van* parked nearby (summer and weekends).

Stage 3: Ribblehead to Whernside Summit

4 miles (6.5 km), 2 hours

From just east of the Station Inn, a dirt road leads north-west towards the Ribblehead Viaduct. When the Settle-Carlisle Line was threatened with closure, this viaduct became

The Other Three Peaks

The Three Peaks of Yorkshire route is not to be confused with the Three Peaks of Britain route. This involves the three highest peaks of England, Wales and Scotland: Scafell Pike, Snowdon and Ben Nevis. Most people do this by driving between the start and finish points at the foot of each mountain: with good planning, good weather and a chauffeur this can be done in a long, hard weekend (without breaking speed laws either). There's even a Three Peaks Yacht Race. It so happens that these three high mountains are all fairly close to the sea, and once a year teams of sailors and runners go from the North Wales coast, to scale Snowdon, then sail to the Cumbria coast to go up and down Scafell Pike, and then sail to Fort William to finish on the summit of Ben Nevis. Once again, this is weekend material for the experts.

If you want to bag the 'Big Three' during your visit to Britain, without the help of a car (or yacht), you can get between them quite easily by public transport – as described in the sections of this book which cover these mountains. However, to do this and nothing else might miss the point of walking in Britain, and miss a lot more besides. ■

the symbol of the fight to keep the line open (see aside). The success of that campaign is commemorated by a plaque, showing a Victorian navvy and a modern railway engineer 'shaking hands across the century'.

Do not go beneath the viaduct, but follow the path running next to the railway line as it curves round to the north-east, to take a small bridge (also carrying Force Gill stream) across the line. You then head for the summit of Whernside round to the north of Greensett Moss and Greensett Tarn.

You reach the wall which runs along the summit ridge, which you follow to the summit trig point. (The path is on the east side of the wall and the trig point is on the west side – you could miss it in mist.)

Stage 4: Whernside Summit to Chapel-le-Dale

2½ miles (4 km), 1 hour

From the summit, follow the path south-west down the ridge for about 1½ miles, before branching left (south) and heading steeply down the hillside and into fields to reach Bruntscar Farm, and a track leading directly to Chapel-le-Dale. The *Old Hill Inn* might be the place for a drink and a rest.

Stage 5: Chapel-le-Dale to Ingleborough Summit

2 miles (3.5 km), 1½ hours

From the Old Hill Inn head up the main road

for about 200m, to reach a gate and signpost on the right. The path goes through fields and a nature reserve of eroded limestone pavement, and past a large funnel-shaped depression called Wife Hole. Beyond here, the path has been boarded. (Even though these boards are unsightly, they cross some severely boggy sections – it makes the walking much easier, and mosses, grass and small flowers are growing peacefully in the mud, rather than being trampled to death under walkers' boots.) The boardwalk turns to stone steps, which climb steeply up to the pathless Ingleborough summit plateau. In clear weather the trig point and large stone wind-shelter are easy to see, but in the mist you could get lost here, so keep your wits (and compass) about you.

Stage 6: Ingleborough Summit to Horton

5 miles (8 km), 2 hours

From the summit, retrace your ascent path for a short distance to reach a fork. Go right (left is where you came up), heading east on a clear path, then south-east. Keep descending, through limestone pavement, until you see Horton down in the valley and the bizarre turquoise lake in Maugham Quarry over to your right (south). You reach Horton near the station. Cross the lines, go straight on, then over the river to reach the car park, the cafe and the finish of the walk.

WHARFEDALE & LITTONDALE

Distance 12¾ miles (20.75 km)
Duration 5 to 6 hours
Start & Finish Kettlewell
Regional Centres Skipton
Area Yorkshire Dales National Park
Summary A good but nonstrenuous circular day-walk along two contrasting dales, in classic scenery, along good, well-signposted paths.

Wharfedale is one of the largest and most well known of the Yorkshire Dales. The River Wharfe rises in Langstrothdale, but soon flows into the valley which bares its name, running southwards through Buckden, Kettlewell, Grassington and Bolton Abbey before leaving the national park and continuing eastwards through Otley, Ilkley and Wetherby, right across England to eventually meet the River Humber and flow into the North Sea. This major valley cuts through the heart of the Yorkshire Dales, and makes a natural line to be followed by the first few days of the Dales Way, which is described in the Northern England – Long-Distance Paths chapter.

In contrast, Littondale is small and hardly known. It lies only a few miles to the east and north of the popular walking areas of Pen-y-ghent (described in the Three Peaks section above) and Malham Tarn, but fewer people approach the hill or the tarn from this side, so the valley is often ignored. The River Skirfare running through Littondale has a short-lived life, fed by several streams including Pen-y-ghent Gill, and flowing into the Wharfe within about five miles. There are two small villages: Arncliffe and Litton.

This walk takes in a section of both dales, linking them with sections of higher ground, which offer fine views of the surrounding landscape. It's not very long, but this is the kind of walk to be done slowly, maybe with a picnic or pub-lunch halfway, so you can properly absorb the Dales scenery and atmosphere.

Direction, Distance & Duration
This circular route as we describe it starts and ends in Kettlewell, because it's relatively easy to reach and has good accommodation options. It can be followed in either direction; we describe it clockwise. Litton is a good place for lunch, so depending what time you leave you may decide which way round you go. It's also possible to start and finish in Buckden, or in Litton itself, although Litton might be harder to reach without your own transport.

The total distance is 12¾ miles. This takes about five to six hours of walking, but you should allow an extra hour or two for stops.

Books & Maps
Books on the area are covered in the Three Peaks and Other Walks in the Yorkshire Dales sections. For this route use the OS Landranger (1:50,000) sheet 98. For more detail, all the route except a short section around Arncliffe is also covered by the OS Outdoor Leisure (1:25,000) sheet 30.

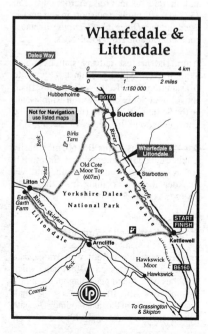

Wharfedale & Littondale

NORTHERN ENGLAND

Places to Stay & Eat

Accommodation and food options in Kettlewell and Buckden (and nearby Hubberholme) are described in the Dales Way section. In Litton, the friendly *Queens Arms Inn* (☎ 01756 770208) is open every day except Monday from noon to 3 pm, 7 pm to 11 pm. They do snacks, bar food and full meals, and have a log fire for when it's cold and a garden for when it's sunny. They also do B&B from £16 per person (£19.50 ensuite). All rooms are £12 per person midweek in winter.

Getting There & Away

Bus There are several buses each day from Leeds, Ilkley and Skipton to Grassington. Some continue to Kettlewell or you may have to change in Grassington. Services on weekdays in school holidays may be more limited, but on summer weekends there are extra services. For more details phone the Yorkshire Dales National Park headquarters and main PIC in Grassington (☎ 01756 752774). All public transport in the area is listed in the *Dales Connections* timetable booklet available from local TICs.

Train The nearest railway stations are at Skipton (from where you must get a bus to Grassington and Kettlewell as described above) or at Settle or Horton-in-Ribblesdale on the Settle-Carlisle Line (for details see the Three Peaks and the Dales Way sections).

Car Kettlewell is on the B6160, most easily reached via Grassington and Skipton if you're coming from the south, and via Buckden if you're coming from the north. There is a car park in the village.

The Route

Stage 1: Kettlewell to Arncliffe

2½ miles (4 km), 1 to 1½ hours

From the west side of Kettlewell Bridge, take a track for 100m then a footpath which branches off left and goes diagonally uphill, signposted to Arncliffe, towards some small limestone cliffs on the near skyline. The path gets steeper near the top with a nice view down over Kettlewell village and the broad Wharfedale valley.

After about 30 minutes the path crosses the broad ridge of the fell, and begins to descend into the Littondale valley. You go through fields and then steeply down through woodland to reach Arncliffe. Cross a lane and go through a small gate opposite and walk alongside the River Skirfare, with the church on the opposite bank.

Stage 2: Arncliffe to Litton

2½ miles (4 km), 1 hour

Cross the bridge over the river then turn immediately right, in front of a cottage and along a track past some old stone barns. After a few minutes, meet the lane again and turn right, over another bridge and then where the road bends left (signposted to Malham) go straight on into fields signposted to Litton and Horton Gill (nearby is a teashop if you need refreshment). The path goes along the level valley floor through meadows and over several stiles and at one stage passes through Scoska Wood National Nature Reserve. A sign informs you that this is the largest ash and rowan woods remaining in the Dales, and that the profusion of wildflowers you may see (if you come this way in spring or summer) is because no fertiliser is used here and the fields are only lightly grazed by livestock.

The path keeps to the south-west side of the river all the way to Litton to meet a track near East Garth Farm. Go right, over the river on a ford and round a few bends (signposted) in the track to meet the tarred lane opposite the *Queens Arms* pub.

Stage 3: Litton to Buckden

4 miles (6.5 km), 1½ to 2 hours

From the pub go left and uphill on a track (signposted 'Bridleway – Buckden') through a farmyard marked on the map as The Hall. The track climbs steadily up to the open fields, with great views over the valley: a classic patchwork of fields and in the distance to the left (east) the bulk of Pen-y-ghent and its neighbour Plover Hill. It takes about 45 minutes to an hour to reach the top of the fell (there's a trig point about 200m to the right), but unfortunately the top is too broad to allow views down into both valleys. So take a last look at Littondale valley and start dropping down again into Wharfedale valley, where a new panorama opens; you can see the villages of Buckden and Starbottom, and the edge of Kettlewell in the distance. The hills behind include Buckden Pike.

The path drops to meet a track which winds down the edge of a wood and through fields near a farm, eventually to meet the lane just west of Buckden village. Turn right and walk along the lane for 500m to reach the bridge over the River Wharfe.

Stage 4: Buckden to Kettlewell
4 miles (6.5 km), 1½ hours

If you need refreshment go into the village. Otherwise, before crossing the bridge, go right over a stile and onto a riverside path heading south-east. You are now on the Dales Way, although following the route against the direction most long-distance walkers take.

Keep to this flat and very pleasant path as it winds through a few patches of woodland, meadows and fields, past stone walls and barns, and over a rather tiring number of stiles, all the way back to Kettlewell. To reach the village you cross back over the bridge; in summer months there's a traditional ice-cream-man here. Otherwise the teashops or pubs will provide any end-of-walk drinks and food required.

OTHER WALKS IN THE YORKSHIRE DALES

In the sections above we have described a long classic peak route, and a less demanding route through two valleys. Of course there are many more opportunities for walking in the Dales. Many of the best walking areas are already partly covered above. Wharfedale, for example, is included in both the Dales Way and the walk along Littondale. A quick look at a map will show you that sections of these walks can be modified to create numerous other circular walks in the area, linking

the villages in the valley with the high moors. Likewise, with a map and some initiative there are many more routes around the Three Peaks.

Information

Useful TICs for the Yorkshire Dales include Ilkley (☎ 01943 602319), Grassington (☎ 01756 752774), Hawes (☎ 01969 667450) and Settle (☎ 01729 825192).

Books & Maps Guidebooks to the Dales area include: the *Pathfinder Guide – Yorkshire Dales Walks* (published by the OS), *Short Walks in the Yorkshire Dales* by John Merrill (Footprint Press), *Complete Dales Walker North* by Geoffrey White and *South* by Colin Speakman (both are published by Dalesman, £7.50), *Walks in the Yorkshire Dales* by Jack Keighley (Cicerone, £3.99), *One Foot in the Yorkshire Dales* by Roland Smith and *Yorkshire Dales Walking – on the level* by Norman Buckley (published by Sigma, £6.95).

For a sense of history, try *Walks in Limestone Country* and *Walks on the Howgill Fells* by Alfred Wainwright (published by Michael Joseph), one of the many classic guidebooks originally produced by the legendary 'old man of the fells' in the 1960s, and not updated since (so you definitely need a modern map too – these are listed under Books & Maps in the walk descriptions above). Some other guidebooks are listed in the Dales Way section of the Northern England – Long-Distance Paths chapter.

General books about walking in this part of Yorkshire include *Walking the Dales*, a fine collection of photos and writings which capture the spirit of the Dales, and their particular attraction for walkers, by Mike Harding, a TV entertainer who also happens to be a Dales-addict and former president of the RA. Another inspirational volume is *Freedom of the Dales* by Paul Hannon (Hillside), describing 40 walks of various distances with maps and beautiful colour pictures.

Guided Walks

The national park organises guided walks in

various parts of the Dales with different distances (easy to strenuous) and themes (wildlife, archaeology, local legends etc). Contact the Grassington PIC (☎ 01756 752774) for a booklet. Cold Keld Farm (☎ 015396 23273), Ravenstone (north of Sedbergh), organises fully inclusive walking weeks from £220. The Swaledale Walking Guides Association, based in Richmond, leads walks around Richmond and the Yorkshire Dales. They leave every Tuesday at 2 pm from the TIC in Friary Gardens in Richmond (☎ 01748 850252).

The Possibilities

An interesting place with lots of potential is the area around the village of Malham – in the south of the national park – although this is one to be avoided if at all possible at weekends and during holidays as it gets very busy. The area is a geologist's paradise, and fascinating for lay-folk too – you can visit the precipitous cliff of Malham Cove, the remains of an ancient waterfall, topped by an area of classic limestone pavement, complete with 'clints' and 'grikes' (see the Glossary of British Terms & Abbreviations for an explanation). Nearby is picturesque Malham Tarn and the waterfall of Gordale Scar. These can all be linked on an excellent eight mile walk from Malham, which includes a scramble up or down Gordale Scar – not advisable when the river is high. Malham has a YHA hostel and several more places to stay, and can be reached by bus. Alternatively, you could walk here from Wharfedale valley along the Mastiles Lane, an old drovers road.

The valleys of the River Twist and the River Doe just north of Ingleton are justifiably popular, but again the stunning scenery attracts many visitors, so come at a quieter time of the year if you can. Those with an interest in history may want to follow the Roman road, known as both the Cam High Road and the Devil's Causeway, from Ribblehead north-east for 12 miles to Bainbridge in Wensleydale.

Ribblehead is on the Settle-Carlisle Railway, which provides a great way for walkers to get into the heart of the Dales (see the aside in the Three Peaks section). Dent station is also on this line, and will get you into Dentdale, another very beautiful valley, as described in the section on the Dales Way.

The Dales Way leads you through here up to Sedbergh, which is a good base from where to explore some largely ignored but very impressive hills, the Howgill Fells. The Howgills are a compact group of big, rounded hills, sometimes likened to a group of squatting elephants. There are not many paths and the tops are completely featureless, making navigation a serious test, even in good weather. However, the actual walking underfoot is easy, the hills are uncrowded and the views of the Lake District mountains, the Yorkshire Dales and the North Pennines are unsurpassed. A walk from Sedbergh over Calders and up to The Calf is an excellent introduction to these hills.

Finally, don't forget Swaledale, in the north of the national park. This is covered in detail in the Coast to Coast Walk, and in various local guidebooks, and can be explored for a day from Keld or Reeth, which both make good bases for other walks in this area.

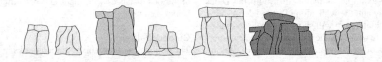

Northern England – Long-Distance Paths

The Coast to Coast Walk

Distance 191 miles (307 km)
Duration 12 to 14 days
Start St Bees Head, Cumbria
Finish Robin Hood's Bay
Regional Centres Whitehaven, Keswick, Northallerton, Middlesbrough, Whitby
Counties Cumbria, North Yorkshire
Areas Lake District National Park, Yorkshire Dales National Park, North York Moors National Park
Summary This is a classic and popular route crossing three well-known national parks in the north of England. The traverse of the Lake District presents the hardest challenge; experience of mountain conditions and fitness is needed. From the Lakes, the route proceeds to less arduous terrain, along easier paths.

Some walkers say the Coast to Coast Walk should be called the Wainwright Way. The route was first described in a book published in 1973 by Alfred Wainwright, Britain's most famous and respected fell-walker. Wainwright started his walking in the 1930s, predominantly in the fells (hills) of Cumbria and the Pennines. He was an ardent and prolific writer of guidebooks, combining a unique, handwritten style and a romantic devotion to wilderness and solitude with a scientific attention to detail in his hand-drawn maps and illustrations.

After many years of reconnaissance and exploration, he created this route across England, which he called A Coast to Coast Walk, implying that it was only one of many possible ways of crossing the country. However, most people doing Wainwright's route these days call it *The* Coast to Coast, and follow the original description closely. The route passes through the finest landscape in England and can be covered in around two weeks, making this long-distance path (LDP) one of the most popular in Britain.

Some sections include several miles of forestry tracks and tarred roads. You might find these tedious at times. However, for the most part it's an imaginative and exciting route which takes walkers from the Irish Sea over the wild and rugged mountains of Lakeland, through the rolling hills of the Pennines and the picturesque valleys and villages of the Yorkshire Dales, over farmland and down quiet rural lanes, and finally across the haunting North York Moors into the tiny east-coast harbour of Robin Hood's Bay, on the North Sea.

It would be hard to imagine a more enjoyable way to learn about British history, geography and society than to embark on this walk. There is the legend (albeit faintly linked) of Robin Hood, the brigand who stole from the rich to help the poor; there are the mines and railways, reminders of a once flourishing industrial age; there are lonely inns on windswept hilltops, medieval travellers' haunts, and above all the wilderness, the space and the bleakness of the mountains and moors which cover the north of England.

DIRECTION, DISTANCE & DURATION

The Coast to Coast Walk can be followed in either direction. However, we recommend starting at St Bees on the Cumbrian coast and following the route from west to east, with the wind and sun behind you (mostly anyway). Although this provides some of the steepest terrain right at the beginning of the walk, it also offers some of the most beautiful, mountainous scenery while you are still fresh and raring to go.

The Coast to Coast is not a national trail and is only waymarked haphazardly, although in some places the signposts are better than on some national trails. You'll need a map.

NORTHERN ENGLAND

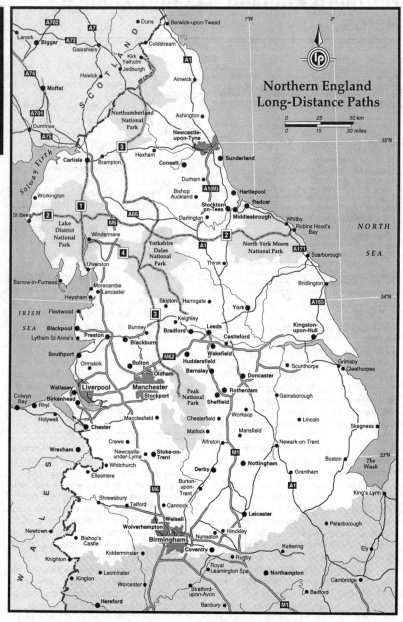

Northern England Long-Distance Paths

**NORTHERN ENGLAND –
LONG-DISTANCE PATHS**
1 The Cumbria Way
2 The Coast to Coast Walk
3 The Pennine Way
4 The Dales Way

The Coast to Coast Walk is 191 miles long and has traditionally been tackled over 12 days. Apart from a couple of days in the middle, most days have some ascents, particularly the Lakes section. This offers some high-level route options if you are feeling fit and confident, if the weather is fine and, above all, if your sack is not too heavy.

STAGES

The itinerary originally devised by Wainwright included 12 days of walking. We have kept with tradition, and split the route into the following stages:

Day	From	To	Distance
1	St Bees	Ennerdale Bridge	14 miles (23 km)
2	Ennerdale Bridge	Rosthwaite	14½ miles (23.5 km)
3	Rosthwaite	Patterdale	17½ miles (28 km)
4	Patterdale	Shap	16 miles (26 km)
5	Shap	Kirkby Stephen	21 miles (34 km)
6	Kirkby Stephen	Keld	13 miles (21 km)
7	Keld	Reeth	11 miles (18 km)
8	Reeth	Richmond	11 miles (18 km)
9	Richmond	Ingleby Cross	23 miles (37 km)
10	Ingleby Cross	Great Broughton	12 miles (19 km)
11	Great Broughton	Glaisdale	18 miles (29 km)
12	Glaisdale	Robin Hood's Bay	20 miles (32 km)

There is no doubt that this route is a demanding undertaking if completed in one go, particularly if you are camping and carrying your own gear. Note that the hours given for each stage in the main route description are walking times only; you should allow an extra hour or two for rests, lunch stops, and so on.

If you prefer a relaxing holiday, you might consider some rest-days on the way, for example at Patterdale (Lake District) and in the Yorkshire Dales, perhaps Keld or Reeth, making it a 14 day venture. You could shorten some days by changing or adding overnight stops, for example including Grasmere, Blakey and Grosmont. Days 4 and 5 could be broken up by ending Day 4 in Bampton and Day 5 in Orton or Newbiggin, possibly nicer overnight stops than Shap.

Fit walkers could cut it to 11 days by linking Days 7 and 8. A few more days could be trimmed by using some of the intermediate accommodation described in this section, but this would make it quite a march. The whole route has even been done as a run in around 39 hours!

If you are not bothered about accolade and only have time to do part of the route, your best bet would be the Lake District section only, finishing at Shap or Kirkby Stephen (which has better transport connections).

It's worth NOT beginning this route on a weekend, which is when most British walkers (with two weeks holiday) start. As well as having a bit more space on the hills, you'll also be out of sync with the 'bed & breakfast bulge' which follows these walkers along the route, and have more chance of easily finding a place to stay.

INFORMATION

The main Tourist Information Centres (TICs) on the walk are: Windermere (☎ 015394 44444), for the Lake District; Whitehaven (☎ 01946 695678), for information on St Bees; Kirkby Stephen (☎ 017683 71199), for the Eden Valley; Richmond (☎ 01748 850252), for the Vale of Mowbray; York (☎ 01904 707961), for the Yorkshire Dales; and Whitby (☎ 01947 602674), for the North York Moors.

In addition, the following National Park Information Centres (PICs) have valuable information: Lake District – Windermere

(☎ 015394 46601); Yorkshire Dales – Grassington (☎ 01756 752774); North York Moors – Helmsley (☎ 01439 770657). For accommodation information two leaflets are available; see the Books section.

Books

The original 'pictorial guide' to this route, *A Coast to Coast Walk* by Alfred Wainwright, is a classic and has been reprinted many times since its first publication in 1973. However, for a long time it was not rewritten or updated to take account of necessary changes to the route and other events (such as new main roads and demolished hotels) which had occurred in that time. Now published by Michael Joseph (at £9.99), since 1994 the book has been slightly revised, describing new and recommended alternatives to Wainwright's route where it had originally strayed from public rights of way, although still keeping the original text for historical completeness.

Alongside this is a larger format picture guide, *Wainwright's Coast to Coast Walk* (Michael Joseph, £14.99), which celebrates the route with Wainwright's characteristic prose and splendid photos by Derry Brabbs. Use it to whet your appetite, or as a souvenir after the walk.

The Coast to Coast Walk by Paul Hannon (Hillside, £7.50) is a pocket-size paperback, conveniently bound in plastic and more practical. It describes the Wainwright route, in similar style, with hand-drawn illustrations, but with printed text. This means it is a little more clearly presented and easier to read. There's also *The Northern Coast to Coast Walk* by Terry Marsh (Cicerone, £7.99), which has made adjustments to the original route in consultation with national parks and conservation officials, keeping to rights of way and avoiding eroded areas.

There are two extremely useful *Coast to Coast Accommodation Guides*. One is produced by Doreen Whitehead (☎ 01748 886374), East Stonesdale Farm, Keld, near Richmond DL11 6LJ, available by post for £2 (include a self-addressed envelope). You can stay on this farm while you're doing the

route: Doreen and her husband are a good source of information on local history and society. The other guide is produced by the North York Moors Adventure Centre (☎ 01609 882571), Park House, Ingleby Cross, Northallerton DL6 3PE (£2.95). It includes campsites and Youth Hostel Association (YHA) hostels and is clearly presented. The Adventure Centre also produces Coast to Coast badges, T-shirts and certificates.

Maps

Deciding which maps to take is tricky. To cover the whole route you need Ordnance Survey (OS) Landranger (1:50,000) sheets 89, 90, 91, 92, 93, 94, 98 and 99. These maps are expensive and heavy. This problem is partially solved by two strip maps, specially designed for Coast-to-Coasters, with extracts from relevant OS Outdoor Leisure (1:25,000) sheets, with Wainwright's descriptions and some of his illustrations alongside. In theory this means no guidebook or other maps are needed, so the expense could be cut down to £5.25 per map. In practice, navigating could be difficult, especially in bad weather, because the maps only show a limited strip of the area you're passing through. We compromised by using a combination of guidebook, strip maps and some of the OS 1:50,000 sheets covering the areas that would cause problems in bad weather. These were sheets 89, 90, 91 and 94. Harveys maps also cover the Lakes. You need the *Western Lakeland* and *Eastern Lakeland* sheets for the Coast to Coast. Another strip map has been produced by Footprint, based in Stirling (☎ 01786 479866). It's cheap at £2.95, but not detailed enough.

GUIDED WALKS & LOCAL SERVICES

The YHA Northern Region (☎ 01629 825850), PO Box 11, Matlock, Derbyshire DE4 2XA, offers a 15 night Coast to Coast walking holiday led by experienced guides. Several other national companies organise walks along all or part of the route; these are listed under Walking Tours in the main

TONY WHEELER

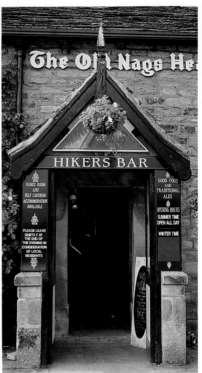

TONY WHEELER

DAVID ELSE

Top Left: High Force Fall, on the Pennine Way
Top Right: The Old Nag's Head Hikers Bar, Edale, the place for a traditional pint before starting the Pennine Way
Bottom: Stile on the Pennine Way, near Bellingham

TONY WHEELER

DAVID ELSE

Left: The well-warn stones of a Roman road, along the Pennine Way
Right: Gully scrambling, in the Lake District

Getting Around chapter. Bee Jay International (☎ 0191 5487060), at 4 Peareth Grove, Sunderland SR6 9NL, specialise in Coast to Coast walking tours between 13 and 16 days long, departing every summer weekend. Even if you don't want to take a tour, you can use its luggage transfer service.

Other luggage transfer services include Coast to Coast Pack Horse (☎ 017683 71680), West View Farmhouse, near Kirkby Stephen CA17 4JH, which runs a daily minibus via set points along the route, April through September. The service is flexible – ideal if you don't want your luggage transported every day or if you want to make on-the-spot decisions. It will also transport passengers if you're tired, blistered or just want a day off, and you can park cars at their depot for the duration of your walk. The White Knight Coast to Coast Luggage Link & Passenger Service (☎ 01903 766475), Lancing, West Sussex BN15 0AE, operates a year-round door-to-door service by taxi for both baggage and passengers but on an advance booking basis only.

PLACES TO STAY & EAT

The route is mostly well served with B&Bs, although this is a popular route through three popular areas, and accommodation prices reflect this. All towns and villages in the itinerary described here have several choices, except Keld where options are limited. For a wider choice, consult the RA Yearbook and National Trail Companion (see the Books section of the Facts for the Walker chapter), and the accommodation leaflets mentioned in the preceding Books section.

YHA hostels can be found in most places, apart from Clay Bank Top, Glaisdale and Robin Hood's Bay (although nearby Whitby could serve as an alternative). Some of the hostels are situated away from the overnight stops recommended here. For example, Ennerdale hostel is five miles on from Ennerdale Bridge at Gillerthwaite (between Ennerdale Bridge and Rosthwaite) and Grinton Lodge is about a mile beyond Reeth, slightly off the route. Enquire when you book. The route is also well served by campsites, usually on farms.

At the end of the day, you will have no trouble finding pubs serving good food and local beer. Restaurants are limited to bigger places. The route passes shops on only several of the days, so being self-sufficient is a logistical headache. For lunch, some days include a midway cafe or pub, but you'll often need to provide your own food.

GETTING THERE & AWAY

Bus

Stagecoach Cumberland (☎ 01946 63222) runs buses from Penrith via Keswick and Cockermouth to Whitehaven daily every two hours (less on Sunday). Twice a day this bus continues to St Bees. From Robin Hood's Bay, the end of the walk, there are buses to Whitby all day, about every hour.

Train

St Bees is on the Cumbrian Coast line between Carlisle and Barrow-in-Furness, with connections from Kendal and Oxenholme. For details phone Cumbria Travel Link (☎ 01228 812812). The nearest station to Robin Hood's Bay is Whitby, from where trains go to Middlesbrough, with connections to the rest of the country.

If you want to 'escape' at Kirkby Stephen, you can either go to Leeds on the famous Settle-Carlisle Line (for details see the Northern England – Short Walks chapter) or catch connections to Manchester from Hellifield, on the same line. The Kirkby Stephen TIC (☎ 017683 71199) will send you a Regional Railways leaflet.

Car

St Bees is reached from the M6 at Penrith, by the A66 to Cockermouth, the A5086 to Egremont and from there along a small country road. If you are leaving your car at St Bees you could catch a lift back from Robin Hood's Bay on the Pack Horse shuttle service mentioned in the preceding Guided Walks & Local Services section.

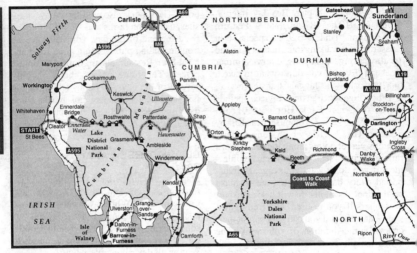

THE ROUTE

This is a suggested itinerary – there are several variations possible with longer days or additional stops. Some of these are detailed in the route description.

The Start: St Bees

The unpretentious village of St Bees could easily be a more lively tourist location if it wasn't for three things: the Sellafield Nuclear Power Station just a few miles south, the Whitehaven chemical works to the north and the closeness of the Lake District which attracts most tourists who come to this part of Britain. However, it bravely stands up to the challenge and proudly boasts its beach, a Royal Society for the Protection of Birds (RSPB) reserve ('one of the largest on the West Coast of England and the only place in the country where Black Guillemot breed') and the historic Priory Church of St Bega (St Bees' original name), to which one of the first Public Schools after Oxford and Cambridge was added in the 19th century. Many of the houses in the village date from the 17th and 18th centuries.

There is no TIC, but the staff in the post office on Main St will be happy to advise you. There are plenty of B&Bs (although many are fully booked during the week with Sellafield workers) and some pubs with accommodation. These include *The Queens Hotel* (☎ 01946 822287), on Main St, with comfortable rooms from £21 per person and good evening food for around £5. Tasty vegetarian meals are served on request. *Stonehouse Farm* (☎ 01946 822224), next to the railway station on Main St, does good B&B from £15 per person. There's also a back garden which can accommodate two or three small tents for £2 per person. Also on Main St is the attractive *Outrigg House* (☎ 01946 822348), from £15, and *Fairladies Barn Guesthouse* (☎ 01946 822718), good value at £14. On High House Rd is the pleasant and interesting *Khandhalla* (☎ 01946 822377), charging £15 per person. Khandhalla means 'Place of Peace and Plenty', named by its first owner, a missionary returning from India in the 19th century.

For food, *The Oddfellows* pub, opposite Fairladies Barn, is recommended. If you fancy something more exotic in this unexotic village, the *French Connection* in the railway station building, offers a special ambience and a more varied menu.

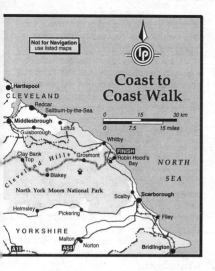

Not for Navigation use listed maps

Coast to Coast Walk

0   15   30 km
0   7.5   15 miles

CLEVELAND
Hartlepool
Redcar
Saltburn-by-the-Sea
Middlesbrough
Guisborough   Loftus
Clay Bank   Cleveland   Hills   Grosmont
Top   Whitby
                    FINISH
            Blakey   Robin Hood's   NORTH
North York Moors National Park   Bay
Helmsley   Pickering   Scalby   Scarborough   SEA
                    Filey
YORKSHIRE
        Malton
    A19   A64   Norton   Bridlington

Day 1: St Bees to Ennerdale Bridge
14 miles (23 km), 6 to 7 hours
This introductory day gives walkers some idea of the contrasts and variety you will encounter on this hike. From the exhilarating sea cliffs high above the shore and the foaming Irish Sea you turn inland to cross an industrial and agricultural plain, passing through patches of forest, quiet valleys and over some high ground with absolutely marvellous views.

On the beach of St Bees, it is customary to dip your boot or toe into the water, a ritual to be repeated at the other end of the hike, marking your passage from 'sea to shining sea'. That done, head for the footbridge at the end of the concrete promenade, going up the steps to the cliffpath leading to St Bees Head and Fleswick Bay. 'CtoC' signposts and yellow arrows are easy to follow until Bell House Farm.

Continue past the farm, through a gate and follow the right-hand path. At a fork, confusing arrows point in both directions; follow the left-hand one, down the field, underneath the Cumbrian Coast railway line, and turn immediately left to zigzag through several fields (and under another railway line – now

dismantled) to pass through the villages of Moor Row and Cleator.

The route continues through fields towards the summit of Dent Fell. On the forestry track, note the sign on the left to 'Dent Fell' and exchange with a sigh of relief the hard-track surface for the soft grassy path, leading right up to the top. The views from its summit make you feel like the journey really starts here, for everything that you are leaving behind and that you are about to enter is laid out at your feet: behind you the glinting sea, the hazy, almost haunting silhouette of the Sellafield nuclear reactors and the bellowing clouds of the Whitehaven chemical works, and ahead of you the imposing, almost intimidating skyline of the Lake District mountains.

Now the best part of the day has begun. After descending through the eerie silence of the dark forest, you enter the enchanting limestone vale of Nannycatch Beck which feels like an oasis after the windswept fell. Passing under Raven Crag and Kinniside Stone Circle, you turn right on a tar farm road, which leads to the main road and the village of Ennerdale Bridge.

Ennerdale Bridge Places to stay include the conveniently located *Old Vicarage* (☎ 01946 861107), providing peaceful surroundings and good B&B for £16 plus camping for £3. Nearby, *Miss Sherwen* (☎ 01946 861917), at 6 Ehen Garth, charges £15. The smart *Shepherds Arms Hotel* (☎ 01946 861249), in the middle of the village, near the post office, charges £22 per person. The bar looks like someone's living room with sofas and a chaise longue. After a rough day on the hills, this feels like heaven. To complete the comfort, they also serve afternoon tea. Further up the road, towards Ennerdale Water, is *Low Moor End Farm* (☎ 01946 861388), which does good B&B for £15, and has fine camping facilities at £2 per person, including hot shower. *Ennerdale Village Campsite* (☎ 01946 861339), just as you leave the village centre on the right, is the same price, also with hot showers.

The *Shepherds Arms* restaurant serves

delicious food. A three-course meal costs around £10. Try the Cumberland Rum Nicky for dessert. The *Fox & Hounds Inn* near the delightful old churchyard also offers reasonable pub meals for between £4 and £5.

Day 2: Ennerdale Bridge to Rosthwaite
14½ miles (23.5 km), 6 to 7 hours

This is a long but easy day, with an exciting section along Ennerdale Water (it's worth leaving yourself plenty of time to savour this), only one short ascent and a good descent to finish.

From Ennerdale Bridge follow the signs to Ennerdale Water, turning right as you enter a plantation along a quiet lane which zigzags to the lake. You stay on this path for over one mile, level with the water, except for a short, interesting and easy scrambling section below Angler's Crag.

At the end of the lake, stiles lead to a footbridge across the River Liza and up the valley, passing Low Gillerthwaite Field Centre (☎ 01946 861229), which also offers camping, and *Ennerdale YHA Hostel* (☎ 01946 861237, £6.75).

Just past here a high-level option over Red Pike and Hay Stacks goes off left, but this is demanding and requires a high standard of mountain-walking experience. In bad weather it should not be attempted unless your navigation skills are excellent. The usual low-level route follows four miles (1½ hours) of flat and fairly boring forestry road to the remote *Black Sail Hut YHA Hostel* (no phone).

Whatever your decision, you will end up eventually on the saddle below Brandreth, heading north towards the Drum House (which once worked trams serving the Honister slate mines in the 19th century). From here, turn east for your descent into the valley of Borrowdale and the small village of Rosthwaite.

Rosthwaite For a place to stay, there's *Borrowdale YHA Hostel* (☎ 01768 777393, £7.45). *Nook Farm* (☎ 01768 777677) does good-value B&B for £14, and *Oak Cottage* (☎ 01768 777236) charges £12.50. *Yew Tree Farm* (☎ 01768 777675) is in a lovely position overlooking the valley, though more expensive at £18. *The Royal Oak Hotel* (☎ 01768 777214) has rooms for £22. This is also the best place to eat. Rosthwaite also has a small general store. One mile along the river, in Stonethwaite, a picturesque and quiet place, the *Langstrath Hotel* (☎ 01768 777239) is better for food and has B&B for £19.50. Mrs Brownlee's at *Stonethwaite Farm* (☎ 01768 777234) is worth trying at £16.50 and *Knotts View* (☎ 01768 777604) is also good for £17 – both offer evening meals. The campsite further up the river belongs to *Stonethwaite Farm*. It's £1.50 per person, with only basic toilet facilities. The water is not safe to drink; it should be boiled. There are more options at Seatoller (see under Scafell Pike in the Lakes District section of the Northern England – Short Walks chapter).

Day 3: Rosthwaite to Patterdale
17½ miles (28 km), 7 hours

On this day you pass through the heart of the Lakes, with several major peaks overlooking the route. If you have the time, it can be broken up into two days by staying at Grasmere (a very popular tourist destination, thanks to its Wordsworth connection, which has two YHA hostels, several teashops and a host of B&Bs), making it not only easier but also more fulfilling in terms of enjoying the scenery. If the weather is good and you are feeling fit you can take in Helvellyn and Striding Edge on the following day and still feel fresh, sauntering into Patterdale.

From Rosthwaite, head just past the bus stop in the Keswick direction, turn into a lane which leads to Hazel Bank, then turn immediately right onto a gravel track to Stonethwaite Beck, going through gates and along a wall to Stonethwaite Bridge. Cross the bridge and turn right to pick up the path along Stonethwaite Beck, past the imposing Eagle Crag, marking the junction with Langstrath Beck, and gradually ascending Greenup Gill to Lining Crag. Here the first pass beckons, Greenup Edge at 600m (2000 ft). In fair weather, the high-level option from here via Gibson Knott and Helm Crag to Grasmere village is a wonderful alternative to Far Easedale Gill. Since you are already high on the pass, this is not strenuous and just makes use of the height already gained.

If you are continuing from Grasmere, too many cream teas may weigh you down on your ascent to Grisedale Tarn. By now, however, you should be well into your stride on the uphills, and may want to consider the path to Helvellyn via Dollywaggon Pike, which starts on the northern side of the tarn. Alternatively, the ascent over St Sunday Crag is easier and very enjoyable. The low option, the valley of Grisedale itself, is a dream come true, with meadows teeming with wildflowers, a melodious stream cutting a silvery trail along the foot of Helvellyn, and lonely barns, hiding secrets of days gone by. It's plain sailing now into Patterdale.

Patterdale This peaceful little village has escaped mass tourism because it is not situated directly on a lake, but there are several places to stay. As you come down the path from Grisedale, *Grassthwaite How* (☎ 01768 482230) is on the left, uphill (if you can still make it); it's basic but quaint and good value at £13. Its only drawback is lengthening tomorrow's distance, and you have to walk into Patterdale for an evening meal. Further down the hill in a beautiful position is *Home Farm* (☎ 01768 482370), charging £15 per person. In Patterdale village itself is the *Patterdale Hotel* (☎ 017684 82231). They cater largely for coach tour groups and have B&B from £25. They also do meals and bar food. The friendly *White Lion Inn* (☎ 01768 482214) does B&B for £27.50 with ensuite rooms. They also do bar food. Nearby is *Noran Bank Farm* (☎ 01768 482201) and *Greenbank Farm* (☎ 01768 482292), both from £15, and the *YHA Hostel* (☎ 01768 482394, £9.10). There's a campsite at *Side Farm* (☎ 01768 482337), charging £3.50. Patterdale also has a post office shop.

Day 4: Patterdale to Shap
16 miles (26 km), 6 to 7 hours
This is a day when you might feel pangs of nostalgia and melancholy, for you are not only leaving the Lake District but also one of the most enchanting valleys of the area. But as you tackle the whaleback ridges, comfort yourself with the fact that for the first part of the day you will be rewarded with magnificent views over Ullswater and the Helvellyn and Fairfield ranges, and by the end of the day excitement at the prospect of the next section will prevail.

From Patterdale, south of the White Lion, turn left into a sideroad, crossing Goldrill Bridge to the end of the lane where a gate marks the beginning of the open fell. The route climbs to Boredale Hause, from where you follow a glorious airy path with wonderful views over the valley and surrounding mountains. You pass to the north of Angle Tarn and skirt The Knott, or you can divert briefly to the summit, where the views are excellent and help you to decide the next bit of your route.

The usual way aims eastwards, over Kidsty Pike, traditionally the 'last Lakeland summit' on this route, and then down to the banks of Haweswater at its southern end. In bad weather precise compass bearings are called for to avoid missing Kidsty Pike.

If you have time and the weather is good, you could take the high-level alternative over High Raise which finally drops down to Haweswater at its northern end. (This is off the OS/Wainwright strip map and should only be attempted with a proper map of the whole area.)

You could stay in Bampton, at *St Patrick Wells Inn* (☎ 01931 713244) for £17.50, or in Bampton Grange, at *Leyton Barn* (☎ 01931 713314), if you want to break up the next day by staying at Newbiggin instead of Kirkby Stephen – a good option. But if Shap is your choice, you'll enjoy a delightful stroll via Haweswater Beck and the River Lowther to the remains of the 12th-century Shap Abbey before entering the village.

Shap While Shap is not the most attractive

village on this walk, it has several B&Bs, including *Pleasant View* (☎ 01931 716336), very reasonable at £13.50; *New Ing Farm* (☎ 01931 716661, £15), with drying facilities; *Fell House* (☎ 01931 716343, £15); *The Rockery* (☎ 01931 716340, £15); and *Brookfield Guesthouse* (☎ 01931 716397, £16) which also offers evening meals. The *King's Arms Hotel* (☎ 01931 716277) on Main St has rooms at £18 and is worth trying for food. The *Crown Inn* (☎ 01931 716229) has a bunkhouse and camping, as well as B&B for £15. *Green Farm* (☎ 01931 716619) also has camping and B&B at £15.

Day 5: Shap to Kirkby Stephen
21 miles (34 km), 8 hours

After the exhilarating experience of crossing England's highest mountain region, this day will feel tame but will perhaps be a welcome respite from the windswept desolation of upland fells. The limestone provides softness in colour and vegetation, and wide and sweeping vistas, at times empty and barren, at other times broken by pockets of woodland and farm settlements. However, this day is long and quite tiring, so ancient stone circles, tumuli and evidence of prehistoric dwellings are welcome distractions. It is important to note that some of the sections on this route have been revised due to changes in the rights of way granted by landowners. It is crucial to keep strictly to the authorised path as signposted.

The route turns off the A6 opposite the King's Arms Hotel and crosses the railway line, taking walkers straight to the M6, an unfortunate reminder of 'civilisation'. The footbridge is crossed in a hurry and a quick escape is made to the moor and Crosby Ravensworth Fell, past the secluded hamlet of Oddendale. Slow down for Oddendale Stone Circle, a superb lookout, and get back in touch with the serenity of ancient sites which abound on this route. Robin Hood's Grave, one of several resting places dedicated to the legendary brigand, is a sudden reminder of the walk's goal, still several more days of hard toil ahead.

Orton is one of many traditional villages on this walk, unspoilt, oozing history and well worth exploring. Leaving Orton on the B6261, you turn off left at the end of a wood to rejoin open country. The path is visible but without waymarks. The next highlight is Sunbiggin Tarn, a Site of Special Scientific Interest, protected as a breeding ground for birds. Its shores are out of bounds for human feet. From Lime Kilne Hill, the views over the Eden Valley to Nine Standards Rigg will help to take your mind off your aching feet and whet your appetite for tomorrow's jaunt. The bustling market town of Kirkby Stephen can be entered via *The Pennine Hotel* – you avoid the main road and end up opposite the marketplace.

Kirkby Stephen The ancient market town of Kirkby Stephen is the largest settlement reached so far on this walk. It has shops, banks, a post office and other signs of civilisation. Camping at *Pennine View Caravan & Camping Park* (☎ 017683 71717) costs £3 with showers, and there's a *YHA Hostel* (☎ 017683 71793, £7.45) on Market St. B&Bs include *Redmayne House* (☎ 017683 71441), in Silver St, an excellent choice. It's a spacious Georgian house in a quiet setting with a large garden, and home-made bread for breakfast, for £15. On the high street is the tastefully furnished *Old Court House* (☎ 017683 71061), comfortable and friendly at £15. Next door is *The Jolly Farmer* (☎ 017683 71063), also good but less personal at £15. *The Pennine Hotel* (☎ 017683 71382) is popular at £15, particularly for its bar meals. More up market is the *King's Arms Hotel* (☎ 017683 71378) with its cocktail bar and rooms from £22.50. *The Old Forge Bistro* (☎ 017683 71832), on North Rd, makes a change from pubs, with meals for around £6. Their B&B costs £15.

Day 6: Kirkby Stephen to Keld
13 miles (21 km), 6 hours

Today is a gem, leading you into the picturesque landscape of the Yorkshire Dales via the ascent of Nine Standards Rigg – a fine hill which marks the Pennines watershed – and the head of the Swaledale valley.

Before leaving Kirkby Stephen, make sure you're stocked up for the day, and possibly the evening, as eating options are very limited on this day. The signposts from Kirkby Stephen's marketplace send you down to Frank's Bridge to embark on a pleasant stroll by the riverside to the delightful village of Hartley. Turn right along the main street through the village, but after a short spell along here turn left down a path to the footbridge, then over to the lane bearing left uphill to Hartley Quarry. The lane ends by a fork on the approach to Hartley Fell. Take the left branch, towards Rollinson Haggs, through a gate and uphill to another gate with a signpost for Nine Standards and the Coast to Coast Walk.

At 662m (2170 ft), Nine Standards Rigg surpasses all other high points in this area and is the highest you'll be for the rest of the walk. The origin of the Nine Standards is a matter of imagination. Are they a 'stone army' meant to ward off invaders, or merely boundary markers? The choice is yours. One thing is certain, the views are magnificent: east to Swaledale, to the west the Lake District, to the north the Pennines and south the long grassy ramp of Wild Boar Fell (reputedly the last place in this country where wild boar were hunted).

On White Mossy Hill, a little way past the view indicator, dedicated to Lady Di's wedding, a signpost marks the way across the moor on a bleak trot down to Ney Gill. This was the original route recommended by Wainwright until 1992. The OS strip map and other guidebooks, however, now advise you to veer left into Whitsundale. In 1992, this new permissible path was devised to avoid serious erosion on the moors. However, it is now beginning to suffer erosion as well. At the junction of Ney Gill and Whitsundale, a little too late for walkers from Kirkby Stephen, a detailed information post announces a system of seasonal rotation. The Whitsundale route should only be used from August to November, the traditional route via Ney Gill from May to July, and in winter the Nine Standards Rigg and the moors should be avoided altogether in

favour of a low-level route from Hartley Fell, via Lamps Moss and Ney Gill to Ravenseat.

The last section beyond Ravenseat (said to be the remotest hamlet in Swaledale) along Whitsundale Beck is a delight. At Low Bridge, just before Keld, some guidebooks send you across the River Swale to follow the B6270 to Keld. A more attractive alternative takes the wide track to *East Stonesdale Farm* (☎ 01748 886374), home to the legendary Mrs Whitehead (mentioned in the Information section at the start of this chapter), where B&B, including a 1st-class breakfast, with real coffee, costs £16, with an evening meal for £8. From the comfortable house you have a perfect view over to Keld nestled in the valley and the moors leading into Wensleydale and Wharfedale towards the south.

Keld If you continue to Keld you'll find a beautiful village, which may stay in your memory for a long time. It's unspoilt, traditional and purely residential, without any public facilities for the traveller, apart from some toilets and two churches.

Places to stay include three *campsites* – one by Low Bridge on the farm, one by the river in Keld and one on the hill by the toilets, overlooking Swaledale – and the *YHA Hostel* (☎ 01748 886259, £6.75). B&Bs are limited to *Greenlands* (☎ 01748 886576), on the road to Reeth, costing £15, and *Catrake Cottage* (☎ 01748 886340), where Betty and David Cox provide a home away from home. They will even give up their own bed and sleep on the floor if you are stuck without accommodation. Their evening meal (£7) deserves a five-star rating. If you take the B6270 to Keld, on the way from Low Bridge, it's up the hill, the second house in the first row of cottages on the left before the turn-off to Keld. (There are no more B&Bs in the vicinity, so book well in advance.)

Keld has no shop, no cafe, no restaurant and no pub (it was turned into a Methodist chapel 40 years ago), so apart from spiritual nourishment you may go hungry unless you eat at your B&B or bring stuff from Kirkby Stephen if you're camping. On sunny

Sundays, you may find afternoon tea and ice-creams for sale on the lawn at the bottom of the village.

Day 7: Keld to Reeth
11 miles (18 km), 5 hours

Apart from being an enchanting, verdant valley, winding a course through a maze of bleak and hostile moorlands, Swaledale is also a site of industrial waste. In the 17th and 18th centuries, lead mines dominated the scenery and the social fabric of the area. Today's Wainwright route from Keld to Reeth will appeal to those with an interest in industrial and economic history, because it guides you on a moorland walk through the ghostly ruins of smelting mills, empty mine shafts, stark chimneys and mounds of debris dug out in search of lead, particularly the section between Blakethwaite and Old Gang Smelting Mill. In mist and rain, this could either fuel a romantic taste for mystery (provided your navigation is up to it) or it could be a downright tedious trot across bleak and barren nothingness. The river walk along the valley floor is more enjoyable, especially in bad weather, forsaking mystery for the friendliness of the dale's lush surroundings. We recommend a compromise by walking over the moor to Blakethwaite Smelting Mill and then descending the east bank of Gunnerside Gill into the valley.

The Coast to Coast leaves Keld in an easterly direction over a footbridge crossing the Swale. This is a junction of Britain's two most popular paths, the Pennine Way and the

Coast to Coast, and you might want to swap experiences.

The top of Swinner Gill is reached after about half an hour, then you follow a wide dirt track towards Blakethwaite. As you approach Gunnerside Gill after about 10 to 15 minutes, the track descends sharply to the right and a narrow footpath branches off through the heather to the left, north-east. You are now contouring above Gunnerside Gill, on course for the ruins of Blakethwaite Smelting Mill. In mist, this will require some care. Blakethwaite, the most haunting of all the mills in Swaledale, is worth a visit. Its ruins evoke the blood, sweat and tears of the men and women who toiled in the bowels of the earth for a meagre subsistence. The way ahead is steep up to a grass track and another cluster of ruins on the east bank of Gunnerside Gill. From here, you can descend to the valley and enjoy the riverwalk to Reeth.

Reeth The 'capital of Swaledale' is a small town, but in contrast to Keld it sports three pubs, three teashops, a post office and a museum.

The *YHA Hostel* (☎ 01748 884206, £6.75) is at Grinton, a mile out of Reeth, in a former shooting lodge, and there's camping at *Wood Yard Farm* (☎ 01748 884251) for £1.50 and at *Town End Hall* (☎ 01748 884377) for £1. B&Bs include *Ewell* (☎ 01748 884406), a large bungalow on Arkengarthdale Rd, recommended at £16 per person. On the same road, past the garage on the left, is *Miss Highmoor* (☎ 01748 884358), at 2 Arkle Terrace,

---

Swaledale Miners
The Yorkshire Dales were formed during the Ice Age by glaciers cutting through the rocks and the mineralised faults, which revealed the lead. Mining in the Dales had probably begun as early as 1000 BC. In the 19th century, the miners were either working for themselves or employed by companies grouped into so-called 'dead men' who developed and prepared the work without producing, 'trammers' who brought out the wagon trains of ore from the mines, and the 'ore getters' who only worked a limited number of hours when the veins were laid bare. The work was arduous and dangerous, but the Dales people were desperately poor. Child labour was common, and diseases like scarlet fever and typhoid were rife. When cheaper foreign ore took over the market in the late 19th century, the mines had to close. The miners, desperate in their search for a livelihood, emigrated to Australia and America. Thus Swaledale's mines and mills gave way to the peaceful farming community of today. ∎

which is very reasonable at £14. The *Arkleside Hotel* (☎ 01748 884200) at the Village Green may be a bit expensive at £28 per person, but it's definitely worth it if you fancy a bit of luxury.

For your evening meal we recommend the *King's Arms Hotel* (☎ 01748 884259) which has an enormous stone fireplace, with a roaring fire on cool evenings, and good beer.

Day 8: Reeth to Richmond
11 miles (18 km), 5 hours

After the bleakness of the moors, this is a day of sauntering through green fields, meadows and woodlands exploding with wildflowers. You pass picturesque, sleepy villages, with converted barn dwellings. It's also a day for making friends with farm animals as you are crossing field after field with cows, sheep and horses.

From Reeth, the route keeps north of the swirling River Swale, until a lane carries you to Marrick Priory. The woodlands on the approach to Marrick village were enjoyed by priory nuns in the 12th century. It certainly makes the option of religious life appear very attractive. As you slowly walk along the paving stones, if the sun is shining and the birds are singing, with the flowering garlic smelling sweet and carpets of bluebells and primulas covering the ground, heaven could be within reach. The view back over the priory is a painter's delight.

From Marrick, the route embarks on a waymarked journey, with fabulous panoramic views over rolling farmland, to the limestone scar of Applegarth. About halfway, in the village of Marske, there is a bench by a phone box under a cherry tree, a vantage point from which to see the world go by, and an ideal opportunity for lunch.

Life is easy now – it's a stroll across to Applegarth Scar, through Whitcliffe Wood and down the road to Richmond.

Richmond Richmond is one of the most intact historic towns in England, unspoilt by modern developments or architectural eyesores. Its elegant Georgian housefronts and cobbled streets blend harmoniously with the powerful-looking Norman castle, occupying a strategic position high above the River Swale. The TIC (☎ 01748 850252) is in Friary Gardens, on the roundabout as you turn right into the town centre from Victoria Rd.

Richmond boasts many ancient buildings, like the 18th-century Georgian Theatre (☎ 01748 823021), which is one of the town's three museums, the Green Howards Museum (☎ 01748 822133), which is a military history museum set in a 12th-century church, and the Richmondshire Local History Museum (☎ 01748 825611).

The first B&B you come to is Kay Gibson's *West Cottage* (☎ 01748 824046) on Victoria Rd on the way into town; it's a great place with friendly people, perhaps the best in Richmond and well worth £16. Other places to try are *Kimber House* (☎ 01748 824105, £17), in Lombard's Wynd, and *Willance House Guesthouse* (☎ 01748 824467), at 24 Frenchgate, in the centre of town. There are more B&Bs in Frenchgate which are all good. *East Applegarth Farm* (☎ 01748 822940) has camping for £2, but there is no shower.

Day 9: Richmond to Ingleby Cross
23 miles (37 km), 8 hours

From Richmond, the Vale of Mowbray separates the Yorkshire Dales from the North York Moors. This is the least attractive section of the walk. It's flat and pastoral, the walking mostly monotonous; you're just covering distance on working farmland and country lanes. If the weather is bad you could take the bus to Northallerton and from there to Osmotherley. It means you still have lots of energy left for the last push over the Moors.

The start of today's walk is pleasant enough, leaving Richmond from the southwest corner of the marketplace and crossing Richmond Bridge for the south bank of the Swale. The view from here over the castle is splendid. The course of the river is more or less followed for a while with sections of woodland and meadow to savour. Beyond Catterick, the famous 900 year old army garrison, bid farewell to the lovely Swale and embark on a long trot for about 2½ hours along country lanes with small clusters of sleepy villages and pockets of plantations breaking up the scenery. Eventually, beyond Oaktree Hill, those who prefer to feel the earth under their feet can sigh with relief.

The crossing of the A19, just before Ingleby Arncliffe beside a service station, is extremely dangerous and requires great care. Cars and trucks travel at high speed on this stretch.

Ingleby Cross & Osmotherley Ingleby Cross is a tiny place with a post office shop and a pub. B&Bs include *Ox Hill Farm* (☎ 01609 882255), at £14 per person, and the *Blue Bell Inn* (☎ 01609 882272, £15), which also serves reasonable pub meals and has camping facilities for £2. *The North York Moors Adventure Centre* (☎ 01609 882517) also does B&B for £14 and offers evening meals. At the centre you can collect your badges, T-shirts and certificates for completing the walk (but no cheating, you've still got three or four days to go!).

Osmotherley is a better place to stay. It's a picture-postcard village, natural and unspoilt, with tiny cottages, colourful gardens and the prettiest public toilets in the whole country. There's a *YHA Hostel* (☎ 01609 883575, £7.45) just out of the village. Recommended B&Bs include *Quintana* (☎ 01609 883258), Back Lane, at £15.50, run by Dr and Mrs Bainbridge who have a wide knowledge of the area and make delicious home-made cakes. Others are *Oak Garth Farm* (☎ 01609 883314, £14) and *Vane House* (☎ 01609 883448, £15), both on North End.

For food, the *Three Guns* pub is recommended. It's a quaint old building, with wooden beams and cosy open fires.

Day 10: Ingleby Cross to Great Broughton
12 miles (19 km), 4 to 5 hours
This day will more than compensate for yesterday's footslogging: it's a rollercoaster stomp through heather, moor and gorgeous woodlands along easy paths. You are walking on the edge of the Cleveland Hills which form the northern part of the North York Moors, overlooking an industrial plain to the north, where the chimneys of Middlesbrough and Stockton-on-Tees take centre stage, and the moors to the south, hiding secrets of a barren but engaging wilderness. The end of today's walk, Great Broughton, is off the route, so add two miles and allow some extra time if you're heading here, but don't arrive too early as this place has few attractions.

From Osmotherley, the Coast to Coast Walk joins the Cleveland Way and together they climb Beacon Hill (299m), from where you can clearly see your path sweeping down the moorside. After a couple more miles or so, Scugdale provides a surprisingly lush and genteel interlude to the empty moors, with its delightful mixed woodlands, abounding in wildflowers and twittering birds.

At the bottom of Cringle Moor, a *cafe* invites rest and reflection. Only two to three hours into the day, you have plenty of time before continuing for another couple of hours to Clay Bank Top.

Clay Bank Top is where the route crosses the B1257. There is no accommodation available there. We recommend heading for Great Broughton, reached by descending through forest and following a quiet country lane. Most B&Bs here offer to bring you back to the start of the walk the next morning.

Great Broughton For a place to stay, try *The Hollies* (☎ 01642 710592), at 98 High St, at the end of a secluded drive on the left. This place is friendly and hospitable, charging £15 for B&B. At *Hilton House* (☎ 01642 712526), a little further down the road on the same side, Mrs Mead charges £17, with strawberries for breakfast if you are lucky. Other choices are *The Mendips* (☎ 01642 713774, £16), at 139A High St, and *Mrs Noble* (☎ 01642 712291, £15), at 4 Manor Grove. You can camp at *White House Farm* (☎ 01642 712148), Ingleby Road, for £3 with shower.

Great Broughton has one shop and three pubs including the *Jet Miners* (☎ 01642 712427), definitely the best for food, in tropical conservatory surroundings or traditional pub atmosphere (this place also has camping for £2 – includes shower), and the more expensive *Wainstones Hotel* (☎ 01642 712268), with B&B at £25.

Day 11: Great Broughton to Glaisdale
18 miles (29 km), 6 to 7 hours

After the initial walk up to Urra Moor, the first half of today's stage covers mostly level walking along the dismantled tracks of the legendary Rosedale Ironstone Railway, which served mines in this area during the 19th century. The second half of the day is more varied – across heather moor and an old horse track leading down to the Esk Valley.

The highlight of the day is The Lion Inn at Blakey (possibly more legendary than the railway), at 400m the highest point of the North York Moors, and a formidable place for lunch, or even for an overnight stop.

From the start of today's walk at the B1257 you follow a wide track up to Urra Moor and continue on this old packhorse route in an easterly direction to Bloworth Crossing. This is where the Rosedale Ironstone Railway once crossed an old road called Ruddland Rigg. There's a big plaque, hard to miss even in fog, which tells the story.

The Cleveland Way turns sharply back on itself in a northerly direction, but you keep on the old railway (which is also the route of the Lyke Wake Walk – see the North York Moors section of the Northern England – Short Walks chapter for more details) for the next five miles. If you are lucky to have views, they will make this day special, for the walking is fairly straightforward. As you stride along, thinking of all the railway songs you've ever known, you may wonder where in the world you might find a similar feeling of space and infinity, of lightness and light. If you are unlucky, enveloped by a void of mist and rain, let your imagination create the hustle and bustle of the iron-ore mines and the whistle of the trains, steaming through blizzards, gales and storms. Don't get too carried away though, or you'll miss the sign at Blakey indicating the left turn for the Lyke Wake Walk, which leads up a narrow heather path to The Lion Inn. The inn itself is not signposted.

The Lion Inn (☎ 01751 417320), a classic walkers' pub, is a fine place for lunch, with a welcome fire and tempting selection of beers. You might possibly stay the night, if you want the fun of sleeping in an inn with a 400 year history. They have small twin rooms from £16.50 per person and double rooms from £22.50 per person. There are also camping facilities with breakfast available at the inn if you don't feel like cooking.

From Blakey, you turn left as you step out of the pub door (if you can still stand up straight) and walk for about 15 minutes along the road to Eskdale until a right turn brings you to the White Cross (also called 'Fat Betty' – you'll see who we mean). Pause for a minute to enjoy panoramic views over a sea of endless moorland. You are now bound east, skirting along the head of Fryup Dale and veering north-east along the incredible endless ridge of Glaisdale Rigg, with wonderful views into the valleys on either side, to finally reach the village of Glaisdale.

Glaisdale Glaisdale has one teashop by the railway station, a general shop, a butcher and three pubs. There is also a bench under a lovely tree overlooking the Eskdale Valley.

For places to stay, B&B is available in some of the farms along the Glaisdale road. (You can come down from Glaisdale Rigg directly, without going into the village, otherwise it's a long tramp back along the road.) These include *Red House Farm* (☎ 01947 897242), nearest to the village, quite smart and also the most expensive at £18; *Egton Banks Farm* (☎ 01947 897289), also good and a bit cheaper at £14, with evening meals on offer; and *Hollins Farm* (☎ 01947 897516), small and quaint, with adequate rooms at £15, and one tiny twin room at £12. They also have camping facilities at £1.50 with shower. In the village, *Ashley House* (☎ 01947 897656) is hospitable and good value for money at £14.50. *The Anglers Rest Inn* (☎ 01947 897070) has bar food, rooms at £18.50 and camping at £3 with shower. You can also get B&B for £15 and evening meals, if booked in advance, at *The Railway Station* (☎ 01947 897533).

Day 12: Glaisdale to Robin Hood's Bay
20 miles (32 km), 7 to 8 hours

And now for the grand finale – a last long haul, exchanging, for a while at least, rugged and bleak moorland for green, rolling pastures and sweet-smelling woodlands, ancient trees and gurgling rivers. This also means abandonment of wilderness and loneliness, as we join bands of tourers and holiday-makers from the nearby coast.

From Glaisdale, the first delight is the stroll through Arncliffe Woods from just below the railway station, along the River Esk, one of many old trade routes in this valley: half an hour of pure luscious indulgence and peaceful calm. Before entering the woods, have a look at the 17th-century Beggar's Bridge, a beautiful witness of travelling days gone by, now rendered useless by the new road nearby.

On leaving the woods (far too soon), a quiet tar lane carries you down to Egton Bridge, another gem on the banks of the Esk and worth lingering over. Egton itself is famous for its annual gooseberry show. From here your acquaintance with the Esk is prolonged for a short while on a pleasant track along its course, until the moors return just beyond Grosmont.

Sleights Moor, just out of Grosmont, has the only advantage of leading into Little-beck, the last sylvan feast on the Coast to Coast. It harbours treasures like an 18th-century hermitage and a waterfall, Falling Foss, plunging from a height of 20m into a leafy ravine. From now on, the walking is fairly boring, along roads and through a caravan site. From here it's a final hour of wonderful clifftop walking, overlooking the sea, until the path deposits you rather uncer-emoniously in the suburbs of Robin Hood's Bay.

Keep going until you meet the main road then go left and downhill, to descend the final stretch of steep cobbles down to the water's edge at the slipway. Naturally, you'll want to dip your boot in the sea, to mark the official end of your walk, but beware of waves that wash up here when the wind's in the right direction. Total immersion would be a tragic end to this most marvellous of long-distance walks.

Robin Hood's Bay The small town of Robin Hood's Bay clings to steep, rugged cliffs, which are gradually breaking away under the power of the North Sea. Full-scale romantics may be disappointed to find out that the link between Robin Hood's Bay and the heroic outlaw is only legendary, and extremely tenuous. At the most, the isolation and seclusion of the harbour may have enticed Robin Hood to leave a boat here, ready for a possible quick getaway from his pursuers. Nevertheless, while roaming the steep and narrow cobbled lanes, with miniature cottages

Grosmont & the North Yorkshire Moors Railway
Grosmont is worth a lunch break or even an overnight stop, particularly if you are coming from The Lion Inn instead of Glaisdale. It is the meeting point of the Esk line (the regular rail link between Whitby and Middlesbrough) and the North Yorkshire Moors Railway (NYMR), the revived Whitby & Pickering line, built by none other than George Stephenson, and first opened in 1836. If you time it right you might take a steam train to Pickering and back – an unforgettable journey through the heart of the North York Moors. The most useful departures are at 11.50 am and 12.50 pm (when lunch is served on board), which will get you back to Grosmont two to three hours later. For more details phone the NYMR headquarters (☎ 01751 472508). ■

and tiny gardens glued to the sloping cliffs, there is nothing to stop you from imagining the bustling fishing community of earlier centuries: a haven for smugglers, shipwrecked sailors and, of course, heroic outlaws. (An early guidebook for the adventurous travellers of the day described the inhabitants of Robin Hood's Bay as 'simple, honest fisherfolk'.) Despite some changes, this is still a perfect place to end a strenuous walk and spend a few days relaxing and sightseeing.

Places to Stay & Eat Robin Hood's Bay is a popular tourist spot, with many B&Bs and some nice teashops. On the outskirts of town, just as you come off the cliffs, is the recommended *Meadowfield Guesthouse* (☎ 01947 880564), on Mount Pleasant North, with B&B at £16. Nearby, the similarly priced *Rosegarth* (☎ 01947 880578) is worth a try. In the heart of the village, through a passage in a secluded corner, is the very quaint *Orchard House* (☎ 01947 880912), with good-value accommodation at £17.50. *The Bay Hotel* (☎ 01947 880278), overlooking the slipway where you ended your walk, charges £22 and is often booked up. It has a Coast to Coast hikers' bar, and good beer, with bar meals around £6. Back up the hill and more up market is *The Victoria Hotel* (☎ 01947 880205), with great sea views and B&B from £25 to £30, plus £7 for an evening meal. There's also good bar food, including vegetarian.

The nearest *YHA hostels* are at Whitby (☎ 01947 602878) and Boggle Hole (☎ 01947 880352), and the only camping is outside Robin Hood's Bay, at *Hooks House Farm* (☎ 01947 880283) for £2.50 without shower. Perhaps it's time to treat yourself to B&B and a hot bath.

The most interesting teashop is in Chapel St, in the old chapel with a second-hand bookshop attached, so you can sit outside on the patio, reading and listening to soothing music, whilst devouring a cream tea for a bargain £1.50. Another temptation is the *Old Bakery* further along above King's Beck at the corner of New Rd.

The Cumbria Way

Distance 68 miles (109 km)
Duration 5 days
Start Ulverston, southern Cumbria
Finish Carlisle, northern Cumbria
Regional Centres Lancaster, Ulverston, Windermere, Carlisle
County Cumbria
Area Lake District National Park
Summary This is a route through the Lake District, one of the most mountainous parts of England, yet keeping mainly to valleys. Although some days are long, conditions are not too strenuous or difficult.

During the great boundary reorganisations of the 1970s, Cumbria was created by joining the two ancient counties of Westmoreland and Cumberland, with some parts of Lancashire and Yorkshire's West Riding thrown in for good measure. Although it's now all one county, local people still talk about the old counties as if they still exist, and within this single unit there's undoubtedly a wide variety of scenery – possibly more than in any other county in England: from the sea-level sands of Morecambe Bay to the summit of Scafell Pike, England's highest mountain, via woodland, farmland, rivers, fells and valleys. And, of course, lakes. For within Cumbria lies perhaps the most famous, and one of the most visited, of all Britain's national parks: the Lake District – more often called simply the Lakes.

This wonderful area, beloved by romantic artists and poets such as Wordsworth in the 19th century, is just as popular today with outdoor fans. (See the Lake District section of the Northern England – Short Walks chapter for more details.)

The Cumbria Way winds through the heart of the Lakes, and shows walkers some of the finest mountain views the area has to offer, without actually going to any summits.

Beyond the popular Lake District are other parts of Cumbria, perhaps not quite as stunning as the high mountain areas, but beautiful nonetheless and far less crowded.

NORTHERN ENGLAND

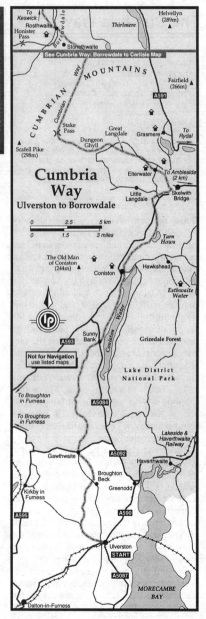

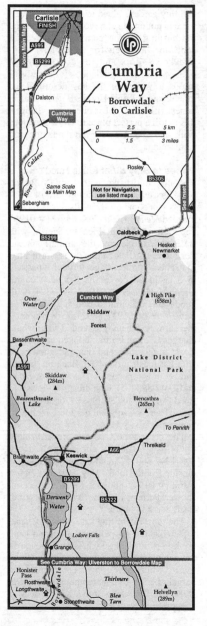

The Cumbria Way goes through some of these areas too, and presents a true cross section of all the county has to offer.

DIRECTION, DISTANCE & DURATION
The route can be followed in either direction, but we recommend starting in Ulverston and going north to Carlisle. This way, you should have most of the wind behind you (although don't bank on it). There are very few specific waymarks indicating the Cumbria Way's route, although the footpath signposting is generally good enough to keep you on the right track when used in conjunction with map and guidebook.

The Cumbria Way is 68 miles long. That's measured on the map, so with the ups and downs it's probably 70 miles or more. Although this is a mostly low-level route, it goes near several tempting mountain tops and the possibilities for diversions are numerous, but they will of course add to your mileage (and time).

Most people take five days to cover the route, although you should allow extra for peak-bagging forays, or simply for sightseeing at places like Coniston and Keswick. Note that the hours given for each stage in the main route description are walking times only: you should allow an extra hour or two for rests, lunch stops, and so on.

STAGES
For a five day walk, as described here, the most convenient places to start and end each day, are as follows:

Day	From	To	Distance
1	Ulverston	Coniston	15 miles (24 km)
2	Coniston	Dungeon Ghyll, Great Langdale	11 miles (18 km)
3	Dungeon Ghyll, Great Langdale	Keswick	15 miles (24 km)
4	Keswick	Caldbeck	13 miles (21 km)
5	Caldbeck	Carlisle	14 miles (23 km)

If you're a fast walker, you could possibly do the whole route in four days, but if you are that pushed for time you should consider cutting the last day instead (see Day 5 for more thoughts on this). Relaxed walkers could easily take six days, overnighting at Coniston, Elterwater, Borrowdale, Keswick or Skiddaw House, Caldbeck and Carlisle. If you plan to branch off the route for some high-level add-ons, you could stay two nights at Coniston, doing the Old Man on the day in-between, then stay at Elterwater two nights and visit Grasmere or Ambleside, or stay at Borrowdale two nights and bag Scafell Pike. Several more day-walks are described in the Lake District section of the Northern England – Short Walks chapter.

INFORMATION
The main TIC for central Cumbria and the Lake District is at Windermere (☎ 015394 46499). Other information centres on the Cumbria Way are Ulverston TIC (☎ 01229 587120), Coniston PIC & TIC (☎ 015394 41533), Keswick (PIC ☎ 017687 72803, TIC ☎ 017687 72645) and Carlisle TIC (☎ 01228 512444). For more about events, transport and accommodation check the *Lake District Guardian*, a free tourist newspaper. Most TICs and PICs have the latest weather reports, or you can dial the local weatherline (☎ 017687 75757).

Books
The original guidebook, which led to the route's creation, is *The Cumbria Way* by John Trevelyan (Dalesman, £3.95). This has good route descriptions and some interesting background information. Proceeds from sales go to footpath conservation. Your other option is the *Guide to the Cumbria Way* by Philip Dubock (Miway), in the Wainwright style with combined hand-drawn maps and text. Some other books on walks in Cumbria and the Lakes are listed in the Lake District section of the Northern England – Short Walks chapter.

Maps
The Cumbria Way is completely covered by

OS Landranger (1:50,000) sheets 96, 90 and 85. If you want more detail, the main part of the route (between Coniston Water and Skiddaw) is covered by OS Outdoor Leisure (1:25,000) sheets 4 and 6 (plus a small bit on sheet 7), with the route clearly marked. However, as the beginning and end of the route are not on these maps, you need all three Landranger sheets anyway. Your other options are the Harveys maps of the Lake District, at 1:40,000 or 1:25,000, although the actual route of the Cumbria Way is not marked.

GUIDED WALKS
Walker's Guided Lakeland Holidays (☎ 01253 592332) organises walking tours on the Cumbria Way and other routes in the area. For details on other local guides see the Lake District section of the Northern England – Short Walks chapter.

PLACES TO STAY & EAT
Because much of this route passes through the touristy Lake District, you're rarely more than a few miles from a hotel or B&B, and often much nearer. The route has several YHA hostels, although there's a big gap between Keswick/Skiddaw and Carlisle. There are also several camping barns (☎ 017687 72803, £3 per person per night, bookings are essential) and campsites. Places to stay are listed in the route description. For a wider choice, as well as the *RA Yearbook* and the *National Trail Companion* (details in the Books section of the Facts for the Walker chapter), South Lakeland District Council Leisure Services Dept (☎ 01539 733333) has a *Cumbria Way Accommodation List*, also available from TICs.

The route is also generally well served by comfortable pubs, cafes and restaurants. Finding something to eat in the evening is no problem, although midday choices are sometimes nonexistent. If you're self-catering, the route passes many villages with shops for resupplying.

GETTING THERE & AWAY
Bus
National Express coaches to Barrow from most parts of the country go via Ulverston. They also run to Windermere, from where local buses run to Barrow, via Ulverston, about six times per day.

Carlisle is well served by public transport, with National Express coaches to all parts of the country. Stagecoach Cumbria (☎ 01946 63222) runs several local services, including the No 555 Lakeslink service, between Carlisle and Lancaster via Keswick, Ambleside and Windermere, about four times per day.

Train
Ulverston is on the Cumbria Coast line, between Lancaster and Carlisle. Lancaster has frequent train services to/from all parts of Britain, and a regional service to Ulverston, every few hours Monday to Saturday, but only twice on Sunday.

At the end of the walk, Carlisle has frequent rail links with most parts of the country, including main-line services to London and Scotland, and the Cumbria Coast line back to Ulverston.

Car
Ulverston is on the A590 which runs from the M6 motorway to Barrow-in-Furness (often shortened to Barrow). Carlisle is on the northern edge of the Lake District, just off the M6.

THE ROUTE
The Start: Ulverston
Ulverston is not a typical Lake District town; the cobbled streets have yet to be lined with teashops and tourist tat. There are however lots of pubs – some get lively on Thursday (market day) and at the weekend. Somewhat bizarrely, Ulverston is also home to a Laurel & Hardy museum (Stan was born here), worth a visit if you're not too anxious to get walking.

The excellent TIC (☎ 01229 587120) is in the town hall. Staff are particularly helpful in making bookings for accommodation along the Cumbria Way. The Furness Rambler gear shop has walking equipment, plus guidebooks and maps.

For a place to stay, the nearest campsite is

Bardsea Leisure Park (☎ 01229 584712), mainly for caravans, but campers can hire a whole pitch from £6, depending on the season. For B&B, *Rock House* (☎ 01229 586879), at 1 Alexander Rd (near the main bus stop), is recommended, at £16 per person. Others to try are *Dyker Bank Guest House* (☎ 01229 582423), at 1 Springfield Rd, also £16, and *Church Walk House* (☎ 01229 582211), near the marketplace, around £19.

For food in the evening, there's a fish & chips shop on King St, and a few of the pubs do food. The *Rose & Crown*, also on King St, has excellent food at very reasonable prices. Consequently, it's often crowded, so go early or late to find a table.

Day 1: Ulverston to Coniston
15 miles (24 km), 6 to 7 hours

This opening day is quite long, but undulating rather than steep, and not too hard. About halfway you enter the national park, but apart from a few more signposts and neater stiles, you won't notice much difference in the path itself. What *is* noticeable, though, is the change in the landscape – from rolling farmland to rugged fells, albeit small on this day, but a taste of the greater things to come. From several high points, you can see the sea behind you, while ahead larger peaks loom on the horizon, and there's even a glimpse of a lake. (Today there are no pubs or cafes for lunch, so stock up in Ulverston.)

The start of the route is at the top of an open area called The Gill (or Ghyll), north of the marketplace, marked by a solitary Cumbria Way sign. Follow a tarred footpath uphill, then (after five minutes) left across a small bridge and up another path to meet a lane. Don't cross the lane but go right, through a squeeze gate, across fields towards Old Hall Farm.

From here the route is mostly straightforward, winding through more fields and farmyards. A place to be alert is Keldray (about two hours from Ulverston), where the route is diverted to the left (west) of the farm, but then seems to fizzle out. To keep on the route, once past the house go left and uphill to reach Gawthwaite.

Continue through fields and some craggy patches of moorland, passing Beacon Tarn, the first of several scenic small lakes near the walk, before dropping to cross the A5084 and reach water. This final section through the lakeside woodland is a wonderful end to the day's walk. You hit civilisation at Coniston Hall Camp Site (see below for details), from where a clear path leads into Coniston town itself. If you want to save a few steps, or just enjoy boating, the Coniston Launch (☎ 015394 36216) stops at Park Coppice jetty (just over two miles before the town) once per hour in the summer, and goes to Coniston.

Coniston Coniston has the manicured look of a classic Lakes tourist town, but the surrounding craggy hills give it an 'authentic' hard edge. Attractions include the John Ruskin Museum. There's a TIC (☎ 015394 41533), a supermarket, a post office, a bank and several smaller shops. Summitreks on the main street has walking gear, maps and books.

Coniston Hall Camp Site (☎ 015394 41223), on the lake about a mile south of town, has pitches from £2.50 per person. *Holly How YHA Hostel* (☎ 015394 41323, £7.45) is on the north edge of town, and *Coppermines YHA Hostel* (☎ 015394 41261, £6.75) is just over a mile away. B&Bs include *Beech Tree* (☎ 015394 41717) on Yewdale Rd, charging from £17 to £22 and dinner at £12, or the nearby (nonsmoking) *Oaklands* (☎ 015394 41245), at £15 to £17. Two others to try, both on Tilberthwaite Ave, are *Lakeland House* (☎ 015394 41303, £14 to £20 per person), and *Shepherds Villa* (☎ 015394 41337, £16 to £20).

The *Black Bull Hotel* (☎ 015394 41335) and the *Yewdale Hotel* (☎ 015394 41280) are smarter inns with ensuite B&B for around £29, and evening bar meals from £5 to £10. Up a grade from here, *Coniston Lodge Hotel* (☎ 015394 41201), the *Crown Inn* (☎ 015394 41243) and the *Sun Hotel* (☎ 015394 41248) all have rooms from £35 per person. They also all do evening meals.

Coniston has a few cafes and teashops,

open during the day and into early evening. Apart from the pubs and inns, another choice for traditional English evening food is the *Pizza Parlour* near the road down to the lake.

Day 2: Coniston to Dungeon Ghyll, Great Langdale

11 miles (18 km), 5 to 6 hours

This day's walk is a wonderful mixture of farmland, woodland, hills and river plains, leading to the top end of Great Langdale, one of the large valleys penetrating into the heart of the high Lake District. However, steep sections are rare, with just a few short sharp shocks right at the end of the day.

The route leaves from the east side of Coniston town and can be tricky to find: from the TIC take Tilberthwaite Ave (towards Hawkshead) for 400m, then go left (signposted to Ambleside), past the football field on the right, to reach a small old stone bridge on the right. Go over this bridge, and immediately left, over a stile to reach a path leading uphill through meadows and into woodland.

From here the route is clear: past Low Yewdale farm and Tarn Hows cottages, then up a lane to reach Tarn Hows, where the route goes west of the tarn, then along a track to reach the A593 main road.

After a short stretch near the road the woodland theme continues as you follow lanes and paths, mostly downhill (with a possible diversion to view Skelwith Force waterfall), to reach Skelwith Bridge, where the route goes through the yard of a slate factory. This is an ideal place to aim for lunch. In the factory showroom (you'd be surprised at just how many things can be made from slate!) is *Chesters Restaurant* with good home-made food at reasonable prices. Nearby is *The Talbot* pub, with sandwiches, and bar meals from £4.

Beyond Skelwith Bridge, the route follows the north bank of the river upstream to Elter Water, a beautiful little lake, with a fine view from its banks up Great Langdale, with rising fells on either side, and the conical Langdale Pikes dominating the head of the valley.

On the north side of Elter Water, the map shows the route branching away from Great Langdale Beck, but you're better off following the new path which keeps to the bank, to arrive at Elterwater village. This is a possible overnight stop, with a *YHA Hostel* (☎ 015394 37245), plus B&B at the traditional *Britannia Inn* (☎ 015394 37210) for £30 per person ensuite, or at *Maple Tree Corner*, run by the Inn, from £23. The village has several other essentials: post office, shop, telephone, public loo and bowling green.

Beyond Elterwater, the route continues along Great Langdale, passing several other places to stay. In Chapel Stile village is the Wainwright's Inn which, despite its title, only does accommodation if you buy a timeshare apartment, but there are some more viable options, including B&B at *Baysbrown Farm* (☎ 015394 37300, £17) (evening meal £8), which also allows camping for £1.80.

Further up the valley is the *Long House* (☎ 015394 37222), a beautifully renovated 17th-century cottage with ensuite B&B for £23. Beyond that, the smart *New Dungeon Ghyll Hotel* (☎ 015394 37666) does B&B for £32.50 (ensuite), and the less refined *Sticklebarn* pub (☎ 015394 37356) has a spartan bunkhouse (no cooking facilities) for £10 per person (both places also serve bar meals, and the Sticklebarn does a good breakfast). Beyond here is the often crowded *National Trust Campsite* (☎ 015394 37668), with pitches for £2.50 per person, and the near-legendary *Old Dungeon Ghyll Hotel* (☎ 015394 37272), universally known as the ODG, where the no-frills Hiker's Bar has good beer and large helpings of food for about £5. The adjoining hotel is far smarter – and often full – with B&B from £29.

Other B&Bs in the Dungeon Ghyll area include *Stool End Farm* (☎ 015394 37615), the last inhabited building as you go up the valley. They charge £16: rooms are nothing special, but staying here cuts tomorrow's distance.

Day 3: Dungeon Ghyll, Great Langdale to Keswick

15 miles (24 km), 6 to 8 hours

Until this point, the Cumbria Way has mostly

followed valleys, but on this day's walk you reach the fells proper, and get a feel of the splendid ruggedness that the Lake District has to offer. In fact, the 'feel' is only a tantalising hint, as the route soon returns to valleys once again, but it may be inspiration enough to sample the day-walks described in this book.

From Great Langdale, aim towards the head of the valley called Mickleden, with a spur called The Band on your left (south) and the towering buttresses of Langdale Pikes on your right. At a fork, go right, up fairly steeply to Stake Pass. From the top you can see back down Mickleden, with a range of wonderfully named peaks spread out behind – Pike of Blisco, Crinkle Crags, Bow Fell – and on the other side the pointed top of Pike of Stickle can also be seen.

All views briefly disappear as you cross the top of the pass, winding through grassy mounds and past the cairn that marks the highest point on this day's walk (about 480m).

Another splendid view opens out as the route descends into Langstrath and Borrowdale to reach Stonethwaite, where this route crosses the Coast to Coast Walk, and there's a welcome teashop. This (or nearby Longthwaite and Rosthwaite) is also a possible overnight stop: with campsites, hostels and several B&Bs (see the places listed in the Coast to Coast Walk section of this chapter).

From here, the route keeps fairly close to the River Derwent (one of many rivers with this name in Britain – so don't be confused) then follows the west bank of Derwent Water. This is reckoned to be one of the most scenic lakes in Cumbria, so make the most of the views because beyond Victoria Bay the route leaves the lake shore and passes through woodland (look out for the three bears sculpture) until it reaches Pontiscale, on the edge of Keswick.

If you want to cut the last few miles, the Keswick ferry (☎ 017687 72263) runs clockwise round the lake (hourly in summer) via several jetties including Victoria Bay and Hawes End. Cruising into Keswick is a splendid way to end the day's walk.

Keswick Keswick is the northern centre for the Lakes and often very busy, but it's been a market town for centuries, and on the tourist map for over 100 years, so it seems to cope with the crowds. The TIC (☎ 017687 72645) is in the central Market Square. Keswick also has plenty of food stores, banks and a main post office, plus several gear shops including George Fisher's.

Cheap places to stay include the *YHA Hostel* (☎ 017687 72484, £9.10) right in the centre, and *Cat Bells Camping Barn*, in Skelgill, on the route a few miles before Keswick. The Camping and Caravanning Club's *Derwentwater site* (☎ 017687 72392) has backpacker pitches for £6 per person.

For cheap B&B, *Bridgedale Guest House* (☎ 017687 73914), at 101 Main St, charges

---

Keswick & Lake District Pencils

Keswick is where Derwent Watercolour pencils are made, and the factory's attached museum tells the story of pencils from the discovery of graphite to the present day. The museum and the world's largest pencil shop (☎ 017687 73626) are open daily from 9.30 am to 4 pm (£2) and worth a visit if you've time.

One of my most vivid childhood memories is a set of colouring pencils. On the lid was written *Lakeland by Cumberland* below a hand-drawn illustration of a range of mountains. My family lived in the south of England, and I'd never seen a real mountain at that time. What struck me about the illustration was that the mountains were not green, but shaded in purple. This image (and the pencil box) stayed with me for a long time. For many years I wanted to go to Lakeland by Cumberland, which I assumed was a place in the north somewhere, to see these amazing purple mountains. Maybe the pencil set planted subliminal signals that got me into walking. These days I understand about artistic licence, but still find Lakeland mountains constantly attractive (even if they are mainly green).

David Else

£13 (£11 without breakfast). There are more B&Bs just to the east of the town, including, on Eskin St, *Allerdale House* (☎ 017687 73891), with excellent rooms for £22.50 per person, *Clarence House* (☎ 017687 73186), charging from £19, and *Braemar* (☎ 017687 73743), from £15. On nearby Southey and Blencathra Sts are several more places: stroll up and down, or visit the TIC first.

For food, Keswick has plenty of cafes and teashops. *Abraham's Tearoom* above Fisher's gear shop has good meals and great views. In the evening, pubs are your best bet. The *Dog & Gun* on Lake Rd is good value, and the *George Hotel* on St John's St is also popular. *Greensleeves Restaurant*, also on St John's St, has good-value meat and veggie dishes for around £5. The nearby *Coriander Restaurant* is similar.

Day 4: Keswick to Caldbeck
13 miles (21 km), 5 to 6 hours

This day is not especially long, but it is potentially the most serious, as it crosses open moorland, including High Pike (658m – the 'summit' of the Cumbria Way), and you are further from civilisation than at any other point on the route. This of course has its benefits: a splendid feeling of space and airy isolation. But it also has its dangers – paths are not always easy to follow, and mist is not at all infrequent. If the clouds are low, or you're not feeling intrepid, the guidebooks describe an alternative route which keeps to easier ground (mostly on lanes).

Leave Keswick centre on Station Rd, over the bridge near the YHA hostel. When the road bears right, take a path straight on, past a swimming pool, to meet Brundholme Rd. Turn left here, ignore a lane coming in from the right, then take an untarred track on the right, over the A66 bypass on a bridge, then uphill into conifer plantation to eventually meet the end of the lane up from Applethwaite.

From here the route strides out across the fells, ignoring the 'motorway' up Skiddaw, taking instead a quieter path along the edge of the steep-sided Glenderaterra Valley to reach the remote *Skiddaw House YHA Hostel* (no phone; £5.50). From here, go down by

Caldew Beck, turning steeply up Grainsgill to Lingy Hut – a mountain shelter. Beyond the hut paths go either side of High Pike. To bag the summit make your own way up. The top is marked by a cairn, and a slate bench – ideal for a rest and admiring the view northwards to the Cheviot Hills and the silvery tongue of the Solway Firth, marking the border between England and Scotland. Below the lookout, the wild fells drop steeply and suddenly to comfortable farmland; the Lake District definitely ends here, almost as if cut by a knife.

To leave the summit use your compass to take a bearing on the hamlet of Nether Row, then drop to meet farm tracks, lanes and a short section of path that leads you into the village of Caldbeck.

Caldbeck The village of Caldbeck has a small choice of places to stay. There's no nearby hostel or campsite, but there is *Hudscales Camping Barn* at Nether Row. B&Bs include *Friar Hall* (☎ 016974 78633), charging £18, and *Height Farm* (☎ 016974 78668, £16), about a mile north of the village. If High Pike has worn you out, phone from the village and they'll come and pick you up. Your other choice is the more up-market *Oddfellows Arms* (☎ 016974 78227), where singles/doubles are £25/45. This is also the only place to get an evening meal (served in the bar or adjoining restaurant) so prices are on the steep side – although the food is undeniably excellent. Another place to find food is the imaginative *Watermill Restaurant* (☎ 016974 78267), but this usually closes at 5 pm. The village shop is open every day (but possibly closed on Sunday afternoon if it's raining).

Day 5: Caldbeck to Carlisle
14 miles (23 km), 5 to 6 hours

After the long upland days across Stake Pass and High Pike, this final day looks deceptively easy on the map. But it's circuitous, with a more than generous helping of stiles and gates, and so is surprisingly tiring. It's tempting to cut this section completely, and if you're short of time and weighing up this day against an extra one in the high fells (based, say, in Coniston or Langdale), then we'd definitely go for the latter. But this is the *Cumbria* Way, not the Lakes Way, and this final bit of the route shows you parts of the county rarely seen by visitors.

From Caldbeck take the path along the west side of the church. Stop to look at the grave of John Peel (the famous huntsman), or the more interesting mill museum nearby. The path crosses a bridge to reach a road, where you turn right. The road soon becomes a track, which you follow through fields into woodland. The map is unclear at this point, so pay attention to your route. Don't be tempted to follow too close to the river, but go left at two forks, gradually uphill, then level through more fields, to reenter woodland on a wide track used by forestry vehicles. A path branches right off this track, marked by a cairn, and goes steeply down to meet the river once again (about one hour from Caldbeck).

The route now follows the river (rarely more than a few hundred metres from it), using faint paths, clear tracks and some sections of busy lane, all the way to Carlisle. The first few hours are through pleasant farmland and even the latter section is surprisingly rural, considering how near you are to a city. At Bridge End, over halfway from Caldbeck, the *pub* does food, and the nearby garage has a small shop (closed Sunday).

Around Dalston is not very pleasant – with overgrown paths full of trash and dog shit – but you might be able to avoid this by keeping to the east side of the river between Buckabank and Cummersdale Bridge. Another option, if you're not a purist, is to catch the train from Dalston into Carlisle – or even back to Ulverston.

On the outskirts of Carlisle, you leave the fields and walk along a street, with houses on your right, passing between two large gas tank towers to meet a main road. Go left here, then swing right over a railway bridge. Take the third left, a pedestrianised shopping street, to reach the old town hall (now the TIC) and the famous Carlisle Cross, a fitting and welcome end to the Cumbria Way.

Carlisle The city of Carlisle is the capital of north Cumbria, with all facilities and a surprisingly pleasant atmosphere. Historically it's fascinating, with Hadrian's Wall nearby,

---

Carlisle

The Romans first built a military station here, probably on the site of a Celtic camp or *caer* (preserved in the modern name Carlisle). Later, Hadrian's Wall was built a little to the north, and Carlisle became the Roman administrative centre for the north-west. Even the mighty Roman Empire was hard-pressed to maintain control, however, and the Picts sacked the town in 181 and 367.

The town survived into Saxon times, but was under constant pressure from the Scots and was sacked by Danish Vikings in 875. The Normans seized the town from the Scots in 1092 and William Rufus began construction of the castle and town walls, although the Scots once again regained control between 1136 and 1157. Forty years later the city withstood a siege by the Scottish King William, and 60 years later it did so again against William Wallace during the Scottish War of Independence.

The cathedral was originally constructed as a priory church in 1123, but it became a cathedral in 1133. It's a small building in north Cumbria's distinctive red sandstone. Life for Carlisle was dangerous and difficult, however, and this is reflected in the fabric of the building. The most serious indignity it suffered was during the 1644-5 siege, when two-thirds of the nave was torn down to provide stone for repairing the city wall and castle. Serious restoration did not begin until 1853, but a surprising amount survives – including the east window and part of the original Norman nave.

The Borders, or the Debateable Lands as they were known, were virtually ungoverned and ungovernable from the late 13th to the middle of the 16th century. The great families with their complex blood-feuds fought and robbed the English, the Scots and each other. The warriors were known as *reivers*, appropriately remembered in the word bereaved. Carlisle was in the middle of this unstable territory, and the city's walls and the great gates that slammed shut every night served a very real purpose. ∎

plus other Roman remains, a cathedral, city walls and a fine castle. The museum is one of the best in Britain.

Carlisle's nearest camping is *Dalston Hall Caravan Park* (☎ 01228 710165), with sites from £5.50, best approached from Dalston. The *YHA Hostel* (☎ 01228 23934) is about two miles from the centre. However, it may have moved by the time you read this, so phone first to check.

For B&B near the centre, Warwick Rd has several options, including: *Cornerways Guest House* (☎ 01228 21733, £13); *East View Guesthouse* (☎ 01228 22112, from £18 with ensuite); and *Calreena Guest House* (☎ 01228 25020, from £15).

More up-market places include the functional *Forte Posthouse* (☎ 01228 31201), with B&B around £35, and the fine old *Royal Hotel* (☎ 01228 22103), right in town, with a range of rooms, most ensuite, from £21 to £46.

For food, possibly an après-route splurge, try *Gianni's Pizzeria*, Cecil St, with pastas and pizzas from £4 to £5, or the similar *Valentino's*, Castle St. *Zapotec*, at 18 Fisher St, has good-quality Spanish and Mexican food, and *Ashuka Tandoori*, at 23 West Tower St, also has a good reputation. For a cheap lunch, visit the *Grape Vine*, at 22 Fisher St, in the YMCA building. Slightly more expensive is the *Priory Restaurant* in the old vaults of the ruined cathedral.

The Dales Way

Distance 84 miles (135 km)
Duration 5 to 7 days
Start Ilkley
Finish Bowness-on-Windermere
Regional Centres Ilkley, Skipton, Sedbergh, Kendal, Windermere
Counties Bradford, North Yorkshire, Cumbria
Areas Yorkshire Dales National Park, the eastern Lake District National Park
Summary This route follows mainly level or undulating ground, on good paths, along some of the most scenic valleys in Northern England, mostly through farmland with one section of exposed moorland.

The Dales Way winds through the Yorkshire Dales, leading to the foothills of the Lake District. These two national parks (covered in detail elsewhere in this book) are among the most frequented walking areas in Britain, and the LDP that links them is naturally very popular too. Major attractions are the scenery – traditional farmland, meandering rivers, ancient villages, rolling hills – and the relatively straightforward route, following clear paths, tracks and even a stretch of Roman road. The Dales Way is also particularly well served by campsites, barns, B&Bs and a great many comfortable pubs. Despite its popularity, however, this route is not well waymarked, so you have to keep an eye on the map to avoid following footpath signs which may lead you astray. The Countryside Commission may be considering proposals to make the Dales Way a national trail. If this does happen, the number of waymarks, and the number of walkers, will no doubt increase.

DIRECTION, DISTANCE & DURATION

We recommend starting in Ilkley and following the route, roughly east to west, to Bowness, near the larger town of Windermere. This direction is more aesthetically pleasing; it's far better to leave Ilkley than to arrive, and the edge of Lake Windermere makes a very precise and satisfying end to the walk.

The Dales Way is 84 miles long. That's measured on the map, so it's a bit more with all the ups and downs.

Most people take six days to cover the route, although you should allow extra for looking around places such as Bolton Abbey or Kendal. Note that the hours given for each stage in the main route description are walking times only: you should allow an extra hour or two for rests, sightseeing, lunch stops, and so on.

STAGES

For a six day walk, as described here, the most convenient places to start and end each day are as follows:

Day	From	To	Distance
1	Ilkley	Grassington	17 miles (27 km)
2	Grassington	Buckden	11 miles (18 km)
3	Buckden	Upper Dentdale	16 miles (26 km)
4	Upper Dentdale	Sedbergh	13 miles (21 km)
5	Sedbergh	Burneside	17 miles (27 km)
6	Burneside	Bowness-on-Windermere	10 miles (16 km)

If you're a fast walker, you could cut the walk to five days. Starting at Bolton Abbey and ending at Sedbergh would be another possibility if your time is limited. If you want to take your time, the route can be done in seven or eight days; for example, by splitting the first day, overnighting at Barden Tower, and breaking Day 3 at Cam Houses.

INFORMATION

The Yorkshire Dales National Park head-quarters and main PIC is in Grassington (☎ 01756 752774), on the Dales Way. Other PICs include Sedbergh (☎ 0153696 20125). There are TICs at Ilkley (☎ 01943 602319), Skipton (☎ 01756 792809), Sedbergh (☎ 015396 20125), Kendal (☎ 01539 725758) and Windermere (☎ 015394 46499). For more information about events, transport and accommodation in the Dales area, check *The Express*, a free tourist newspaper, or *The Visitor*, a freebie produced by the Dales National Park.

Books

The Dales Way by Colin Speakman (Dalesman, £4.95), first published in 1970, originally inspired the route's creation. Although the terminology is slightly quaint, it contains a great deal of good background information. *The Dales Way Route Guide* by Colin Speakman and Arthur Gemmell (Stile, £2.80) includes details of the main route, plus several circular day-walks taking in

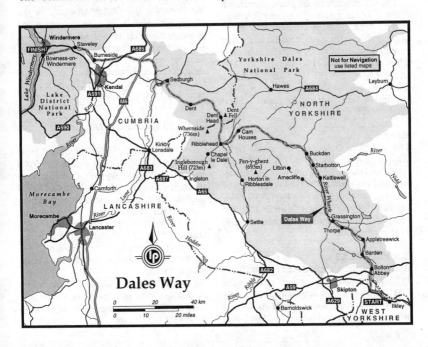

Dales Bunkhouse Barns

The Dales Bunkhouse Barns scheme is run by the Countryside Commission and the national park authorities, converting traditional barns and farm buildings, which would otherwise be disused, into simple overnight accommodation for walkers. Facilities at each bunkhouse barn include straight-forward sleeping areas (own sleeping bag required), toilet, shower, cooking facilities (including pots, pans, plates etc), eating area and drying room. Overnight fees are around £5 per night. Advance bookings are preferred, direct to the farmer. Dairy produce can often be ordered in advance. Useful bunkhouse barns on the Dales Way are at Bardon Tower, Skirfare Bridge, Hubberhulme (near Buckden), Outashaw, Cam Houses, Ribblehead and Catholes (near Sedbergh). ∎

sections of the Way. *The Dales Way Companion* by Paul Hannon (Hillside, £5.50) is lovingly hand-crafted in the Wainwright tradition, combining pen-and-ink text and illustrations, plus just enough background information to entertain without distraction. All these books have hand-drawn maps of varying quality, but they should nevertheless be used with a properly surveyed map (see below).

The exceedingly useful *Dales Way Handbook*, published annually by the RA West Riding Area, contains accommodation listings, public transport details and other essential information. It's available in most TICs or by post from 27 Cookeridge Ave, Leeds LS16 7NA (£1.50). Other books on the Dales are listed in the Yorkshire Dales section of the Northern England – Short Walks chapter.

Maps

The Yorkshire Dales, and the whole Dales Way, are covered mostly by OS Landranger (1:50,000) sheets 98 and 99, with the start on 104, and the end on 97. The central parts of the route are also shown on the OS Outdoor Leisure (1:25,000) sheets 2, 10 and 30, but you'll still need Landranger sheets 104 and 97 at each end.

GUIDED WALKS

Walker's Guided Lakeland Holidays (☎ 01253 592332) organise walking tours on the Dales Way and other LDPs in the area. For details of day-walks organised by local guides and national park rangers see the Yorkshire Dales

section of the Northern England – Short Walks chapter.

PLACES TO STAY & EAT

You can cover the entire Dales Way using B&Bs, YHA hostels and bunkhouse barns (see aside). We provide some suggestions in the route description. For a wider choice, use the *RA Yearbook* and the *National Trail Companion* (details in the Books section of the Facts for the Walker chapter), or the *Dales Way Handbook* (see the preceding Books section). If you prefer to camp and self-cater, there are several campsites on or near the route, and you pass many village shops for resupplying. There are also numerous pubs, cafes and teashops: if you stopped in them all you'd never make it to Bowness.

GETTING THERE & AWAY
Bus

Ilkley is served by frequent buses from Leeds and Skipton, both easily reached from anywhere in the country by National Express coach. If you start at Bolton Abbey or Grassington, these places can also be reached from Leeds (three times per week) or Skipton (daily) on buses run by Harrogate & District (☎ 01423 566061). All public transport in the area is listed in the *Dales Connections* timetable booklet available from local TICs.

From Windermere, the end of the route, local buses go to all parts of the Lakes, and National Express coaches go to all parts of the country. (For more details see the Lake

District and Cumbria Way sections of this book.)

Train

Services run by West Yorks Metro (☎ 0113 245 7676) go between Ilkley and Leeds at least once an hour. From Windermere there are hourly trains to Kendal, from where you can reach the rest of the country.

If you decide to start or end your walk somewhere along the route, the trains on the Settle-Carlisle Line, and the connecting buses, are very useful. For details see the Yorkshire Dales section of the Northern England – Short Walks chapter.

Car

Ilkley is on the main A65 road between Leeds and Skipton. Windermere is on the eastern edge of the Lake District, reached from the M6 motorway along the A591.

THE ROUTE
The Start: Ilkley

Originally established as a village on the main packhorse route across the Dales, Ilkley in the Middle Ages grew to a wealthy market town, with much of the trade based on wool. Today, Ilkley still exudes an air of quiet comfort, with hanging baskets and antique shops, perennial symbols of well-to-do towns, much in evidence.

Ilkley's TIC (☎ 01943 602319) is in the town hall, opposite the bus and railway stations. They run a Dales Way book-a-bed-ahead service. There are plenty of B&Bs in Ilkley, including *Mrs Terry* (☎ 01943 607598, £13.50), at 2 Victoria Ave, and *Mrs Roberts* (☎ 01943 817542, from £16), at 63 Skipton Rd. The TIC can help with more addresses. There's a campsite near the route at Addingham (see Day 1 route description). The town also has a good selection of places to eat, including the famous and smart *Betty's Cafe*, and some pleasant *pubs*.

Day 1: Ilkley to Grassington
17 miles (27 km), 6 to 8 hours

This first day is probably the most 'populated' section of the route, used more by afternoon strollers than by long-distance walkers. The route from Ilkley to Bolton Abbey, although not unpleasant, is neither scenic nor particularly interesting, so you could miss it without feeling guilty. Some walkers also miss the section around Bolton Abbey because it gets crowded on summer weekends, with ice-cream stalls and a 'Pavilion' selling teas and postcards. If you're setting off to cover the route, kitted out with boots and rucksack, you feel a bit of a berk surrounded by people in beachwear, kids in pushchairs and grannies on zimmer frames. Nevertheless, this is a really beautiful bit of the valley and a shame to miss. Try to do it on a weekday.

If you do begin in Ilkley, to reach the start from the bus station, face the town hall and turn right, then first right, down to the 'new' bridge (built 1904) over the River Wharfe. Do not cross the bridge but go left down some steps and along the river to reach the attractive Old Bridge, the official start, marked by a single Dales Way signpost (which says, misleadingly, 'Bowness 73 miles').

Continue along the south bank, through woodland, past a tennis club, then across flat meadows, to enter more woodland next to the river once again. Although the main road is nearby, it's surprisingly quiet; the sound of traffic is not enough to drown out the birdsong. The path continues alongside the river to Addingham, then Bolton Bridge, before thankfully returning to meadows, to reach Bolton Abbey village, and the ruins of Bolton Priory.

The route continues through woods above The Strid, a narrow gorge, to reach Barden Bridge and Barden Tower, a 15th-century hunting lodge. Next to the tower is an 'olde worlde tea-shoppe', and *Barden Tower Bunkhouse Barn* (☎ 01756 720630). From here you follow the river through farmland, passing close to Appletreewick with several B&Bs, a couple of *pubs* and a *campsite*, which all get very crowded at summer weekends. Much less frenetic is Burnsall, about two miles upstream; B&B at the comfortable *Red Lion* (☎ 01756 720204) costs £37 and

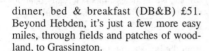

Bolton Priory

Bolton Priory is often mistakenly called Bolton Abbey, but Bolton Abbey is the name of the tiny village in which Bolton Priory stands. The ruined priory occupies a superb site overlooking the River Wharfe. It was built in the 12th century by Augustinian monks, also known as the Black Monks, who had been given the land by one Norman de Romilles of Skipton, after moving here from nearby Embsay. During the dissolution of the monasteries the nave of Bolton Priory was spared and is used today as the parish church of St Mary & St Cuthbert. The spectacle of these grand ruins in such beautiful surroundings has inspired poets, writers and painters such as Wordsworth, Turner and Landseer. The priory is open to visitors every day and admission is free, although contributions towards the upkeep are always welcomed. ■

dinner, bed & breakfast (DB&B) £51. Beyond Hebden, it's just a few more easy miles, through fields and patches of woodland, to Grassington.

Grassington This is a very attractive village and a popular base for exploring the Dales. Once a lead-mining centre, today the major industry is tourism, with several pubs, cafes and craft shops, and heavy crowds on summer weekends. The Mining Museum is worth a visit. Grassington also has a small supermarket, a bank and Field & Fell gear shop. Places to stay include *Linton YHA Hostel* (☎ 01756 752400, £8.25), just south of Grassington. About one mile west, at Skirethorns, is *Wood Nook Campsite* (☎ 01756 752412). For B&B, *Raines Close* (☎ 01756 752678), at 13 Station Rd, charges £20 to £23. Smarter is the *Foresters Arms* (☎ 01756 752349), an old coaching inn on Main St, with B&B from £16, and also serving bar meals. More up market again is the *Grassington House Hotel* (☎ 01756 752406), on Market Square, with good food and comfortable ensuite rooms from £26 per person and DB&B from £36.50.

Day 2: Grassington to Buckden

11 miles (18 km), 4 to 5 hours

On this day, the Dales Way continues up Wharfedale, but leaves the valley floor for the first time, crossing grassy fields and some beautiful sections of limestone pavement, before dropping again to wind through

several picturesque villages, most with lunch or overnight stop possibilities.

From the centre of Grassington go up the main street, left into Chapel St, through the 'suburb' of Townhead. The Way leads through a farmyard which is almost impassable, with gates, cows and slurry strategically positioned. Look carefully for the signs (to Grass Wood and Conistone) and wade through, or take a more pleasant alternative by turning right up Bank Lane (untarred, signposted to Bycliffe Rd) just before the farm, to rejoin the Way about one mile north of Grassington.

Above the village, the route passes some old lead mine entrances (there are also many shafts in this area – take great care if you lose the path in mist), to cross the Bycliffe Rd bridleway. On the other side of the valley is Kilnsey Crag – a rock-climbers' test-piece. Below the crag is a *campsite* and *Skirfare Bridge Bunkhouse Barn* (☎ 01756 752465).

The route drops to meet a lane about one mile south of Kettlewell, then soon branches off right (north), but if the lane is quiet you might as well head straight into the village, which has *Fold Farm Campsite* (☎ 01756 760886), charging £2.50 per person, a *YHA Hostel* (☎ 01756 760232, £7.45) and three *pubs*, all with accommodation and evening food (*The Racehorses* has a hikers' bar). The smart *Dale House Hotel* (☎ 01756 760836) offers B&B from £25, or a more up-market DB&B package for £42. The proprietor often leads guided walks in the area. *The Cottage Tearoom* (☎ 01756 760405), as well as meals, snacks and drinks, does ' four-poster B&B' for £19.50 midweek, £22.50 weekends. There are also several more B&Bs, a few grocery stores, Over & Under gear shop, and a post office.

Beyond Kettlewell the path follows the river, sometimes near the bank, sometimes a few fields away from it, through classic Dales scenery, over stiles, past drystone walls and barns, and through a few patches of woodland to reach Buckden.

Buckden For B&B, *Beck Cottage* (☎ 01756 760340) charges £15 per person, with nearby *West Winds* (☎ 01756 760883) also at £15. The village shop stocks enough for lunch, or overnight if you're camping, and next door is a teashop, with the *Buck Inn* and *White Lion* pubs nearby. Upstream from Buckden is Hubberholme with more B&Bs, including the friendly *George Inn* (☎ 01756 760223), from £25 (also good bar meals), *Grange Farm* (☎ 01756 760259), from £15 (also a *bunkhouse barn*, £5), and the smarter *Kirk Gill Manor Guesthouse* (☎ 01756 760800, £24).

Day 3: Buckden to Upper Dentdale
16 miles (26 km), 7 to 9 hours

Dentdale is actually about nine miles long, and this day's walk ends at its eastern end, between the settlements of Dent Head and Cowgill. This is a long day, and includes the wildest, and potentially most serious, bit of the whole route. You could shorten it slightly by finishing the previous day at Hubberholme. Another option is to break the day into two, and stay at Cam Houses.

After Hubberholme (where the old church is well worth a look around) the valley is called Langstrothdale, but the river is still the Wharfe, getting smaller and more streamlike as it nears its source. The path crosses the river a few times, passing through the lonely farmsteads of Yockenthwaite, Deepdale and Beckermonds, where you take a tarred lane northwards towards Hawes. Just after the hamlet of Oughtershaw, the Way branches off left (westwards). Although the source of the Wharfe is close, the valley gets broader, and the landscape more exposed.

When the wind blows up here you really know about it, and even on calm days there's a feeling of remote emptiness.

The route climbs slightly to reach *Cam Houses Farm* (☎ 0860 648045), where the friendly owners sell hot drinks and home-made cake, do B&B (£16.50) and run an excellent bunkhouse barn (£6.50). In bad weather this is a real haven. But if you're pushing on, follow the waymarks round the north-east corner of Cam Woods (taking care not to take the farm track which leads steeply north up the hill) then up a final slope to a cairn. Here you meet Cam High Road, part of an old Roman road, also followed by walkers on the Pennine Way, and (unfortunately) by 4x4 enthusiasts who have badly rutted this ancient track in places.

But apart from the ruts this is an excellent section of the route. Put the map away for a while and stride out like a centurion, taking in the splendid panoramas of Ingleborough and Whernside (see the Yorkshire Dales section of the Northern England – Short Walks chapter for more details). At a second cairn, the Pennine Way branches off left, but you keep right, descending to meet the B6255 road at Gearstones. Turn left, and follow the road for 100m, then go up the first farm track on the right (signposted Dent Head) to Winshaw House where drinks are sold. (Opening hours are informal. Knock on the door – if they're in, they'll serve you.) From here, the path leads through fields and the moorland edge to meet a lane, just south of the grand Dent Head Viaduct.

From here to Cowgill (three miles) the Way follows the lane, but traffic is light. Going down the valley, with the fledgling River Dee on your left, you pass *Dentdale YHA Hostel* (☎ 015396 25251, £7.45) a couple of B&Bs, including the exceedingly pleasant *Sportsman's Inn* (☎ 015396 25282) with log fires, fine beers, and comfortable rooms for £19 per person. Nearby is *Habourgill Farm Campsite* and *Ewegales Farm Campsite*.

If you're leaving the route here, Dent railway station is also nearby. Trains head north to Carlisle or south to Settle and Leeds. There's even a bus running between Dent village and Dent station, via Cowgill, so you don't have to walk up the hill.

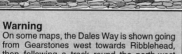

> **Warning**
> On some maps, the Dales Way is shown going from Gearstones west towards Ribblehead, then following a track round the north-west shoulder of Whernside to come into Dentdale near Mill Bridge, just east of Dent. As far as we know, this section is no longer included in the Dales Way, which goes down Dentdale as described in this book. On OS 1:25,000 maps this section is called the Craven Way. However, if you weren't staying at Dent Head, it would be an interesting, though longer, alternative route.

Day 4: Upper Dentdale to Sedbergh

13 miles (21 km), 5 to 6 hours

This is a fairly easy day, as the Way meanders down the picturesque Dentdale Valley, through fields and woodland, all the way to Sedbergh. The scenery is once again classic Yorkshire Dales (even though you're now in Cumbria), familiar and comfortable after yesterday's brief fling with the Cam High Road 'wilderness'.

About two miles beyond Cowgill, the path meets a track below a farm called Low Laith Barn (shown as Laithbank on the OS 1:25,000 map). Here the waymarks and map disagree about the Dales Way route: you can either follow the signs, down the farm track, across the lane and some fields to the river, where you cross a footbridge to the north bank, then another back again; or you can follow the yellow waymarks, left of the farm, to meet the lane at Sike Fold House. Either way, you continue to Mill Bridge, then follow a pleasant riverside path to Church Bridge, near the large village of Dent. This is an interesting place to look around, with narrow cobbled streets and a fine old church, and a good place to stop for lunch, with pubs, teashops, and a store open every day.

If you want to overnight here, campsites include *Conder Farm* (☎ 015396 25277) and *High Laning Farm* (☎ 015396 25239). B&Bs include *Little Oak* (☎ 015396 25330, £15) with evening meals for £7; *Smithy Fold* (☎ 015396 25368), from £14, evening meals at £8; and *Stone Close* (☎ 015396 25231), also an excellent teashop, from £15. The *George & Dragon* (☎ 015396 25256) does B&B from £19, plus lunches and evening meals, and we've heard good reports of the *Sun Inn* (☎ 015396 25208) with B&B for £16.50, and bar meals for lunch or dinner.

From Dent, return to the riverbank, and continue on paths through fields or along quiet tarred lanes between hedgerows. There's one final hill, with fine views from the summit, before dropping into the town of Sedbergh.

Sedbergh This is a market town, with shops, banks, pubs and a good selection of B&Bs, including *Stable Antiques* (☎ 015396 20251), Back Lane, from £16, and *Marshall House* (☎ 015396 21053), Main St, from £23 ensuite plus a drying room. The *Bull Hotel* (☎ 015396 20264) does lunches and evening meals, plus B&B for £19 to £21. Sedbergh is well served with campsites; most convenient is *Pinfold Caravan Site*, with plenty of facilities, including a laundrette, for £3 per person. There's also *Catholes Farm Bunkhouse Barn* (☎ 015396 20334), near the Way before you reach Sedbergh. The TIC can help with other campsite and B&B addresses.

Day 5: Sedbergh to Burneside

17 miles (27 km), 6 to 8 hours

This is a day of transition: the Way leaves the valleys of the Yorkshire Dales, and you pass through the gently rolling landscape of the Eden Valley. The route leaves Sedbergh along the River Rawthey, which flows into the beautiful River Lune, and this is followed, through fields and meadows (and, at Hole House, almost through someone's kitchen!), all the way to Crook of Lune Bridge. To your right, the velvety humps of the Howgill Fells dominate the scene for the whole morning. The route is not well waymarked or signposted, so you need to keep a close eye on your map as you pass through farmyards, old lanes and a great number of stiles and kissing gates. (As well as the river, this morning's walk passes near a disused railway. Where our route crosses it there are splendid viaducts, seemingly out of scale for what was a fairly minor branch-line.)

After crossing the ancient Crook of Lune Bridge, and the less scenic footbridge over the M6, you enter farmland once again. You also cross the main railway line at a level crossing. The signs say 'Beware Trains – Stop Look and Listen'. You'd better – they fly along here.

Burneside Continue through fields, past Black Moss Tarn, along lanes, paths and farm tracks, to finally reach Burneside. B&B options include *Strickland Ketel Guest House* (☎ 01539 729324) and the nearby *Jolly Angler's Inn* (☎ 01539 732552), both charging £14 to £28, depending on facilities, and *Garnet House Farm* (☎ 01539 724542, £16.50). The nearest campsite is between Burneside and Stavely, at *Ashes Lane* (☎ 01539 821119), closed between mid-January and mid-March. If you choose to leave the Dales Way here, Burneside is on the line between Windermere and Oxenholm (where you can connect to the rest of the country), with trains to each about once every two hours.

As Day 6 is short, you could consider cutting some of Day 5 and stopping before Burneside. Options include B&B at *High Barn* (☎ 01539 824625), near Patton Bridge (the Dales Way goes through the garden), charging £14 B&B and £8 evening meal, and *Goodham Scales*, also right on the route, £15, with a free lift provided into Burneside if you want to go there for an evening meal.

Day 6: Burneside to Bowness-on-Windermere
10 miles (16 km), 3 to 4 hours
This final section of the walk is an easy day

alongside rivers and through rolling farm-land, leading gradually down to Bowness on the edge of Lake Windermere. The waymark-ing is generally good on this day's walk, but there are still a few tricky bits where you need to watch the map, particularly in the last few miles, where the route winds through gardens and narrow farm lanes. Just before the end, you're treated to the first view of Lake Windermere, and below this lookout is a slate bench with a plaque marking the 'official' end of the Dales Way. But it's more pleasing to continue down through the streets of Bowness to the lake shore itself, where you can reach the waters between crowds of holidaymakers and boats moored at The Pier, and dip your toe in to mark the end of your walk.

Bowness & Windermere Bowness is on the lake, and the larger town of Windermere is a short distance 'inland', with the main rail and bus station. The two towns merge: from The Pier to the station is about 1½ miles. Windermere's excellent TIC (☎ 015394 46499) is near the station. There is also a TIC in Bowness (☎ 01539 442895) by The Pier, right near the end of the route. It's closed from October to March, but has a list of local B&Bs (with prices and phone numbers) posted in the window. There's a public phone box nearby, so you can easily ring around and find a place to stay. There's also a bus stop and taxi rank by The Pier.

Places to Stay & Eat If any house in Bowness or Windermere doesn't do B&B, it's probably abandoned. Or at least that's how it seems in this busy tourist honeypot. Having said that, in high season, you may still have to do a bit of phoning around to find a bed for the night.

Hostellers can head for the very pleasant *YHA Hostel* (☎ 015394 43543, £7.45), near Troutbeck Bridge about two miles north of Windermere. Numerous buses run from The Pier to Ambleside, via Troutbeck Bridge, or you can get the YHA shuttle bus (☎ 015394 32304) from Windermere station.

For B&B in Bowness, places right at the end of the route include *Blenhiem Lodge* (☎ 015394 43440) and the *Fairfield Hotel* (☎ 015394 46565), both smart, comfortable and charging £25 to £28 per person. Other places to try include *Elim House* (☎ 015394 42021), Biskey Howe Rd, away from the traffic and town noise, with beautiful gardens and rooms from £22.50 per person ensuite, or the nearby *Langdale View Guest House* (☎ 015394 44076) at 114 Craig Walk. If you want a blow-out at the end of your walk, try *The Old England* (☎ 015394 42444), in the heart of Bowness overlooking the lake, where DB&B ranges from £54 per person midweek in winter to about £82 in high summer, but this is for a minimum of two nights. Take your boots off before checking in though!

In Windermere, two places by the station are very popular with budget travellers: the 'world famous' *Brendan Chase* (☎ 015394 45638), at 3 College Rd, £12.50 to £22 for B&B; and the 'totally funpacked' *Lake District Backpackers Lodge* (☎ 015394 46374), almost next door, complete with hammocks and jossticks, charging £9.50 for a bed in the dormitory, including use of the kitchen. Also doing good-value B&B is the central *Elleray Hotel* (☎ 015394 43120), from £15.50. Other places to try include: *Lingmoor* (☎ 015394 44947), at 7 High St, nonsmoking, from £15; *Denehurst* (☎ 015394 44710), at 40 Queens Dve, £18 to £20; and *Applegarth* (☎ 015394 43206), £25 to £35).

For more choice, stroll along Lake Rd, linking Bowness and Windermere, the main run for small hotels. Most have rooms around £20 a night, but competition is stiff and many places show their prices at the front, so you can do comparisons on the hoof.

For something to eat, Bowness and Windermere have more teashops, cafes and takeaways than you can shake a stick at, plus several pubs doing meals, not to mention a batch of classy restaurants. Stroll around for 10 minutes and you'll soon find a place to suit your tastebuds and pocket.

The Pennine Way

Official Name The Pennine Way National Trail
Distance 259 miles (417 km)
Duration 16 to 20 days
Start Edale
Finish Kirk Yetholm
Counties/Regions Derbyshire, West Yorkshire, North Yorkshire, County Durham, Northumberland, Roxburgshire (Borders Region)
Areas Peak District National Park, Yorkshire Dales National Park, North Pennines and the Cheviot Hills, Northumberland National Park
Summary This route follows the exposed central spine of Northern England into Scotland. It's regularly claimed to be the toughest walk in Britain but recent improvements have made the long, muddy stretches of moorland much more manageable.

It's frequently said that Mt Everest wouldn't be so difficult and dangerous to climb if it wasn't so bloody high. Much the same can be said of the Pennine Way. Long though it is, it wouldn't be the toughest and most difficult walk in Britain if it wasn't so often wet, misty and muddy.

Global warming apart, the wet and misty description is likely to continue but various improvements, required to repair the damage from too many passing hikers' boots, have made the Way into a bit of a paper tiger, its fearsome reputation somewhat overstated. This doesn't mean you should underestimate the Pennine Way – swift weather changes can still bamboozle even the most experienced walker – but across some of the most difficult stretches neatly laid flagstones have totally eliminated navigational difficulties, and tales of walkers struggling for hours through thigh-deep sticky mud are ancient history.

The Way has had a long and chequered history. First proposed by Tom Stephenson in 1935, the idea of the Pennine Way played a key part in the 'public access' struggles of the 1930s which allowed walkers to cross private land. Although the Way was mapped out by the Ramblers' Association (RA) in the late 1930s, it was not until 1949 that parliament approved the concept and only in 1965 that the Pennine Way officially opened as the first of what became the national trails.

Along its route the Way crosses some of the highest, and often bleakest, country in Northern England, touches on the literary connections of Bronte country, explores beautiful stretches of the Yorkshire Dales, makes a short foray along Hadrian's Wall and finally crosses empty moorland through the Cheviot Hills to end across the border in Scotland.

DIRECTION, DISTANCE & DURATION

The Pennine Way is traditionally walked south to north. The prevailing winds are at your back and the various guidebooks are all written with that direction in mind. The route is waymarked with arrows and national trail acorn symbols, but not uniformly. Some stretches will have indicators every few steps, others will leave you standing bewildered at unclear junctions, and in some places the picture is complicated by conflicting signs for other walking routes.

There are lots of alternative distances quoted for the Pennine Way, complicated by the many short variations encountered along the route. The permanent-looking sign at the very start of the walk announces there are 275 miles to go, Wainwright insists it's 270 miles, the official OS distance is 256 miles but the summary that follows totals 259 miles. Optional forays off the route will extend that distance. You can sprint the Way in less than two weeks or stroll it in three.

STAGES

The route description that follows covers the walk in 16 days, averaging 16 miles each day with just one long day right at the end (which can be split into two more manageable stages). There are numerous alternatives for reducing the total number of days.

Day	From	To	Distance
1	Edale	Crowden	16 miles (26 km)
2	Crowden	Standedge	11½ miles (18.5 km)
3	Standedge	Hebden Bridge	15 miles (24 km)
4	Hebden Bridge	Lothersdale	19 miles (30.5 km)
5	Lothersdale	Malham	15 miles (24 km)
6	Malham	Horton-in-Ribblesdale	14 miles (22.5 km)
7	Horton-in-Ribblesdale	Hawes	14 miles (22.5 km)
8	Hawes	Tan Hill	16 miles (26 km)
9	Tan Hill	Middleton-in-Teesdale	17 miles (27 km)
10	Middleton-in-Teesdale	Dufton	20 miles (32 km)
11	Dufton	Alston	20 miles (32 km)
12	Alston	Greenhead	18 miles (29 km)
13	Greenhead	Once Brewed	7 miles (11 km)
14	Once Brewed	Bellingham	15½ miles (25 km)
15	Bellingham	Byrness	15 miles (24 km)
16	Byrness	Kirk Yetholm	26 miles (42 km)

INFORMATION

There are TICs and PICs at a number of places along the route, including Edale, the starting point. The various leaflets available include *Accommodation & Services*, which you can get from TICs, and John Needham's *The Pennine Way Accommodation & Camping Guide*, a 90p booklet available along the route or from the Pennine Way Association, 23 Woodland Crescent, Hilton Park, Manchester M25 9WQ.

Books

The two-volume National Trail Guide, *Pennine Way South – Edale to Bowes* and *Pennine Way North – Bowes to Kirk Yetholm*, by Tony Hopkins (published by Aurum Press) utilises OS maps and, as long as you don't get too far off the route, almost allows you to dispense with normal maps. The classic Pennine Way guide, however, is A

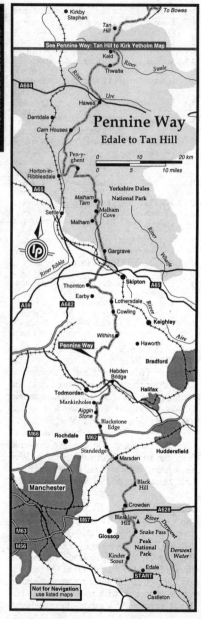

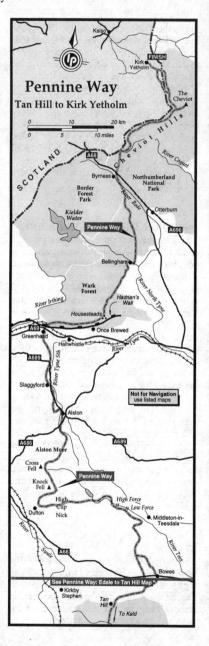

Day Stops along the Pennine Way

A rest stop somewhere along the route can be a good investment. From the south, Hebden Bridge is the first good possibility; it's an interesting small town with shops, cafes, pubs and restaurants, and several good short walks in the vicinity. A day further north, many walkers divert to pay homage to the Bronte sisters at Haworth, where there are enough literary distractions to justify a day's pause. Reached on Day 5, Malham is a major tourist centre in the Yorkshire Dales, with numerous short walks in the vicinity and a variety of facilities in the village. (For more details see the Yorkshire Dales section in the Northern England – Short Walks chapter.) In the North Pennines, Dufton is one of the prettiest little villages along the Way, again with some interesting short walk possibilities. Walkers interested in coming to grips with Hadrian's Wall and the numerous Roman remains in its vicinity may want to pause for a day in this area. (More details on Hadrian's Wall are given in the Northumberland section of the Northern England – Short Walks chapter.) ∎

Wainwright's idiosyncratic *Pennine Way Companion* (published by Michael Joseph). It's fun but not always easy to use; for a start it goes backwards! The reasoning behind this is that since you walk north, each map should continue off the top of one page and on to the bottom of the previous page. Furthermore the text is (neatly) handprinted rather than typeset. And the amazingly intricate maps showing every stile, gate, ditch and cow pat from Edale to Kirk Yetholm are wonderful if you're absolutely on track, but useless once you're five steps off it. Other books include *A Guide to the Pennine Way* by Christopher John Wright (Constable) and *Walk this Way – The Pennine Way* by Peter Gorring (Gotham Press, £4.99), a practical guide aimed at those camping and using bunkhouses.

Maps

The handy little Footprint strip maps to *The Pennine Way* cover the walk in two sections, *Part One – Edale to Teesdale* and *Part Two – Teesdale to Kirk Yetholm*. These may not be detailed enough for tricky navigation but they're terrific for keeping track of what you're doing over a whole day's walking, and to judge how much more ground you've got to cover. Last revised in 1990 and 1992, they're a bit out of date for the most recent route changes. If you want to be fully equipped with OS maps you will need nine Landranger (1:50,000) sheets: 74, 80, 86, 91, 92, 98, 103, 109 and 110.

LOCAL SERVICES

Some overnight stops have only the most basic supplies but places with more comprehensive shopping facilities are mentioned in the route description. If you need walking equipment, Malham, Horton-in-Ribblesdale and Hawes all have gear shops. Hebden Bridge, Hawes, Alston and Bellingham have banks with cash machines.

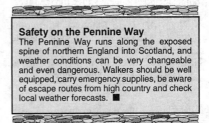

Safety on the Pennine Way

The Pennine Way runs along the exposed spine of northern England into Scotland, and weather conditions can be very changeable and even dangerous. Walkers should be well equipped, carry emergency supplies, be aware of escape routes from high country and check local weather forecasts. ∎

PLACES TO STAY & EAT

There are B&Bs, hostels and campsites regularly spaced along the route, and a selection is detailed in the route description. Many Pennine Way walkers book accommodation well in advance and this may be wise at the height of the season. With the odd compromise and short diversion off the Way it's possible to make the entire walk from one YHA hostel to another – this can be booked through the YHA Pennine Way Bureau

(☎ 01729 823844), Mearbeck, Bridge End Mill, Settle, North Yorkshire BD24 9JS. Finding a place to buy lunch can be more problematic, however, and it's often wise to bring sandwiches or other sustenance.

GETTING THERE & AWAY
Bus
You can reach Edale circuitously by bus, changing at Castleton, but the easiest transport for walkers is the train service between Sheffield and Manchester which stops at Edale 10 to 15 times a day. Either way it takes around half an hour and costs £3. At the other end count on about five hours travel time for the buses between Kirk Yetholm and Kelso, and then two hours for Kelso to Berwick. The last bus from Kirk Yetholm leaves at around 6 pm. If you miss the bus (the last day's walk is long), a taxi to Berwick from Kirk Yetholm should be less than £20.

Train
Berwick is on the main railway line between Edinburgh and London. If you want to break the walk along the way, more accessible points include Hebden Bridge (on the Liverpool to Manchester to Leeds railway line), Malham (buses to Skipton), Horton-in-Ribblesdale (on the Leeds to Settle-Carlisle Line), Middleton-in-Teesdale (buses to Darlington) and Once Brewed (buses to the Newcastle to Carlisle railway line).

Car
Edale lies to the north of the A625 road between Sheffield and Chapel-en-le-Frith. There is a car park, but this is a very popular walking area, so it's frequently full. If you're doing more than a day's walk on the Pennine Way, public transport is a far better option.

THE ROUTE
The Start: Edale
The pretty village of Edale is the beginning of the Pennine Way. A predeparture pint at the traditional starting point, the Old Nag's Head, is part of the ritual. Opposite the pub, the Pennine Way route starts off due west, with a sign announcing you've got 275 miles

to go. (The Pennine Way originally headed north up Grindsbrook Clough then curved round to the west to cross Kinder Scout and meet the new route at Kinder Downfall. If you arrive in Edale with spare time on the day before you set off, it makes an interesting leg stretcher to walk up the old route to Grindslow Knoll and then turn west around the edge of the Kinder Scout plateau before dropping back down to Edale, having worked up a bit of a thirst for that Old Nag's Head pint.) The PIC is open daily, 9 am to 1 pm and 2 to 5.30 pm; November to March it closes at 5 pm.

Places to Stay & Eat The small *Fieldhead Campsite* (☎ 01433 670386) next to the PIC costs £2.85. Showers are another 50p. At the top of the village *Cooper's Camp* (☎ 01433 670372) charges £2.25. The large *YHA Hostel* (☎ 01433 670302, £9.10) is at Nether Booth, about two miles east of the village. The *Rambler Inn* (☎ 01433 670268) by the railway station offers B&B at £22 per person. Up the road past the church, *Stonecroft* (☎ 01433 670262) does B&B from £23 to £25.

East of the village, there's B&B at *Ollerbrook Barn* (☎ 01433 670200) for £16 per person. The *Old Nag's Head* (☎ 01433 670291) and the *Rambler Inn* both do straightforward pub meals in the £5 to £6 bracket from an identical menu. There's a cafe just south of the railway station and a small shop and post office at Cooper's Camp. There are more options in the nearby villages of Castleton or Hope, 10 minutes east on the railway line. For more details see the Peak District Edale Skyline section of the Northern England – Short Walks chapter.

Day 1: Edale to Crowden
16 miles (26 km), 6 to 7 hours
This first day is not too demanding, but no walk in the park either, especially if you're not limbered up. It takes you round the edge of Kinder Scout, then over the moors of Bleaklow. There's nowhere for supplies on this first day of the route so bring something for lunch.

The trail heads west out of Edale across fields before dropping down to a lane at Upper Booth. It follows the lane to Lee Farm then follows the Noe River, and climbs steeply up Jacob's Ladder to Edale Rocks and Kinder Low.

Once on the Kinder plateau, the route sticks right to the edge. Kinder Downfall is an impressive jumble of rocks where, when the Kinder River is in full flow, a waterfall tumbles down. The trail keeps to the plateau edge before dropping down to a signpost at a junction and then climbing up to the cairn and post at Mill Hill, where the route turns to the north-east and strikes out towards Moss Castle. This was once a Pennine Way horror story, a confusing scramble through sticky mud where it was easy to get lost in poor visibility. Now it's an easy doddle along a flagstoned path all the way across Featherbed Moss to the A57 Snake Pass road.

Continuing along the Devil's Dyke and Hern Clough, the trail then wanders across Bleaklow, although frequent trail markers and lots of bootprints make even this stretch relatively easy to follow. The interesting shapes of the Wain Stones are just west of the

trail which soon joins the little stream of Wildboar Grain. The trail stays fairly level until it descends steeply to Torside Reservoir and crosses the dam to the north shore. The Way soon leaves the reservoir side and climbs up to Crowden.

Crowden Campers can use the well-equipped CCC *campsite* (☎ 01457 866057), charging around £3, or £2 in the low season. The *YHA Hostel* (☎ 01457 852135, £6.75) is nearby. Breakfast (£2.80) and dinner (£4.15) are also available for nonresidents. There are no other facilities at Crowden; the nearest pub is four miles away.

Day 2: Crowden to Standedge
11½ miles (18.5 km), 5 to 6 hours
This is a short day, but pleasant, over the wild moors squeezed between Manchester and Huddersfield. If you're a mile-eater, you could head for Mankinholes or Hebden Bridge.

The Way starts out climbing up beside Crowden Brook, then steeply emerges on the edge of Laddow Rocks with fine views down to the stream and reservoir. Up on the plateau

Peat, Bogs & Bog Trotting
For a couple of thousand years, from perhaps 5000 BC to around 3000 BC, Britain (and Ireland for that matter) were rather wetter places than they've been for the last few millennia. Much of Ireland and a large swathe of central Northern England became so waterlogged that dead vegetation simply did not decay as quickly as it accumulated. The result was a deep concentration of vegetable matter which eventually became a metre-thick blanket of peat bog.

Peat is a problem for walkers: drop a mist down over it to hide landmarks and the rolling peat is like the sea; it's easy to get lost. Mist or not, peat all looks the same – the next footstep can be springy, sticky and muddy, or drop straight into thigh-deep primordial ooze.

Equally, walkers are a problem for peat: whatever its consistency, a succession of walkers' boots will soon convert even the springy variety into a disgusting morass. When this happens, walkers seek drier footing to one side, and soon convert that into bottomless mud as well. A neat walking path a couple of boots wide quickly becomes a motorway of mud.

There are two solutions to this problem and you'll see both of them on Day 1 between Edale and Crowden. One is to avoid the most fragile areas. From Edale to Kinder Downfall the Pennine Way now skirts around the rockier edge of the Kinder Plateau rather than striking straight across the moors. Most walkers will find the plateau-edge views a very acceptable substitute.

The other solution is to confront the bog head on and build a path over it. This is definitely less acceptable to the purist *bog trotter*, and it certainly takes the challenge out of crossing the moors, if your idea of challenge is plodding through a sticky, glutinous porridge of oozy mud. Whatever the pros and cons, the previously harrowing traverses of some of the Way's toughest moors have now become easy strolls along yellow brick roads of flagstones. ■

is another one-time horror story. Today a yellow-brick road of flagstones winds across the soggy moors to Black Hill, but until the paved footpath descends from Black Hill as well, it can still be difficult to find the route.

The old Pennine Way heads off north-west; the newer realignment goes more north-east before bending north-west and dropping down to Dean Clough stream and climbing back up to cross the A635 at Wessenden Head. *Snoopy's Food Van* can usually be found close to the junction.

The next stretch passes several reservoirs, with a picturesque climb up from Wessenden along Blakely Clough and across a soggy patch of moor (no doubt soon to be paved) to Swellands and Black Moss Reservoirs before crossing the A62 at Standedge.

Standedge *Globe Farm* (☎ 01457 873040) is just off the route, charging £18 for ensuite B&B. They also have a *bunkhouse* equipped with kitchen for £6. Camping is £2. Campers and bunkhousers can get breakfast for £4 and dinner is £6.50. The *Floating Light* pub, on the A62, is closer to the route; it does B&B at £14 and dinner around £5. A little further east of the Way on the A62 are two other pubs, the *Great Western* and the *Carriage House*, with an interesting Turkish menu.

Day 3: Standedge to Hebden Bridge
15 miles (24 km), 6 to 7 hours

Today's walk takes you over several moors, and past many reservoirs built to supply the surrounding industrial cities. You should be self-sufficient for lunch; one pub is encountered but it's targeted at motorists, not walkers.

From Stangedge, the first section of the route can be confusing, with a mesh of crossing paths, and it's remarkably easy to find yourself on the wrong track. As you come off the moor, make absolutely certain you're passing to the east of Readycon Dean Reservoir. The Way climbs up and over another stretch of moor, then drops down to cross the A672 with the towering Windy Hill TV mast as a prominent marker. Almost immediately the route comes to the M62, hidden away in

a cutting, and crosses on its own elegant walkers' bridge.

Then it's up Redmires, tamed by flagstones, to rocky and dramatic Blackstone Edge. On the other side the Way drops down to the enigmatic Aiggin Stone, an ancient route marker where the route turns 90° from north to west and follows a 'Roman road' for a short distance, although the road's history is as uncertain as the marker stone's.

The route soon turns north again and crosses Blackstone Edge Moor down to the A58. The Way goes in front of the large and rather impersonal *White House Inn* before turning north past the Blackstone Edge Reservoirs. Off to the north-west, and later to the north-east as well, stands of wind-power generators can be seen whirling gently on the horizon.

After two more reservoirs the Way traverses another stretch of moor, then edges around Coldwell Hill, with fine views down to Mankinholes and on to the Woodley Pike Monument, a prominent target along the route.

Hostellers overnighting at *Mankinholes YHA Hostel* (☎ 01706 812340, £6.75) can take the beautifully crafted path known as the 'Long Drag' down from Withins Gate, a 19th-century cotton famine relief project. Continuing on the Way, there's the Woodley Pike Monument, built during the Napoleonic Wars. Construction was halted when Napoleon escaped from Elba and it was completed in 1815, but despite its monolithically solid construction the monument collapsed in 1854 and again in 1918.

From the monument the Pennine Way wanders across the high ground then drops down through woods towards Hebden Bridge. There's a short cut straight to the town but the Way continues to descend gradually, eventually crossing the Rochdale Canal and the Calder River before arriving at the A646 a mile or so west of the centre of Hebden Bridge.

Hebden Bridge For some reason, Hebden Bridge is roundly condemned by most Pennine Way guidebooks when in fact it's a surprisingly attractive, slightly trendified mill town with lots of pubs, B&Bs, hotels and interesting little shops. It's definitely worth arriving early enough to wander around.

The town is wedged into a narrow and steep-sided valley, with a road, river, canal and railway all running through it. You can wander along the canal path into town.

The TIC, on the main road where it crosses the river, will book accommodation and has a list of local B&Bs posted in its window. It's open Monday to Saturday, 10 am to 5 pm; Sunday, 11 am to 5 pm.

Places to stay and eat include the *Woodman Inn* (☎ 01422 842458), with rather scruffy and uninviting rooms at £12.50. You can camp here for £2 although facilities are pretty basic. They also do food. Continue a little further towards town and double back up Oakville Rd to *Four Winds* (☎ 01422 843490), 10 Turret Royd Rd, where B&B is £12 to £15.

A little further towards town is Savile Rd, where *Prospect End* (☎ 01422 843586) at 8 Prospect Terrace is a very genteel B&B with ensuite rooms for £20/34 a single/ double. Nearby is the *Stubbing Wharf* pub; pleasantly relaxed, with reasonable food.

It's a further 10 minutes walk along the canal towpath (more pleasant than the road) into town, where there are a host of accommodation possibilities including a couple of pricier hotels, such as the *Carlton Hotel* (☎ 01422 844400) on Albert St, with rooms from £46 to £89.

For food, apart from the pubs mentioned above, Hebden Bridge has plenty of cafes and restaurants. If you feel your walking efforts deserve it, try *Kittie's Restaurant* (☎ 01422 842956) at 52 Market St, open Tuesday to Saturday, with interesting main courses in the £9 to £13 range.

Day 4: Hebden Bridge to Lothersdale
19 miles (30.5 km), 8 to 10 hours
Today's walk leads across more fine northern moors, as you begin to leave the large industrial towns and cities further in the

distance. There's also a literary taste to the walk, as you pass Wuthering Heights.

For most walkers potential pubs for lunch are encountered too early or too late in the day, so bring something to eat. From Hebden Bridge, walk back to the point where the Pennine Way crosses the A646, and the route goes up Underbank Ave, underneath the railway bridge, switchbacking steeply up to Colden. You drop down to Colden Water, with a perfect-looking campsite, complete with emphatic 'No Camping' sign, and a very solid stone footbridge. Up the other side is *May's High Gate Farm* (☎ 01422 842897); it's just off the Way and has supplies and camping facilities.

From here the Way heads north-west across a stretch of moor, passing a ruined farmhouse, where it's important to stay up high and not get distracted down towards the road and river by alternative footpaths.

Continue along the moortop until a sharp right (north) turn takes you down past a reservoir channel and steeply down to the Graining Water stream, then back up the other side. The *Pack Horse Inn* is just right (east) along the road but it's too early for lunch.

The route leaves the road and passes the first two Walshaw Dean Reservoirs before heading off north-east across moors, again by easily followed paths or along flagged walkways, to the ruins of Withins or Top Withins. This is the first clear sign of Bronte country, for Withins is generally held to have had some connection with the Earnshaw house in *Wuthering Heights*.

A wide track continues towards Haworth (the Bronte's village), a popular detour 2½ miles off the route, where there's a *YHA Hostel* (☎ 01535 642234, £8.25). The numerous Way signs on this stretch are in Japanese as well as English. Past two farmhouses the Way turns sharply left and drops down to Ponden Reservoir. *Ponden Hall* (☎ 01535 644154) has B&B at £16. At the west end of the reservoir the Way turns north, climbs up to the road before turning off, and then takes a confusing left turn to head across the bleak Ickornshaw Moor, although, once again, navigational difficulties and hard work have been eliminated by a stone walkway. Across the moor, the trail drops down to Ickornshaw. There are camping facilities close to the road at *Winter House Farm* (☎ 01535 632234), cheap pub food and equally bargain-priced B&B at the friendly *Black Bull Inn* (☎ 01535 630418), and more B&B at *The Hawthorns* (☎ 01535 633299, £15). There are further possibilities at neighbouring Cowling, so this could be a good place to call a halt, except that Lothersdale is only two miles away and more attractive. The Way follows a mix of country lanes, field paths and stream crossings as it wends its way into this picturesque little mill town.

Lothersdale From where the Way emerges into the town it's only a few steps left (west) to *Old Granary Cottage* (☎ 01535 636075) and *Meriden* (☎ 01535 632531), almost directly behind it, with B&B in the £14 to £18 bracket. Nearby, the *Hare & Hounds* does good no-frills pub food. The adjacent *Burlington House* (☎ 01535 634635) does B&B. Near the Way's exit point from Lothersdale is *Lynmouth* (☎ 01535 632744), with B&B for £20/£30.

Day 5: Lothersdale to Malham
15 miles (24 km), 7 to 8 hours
On today's green and pleasant walk, you enter the Yorkshire Dales National Park. You'll notice a change in scenery and an increase in good lunch opportunities. From Lothersdale, after a short distance along lanes, the Way runs across open moors past Pinshaw Beacon before dropping across fields (a bit confusing past Brown House Farm) and past a disused railway to Thornton-in-Craven on the busy A56.

A mile west is *Earby YHA Hostel* (☎ 01282 842349). From Thornton-in-Craven it's across fields again before emerging on the Leeds & Liverpool Canal towpath. An unusual double-arch bridge crosses the canal at East Marton.

Up on the busy road there's the *Cross Keys* pub, or you can continue along the canal to

the next bridge to find the very pleasant little *Abbot's Harbor* restaurant and cafe. It's a great place for a tea or coffee break, with a tempting assortment of cakes and lunches. If you want dinner (main courses at £4 to £5.50) and an overnight stop there's B&B for £16 in the adjacent *Sawley House* (☎ 01282 843207), where you can also camp for £2 per person.

If you're continuing, the Way leaves the canal and heads through small woods and fields to Scaleber Hill, with St Andrew's church in Gargrave a useful target ahead. As you arrive in Gargrave, across from the church there's pub food at the *Mason's Arms*.

Cross the River Aire into the busy centre where B&Bs include *Dale House* (☎ 01756 749809, £15), at 28 South St, and *Kirk Syke Hotel* (☎ 01756 749356, £21 to £29), at 19 High St. On the way out of town there's B&B at *Old Hall Cottage* (☎ 01756 749412). *Eshton Rd Caravan Site* (☎ 01756 749229) has camping for £3.

For food some interesting dishes are available in the £5 to £6 range at the *Old Swan Inn* (☎ 01756 749232). If you decide to overnight here and want a real restaurant for a change there's *Wood's Bistro* (☎ 01756 749252), open Tuesday to Saturday with main courses around £8.

Leave Gargrave by West Rd, cross the canal again and continue beside a patch of wood for a while before angling off across fields for a mile, then turning gently down to a bridge over the River Aire. It's easy to miss the turn as the path continuing along the wall appears more prominent.

The Way then follows the river for the next four miles, a very pretty and gentle stroll. The route finally turns away from the river by Hanlith Hall and Badger House (look for the windvane) and climbs uphill, then leaves the road to run across fields, above the river, before dropping down into Malham. If your legs completely give out, with Malham almost in sight, there are overnight possibilities at Airton, Kirby Malham and Hanlith.

Malham This busy village has lots of places to stay and eat and some interesting short excursions nearby. There's also a PIC, open daily, 9.30 am to 5 pm; in July and August, 9 am to 5.30 pm. The village shops include the Cove Centre with a wide range of walking equipment. There's a *YHA Hostel* (☎ 01729 830321, £9.10), and campers can head a mile east of town to the *Gordale Scar House Campsite* (☎ 01729 830333), charging £2.50 per person. Beyond the village, northwards along the Way, *Hill Top Farm Bunkhouse* (☎ 01729 830320) charges £6. Across the road is *Town Head Farm* campsite.

B&Bs include *Miresfield Farm* (☎ 01729 830414, £16); *Town End Cottages* (☎ 01729 830487, £15); *Sparth House Hotel* (☎ 01729 830315, £18.50 to £25); *Eastwood House* (☎ 01729 830409, £12 to £16); and the *Malham Café & B&B* (☎ 01729 830348). Just past the centre, *Beck Hall* (☎ 01729 830332) is wonderfully situated right by the river and has B&B at £16, or £20 ensuite.

For luxury, try the *Buck Inn* (☎ 01729 830317) where singles/doubles are £31/52. For food, the *Buck Inn* has a standard pub menu at £5 to £6, plus a pricier menu with meals in the £10 to £12 range and a fancy dining room to enjoy it in. The *Lister Arms* has a similar £5 to £6 menu but with some much more imaginative additions like spicy Mexican enchilada, lime and coriander chicken, lamb, apricot and almond casserole or Louisiana blackened chicken – as good as they sound.

Day 6: Malham to Horton-in-Ribblesdale
14 miles (22.5 km), 7 hours

Today's enjoyable walk winds through the heart of the Yorkshire Dales, finishing with an ascent of Pen-y-ghent Hill, a famous Pennine Way landmark. You pass no villages and only a few small roads, with no cafes or pubs for lunch. Out of Malham the Way climbs steeply up the west side of the cliffs of Malham Cove, then edges right across the top of the curve – a textbook stretch of limestone pavement with wonderful views back down to Malham.

At the east end of the pavement, go sharp left and head north up the increasingly narrow Watlowes Valley. At the head of the valley signs confusingly point to Malham Tarn in both directions; take the southward option, which soon curves round Comb Hill to head north along a valley which opens out before the tarn.

After so many artificial reservoirs a real honest-to-God lake is a small surprise, and the Way edges around the east side of the tarn before heading into a small forest past Malham Tarn House, now a Field Studies Council centre, then turns north off the road just before some houses. For a mile the Way crosses fields, then turns east to cross a road by the prominently signposted Tennant Gill Farm.

Leaving green fields for darker moor, the Way climbs up to Fountain Fell, over a series of ridges, each hinting that maybe it's the top, and past a scattering of disused mineshafts to a bleak stone-walled summit before dropping steadily downhill to meet the equally bleak Silverdale Rd. All the way down you can look across at what you'll shortly have to climb on the other side. The long hump of Pen-y-ghent parallels the road, and the Way marches alongside it for about a mile, past Rainscar House, as if to give walkers plenty of time to contemplate what they have to tackle.

Finally the route turns west past Dale Head Farm, where you may be able to buy a welcome cup of tea, then across to the base of Pen-y-ghent. After all this foreplay the peak turns out to be a bit of a disappointment: a couple of short sharp pushes and you're on the top, crossing a wall at the high point (694m, 2277 ft) and dropping down the other side, along a winding but extremely clear path, the result of some major restoration work on a heavily used section.

The village of Horton-in-Ribblesdale is clearly visible to the south, with an ugly quarry scarring the hillside behind it, but when you turn from west to south-west it's still 1½ miles along a green road, neatly fenced off by stone walls, before you reach civilisation.

Close to the turn are Hunt Pot and Hull Pot, two impressive potholes. Continuing

downhill you pass Tarn Bar, a perfect miniature replica of Malham Cove. Finally the
Way emerges on to the B6479, just before the
Pen-y-ghent Cafe, one of the Pennine Way's
most popular bottlenecks.

Horton-in-Ribblesdale The village is on a
major railway line, so it's a good place to join
or leave the Pennine Way if you have to do
the walk in sections. There's also a good
range of places to stay and eat, plus a village
shop and post office. For full details see the
Yorkshire Dales, Three Peaks section in the
Northern England – Short Walks chapter.
The local TIC is in the Pen-y-ghent Cafe.

Day 7: Horton-in-Ribblesdale to Hawes
14 miles (22.5 km), 6 hours
Another wonderfully wild Yorkshire Dales
day, through 'karst' country, riddled with
limestone caves, and a mecca for local potholers. Once again there's nowhere to get
food. Bring some supplies from the Pen-y-
ghent Cafe.

The Way departs Horton-in-Ribblesdale
along the same route it arrived on, along a
stone-walled green road that climbs up onto
Birkwith Moor. Three miles north of the
village, the Way turns sharply to the west and
shortly afterwards back north again, passing
Old Ing Farm. As it's hidden behind a stone
wall, you could easily miss the attractive stream
tumbling into the mouth of the Calf Holes cave.
Only a quarter of a mile along the Way a short
excursion past the barn to the left of the road
will bring you to Browngill Cave, where the
stream reemerges. Potholers revel in following
this watery underground route.

It's only a mile past the farm to the pretty
little Ling Gill Gorge, and although you
cannot enter the steep-sided valley, the riverbank makes a pleasant picnic spot and there's
an interesting old bridge at the head of the
gorge. The Way climbs up to Cam End and
starts a lonely trudge north-east along the
Roman road route of Cam High Road, coinciding for a spell with the Dales Way
(described elsewhere in this book), before
turning off to the north to edge around Dodd
Fell. The route overlooks a wide and deep
valley, a popular spot for hang-gliding
enthusiasts. Finally the Way drops down
through fields and farms, following Gaudy
Lane to a slightly confusing route through
the village of Gayle to reach the town of
Hawes.

Hawes On the busy A684, Hawes is a surprisingly bustling little centre with a wide
variety of shops, including a supermarket, a
number of banks, half a dozen pubs, a YHA
hostel and a choice of more than 20 B&Bs,
guesthouses and hotels, although despite this
seemingly plentiful supply you can still find
a lot of 'No Vacancy' signs. There's a TIC
(☎ 01969 667450) in the Dales Countryside
Museum on the eastern side of the town, and
they post a notice showing where rooms
were available when they closed for the day.
The same notice is posted outside the library
in the town centre.

The *YHA Hostel* (☎ 01969 667368, £8.25)
is on the western outskirts of the town. There
are numerous B&Bs lined up through the
town and out to the eastern side, and there
are also one or two as you come through

The Pen-y-ghent Cafe & the Three Peaks Challenge
The Pen-y-ghent Cafe is a classic Pennine Way feature. Walkers heading north or south stop here to
sign the guest book, enjoy a snack or meal and perhaps buy new socks, the next map or other
equipment. It's also the starting and finishing point for a piece of local masochism – the Three Peaks
challenge. All you have to do is walk out the front door of the cafe, pop up to the top of Pen-y-ghent,
and the 'neighbouring' hills of Whernside and Ingleborough (a total distance of around 26 miles – all
on foot of course), and walk back in through the front door again within 12 hours. For full details see
the Three Peaks section of the Northern England – Short Walks chapter. ■

adjacent Gayle. *Steppe Haugh Guest House* (☎ 01969 667645) at £16 and *Old Station House* (☎ 01969 667785) at £17 to £20 are just two of this wide selection.

There are plenty of pubs ready to feed hungry walkers, including the *Fountain,* the *Crown* and the *White Hart*, but the real surprise is the *Bulls Head Inn* with a very sophisticated menu offering some of the most interesting dishes you'll find along the whole Pennine Way. Other Hawes dining possibilities include a fish & chips shop, a pizzeria and the *Rose House Restaurant*.

Day 8: Hawes to Tan Hill
16 miles (26 km), 7 hours
The route takes you over more lonely high ground, but if you're tired of sandwiches, there are a couple of lunch-stop options along the way.

After leaving Hawes, it's only a mile to Hardraw where most walkers make a short diversion through the front door of the *Green Dragon Inn* (☎ 01969 667392). After paying 60p, you can follow the path to Hardraw Force, the highest waterfall in England. (The inn does B&B for £18 and camping is also possible, and there are several other options in Hardraw.)

From Hardraw the Way soon abandons green fields for lonely moorland, often following stone-slabbed paths as it leads up to Great Shunner Fell (716m). Off to the east a curious collection of spikey cairns can be seen above Pickersett Edge. From the summit the Way drops down to more fields around the small village of Thwaite, where the *Kearton Café & Restaurant* (☎ 01748 886277) makes an excellent lunch break and offers B&B for £19.50. Almost next door is *Thwaite Farm* (☎ 01748 886444) with B&B at £15.

From Thwaite the path climbs high above the River Swale with wonderful views across the valley. Just before the village of Keld, the Way drops to cross the river, briefly coinciding with the Coast to Coast Walk (described at the start of this chapter). After climbing up the other side of the valley, it's a short diversion downstream to Kisdon Force waterfall.

Keld is another overnight possibility, although walkers who appreciate their end-of-day pint may be disconcerted to note the lack of a pub. (For more details see the Coast to Coast section.)

Tan Hill From Keld the route climbs back on to the moor, and although the road is never far to the west it can be a lonely trudge the last four miles (take care if it's misty, there are numerous unfenced mineshafts close by) to the *Tan Hill Inn* (☎ 01833 628246), where B&B costs £19.50 or you can camp for £1. At 528m this is the highest pub in England, but there's no other place to stay anywhere near, so it's wise to phone ahead and make sure they have space.

Day 9: Tan Hill to Middleton-in-Teesdale
17 miles (27 km), 7 hours
The route bids farewell to the Yorkshire Dales and enters another relatively wild area of Britain known as the North Pennines. In fact, this Area of Outstanding Natural Beauty probably retains some of its wildness precisely because it *isn't* a national park. For many walkers, the next few days epitomise the essence of the Pennine Way. As befitting a wild area, there are of course no places to buy lunch, so it's back to the butties.

From the lonely Tan Hill Inn the route slouches across equally lonely Sleightholme Moor for five miles. If the weather is dry, the walk along the stream can be quite pleasant. If it's wet, it can be a dishearteningly muddy experience and the alternative of following the lane and rejoining further on may be preferable. From the end of the moor the diversion to Bowes, an off-route overnight possibility with a pub, B&B and shop, adds a couple of miles to the walk.

If you're continuing on the main route, there's a brief farmland interlude before you descend to the River Greta, crossing it by a natural stone slab known as God's Bridge. A short, and highly advisable, detour leads to an underpass under the busy A66 before another stretch of bleak moorland.

The diversion to Bowes rejoins the main route at Baldersdale with its reservoirs and the *YHA Hostel* (☎ 01833 650629, £6.75) at the halfway point on the Pennine Way. There are farmhouse B&Bs in the vicinity as well.

The Way climbs up, then drops down to more reservoirs before climbing again to take a slightly confusing route through a maze of fields before descending to Middleton-in-Teesdale.

Middleton-in-Teesdale The River Tees flows past this handsome little grey stone town. There are shops, a supermarket, pubs and B&Bs but no cash machines in the banks.

On the west side of the Tees, just before the town, camping costs £2.50 at the *Daleview Caravan Park* (☎ 01833 640233) or there's B&B for £15. Just past the centre of town on the Alston Rd, *Kingsway Adventure Centre* (☎ 01833 640881) also has camping space, plus rather basic bunkroom accommodation which is no bargain at £11 including breakfast, plus another £2 for bedding. On Market Place in the centre of town, *Blue Bell House* (☎ 01833 640584) has pleasant rooms with bathroom for £21/32. Across the road is the pricier *Brunswick House* (☎ 01833 640393) at £27.50/40. Walkers who feel they deserve real luxury might want to look at the *Teesdale Hotel* (☎ 01833 640264) with rooms at £38.50/60.50, although discounts are often available. There are a number of cheaper B&Bs in town.

The town's pubs include the *Bridge Inn, Talbot Hotel* and *King's Head*, but the *Teesdale Hotel* has a fancy restaurant, good standard pub food in the bar (from £5, up to £12 for specials) and a cheaper tapas bar section round the back.

Day 10: Middleton-in-Teesdale to Dufton
20 miles (32 km), 8 hours

Today's long but varied walk is one of the most interesting along the Way, through classic North Pennine landscape and past a couple of impressive waterfalls.

For the first eight miles the route follows the peat-stained waters of the pretty River Tees, past Low Force waterfall and then the

much larger and more impressive High Force, where a short detour could be made to the *High Force Hotel* if an early lunch was needed.

Beyond the waterfalls the Way briefly abandons the Tees to pass close to Langdon Beck, which has a pub and *YHA Hostel* (☎ 01833 622228, £8.25). The Way turns north to cross Harwood Beck, on a bridge with a sign indicating how far you've come and how much further you have to go, before it rejoins the Tees just before Widdybank Farm, where snacks and light meals may (or may not) be available. The Way then follows a rocky path through a narrow gorge, which can be dangerously slippery if wet. The gorge widens out under the impressive Falcon Clints before the route clambers up the rocky hillside beside the forceful Cauldron Snout waterfall.

Climbing back on to the moors for several miles, the route is bordered by signs warning of an adjacent army artillery range, and then for a couple more miles it follows the sparkling waters of Maize Beck. You suddenly arrive at High Cup Nick, a stunning valley running straight up into the high country, with a steep drop shelving down, down, down to a silvery stream winding off into the distance. This would be a breathtaking view from any angle but the sudden arrival, without advance warning, is superb. From here it's just a few more miles downhill (remembering all the time that all this downhill will be paid for tomorrow morning with a balancing uphill stretch) into the bright little village of Dufton, where houses bear dates from the 17th and 18th centuries.

Dufton Coming down from High Cup Nick, *Bow Hall* (☎ 017683 51835) is about a mile before the village and has B&B for £15. Almost immediately after turning on to the village street there's *Ghyll View* (☎ 017683 51855), similarly priced, while the *Stag Inn* (☎ 017683 51608), on the neatly cropped little village green, charges £18.50. Nearby, *Dufton Hall Farm* (☎ 017683 51573) does B&B at £15. Dufton also has a *YHA Hostel* (☎ 017683 51236, £7.45) and a *campsite*

(£2).The friendly *Stag Inn* welcomes walkers, with good pub food at £5 to £7 (and king-size desserts). The village shop has other basic supplies.

Day 11: Dufton to Alston
20 miles (32 km), 8 hours

Today's route can be one of the most serious sections so far encountered, going over Cross Fell, the route's summit, where weather conditions can be notoriously bad. Garrigal, the only place for supplies along today's walk, is reached quite late, so make sure you've got enough to survive the day.

The Way wanders out of Dufton along farm lanes then starts to climb, first to Knock Fell (794m), then to Great Dun Fell (848m), with its air traffic control radar station (including a giant golf ball) visible from far away. The trail drops, then climbs, often along stone-slabbed pathways, to Little Dun Fell and finally Cross Fell (893m), the highest point along the entire Pennine Way. An 18th-century article on the region commented that Cross Fell was covered in snow for 10 months of the year and cloud for 11.

A series of tall and wobbly looking cairns leads across this bleak summit before the Way drops down to the Corpse Road (so-called because this was once a lead-mining area, and bodies of dead miners were once carried along the route) and then to Greg's Hut, a mountain refuge which could be useful if one of those sudden midsummer snowfalls occurs.

From here it's six weary miles across the moors along a road which is easy to follow but uncomfortably covered in awkward, sharp-edged stones. Reaching the tarred road at Garrigal is a considerable relief. Garrigal has the *George & Dragon* pub, several B&Bs and a small shop, but it's less than four miles along a pleasant path beside the South Tyne to Alston.

Alston This busy little town has places to stay, a selection of pubs, a variety of shops and several banks (two at least with cash machines). The modern *YHA Hostel* (☎ 01434 381509, £7.45) is beside the river

just as you reach the outskirts of town. Campers can head for *Tyne Willows Caravan Site* (☎ 01434 381318), charging £2.50 per person.

On Market Place in the town centre *Blueberry Tea Shop & Guest House* (☎ 01434 381928) has B&B for £17.50/29. A few steps further up the road is the *Victoria Inn* (☎ 01434 381194) with B&B at £14, or £18 ensuite. Rooms are available at several other pubs and hotels, including the *Blue Bell Inn* (☎ 01434 381566), from £13, and the *Hillcrest Hotel* (☎ 01434 381251) from £18.

Food is available in most of the town's plentiful supply of pubs, including the cosy *Angel Inn*, the *Blue Bell Inn*, which has straightforward pub and a more expensive restaurant sections, and the pleasant *Turks Head Inn* on the marketplace, which has good food at £5 to £7 including some more imaginative dishes. Other food possibilities include Chinese at *Ho's House*.

Day 12: Alston to Greenhead
18 miles (29 km), 7 hours

This is another transition day, as you approach Northumberland National Park, and the ancient Roman boundary of Hadrian's Wall. The route keeps to the South Tyne Valley, frequently crossing the main A689, but there's only one potential spot to get lunch, the pub at Knarsdale, and even that's a mile off the Way. There are, however, some great picnic spots along the route.

Leaving Alston, the Way makes a pleasant start with a long stretch through green farm country, passing beside the distinct embankments of a Roman fort. It also passes the route of an abandoned railway line. Completed in the 1850s to transport lead ore from the area's mines, the line became uneconomic by the end of the century and was finally closed in 1976. A number of spectacular viaducts remain: imposing examples of sturdy Victorian railway engineering. In Slaggyford there's a short section of the old line still standing beside the road, but in contrast to those mighty viaducts the line itself is a puny toy-train affair.

Slaggyford has the *Fellview Caravan*

Park and a couple of B&Bs, and a mile up the road in Knarsdale there's the pleasant *Kirkstyle Inn* (☎ 01434 381559), where B&B is also available. From Slaggyford the Way continues to flirt with the old railway line, then follows the route of a Roman road before embarking on a series of field crossings and a brief section of moorland. Late in the day the walk becomes a little tedious before crossing under electricity pylons, over the A69, wandering around a golf course and finally reaching the small settlement of Greenhead in the shadow of Thirlwall Castle and Hadrian's Wall.

Greenhead Greenhead has a limited selection of places to stay; the options include a campsite, YHA hostel and B&Bs. For more details see under Places to Stay in the A Hadrian's Wall Walk section of the Northern England – Short Walks chapter. For eats, during the day *Ye Olde Forge Tearoom* has snacks and light meals, while at night there's the *Greenhead Hotel*. There's more choice at the towns of Haltwhistle and Gisland, not far away by bus or taxi.

Day 13: Greenhead to Once Brewed
7 miles (11 km), 3 hours

Today's walk is very short but there's enough to see on the rollercoaster route along Hadrian's Wall, including a museum and the remains of a large fort, to use up the day very easily. The sites have places to eat. From Greenhead, regain the Way at the ruins of Thirlwall Castle. Constructed with blocks purloined from Hadrian's Wall, the 700 year old castle is a stark reminder of how this border region remained perilously unstable for 1000 years after the Roman departure. A mile further along the Way nothing remains of the fort at Carvoran, but the Roman Army Museum is well worth a visit. The small cafe is only open to museum visitors.

The disused Walltown Quarry takes a large bite out of the wall, but then there's a good-quality section as the Way follows the ridge edge to Aesica or Great Chesters, a Roman fort now overlapped by a farm building. Cawfields Quarry is now a picnic site

and car park; there may be an ice-cream van parked here. From here the Cawfield Crags and Winshield Crags sections of the wall comprise one of the best preserved stretches. From Steel Rigg a road drops down to the YHA Hostel and pub at Once Brewed.

Once Brewed On the busy B6318 Military Road, a half a mile south (and downhill) from the Way, the *YHA Hostel* (☎ 01434 344360, £8.25) is open all day. A short stroll west is the *Twice Brewed Inn* (☎ 01434 344534), with B&B at £17 and good food at £5 to £7. A little further along the road is the *Vallum Inn* (☎ 01434 344248) at £19 to £25. There are some farmhouse B&Bs near Housesteads, but all of them are some distance off the Way.

Once Brewed also has a very good PIC/TIC, full of information, maps and books about the Wall.

If you've got plenty of time, it's worth parking your pack and going back to the Wall to visit Housesteads Fort. You could even do a circular walk tying in with Vindolanda. For more details see the A Hadrian's Wall Walk section in the Northern England – Short Walks chapter.

Day 14: Once Brewed to Bellingham
15½ miles (25 km), 7 hours

Today's route keeps to Hadrian's Wall for a few miles more, then branches into Northumberland National Park and the wilds of the Wark Forest. If it's midge season, this is where they really start to be a nuisance.

From Once Brewed, having regained the Way you head east along the Wall's ridgetop route, overlooking Crag Lough directly below, before leaving at Rapishaw Gap and heading northwards. Housesteads Fort is less than a mile further east and justifies a visit if you did not make it yesterday.

The Way crosses marshy country between two loughs (lakes) and takes a rather confusing route into South Wark Forest, a conifer plantation, before finally emerging to cross farmland, dropping down to Warks Burn and climbing up to Horneystead Farm, where sandwiches and drinks are usually available.

Another mile brings the Way to Lowstead, a fine example of a fortified 16th-century bastlehouse, reminders of that unsettled era when a family had to be prepared to withstand outlaw onslaughts. The Way goes right through the garden of the house, emerging on a lane. For the rest of the way to Bellingham the route alternates between farm and lane, finally crossing the North Tyne and following a riverbank path into the town centre.

Bellingham Pronounced 'Belling-jum', the neat little village has a TIC, banks (one with a cash machine), shops, two pubs, an excellent bakery and the historic St Cuthbert's Church. Bellingham is the last place for more than the most basic supplies until the end of the Way.

The elderly and rather basic *YHA Hostel* (☎ 01434 220313, £6.10) is on the far side of the village. Just beyond the centre you can camp at *Demesne Farm* (☎ 01434 220258) for £2.

B&Bs include *Crofters End* (☎ 01434 220034) at £13, *Victoria House* (☎ 01434 220229) at £13 and *Lynn View* (☎ 01434 220344) at £15, across from the tourist office. *Lyndale House* (☎ 01434 220361), between the marketplace and the river, has ensuite B&B for £17. The *Rose & Crown* has food but it's better at the *Black Bull* despite a 100% 'with chips' menu.

Day 15: Bellingham to Byrness
15 miles (24 km), 6 hours
Today is a relatively easy walk through the contrasting moorland and forest of the national park, before the final day's long slog. There's no place to get food, so make sure you take advantage of Bellingham's facilities.

From Bellingham, the Way goes past a couple of farms and then for about five miles across a wonderfully lonely sweep of heather moor before dropping down to the start of a forest plantation. Sheltered by a wall, the Way climbs steeply, and muddily, up the edge of the plantation before levelling out and for some distance marching resolutely

along with forest to the left, moor to the right. A succession of marker stones along the fence line bear the letters GH; Gabriel Harding was the High Sheriff of Northumberland and these reminders of the extent of his lands have stood on this remote moor for nearly 300 years.

Finally the Way dives into the forest and most of the remaining miles to the small settlement of Byrness are through fir plantations. Signs along the trackside indicate the type of trees and when the various stands were planted. The tiny settlement of Blakehopeburnhaugh marks the boundary of the plantation and the final two mile stretch includes a pleasant riverside stroll.

Byrness The *Byrness Caravan Park* (☎ 01830 520259) is at Cottonshopeburnfoot, on the Way but about a mile before it reaches the A68, with camping space from £3, a bunkhouse at £6 and also B&B. The *Byrness Hotel* (☎ 01830 520231) is on the A68, right by the Way, offering B&B at £17.50 and reasonable food. Across the road is a petrol station and a small cafe with a few basic supplies. The village of Byrness itself is half a mile north-west of the Way's junction with the A68, but there's little to it apart from the *YHA Hostel* (☎ 01830 520519, £6.10). There's also a B&B in the village and another back at Cottonshopeburnfoot Farm.

Day 16: Byrness to Kirk Yetholm
26 miles (42 km), 10 hours
Today's walk is the longest and loneliest stretch on the whole Pennine Way, and can be hard going if the weather is bad. The alternatives to covering the distance in one long slog are rather limited. If you have camping equipment you can spend the night under canvas, and with a sleeping bag and some supplies you can overnight in one of the two mountain refuges along the Way, but the first (at nine miles) is probably too early and the second (at 19 miles) is probably too late. Or you can leave the Way and descend to a farmhouse B&B, although this will add some distance and entail some descent and ascent. The most convenient halfway stop is

Uswayford (☎ 01669 650237) which is only 1½ miles off the Way from about the 15 miles mark. It offers B&B and an evening meal for £22. Weary walkers should note the proprietor's enthusiasm for practical jokes: 'Uswayford farm? No that's another five miles down the valley. You've booked a bed? Never heard of you and we're full up tonight.'

From Byrness, the route starts from just west of the Byrness Hotel and after a few steps along a driveway turns and heads straight up the hill. A swift 150m ascent gets the blood moving but the next few miles are gentle, along the wide ridge overlooking the valley of Cottonshope Burn. The route splits, one direction keeping high while the other drops down to explore the Roman encampment at Chew Green. More moorland follows before the first mountain refuge hut is reached. From there the Way climbs and drops over Beefstand Hill and Mozie Law, keeping close to the English side of the border fence. The Street, an ancient drovers road as much as 1000 years old, comes up from the Coquetdale Valley to meet the Way at this point.

Russell's Cairn, a huge pile of stones from the Bronze Age, marks Windy Gyle, where another track comes up to meet the Way. The track down to the Uswayford B&B turns off the Way about a mile further on; it's signposted.

More rising and falling moor follows before the Way climbs up to the head of a valley at Cairn Hill. From there it's a 2½ mile round trip diversion to the 785m summit of The Cheviot, but although the ascent is now much easier, with stone-slab paths over the muddiest sections, the view is still rather dull.

The Way drops to spectacular Auchope Cairn and then steeply to the second mountain refuge hut. (Look back to see the glacial hanging valley at Hen Hole.)

From here it's almost easy street. There's one final slog up The Schill before the Way finally abandons the border fence and crosses decisively into Scotland.

Four miles from the end there's a choice of routes, one staying low in the valley while the other goes through the hills for the final stretch. You may not want to be bothered with decisions at this stage, but the high route doesn't take much longer. The two routes meet half a mile from the end to follow a road into the village of Kirk Yetholm. The traditional finishing point is the bar of the Border Hotel on the village green. Have a drink to celebrate – you've probably earned it!

Kirk Yetholm The cheapest accommodation is at *Kirk Yetholm SYHA Hostel* (☎ 01573 420631, £5.40). Just as you enter town the *Valleydene Guest House* (☎ 01573 420286) is friendly, comfortable and stylish, and the £16 cost includes one of the best breakfasts along the entire Pennine Way. The *Border Hotel* (☎ 01573 420237) also does B&B from £18, plus good food. Another place to try is *Blunty's Mill* (☎ 01573 420288), with B&B from £16. There are a few other B&Bs in the village and more at Town Yetholm, half a mile away, which also has a small shop. If you need a bank, the nearest is at Kelso – 30 minutes by bus.

OTHER WALKS IN THE NORTH PENNINES

After leaving the rounded hills and valleys of the Yorkshire Dales, the Pennine Way winds across the higher, wilder and altogether more severe mountains of the North Pennines. This is another of those areas like Mid Wales, wedged between two more-famous areas (in this case the Dales and Hadrian's Wall) and often overlooked. It is not a national park, although its landscape is more impressive and its population more thinly dispersed than some other areas with full national park status. It is however an Area of Outstanding Natural Beauty. The local tourist board bills it as 'England's Last Wilderness', and some cynics say it has probably remained wild and relatively little-visited precisely because it *isn't* a national park.

Whatever – the North Pennines have some marvellous walking areas. One of the best is Teesdale, the valley of the River Tees. The stretch from Barnard Castle to Langdon Beck offers the potential for some excellent walking, and is easily accessible, lying on the bus route from Barnard Castle up to Alston. A good place to base yourself would be Middleton-in-Teesdale or at the YHA hostel at Langdon Beck. From here the impressive waterfalls of High Force and Cauldron Snout are within striking distance. An excellent circular walk of 13 miles starts at Langdon Beck then goes over Wool Pits Hill and High Beck Head to cross the B6277 at Holwick Head Bridge. Then it heads west past High Force, over Cronkley Fell and on to Cauldon Snout. (An alternative route at this point would be to follow the Pennine Way along a lovely stretch of the River Tees between High Force and Cauldron Snout.) Here it bears north up to Cow Green and then east again along a minor road back to Langdon Beck.

The Teesdale Way is a recently completed LDP of 90 miles. Officially it starts at Middleton-in-Teesdale, but a good start to the route would be to follow the Pennine Way east from Dufton up to High Cup Nick and over to Maize Beck, which runs into the River Tees. Leaving the Pennine Way at Middleton, the Teesdale Way proper follows the Tees through Barnard Castle and east to finish at Teesmouth on the coast. The first half of the walk is particularly good and doesn't hit urban developments until it reaches Middlesbrough. The official *Teesdale Way Guide* is published by Cicerone Press.

The other major river valley in the North Pennines is Weardale, also lovely and less frequently visited than Teesdale. Upper Weardale offers more excellent walking, combining riverside paths, wild moorlands, and evidence of the area's industrial heritage with old mining sites and disused railways. It will come as no surprise to learn that another LDP, the Weardale Way, runs along this valley, from Allenheads to the North Sea coast. More information on this walk is available from Stanhope TIC (☎ 01388 527650).

The village of Dufton is another good base for walking, from where walks along the Pennine Way up to High Cup Nick and to Cross Fell are very worthwhile in their own right. You could also consider staying at Alston, a fascinating old market town, surrounded by moors which at one time were the site of a major lead-mining industry. Long since gone, the lead mines have left their mark on the moors, which having returned again to their former wild state would be worth exploring. Both Dufton and Alston are on the Pennine Way, with good accommodation choices. Useful TICs for this area include Alston (☎ 01434 381696), Barnard Castle (☎ 01833 690909) and Appleby-in-Westmoreland (☎ 017683 51177).

Books on the area include *Walking in the North Pennines* by Paddy Dillon (Cicerone, £6.99) and *Teesdale* by Paul Hannon (Hillside, £4.99). There's also a useful OS Outdoor Leisure (1:25,000) *North Pennines* map.

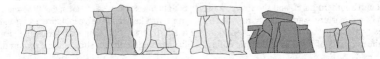

Southern England – Short Walks

Dartmoor

Dartmoor is a spectacular, if frequently gloomy, expanse of peat-covered moorland dotted with piles of granite rocks (called 'tors') looking for all the world like abstract sculptures or the remains of fantastical castles. Dartmoor is also covered by many genuine ancient remains, including prehistoric burial mounds, hut circles and boundary rows. In fact, Dartmoor has the largest concentration of Bronze Age remains in Britain. You can also see clapper bridges (made of slabs of rock) and medieval crosses (from the days when monks would walk over the moor between the various surrounding abbeys), while abandoned mines and dismantled tramways are reminders of the area's more recent, but now-forgotten, industrial days.

Despite being heavily populated many centuries ago, Dartmoor today is the emptiest, highest and wildest area in Southern England. In its remote parts you can be further from a road or village than anywhere in Britain outside Scotland. For keen walkers this is of course its attraction, but the high moor peat bogs and notoriously fickle weather patterns (with mist, rain, and even snow being common hazards) make some of the walking surprisingly challenging. There are few trees (and consequently little shelter) but gorse and heather grow in profusion. There is a great feeling of space and openness. For the less hardy, the lower fringes of Dartmoor, with homely villages and quiet country lanes, offer easier options.

Most of Dartmoor is contained within the 365-sq-mile Dartmoor National Park, and can be divided into the higher, wilder northern and southern parts, and the lower, more inhabited eastern part. The north-western area is the highest part of the moor (peaking at the summits of Yes Tor and High Willays

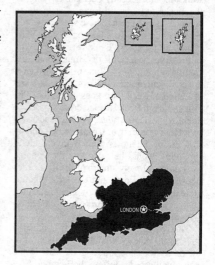

– the highest points in Southern England – both over 600m (2000 ft), although much of this is a military firing range and closed to the public at certain times. The south-western area is also quite high (mostly between 400m and 500m) with a particularly good collection of ancient remains, and no access problems.

The main jumping-off cities for Dartmoor are Exeter and Plymouth. From here by public transport you can easily reach any of the main 'border towns' around the moor itself – Tavistock, Okehampton or Buckfastleigh – which are good bases for local exploration, with plenty of accommodation options. Another possible base is Princetown, at the centre of the moor, which is also the site of the national park's main visitor centre.

The routes we describe in this section are both in this south-western area, easily reached from Buckfastleigh. We've included a long and a short route, but each has variations for further lengthening or shortening if required.

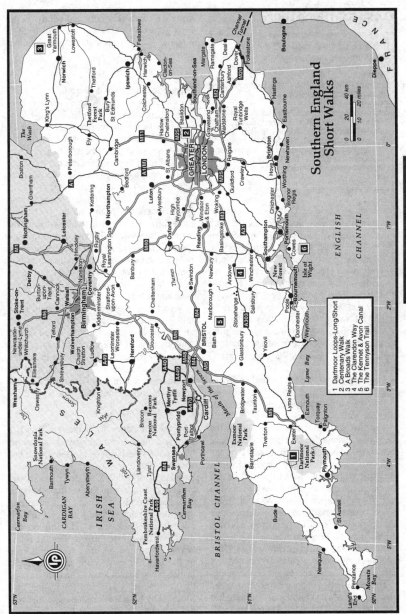

SOUTHERN ENGLAND

Southern England
Short Walks

1 Dartmoor Loops-Long/Short
2 Centenary Walk
3 A Broads Walk
4 The Clarendon Way
5 The Kennet & Avon Canal
6 The Tennyson Trail

A LONG DARTMOOR LOOP

Distance 14 miles (22.5 km)
Duration 7 to 8 hours
Start Ivybridge
Finish Buckfastleigh
Regional Centres Plymouth, Buckfastleigh, Newton Abbot, Exeter, Totnes
County Devon
Area Dartmoor National Park
Summary A long walk over high ground, past many of Dartmoor's ancient historical sites. One steep ascent, then mostly flat for much of the way, but routefinding on the featureless moor could be tricky in bad weather. Suitable gear, plus map and compass skills, are essential.

The wide expanse of Dartmoor is crossed and circled by a number of long-distance walking routes. These include the Two Moors Way which stretches from Ivybridge in South Devon to Lynmouth on the North Devon coast, traversing Dartmoor and Exmoor – a distance of 102 miles. To walk it all takes most people a week to 10 days. However, a very enjoyable day-walk can be had by following the first section of the Two Moors Way from Ivybridge and then looping back eastwards, along part of another long route called the Abbot's Way, to Buckfastleigh.

You can base yourself in either Buckfastleigh or Ivybridge, travelling between the two by public transport, either before or after the walk.

The first section of this walk follows the route of a dismantled tramway, which once transported china clay from a quarry on the high moor to a works near Ivybridge. Even in the worst visibility it's hard to get lost on this bit, but problems can arise when you need to turn off west along the Abbot's Way as the route is less defined and important landmarks are hard to spot in the mist. Consequently, this walk should only be done on a clear day unless you're confident with map and compass. If the weather changes unexpectedly you should turn back rather than risk getting lost on the moor.

There's a better chance of good weather from around May to September (although it can never be guaranteed on Dartmoor!) and,

since it's often very cold and windy on the high ground, it's unlikely you will want to embark on this walk outside peak summer months.

Direction, Distance & Duration

This linear route can be done in either direction. There's not much in it, but Ivybridge makes a better starting point, because the waymarking here ensures you can make a good start, so we describe it from here. Once you're out of Ivybridge and onto the moor proper, there are very few signs and you must rely on your own map and compass skills. With this in mind, you might prefer to start from Buckfastleigh and get the potentially more difficult bit done first, knowing that the disused tramway will hold few surprises. Your decision is most likely to be based on public transport timetables, rather than anything else, as you need to use the bus to get to the start of the walk, or get back to your base afterwards.

Whichever way you go, this walk is 14 miles. You ascend to around 425m from just about sea-level, so the route requires a walking time of seven to eight hours. Most reasonably fit people should be able to complete it in eight to 10 hours, allowing for lunch, map-reading and investigating the various historical sites along the way.

Shorter & Longer Alternatives This is a long and quite committing walk across the high moor, which can be challenging in bad weather. There are no short cuts. If you're based in Buckfastleigh, we describe a shorter circular option later in this section. If you're based in Ivybridge and want a short taste of the moor in relative safety, the best thing is an out-and-back walk, staying on the tramway. If you want to lengthen the route, beyond Huntingdon Cross you could keep on the Two Moors Way and return to Buckfastleigh via the hamlet of Scorriton. Beyond that, of course, you could follow the Two Moors Way for a week or longer all the way to Lynmouth.

Information

Ivybridge TIC (☎ 01752 897035) in Leonards Rd, can book accommodation for you. There are also village information points in the Holne Post Office, and The Fruit Basket in Buckfastleigh. There are also park information centres (PICs) at Newton Abbot (☎ 01626 67494); Okehampton (☎ 01837 53020); Postbridge (☎ 01822 890414); and Tavistock (☎ 01822 612938). The free *Dartmoor Visitor* newspaper contains lots of useful information and addresses.

> **Warning**
> Although the routes described in this section are well away from Army firing ranges, you should beware of unidentifiable metal objects lying in the gorse and bracken. If you do find anything suspicious, don't touch it. Make a note of the position and report it to the police after your walk.

Books & Maps TICs and PICs stock the Countryside Commission's introductory leaflet to the Two Moors Way which contains very basic maps and descriptions. If you wanted to continue along this route for a few more days, Helen Rowett's *Two Moors Way Official Guide* would be useful. If you can't find it, contact J Turner, Two Moors Way Committee, Coppins, The Poplars, Pinhoe, Exeter EX4 9HH, enclosing £2.70 plus 50p for postage and packing.

Cicerone Press publishes *The Two Moors Way – 100 Miles Across Dartmoor and Exmoor*, by James Roberts (£5.99) which also gives a brief description of the Abbot's Way connection to Buckfastleigh, and *Walking on Dartmoor* by John Earle (£6.99), which describes a wide selection of shorter routes, including several in the south-west area described here, with good background notes on the historical sites.

The Ordnance Survey (OS) Landranger 1:50,000 sheet 202 covers the southern part of Dartmoor including the routes in this section. For more detail, OS Outdoor Leisure (1:25,000) sheet 28 covers the whole of Dartmoor.

Guided Walks

The national park organises a series of guided walks throughout the year in all parts of Dartmoor. Details are listed in the *Dartmoor Visitor*.

Places to Stay & Eat

Buckfastleigh is an old market town near the Upper Dart Valley which used to be a centre for the manufacture of woollen cloth. Two miles north of Buckfastleigh is Buckfast Abbey, which was founded in 1016 and flourished until it was abandoned, after the Dissolution of the Monasteries, in 1539. In 1806 the ruins were levelled and a mock-Gothic mansion erected, which was bought by a group of exiled French Benedictine monks in 1882. The abbey church was built between 1906 and 1932.

Places to stay in Buckfastleigh include *Bridge House* (☎ 01364 642135) where B&B costs £12, and *Woodholme Guesthouse* (☎ 01364 643350, £16). You could also try *The Globe* (☎ 01364 642223) or *The Watermans Arms* (☎ 01364 643200), which both charge from £15. Smarter is the *Dartbridge Inn* (☎ 01364 642214), Totnes Rd, with B&B from £50 for an ensuite double. Campers can head for the pleasant site at *Churchill Farm* (☎ 01364 642844), at nearby Buckfast, charging £2.50. Most of the pubs in town do bar food, and you can get lunch or tea in the restaurant at Buckfast Abbey.

About 3½ miles north of Buckfastleigh is the village of Holne, which has several more options. B&Bs include *Church House Inn* (☎ 01364 631208), built in 1329 as a resting place for passing monks, and now offering good B&B for £25 per person in ensuite rooms. Evening meals are available and, with sufficient notice, the owner will collect you from the bus or railway station in Buckfastleigh. Another place is *Hazelwood* (☎ 01364 631235) where B&B is £15, and

SOUTHERN ENGLAND

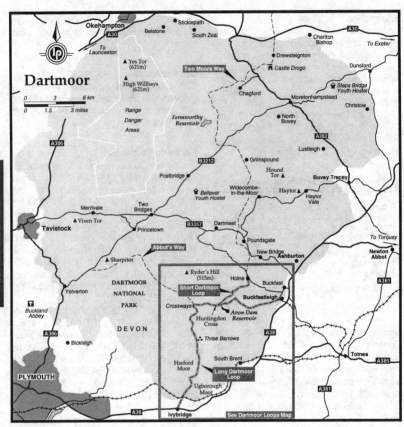

camping in the paddock costs £2. Another cheap choice is the camping barn at *Holne Court Farm* (☎ 01364 631271) charging £3.50 per person. You can also pitch a tent here for £2.

In Ivybridge, B&Bs include *The Toll House* (☎ 01752 893522), nonsmoking, in Exeter Rd for £13 per person, or £17 ensuite, and *Whiteoaks* (☎ 01752 892340) with a range of rooms between £13 and £25, plus evening meals and camping. *Strashleigh Farm* (☎ 01752 892226) also offers B&B.

There is nowhere to get food or drink along the actual walk, so take everything you need for the day.

Getting There & Away

Bus Exeter and Plymouth are both served by National Express coaches from London, Bristol and other parts of the country. A Stagecoach (☎ 01392 427711) express bus (No X39) runs four times per day in each direction between Exeter and Plymouth (less on Sunday). It stops in the centre of Buckfastleigh, but only on the main road about a mile outside Ivybridge (not in the centre itself). There's also a local service three times per day in each direction between Plymouth and Newton Abbot which stops in both Buckfastleigh and Ivybridge.

Train Ivybridge is on the main line between Exeter and Plymouth (which are both connected to London), although not all trains stop here: you may have to change at Exeter or Plymouth. The privately run South Devon Railway (☎ 01364 642336) links Buckfastleigh and Totnes (every 1½ hours, 25 minutes, £5.90 return) on a steam-operated branch line. The service operates daily from mid-May through September. Totnes is also on the main line between London and Plymouth.

Car Both Buckfastleigh and Ivybridge are on the A38 between Exeter and Plymouth, although you have to turn off the main road to reach the town centres.

Taxi From Buckfastleigh, C&M Cars (☎ 01364 43171 or ☎ 0860 565979) will transport you to Holne for £5 and to Ivybridge for £10.

The Route
Stage I: Ivybridge to Crossways
8 miles (13 km), 4 to 4½ hours

From the centre of Ivybridge, on the east side of the river, aim northwards, signposted to Harford, over the railway at Stowford Bridge. (If you've come by train, from Ivybridge Station follow the footpath heading west beside the south side of the railway line to meet Cole Lane, which you follow to reach Stowford Bridge.) The Two Moors Way crosses the bridge and continues for another 250m towards Stowford Farm (B&B available), where you follow the sign reading 'Bridlepath to the moor, ½ mile' uphill along a green lane between hedges. At the top, a gate leads onto the moor. A path then leads upwards between bracken, with views of the cairns on Butterdon and Weatherdon Hills ahead. Within half a mile of the gate you'll meet the old dismantled tramway crossing the path. Turn left (north); the route runs between Harford Moor and Ugborough Moor.

The tramway was constructed in 1910 to carry clay from the quarry at Redlake to a factory near Ivybridge. It was closed down in 1932, but now provides a firm footpath for the six miles. It takes a rather circuitous

route, contouring where possible, so there are some more direct short cuts but they don't save much time.

The tramway continues northwards, passing to the west of Hangershell Rock, then intersects a stones row (ancient boundary), which keeps roughly parallel to the tramway for the next few miles. You pass the Three Barrows, a cluster of huge burial mounds, to the right, then after about half a mile you reach Clay Bridge, with the Leftlake Mires to the right. This is the first relatively sheltered spot encountered – better than nothing in bad weather.

The Two Moors Way continues to follow the tramway, but you could divert briefly to the left (east) to inspect Dartmoor's longest stone row and assorted hut circles on Erme Plains.

The tramway then does a distinct S-curve and intersects with another tramway (running between Red Lake and Shipley Bridge) at a point called, naturally enough, Crossways. At this point you're also on the Abbot's Way, which is so-named as monks once used it to walk between the abbeys at Buckfast and Buckland, near Yelverton.

Stage 2: Crossways to Buckfastleigh
6 miles (10 km), 3 to 3½ hours

Turning east you follow the combined Two Moors Way and Abbot's Way until you're passing along the south bank of a stream called the River Avon. You cross the stream at Huntingdon Cross, a standing stone; it was used as a boundary marker in medieval times, but may have been in use earlier than this as a route marker for people crossing the moor. If the water is high, you can cross at the clapper bridge about 750m back upstream (the bridge is well worth a look anyway). North of here are the rounded slopes of Huntingdon Warren – once a rabbit farm, with the remains of artificial burrows (marked as 'pillow mounds' on the OS 1:25,000 map) built for the rabbits, and stone huts for the 'warreners' who looked after them.

From Huntingdon Cross, the path follows the north bank of the River Avon downstream, and then across the slopes above the Avon Dam Reservoir. To your left (north) are

SOUTHERN ENGLAND

SOUTHERN ENGLAND

several Bronze Age hut circles and other remains in good condition. The path crosses Brockhill Stream: make sure you keep heading east, steeply up the hillside opposite (there's no clear path on the ground). At the top, you cross a small featureless plateau called Dean Moor then drop to Water Oak Corner. This is the border with private farmland, and if you lost the exact path on the plateau you may have to follow the boundary fence until you meet a gate and well signposted continuation of the Abbot's Way. This leads to a small road junction at Cross Furzes, where you turn right (south-east) to follow the quiet lane down to Buckfastleigh.

(If you are staying at Scorriton or Holne, at Cross Furzes you should turn left and follow the lane northwards through Combe. Alternatively, to reach Holne from Huntingdon Cross it is quicker to stay on the Two Moors Way, via Hickaton Hill and Chalk Ford.)

A SHORT DARTMOOR LOOP

Distance 9 miles (14.5 km)
Duration 4 to 4½ hours
Start Holne
Finish Buckfastleigh
Regional Centres Plymouth, Buckfastleigh, Totnes
County Devon
Area Dartmoor National Park
Summary A shorter alternative to the Long Dartmoor Loop described above, although still passing some ancient historical sites and still reaching the high ground where routefinding can be tricky in bad weather. Suitable all-weather clothes and boots, a good map and a compass are musts.

This route starts in Holne and follows a section of the Two Moors Way through pleasant farmland then across a trackless part of the moor to Huntingdon Cross, an ancient route or boundary marker, which has several interesting sites nearby. It returns to Buckfastleigh along a section of the Abbot's Way. All these routes and places are described in more detail in the section above.

As described here, it's a V-shaped route, but you could easily turn it into a circular route (longer or shorter) by following the

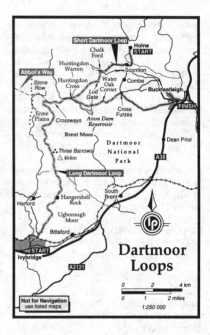

quiet country lanes between Buckfastleigh and Holne.

Direction, Distance & Duration

This route can be done in any direction. Which way you do it, and where you start, will depend on where you stay. The distance between Holne and Buckfastleigh, via Huntingdon Cross, is nine miles, which requires a minimum of four to 4½ hours walking, but with stops you should allow five to six. The direct distance between Holne and Buckfastleigh, along the lanes, is 3½ miles. This makes a total of 12½ miles for the complete circular walk.

Shorter Alternatives If you are staying in Buckfastleigh, there is no need to go to Holne to start this walk; you can pick it up at Scorriton, which cuts about 1¾ miles off the total. If you're staying at Holne, to finish there's no need to go to Buckfastleigh at all; when the Abbot's Way brings you down to Cross Furzes, head north for Holne through

Combe. The total for this shorter circle is 8½ miles.

All other details, such as Places to Stay, Information, Maps and Getting There & Away are covered in the section above.

The Route
Stage 1: Holne to Huntingdon Cross
4 miles (6.5 km), 2 to 2½ hours

From the centre of Holne, with the village hall on your left, head south and take the first left turn. After 100m, turn left again down a track marked 'Unsuitable for Motor Vehicles'. Meet a lane, then cross the river, keeping right to enter the village of Scorriton. In the village, turn right then almost immediately left up a lane which soon deteriorates into a track. About 20 minutes from Scorriton, you reach a fork. Keep left, before soon reaching an access point to the moor. Ignore this and follow signs to Chalk Ford, where a footbridge crosses the river.

From Chalk Ford, various paths go up the hillside. Aim south through the bracken. After about 20 minutes a low building in the trees to your left marks the access point at Lud Gate. From here you aim south-west over the trackless terrain of Hickaton Hill. We were caught in a storm on this bit and found it easier to follow the vague track which goes east towards Huntingdon Warren to meet a stream (Western Wella Brook) south to its confluence with the River Avon at Huntingdon Cross.

Stage 2: Huntingdon Cross to Buckfastleigh
5 miles (8 km), 2 hours

This route follows the latter part of Stage 2 of the Long Dartmoor Loop described in the section above.

Epping Forest

Epping Forest, on the northern edge of London, is a remnant of the royal forest which in the 12th century covered much of the county of Essex. In following years, as kings lost interest in hunting,

the forest diminished until by the 1850s little remained . The possible loss of a much used recreation area (allied to early stirrings of the environmental movement) caused the City of London to promote legislation in 1878 where they became owners ('conservators') of the forest, to keep it public and to preserve its natural aspect. Since then, the forest has remained popular, particularly with walkers as the area contains a network of paths and bridleways. It was to celebrate the hundredth anniversary of the Epping Forest Act that the Centenary Walk described here was devised in 1978.

The forest has a continuous biological history as woodland dating from the last Ice Age, but for more than 1000 years it has been managed to maximise firewood and timber production, to provide grazing for animals and to deliver hunting opportunities for the monarch. Beech, oak and hornbeam are the common trees of Epping Forest, many of which have been pollarded ('beheaded' at around three metres to produce a cluster of branches which can be later relopped for firewood). Pollarding mostly ceased in the last century but left a remarkable legacy of weirdly contorted trees which are seen throughout the route.

THE CENTENARY WALK

Distance 15 miles (24 km), with an optional extension on Essex Way of 8 miles (13 km)
Duration 5½ to 7½ hours (extension 3 to 4 hours)
Start Manor Park, East London
Finish Epping town (extension Chipping Ongar)
County Essex
Area Epping Forest
Summary A linear walk mostly on tracks, some of which can be muddy in rainy periods. Flat in the south becoming undulating in the north. Can be done by any reasonably fit walker. The extension from Epping to Chipping Ongar is on waymarked paths through farmed countryside and sizeable woodlands.

The Centenary Walk through Epping Forest offers good walking surprisingly close to the centre of London. The starting point at

SOUTHERN ENGLAND

SOUTHERN ENGLAND

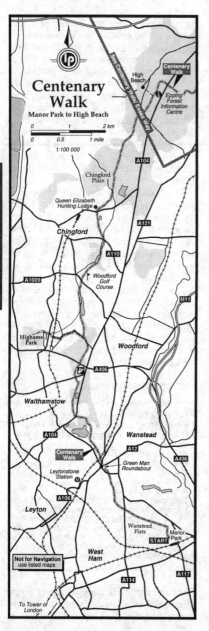

Manor Park is a mere five miles from St Pauls Cathedral, and the route goes through the suburbs of Leyton and Chingford, so the Forest is undeniably embedded in urban development in the south, but its fringes get much more rural further north. Some areas are heavily used on summer Sundays, so if you prefer a fairly solitary walk choose another day.

The one day route we describe here ends at Epping town. Beyond here the full Essex Way long-distance path (LDP) extends 81 miles to the North Sea port of Harwich, but our optional extension offers an opportunity to sample the quiet pleasures of the Essex countryside as far as the ancient market town of Chipping Ongar.

Direction, Distance & Duration

This linear walk can be done in either direction, but we recommend going south to north since it is more pleasing to head out of town into the countryside beyond. From Manor Park to Epping is 15 miles, which requires about five to six hours of walking. With stops for lunch, visiting places of interest and so on, you should allow seven to eight hours.

Shorter & Longer Alternatives There are no real short-cuts on this linear route but starts can be made at Leytonstone or Chingford which reduces the distance to 12 miles or seven miles respectively. A start at Chingford also puts Chipping Ongar within a comfortable day's walk of 15 miles if you want to avoid the southern, more urban, part of the route.

The whole route, from Manor Park to Chipping Ongar is 23 miles, and needs eight to 10 hours of walking (10 to 12 hours in total). In summer this could be done in one long day, but most walkers would probably prefer a two day route, overnighting in Epping.

Information & Guided Walks

The Epping Forest Information Centre (☎ 01815 080028) at High Beach has a wide range of information plus a bookshop and a permanent educational display. It runs an extensive programme of guided themed walks on forest topics.

Books A *Centenary Walk* booklet, published by the Epping Forest Conservators, and *The Essex Way* booklet published by Essex County Council (☎ 01245 492211) are available at the Information Centre and can be posted on request. When ordering, ask for an updated accommodation list. For more options *Short Walks in Epping Forest*, published privately by Fred Matthews, describes 24 routes. For background, try *Epping Forest Through the Ages*, published privately by Georgina Green, or the *Official Guide to Epping Forest* describing its history and management.

Maps The OS Landranger (1:50,000) coverage of Epping Forest spreads over sheets 167 and 177, but a special OS (1:25,000) edition covering the whole forest, and an inexpensive pictorial map of the Centenary Walk, is available from the Information Centre. Almost all of the Essex Way is covered by OS sheets 167 and 168 and for the last few miles into Harwich the map in the Essex Way booklet is sufficient.

Places to Stay & Eat

We have not listed accommodation in London (see one of the general guidebooks listed in the main Books section), but it is easy to return there from Epping by public transport after your walk. If you are doing the two day option, the charming *Epping Forest YHA Hostel* (☎ 0181 5085161, £6.75) at High Beach is well placed. In Epping, B&Bs include *Uplands Guesthouse* (☎ 01992 573733, £15), or the more expensive *Thatched House* (☎ 01992 578353) and *Post House Hotel* (☎ 01992 573137) at Bell Common. In Chipping Ongar the *King's Inn* does B&B for around £20.

There are many pubs along the route serving food, but not entirely of the bar food variety. Epping and Chipping Ongar also have restaurants as well as many more pubs.

Getting There & Away

Epping Forest's location and the linear nature of the Centenary Walk mean cars and buses are not much use, and train the easiest way to go. Both train and 'tube' (underground) services start early in the morning and end late in the evening, with several an hour, although with a reduced service on Sunday. Manor Park Station is reached from Liverpool St (from where you also get trains to Chingford). Tube trains on the Central Line go to Leytonstone and Epping (the terminus). If you finish at Chipping Ongar the No 201 bus goes a few times a day back to Epping (check the timetable there on your way out or phone ☎ 01277 215526 or ☎ 0345 000333).

The Route
Day 1, Stage 1: Manor Park to Green Man Roundabout

3 miles (5 km), 1 to 1½ hours

From Manor Park Station turn left along Forest Dve soon coming to a large grassy open space on the left called Wanstead Flats. Head diagonally across the grass aiming towards twin high-rise buildings in the distance. After a mile, cross a road and continue towards the left edge of houses on the far side of another road which you also cross. Go along a track with grassland on your left. Turn half right ahead through woodland and then left and right around a brick wall to reach a busy main road and Green Man Roundabout (named after a nearby pub). (The walk could be joined here from nearby Leytonstone (tube) Station.)

Stage 2: Green Man Roundabout to Queen Elizabeth Hunting Lodge

5 miles (8 km), 2 to 2½ hours

On the opposite side of the roundabout is Leyton Flats – another largely grassland area. Head across this, through a belt of trees, past Hollow Pond, and straight ahead through woodland to a road which you cross. Pass a pond and attractive houses to the right to enter a road called College Place. At its end go leftish through the Forest, crossing a road to reach the *Rising Sun Pub*, entering woodland with Bullrush Pond on the right. Turn right and along a white posted track (marking forest horse rides). A narrow path on your left leads up a grassy bank to cross a footbridge over a road, from which there are panoramic views over the city and suburbs of London.

Fork left, following posts through a subway under the North Circular Rd into Walthamstow Forest. The track leads through the woods past an area where in 1992 the Epping Forest Conservators repollarded trees as an experiment. For perhaps a thousand years much of the Forest would have looked like this.

Cross a road and continue with a high-rise building on the left. Keep left going downhill and then over a road to the right side of Highams Park Lake. At its end go uphill through trees to pick up a grassy track leading onto and over a road to Woodford Golf Course. Continue on the track, later with a fairway on the right. Go uphill and through trees along a wide grassy strip. Cross a road to Whitehall Plain and continue alongside the little River Ching, turning left over a bridge. Go uphill on a grassy posted track to the left of Warren Pond. To the left is the *Royal Forest* pub and on the right is *Butlers Retreat*; both provide refreshments. In between is the distinctive Queen Elizabeth Hunting Lodge.

Stage 3: Queen Elizabeth Hunting Lodge to High Beach
3 miles (5 km), 1 to 1½ hours

(The route can be joined here, from nearby Chingford Station.) From the Hunting Lodge go towards a fountain behind Butlers Retreat and turn right (with a pond on the right) and down a wide grassy posted track leading down to the right of Chingford Plain. Cross a ditch and turn left along a wide surfaced track through woods and over a junction of tracks. Continue uphill round an overgrown pond on the right and on through forest for 1½ miles. Follow the track out to a large grassy area called Fairmead Bottom, then left uphill. The track winds through beech-woods, crosses a small road and becomes Up and Down Ride, for obvious reasons!

Take a left fork after about 800m and then left again down a hard track to reach Epping Forest Information Centre at High Beach, where Queen Victoria dedicated the Forest to the people in 1882. Years later, the dedication remains unforgotten and this area is busy and noisy at weekends. The *King's Oak* pub and green *tea hut* are nearby: try the slab cake in the latter!

Stage 4: High Beach to Epping Station
4 miles (6.5 km), 1½ to 2 hours

Leave the Centre, retracing your steps on the hard track and then left at the fork. Cross the main road to a car park and continue ahead on a surfaced track, which after 500m joins another main track where you turn left. This is Green Ride, cut through the forest in 1880 so the Queen could go on a commemorative carriage ride after her dedication visit. There is some doubt about whether she ever made the journey, but the route has benefited later users. For the next 2½ miles follow the Green Ride through varied woodland and across two roads

After the second road and 200m beyond another track coming in from the left, it is worth a short detour slanting left into the woodland to the impressive Ambresbury Banks earthworks – an Iron Age defensive

---

Queen Elizabeth Hunting Lodge
The Queen Elizabeth Hunting Lodge, despite its name, dates from Henry VIII's time (mid-16th century). It is open to visitors on afternoons from Wednesday to Sunday. Tradition says that Henry waited here to hear the cannon signalling that Ann Boleyn had been beheaded at the Tower of London. And then went hunting! ■

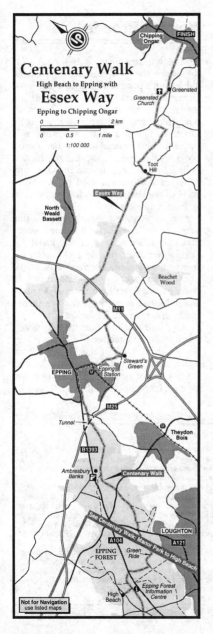

Centenary Walk

High Beach to Epping with

Essex Way

Epping to Chipping Ongar

0   1   2 km
0   0.5   1 mile

1:100 000

Not for Navigation
use listed maps

structure dating from around 500 BC. According to local legend, a British uprising led by Queen Boudicca was put down here by the Romans in 60 AD.

Eventually the track arrives at a grassy area with a cricket pitch to the left. (In the 1970s the Forest here was threatened with the construction of the M25 motorway and access roads. Major environmental battles were fought to prevent the Forest being severed and as a result the motorway is in a tunnel a couple of metres beneath your feet.) Go past the cricket pavilion to a gravel track and turn right on a footpath with a pond on the left. Follow this over a road (the excellent *Forest Gate* pub is to the right) and continue over Bell Common – a narrow strip of scrub, grass and trees between a main road to the left and houses to the right.

At the end of the Common follow Hemnall St (past a little house, which may be visited, where Lucien, the son of Camille Pissarro the French impressionist painter, lived for many years) eventually out to Station Rd, then right to Epping Station.

Day 2, Stage 1: Epping Station to Toot Hill
5 miles (8 km), 2 to 2½ hours

If you are continuing along the first section of the Essex Way, take the footbridge over the railway and then a path past Bower Crt soon leading across fields. On reaching houses, Steward's Green Lane (in medieval times part of the main road between London and East Anglia) leads in about half a mile to the *Theydon Oak* pub. A little beyond the pub turn left on a gradually rising path, the attractions of which are not entirely spoilt by the M11 motorway over to the right. Ahead there lies around two miles of interesting ancient woodland. You also cross the motorway (fortunately a bridge is provided).

Look out for the ditch and banks marking the boundary of Ongar Great Park, the first recorded deer park in England, mentioned in early 11th-century documents. Most of the way to Toot Hill – the name means lookout post – the marked path goes over the grounds of this ancient park. The *Green Man* pub (like its namesake in Stage 1 on Day 1, named after the ancient legendary spirit of the woods) in Toot Hill is OK for a drink and snack but full meals can be pricey.

Stage 2: Toot Hill to Chipping Ongar
3 miles (5 km), 1 to 1½ hours

Just past the end of the village a footpath leads across fields alongside a hedge. At a left turn by Widows Farm a right of way goes straight ahead to the isolated but welcoming *Drill House* pub, with reasonably priced meals. The main path goes across a lane and first by a wood and then hedged fields to Greensted Church, a remarkable survivor from the 10th century or earlier and possibly the oldest wooden church in the world. Behind the church a fine descending path known as the Avenue – a double row of stately elm trees failed to survive Dutch Elm Disease in the 1970s but replanting has been done – goes directly to the heart of Chipping Ongar. This small town has a range of interesting features, including an 11th-century church and castle and some attractive old houses. The return bus to Epping leaves from where the Essex Way meets the main road near Budworth Hall. Instead of standing at the bus stop, you could have a celebratory drink at the *Cock Tavern* or the nearby *King's Inn*.

Norfolk Broads

Norfolk is a large county in East Anglia, off the beaten track for most foreign visitors, although it's popular with holidaying Brits. Between Norwich (the county capital) and the coast lie the Broads, a vast network of navigable rivers and lakes surrounded by farmland. This area is not renowned as a major walking destination: it is flat, there's not a mountain in sight, and the highest point, How Hill near Barton Broad, is only about 12m above sea level (ASL). Some parts of the Broads are so low that they're actually below sea level.

Many more people come here for boating than for walking. Official figures record about 11 million visitors per year, and if you come to Wroxham (the Broads' 'capital') in high summer it seems like they've all arrived at the same time. On a popular stretch of water like the River Bure, there are so many motor boats cruising up and down there's hardly enough room for the ducks.

But if you step back from the busy waterways you'll find another world where very few visitors go, with fields, woods, dykes, water meadows and salt marshes, and the many kinds of birds, butterflies and water-loving plants that inhabit them. There are

SOUTHERN ENGLAND

Broads Nomenclature & Origin
In this area *broads* are open stretches of water; either separate lakes or ponds, or places where the rivers simply widen out. Drainage ditches, originally dug to turn marshes into agricultural land, are called *dykes* or *dikes*. These empty into larger waterways called *fleets*. Larger canals (for boats) are called *cuts*, and the place where boats tie up is called a *staithe*.

For many years the origin of the Norfolk Broads was unclear. The rivers were undoubtedly natural and many people thought the lakes were too – it's hard to believe they're not when you see them – but no-one could explain how they could have been formed. The mystery was solved when records were discovered in the remains of St Benet's Abbey (on the River Bure). They showed that from the 12th century, certain parts of land in Hoveton Parish were used for peat digging. The area had little woodland and the only source of fuel was peat. Since East Anglia was well populated and prosperous, peat digging became a major industry.

Over a period of about 200 years, approximately 2600 acres (1040 hectares) were dug up – leaving big holes. However, water gradually seeped through, causing marshes, and later lakes, to develop. The first broad to be mentioned in records is Ranworth Broad (in 1275). Eventually, the amount of water made it extremely difficult for the diggers, and the peat-cutting industry died out. In no other area of Britain has human effort changed the natural landscape so dramatically. ■

picturesque villages, with thatched cottages, ancient churches and comfortable pubs, and everywhere you look there are windmills (actually, most of them are *wind pumps*) – some ruined, but others in marvellous condition, standing proud above the surrounding marsh and flatlands. And of course, as in any ancient rural area, there's a network of tracks and footpaths which make for some wonderful walking.

Thus the Broads is not a place for peak-baggers, or for hardy hill-walkers looking for airy lookouts and combat with the elements. Rather it should be walked through slowly and savoured.

There are a many short walking routes and several LDPs in Norfolk (see Long Walks in Norfolk at the end of this section), and the day-walk we describe here follows part of one of them: the Weavers Way, taking in several Broads highlights, with their accompanying crowds, and also discovers several quieter spots, where your only companions will be cows, birds or great crested newts.

A BROADS WALK

Distance 16 miles (26 km)
Duration 6 to 8 hours
Start Great Yarmouth
Finish Potter Heigham
Regional Centres Norwich, Great Yarmouth
County Norfolk
Area Broads Special Area
Summary A nonstrenuous walk on clear paths and easy ground alongside rivers and through farmland, with several points of interest, and options for short cuts, along the way.

This walk mostly follows a section (a thread?) of the Weavers Way, and is an ideal introduction to Broads walking, showing many varied aspects of the area. It goes from Great Yarmouth (usually shortened to Yarmouth) – which manages to be a busy

Broads Conservation

The marshes such as Halvergate Marshes are areas of wetland, which over the years have been extensively affected by humans. Local people needed grazing lands for their animals, and drained large areas of marshland by creating an intricate system of dykes. Windpumps were then built, moving water along the dykes and into the rivers; drying out the land sufficiently for grazing animals. With the advent of steam and then electric pumps it became possible to dry the land so efficiently that it could be much more profitably used for arable farming.

With the drying of the land and ever-decreasing water levels in the dykes, rare plants such as the Water Soldier, and the seemingly endless varieties of butterflies and dragonflies started to disappear. Realisation of the grave threat to this very special wildlife habitat finally dawned, and in 1986 the Broads became Britain's first Environmentally Sensitive Area (ESA). This is a voluntary scheme which encourages farmers to restore and keep their grazing marshes, in return for Government grants for each acre of land farmed traditionally. Halvergate Marshes are an excellent example of the results of this scheme which has been so successful in combining the needs of the farmers with the conservation of wildlife.

Surrounding some of the broads and the rivers are wet grassland areas known as 'fens', which consist principally of reed and sedge. In the past, the reed and sedge were used for thatching roofs and regular cutting of them for this purpose kept the fens in good condition. In recent times, however, thatched roofs have become less popular – owing mainly to their expense and their tendency to burn down! As a result, the fens were neglected and seedlings were allowed to grow into bushes and trees. Trees tend to dry out the land and also shade out small plants, altering the habitat to such an extent that it discourages the survival of birds, butterflies and dragonflies that rely on the wet marshy conditions. Conservation programmes now operate to keep areas of the fens cut and so encourage the survival of such birds as the marsh harrier and the bittern, as well as the swallowtail butterfly, the Norfolk Hawker dragonfly and the Fen Orchid.

If you want to learn more, The Broads Authority (☎ 1603 610734), Thomas Harvey House, 18 Colegate, Norwich NR3 1BQ, can supply information about the conservation centres and RSPB bird-watching hides at Berney Marshes, Ranworth, Bure Marshes, and various other sites around the Broads. ∎

commercial port, boating centre and seaside resort all at the same time – along Breydon Water, the largest of the broads and an important nature reserve, through the pretty villages of Halvergate and Thurne, past splendid windmills, including the seven-storey giant at Berney Arms, and over the famous bridges at Acle (pronounce Ay-cle) and Potter Heigham.

The Broads Special Area is effectively a national park, although relatively low-key with little in the way of visitor centres and other facilities once you get away from the water-ways themselves. There's a laudable policy here encouraging walkers to explore with only a little help, and thus discover things for themselves. Within the area are several smaller zones, designated SSSI or ESA (see glossary), where endangered plants or animals get special protection. Don't rush this walk, a lot of the interest is at your feet or just nearby, but it takes a bit of spotting.

Direction, Distance & Duration

This linear walk can be done in either direction. We recommend starting in Great Yarmouth and ending at Potter Heigham, because the city skyline is better behind you than in front. If you stay the night at Yarmouth you can get back there quite easily from Potter Heigham. Or, if you stay in Potter Heigham, it's even easier to get into Yarmouth in the morning. For most of the route you can follow the Weavers Way waymarks, but there are many signposts and yellow circular markers in the area which show other paths. The route is 16 miles and nonstop you could do it in six hours or less, but allowing extra for lunch and photos,

bird-spotting or for visiting windmills, you'll probably need about eight to nine hours.

Shorter & Longer Alternatives

If you spend more time spotting than walking, the route can be finished at Acle instead of Potter Heigham, reducing the distance to about 10 miles. You can then get back to Yarmouth or Potter Heigham by bus. Another way to shorten the route is to take the train from Yarmouth to the station at Berney Arms. From here to Potter Heigham is 11½ miles. An even shorter option is to go from Berney Arms to Acle which is 5½ miles.

If you want to see more of the Broads, and you've got time, you can continue along the Weavers Way for another day or two (see the Books section). Transport back to Yarmouth is straightforward from several points along the route.

Information

Yarmouth's main TIC (☎ 01493 846345) is in the town hall, not far from the railway station, with useful leaflets plus walking guidebooks and maps. There's another TIC (☎ 01493 842195) near Britannia Pier on the seafront (summer only). The Broads Authority headquarters is in Norwich (☎ 01603 610734). In Yarmouth there's an information centre (☎ 01493 332095) open late July to September, in the North West Tower near the River Bure road bridge. Local events, places to stay and hire boats are listed in *The Broadcaster*, a free tourist paper. For specifics on the Weavers Way contact Norfolk County Council Country-side Unit (☎ 01603 222774).

Norfolk Local Architecture

The distinctive architectural character of the region was determined by the lack of suitable building stone. Stone was occasionally imported for important buildings, but for humble churches and houses three local materials were used: flint, clay bricks and oak. Flint can be chipped into a useable shape, but a single stone is rarely larger than a fist; it is used in combination with dressed stone or bricks to form decorative patterns. ∎

Books As this walk follows part of the Weavers Way, you might like to get a copy of the *Peddars Way, Norfolk Coast Path & Weavers Way* leaflet produced by the Peddars Way Association (see the Peddars Way section of this book), a brief guide to these routes, with transport and accommodation details.

Other guidebooks covering walks in this area include *Pub Walks in Norfolk* by Liz Moynihan (Countryside, £4.95) and the *Pathfinder Guide to Norfolk & Suffolk Walks*, published by OS & Jarrold, with the usual good selection of walks and maps. The Broads Authority publishes a nice set of route cards, called *Broad Walks in the Bure Valley* describing several short circular routes in the area. Some of these overlap the route described here and give a lot of extra background information.

Maps The Broads and the southern half of the Weavers Way are covered by OS Landranger (1:50,000) sheet 134, which is adequate for this route, as landscape features are not too complex. A series of local Footpath Maps, researched, written and drawn by Wilfred George, are available for the bargain price of £1 from local TICs; *Caister & Acle* shows the route from Yarmouth to Oby, plus other paths and tracks in the area. If you're combining walking and boating *The Broads* map by GeoProjects (£3.75) shows all navigable areas in great detail and has some walking routes marked also.

Places to Stay & Eat

Yarmouth is one of Britain's most popular seaside resorts, so along with all the tacky trimmings such as amusement arcades and giftshops, are many places to stay and eat. The *YHA Hostel* (☎ 01493 843991, £8.25) is near the beach, three-quarters of a mile from the railway station. Campers are probably better off at Potter Heigham, as the sites around Yarmouth are generally large caravan parks or holiday resorts, not for passing backpackers. For B&B there's a huge choice, although spaces fill quickly at the height of

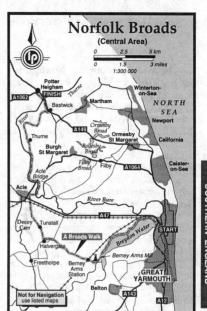

summer, so it's easiest to visit or phone the TIC (number below) for suggestions.

Unless you like busy seaside resorts, however, we'd recommend Potter Heigham. This place has two 'centres': the Village, which straddles the main A149 road between Cromer and Yarmouth; and the Old Bridge. (The A149 bypasses to the east, crossing the river on, you've guessed it, the New Bridge.) At the Old Bridge is the boatyard, supermarket, fish & chips shop, a pub, several cafes and stores, and even an amusement hall in case the natural scenery bores you. Between the Old Bridge and the Village is *Causeway Cottage* (☎ 01692 670238), where pitches (ie a tent, car and up to four people) are £8 and there's also B&B for £15. Smaller and friendlier is *White House Campsite* (☎ 01692 670403) south of the Old Bridge, near the village of Bastwick, where a pitch is £6. The comfortable *Falgate Inn* (☎ 01692 670003), about half a mile north of the Old Bridge, has B&B for £17 per person (£21 ensuite), with lunches and evening meals from £4.

Getting There & Away

Bus Norwich (pronounced 'Norridge') is easily reached by National Express coach from all parts of the country. An hourly Eastern Counties (☎ 01603 622800) service runs between Norwich and Yarmouth, and there are several other operators on this route.

Eastern Counties and Neaves (☎ 01692 580383) jointly run services about every two hours (except Sunday) in each direction between Potter Heigham and Yarmouth via Ormsby or Winterton and Caister. From Potter Heigham, the handiest service for walkers is Neaves' morning 'shoppers special' which goes to the Asda supermarket in Yarmouth where the route begins.

There are about six buses per day (except Sunday) between Acle and Yarmouth. The last one departs Acle about 5.30 pm. (There's no direct bus from Acle to Potter Heigham – you have to go via Yarmouth.)

For more details, phone the Norfolk County Public Transport information line (☎ 01603 613613).

Train Norwich has services to/from all parts of the country, with hourly trains to/from Yarmouth.

If you plan to shorten the route by taking the train from Yarmouth to Berney Arms, there are two trains per day (more on Sunday), but tell the conductor you want to get off here before the train leaves Yarmouth.

Car Yarmouth is reached by the A47 from King's Lynn and Norwich, the A12 from Lowerstoft, or the A149 from Cromer. Potter Heigham is on the A149 between Cromer and Yarmouth.

The Route
The Start: Great Yarmouth

The route starts at Vauxhall Bridge, on the western side of Yarmouth city centre, near the railway station and the giant Asda supermarket. This is a disused railway bridge

(from the days when the trains used to run right into the dock area), but now it's for pedestrians only. A signpost indicates that this point is the junction of the Weavers Way and the Angles Way, and there's an information board about the routes.

Stage 1: Great Yarmouth to Berney Arms

4½ miles (7 km), 1½ to 2 hours

Keeping the river to your left, follow an embankment round the edge of the car park, under the swingbridge to immediately reach the banks and salt marshes of Breydon Water. The path follows a narrow strip of land between the water and the railway line, then a seawall separating Breydon Water from the fields and marshes on the right (north) side. To your left, boats of all sizes stream up and down the centre of the Water, but little disturbs the tidal mudflats at the Water's edge, so this is a good area for wading birds.

Where the route passes close to the railway again, keep close to Breydon Water. Ahead the large Berney Arms windmill is a clear landmark. To your right, this area of flat lands is called Halvergate Marshes. At Berney Arms, Breydon Water narrows to become the River Yare. The windmill (an EH property, open to the public) is one of the largest remaining in Norfolk. It is in excellent condition, with an interesting display and great views from the seventh floor 'balcony'.

The *Berney Arms* pub is nearby. It opens at 11 am, so you might be just in time for morning coffee or a prelunch aperitif. The next-door shop sells drinks and snacks.

Stage 2: Berney Arms to Acle Bridge

5½ miles (9 km), 2 to 3 hours

From the windmill the route leaves the river aiming north-west, and over the railway near the tiny Berney Arms Station. On OS maps, the Weavers Way goes between Manor Farm and Halvergate village, but the waymarks lead you across fields, over stiles and several small bridges, passing south of Manor Farm Windmill, to meet the farm track which leads to the lane between Halvergate and Stracey Arms. A mischievous farmer has painted arrows, pointing in every direction, on just about every gatepost. Ignore these, follow only the Weavers Way signs and keep an eye on the map.

Aim west through Halvergate village, past several traditional houses and the *Red Lion* pub (a lunch possibility), and then right into Squires Lane. This becomes a gravel track, which you follow straight on through fields to Tunstall, over one of the highest points on the route so far – a dizzying 15m ASL – but with very good views over the marshes to the east. In Tunstall turn left and pass the old church on your right. Don't follow the concrete farm track, but head northwards on the footpath across the field to meet the lane. Keep on this, passing Staithe Farm to your left, to reach a small junction where a track leads off left (west) towards Acle.

This is now one of the Broads Walks (described in the Books section above: look for the blue waymarks), a very pleasant stretch of the route, through lush fields, along the edge of Decoy Carr woodland, and past old dykes where reeds and lilies grow, and (in the summer) butterflies and dragonflies energetically do their stuff.

This idyll is suddenly truncated by the railway and the main A47, both of which you cross (with care) to reach Acle Cut boatyard. Go along the north side of the cut to meet the River Bure (pronounce Byure). Turn left (north) and follow the towpath to reach Acle Bridge.

About a thousand years ago this was the lowest fording point on the Bure, before it spread out into a marshy estuary that ran all the way to Yarmouth. The marsh was progressively drained from 1100 AD, and a series of bridges were built over the following centuries. The current model (high enough for pleasure craft to pass) dates from the 1950s, but a new one is due some time before 2000. Nearby are a couple of shops and the vast and busy *Bridge Inn*, catering almost exclusively for the boat trade, with drinks at holiday prices and a not unreasonable range of bar food.

If you end here, buses go to Yarmouth and Potter Heigham. If you miss the bus, you could consider a taxi from Acle Private Hire (☎ 01493 750455) or try hitching on a boat.

Stage 3: Acle Bridge to Potter Heigham Old Bridge
6 miles (10 km), 2½ to 3 hours

Cross to the north side of Acle Bridge, then head west along the towpath keeping the river to your left. Few people walk this way, so in high summer it may be overgrown. About 45 minutes from Acle you reach Oby Cut. At the end of the cut, go through the car park and up the track towards Manor Farm, turning left down another track about 50m from the car park. (The signpost is hard to see.) Pass through the yard of another farm, then across fields, following signs, to reach a track just east of Boundary House. Go left onto the track, then (just before the gates into Boundary House) right onto a path that leads you to Thurne Church.

As with so many Broads villages, the church was built on high ground – an island in what would have been a 'sea' of marsh and river. Although only nine metres ASL, these are the best views on the route: west across the bend in the Bure, and across the broads and woodland around Horning, to the town of Wroxham in the distance; south and east back towards Acle and the Halvergate Marshes, with Yarmouth still visible on the horizon.

Facing the church, go left, round the corner, into Thurne village 'centre', at the eastern end of Thurne Cut (full of boats). There's a *pub* and shop here and the classic white Thurne Mill, a frequent feature in Broads promo material.

The path alongside this river can now be followed back to Potter Heigham Old Bridge, but a more pleasing route is available: from Thurne centre go north along the lane for 500m to reach a T-junction, where you go right (east), past a couple of cottages and through a lovely stretch of woodland, to cross Shallam Dike, then north across a large field to reach the edge of Repps village, from where another path leads through fields to Bastwick. Turn left here to meet the main A149. Turn left again, passing White House campsite on your right, then branch off the

Further Travels in the Broads

Having seen the Broads 'land-side' you may want to take to the waters. Most boats you see have motors rather than sails, and most people in them are not well-to-do yachty types, but normal hoi poloi, cruising up and down, using the boat like a movable beach, with radios on and most clothing off whenever there's a glimpse of sun. If you want to join the fun, boating holiday companies include Blakes (☎ 01603 782911) and Hoseasons (☎ 01502 501010). Costs depend on the boat size, the facilities, the time of the year and the length of the holiday. A boat for two to four people is about £400 for a week – fuel is extra, though you're unlikely to use much. Short breaks (three to four days) during the off season are much cheaper. Many boatyards (particularly in Wroxham and Potter Heigham) have a variety of boats for hire by the hour, half day or full day. Charges still vary according to the season and the size of the boat, but they start from £8 for one hour, £24 for four hours and £40 for a day. No previous experience is necessary, but remember to stay on the right side of the river and to stick to the speed limit – you can get prosecuted for speeding. If you don't feel like piloting your own boat, Broads Tours (☎ 1692 670711) runs pleasure trips from Potter Heigham with a commentary, from April to September, from £5 per person. ∎

main road to reach Potter Heigham Old Bridge.

LONG WALKS IN NORFOLK

Elsewhere in this book we describe the Peddars Way & Norfolk Coast Path which starts in Knettishall Heath, near Thetford and passes far to the west and north of the Broads, ending at the coastal resort town of Cromer. From Cromer, the Weavers Way LDP runs inland through the heart of north-east Norfolk, to end (or start) at Great Yarmouth, where the Broads meet the sea. (The day-walk in the section above follows a section of the Weavers Way, between Yarmouth and Potter Heigham.) Also at Great Yarmouth, another LDP called the Angles Way runs through the southern Broads, linking Yarmouth with Knettishall Heath – the start of the Peddars Way – thus completing a huge circular route around the county.

The whole Round-Norfolk route measures 230 miles and could be done between two and three weeks. More information is available in the *Peddars Way, Norfolk Coast Path & Weavers Way* leaflet produced by the Peddars Way Association (see the Peddars Way section of this book). There's also a booklet on *The Angles Way* produced by the Ramblers' Association, £1.20. *Langton's Guide to the Weavers Way & Angles Way*, and another on *The Peddars Way & Norfolk Coast Path* are more detailed, but more expensive, alternatives.

Alternatively, the seriously historically motivated could continue heading west from Knettishall along the Icknield Way to Ivinghoe then follow the ancient tracks of the Ridgeway Path to Avebury Stone Circle in Wiltshire, taking in some fascinating sites of English history along the way. More details in the Ridgeway and Other Walks in Wessex sections.

Wessex

There's officially no such place as Wessex. In the 9th century it was one of several ancient British kingdoms, ruled by King Alfred the Great from his capital at Winchester. (The name is a derivation of 'west', hence also Essex, Sussex and Middlesex – although no Nossex). Today, Wessex is generally regarded as the counties of Dorset, Hampshire and Wiltshire, with just a dash of Somerset thrown in for good measure. The Wessex name was resurrected and immortalised by the writer Thomas Hardy (1840-1928) who based his pastoral novels, including *Tess of the Durbervilles* and *Far from the Madding Crowd*, in this part of Britain.

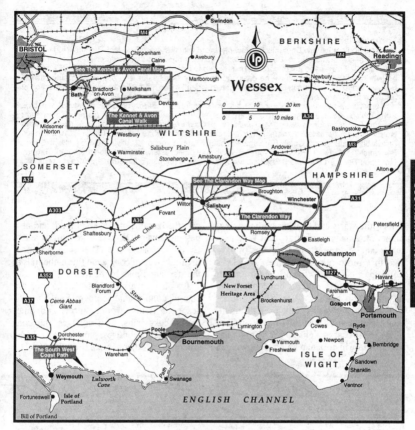

Wessex is still a rural region and, although real wilderness areas are limited, there are many opportunities for walking. Most routes are easy to reach, usually straightforward, often spectacular without being overbearing, and can be walked at any time of year. For walkers, notable features of Wessex include its coastline, followed by the South West Coast Path LDP, and the 'walker-friendly' Isle of Wight. In this section we include as samples: the Clarendon Way, linking Winchester (Alfred's capital) and Salisbury; and a fascinating taste of Britain's early industrial heritage along the Kennet & Avon Canal.

THE CLARENDON WAY

Distance 27 miles (43.5 km)
Duration 9 to 11 hours (over one or two days)
Start Salisbury
Finish Winchester
Regional Centres Salisbury, Winchester, Southampton
Counties Wiltshire, Hampshire
Area Wessex
Summary An easy walk, mostly on good paths and tracks, through woods, farmland and villages, and over some downs.

SOUTHERN ENGLAND

Thomas Hardy

Wessex, and particularly Dorset, is inextricably linked with the life and work of Thomas Hardy, one of Britain's best-known authors. Born in 1840, he started work at an architect's office in Dorchester in 1856. In 1862 he moved to London, but he returned to Dorset in 1867 for health reasons. From 1885 he lived in Max Gate, the house he designed himself in Dorchester. You can visit his birthplace at Higher Bockhampton, and in Dorchester, where he spent much of his life, there's a reconstruction of his study in the museum.

Dorset was the setting for most of his work, recreated as the fictional county of Wessex. Although some place names were unaltered, many others were renamed; for example, Dorchester became Casterbridge (a setting for *The Mayor of Casterbridge*). Other real place names and their Hardy versions include Bournemouth (Sandbourne), Cerne Abbas (Abbot's Cernel), Chesil Beach (the Pebble Bank), Corfe Castle (Corvsgate Castle), Exeter (Exonbury), Lulworth Cove (Lulwind Cove), Penzance (Penzephyr), Poole (Havenpool), Salisbury (Melchester), Taunton (Toneborough), Torquay (Tor-upon-Sea), Truro (Trufal), Shaftesbury (Shaston), Weymouth (Budmouth) and Yeovil (Ivell). ■

This route starts and finishes at the ancient cathedral cities of Salisbury and Winchester. It can be done in one long day, or over two in a more relaxed manner. Access is good, particularly to/from London, and it makes an ideal weekend break from the city.

The route derives its name from the medieval Clarendon Palace; the ruins are passed a few miles east of Salisbury. The route has several more historical features, following in part the remains of a Roman road, and also passing several Bronze Age tumuli and a Civil War battle site. The main historical highlights are of course the fine cathedrals at the start and finish of the route.

It's also a walk through Britain today; a classic, comfortable southern-English landscape of fields, woods, farms and quiet rivers, cosy pubs, neat cottages and converted manor houses, and narrow lanes where every other car is a flash new 4WD.

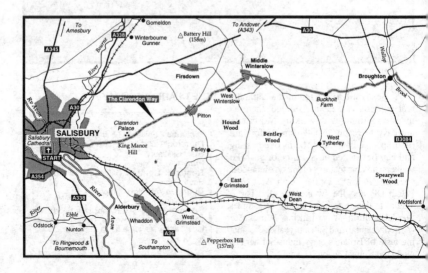

Direction, Distance & Duration

The walk can be made in either direction. East to west gives better views of Salisbury as you approach the city, but west to east may be more comfortable weather-wise, so that's how we describe it here. (You can always turn round and look back at Salisbury now and again.)

The 27 miles requires between nine and 11 hours walking time. This can be a push to cover in one day, particularly if you make any sightseeing pauses or excursions. Most walkers may prefer to stretch it out over two.

Waymarking is reasonable, but no substitute for a map. The route's symbol is a bishop's mitre (hat).

Shorter Alternatives There are no short cuts on this linear walk, but the mileage can be reduced by doing just one part of the route, starting or ending at Stockbridge, near King's Somborne – the halfway point.

Information

There are large and efficient TICs at both ends of the walk: Salisbury's (☎ 01722 334956) is behind the Guildhall; Winchester's (☎ 01962 840500) is on Broadway. Both have com-

prehensive *Where to Stay* lists and will make free bookings.

Books & Maps *Walks in Wessex: The Test Way & The Clarendon Way* is a Hampshire County Council publication by Barry Shurlock. It describes the way in detail, with extracts from the relevant OS maps and covers accommodation and food possibilities. OS Landranger (1:50,000) sheets 184 and 185 cover the route.

Places to Stay & Eat

Salisbury's *YHA Hostel* (☎ 01722 327572, £9.10) is an attractive, old building in two acres of garden, an easy 15 minute walk from the centre. *Ron & Jenny Coats* (☎ 01722 327443), at 51 Salt Lane, close to the bus station, is an independent hostel where a bed in the dorm is £9, breakfast £1.50. Up the scale from here, Castle Rd (the A345 north from Salisbury, between the ring road and Old Sarum) has a wide choice of small hotels doing B&B; these include *Leena's* (☎ 01722 335419) at No 50 with singles/doubles from £18/38, and *Victoria Lodge* (☎ 01722 320586) at No 6, from £29.50/42 (ensuite). Near the railway station, *Clovelly Guest*

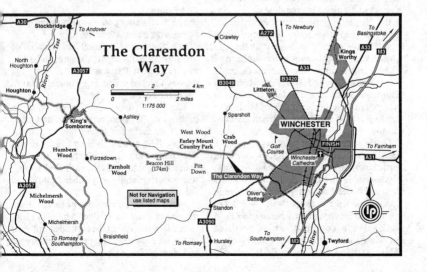

House (☎ 01722 322055), at 17-19 Mill Rd, has rooms from £25/42. Just beyond the ring road and the youth hostel, is *Byways House* (☎ 01722 328364), at 31 Fowlers Rd, where ensuite rooms cost from £23.10 per person.

For something a bit more stylish the *White Horse Hotel* (☎ 01722 327844), at 38 Castle St, charges £40/55, and the *Coach & Horses* (☎ 01722 336254), on Winchester St, charges £40/50. Salisbury has a wide range of places to eat from fast-food outlets to fine restaurants.

Winchester's *YHA Hostel* (☎ 01962 853723, £7.45) is in a beautiful 18th-century restored water mill at the east end of Broadway. There are plenty of B&Bs and small hotels. Try *Mrs Sullivan* (☎ 01962 862027, £14), at 29 Stockbridge Rd, near the railway station; *Mrs Wright* (☎ 01962 855067, £15), at 56 St Cross Rd; or *Florum House Hotel* (☎ 01962 840427, from £36/54 for ensuite singles/doubles), at 47 St Cross Rd. Up from here is the central *Portland House Hotel* (☎ 01962 865195, ensuite rooms for £38/48), at 63 Tower St.

For food in Winchester you have a wide choice. Try *Pizza Express* in a renovated 18th-century building, light years away from the usual plastic and vinyl. The *Eclipse Inn*, near the Cathedral, serves homely food in quaint but cramped surroundings.

If you fancy pursuing the ecclesiastical trail, you can dine more luxuriously and significantly more expensively at the *Old Chesil Rectory* restaurant at the junction of Chesil and Bridge Sts. For après route refreshment try the *Wykeham Arms* on Kingsgate St, or let a sign lead you down a narrow alley on the north side of High St to the *Royal Oak* with over a dozen beers to sample.

On the route, there are pubs serving lunch at the villages of Broughton and King's Somborne, neatly bracketing the halfway point of the walk. If you want to spread the walk over two days there's also B&B accommodation available in Broughton at *Yew Tree House* (☎ 01794 301227), opposite the Greyhound pub from around £19. In Stockbridge, a couple of miles north of Broughton, there's the pricier *Carbery Guest House* (☎ 01264 81071) with B&B from £23

(and a heated swimming pool) or the *White Hart* (☎ 01264 810663) the singles/doubles at £30/50. For more places, check with the TICs in Winchester and Salisbury.

Getting There & Away

Bus Winchester and Salisbury are linked by regular National Express coaches to London and Heathrow Airport. Local buses (☎ 01722 336855) run between Winchester and Salisbury, roughly every two hours (slightly less frequently on Sunday); all go via Stockbridge, some via Broughton, and some via King's Somborne. If you want to cut the first few miles, buses from Salisbury and Andover stop at Middle Winterslow.

Train This is the outer edges of London commuter country, so there are frequent trains to/from Winchester and Salisbury.

Car Winchester lies just off the M3 between London and Portsmouth. Salisbury is on the A30, also easily reached from London. The two cities are linked by the A30 and the B3049, which goes through Stockbridge.

The Route
Stage 1: Salisbury to King's Somborne
14 miles (22.5 km), 4½ to 5½ hours
Start at Salisbury Cathedral and head out of town along Milford St, passing under the ring road, past the youth hostel, over the railway line and surprisingly quickly you're out in the country.

The route crosses the Bourne River, a tributary of the Avon, turns off along Queen Manor Rd and soon leaves the road to cut across a field and climb King Manor Hill to Clarendon Park. Looking back, the path points straight towards the cathedral's spire, still towering above any other building in Salisbury.

After three miles you pass the bare remains of Clarendon Palace where, in 1164, Henry II hosted one of the earliest skirmishes in the long power struggle between crown and church. The 'turbulent priest' Thomas à

Salisbury & The Cathedral

Salisbury is justly famous for its cathedral, but this bustling market town (officially a city) is not just a tourist trap. Markets have been held twice weekly for over 600 years and the jumble of stalls still draws a large, cheerful crowd. Before the cathedral was built, Salisbury did not exist, although there was a major settlement at Old Sarum two miles north. (The original cathedral at Old Sarum was completed in 1092 by St Osmund, who arrived in England with William the Conqueror.) The town's architecture is a blend of every style since the Middle Ages, including some beautiful, half-timbered black-and-white buildings.

Salisbury Cathedral, correctly the Cathedral Church of the Blessed Virgin Mary, is one of the most beautiful and cohesive in Britain. The style is uniformly Early English, a period characterised by the first pointed arches and flying buttresses and a rather austere feel. The cathedral owes its uniformity to the speed with which it was built – between 1220 and 1266. Only the magnificent spire, at 121m (404 ft) the highest in Britain, was added as an afterthought between 1285 and 1315. Amazingly, there had been no earlier plan to add this considerable construction, so the four central piers of the building had to carry an additional 6400 tons.

The cathedral is open May through October, 8 am to 8.15 pm, and the rest of the year until 6.30 pm; a donation of £2.50 is requested. ∎

Becket was present at the council and was killed at the king's behest six years later. An overgrown stretch of a wall's foundation is all you'll find of this once important place.

The way continues through woodlands before crossing a road by a group of houses and, after another woodland jaunt, emerging through the village school yard into pretty little Pitton. Continue, over a down, through the villages of West Winterslow and Middle Winterslow before joining the straight track of a former Roman road which originally ran from Old Sarum to the port of Clausentum, near Southampton. At Buckholt Farm the route goes up and over the down and along a pathway lined with yew trees into Broughton where a pair of *pubs* await the weary and thirsty walker.

St Mary's Church in the middle of the village has a fine dovecote in its churchyard. Battery chickens are hardly a new invention, as battery pigeons were raised in this circular structure in medieval times. Apparently, over 3½ tons of young pigeons were slaughtered in one year.

The route leads out of Broughton, over Wallop Brook and behind some large houses, then across fields and past farms (where pigs get the battery treatment) before reaching Houghton and crossing the crystal clear waters of the River Test. A rash of 'private'

and 'no fishing' signs indicate that this is one of England's premier trout rivers. If there's one thing the English value more than their privacy it's their fishing rights. Rumour has it that even Prince Charles had to join a waiting list for membership of the local angling club.

Just after the river, our route crosses the Test Way (an LDP through Hampshire) on an old railway track. If you want to call it a day here, turn left to reach Stockbridge, with *B&Bs* and buses to Winchester or Salisbury.

The way climbs out of the Test Valley then drops down to the pretty village of Somborne (correctly King's Somborne) straddling the busy A3057 road. Again there's a *pub* to slake any walking thirsts.

Stage 2: King's Somborne to Winchester

13 miles (21 km), 4½ to 5½ hours

The route climbs steeply out of the village and runs through fields and woods to fine views from Beacon Hill before reaching Farley Mount where the 174m hill is topped by a curious pyramid-like monument marking the burial place of a horse which, in 1733, tumbled 7.5m into a local quarry during a hunt. Horse and rider survived to

Winchester & The Cathedral

Winchester is a beautiful city surrounded by water meadows and rolling chalk downland. If one place lies at the centre of English history and embodies the romantic vision of an English heartland, it is Winchester. Despite this it seems to have escaped tourist inundation – certainly compared to nearby Salisbury and theme parks like Bath.

Alfred the Great and many of his successors made Winchester their capital, and William the Conqueror came here to claim the crown of England. The Domesday Book was also written here, but much of the present-day city dates from the 18th century, by which time history had bypassed Winchester and the town had settled down as a prosperous market centre.

Winchester's first church, the Old Minster, was built in 648, and by around 1000 it was one of England's largest. The Norman conquest in 1066 brought sweeping changes and the new cathedral was built between 1079 and 1093. In the 13th century the east end of the cathedral was extended in the Early English style, and from the mid-14th century the Norman nave was completely rebuilt in Perpendicular style. But there have been no further major changes. Winchester Cathedral's internal detail outshines the comparatively mundane exterior and makes an interesting contrast with Salisbury Cathedral where the exterior is wonderful, the interior less inspiring.

The cathedral is open daily from 7.15 am to 6.30 pm and a £2 donation is requested. ■

win a race the following year, carrying the name 'Beware Chalkpit' to victory.

If it's a weekend you may meet lots of people for the next couple of miles as the way crosses the Farley Mount Country Park, with a rather confusing tangle of walking tracks, bridleways and interspersed car parks.

The way runs past a golf course then enters the suburbs of Winchester, detouring to Oliver's Battery from where Cromwell forced the city to surrender during the Civil War. You get a quick glimpse of the cathedral, much less dominant than Salisbury's soaring spire, before another stretch of country ends with a footpath over the main London-Southampton railway line. You meet the busy A333 road at St Cross' Hospital, a charitable home founded in 1137 for 'thirteen poor impotent men so reduced in strength as rarely or never able to raise themselves without the assistance of one another'. The final pretty pathway leads across water meadows, beside the trout-famed River Itchen and through the narrow streets and arches around ancient Winchester College, into the heart of the city to finish at Winchester Cathedral.

If you've got an afternoon to spare before leaving Winchester, we describe a short walk on the outskirts in the South Downs Way section of this book.

THE KENNET & AVON CANAL

Distance 10 miles (16 km) from Bath to Bradford-on-Avon, plus 11½ miles (18.5 km) to Devizes
Duration 4 to 5 hours, plus 5 to 6 hours on the second day
Start Bath
Finish Bradford-on-Avon (or Devizes)
Counties Somerset, Wiltshire
Area Wessex
Summary This National Waterway Walk is generally flat, following the canal towpath, which is for the most part shale surfaced, making for easy walking conditions.

The Kennet & Avon Canal was built between 1794 and 1810 to join London and Bristol, two of the most important ports and cities in the country, by linking the navigable sections of the River Avon and the River Kennet, which joins the Thames at Reading. The project was completed before the days of mass mechanisation, so most of the construction was done by workmen called navigators (or 'navvies') using little more than picks, shovels and wheelbarrows. Goods were carried along the canal in 'narrow-boats' pulled by horses, so a towpath was also constructed along the length of the canal.

In the late 19th and early 20th centuries, canals all over Britain came under increasing competition from train transport, and then road transport, for the movement of freight. By the 1960s, much of the Kennet & Avon canal had been neglected and was in an unusable state. But since the early 1980s, dedicated enthusiasts have rebuilt the canal and its towpath, giving this wonderful industrial artery a new lease of life and creating leisure and pleasure features that could never have been envisaged by the original navvies.

Using the towpath, walkers can follow the whole length of the canal, from Bath all the way to Reading (where you can join the Thames Path – described elsewhere in this book – and continue to London if you so desire). But one of the most interesting sections is from Bath to Bradford-on-Avon, which can be easily done in a day. Both Bath and Bradford are easy to reach, and Bath especially has a good choice of places to stay.

This day-walk is an ideal way to enjoy the North Wessex countryside. From the centre of the historic city of Bath you walk through a rural landscape, with the Mendip Hills to the south and the Cotswolds to the north. Although the railway and roads came later, they followed the same route down the Avon Valley, seeking easy gradients. As you walk this route today you see river, canal, road and railway almost side-by-side, frequently crossing and recrossing each other, using a fascinating series of bridges, tunnels and incredibly impressive aqueducts. Other attractions include canal-boat activity, canalside pubs, and good birdlife.

If you've got more time to spare, we describe a second day's walk along the canal, onwards from Bradford to the ancient market town of Devizes. Here, the countryside changes as you enter flat land to the north of Salisbury Plain and, near the end of the walk, you pass the Caen Hill flight of 16 closely stepped locks – one of the most spectacular features on the entire British inland waterway system.

Direction, Distance & Duration

This linear route can be done in either direction. We describe it from Bath to Bradford, assuming you'll come back to Bath by train.

If you want to dawdle and not have to clock-watch, you may prefer to take the train to Bradford first and walk this route in reverse.

From Bath to Bradford is a flat 10 miles, which takes about four to five hours of walking. Add a bit extra for lunch and admiring the aqueducts, and you will probably need about six hours. If you decide to stay in Bradford and carry on to Devizes next day, this is another 11½ miles, requiring five to six hours of walking – about eight hours in total.

Shorter Alternative If you don't want to go all the way to Bradford, you can, of course, simply walk up the towpath for as long as you want, then turn around and come back. Alternatively, walk as far as Avoncliff (8½ miles from Bath), from where you can catch a train on to Bradford or back to Bath.

Information

There are TICs along this route at Bath (☎ 01225 462831), Bradford-on-Avon (☎ 01225 865797) and Devizes (☎ 01380 729408). If you need more specific information, the canal is administered by British Waterways (☎ 01380 722859) and much of the restoration work has been due to the efforts of the Kennet & Avon Canal Trust (☎ 01380 721279).

Warning
Note that cyclists can ride on the towpath. There should be plenty of room for all considerate users.

Books & Maps *The Kennet & Avon Walk* by Ray Quinlan (Cicerone, £6.99) covers the whole route along the canal, plus river walks at either end, from the mouth of the Avon, near Bristol, to Westminster in the heart of London.

The OS Landranger (1:50,000) sheets 172 and 173 cover the route described here and

SOUTHERN ENGLAND

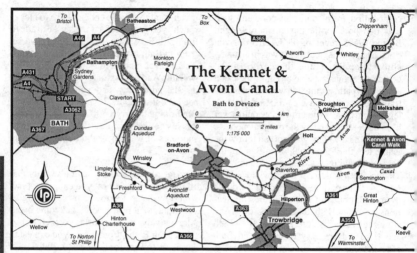

much of the surrounding area. For more detail on the whole canal, and a barge-full of useful and interesting information, get the *Kennet & Avon Canal* map and guide, published by Geo Projects (£3.75).

Places to Stay & Eat

As a major tourist destination, Bath has facilities for all tastes and budgets (listed in the Cotswold Way section of this book). If you're making an early start, *Tasty 1* opposite Bath Spa Station entrance, provides drinks and food from 7 am.

Bradford-on-Avon has a choice of places to stay including the *Barge Inn* (☎ 01225 863403), near where this route leaves the canal, charging from £35 per person, and the central *Riverside Inn* (☎ 01225 863526), with a pleasant setting and simple ensuite single/double rooms from £27.50/45. Smarter is the nearby *Swan Hotel* (☎ 01225 868686), charging from £40/52.50 for singles/ doubles. They also do bar food and have a restaurant. Up from here, in price and position, is the *Bradford Old Windmill* (☎ 01225 866842), a beautifully converted mill, charging from £30/55 to £55/70, but the

views, the atmosphere and the friendly welcome are worth it.

Places to eat in Bradford include the *Canal Tavern* and the *Tight Squeeze Cafe*, mentioned in the route description. In the town centre, by the TIC, is the *Scribbling Horse Cafe*, a 17th-century *tearoom* and a *wholefood store & snackbar* – which between them should provide something for everyone.

If you go for the two day option, places to stay in Devizes include *The White Bear* (☎ 01380 722583), with B&B from £17, and *The Castle Hotel* (☎ 01380 729300), with ensuite rooms for £40/55. Both pubs also do food, and the town has several other cafes and restaurants. Campers can go to *Lower Foxhangers Farm* (☎ 01380 828254), on the canalside, charging from £5. They also do B&B.

Getting There & Away

Bus Bath is regularly linked to all parts of the country by National Express coaches, while local buses serve surrounding towns. At the end of the route, occasional buses go from Bradford back to Bath, but it's far easier to use the train (see following section).

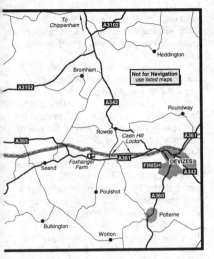

Not for Navigation
use listed maps

If you walk to Devizes and need to get back to Bath, there's at least 10 buses per day in each direction (four on Sunday), going via Sells Green, which is also on the route. Alternatively, from Devizes buses go about five times per day (less on Sunday) to Swindon, which is on the main rail line (see below). Alternatively, you may like to use the same bus to travel onwards from Devizes to Avebury Stone Circle (described in the Ridgeway section of this book). For more details phone the Wiltshire Bus Line (☎ 0345 090899).

Train Bath (the station is called Bath Spa) is served by mainline trains, with regular connections to/from London, Swindon and Bristol. (More details in the Cotswold Way section.) There are about eight trains per day each way between Bath and Bradford (five on Sunday).

Car Bath is on the A4 east of Bristol, and south of the M4 motorway. Bradford-on-Avon is on the A363 between Bath and Trowbridge. Devizes is south of the A4, on the junction of the A361 and A342.

The Route
Day 1: Bath to Avoncliff
10 miles (16 km), 4 to 5 hours

With your back to Bath Spa Station entrance, turn right. Opposite the *Royal Hotel* follow the footpath sign under the railway arches to cross Widcombe Bridge, a footbridge over the River Avon. Turn left at the main road, then after 50m left again to Thimble Mill and the start of the canal. Follow the canal path, with a large basin and *Stakis Hotel* on your left. Within a few metres you reach the first lock and cross a main road, then follow a section through houses. There are several benches provided here, but it's a little early in the journey for a rest. There are two more roads to cross, then you have no further need to leave the path.

There can be few quieter, or more attractive, ways of leaving Bath, The path passes below Cleveland House, straddling the canal, and then through Sydney Gardens, at one time a very fashionable part of Bath, so two more bridges were built to hide the canal from sensitive aristocrats.

Beyond here, the canal is less enclosed, and you soon reach Bathampton (2½ miles from the start), where *The George Inn* serves drinks and specialises in Thai food. But if it's too early for a stop, continue down the path, now heading south. After Bridge 181 (they are numbered from Reading) the canal-side is forested on the right, while a beautiful stretch of North Somerset countryside unfolds to your left.

About five miles from Bath, you reach Dundas Wharf and cross to the other bank. There is usually some activity in this basin, where the K&A is joined by the Somerset Coal Canal. A small section has been renovated and can be viewed just before crossing the River Avon on the remarkably ornate Dundas Aqueduct, named after the first chairman of the canal company but designed by John Rennie, the canal's principal engineer. The *Viaduct Inn*, on the road above the basin, might be a good place to stop for refreshment.

Alternatively, continue on the towpath through a wooded section and at Bridge 175,

SOUTHERN ENGLAND

above Limpley Stoke, leave the canal for the *Hop Pole Inn* (500m off the path), where hot and cold lunches are available, with special rates for senior citizens. Much nearer, 100m past the bridge and adjacent to the path, you may find a tea garden open.

Another few miles will bring you to the Avoncliff Aqueduct, longer, higher and even more splendid than Dundas. You have to go under the canal here to reach the other bank, past *Teasels Coffee Shop* (open weekends only to 5.30 pm). Nearby is the *Cross Guns* pub and the small Canal Bookshop.

The last 1½ miles takes you into Bradford-on-Avon. If you want a change from the towpath, you can walk through the country park that parallels the canal. Whichever way you go, the famous Tithe Barn (see aside) is well worth a visit.

The end of this walk is marked by the *Canal Tavern*, doing a fair range of bar meals, and the *Tight Squeeze Cafe*, where the Boatmans Breakfast is offered as a challenge as much as a meal. There are also cycle and canoe hire facilities, which may provide an alternative way of covering the route.

Take the lane between the pub and the cafe to reach the road. (Before leaving the canal it is worth crossing the road to see the lock, basin and dry dock.) Go left, and a walk of 300m will lead to the *Three Horseshoes* and another left turn takes you in to the railway station.

Day 2: Bradford-on-Avon to Devizes

11½ miles (18 km), 5 to 6 hours

If you are carrying on for another day to Devizes, today's route starts at the bridge by the Canal Tavern, which marked the end of yesterday's stage. The first section of the walk is one of contrasts, taking you through fancy new marinas (one fast taking on the appearance of Costa del Canal), then close to some industrial premises before reaching the comparative tranquillity of the open country beyond Hilperton. Midweek this stretch of path should be quiet, increasing your chances of seeing birdlife at close quarters.

Places to stop for a drink or lunch (depending what time you left Bradford) include the *Kings Arms* at Hilperton Bridge, or the *Somerset Arms* at Semington (five miles from Bradford). Just beyond here is a set of locks, then you pass through an open stretch to Seend where the old *Barge Inn* (now modernised) provides good food. Three miles beyond here, at Sells Green Bridge (No 149), a signposted diversion to

Things to See in Bradford-on-Avon

The old country town of Bradford-on-Avon holds plenty of interest, so it's worth looking around before catching your train. For advice on sights and accommodation, should you wish to linger longer or continue to Devizes tomorrow, the TIC (☎ 01225 865797) is on Silver St, beyond the Town Bridge. The bridge dates from 1610, and the small 'lockup' (or prison) built into its central pier has become a symbol of the town.

Although Bradford-on-Avon dates back to the first millennium, it reached its peak in the 17th and 18th centuries as a weaving centre, when West Country wool was highly prized across Britain and Europe. Some magnificent mill buildings remain alongside the river, with imposing stone houses of the town's wealthy clothing entrepreneurs and humbler workers' dwellings stacked in rows on the steep hillsides above.

Other things to see include The Shambles, the town's original marketplace, Westbury House, where a riot against the introduction of factory machinery in 1791 led to three deaths, and the Bradford-on-Avon Museum in the library building by the river. Also don't miss the medieval Barton Packhorse Bridge, over which produce used to be carried to the immense Tithe Barn near the canal, built in 1341 with 100 tons of stone tiles on the roof.

Up on the hill overlooking the town is the tiny Saxon church of St Laurence. It was founded around the 7th or 8th century, but when a new church was constructed it was put to secular use and eventually forgotten. Its rediscovery around 1856 resulted in an interesting restoration and the church has been returned to its original condition. ■

the left will take you to the *Three Magpies* pub which has a reasonably priced daytime menu and a campsite. By this time the locks come more frequently, as the canal starts to work its way uphill towards Devizes.

Canal-side activity also increases as you pass Foxhanger Wharf and cross to the other side of the canal; anglers use the wider and deeper waters, with some very large specimens being brought to the bank. *Foxhanger Farm* (B&B and camping) has an entrance alongside the path.

You pass under a small road bridge and reach the bottom of Caen Hill Flight. This chain of 16 closely stepped locks are just part of the 35 needed to take the canal from 40m ASL at Semington to 130m at Devizes. For an artificial waterway this is a spectacular height-gain of 90m in just over six miles. As you walk up the hill, with luck you'll see some narrow boats negotiating the long haul through the locks. (Beyond here the canal crosses the comparatively flat Vale of Pewsey, with a final peak near Crofton, before the long descent to the Thames at Reading.)

At the top of the flight continue under the main road, and at the next bridge go up the ramp to the road, turn right and right again, taking the path on the other bank which leads to The Wharf. One more bridge crossing takes you to the Wharf Centre, which houses a Canal Exhibition and shop (☎ 01380 729489), open from 10 am to 5 pm, March to Christmas, a theatre and the *Wharfside Restaurant*, tucked into the corner, but a fine place to mark the end of this walk.

Devizes This is an old market town, with a regular Thursday market in The Square that has formed the background to various films of Hardy's stories. There are half-timbered buildings, quiet 'ginnels' (alleys) and plenty of pubs providing food. The TIC, plus a choice of teashops and restaurants, is in the Market Square area, which is also where buses arrive and leave. Things to see include the market cross, which tells the story of one Ruth Pierce who, in 1753, asked God to strike her dead if she lied about the price of corn – and was struck down immediately. There's also the Old Town Hall, dating from 1750, the Elizabethan houses of St John's Alley, and the Devizes Museum (☎ 01380 727369), which also has displays about Stonehenge and Avebury – useful if you're heading that way next.

OTHER WALKS IN WESSEX

Parts of Wessex which lend themselves to walking include the rolling grassland and steep escarpments of Salisbury Plain, and the quiet farmland and heath of Cranborne Chase, east of Shaftesbury, which along with the West Wiltshire Downs is a designated Area of Outstanding Natural Beauty. Also good are the chalky and sparsely wooded hills of the North Wessex Downs in the area between Devizes and Marlborough. These downs (also called the Wiltshire Downs and the Marlborough Downs) are traversed by the Ridgeway National Trail which starts near Avebury and is described elsewhere in this book. Several day-walks are possible taking in a section of the Ridgeway. Alternatively, to the west of Avebury, just south of the A4 road between Marlborough and Calne, is Cherhill (pronounced 'Cheril') – a fine down, topped by a monument and white horse figure carved in the chalk.

South of Avebury is the small town of Pewsey, which makes a good base for exploring the area. It's also on the main rail line between London and the West Country – so access is quite easy. Within walking distance are two more white horses, several tumuli and other prehistoric remains and the more recently constructed Kennet & Avon Canal, which is described above. One suggested way of reaching the start of the Ridgeway is from Pewsey, so it might be worth spending a day or two here 'limbering up' before setting out for Avebury and the long-distance path.

Salisbury Plain

To explore Salisbury Plain you could base yourself in the city of Salisbury itself (covered in the Clarendon Way section), which is easy to reach and has a good range

SOUTHERN ENGLAND

Wessex Chalk Figures

Much of the rolling downland and farming country of Wessex covers a large area of chalk. The vegetation is only a thin green cloak covering the white substructure, and the practice of cutting pictures into hillsides in this area has a long history. The technique is simple: mark out your picture and cut away the green grass and topsoil to reveal the white chalk below. The picture will need periodic maintenance, but not much – some of the chalk figures may date back to Bronze Age times, although the history of the oldest figures is uncertain.

Wessex has many chalk figures, and Wiltshire has more than any other county. Most are horses, and include those at Cherhill and Uffington (near the Ridgeway – which lends its name to the nearby Vale of the White Horse), plus several more near Pewsey and Westbury. There's another good one at Osmington near Weymouth.

The tradition has continued into the 20th century. During WWI, soldiers based at Fovant, west of Salisbury, cut a series of army regimental badges into a nearby hillside, and a New Zealand regiment left a gigantic kiwi on a hillside at Bulford, near Amesbury in Wiltshire, a few miles east of Stonehenge.

Although Wiltshire goes for sheer quantity, in other parts of Wessex the locals go for sheer style. Probably the most impressive chalk figure is Dorset's 180-foot-tall Cerne Giant (on a hillside near the village of Cerne Abbas in Dorset), with his even more notable 30-foot penis. ■

of places to stay and eat, as well as several sites of interest. The TIC sells local walking guides and can provide leaflets and advice about walking on and around Salisbury and the Plain. Note that much of the area is an army firing range and closed to the public at certain times, so most options for walkers keep pretty much to the edge of the Plain rather than crossing it. You have to choose your routes carefully.

However, while you're in the area, ask about the Sarcen Way, a 26 mile route across the rarely visited heart of the Plain linking the Stone Circles of Stonehenge and Avebury. Unfortunately, it's only open on certain days of the year, but if you happen to coincide with these it would be well worth doing. (There's also an annual run along this route called the Neolithic Marathon.) If all this sounds too much, the quiet villages and classic English farmland of the Hampshire Avon Valley north of Salisbury towards Amesbury and Stonehenge offers a comforting contrast to the wide open plains.

Another way to explore Salisbury Plain might be from Warminster, a large town about 20 miles north-west of Salisbury, on the edge of the Plain. From here a 20 mile circular walk called the Imber Perimeter Path, loops round the army area, via the villages of Bratton, West Lavington,

Tilshead and Chittern. (The village of Imber itself is in the heart of the range. The people were moved out in 1943 and since then the village has remained closed to the public, except for a few days each year.) If you don't want to do the whole circuit, a short out-and-back walk on the hills above Warminster takes you to the white horse and Iron Age fort above Westbury. Another nearby attraction is Cradle Hill, where many UFO sightings have been claimed by enthusiasts.

New Forest

South of Salisbury is the New Forest. Visitors to Britain love this name, as the area is more than a 1000 years old (William the Conquerer christened it), and there aren't *that* many trees. But apart from these minor matters, it's a wonderful place with several good walking opportunities. The area covers 145 sq miles, of which 105 sq miles is forest and woodland; the rest is occupied by villages and farmland. The forest trees include fine stands of oak, beech and holly, plus some conifer plantation and a lot of open heath and gorseland (many trees were cut down to supply the navy shipyards at Portsmouth and Southampton in the days of wooden boats). Animal life features deer, badgers, foxes and, most particularly, the famed semi-wild New Forest ponies.

The New Forest is designated a 'Heritage Area' which gives it protected status. There's a chance it will be made a full-blown national park in future. Lyndhurst or Brockenhurst make good bases, with a choice of B&Bs and campsites. The New Forest Visitor Centre (☎ 01703 282269) in Lyndhurst is open daily, with plenty of information on transport, places to stay and walks in the area.

Long Walks in Wessex

If you're searching for something a bit harder, long-distance routes in Wessex include, on the northern and eastern outer fringes, the Thames Way, the South Downs Way and the Ridgeway national trails, which are all described in this book. The highlight of the southern part of Wessex is the English Channel coast of Dorset and South Devon, parts of which are billed as the English Riviera, on account of its mild climate (although don't expect Cannes). This stretches from Poole Harbour to Exmouth, via Weymouth and Lyme Regis, and for walkers this is the route followed by the Dorset Coast section of the South West Coast Path, described in the Southern England – Long-Distance Paths chapter.

The Wessex Ridgeway is an excellent 140 mile route between Marlborough in Wiltshire and Lyme Regis in Devon. This route takes in several of Wessex's special highlights, including Avebury Stone Circle, the northern and western edge of Salisbury Plain and a section of the picturesque Wylie Valley (running parallel to the Imber Perimeter Path, mentioned above), Cranborne Chase, the huge chalk giant of Cerne Abbas, then runs through the heart of Thomas Hardy country to finish on the South Devon coast at Lyme Regis – famous for its fossils. The Ramblers' Association produces a handy *Wessex Ridgeway Guide* by Alan Proctor which tells you more

A glance at the map will show you that Lyme Regis is also on the South West Coast Path, so parts of this and the Wessex Ridgeway could be combined into a shorter stroll of between one and four days so you can see something of the Wessex coast and

'hinterland'. If you're into really long walks, it won't have escaped your notice that the Wessex Ridgeway links neatly with the Ridgeway National Trail at Avebury, which in turn runs into the Iknield Way and then the Peddars Way (also described in this book), allowing you to follow Neolithic, Roman and medieval footprints all the way across England from the Channel to the North Sea.

The Isle of Wight

The Isle of Wight, 23 miles (37 km) long by 13 miles (21 km) wide, lies only a couple of miles off the Hampshire coast. Its name is thought to come from 'wiht', an ancient word meaning 'lifted', ie rising from the sea. During their occupation of Britain, the Romans named the island Vectis and built several villas here. Perhaps the mild and sunny climate was as near as they could get to Mediterranean.

The pleasant weather still attracts visitors and the island is a popular day trip from the mainland. Many people also come for longer holidays, particularly to the busier eastern side of the island. For walkers there's a marvellous network of footpaths, and you could easily stay a week or longer exploring them all. As our sample route we describe a popular trail through the heart of the western side of the island, and at the end of the section we outline several other walking routes (longer and shorter) on the island.

THE TENNYSON TRAIL

> **Distance** 14 miles (22.5 km)
> **Duration** 5 to 6½ hours
> **Start** Carisbrooke, near Newport
> **Finish** The Needles & Alum Bay
> **Regional Centres** Newport (Isle of Wight), Lymington, Portsmouth, Southampton (mainland)
> **Area** Isle of Wight
> **Summary** Easy walking on clear paths through woods and farmland and across rolling coastal downs.

SOUTHERN ENGLAND

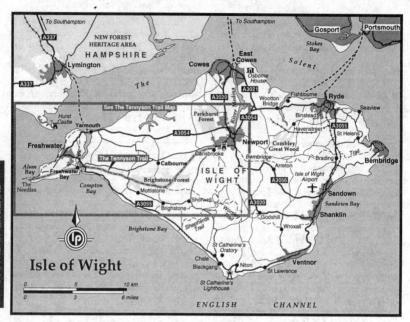

The Tennyson Trail is named after the 19th-century poet, Alfred Lord Tennyson, who lived on the Isle of Wight. As a lover of the outdoors, he'd have probably approved of this route which runs along a chalk ridge through the quieter western side of the island, and finishes on high sea-cliffs, where fine views and a spectacular lighthouse are the principal attractions.

Direction, Distance & Duration

This linear route runs for 13 miles from Carisbrooke, near Newport in the centre of the island, via Freshwater Bay, to the Needles at the extreme western end. From there it's another mile to Alum Bay where the route ends and you can find transport back to the start. You could do it in either direction, but a finish on the cliffs is more pleasing. The walk takes five to 6½ hours of walking, so with stops for lunch and gazing out to sea, you should allow about seven to eight hours. For this walk, you could base yourself in Newport and return there by bus at the end. But Freshwater (on the coast just north of Freshwater Bay) seems a more pleasant place to stay, so you could catch an early bus to Newport, then walk back.

Shorter Alternatives There's no real way to shorten this linear route, unless you end at Freshwater Bay, which misses the best bit of the walk. We recommend some short routes in the Other Walks on the Isle of Wight section.

Information

Newport's TIC (☎ 01983 525450) is on South St. The nearest TIC to Freshwater is Yarmouth (☎ 01983 760015), on the ferry quay.

Books & Maps The TICs have a very good selection of leaflets and booklets on walking routes all over the island. The one on the Tennyson Trail is unfortunately tedious, full of arcane grid references for the junctions, but some of the others are very informative and user-friendly. OS Landranger (1:50,000) sheet 196 and Outdoor Leisure (1:25,000) sheet 29 both cover the whole island.

Places to Stay & Eat

There's a plentiful supply of places to stay. Freshwater has *Heathfield Farm Campsite* (☎ 01983 752480) on the north side of town, mainly for caravans, but backpacker tents are charged £3.25 per person, and *Totland Bay YHA Hostel* (☎ 01983 752165, £8.25), very handy for the end of this walk. Places doing B&B in Freshwater (and its 'satellites' – Totland and Colwell) include *Sandford Lodge* (☎ 01983 753478), The Avenue, charging from £22 per person B&B and £32 per person B&B including dinner; the *Ontario Hotel* (☎ 01983 753237), Colwell Common Rd, from £21; and the *Nodes Country Hotel* (☎ 01983 752859, £25), Alum Bay Old Rd, overlooked by Tennyson Down. Or try the *Royal Standard Hotel* (☎ 01983 753227, £20), on School Green Rd. All these places do evening meals.

In Newport, B&Bs which welcome walkers include *Fairways* (☎ 01983 522254) and *Salween House* (☎ 01983 523456), both from £18, and *Newport Quay Hotel* (☎ 01983 528544) which has a range of rooms from between £20 and £55 per person.

Both Newport and Freshwater Bay have a good selection of places to eat, including restaurants, pubs and teashops. For a meal or drink in a fine location, the *Waterfront Restaurant* (☎ 01983 756969) down on the beach overlooking Totland Bay has snacks from £2, light meals around £5, and main courses from £5 to £10

If you arrive on the ferry from Lymington, and don't feel like going on to Freshwater, there are plenty of places in the pleasant little town of Yarmouth. *Westport Cottage* (☎ 01983 760751), charging £16 and *St Hilda's* (☎ 01983 760814), charging £14, are two recommended B&Bs. There are also smarter inns and hotels. The TIC (☎ 01983 760015), on The Quay, where the ferry docks, will be able to set you up. Around The Square are plenty of places to eat, catering for all budgets.

The only place along the walk for food or refreshments is at Freshwater Bay where there's a pub, cafe, tearoom and shops. In summer there may be ice-cream vans or other moveable feasts at the National Trust car park at Mottistone Down.

Getting There & Away

Ferry Nearly all visitors reach the Isle of Wight by ferry (although it is possible to fly). To reach the western side of the island, there's Red Funnel (☎ 01703 220099) high-speed passenger service between Southampton and West Cowes every half hour for much of the day (£9 return), and the Wightlink (☎ 01705 827744) between Lymington and Yarmouth (near Freshwater), hourly, for a slightly cheaper fare.

Bus There are regular National Express coaches to Southampton, although fewer to Lymington, from where you can catch the ferry. Isle of Wight buses are operated by Southern Vectis (☎ 01983 562264). There are regular buses between West Cowes and Newport, and between Alum Bay and Newport (via Yarmouth). Timetables are posted at the Newport bus station and at the Alum Bay terminus, which list all the relevant schedules. If you're staying for a few days, they have various money saving passes available.

Train Southampton has very frequent train services to/from London and can easily be reached from other parts of the country. Trains on the Isle of Wight cover only the east of the island, and are not used for this route.

Car Both the ferry services above also carry vehicles, but prices depend a lot on the size of car and the time of year. At both mainland ports there are big car parks, where you can leave your car for a couple of days and go on the ferry as a foot passenger.

SOUTHERN ENGLAND

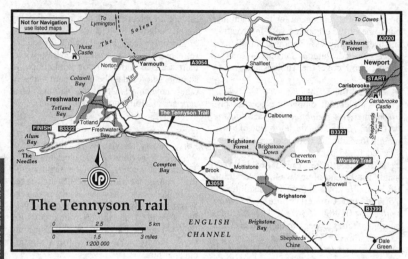

The Tennyson Trail

Not for Navigation
use listed maps

ENGLISH
CHANNEL

0   2.5   5 km
0   1.5   3 miles
1:200 000

The Route
Stage 1: Newport to Freshwater Bay
8½ miles (13.5 km), 3 to 4 hours

It's only a mile from Newport to the official trail start at Nodgham Lane, Carisbrooke, just north of Carisbrooke Castle. The trail goes up Down Lane almost immediately; don't miss the turn-off with its slightly hidden sign pointing along the bridleway towards Freshwater Bay. (Despite the island's thoroughly developed character there is no habitation until you reach Freshwater Bay, so if you want lunch earlier you'd better bring it with you.)

Down Lane quickly becomes a narrow path lined by trees and hedges, but it soon gives way to the field-side trails which characterise the first part of the walk. There are a variety of signposts – follow those towards Brighstone Forest. A towering BBC TV transmitter mast pops up to the north of the trail but otherwise the views are relatively circumscribed until you emerge onto Brighstone Down. Its 214m (702 ft) summit is not the highest point on the island, but there are fine views taking in the south coast from St Catherine's Point in the east to Freshwater Bay in the west.

The trail crosses the first road encountered on the walk to arrive at a National Trust car park. From this dip the trail climbs again to Mottistone Down, past a series of Stone Age burial mounds with fine views all the way to the north and south coasts of the western end of the island and to Tennyson Down with its towering chalk cliffs, west beyond Freshwater Bay. It's a 450m detour south down the slope of the down to the Long Stone, a 4000 to 5000 year old stone megalith, the only one found on the island. The chimneys of Mottistone Manor can be seen further down the slope. The gardens of the National Trust owned property are open to the public on Wednesday afternoons.

The trail dips down again to cross the B3399 then immediately climbs to cross a series of downs, teetering along the top of the ridge through a long and narrow golf course. The western end of the golf course ends right at the beginning of Freshwater Bay, which is a good place for a lunch stop at one of the cafes, or the bar in the *Albion Hotel*, or just beyond the bay the *Fort Redoubt Tearoom* inside the 1875 coastal fort. You can sip your tea while keeping a weather eye to the south for French invaders.

Stage 2: Freshwater Bay to Alum Bay
5½ miles (9 km), 2 to 2½ hours

Alfred Lord Tennyson lived near Freshwater Bay for 16 years from 1853. It's recorded that he walked almost every day on the Tennyson Down, the next bit of this route (which also shares the Coast Path). The Tennyson Monument marks the 145m (482 ft) high point of this coastal down with its impressively sheer cliffs tumbling straight into the sea.

At the western end of the downs are the Needles – the postcard symbol of the Isle of Wight. A series of chalk outcrops stepping out to the lighthouse, they included a really needlelike cousin until it tumbled into the sea in 1764. The Old Battery overlooking the Needles was another mid-19th-century outpost built to forestall a feared French invasion. Now operated by the National Trust, it's open daily in July and August; Sunday to Thursday from April to October.

From the Needles follow the Coast Path back on the northern side of the peninsula, to drop down to the amusement park and shops at Alum Bay from where buses will take you back to the starting point. If you've got time to kill, you could take a cable car down the cliff to see (or bottle) some of the famous multi-coloured sand.

OTHER WALKS ON THE ISLE OF WIGHT

The Isle of Wight County Council have put a lot of effort into designing, publicising and signposting a network of footpaths and trails all over the island. All TICs on the island have leaflets. Most are linear and can be done in a day; using the island's excellent bus service you can always get back to your starting point. These include: the Shepherds Trail from Carisbrooke south over downland to the coast at Shepherds Chine; the Bembridge Trail from Newport west to the coast, through villages, past manor houses and Roman villas; and the Wolsley Trail, from Brighstone over more downs to the holiday town of Shanklin. (There's also a Clarendon Trail – not to be confused with the Clarendon Way between Salisbury and Winchester described in the section above).

A good circular day-walk from Freshwater takes in a section of the Coastal Path south to Alum Bay and the Needles, then follows a section of the Tennyson Trail over Tennyson Down to Freshwater Bay (an early lunch), heading through Aston and along the eastern Freshwater Way to join the old railway track beside the Yar Estuary to Yarmouth (a late lunch), then back to Freshwater via the coast and Fort Victoria Country Park.

And for the mile-eaters there's the whole Coastal Path; 77 miles (124 km), which takes anywhere between four and eight days, although, as with the rest of the island, the western side is quieter with fewer holiday resorts, so you might consider just doing part of it, eg from Cowes or Yarmouth to St Catherine's Point. This route is covered by a very handy set of four leaflets available in local TICs, and by the *Isle of Wight Coast Path* booklet by John Merrill (JNM Publications, £4).

Walking tours and holidays (short or long, guided or self-guided) are run by the *Hambledon Hotel* (☎ 01983 862403) in Shanklin, on the east side of the island. The proprietors are keen walkers, and the hotel loans out maps and walk-notes, and gives you full run of the boot-drying facilities.

SOUTHERN ENGLAND

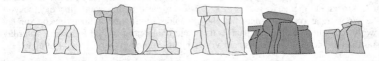

Southern England
– Long-Distance Paths

SOUTHERN ENGLAND

The Cotswold Way

Distance 103 miles (164.5 km)
Duration 6 to 8 days
Start Chipping Campden
Finish Bath
Regional Centres Stratford upon Avon, Cheltenham, Gloucester, Stroud, Bath
Counties Gloucestershire, North Somerset (Avon)
Areas The Cotswold Hills Area of Outstanding Natural Beauty
Summary An easy walk through classic southern English countryside.

The Cotswold Way runs along the western edge of the Cotswold Hills from Chipping Campden (just south of Stratford-upon-Avon) to Bath; providing a link between two of the most touristy towns in Britain. The Way crosses land that has been tamed for many centuries, but it's very pretty countryside, and some of the villages, with their honey coloured stonework, are a delight.

The Way is also a walk through England's history, with numerous prehistoric hillforts and ancient burial barrows. There are Saxon and Civil War battle sites, reminders of the Romans, some fine stately homes, the ruins of a magnificent medieval monastery and many other ancient monuments. The character of the Cotswolds is all due to wool. In the 13th century there were half a million sheep here, producing a large slice of medieval England's wealth. Wool merchants were extremely wealthy and the Cotswolds fine stone houses and churches are symbols of that era. The wool trade died in the 17th century, the industrial revolution bypassed the Cotswolds and the region has since been virtually frozen in time.

The wool trade may be gone, but the Cotswolds are still a patch of England at its most affluent. The pretty-as-a-postcard villages exude a heady aroma of solid bank accounts. This is an area of expensive public schools and lots of golf courses.

Hills is technically the wrong term to define the Cotswolds. The region is actually a long escarpment, sloping up gently from the east and dropping off steeply to the west. The Cotswold Way mainly follows the sharper western edge, but compared to some of the wilder options described in this book, it's a comfortable walk. The weather in this favoured quarter is not viciously changeable and at night there's always a handy B&B and a welcoming pub to aim for.

DIRECTION, DISTANCE & DURATION
The walk can be done in either direction, although we describe it north to south (Chipping Campden to Bath). Waymarking is quite good, with small arrows with a white dot in the centre or beside the arrow, but it's still possible to miss turns simply because there are so many of them. The Way often cuts straight across fields and circular 'targets' are often useful in these situations. Note that the Cotswold Way is earmarked to be upgraded to full national trail status; waymarking may change and improve.

The Cotswold Way is about 100 miles long – you can add a few miles by taking alternative routes to avoid roads, or reduce it by taking short cuts.

Although there are steep ascents and descents they never go on for long as the highest point on the Way is only 330m high. The *Cotswold Way Handbook* estimates you climb around 3900m over the 100 miles, although at times you may feel you've ascended Everest by stile!

The following itinerary covers the route in seven days, with a short first day, so you could start the walk at lunch time on Sunday and complete it on the following Saturday night – although there are a lot of churches, houses, villages and other distractions to stretch the walk to more than a week if you've got the time. Note that the hours given for each stage in the main route description are walking times only: you should allow an extra hour or two for rests, lunch stops, and so on. Except for night three in Cheltenham all the overnight stops are right on the Way. Other possible halts are suggested in the route description.

STAGES

For a seven day walk, as described here, the most convenient places to begin and end each day are:

Day	From	To	Distance
1	Chipping Campden	Broadway	6 miles (9.5 km)
2	Broadway	Winchcombe	12 miles (19 km)
3	Winchcombe	Cheltenham	11 miles (17.5 km)
4	Cheltenham	Painswick	19 miles (30.5 km)
5	Painswick	Dursley	16 miles (25.5 km)
6	Dursley	Old Sodbury	20 miles (32 km)
7	Old Sodbury	Bath	19 miles (30.5 km)

INFORMATION

Additional information on the Cotswold Way can be obtained from the Cotswold Countryside Service (☎ 01452 425674), Gloucestershire County Council, Gloucester GL1 2TN. You may meet volunteer wardens with their distinctive armbands along the Way.

Books

The Cotswold Way by local expert Mark Richards (Reardon Publishing, £3.95) is an affectionate step-by-step account of the walk with detailed information on features along the route. It's complemented with informative and attractive hand-drawn maps. The same author has another guide describing the Way south to north (Bath to Chipping Campden), published by Penguin. Another guide is *The Cotswold Way* by Kev Reynolds (Cicerone, £6.99).

Maps

The Ordnance Survey (OS) *Cotswold Touring Map* (1:63,360) covers the first two-thirds of the Way from Chipping Campden to just beyond Painswick. For more detail, OS Landranger (1:50,000) maps 150, 151, 162, 163 and 172 cover the whole Way (162 and 172 cover the parts not on the Touring Map). The Ramblers' Association (RA) has two 1:25,000 maps based on OS maps which cover part of the route.

PLACES TO STAY & EAT

The Cotswold Way can offer classy hotels and gourmet food, and is admirably equipped with B&Bs, although these generally cost a bit more than the British average; around £16 to £22 per person.

Choice is more limited if you're trying to do it on a budget. There are not many campsites, but there are plenty of inviting looking fields. Prospective campers should always politely request permission before setting up tent. Hostel possibilities are not so good either. There's a YHA hostel right by the Way at Cleeve Hill, but otherwise hostels require off-the-way excursions by bus or taxi, until you reach Bath.

Pubs, shops and cafes along the route make lunches fairly easy, although it's worth carrying something, just in case planned stops don't work out perfectly.

Places to stay are listed in the route description. For further information, as well as the *RA Yearbook* and the *National Trail Companion* (see the Books section of the Facts for the Walker chapter), the annually published *Cotswold Way Handbook* lists accommodation and other details, available for £1 from the RA or from local Tourist Information Centres (TICs).

GETTING THERE & AWAY
Bus & Train

Oxford, Statford and Evesham can all be reached by rail or National Express coach.

SOUTHERN ENGLAND

SOUTHERN ENGLAND

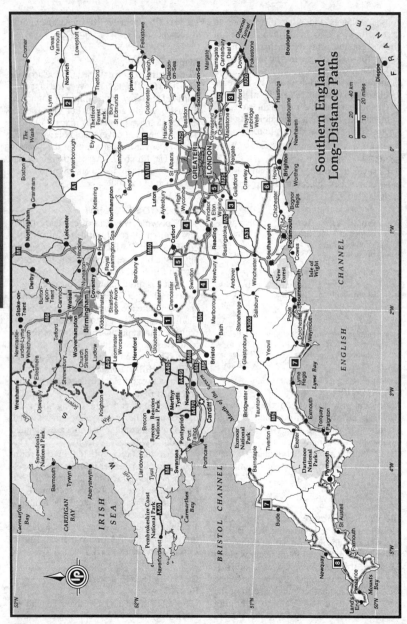

Southern England
Long-Distance Paths

There are regular buses from all three towns to Chipping Campden.

The southern end of the route is right in the heart of Bath. Bath is on the main railway line between London and Bristol, and is also linked by National Express to other points around the country.

Car

Chipping Campden lies north of the A44 between Evesham and Oxford, about 12 miles south of Stratford-upon-Avon. Bath, at the end of the route, is south of the M4 motorway between London and Bristol.

THE ROUTE
The Start: Chipping Campden

The stonework in the houses of Chipping Campden is said to be the finest in the Cotswolds, so it makes a fitting starting point. Buildings of interest include the medieval town hall, St James' Church and the 1627 market hall. Further up the street, William Grevel's late-14th-century house can lay claim to being the oldest and the finest in the village. Also worth a visit is the Ernest Wilson Memorial Garden with an international collection of plants from East Asia.

Chipping Campden has a good selection of B&Bs. Those near the start of the path include *Sandalwood House* (☎ 01386 840091), charging between £20 and £25. Others to try are *Haydon House* (☎ 01386 840275), with comfortable single/double ensuite rooms for £23/45, and the similar *Sparlings* (☎ 01386 840505, £26.50/43.50). At Dover Hill, on the route just outside the village, is *Weston Park Farm* (☎ 01386 840835), with a single for £25, and large

ensuite double for £40. The people here are friendly, and let you park your car here while you're doing the Cotswold Way. The village is well supplied with pubs; most do food. The *Eight Bells* (☎ 01386 840371) in Church St does delicious dishes like king prawns in garlic for £7.50. Other places to try are *Badger Bistro* (☎ 01386 840520) in The Square, and *Joel's Restaurant* (☎ 01386 840598) in the high street with pasta from £4.95 and main dishes for £6 to £13.

Day 1: Chipping Campden to Broadway
6 miles (9.5 km), 2½ to 3 hours

This short half day technically begins from the town hall, but St James' Church probably makes a more appropriate starting point, since it's visible for many miles from the village.

The path climbs up Hoo Lane to Dover Hill with fine views to the west. This is the start of the Cotswold Edge, the escarpment which the Way sticks to for most of its distance. Dover Hill takes its name from Robert Dover who instituted a local 'Olympick Games' in 1612, featuring such fine sports as 'shin kicking'. From here the route runs fairly level along a long, narrow field known as the Mile Drive. It then crosses fields and a road beside the *Fish Inn* pub, and climbs gently to Broadway Tower, an elegant 1798 folly on Beacon Hill.

The view from the top is not much better than the fine view from ground level, but the tower does house interesting exhibits on its 19th and 20th-century inhabitants. From the tower the Way descends steeply, crossing a number of stiles, to the very touristy village of Broadway.

Broadway The village started life as part of a nearby monastery and expanded during the 17th and 18th centuries and became an important stop for stagecoaches. The 12th-century St Eadburgh's Church, a survivor from the old monastery, is half a mile away. The picturesque high street houses are constructed of golden stone with the typical Cotswold mix of tiled and thatched roofs.

SOUTHERN ENGLAND

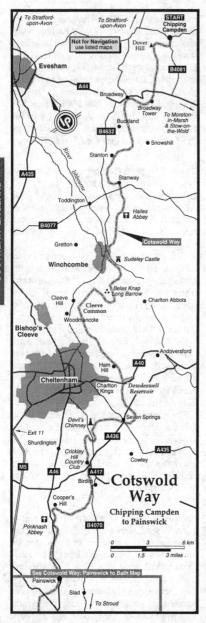

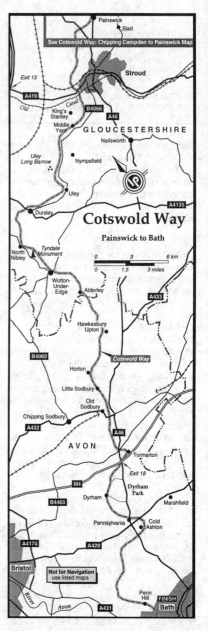

Shakespeare Cottages on Flea Bank are a particularly photogenic group.

For a place to stay, you might consider the deluxe *Lygon Arms* (☎ 01386 852255) (pronounced 'liggon'). It was converted from a home to an inn in the 16th century and renamed by General Lygon, a Waterloo hero, around 1830. Today it's one of the best known country hotels in Britain; singles/doubles start from £103/153 but you'd better have a tie in your backpack if you want dinner. If you're already tiring of the walk you could call for a helicopter, as the hotel has its own landing pad.

If your credit card won't stretch to the Lygon Arms there are plenty of less expensive options. Camping is available at *Leedon's Park* (☎ 01386 852423) for £7 per tent. B&Bs include *Olive Branch Guest House* (☎ 01386 853440), at 78 High St, charging from £17, up to £45 for an ensuite double, and *Southwold House* (☎ 01386 853681), Station Rd, from £20 to £25.

The excellent *Cinnibar Cottage* (☎ 01386 858623), at 45 Bury End, about half a mile from the centre, charges £33 a double. Pubs include the *Crown & Trumpet* (☎ 01386 853202), with B&B from £20, and good food.

Other places to eat include the comfortable *Luigi's* and *Goblet's*, part of the Lygon Arms, but with fine pub food at surprisingly reasonable prices. The TIC (☎ 01386 852937), at 1 Cotswold Crt, can help with more accommodation options if the ones suggested here are full.

Day 2: Broadway to Winchcombe
12 miles (19 km), 4½ to 5½ hours

The route climbs to Broadway Coppice, a small patch of wood, then skirts the village of Buckland. If it's open, consider a diversion to Snowshill Manor, which has an amazing collection of odds and ends assembled by its last owner. The Way climbs to Shenbarrow, an Iron Age hillfort, and cuts right through the fort's embankments to drop steeply down to the pretty village of Stanton. This is a possible place to overnight or pause for a pint at the pleasant *Mount Inn*.

The Way cuts across fields to Stanway House (open Tuesday and Thursday). Near the church is a 14th-century tithe barn. The *Old Bakehouse* does teas and snacks, but not every day.

The route climbs to Beckbury Camp, a large Iron Age fort, then drops to Hayles Fruit Farm where you can get tea and snacks or farm produce and other refreshments. Just beyond the farm are the ruins of Hailes Abbey, which once attracted streams of medieval pilgrims to see its famed sample of Christ's blood – later proved to be coloured honey! Nearby, the tiny St Nicholas Church predates the abbey and has walls decorated with fading, but still discernible, 13th-century murals.

The Way follows the old pilgrims' route to Winchcombe.

Winchcombe The small township of Winchcombe was once a medieval abbey, but after Henry VIII conducted his monastic land-grab in 1539 it completely disappeared. Historic sites remaining include St Peter's Church (1465), which is noted for its amusing collection of gargoyles. Just outside the town, Sudeley Castle is open daily during the summer months. It was the home of Henry VIII's sixth wife, Catherine Parr, but it was deliberately damaged after the Civil War and not rebuilt until nearly 200 years later in 1863-67. Winchcombe also has a museum and a TIC (☎ 01242 602925) in the old town hall.

Places to stay include *Courtyard House* (☎ 01242 602441), at 18 High St, with double rooms for £35, and *Cleevely Cottage* (☎ 01242 602059), at Wadfield Farm, which is on the Way, and charges £20/36 for singles/doubles. *Gower House* (☎ 01242 602616), at 16 North St, charges between £16 and £20 per person. Further out, *Blair House* (☎ 01242 603626), at 41 Gretton Rd, charges £16/32. *Sudeley Hill Farm* (☎ 01242 602344), overlooking the castle, about a mile from the centre, charges from £21. For eats, *Pilgrims Bistro* (☎ 01242 603544), round the corner from the TIC at 6 North St, has main dishes from £6 to £13.

Petticoat Tails (☎ 01242 603578), at 7 Hailes St, does soup with tasty rosemary and raisin bread for £2.20 and a set tea for £3.95. Pubs doing food include the 15th-century *Old White Lion*, the *White Hart Inn* on the main street, and the *Plaisterer's Arms*, which also does good B&B from £15 to £18 per person.

Day 3: Winchcombe to Cheltenham
11 miles (17.5 km), 4½ to 5½ hours

This day's walk finishes off the Way due to limited accommodation options on the route.

From Winchcombe the Way goes along Vineyard St (formerly known as Duck St as disobedient women were once ducked in the river here!) then passes the castle, to cut across fields with footpath markers like targets to aim for. The route climbs past Wadfield Farm (no sign of the nearby Roman villa) and continues to climb steadily and rather circuitously to Belas Knap, a 4000 year old Neolithic long barrow.

The Way then makes a circuit around Cleeve Common. You could save several miles by cutting straight across, but if you go the long way you reach Cleeve Hill, perched on the edge of the Cotswolds, with excellent views. This also makes a possible overnight stop, with comfortable *Inglecroft* (☎ 01242 673558) charging £15 per person, and the *Rising Sun Hotel* (☎ 01242 676281) £75 per room; there are several other places. There's good food in the *High Roost* pub or excellent food in the *Rising Sun's* restaurant.

From Cleeve Hill the Way continues around the edge of the common, passing an Iron Age earthwork dubbed, for obvious reasons, The Ring, then down Happy Valley out of Cleeve Common. You meet a road, where a sign points towards the *Ham Hill Farm B&B* (☎ 01242 584415). The route drops steeply down to Dowdeswell Reservoir, where B&B is available at *Langett* (☎ 01242 820192) from £16 per person. Just beyond here you meet the main A40. On the other side of the road is the *Reservoir Inn*. From here it's about one mile to Charlton Kings, a smart suburb of Cheltenham with

some places to stay, or three miles into Cheltenham itself where there is plenty of accommodation.

Buses run along the A40, or taxis are available from Central (☎ 01242 52611 or ☎ 01242 523219) or Cheltax (☎ 01242 525191 or ☎ 01242 522280).

Cheltenham Places to stay in Charlton Kings include the *Old Stables* (☎ 01242 583660), at 239A London Rd, charging from £15 for B&B. An alternative is the *Charlton Kings Hotel* (☎ 01242 231061), just half a mile off the Way. It's a fairly smart place, but they welcome walkers, with B&B in an ensuite double at £82, and single rooms from £49, plus £5.50 for breakfast. Evening meals are around £10 to £15.

Essentially a very elegant Regency town, Cheltenham has not survived the 20th century as well as Bath, so handsome squares, colourful public gardens and elegant architecture are interspersed with dreary contemporary shopping areas. However, with plenty to see and a good selection of places to stay and eat, Cheltenham makes an ideal rest-day, and is also a handy 'escape' point, as transport to other parts of the country is good.

The helpful TIC (☎ 01242 522878) is on The Promenade – a wide street decorated with hanging baskets full of flowers in summer, and described as Britain's most beautiful thoroughfare.

If you're on a tight budget, cheap places to stay include the *YMCA* (☎ 01242 524024), at 6 Vittoria Walk, with singles from £13. Over Easter and the summer vacation *Cheltenham & Gloucester College* (☎ 01242 532774) lets out student rooms from £18 per person. The nearest place to pitch a tent is *Longwillows Caravan & Camping Park* (☎ 01242 674113), three miles from the town on Station Rd, Woodmancote (near Bishop's Cleeve), charging £2.75 for backpackers. The best place to search out cheaper B&B is the Montpellier area, just south-west of the centre. Along Park Place, there's *Segrave* (☎ 01242 523606), at No 7, and *No 32* (☎ 01242

582889) both from £16. *Micklinton Hotel* (☎ 01242 520000) at 12 Montpellier Dve, has ensuite doubles for £38. Nearby is *Lonsdale House* (☎ 01242 232379) from £18 per person, and *St Michael's Guest House* (☎ 01242 513587) for £22/35. Also centrally located, the friendly *Brennan Guest House* (☎ 01242 525904), at 21 St Lukes Rd, has six rooms for £18/34, mostly with common bathroom. More expensive places include *Lypiatt House* (☎ 01242 224994), in Lypiatt Rd, from £48/55, and the *Hallery House Hotel* (☎ 01242 578450), at 48 Shurdington Rd, south of the centre, with ensuite rooms from £45/65 (and cheaper rooms without ensuite from £21/42). Nearby *Beaumont House Hotel* (☎ 01242 245986) has rooms from £25/40.

Further up the scale, the gracious Victorian *Queen's Hotel* (☎ 514724) stands at the top of The Promenade, with rooms from £54/104. Previous guests include Edward VII, Edward Elgar and Arthur Conan Doyle, but it's not clear if they were all walking the Cotswold Way. Between the town centre and Pittville Park, the luxurious Regency *Hotel on the Park* (☎ 01242 518898) charges £76/99.

For places to eat, Cheltenham has a very good choice for all budgets. Around the bus station are several cheap cafes; try *Muffin Man*, at 3 Crescent Terrace, or *Le Café*, at 1 Royal Well Rd. *Pizza Express* in Belgrave House, Imperial Square has live jazz on Wednesday evenings. Other places to try include *Pepper's* (☎ 01242 234232), at 317 High St, an inviting vegetarian restaurant where a nut roast and salad costs less than £5. Other places worth a mention are *Below Stairs* (☎ 01242 234599), at 103 The Promenade, a popular bistro specialising in seafood with main courses between £8 and £18. Nearby, the *New Land* (☎ 01242 525346) is a good Vietnamese restaurant. In Montpellier, *Flynn's* (☎ 01242 252752), at 16/17 Courtyard, is a convenient and moderately priced brasserie. The excellent *Indus* (☎ 01242 516676), at 226 Bath Rd, is most probably the best of the town's Indian restaurants.

Day 4: Cheltenham to Painswick
19 miles (30.5 km), 8 to 9 hours

From Cheltenham or Charlton Kings, return to the Cotswold Way at the Reservoir Inn. The Way leaves the road and crosses an old railway, to climb through the pretty Lineover Wood, up a grassy bank and across to the A436.

Here there's a choice of a one mile slog along the busy road or a two mile country route.

Whichever you choose you'll end up at a confusing road junction close to the *Seven Springs Inn*. The springs are the source of the River Churn which eventually joins the Thames; some claim this is the Thames' real source. From the junction the Way passes Windmill Farm, with a decrepit miniature version of an Australian windmill, and then makes another foray along the edge of a plateau. At Leckhampton Hill the intriguing Devil's Chimney is just north of the Way, off the edge of the plateau. This rock pinnacle 'natural feature' is actually the product of Victorian quarryworkers with a sense of humour!

After passing a golf course the Way runs through a wood to Crickley Hill Country Club with the site of a large Iron Age hillfort and more modern quarries. A short detour just before entering the park will take you into Shurdington, a village on the southern fringe of Cheltenham where the accommodation possibilities include the luxurious *Greenway Hotel* (☎ 01242 862352).

Just beyond the park the *Air Balloon* pub serves snacks and meals. The Way soon leaves the road. After pausing for the view at Barrow Wake you follow the path through woods to a promontory lookout at the Peak. It's a short, but very steep, detour from the Way into the small village of Birdlip with B&Bs including the *Beechmount Guest House* (☎ 01452 862506), the *Royal George Hotel* (☎ 01452 862262) and the *Kingshead House Restaurant*, a critics' favourite which also does fairly expensive B&B. From Birdlip, the Way makes a long foray through woods, passing close to the remains of a Roman villa at Great Witcombe, then continues along the edge of the woods to Cooper's Hill where scones and jam at the *Haven Tea Garden* is a Cotswold Way ritual. It also offers B&B and camping, and the 'closed' sign is not 100% reliable!

The Way climbs up beside an extremely steep, rolling field (site of the annual Spring Bank Holiday cheese-rolling contest, a rough and ready pursuit dating from medieval times) then runs through woods, passing close to Prinknash Abbey where the monks run a teashop. *St Mary's Lodge* (☎ 01452 813222) in Prinknash has B&B and some camping space.

The Way continues through woods and across a golf course beside Painswick Beacon, another Iron Age hillfort, much chopped around by quarrying, then enters the pretty village of Painswick.

Painswick The tourist town of Painswick has heavy traffic and jostling crowds at weekends, but it's definitely a town with a history: New St was 'new' in 1253, and the timber framing on the post office dates from 1428. Other attractive buildings line the convoluted streets, but the typical Cotswold stone is a little greyer, a little less golden, than further north. St Mary's Church dominates the centre of the village and is noted for its large collection of table-top tombs and for the 99 neatly trimmed yew trees that line the paths through the churchyard.

Painswick has a very wide choice of accommodation, pubs and restaurants. In Edge Rd *Hambutt's Mynd* (☎ 01452 812352) is a pleasant place catering especially for Cotswold Way walkers for £21/39. Nearby is *The Cottage* (☎ 01452 812352) with B&B at £21/39. You can camp beside Edge Rd at *Hambutt's Field* (☎ 01452 812495) for £2; enquire at Rudge House on Edge Rd. Other B&Bs to try include *Upper Dorey's Mill* (☎ 01452 812459), £38 a double, *Brookhouse Mill Cottage* (☎ 01452 812854), Tibbiwell Lane, around £19 per person, and *Thorne* (☎ 01452 812476), Friday St, one of the town's oldest buildings, with doubles for £36. Luxurious accommodation can be found at the *Painswick Hotel*

(☎ 01452 812160) with rooms for £70/98, many with views over the valley.

For food and drink, the *Royal Oak* in St Mary's St is a popular local. The *Falcon Inn* (☎ 01452 812819) on New St, has a good-value set menu. Nearby, the pricier *Country Elephant Restaurant* (☎ 01452 813564) has main dishes from £6.50 to £16, and a cheaper set menu.

Day 5: Painswick to Dursley
16 miles (25.5 km), 6½ to 7½ hours

From Painswick the Way cuts across fields, crosses the B4072 by the *Edgemoor Inn*, then runs through woods before climbing to Haresfield Beacon at the end of a promontory. A mile further on it runs out to another promontory lookout point, then continues through Standish Wood with a National Trust (NT) *campsite*. The route steadily drops through woods and across more fields before crossing a railway line and the A419, where a sign indicates the way to a nearby *B&B*. It then crosses the disused Stroudwater Canal and the Frome River.

The Way skirts around King's Stanley but goes through Middle Yard; there are *B&Bs* in both locations, and Middle Yard also has a shop. The route then climbs steadily through woods and alongside the B4066 to pass the Nympsfield long barrow, a prehistoric burial site. A mile or so further on is the more impressive barrow called Hetty Pegler's Tump, but it's slightly off the route and you may have to detour to Crawley Barns to borrow the keys.

There are several B&Bs close to the Way at Nympsfield and Uley. The elegant and expensive *Calcot Manor* (☎ 01666 890391) is at nearby Calcot.

The Way descends by the Uleybury hillfort, looking like a large flat field atop a plateau.

From the ponds at the bottom there's a steep climb across fields to Cam Long Down and then an undulating walk along the top of this long ridge. A final up and down jig takes you over the flattened top of Cam Peak (popular with hang-gliders) and down into Dursley.

Dursley Remarkably little of the town dates from the wool trade boom era. The 1738 Market House, standing squarely in the centre of town, is virtually the only survivor. Facing the hall is St James' Church, minus its spire. In January 1699 a peal of bells was rung to celebrate the completion of major repairs, but the vibrations of the bells brought the whole lot tumbling down, wrecking the end of the church and killing a number of spectators. Queen Anne, who helped pay for the repairs, was rewarded with a statue in a niche in the Market House.

There are several hotels and B&Bs including *Claremont House* (☎ 01453 542018), at 66 Kingshill Rd, well used to Cotswold Way walkers, with B&B from £17.50. On Long St, the *Old Bell Hotel* (☎ 01453 542821) does B&B from £20. Just outside the town, on the Way near Stinchcombe Golf Course, is *Highlands* (☎ 01453 542539) with B&B from £20. For eats, a host of bakeries and cafes can be found along Parsonage Lane, the pedestrianised shopping street directly behind the Market House. For something more filling, try *Dil Raj Tandoori* (☎ 01453 543472), on Long St, or the *Old Spot Inn*, a popular pub on May Lane.

Day 6: Dursley to Old Sodbury
20 miles (32 km), 8 to 9 hours

The next 20 miles offers a number of good alternative places to overnight. The Way turns out of Dursley's pedestrianised main street, turns again by the *Old Spot* then climbs steeply to the golf course. You can follow the Way around the edge or cut a couple of miles out by simply walking across – a fine idea if you've had your fill of Cotswold tees and greens. The circuit does, however, take you to the summit of Stinchcombe Hill. The route descends to North Nibley where there's a host of B&Bs including the *Black Horse Inn* (☎ 01453 546841), at £27.50/40.

From the village the route ascends steeply and a little confusingly to the Tyndale Monument. Looking like a squared off lighthouse, erected in 1866 to commemorate William Tyndale who was born in North Nibley and made the first translation of the Bible into English in the 16th century. In 1538 Henry VIII passed a law that every church in England must have a Bible in English. Could have been a good earner for William but, unfortunately, he had been burnt at the stake for heresy in 1536. You can ascend the monument, but first you must borrow the key from the shop in North Nibley at the bottom of the hill. And return it afterwards!

The Way runs on a wide, easy path through Westridge Woods emerging to a lookout above Wotton-under-Edge at the curious Jubilee Clump, a circular walled-in enclosure of trees planted in 1815 to commemorate the Battle of Waterloo. The route drops steeply down to Wotton-under-Edge, another good overnight stop.

Wotton is another once-prosperous wool town. The fine St Mary the Virgin Church dates from at least 1283, possibly even earlier. On Church St, Hugh Perry's Alms-houses have a daunting list of regulations above the entranceway. Just off Long St in Orchard St, Isaac Pitman invented a system of shorthand writing in 1837 and immortalised his name for the secretarial profession. On summer Tuesday to Sunday afternoons the now disused Tabernacle Church is open to show the wonderful reproduction of a Roman mosaic pavement.

The *Wotton Coffee Shop* (☎ 01453 843158), at 31A High St, is a good B&B which looks after walkers well, charging £20/35. Wotton also has several pubs including the *Falcon Inn* and the *Royal Oak* which serves up food in big enough quantities for any walker's well-honed appetite. Alternatively, try *Wotton Indian Cuisine* on Church St.

From Wotton, the route climbs to a lookout above the engagingly named Nanny Farmer's Bottom, then drops down to Alderley. From there it runs along a small lane with some attractive old houses beside a pretty stream, then climbs through woods and fields to join a road just before the towering 1846 Somerset (or Hawkesbury) Monument, commemorating a Battle of

Waterloo hero. Hawkesbury Upton has a pub and shop but the route peels off just as it enters the village and runs for a couple of miles beside fields before turning into woods to skirt Horton Court, part of which dates from the 12th century. The Way then follows a lane to the village of Horton.

The Way continues to Little Sodbury where Tyndale worked on his Bible, then climbs to cross the very prominent ramparts of the Sodbury hillfort which dates from the Iron Age, but was also used by the Romans and Saxons. A few minutes more walking leads to Old Sodbury.

Old Sodbury Despite its busy location on a main road, and uninspiring name, Old Sodbury has a plentiful supply of B&Bs including *Dornden Guest House* (☎ 01454 313325), Church Lane, charging £25/40 for singles/doubles (£36/50 for ensuite), *Crofton* (☎ 01454 314288), Chapel Lane, from £16, and *Mrs Rees* (☎ 01454 314688), at 1 The Green, charging £19 per person (or £23 for ensuite). The *Dog Inn* does good food, and has B&B from £15 to £18. *The Bell* also has food.

Day 7: Old Sodbury to Bath
19 miles (30.5 km), 7½ to 8½ hours

The walk continues through fields, passing very close to but without actually catching a glimpse of Dodington House, crossing the A46 and a succession of stiles as it threads through Tormarton; there the *Portcullis Inn* (☎ 01454 218263) charges £38 a double, and a couple of other places offer accommodation. The church of St Mary Magdalene in Tormarton dates from Norman times and has a number of interesting memorials. After dodging round the M4 motorway exit roundabout, the Way soon heads into fields again before crossing the B4465 and skirting Dyrham House's deer park. (The main entrance to Dyrham House is on the A46, but there's a back gate from the parish churchyard.)

From Dyrham it's more fields and woods before the Way crosses the A46 again at Pennsylvania where there's the *Swan* pub.

Another couple of field crossings bring you to the *White Hart* on the A420 and the village of Cold Ashton. There are several *B&Bs* in Cold Ashton and several more in nearby Marshfield offering a lift service. A five mile diversion from here will take you to *Lucknam Park* (☎ 01225 742777), the final opportunity for luxury overnighting along the Way.

The route crosses a series of fields, and one fine lookout, which also features a fine seat, courtesy of a thoughtful local farmer. The Granville Monument commemorates a 1643 Civil War battle at this site where, the inscription notes: 'more officers and gentlemen of quality than private soldiers were slain'. The Way skirts another golf course, fortunately without making it the excuse for a long excursion, then cuts through the Little Down hillfort.

The Way follows tracks – with occasional glimpses of Bath below – to Penn Hill, then descends a hill, cuts across a recreation ground and surprisingly suddenly deposits you in the suburban sprawl of Weston. After strolling down the suburb's shopping street, however, the Way dives off to the other side of the valley and has a final semirural fling, complete with a couple of stiles and gates, before crossing yet another small golf course and Royal Victoria Park, then emerging on The Royal Avenue past The Royal Crescent. From here several twists and turns take you through the centre of Bath to the Abbey, and the end of the Cotswold Way.

Bath Beautiful Bath is one of the 'must sees' on any first-time visitor's list, and it makes a splendid finale to your walk down the Cotswold Way. For more than 2000 years, the city's fortune has revolved around its hot springs and the tourism linked to it. It was the Romans who first developed a complex of baths and a temple to Sulis-Minerva on the site of what they called Aquae Sulis. Today, however, Bath is just as famous for its glorious Georgian architecture, which has won it World Heritage Site status from UNESCO.

Throughout the 18th century, Bath was the

most fashionable and elegant haunt of English society. Aristocrats flocked here to gossip, gamble and flirt. Fortunately, they had the good sense and fortune to employ a number of brilliant architects who designed the Palladian terraced housing, the circles, the crescents and the squares, that dominate the city.

Like Florence in Italy, Bath is an architectural gem. It too has a much-photographed, shop-lined bridge, and like Florence, the town can sometimes seem little more than an up-market shopping mall for wealthy tourists. However, when sunlight brightens the honey-coloured stone, and buskers and strollers fill the streets and line the river, only the most churlish would deny its charm.

The best known sites in and around Abbey Courtyard receive too many visitors for their own good. Away from the centre, however, smaller museums fight for the droppings from their more famous neighbours' tables, and are genuinely pleased to see those who trouble to seek them out.

Inevitably, Bath also has its share of residents for whom affluence is somebody else's story. Alongside the glitz, you'll see beggars on the streets. The legacy of 1980s boom-bust economics also lingers in abandoned shops and hotels, even in the city centre.

Information & Guided Walks The TIC (☎ 01225 462831) in the Abbey Churchyard, is open Monday to Saturday until 7 pm, and until 6 pm on Sunday from mid-June to mid-September. For the rest of the year it closes at 5 pm, and 4 pm on Sunday. It has a *bureau de change*. If you're still feeling fit after the Cotswold Way, fascinating walking tours (free) leave from the Abbey Churchyard at 10.30 am (except Saturday).

Bath Festival From mid-May to early June the Bath Festival is in full swing with artistic and cultural events all over the city. Details are available from the Festival Box Office (☎ 01225 462231), at 1 Pierrepont Place, from February each year. Accommodation is likely to be particularly hard to find during the festival.

Places to Stay Bath is a popular tourist destination with something for every taste and budget. Advance booking over holiday periods is highly recommended.

The new *Bath Backpackers Hotel* (☎ 01225 446787), at 13 Pierrepont St, is Bath's most convenient budget accommodation: less than 10 minutes walk from the bus and railway stations. B&B in dorm rooms

Prehistoric Camps

Prehistoric camps on the hills around Bath indicate settlement before the Romans arrived, and legend records King Bladud founding the town after being cured of leprosy by a bath in the muddy swamps. The Romans seem to have established the town of Aquae Sulis (named after the Celtic goddess Sul) in 44 AD and it was already a spa, with an extensive baths complex, by the reign of Agricola (78-84). When the Romans left, the town declined and was captured by the Anglo-Saxons in 577. In 944 a monastery was set up on the site of the present abbey and there are still traces of a medieval town wall in Borough Walls St. Throughout the Middle Ages, Bath served as an ecclesiastical centre and a wool trading town.

However, it wasn't until the 18th century that the city came into its own, when the idea of taking spa water as a cure for assorted ailments led to the creation of the beautiful city visitors see today. Those were the days when Ralph Allen developed the quarries at Coombe Down and employed the Woods (father and son) to create the glorious crescents and terraces; when Doctor William Oliver created the Bath General Hospital for the poor and gave his name to the Bath Oliver biscuit; and when the gambler Richard 'Beau' Nash became the arbiter of fashionable taste.

By the mid-19th century, sea bathing had become more popular than visiting spas and Bath fell from favour as a place to stay. Curiously, even in the 1960s few people appreciated its architecture and many houses were pulled down to make way for modern replacements, before legislation was introduced to protect what remains. ■

SOUTHERN ENGLAND

with up to eight beds costs £9.50. There's a lounge and cooking facilities and even a spa bath. The *YMCA International House* (☎ 01225 460471) is also central, takes men and women, and has no curfew, but is often full, especially in summer. Singles/doubles with continental breakfast are £12.50/23, dorms are £10. *Bath YHA Hostel* (☎ 01225 465674, £9.10), is out towards the University of Bath, a good 25 minute walk, or catch Badgerline bus No 18 (75p return) from the bus station. The nearest campsite is three miles west of Bath, at Newton St Loe; *Newton Mill Touring Centre* (☎ 01225 333909), charges £7.95 for a tent and two people.

B&B in Bath doesn't come cheap. In summer, most places charge at least £18/32 for singles/doubles. The main areas are along Upper Bristol Rd (A4) and Newbridge Rd to the west, Wells Rd to the south, and around Pulteney Rd in the east. *Henry Guest House* (☎ 01225 424052), at 6 Henry St, is a bargain at £16 per person, and very central: just a few minutes walk from the bus and railway stations. *No 9 Charlotte St* (☎ 01225 424193) is also central, and good value from £30 for a double. *Ashley House* (☎ 01225 425027), at 8 Pulteney Gardens, charges from £20 to £25 per person. *No 14 Raby Place* (☎ 01225 465120), off Bathwick Hill, off Pulteney Rd, is a nonsmoking establishment charging £18 to £21. Continue along Bathwick Hill over the canal to *No 14 Dunsford Place* (☎ 01225 464134), a small B&B that charges from £15.

There are several places along Henrietta St, near Henrietta Park. At No 34, the *Georgian Guest House* (☎ 01225 424103) has a range of rooms from £20 for a simple single to £35/45 ensuite singles/doubles. The *Henrietta Hotel* (☎ 01225 447779) is next door at No 32; during the week, rooms cost from £25/35, and rise to £35/55 or more at weekends. All rooms have attached bathroom and a buffet breakfast is included.

In an idyllic location beside the River Avon, the *Old Boathouse* (☎ 01225 466407), Forester Rd, is within walking distance of the centre. Comfortable non-smoking ensuite rooms cost from £20 per person. If you want to celebrate the end of your walk in style, or have had your appetite for luxury whetted by all those fancy Cotswold inns, Bath also has several luxurious small hotels. These include *Somerset House* (☎ 01225 463471), at 35 Bathwick Hill, which is a comfortable nonsmoking Georgian restaurant with rooms with views over Bath. Rooms cost from £43/100 at weekends. The nonsmoking award-winning *Holly Lodge* (☎ 01225 424042), at 8 Upper Oldfield Park, is a 10 minute walk from the centre, with views over the city, and rooms from £46/75. Bath's top place to stay is the grand *Royal Crescent Hotel* (☎ 01225 319090), where rooms are officially from £98/120, but if it's low season and midweek you can ask about special rates.

Places to Eat With so many travellers passing through, Bath overflows with pleasant eating and drinking places. In Manvers St near the bus station *Bloomsbury's Café-Bar* (☎ 01225 311955) has a good choice of vegetarian dishes from £4. Near the abbey *Café Retro* (☎ 01225 339347) in York St does three-course meals for around £10, although you can snack for much less. *Demuth's* (☎ 01225 446059) in North Parade Passage serves vegetarian/vegan meals from about £4.50. *Pierre Victoire* (☎ 01225 334334), at 16 Argyle St, does a popular three-course set lunch for £4.90. Nearby, at 2 Grove St, *Bathtub Bistro* (☎ 01225 460593) is a good-value place serving interesting dishes from around £5.

In the centre, on Walcot Rd, there are several restaurants upstairs in the modern Podium shopping complex; choose from Tex-Mex at *Footlights*, spicy Szechuan-style Chinese at *Just Duck* or Italian at *Caffe Piazza*. There's also a very popular branch of *Carwardine's Coffee House*. The central area has loads of cosy pubs, many doing food.

These include the *Moon & Sixpence* (☎ 01225 460962), at 6 Broad St, with two-course all-you-can-eat lunches for £5, and the *Crystal Palace* (☎ 01225 423944),

DAVID ELSE

TONY WHEELER

DAVID ELSE

Top: Along the scenic Kennet & Avon Canal in Wessex
Middle: Looking across to Freshwater Bay, on the Tennyson Trail, Isle of Wight
Bottom: Right of way through cornfields, in the Norfolk Broads

DAVID ELSE

DAVID ELSE

DAVID ELSE

Top: Wells-next-the-Sea, East Anglia
Middle: Berney Arms windmill, Norfolk Broads
Bottom: Sheringham, Norfolk Coast Path

Abbey Green, has a beer garden, traditional ale and lunch or evening meals from £4.50. This last place is just south of the Abbey itself and a good place for an end-of-Way celebratory pint before going off to your accommodation.

Peddars Way & Norfolk Coast Path

Official Name Peddars Way & Norfolk Coast Path National Trail
Distance 88½ miles (142.5 km)
Duration 6 to 8 days
Start Knettishall Heath
Finish Cromer
Regional Centres Norwich, Thetford, Swaffham, King's Lynn, Cromer
County Norfolk
Area East Anglia
Summary A generally level route, on good paths with some minor roads, through rolling farmland and coastal areas. Generally firm underfoot, although on the coast soft sand and pebbles may slow progress.

This national trail through East Anglia combines two contrasting routes into one. The Peddars Way is a Roman road, originally built around 60 AD as part of Rome's battle against the legendary British Queen Boudicca (see aside). As a military road, Peddars Way did not connect settlements, and generally speaking that's still the case today; when walking here you're unlikely to meet more than a handful of people, even on a sunny summer's day.

The Norfolk Coast Path tends to be more populated, and also offers plenty of history. Villages claim a maritime tradition that saw them send fighting ships to repel the Spanish Armada of 1588. Lord Nelson, one of the greatest English admirals (Battle of Trafalgar, 'Kismet Hardy' and all that) hailed from Burnham Thorpe, just a little way inland.

The Norfolk coast boasts some of the finest sections of sweeping, sandy beaches in Britain, and although in summer it can get pretty busy around the towns, a walker can quite quickly get away from the crowds and enjoy spectacular vistas of sky and sea. This area is also about the richest in Britain for birdwatching, with some internationally important reserves. You'll meet bird-watchers along the way who will be pleased to tell you what's new in the area, so, even if you're not that keen, it's worth packing a pair of binoculars.

DIRECTION, DISTANCE & DURATION

The route starts at Knettishall Heath, around five miles east of Thetford, then runs roughly north-west to the coast at Holme-next-the-Sea. As befits a Roman road, Peddars Way is often literally straightforward to follow, although it does occasionally deviate, so a map is essential. From Holme the route heads eastwards, often with saltmarshes between you and the sea, but you'll soon get the hang of a coastal walk that may not involve sea views for several miles.

The whole route is generally well way-marked, with the standard national trail acorn symbol and straightforward yellow

Peddars Way

Peddars Way is a Roman road, constructed around AD60 in order to move troops around quickly to deal with the rebellious locals. Queen Boudicca (or Boadicea) led the Iceni in a violent and briefly successful uprising against the occupying Romans, taking the modern-day towns of Colchester, St Albans and London. The Roman governor Paullinus eventually defeated the Iceni, and the new road was built to establish a link between the Lincolnshire coast, from where his troops were ferried across to Holme, and newly built garrisons responsible for maintaining the military presence.

There is no recorded Roman name for Peddars Way, which probably derives from a much later word for 'path'. ■

arrows, although signposts are not standard throughout.

Peddars Way is 46½ miles from Knettishall to Holme, and the Coast Path a further 41½ miles to Cromer, making a total of 88½ miles. There are no short cuts, but it is possible to finish before Cromer, or not start at the true beginning (given the awkward situation of the start, this could be quite a good idea).

The Coast Path actually starts at Hunstanton, west of Holme. If you're a real purist you should cover this too, bringing the total distance up to 93 miles.

Most people take three or four days to complete each half of the route; so it'll take six to eight in total. The availability of accommodation will be your prime consideration. If time is short and you are a strong walker, Day 1 and Day 2 can be merged. It's even possible to burn up the entire route in four days, stopping at Castle Acre, Holme and Wells, but you won't see much of your surroundings and, given the remarkable sense of space that the landscape confers, this would be a shame. Some guidebooks suggest additional stops at Sedgeford (before reaching the coast), and breaking the coastal path (where there's a wider accommodation choice) into four sections by stopping after Holme in Burnham Overy Staithe, Stiffkey and Weybourne. If you like to amble, paddle in the sea, eat ice-cream and watch birds, then do this.

STAGES

For a six day walk, as described here, the most convenient places to start and end each day are:

Day	From	To	Distance
1	Knettishall	Little Cressingham	14½ miles (23 km)
2	Little Cressingham	Castle Acre	12 miles (19 km)
3	Castle Acre	Holme-next-the-Sea	20 miles (33 km)
4	Holme-next-the-Sea	Wells-next-the-Sea	19 miles (30.5 km)
5	Wells-next-the-Sea	Cley-next-the-Sea	10 miles (16 km)
6	Cley-next-the-Sea	Cromer	13 miles (21 km)

Books & Maps

The walk description in this book, combined with a map, should get you from Knettishall to Cromer, but for more detail on the route and the places of interest on the way, a few guidebooks are recommended. These include the 'official' *Peddars Way & Norfolk Coast Path National Trail Guide* by Bruce Robinson, a thorough and well-presented guide, with excellent colour OS strip maps, photos and plenty of interesting background information. *Peddars Way & Norfolk Coast Path* by Andrew Durham (Langton, £9.99) is a very detailed route guide, which also includes accommodation, transport and shop information. Most useful is the cheap and regularly revised *Guide & Accommodation List* produced by the Peddars Way Association. It has a very handy list of telephone numbers for booking accommodation.

The whole route is covered by the OS Landranger (1:50,000) sheets 144, 132 and 133.

INFORMATION

There are TICs in Thetford (☎ 01842 752599), Wells (☎ 01328 710885), Sheringham (☎ 01263 824329) and Cromer (☎ 01263 512497), but these are open only in summer. King's Lynn (☎ 01553 763044) or Norwich (☎ 01603 666071) are open all year.

GUIDED WALKS

National companies organising tours along LDPs are listed in the main Getting Around chapter. Local companies specialising in this area include *Windmill Ways* (☎ 01603 871111).

PLACES TO STAY & EAT

There are B&Bs along the whole route, although on the Peddars Way (which was never built to connect settlements, and to a large extent still doesn't) options are limited. There are more places to stay on the coast, but many of the villages are small and this is a popular holiday destination, so advanced booking is often advisable, even in spring and autumn, when the birdwatching is especially good. Camping is also possible, but again there are fewer sites than you'd expect. Places to stay are listed in the route description. For a wider choice, as well as the *RA Yearbook* and the *National Trail Companion* (see the Books section of the Facts for the Walker chapter), an accommodation guide is available – see the earlier Books & Maps section.

For food along the way, there are some excellent pubs, and cafes on the coast. If you are self-catering there are also shops where you can restock, but detours may be required on the Peddars Way.

GETTING THERE & AWAY
Bus
Norwich, Thetford and Cromer are all on the National Express network. For local buses though, it's absolutely vital to check timetables. Buses along the coast only operate in summer, so if you plan to finish in, say, Wells and get back to Norwich in February, you'll have an uncomfortably long wait. Likewise, buses do not necessarily run every day in some parts of Norfolk, so if you plan to start in Castle Acre, you will need to catch one of the twice-weekly shoppers' buses from King's Lynn (Tuesday and Saturday). The Norfolk Bus Information Centre (☎ 0500 626116) is open from 8.30 am to 5 pm, Monday to Saturday and staff are very helpful. There is no bus service to Knettishall Heath, so it's either a five mile walk from Thetford, or a sneaky start in a taxi. *Baz Cabs* (☎ 01842 753232) will get you there for £6.00.

Train
Thetford and Cromer have railway stations which connect through Norwich, and trains are fairly regular, although you should still check in advance, especially if you want to travel on a Sunday. Worth bearing in mind for the start of the walk is the station at Harling Road, east of Thetford (near the village of Larling, south of the A11), from where it is a far nicer walk to join the Peddars Way than the five miles of busy roads from Thetford.

Car
Knettishall Heath is a small country park, five miles east of Thetford, on a small road between Rushford and Hopton. There is a car park here, but it's a quiet spot and security may not be good. You should advise the Country Park Warden (☎ 01953 688265) if you are planning to leave your car here.

THE ROUTE
This is a suggested itinerary, but there are any number of variations possible with longer

SOUTHERN ENGLAND

Norfolk Windmills & the Link with Europe
Historically, East Anglia has always had close links with the European mainland. In the 6th and 7th centuries it was overrun by the Norsemen. From the late Middle Ages, Suffolk and Norfolk grew rich trading wool and cloth with the Flemish; this wealth built scores of churches and helped subsidise the development of Cambridge. The windmills, the long, straight drainage canals and even the architecture (especially in King's Lynn) call the Low Countries to mind. To this day, Harwich and Felixstowe are major ports for European traffic.

Windmills first appeared in eastern and Southern England towards the end of the 12th century, and by the 1850s there were about 240 working windmills in the Norfolk Broads. These were more accurately called windpumps, since their purpose was to drain the marshland, so making it suitable for animal grazing. Today, approximately 70 windpumps remain standing, and a few are still in working order. Probably the best example is Berney Arms windmill, passed on the Broads Walk route described in the Southern England – Short Walks chapter.

Throughout Norfolk are many more 'true' windmills, used for grinding corn. Bircham Mill, just off the Peddars Way, is well worth a visit. It is a working mill, complete with a complex system of gears to keep the sails facing the wind and an attached bakery – still using the original oven, which has capacity for 100 loaves. ■

SOUTHERN ENGLAND

days or additional stops. Some of these are detailed in the route description.

The Start: Knettishall Heath

The path officially begins in the Country Park car park, but your start is wherever you have spent the night before. There are B&Bs and pubs in Thetford, which is a small and quiet market town. Norwich might be a better choice; it's a lively and fascinating city, with plenty of places to stay. You can reach Thetford or Harling Road by train in the morning of your first day, and easily get back to Norwich from Cromer at the end of your walk.

Day 1: Knettishall Heath to Little Cressingham

14½ miles (23 km), 5 to 7 hours

The first day follows pleasant paths through oak and birch, with a brief but very pretty stretch beside the River Thet, and some open stretches of heath and farmland. The Way crosses a couple of major roads and a military range, but only one village (Stonebridge) with a pub and shop, so take enough drinking water and food.

From the official start at Knettishall Heath the path is clearly marked, leading into the woods and across a small bridge over the Little Ouse, the border between Suffolk and Norfolk.

It is very important to keep a look out for the waymarks on this early stage, but once beyond the Forestry Commission's Thorpe Woodland, the route settles into its long, straight stride. You will soon become familiar with the linear mound that marks the line of the old Roman road, which you follow, cross and recross, for the next three days.

Take great care crossing the A11 dual carriageway about four miles from the start. A sign declaring 'Danger – MOD range' may also increase your pulse rate at this stage, but so long as you keep to the path you'll be perfectly safe.

The Dog & Partridge pub in Stonebridge (which is also known as Wretham), is a potential lunch stop before the way crosses more

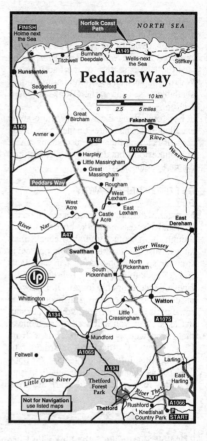

military ground, and then follows a stretch of the 'Great Eastern Pingo Trail'. Dating from the last Ice Age, a pingo is a lens-shaped mass of ice which forms under the ground, forcing the earth upwards, then melts to form circular hollows. Apart from its unusual geology, this area is interesting for its flowers and insects.

Emerging into more open farmland, traces of the Roman road have been lost. You pass Home Farm, and after one km a turning on the left takes you down a green lane and a final mile along a tarred road into Little Cressingham.

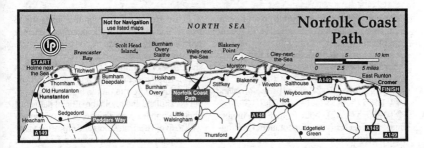

SOUTHERN ENGLAND

Little Cressingham In Little Cressingham *The White Horse* (☎ 01953 883434) is a friendly pub offering good food and accommodation from £15. Other options include B&B at *Sycamore House* (☎ 01953 881887), and *camping* by the village hall (☎ 01953 883716) at £3 per person.

Day 2: Little Cressingham to Castle Acre
12 miles (19 km), 3 to 5 hours

Almost all of this day's walking is on minor roads, with grass verges and light traffic, so it's easy to make good time through undulating farmland with good views of typically English scenes of cornfields, copses and combes.

Leave Little Cressingham by Pilgrims' Way, opposite the pub, and continue along the lane for about three miles. The path then runs behind a hedge parallel to the lane, before it zigzags across fields to North Pickenham (where *The Blue Lion*, just off the route on the main street, might do for an early lunch).

Two miles on from here, after a welcome stretch of green lane, the route suddenly emerges onto the busy A47, where the even more sudden appearance of a McDonalds could be traumatic for the unprepared (although it does make a suitable refuelling stop for hungry walkers).

On the far side of the main road the route follows a narrow tarred road known as Procession Lane. The route goes past Palgrave Hall and round a few corners (all signs of the Roman road having been temporarily lost) on a short tarred road to reach a crossroads with the main Castle Acre to Swaffham road.

Go straight over towards West Acre, then take a delightful lane marked 'Ford – unsuitable for motors' into the village of Castle Acre.

Castle Acre Castle Acre is well worth exploring, with its ruined 11th-century castle, Cluniac priory and church. One reference source intriguingly remarks that 'a series of scandals suggests that by the 14th century discipline at Castle Acre was slack'.

The traveller today will find a picturesque village with plenty of places to eat and stay, including *Gemini Guesthouse* (☎ 01760 755375) and *The Ostrich Inn* (☎ 01760 755398), both with B&B from £15, and the *Old Red Lion Independent Hostel* (☎ 01760 755557), with B&B at £10. Camping is allowed at the Ostrich.

Day 3: Castle Acre to Holme-next-the- Sea
20½ miles (33 km), 7 to 9 hours

This is a long day, rewarded by arriving at the seaside and the halfway point. The route's Roman ancestry is confirmed by a remarkably straight 16 miles or so, initially on or beside a tarred road, but then following a good path through chalky farmland, with only gentle gradients. The Way passes through no villages, although there are a few pubs and shops a mile or so off the route.

The route leaves Castle Acre by the Great Massingham road, passing a useful shop just before it leaves the village. After about three miles, at a trig point, the road swings right, but the Peddars Way continues its line along a grassy lane. There is a fine sense of space, with open views which include, on Harpley

Common, some ancient tumuli to remind us that the Romans were relatively recent inhabitants.

You might make a detour into Sedgeford, where *The King William* pub serves excellent meals. Some walkers break this stage by staying here. B&Bs include *Parkview* (☎ 01485 571352) or *Dovehill Cottage* (☎ 01485 571642), both from £15. Another fine pub, *The Gin Trap*, is encountered in Ringstead, and there's also *Courtyard Farm Bunkhouse* (☎ 01485 525369), about one mile along the road towards Docking, charging £4 per person. You may get permission to camp.

Holme-next-the-Sea By now it's only about two miles to Holme and, although the purist route veers off left past a disused windmill, you may as well stick to the road, which will take you directly into the village. The beach is a further half mile. Holme marks the halfway stage of this route, and also a distinct change of scenery. Give yourself some time to savour your first encounter with the North Norfolk coast. The vast skies and acres of sand create a profound atmosphere, especially after the trippers have gone home or if you walk beyond the car parks.

Holme has *Inglenook Campsite* (☎ 01485 525598), charging around £3. B&Bs include *Eastgates Cottage* (☎ 01485 525218), from £22.50. *The White Horse* pub serves meals, and there is a shop open seven days a week. There are many more accommodation options in nearby Hunstanton – including *Courtyard Farm Bunkhouse* (☎ 01485 525369) – Old Hunstanton, Ringstead and Thornham.

Day 4: Holme-next-the-Sea to Wells- next-the-Sea
19 miles (30.5 km), 7 to 9 hours
Today is a long walk with wide open vistas, empty sandy beaches and salt marshes. The sound of waves, gulls and the flapping of rigging against mast in the harbours will be your soundtrack for the day. In a few places walking is soft underfoot and slower than usual. Attractions include good swimming beaches and bird reserves, so you might want to break this stage in two rather than hurry.

Leave Holme by the road that leads to the beach. You can either walk along the beach or follow a sandy path which soon gives way to a boardwalk through a nature reserve on the shore side of the dunes. (The dunes themselves are a fragile ecosystem and shouldn't be walked on.) If you're on the beach, be sure to cut back inland and rejoin the official path after about two miles; you need to be up on the sea wall to avoid deep channels and enjoy the view.

The path heads inland towards Thornham, turning left to cross a small bridge by the remains of a windmill. A parallel road a further 100m along will take you past *The Lifeboat Inn*, which is well known for excellent meals. Sadly, it may be a little early in the day for lunch here or in *The Kings Head* (☎ 01485 525598) or *The Chequers* (☎ 01485 512229), both of which also offer B&B from £18.00 and £24.00 respectively. Thornham also has a shop.

Next comes the inland section. Take the main road through the village, then turn right along a lane signposted to Chosely, turning left by a copse and following signs through fields, eventually leading to Brancaster. (This detour avoids impassable saltmarsh, but also misses the bird reserve at Titchwell. If you're into birdwatching, you can get here from the main road, and after a spot of 'twitching' carry on along that road to rejoin the route in Brancaster.)

The Ship Hotel (☎ 01485 210333), in Brancaster, serves meals, and provides B&B from £20.00. There are a couple of other B&Bs: *Mrs Townshend* (☎ 01485 210501) and *The Old Stores* (☎ 01485 210279), both from £17.00. There's also a village shop.

The path runs by the edge of the saltmarsh into Burnham Deepdale – where *Granary Bunkhouse* (☎ 01485 210256) charges from £6 – and then along the top of a sea wall, although the sea is now more than a mile away. Much of the marshland on your left forms part of the Scolt Head nature reserve. In Burnham Overy Staithe *The Hero* pub, named in honour of Lord Nelson, serves meals. B&Bs in the village include *Domville House* (☎ 01328 738298) and *Uptop* (☎ 01328 730237), both from £17.00. For those who have enjoyed a leisurely walk, or indulged in some birdwatching, this is the obvious place to spend the night, as the next opportunity will be in Wells, another six miles away along one of the best stretches of beach you'll meet.

Leave Burnham Overy Staithe by the sea wall, and follow the path through the dunes and onto the beach. The view can only be described as 'big' here, and with firm sand underfoot it's a joy to walk along to Holkham Bay (unless the tide's right in, when the soft sand is a bit of a slog). With a huge nature reserve to your left and the nudist beach near Holkham Gap, there's no shortage of interest. On a warm day the sea is very inviting, too.

Holkham Hall, two miles inland from here, is a pretty sumptuous stately home, built between 1734 and 1762. If you're into stately piles, this could be an interesting diversion, but check with local TICs (numbers in the earlier Information section) for days and times of opening before planning this detour.

From Holkham Gap, the path runs on the inland edge of some pine woods, but walking along the beach will also bring you to the large car park near the lifeboat station at the end of a very straight road into Wells-next-the-Sea.

Wells-next-the-Sea Wells is a lively resort in the summer months, with several cafes and takeaways. (Wells is also a working harbour, so the fish is always fresh.) *The Edinburgh* pub serves meals and provides B&B from £20.00. There are several other cafes and B&Bs, including *Eastdene* (☎ 01328 710381), from around £18.00. There's also a campsite at *Pinewoods* (☎ 01328 710439, £4.75) on the beach road.

Day 5: Wells-next-the-Sea to Cley-next-the-Sea

10 miles (16 km), 4 to 6 hours

This day is a coast walk without much sight of the sea, but away from the beaches and holiday-makers it's a much wilder experience than yesterday. Sea birds soar over one of the largest surviving areas of saltmarsh in

the UK, and there are views out to Blakeney Point where the seal colony is often visible at low tide. The going is firm underfoot, and the distance isn't far, so there's plenty of time to enjoy the airy views from the sea wall.

Leave Wells by the road from the harbour, and where it starts to cut inland, the route goes between some sheds, which will reveal the path up onto the sea wall.

The path passes north of Stiffkey, which has a *campsite* (☎ 01328 830479), charging £3 to £5, and B&Bs including *Warborough House* (☎ 01328 830217) charging £22 per person, and *The Manor House* (☎ 01328 830439), and also *The Red Lion*, which serves meals.

At Morston the route crosses the boatyard, with the NT information centre on your left. You can take boat trips from here out to Blakeney Point seal colony. Boatmen include John Bean (☎ 01263 740038) and Jim Temple (☎ 01263 740791), among others, advertising here.

Following the sea wall will bring you into Blakeney, where you will find several pubs for a late lunch. *The Kings Arms*, to the right as you meet the road, serves meals all day, and has an interesting mix of showbusiness and local-history pictures on the walls, should the art of conversation have deserted you. There are seal-watching opportunities from Blakeney, with Bishops Boats (☎ 01263 740753) and Graham Bean (☎ 01263 740505) advertising on the quay.

From Blakeney to Cley is a three-sides-of-a-square walk along the top of the sea wall. The tired and emotional could simply follow the road and reduce the time by an hour or so, but to do this would mean missing a particularly open (and in some weather, distinctly wild) stretch, right on the edge of the marsh. Don't be tempted down onto the marsh, even less to try to cross over to the spit of land which now lies between you and the sea: there is no way through and the marshes can be treacherous.

Cley-next-the-Sea Cley, along with its neighbours Blakeney and Wiveton, were the richest towns in the area during the 15th

SOUTHERN ENGLAND

century, when their coastal trade was at its height. Ships took corn and salt to Newcastle, returning with coal, and fish from here supplied London markets. Cley and Wiveton's downfall began in the 17th century when landowners built the first sea walls (upon which you will be walking) in order to drain the marshes for pasture, and the estuary of the River Glaven began to silt up.

Places to stay include *The George & Dragon* (☎ 01263 740652) with B&B from £27.50 and good meals, plus *Marshlands* (☎ 01263 740284), in the old town hall, and *Rhu-Sila* (☎ 01263 740088) both with B&B from £16.

Although the next day's walk goes around the famous bird reserve, the only real way to see it is to walk through the village on the main road and find the Information Centre on the right. You'll get advice there on what you may see, and whereabouts on the reserve to go. This is a particularly popular place in spring and autumn, as migrating birds follow the Norfolk coast and birds not normally seen in this part of Britain frequently pass through.

Day 6: Cley-next-the-Sea to Cromer
13 miles (21 km), 5 to 7 hours

After nearly a week of enjoying the flatness of Norfolk, this day's walk actually involves some height!

To leave Cley, unlikely looking alleyways either side of the old town hall (*Marshlands* B&B) bring you to an equally unlikely path along the backs of houses, which leads beyond the old windmill, onto the sea wall and out towards the sea. The path runs through a car park on the landward side of the shingle sea defence. You can walk along the beach, but it's slow shingle, and you'll make better progress on the proper path. Walking along the sea defence is not encouraged as it's erosive (and hard work on even deeper shingle). To your right here is the nature reserve, although you are a bit too far from the lagoons to be able to differentiate your Redshanks from your Greenshanks.

A little further along, work may still be progressing to clear the beach of landmines laid during WWII, so be vigilant! You may

also see signs of army activity as you pass the Muckleburgh Collection, a military vehicle museum, possibly worth a visit if you're into tanks and jeeps.

You pass near Weybourne, which has a pub, a shop and some places to stay. Beyond here the path climbs steadily onto the clifftops. Signs now warn about the dangers of crumbling cliffs, and they mean it: you'll have to skirt around a line of houses, perilously close to the edge and destined one day to topple.

The route descends into Sheringham – a tourist town, with any number of cafes, pubs and fish & chips shops to choose from, plus plenty of places to stay. There is a *YHA Hostel* (☎ 01263 823215) costing £8.25, and a number of B&Bs, about which you can get advice in the TIC. From the main railway station, there are trains to Cromer and Norwich roughly every hour. From the North Norfolk Station, a restored steam engine can take you to Holt and back.

Leave Sheringham along the promenade and over Beeston Hill, which offers marvellous views of the surrounding caravan parks, and shows you why the path turns inland into woods, and past the fraudulently named Roman Camp (some strange earthworks are probably the work of medieval iron-smelters). This is some of the highest ground in Norfolk, almost reaching the dizzy altitude of 100m!

The Way is well signposted into Cromer; just as well, as it twists and turn a few times descending from the woods. On the outskirts, the route passes close to *Seacroft Campsite* (☎ 01263 513339), which costs from £3.00 (but is only open between March and October), and then meets the main A148 near the railway station (which has regular trains to Norwich). The route seems to fizzle out here, but it would seem a shame not to walk back to the sea for a final paddle or an ice-cream on the prom.

Cromer This seaside town has a lot of places to eat, drink and stay. Prices start at £16.50 at the walker-friendly *Carrolls Guesthouse* (☎ 01263 511254), which charges £16 per person (or £18 for ensuite), and *Birch House*

(☎ 01263 512521), which charges £16 (or £19 for ensuite). At *Morden House* (☎ 01263 513396) prices start from £21.00, and you can also get an evening meal here from £11.00. If these are full, the TIC, in the centre of the town, can provide more addresses.

The North Downs Way

Official Name The North Downs Way National Trail
Distance 130 miles or 123 miles (208 km or 197 km)
Duration 8 to 11 days
Start Farnham
Finish Dover
Regional Centres Guildford, Sevenoaks, Rochester, Ashford, Canterbury, Folkestone
Counties Surrey, Kent
Areas The Surrey Hills and Kent Downs Areas of Outstanding Natural Beauty
Summary A route through the finest countryside of south-east England with continual ascents and descents, some steep. Generally on well-waymarked paths. Some parts can get muddy after rain. Suitable for fairly fit walkers.

The North Downs are a succession of chalk ridges which run between Farnham and Dover. The walk follows this natural line passing almost entirely through two Areas of Outstanding Natural Beauty made up of woods, grassy downland, nature reserves, farmland, orchards, vineyards, white cliffs, and much more, often with panoramic views. There are lots of interesting things to see on the way including Neolithic long barrows, castles, eccentric follies, Kentish oast houses, and chalk motifs cut out of hillsides.

For a lot of the time the North Downs Way (NDW) runs parallel to and sometimes joins the Pilgrims' Way – an ancient route which it is believed the Pilgrims took in the 14th century – and there are many references to this throughout the walk. On a small-scale map the NDW can appear caught up in London's cobweb of roads, but in reality the route bypasses most towns and villages and you usually feel deep in the English countryside, not infrequently the only one on the trail.

DIRECTION, DISTANCE & DURATION

The walk starts in Farnham and follows the Downs north-east to Rochester and then south-east to Dover. Near Ashford, the route splits in two and you can walk via Canterbury or Folkestone.

The NDW is described as 153 miles long but this is counting both routes. In reality, if you choose the Canterbury loop it is 130 miles and if you walk via Folkestone it is 123 miles.

Ideally you should allow 10 or 11 days so you can spend a day or two sightseeing, possibly at Leeds Castle or in Canterbury. If you wanted to do the walk in one go you could fit it into seven days, but this would be pushing it. Being so well served by public transport, if you were short for time, it would be better to do the walk as a series of day or weekend trips.

STAGES

For a 10 day walk, as described here, the most convenient places to start and finish each day are:

Route via Folkestone

Day	From	To	Distance
1	Farnham	Guildford	11 miles (17.5 km)
2	Guildford	Dorking	13 miles (21 km)
3	Dorking	Merstham	10 miles (16 km)
4	Merstham	Oxted	8 miles (13 km)
5	Oxted	Otford	12 miles (19 km)
6	Otford	Rochester	17 miles (27 km)
7	Rochester	Hollingbourne	15 miles (24 km)
8A	Hollingbourne	Wye	15 miles (24 km)
9A	Wye	Folkestone	16 miles (25.5 km)
10A	Folkestone	Dover	6 miles (10 km)

Route via Canterbury

8B	Hollingbourne	Boughton Lees	(21 km)
9B	Boughton Lees	Canterbury	13½ miles (21.5 km)
10B	Canterbury	Dover	17½ miles (28 km)

SOUTHERN ENGLAND

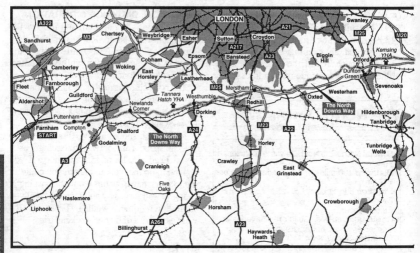

INFORMATION

Surrey County Council (☎ 0181 5418800) and Kent County Council (☎ 01622 671411) have a lot of information about the trail specific to their region, including transport options, accommodation and places of interest. For information on the area covered by the whole walk, contact the South-East England Tourist Board (☎ 01892 540766) in Tunbridge Wells. In addition, there are TICs at Farnham (☎ 01252 715109), Guildford (☎ 01483 444333), Sevenoaks (☎ 01732 450305), Rochester (☎ 01634 843666), Maidstone (☎ 01622 673581), Ashford (☎ 01233 629165), Canterbury (☎ 01227 766567), Folkestone (☎ 01303 258594) and Dover (☎ 01304 205108).

Books

For a detailed route description you need the *North Downs Way National Trail Guide* by Neil Curtis, published by Aurum Press with the Countryside Commission (CC) and OS. Also interesting is *Discovering the North Downs Way* (Shire Publications), a pocket-sized book full of fascinating historical anecdotes and facts. *A guide to the Pilgrims' Way and North Downs Way* by Christopher John Wright (Constable) is good as background reading.

Maps

The whole walk is covered by OS Landranger (1:50,000) maps 186, 187, 188, 178, 189 and 179 (in that order). For the complete route try the *Leisure Map of South-East England* (Estate Publications), available from the South-East England Tourist Board (£3.25).

GUIDED WALKS

All year round various organisations in both Surrey and Kent arrange walks, some of which include or take in sections of the NDW. Details of these are published by the county councils in their free brochures or newspapers.

PLACES TO STAY & EAT

There is some accommodation actually on the route, but most B&Bs, guesthouses, hotels and YHA hostels are a mile or so from it. There are campsites in the vicinity of all overnight stops except Farnham, Merstham and Oxted, but some are very basic. A booklet called *North Downs Way – A Practical Guide* combining accommodation and eating options with other facilities along the path is published by Kent County Council

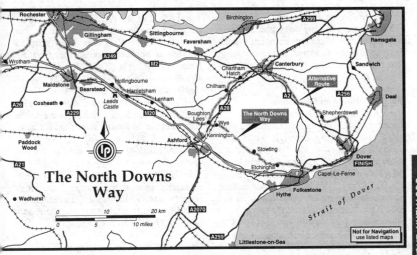

The North Downs Way

Not for Navigation
use listed maps

(☎ 01622 671411) and costs £1.95. At the end of each day there are always places to eat, whether it be pubs, restaurants or cafes, but on some of the walks midday options can be sparse and it can be best to take a packed lunch.

GETTING THERE & AWAY
Bus
From London there are two National Express buses a day to/from Farnham on the London-Portsmouth and London-Bournemouth line. Between London and Dover there are National Express buses almost every hour. Local bus services in Surrey and Kent are excellent. For details ring Surrey Traveline (☎ 01737 223000) or Kent County Council Travel Line (☎ 0800 696996); both operate every day.

Train
There are around two trains an hour between London Waterloo and Farnham. Between a number of London stations and Dover there is a similarly frequent service. All places recommended as overnight stops have railway stations with the exception of Boughton Lees, where the nearest one is Wye, and there is also a North Downs Line

between Guildford and Redhill. This means that walking the NDW in sections using public transport either to get there and back or else to return to a parked car is very easy.

Car
Farnham is just off the A31, which runs between Winchester and Guildford. At the end of the route, Dover is reached via the A2 from Canterbury or the A20 from Folkestone.

THE ROUTE
The Start: Farnham
Farnham is an old market town with some attractive Tudor buildings and red-brick Georgian houses and facades, as well as a castle with a Norman keep. The TIC (☎ 01252 715109) is in the library, at 28 West St.

Farnham has a lot of accommodation options. Close to the start of the walk is *Mrs Diment* (☎ 01252 721930), at 1 Broomleaf Corner where B&B costs £18/32. At 48 West St, along from the TIC, is the very reasonable but basic *Meads Guest House* (☎ 01252 715298) where B&B costs £15. *The Bush Hotel* (☎ 01252 715237) at the Borough dates from the 17th century and is a charming, old-fashioned place to stay. From

Sunday to Thursday singles/doubles cost £70 per room and on Friday and Saturday nights £44.50. Many of Farnham's pubs serve good-value food and, if you're staying near the station, *The Waverley Arms* does evening meals.

Day 1: Farnham to Guildford
11 miles (17.5 km), 4 to 6 hours

For most of the day you are clambering over stiles and walking through woodland, meadow and open fields. For the first six miles or so, the trail is fairly easy and level, except for a steep, uphill section after crossing the River Wey, and another before Puttenham – here *The Good Intent* on the main street is ideally placed for lunch.

From here you pass under the A3 and an old bridge with crosses strapped to either side – a reference to the Pilgrims' Way – before coming out at the Watts Gallery and busy teashop at Compton.

The last three miles are almost straight uphill, passing through Losely Estate where there's very basic camping at *Losely Park Farm* (☎ 01483 304440), until you descend steeply towards the River Wey. Here there's a path off to the right leading to the remains of St Catherine's chapel. After the bridge the trail dissolves into Shalford Park, which is about one mile south of Guildford. There is a bus stop beside the park and plenty of buses.

Guildford Guildford, the capital of Surrey, has some fine old buildings, cobbled streets and a ruined castle with 12th-century keep.

The TIC (☎ 01483 444333) is at 14 Tunsgate. There's plenty of accommodation, but close to the NDW is *Mrs Web* (☎ 01483 573885) at Mulberry Corner, East Shalford Lane, where B&B is £20/32. Near the castle is *Mrs Braithwaite* (☎ 01483 563324), at 11 Castle Hill, and *Greyfriars* (☎ 01483 561795), at 9 Castle Hill. Both charge £14 per person for B&B. In the centre of Guildford, close to the bus station, at 14 Bridge St, is *The 'Y' Centre* (☎ 01483 32555) charging £27/39.50 for B&B. At Shalford there's a supermarket and you can eat at the *Sea Horse Inn*.

In Guildford there are tons of places to eat, especially around the castle. *The King's Head* (☎ 01483 575004), in Quarry St, is the most historically interesting, and the food's so good it is wise to book ahead.

Day 2: Guildford to Dorking
13 miles (21 km), 5 to 6 hours

It can get crowded up on the trail today, which is not surprising as there are some great views to be had and you really start to feel like you're out on the Downs.

The first two to three miles are the hardest in terms of uphill sections as you climb St Martha's Hill to the isolated 12th-century church on top, followed by an ascent of Albury Downs to the popular beauty spot of Newlands Corner. Here there's a Countryside Information Centre, toilets, car park and a takeaway snack bar – this is the only place to eat or drink all day without a significant diversion.

The only confusing part of the day is following the official route down from St

---

The Watts Gallery & Mortuary Chapel

In his time, George Frederic Watts (1817-1904) was a fairly successful sculptor and artist. He is probably best known for his painting *Hope* which is in the Tate Gallery in London. This gallery and workshop was built by his wife, Mary Watts, for the express purpose of showing her husband's work. It is open Monday, Tuesday, Friday and Sunday from 2 to 6 pm, on Wednesday and Saturday from 11 am to 1 pm and between 2 and 6 pm, and closed all day Thursday. Admission is free.

Five minutes down the road is the little-known and very unusual Mortuary Chapel designed and built by Mary Watts in around 1900. It is beautiful both inside and out, but its interior is extraordinary for its richness and intricacy of art nouveau design. The chapel is open every day until dusk. ■

Martha's church; it is actually easier to descend via the very obvious sandy track to the east of the church. At the bottom of the hill there's an LDP called the Downs Link, which joins the NDW with the South Downs Way (described elsewhere in this book).

From here the path levels out and becomes easy walking through enclosed woodlands and downlands (with good views), until you reach St Barnabas' church at Ranmore Common. This is the church of the North Downs Way, built in 1859. From here a gravel track descends through the vineyards of Denbies Wine Estate, to Westhumble on the A24, just over a mile north of Dorking.

Dorking For most accommodation, eating options and facilities you'll need to go into Dorking, which is an old, fairly nondescript dormitory town. However, in Westhumble there is *Mrs Wade* (☎ 01306 882734), Danesmore, Pilgrims' Way, where B&B costs £37.50 a double, and good meals at the *The Stepping Stones* pub. In the woods at the far end of Ranmore Common is the basic *Tanner's Hatch YHA Hostel* (☎ 01372 452528). Costing £6.10, it has no electricity and is self-catering only.

In town is *Fairdene Guest House* (☎ 01306 888337), Moores Rd, which has B&B for £20/35. Another option is *Mrs Chisman* (☎ 01372 375050), Old House Cottage, Mickleham, where B&B is £30 a double. She will collect you from the Burford Bridge Hotel, north of the NDW. There's a very basic campsite at *Lower Boxhill Farm* (☎ 01306 882968) about one mile east of Dorking.

Day 3: Dorking to Merstham
10 miles (16 km), 4 to 5 hours
The first half of today's walk runs through open countryside, while the second part edges close to the M25. There are also some steep uphill and downhill sections, often made easier by wooden steps.

From Dorking, the walk starts by crossing the Mole River on stepping stones (there is a bridge if you prefer) before steeply climbing to the top of Box Hill, a popular beauty spot with wonderful views. At the top is a NT

Information Centre, car park, toilets, a snack bar and an interesting Victorian Fort built in 1899. The trail then passes close to *Boxhills Tavern*, the highest pub in Surrey, before heading downhill through woodland and past some working chalk quarries. After another steep climb up Colley Hill you emerge onto an area of open downland close to the M25. To the left is an interesting red-brick water tower dating from 1911 and a little further on a graceful hexagonal temple structure with a mosaic ceiling built in 1909. At Reigate Hill there's a car park with refreshments and an easy downhill walk to Quality St in Merstham village.

Merstham Merstham has a number of pubs, two supermarkets and a post office. There are only two places to stay, both on the main road to Redhill. The closest is *Rookwood House Hotel* (☎ 01737 643207), at 13 London Rd South, where rooms cost £25/35 for B&B. The hotel has a restaurant. Further away is *Lynwood House* (☎ 01737 766894), at 50 London Rd, where B&B costs £25/40; they will collect you from the village.

Day 4: Merstham to Oxted
8 miles (13 km), 3 to 4 hours
As today's walk is fairly short, you might add it onto another day, but be warned, there's nowhere convenient to stay or eat until you reach Oxted. The way out of Merstham isn't pleasant as you negotiate a number of main roads, but after this it's uphill across fields to the top of the ridge where the walking becomes flat and easy as you follow country lanes through farmland to Gravelly Hill.

For much of the day, though, you can hear traffic from the nearby M25. At the beginning of War Coppice Road there's an unusual folly on the left. Skirting the hill, you descend into woods which, surprisingly, lead to a small rubbish tip where you think you've gone wrong; you haven't. From here wooden steps lead to a vineyard, then a hilly woodland path crosses the Oxted Downs before descending steeply towards the M25 and Chalkpit lane, about one mile north of Oxted.

Oxted The small town of Oxted has some wonderful 16th-century buildings as well as newer residential and shopping areas. Accommodation is a bit thin on the ground and these are the only options. Within walking distance are *Rosehaven* (☎ 01883 712700), at 12 Hoskins Rd, where B&B is £18/35, and *Pinehurst Grange Guesthouse* (☎ 01883 716413), East Hill, where B&B costs £24/39. About three miles away are *Mrs Mills* (☎ 01883 715969), Old Forge House, Merle Common, and *The New Bungalow* (☎ 01342 892508), Old Hall Farm, Tandridge Lane, where B&B is £17/32 and £22/35 respectively. Either will pick you up from Chalkpit Lane if you ring from the phone box. In Oxted there are a variety of places to eat, including nearby pubs.

Day 5: Oxted to Otford
12 miles (19 km), 5 to 6 hours

Despite ascending Botley Hill (265m), the highest point on the NDW, the rest of this segment is fairly flat, easy walking as good woodland paths and country lanes take you from Surrey into Kent.

From The Avenue, about four miles into the walk, the trail loops through fields and farmland where if the waymarking wasn't so good you could get lost. There is a slight change in the route just past Knockholt Pound (before you see Chevening House) where you now turn left at the kissing gates, instead of passing through them. From here you gently descend through fields before negotiating the busy roads at Dunton Green (there's no change to the NDW route here). On the A224 there's a campsite at the house called *Chaddesden* (☎ 01732 462868) and a good restaurant at the nearby *Rose and Crown* – the only eating option you'll come across all day. From here it's only one mile or so across fields and woodland to Otford.

Otford The NDW runs through Otford and past numerous historical buildings, some of which date from the 14th century. There is also the remains of an Archbishop's Palace and an unusual village duckpond-cum-roundabout. There are several B&Bs in the village, plus all the usual facilities. *Mrs Smith* (☎ 01959 523596), at 9 Warham Rd, does B&B for £18 and nearby *Mrs Laundon* (☎ 01959 522139), at 1 The Butts, charges £16. In Kemsing, about two miles further along the NDW, is a *YHA Hostel* (☎ 01732 761341), charging £8.25. *East Hill Farm Caravan Park* (☎ 01959 522347) is just under two miles from the top of Otford Mount. In Otford both *The Crown* and *The Bull* pubs do excellent food.

Day 6: Otford to Rochester
17 miles (27 km), 7 to 8 hours

Today is long and tiring with quite a few hills to climb and in wet weather some very muddy sections. It is also quite a populated stretch of the NDW.

After the climb up Otford Mount the first seven miles are mostly on the flat through woodlands, fields and a nature reserve, passing a wooden cross on the Downs above Kemsing (great views), and a NDW milestone (Farnham 60 miles, Canterbury 54, Dover 65). Descending into Wrotham, there are some good pubs for food and some B&Bs including *Mrs Jolliffe* (☎ 01732 883069), Green Hill House, on the high street, and *Mrs Thomas* (☎ 01732 822564), Hillside House, Gravesend Rd; both charge from £16. You then have to negotiate an unpleasant tangle of main roads before ascending to the *Vigo Inn* – good for a drink but not food.

Just over a mile from here the woodland path descends sharply and there's a sign for Coldrum Long Barrow (c. 2000 BC), over in the fields. The last six miles pass through hilly woodland and fields before descending towards the Medway Bridge, over a mile south of Rochester. For a taxi into town, or over the bridge, try Windmill taxis on freefone ☎ 0800 582582.

Rochester Historic Rochester, with its Norman castle, cathedral, and connections with Charles Dickens is definitely worth a visit. The TIC (☎ 01634 843666) is at Eastgate Cottage on the main Street. Accommodation includes a *YHA Hostel* (☎ 01634 400788, £8.25) which is at Capstone Farm Country Park in nearby Gillingham. Closest to the NDW are the three B&Bs in the Borstal area, just over and to the left of the Medway Bridge. The nearest is *Walnut Tree House* (☎ 01634 849355), at 21 Mount Rd, where B&B costs £16. *St Ouen* (☎ 01634 843528), at 98 Borstal Rd, and *St Martins* (☎ 01634 848192), at 104 Borstal Rd both do B&B for £15. The nearest campsite is *Woolmanswood Caravan Park* (☎ 01634 867685) at Bridgewood, over two miles further on from Borstal. For something to eat it is best to go into Rochester where there's a good choice.

Day 7: Rochester to Hollingbourne
15 miles (24 km), 6 to 7 hours

For the first half of today's walk you are mostly on lanes, minor roads or tarred footpaths and, apart from the ascent through fields from the Medway Bridge, the Way is fairly flat. After Blue Bell Hill, a popular picnic spot, the NDW runs close to the A229 for a mile or so where you'll find Kits Coty ('tomb in the woods' in Celtic) – the remains of a Neolithic long barrow from around 2000 BC. A little further on, and very close to the trail, is Little Kits Coty.

From the A229 underpass to Detling the NDW ascends steeply, passing through exposed farmland and woodland where it levels out before descending quickly towards the busy A249. This road has four lanes of traffic, so take care as you walk beside it for a short while before crossing it without either a bridge or an underpass. On the other side the view is magnificent as you ascend and descend the Downs to Hollingbourne. During the day there's nowhere to lunch or buy supplies unless you count Detling which can be quite difficult to get to because of the A249.

Hollingbourne Hollingbourne is a long, pleasant village, close to beautiful Leeds Castle. It has all the usual facilities and several B&Bs. At the top of the village, the NDW passes very close to *Manorfield* (☎ 01622 880373) on the Pilgrims' Way, where B&B costs £35/45 a double/triple. About a mile into the village is *Mr & Mrs*

Reed (☎ 01622 880554), at 53 Eyhorne St, where B&B is £16. At No 49 is the 17th-century, timber-framed house of *Mr & Mrs Woodhouse* (☎ 01622 880594), where B&B costs £17. The nearest place to camp is *Hogbarn Caravan Park* (☎ 01622 859648) at Harrietsham. There are a number of pubs in the village which do food, but the best is the *Dirty Habit* on the Pilgrims' Way.

Day 8A/B: Hollingbourne to Wye or Boughton Lees
13/15 miles (21/24 km), 5/6 hours

As the NDW splits at Boughton Lees, today you have to decide which branch to take. Do you want to visit the sights of ancient Canterbury or would you prefer the breathtaking clifftop walk between Folkestone and Dover?

Today is easy walking as the NDW joins the bridleways, tracks and lanes of the Pilgrims' Way through open farmland, fields and woodland, with good views. This is quite a popular stretch, possibly because there are very few hills (only gentle ups and downs) and some interesting things to see. You can even start the day off with a visit to Leeds Castle as there's a footpath from Hollingbourne into the grounds which joins the NDW at Harrietsham. About two miles further on there's a chalk cross carved out of the downs above Lenham and a similarly large crown cut into those above Wye. The best place for lunch is Charing, about eight miles into the walk and about half a mile from the path.

Wye If you are walking via Folkestone then it's another two miles through fields and orchards to the pretty town of Wye where there's more accommodation and places to eat. With the largest number of rooms and a good restaurant is *The New Flying Horse* (☎ 01233 812297), Upper Bridge St, where B&B costs £37.50/47.50. Less expensive is *Mr & Mrs Morris* (☎ 01233 812133), at 38 High St, where it's £20 for B&B.

Boughton Lees Boughton Lees is a small hamlet with no shops but, if you're taking the Canterbury route, it is the best place to stay.

There's basic camping at *Dunn Street Farm* (☎ 01233 712537) just before you cross Eastwell Park. Otherwise there are only two affordable options: the 15th-century *Flying Horse Inn* (☎ 01233 620914), which costs £20/35 and *Warren Cottage* (☎ 01233 740483), where B&B is £13.50. The pub does excellent food. There is also plenty of accommodation in and around Ashford.

Day 9A: Wye to Folkestone
16 miles (25.5 km), 6 to 7 hours

Most of today's walking is on exposed downland or open farmland with wonderful views all around. In the first six miles there are a few short woodland sections, including the Wye National Nature Reserve, and no major inclines.

At Stowting the route descends and passes the *Tiger Inn*, which is a good place for lunch, and *Water Farm* (☎ 01303 862401), with B&B for £16. There's a steep climb out of the village up Cobb's Hill to Farthing Common where *Miss Wadie* (☎ 01303 862391) does B&B for £15. On the Downs above Postling it can be easy to lose your way, but your book and maps will get you through. After a steepish climb up Tolsford Hill, the NDW joins the Saxon Shore Way and you follow signs for both, descending through woods towards Etchinghill, where there's a pub but no accommodation. From here the trail ascends sharply and loops through fields before joining the Pilgrims' Way close to Folkestone, from where you can see the Channel Tunnel terminal. At the A260 you're just under two miles from the town.

Folkestone Folkestone's TIC (☎ 01303 258594) is in Harbour St. There's lots of accommodation, much in Cheriton Rd. At No 38 is the *Folke-Leas Guest House* (☎ 01303 251441), at No 39 *Normandie Guest House* (☎ 01303 256233) and at No 85 *Sunny Lodge Guest House* (☎ 01303 251498); all do B&B for around £15. Much closer to the trail, but two miles further on from Folkestone at Capel-le-Ferne, there's *Mrs Strutt* (☎ 01303 257956), at 18 Alexan-

dra Rd, where B&B costs £13, and camping at *Little Satmar Holiday Park* (☎ 01303 251188) in Whinehouse Lane. In Folkestone there's a fair selection of eating options, including *Emilio's Restaurant* at 124A Sandgate Rd, which is very good.

Day 10A: Folkestone to Dover
6 miles (10 km), 2 to 3 hours

The final stretch of the NDW is a short, dramatic, coastal walk. It's not for vertigo sufferers, as the route climbs up to the white clifftops and sticks frighteningly close to their edge. Needless to say, this section of Heritage Coastline is very popular. Far below you to the right is the sea, to your left the busy A20, and the views are spectacular as a well-marked path steeply ascends and descends through tufty grasslands and wild gorse bushes towards Dover. Just before Capel-le-Ferne you pass a Battle of Britain memorial with museum and at regular intervals you see deserted pillboxes, left over from WWII. Refreshments are found at the *Cliff Top Cafe* and the *Capel Court Hotel* along the way. For accommodation see the end of this section.

Day 9B: Boughton Lees to Canterbury
13½ miles (21.5 km), 6 to 7 hours

Today the NDW passes through many more hamlets or villages than usual and is also quite populated. After ascending the Downs, the first half of the walk is on a good flat path through King's Wood, which then descends into the pretty village of Chilham. Here you can lunch at the *White Horse Inn* or the *Copper Kettle Tearooms* and visit the grounds of the castle (really a Jacobean House). There's also quite a lot of accommodation including *The Woolpack* (☎ 01227 730351) where B&B costs £37.50/47.50. The next four miles to Chartham Hatch crosses rolling arable land, orchards and hop fields. At the village you pass the *Chapter Arms* pub and *Wysteria Lodge* (☎ 01227 738654) were B&B costs £20. The rest of the route passes through wood and scrubland to Canterbury.

Canterbury The ancient walled city of Canterbury, famous for its magnificent cathedral, is on every tourist's itinerary. The TIC (☎ 01227 766567) is at 34 St Margaret's St. There's lots of accommodation and the NDW follows London Rd where most of it is found. To name but a few, at No 59 is the *Victoria Hotel* (☎ 01227 459333) where room only rates are £31.50. At No 62 there's *Derwent House* (☎ 01227 769369) and at No 14 *London Guest House* (☎ 01227 765860), both with B&B from £17 per person.

There is also a *YHA Hostel* (☎ 01227 462911) for £9.10 at 54 New Dover Rd, *Kipps Independent Hostel* (☎ 01227 786121), at 40 Nunnery Fields, charging £10 to £13, and the Camping & Caravanning Club's (CCC's) *Camping & Caravan Site* (☎ 01227 463216) at Bekesbourne Lane, where backpackers pay around £5. Canterbury has lots of nice places to eat, but for a great vegetarian meal try *Fungus Mungus* at 34 St Peters St.

Day 10B: Canterbury to Dover
17½ miles (28 km), 7 to 8 hours

This last section is rather monotonous because you're mostly on good paths either through flat, open, arable land or fields. There are very few hills and hardly any views. After the tiny village of Patrixbourne, the NDW runs parallel to the busy A2 for a mile or so before leaving it and ascending to the larger village of Shepherdswell or Sibertswold. At around the 10 mile mark, the *Bell Inn* is almost on the path and a good place to eat. Opposite is *Sunshine Cottage* (☎ 01304 831359) where B&B costs from £38 a double. After crossing the A256, you get onto the long, straight Roman road (or sunken pathway) which takes you the last three or so miles into Dover. The Way is signposted through the town, linking up with the alternative route via Folkestone. Kent County Council has commissioned a statue to mark the end of this LDP, but at present they are not sure where it will be placed.

Dover Dover is a very busy passenger port, best known for its white cliffs and medieval castle. The TIC (☎ 01304 205108) is on Townhall St near the seafront. It has two YHA hostels: *Dover Central* (☎ 01304 201314, £9.10), at 306 London Rd, and the *Dover Annexe* (☎ 01304 201314), at 14 Godwyne Rd. Otherwise, the main area for B&Bs is Park Ave leading to Mon Dieu Rd, on the Canterbury NDW route. These include: *Chrislyn's Guest House* (☎ 01304 202302), at 15 Park Ave, where B&B is £16 per person; *Mon Dieu Guest House* (☎ 01304 204033) at £20/30; and *Penny Farthing Guest House* (☎ 01304 205563), at No 109, costing £22/32. One of the best places to eat is the *Red Lion* pub at Charlton Green, near the central YHA hostel.

The Ridgeway

> **Official Name** The Ridgeway Path National Trail
> **Distance** 89 miles (142 km)
> **Duration** 6 days
> **Start** Overton Hill, near Avebury
> **Finish** Ivinghoe Beacon, near Aylesbury
> **Regional Centres** Swindon, Marlborough, Wantage, Goring, Aylesbury
> **Counties** Wiltshire, Oxfordshire, Berkshire, Buckinghamshire, Hertfordshire
> **Areas** North Wessex Downs and Chilterns Areas of Outstanding Natural Beauty
> **Summary** A straightforward route, mostly well signposted, through contrasting countryside of high, open rolling chalk hills and wooded farmland, with a rich historical background.

The Ridgeway is dubbed 'Britain's oldest road'. This may be tourist-board hype, but archaeological evidence does suggest that much of the route followed by the modern national trail has been used for at least 5000 years. The original Ridgeway evolved as a route because it follows a ridge of high chalkland, making travel easier for the Neolithic peoples who used it, avoiding the forested low plains and valleys. Various theories put the Ridgeway as part of a large network of ancient routes linking the west of England with the east coast, which in turn was the 'gateway' to mainland Europe and Scandinavia.

For today's walker, the Ridgeway follows

the same high ground across the Wiltshire Downs and North Wessex Downs through marvellous open country, with few roads and villages, and excellent views when the skies are clear. The route is certainly rich in history, passing many ancient sites including Stone Age burial mounds, Iron Age 'castles' (more accurately forts – usually circular turf mounds and ditches, often with spectacular views), the enigmatic Silbury Hill and the massive stone circle at Avebury.

Beyond the Thames Valley, which cuts the route neatly into two main sections, the Ridgeway follows the river itself for several miles before winding through the farmland, woods and villages of the Chiltern Hills. The scenery on this second section is less 'wild', but more typically 'English'. Both the North Wessex Downs and the Chilterns have been officially designated areas of outstanding natural beauty.

The Ridgeway is an ideal summer route, when mild gradients and dry paths make the walking effortless and enjoyable. In winter the paths can be muddy, but still not at all difficult, and the Ridgeway is an attractive destination when some other parts of Britain become too serious for walkers due to bad weather.

DIRECTION, DISTANCE & DURATION

The Ridgeway is a linear route, running roughly west to east, but can of course be followed in either direction. We recommend west to east, as the wind is mostly behind you, and this has always been the traditional direction. As a national trail the route is well waymarked with acorn symbols and specific signs.

The original Ridgeway was a series of tracks keeping roughly to the crest of the high ground. In more recent times some of these tracks were farmed over, but much of the ancient route remains and is marked on OS maps (usually in 'archaic' lettering). Today's Ridgeway Path National Trail mostly follows the original Ridgeway, but in some places it deviates, because the ancient route now crosses private property, or simply

because the new version is a better walk. When map-reading, remember to follow the modern Ridgeway path, rather than the ancient Ridgeway.

The total official distance is 89 miles, although you will need to add a few extra for leaving and rejoining the route to/from your accommodation. When we did the route, the measurements came to 95 miles.

Most people do the walk in six days. Hours given in the description are walking times only: add extra for lunch, sightseeing, rests etc. If you're short of time, either the western or eastern half of the route can be done as a self-contained section, with Goring (the halfway point) easy to get to/from by bus or train.

STAGES

For a six day walk, as described here, the most convenient places to begin and end each day are:

Day	From	To	Distance
1	Avebury	Ogbourne St George	9 miles (14.5 km)
2	Ogbourne St George	Court Hill	21 miles (33.5 km)
3	Court Hill	Goring	14 miles (22 km)
4	Goring	Watlington	15 miles (24 km)
5	Watlington	Princes Risborough	12 miles (19 km)
6	Princes Risborough	Ivinghoe Beacon	18 miles (29 km)

INFORMATION

The Ridgeway is managed by the Department of the Ridgeway Officer (☎ 01865 810224), Leisure & Arts, Holton, Oxford OX33 1QQ. The department gives specific information on the route. For general accommodation and transport enquiries contact a TIC on or near the route: Avebury (☎ 01672 539425), Wantage (☎ 01235 760176), Wallingford (☎ 01491 826972), Princes Risborough (☎ 01844 274795), Wendover (☎ 01296 696759) and Tring (☎ 01442 823347).

Hikers, Bikers & 4x4s

The whole western section of the Ridgeway, between Overton Hill and Streatley, and a few parts of the eastern section, are rights of way defined as 'Byway' or 'Road Used as Public Path' (RUPP). This means walkers share the route with cyclists and horse-riders, which doesn't cause too much of a problem, although hooves and mountain bike tyres can churn up the ground in wet weather, making walking tricky. More important though, the Byway and RUPP status means walkers share the Ridgeway with 4x4 'leisure vehicles', which can make things really difficult – these heavy vehicles do a lot of damage and some drivers take great delight in speeding along this ancient highway. In several parts of the trail, separate narrow footpaths run parallel to the main track giving walkers a chance to avoid these vehicles and the ruts they make in bad weather. A new Code of Respect for all Ridgeway users has been introduced and this is clearly posted at places where the Ridgeway crosses conventional roads. The Friends of the Ridgeway (90 South Hill Park, London NW3 2SN) is a voluntary organisation campaigning for the long-term preservation of the route, and particularly against the use of motor vehicles on it. In other words, they try to ensure your walk is enjoyable. By way of thanks, you could send them a small donation or a letter of support.

For more information on Byways and RUPPs, see the Terms & Definitions Used in This Book section of the Facts for the Walker chapter. ■

Books

The most useful item you can have is the *Ridgeway Information & Accommodation Guide* (published by the Department of the Ridgeway), available from local TICs for a bargain £1.50; it has details on public transport, places to stay, places to water your horse, and so on. The *Ridgeway Information Pack* contains the *Guide* plus a batch of other leaflets about places of interest in the area. More elaborate guidebooks include *The Ridgeway National Trail Guide* by Neil Curtis, which contains sections of all the OS maps covering the route, and saves buying several individual sheets.

After your journey, if you've been caught up by the atmosphere – especially on the section between Avebury and Streatley – then *The Ridgeway – Europe's Oldest Road* by Richard Ingrams (Phaidon) is a must. The book includes an essay on the various writers who have lived near and been influenced by The Rudge (its local name), but its main content is the work of a group of artists who have recorded the Ridgeway in their own varied styles.

Maps

The western section of the Ridgeway is covered on OS Landranger (1:50 000) sheets 173 and 174; because the going is straightforward these maps are fine. The eastern section of the route is on Landranger sheets 175 and 165. For more detail on this section of the route you could use the OS Explorer (1:25 000) map sheets 2 and 3.

GUIDED WALKS

National companies organising walks along the Ridgeway are listed in the main Getting Around section. Local organisations, such as the Friends of the Ridgeway, county councils and the NT also arrange guided walks on or around the Ridgeway throughout the year. TICs have details.

PLACES TO STAY & EAT

The Ridgeway is served by three YHA hostels and plenty of B&Bs, although many of these are a mile or two off the actual route (some places do a pick-up-drop-off service). Your choices are limited on the western section as there are few villages.

The route does not lend itself to camping, although there are sites near Avebury, Ogbourne St George, Wantage and Watlington. Camping is also allowed at Ivinghoe YHA Hostel. To fill the gaps, determined campers may find farmers willing to allow

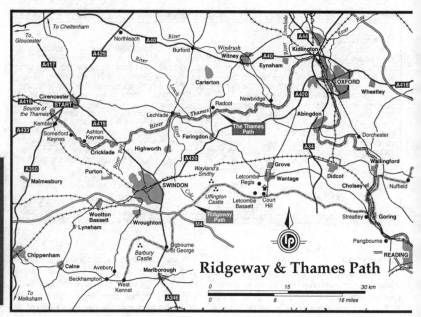

Ridgeway & Thames Path

one-off overnight stops at other points along the route.

For food along the way, the western part of the route goes through just two villages, with no handy cafes and pubs for midday stops; it's best to carry lunch supplies. Most villages mentioned as overnight halts have small food shops. It's also important to carry enough water (especially in summer) as the western part of the route is above the spring line and there few opportunities for refills. (We highlight some in the route description.) In the eastern section, the route passes through several villages, so midday refuelling (with food, water or beer) is easier.

GETTING THERE & AWAY

The official start of the Ridgeway is Overton Hill, on the main A4 road west of Marlborough. There is a car park and an information board, but it's not a very inspiring start to this fine ancient route, so we suggest starting at histori-

cally fascinating Avebury Stone Circle, and joining the Ridgeway from there, missing the first few miles of the official route.

A free booklet with comprehensive details of all public transport serving the Ridgeway is available from the Ridgeway Officer (address in Information) and from local TICs.

Bus

Swindon, Marlborough and Salisbury can all be reached from most parts of the country by National Express coach. The easiest way to reach Avebury is on the bus which runs between Swindon and Salisbury, three times per day in each direction (four on Sunday). The main operator is Wilts & Dorset (☎ 01722 336855). Services run by Thamesdown Buses (☎ 01793 428428) go between Swindon, Devizes and Marlborough via Avebury.

On Sunday, from early May to early October, the Ridgeway Explorer bus runs

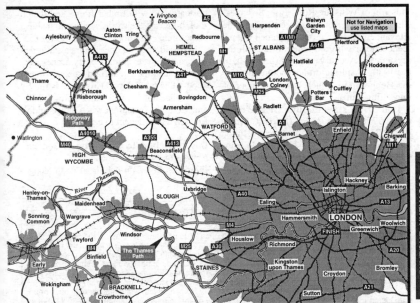

between Swindon and Reading, via many points along the national trail. For more details check the local public transport info line (☎ 0345 090899).

From Ivinghoe village at the end of the route, buses run by Aylesbury Bus Co (☎ 01296 23445) go to Tring, Aylesbury or Luton – from where National Express coaches go to London and most other parts of the country. For timetable details you can phone the local transport information line (☎ 01734 234524).

Train

No trains go to Avebury, but many go to Swindon and Salisbury from where you can catch a bus. You can also get a train to Pewsey, from where Avebury is a six mile scenic walk – details are in the *Ridgeway Information & Accommodation Guide* (see Books). The nearest stations to the end of the route are at Tring, Berkhamsted and Aylesbury, which all have frequent services to London.

Car

Avebury is two miles north of the main A4, about 10 miles south of Swindon, easily reached from most parts of the country on the M4 motorway. There's a large car park on the edge of the village. At the end of the route, Ivinghoe Beacon is near the small village of Ivinghoe, about eight miles east of Aylesbury.

THE ROUTE
The Start: Avebury

Although the Ridgeway officially begins at Overton Hill, we suggest starting at Avebury, because it's easier to get to, is well worth a visit in its own right, and is a very appropriate introduction to this walk through ancient British history.

The village is surrounded by a gigantic stone circle, larger than Stonehenge, and almost as old, plus several other historic sites and burial chambers. Other places of interest in the village are the Great Barn, dating from the late 17th century and now the TIC and

Museum of Wiltshire Rural Life; St James' Church, dating from Saxon times; and the Alexander Keiller Museum, named after a local scholar who did much to unearth the mysteries of Avebury (in fact he bought it) in the 1930s. Aspiring druids should head for the Henge Shop, which has all manner of interesting items.

Places to stay include *St Andrew's* (☎ 01672 539247) or *Hollis Cottage* (☎ 01672 539200) charging around £16, or the *Old Vicarage* (☎ 01672 539362) from £38, all on Avebury's main (and only) street. *The Red Lion* (☎ 01672 539266), a picture-postcard pub with timber frame and thatch roof, billed as 'the world's only pub inside a stone circle', also does ensuite B&B for £35.

For food, the pub does bar meals at lunch time and in the evening – or try *Stones Restaurant*, near the Great Barn, specialising in good-value wholefood. This place is run by two archaeologists who came here on a dig and set up the restaurant when they couldn't find anywhere decent to eat.

Day 1: Avebury to Ogbourne St George
9 miles (14.5 km), 4 to 5 hours
From the *Red Lion* pub, head north along a

Avebury Stone Circle
The stone circle at Avebury dates from around 2600 to 2100 BC, between the first and second phase of construction at Stonehenge. With a diameter of about 350m, the circle is one of the largest in Britain. The site originally consisted of an outer circle of 98 standing stones, many weighing up to 20 tons. The stones had been selected for their size and shape, but had not been worked to shape like those at Stonehenge. They were surrounded by another circle formed by an six-metre-high earth bank and a deep ditch. Inside were smaller stone circles to the north (27 stones) and south (29).

The circles remained largely intact right through the Roman period, when the site may have been a Roman tourist attraction. A Saxon settlement grew up inside the circle from around 600 AD but in medieval times, when the power of the church was strong and fear of paganism even stronger, many of the stones were deliberately buried. Worse was to come in the late 17th and early 18th century when the village began to expand rapidly and stones were systematically removed and broken up for building material. Fortunately, William Stukely (1687-1765) extensively surveyed the site around this time.

Modern archaeological surveys of the site commenced this century. In 1934, under the supervision of Alexander Keiller, buried stones were located and resurrected, and markers were placed where stones had disappeared. The wealthy Keiller actually bought Avebury in order to restore 'the outstanding archaeological disgrace of Britain'.

The modern roads into Avebury neatly dissect the circle into four sectors. To see everything, start from High St, near the museum and car park, and walk round the circle in an anticlockwise direction. There are 12 standing stones in the south-west sector, one of which is known as the **Barber Surgeon Stone**. The skeleton of a man was found under this stone. From the equipment buried with him, he appeared to have been a medieval travelling barber-surgeon (the two jobs were often combined in those days). He was killed when a stone accidentally fell upon him when it was being buried.

The south-east sector starts with the huge **portal stones** which marked the entry point into the stone circle from West Kennet Ave. The **southern inner circle** stood in this sector and within this circle was the **Obelisk** and a group of stones known as the **Z Feature**. Just outside this smaller circle, only the base remains of the **Ring Stone**. Few stones, standing or fallen, are to be seen around the rest of the south-east or the north-east sector. Most of the northern inner circle was in the north-east sector. The **Cove**, made up of three of the largest stones at Avebury, marked the centre of this smaller circle.

The north-west sector has the most complete collection of standing stones, including the massive 65-ton **Swindon Stone**, the first stone encountered, which is one of the few never to have been toppled.

The Alexander Keiller Museum helps explain the purpose, construction and subsequent decay and destruction of the Avebury Circle. It also houses a collection of finds from the sites in what was originally Keiller's private museum. The museum is a good place to start your exploration. It's located in the former stables of Avebury Manor and is open April through October, daily from 10 am to 6 pm, and the rest of the year, Wednesday to Sunday from 10 am to 4 pm. Entry is £1.35. ■

narrow lane, which soon becomes an unsurfaced track, leading uphill through fields to meet the Ridgeway at a junction. Turn left here and keep going for six days!

This first day's walk is through classic Wiltshire downland: rolling hills of grass and wheat, with occasional clumps of trees on the skyline and the whole area dotted with mysterious mounds and standing stones. The route itself is wide and easy to follow, but take care not to be sidetracked onto 'vehicle only' diversions. Just after Barbury Castle (an Iron Age hillfort) there are toilets and a very welcome cafe at the warden's bungalow. There's also a water tap.

Beyond Barbury the route approaches the northern edge of the downs and the views get better: across to the giant town of Swindon and the more scenic Vale of the White Horse. You follow Smeathes Ridge across open farmland and descend past Aldbourne reservoir to the road. Turn right to the village of Ogbourne St George.

Ogbourne St George The path goes straight on at the sign for the *Old Crown Inn*; you follow the road left to reach the pub and village proper. Places to stay include *Elm Tree Cottage* (☎ 01672 841408) with B&B for £30 a double and *Foxlynch* (☎ 01672 841307) on Bytham Rd with B&B at £13.50 per person. Camping here costs £3 per person. *The Old Crown Inn* (☎ 01672 841445) on Marlborough Rd charges £30 per ensuite double, and also does meals, or try the smart *Parklands Hotel* nearby.

If you've got the cash and energy, continue down the Ridgeway for another mile, across the busy A345 to reach *Laurel Cottage* (☎ 01672 841288), a 16th-century guesthouse charging £45 to £50 per night.

Day 2: Ogbourne St George to Court Hill
21 miles (33.5 km), 8 to 10 hours

This is a long day; the scenery, surface and landscape vary, but the route is straightforward. With an early start you should have no problems.

From Ogbourne, follow the tree-lined path out of the village, over the A345. The first ascent of the day starts on a rough track, again tree-lined, passing through an old railway line, which now serves as a cycle way alternative to the A346. The path continues up to Liddington Hill, the trail summit at 277m. Nearby is Liddington Castle, reached by an overgrown permissive footpath, which offers a fine panorama, spoilt only by the scar of the M4 motorway. You descend a chalky track, then walk along a busy road, before turning right to cross the M4 on a bridge towards Fox Hill.

At the crossroads is the *Shepherds Rest*, the last pub actually on the route until Streatley, and 200m from here the Ridgeway resumes its unsurfaced track, varying on the next few miles to grass, shale, tar and back to gravel, as you pass through high ground with more sweeping views. (There's a water tap 10m north of where the route crosses the road to Idstone.)

Further on is Wayland's Smithy (a 'chamber barrow' burial site) and beyond here Uffington Castle. The lookout here has views of the Vale

---

Archaeological Sites Around Avebury
If you've got time before starting your Ridgeway trek, there are a number of important sites around Avebury which are connected by excellent short walks, starting with Silbury Hill and West Kennet Long Barrow (three miles there and back). Silbury Hill is one of the largest artificial hills in Europe, similar in size to the smaller Egyptian pyramids. Like a truncated cone, its 39m-high summit ends in a flat top that is 33m in diameter. It was constructed in stages starting from around 2500 BC, but its purpose is a mystery. Or try Windmill Hill, a Neolithic enclosure or 'camp', dating from about 3700 BC, about three km north-west. There's also a fine walk of about six miles from Avebury to Marlborough via a dolmen known as the Devil's Den. ■

of the White Horse, with the chalky outline of the aforesaid animal just below. As you continue, do stop occasionally and look back – the views are still stunning.

Court Hill Soon after Letcombe Castle, you reach the A338 Wantage road. About 500m north is Court Hill, the Ridgeway Information Centre, which contains an interesting exhibition, and *YHA Hostel* (☎ 012357 60253, £7.45), where camping is also permitted.

If you're not hostelling, there's B&B at Letcombe Regis, about 1½ miles north, including: the thatched *Quince Cottage* (☎ 01235 763652) and *Court Hill House* (☎ 01235 763052) both charging £18.50. If these are full, the nearby town of Wantage (famous for being the birthplace of King Alfred the Great) has a wider choice.

Day 3: Court Hill to Goring
14 miles (22.5 km), 5 to 6 hours

This day is one of transition; your final miles on the high, open downland before dropping to the more enclosed surrounds of the Thames Valley.

From the hostel, Letcombe Regis or Wantage, retrace your steps to the Ridgeway and continue along the northern edge of the downs, following the route of an ancient defensive dyke called Grim's Ditch. You will soon be walking on a wide, grassy track to the Lord Wantage Monument (about 500m past the monument there is a water tap). You'll see signs of the racehorse activity for which this area is famous, as well as the cooling towers of Didcot power station and the former Atomic Energy Research Establishment at Harwell to the north, but this need not affect the calmness of the downland through which you are walking.

About 6½ miles from the start, the Ridgeway goes under the busy A34 by way of a tunnel (there are even some murals added for your enjoyment) and, one mile beyond here, the byway is paved with concrete, although there is a broad grass verge alongside. Look for the sharp left turn off this road. The route deteriorates, with rutted grassy, then chalky, paths for the next 2½ miles.

After Warren Farm you are faced with three miles of almost continuous descent through Streatley Warren. Initially, the track is loosely surfaced, but on reaching another Warren Farm, it's tarred. After the remoteness of the last few hours, the first sign of civilisation (an organic food produce stall) may be a shock, but you'll soon be passing houses and a golf course, before reaching a road junction with the busy A417. Turn right to reach the next junction with the even busier A329 and then go straight into Streatley, where a left turn at the traffic lights will lead across the River Thames into Goring.

Streatley & Goring For a place to stay, there's *Streatly On Thames YHA Hostel* (☎ 01491 872278), costing £9.10. In a different league is *The Swan* (☎ 01491 873737) with prices ranging from £52 for a single room.

In Goring, just on the other side of the river, B&B options include: *14 Mountfield* (☎ 01491 872029; also a taxi service), on Wallingford Rd, from £20, *The Queen's Arms* (☎ 01491 872825), near the railway station, for £20, and *The Miller of Mansfield* (☎ 01491 872829) from £27.50. For food, the *Riverside Tearooms*, near the bridge, does cakes, home-made pasties and meals until 6 pm. Pubs for evening food include those just mentioned, and *The John Barleycorn*. There's also a *Chinese takeaway*, open in the evening, offering the cross-cultural speciality of Mandarin fish & chips.

Day 4: Goring to Watlington
15 miles (24 km), 5 to 7 hours

Beyond Goring the nature of the Ridgeway changes dramatically. For the next three days you pass through woods, farms and villages – an interesting contrast to the rolling Wessex downland already covered.

Today's walk has three distinct phases. The first six miles are flat, following the River Thames upstream (north). Then after passing Carmel College, a Jewish public school, you turn 'inland' once again along the route of Grim's Ditch ascending to the highest point of this part of the Chiltern Hills, at 212m. After the village of Nuffield the walk changes again, crossing lush valleys and woods until it joins the foot of the Chilterns escarpment just before Watlington.

If you have an interest in churches then you will have a productive day: South Stoke, North Stoke, Nuffield and Swyncombe all have fascinating and historic specimens. If, however, you have an interest in finding places to eat and drink you will be disappointed.

About two miles north of Goring you pass the excellent pub and restaurant, *The Leatherne Bottle*, but after that there is no opportunity to obtain sustenance until Watlington. You will need to carry your own food, but drinking water is readily available at Nuffield Church.

You also pass near several alternative accommodation options. In Wallingford, about two miles off the route, you could try *The Studio* (☎ 01491 837277), costing £16 with a free foot bath and foot massage. At Nuffield, between Wallingford and Watlington, *The Rectory* (☎ 01491 641305) charges £18 to £20 for B&B (and £2 a tent for camping). At Park Corner, a hamlet east of the Ridgeway, north of Nettlebed, *Park Corner Farm House* (☎ 01491 641450) charges around £18. The *Crown Inn* in Nuffield does evening meals.

Watlington If you are staying in Watlington then it's worth turning off the Ridgeway at Lys Farm House, and taking the footpath across the fields into Watlington, thus avoiding one mile of walking on main roads. In Watlington *The Fox & Hounds* (☎ 01491 612412) provides B&B from £25, and serves a wide range of evening meals. The other main option for food is *The Prince of India* in the high street.

Day 5: Watlington to Princes Risborough
12 miles (19 km), 4 to 6 hours
The Ridgeway continues along the foot of the escarpment, which is a wide, rutted bridleway, lined much of the way by trees. It is reminiscent of earlier sections of the route, although the peace is disturbed for some miles by the whine

of traffic from the nearby M40 motorway and, as you approach Chinnor, a cement works dominates the view. If you look to your left as you pass under the motorway you will see Beacon Hill and a nature reserve which has been sliced in two by the road.

Chinnor is a convenient place to stop for lunch and as you walk into the town, you pass a number of pubs. *The Crown*, at the first main crossroads, provides good bar food. If your lunch was particularly good, a weekend steam train service (☎ 01844 353535) runs six trips a day from Chinnor to nearby Princes Risborough.

Princes Risborough After Chinnor the Ridgeway climbs and weaves its way over chalk hills to Princes Risborough, where places to stay include *The Black Prince* (☎ 01844 345569) on Wycombe Rd, right on the route, charging £23.50 to £36 for B&B and also doing evening bar meals. In Askett, just north of Princes Risborough, *Bell House Barn*, (☎ 01844 346107) charges £14 for B&B. The village also has two pubs doing food.

If you want to shorten the final day, to finish the route and travel onwards, you could extend this day by overnighting in Wendover. Places to stay here include *26 Chiltern Rd* (☎ 01296 622351) right on the route, charging £12 for B&B, with kitchen facilities available. Or try *46 Lionel Ave* (☎ 01296 623426), less than half a mile from the route, charging £18 for B&B. The *Red Lion* does good evening food.

Day 6: Princes Risborough to Ivinghoe Beacon
18 miles (29 km), 7 to 9 hours
Today involves plenty of hills, but your effort is rewarded with some spectacular views. There is a wide variety of scenery and it makes for an interesting day of walking. It seems as if the paths get busier at this end of the Ridgeway, which is not too surprising as by now the route is within the London commuter belt. Ivinghoe Beacon attracts large numbers of visitors, most of whom park nearby and walk one mile to the top. In

places there is noticeable erosion of the chalk land surrounding the paths. Ivinghoe Beacon is a fitting end to the walk, with 360° views across the heart of England.

There are plenty of opportunities to stop for refreshments on today's walk, including *The Plough* at Lower Cadsden, a useful morning coffee stop. At Wendover we found *Le Petite Café* very welcoming, serving a wide range of food. *The Railway Hotel* at Tring Station serves food and can be a useful place to wait if you plan to catch a train to London at the end of your walk. There is a wide choice of accommodation in the area, including the *YHA Hostel* (☎ 01296 668251) for £7.45 in Ivinghoe. The nearby *Rose & Crown* pub does food.

For B&B, in Edlesborough, one mile beyond the Beacon, the appropriately named *Ridgeway End*, 5 Ivinghoe Way (☎ 01525 220405) charges £18. The village also has two pubs doing food. In Ringshall village, 1½ miles south-east of the Beacon, *12 Ringshall* (☎ 01442 843396) charges £13. There are also several B&Bs in Tring.

The Thames Path

> **Official Name** The Thames Path National Trail
> **Distance** 173 miles (276.5 km)
> **Duration** 10 to 15 days
> **Start** Trewsbury Mead, near Cirencester
> **Finish** Thames Barrier, London
> **Regional Centres** Cirencester, Oxford, Maidenhead, Windsor, London
> **Counties** Wiltshire, Gloucestershire, Berkshire, Buckinghamshire, Oxfordshire, Surrey
> **Area** Chilterns Area of Outstanding Natural Beauty
> **Summary** Primarily a towpath walk, level and undemanding, although some sections are muddy and uneven.

The Thames Path takes the walker through a rich vein of English countryside, history and culture. It follows the River Thames from its source – an indentation in a meadow in the midst of rural Gloucestershire – then through the heart of Southern England, past unspoilt

pastures and market towns, crossing broad flood plains and slicing through large settlements. Eventually you end up in the heart of 'the big smoke': London.

The Thames is described as a lowland river, and the source is a mere 107m above sea level. Geological barriers have been few, so the river has an easy time of it, flowing mostly over its own riverine deposits. It ambles towards the sea, losing height slowly with no tumbling falls or rapids rippling its surface.

While the views and scenery around the river can be beautiful if unspectacular, the history is fascinating. Some of the most historically significant towns and villages of Southern England grew up in the vicinity of the Thames and are often worth a brief diversion. Within the first few miles the young river has been diverted to provide water for millponds, and later for locks, weirs and cuts (canals), all customising the river for human use. Having said that, as you walk down the river there is evidence of occasional rebellion when the river has broken out of its artificial straightjacket and flooded the surrounding lands. Regular commemorative stones mark high floods, particularly in 1897 and 1947 when enormous devastation was caused.

DIRECTION, DISTANCE & DURATION

The route described here takes you from the source to the Thames Barrier. It can be walked in either direction, but going downstream is more satisfying, since you follow the remote and rural stream as it develops into a magnificent river. The Thames Barrier is a fitting end to the walk whereas arriving at the source, an indistinct depression in a field, can be an anticlimax.

Waymarking is erratic, often poor to nonexistent, and occasionally misleading when the path detours away from the river. For long stretches the only signs you will see which refer to the Thames Path are those put up by weary landowners who have clearly had too many walkers take a wrong turning through their land. As the route continues to be improved, the signing will probably improve too.

The History of the Thames Path National Trail

The Thames Path National Trail was officially opened in 1996 (and is still being routed in some places), although the idea of an LDP along the river was first mooted in the 1920s. The plan was debated for some decades, but only in the past ten years have serious efforts been made to develop the trail. This process, promoted by the Ramblers' Association (RA) and sponsored by the Countryside Commission (CC), has involved the cooperation of six local authorities as well as the National River Authority (now the Environment Agency) and the Port of London Authority. You will notice as you walk down the path that some authorities have taken their responsibilities more seriously than others.

The trail is loosely based upon the towpath that used to run beside the navigable river. Unfortunately, in past centuries the establishment of the towpath was hindered by powerful riverside ('riparian') landowners many of whom obstructed the efforts of the Thames Commissioners who, in the 17th century, were given responsibility for developing the Thames as a business route. Thus the towpath frequently jumps over the river to avoid the land of some uncooperative aristocrat. Until earlier this century ferries operated at these points, but these are now redundant and the walker has to endure some lengthy diversions away from the river, some of which are poorly signposted. New sections of path are planned to avoid some of the diversions, but these are slow in being agreed to and implemented. ■

SOUTHERN ENGLAND

The distance from the source to the Thames Barrier is officially measured at 180 miles. You will see references in some books to distances of over 200 miles, this includes the length of path in London where the official route runs along both sides of the river simultaneously. Many of the guidebooks stop (or start) the walk at Kew or Richmond, on the outer limits of Greater London. This misses a large section of the walk through London, which, although built up and urban, provides the visitor with views and experiences not found on the standard walking trails.

The meanders on the river provide opportunities for short cuts. Some can be a few hundred metres, others can cut out miles. If you do spot an opportunity to cut across a loop please keep to footpaths or roads – most of the land you walk through is private, and often intensively farmed. From Windsor to the Thames Barrier, you can take boat trips downstream and save a few miles.

This book describes a 12 day walk. The first two days are 10 miles. Subsequent days average 15 miles. Hours given for each day's distance are walking times only. You will need to add extra for lunch, sightseeing etc. The first two days could be combined, but it makes for a long and tiring first day over rough paths. In the more populous sections, downstream of Oxford, there is plenty of scope to extend or shorten the distances. Some of the towns you pass, such as Windsor, deserve lengthy visits, and where the paths are good you may wish to extend the distance.

STAGES

For a 12 day walk, as described here, the most convenient places to begin and end each day are:

Day	From	To	Distance
1	Thames Head	Cricklade	10 miles (16 km)
2	Cricklade	Lechlade	11 miles (17.5 km)
3	Lechlade	Newbridge	16 miles (25.5 km)
4	Newbridge	Oxford	14 miles (22.5 km)
5	Oxford	Dorchester	16 miles (25.5 km)
6	Dorchester	Pangbourne	16 miles (25.5 km)
7	Pangbourne	Henley-on-Thames	15 miles (24 km)
8	Henley-on-Thames	Maidenhead	15 miles (24 km)
9	Maidenhead	Staines (via Windsor)	14 miles (22.5 km)
10	Staines (via Windsor)	Kingston-upon-Thames	15 miles (24 km)
11	Kingston-upon-Thames	Battersea	15 miles (24 km)
12	Battersea	the Thames Barrier	16 miles (25.5 km)

INFORMATION

As the walk passes through so many different local authority areas, further information needs to be obtained from a string of sources. There are TICs at most major towns; telephone numbers are listed in the text. The Environment Agency (☎ 01734 535000) can provide information about the river and locks, as well as a list of 30 riverside campsites.

Books

The Thames Path National Trail Guide by David Sharp is the most recent and comprehensive guide available, with the route from the source to the Thames Barrier depicted on sections of maps. Also by David Sharp is *The Thames Walk* (published by the RA), a booklet which describes the route from the other direction. Despite a 1995 publication date, the main text was written in 1985 and some sections haven't been updated which is, at times, misleading.

Easy to use and informative is *The Thames Path* by Helen Livingston, which follows the route from the source to Richmond using aerial photographs. *The Thames OS Guide* (Nicholsons, 1994) is a handbook of the river. It does not focus on the Thames Path although it does include some information for walkers. It is particularly useful for identifying places to visit, eat and drink, as well as general information.

A classic of English literature is *Three Men in a Boat* by Jerome K Jerome, a whimsical tale of a trip up the Thames. There are many other literary associations with the river which you will be reminded of as you pass the relevant town or inn.

Maps

OS Landranger (1:50,000) sheets 163, 164, 175, 176 and 177 cover the whole route. A single map showing the whole river as far as Tower Bridge is the very useful *Thames, the River and Path*, published by Geo Projects. It is not quite detailed enough to be relied upon at tricky, poorly signed sections, but it includes a wealth of background information and many useful phone numbers.

GUIDED WALKS & LOCAL SERVICES

Various organisations offer guided walks in Oxford, Windsor and London; TICs have details. For boat trips on the river, the Upper Thames Passenger Boat Association run by French Brothers (☎ 01753 851900) in Windsor will provide details of passenger cruises and river buses which run between Windsor, Richmond, Kew, Westminster and the Thames Barrier. In Oxford there are local cruises run by Salter Brothers (☎ 01865 243421). If you want to explore the river alone, boats can be hired for the day from Hobbs & Son (☎ 01491 572035) in Henley, and from French Brothers in Windsor.

PLACES TO STAY & EAT

The Thames, having being a major trading route, retains a legacy of inns, hotels, guesthouses and B&Bs. These are less common in the early sections (the un-navigable part of the river), but once you pass Lechlade the options increase. There are YHA hostels at Oxford, Streatley and Windsor. If you want to camp there are plenty of sites; a list is available (see Information section). Some farmers may allow camping on their land – always seek permission. Even in the early rural stages, a village or town is never far away, so stocks and supplies should not present any problems.

GETTING THERE & AWAY

The start of the walk is approximately two miles from Kemble, and four miles from Cirencester. Public transport can take you to both towns, but you will then need to either walk to the source or take a taxi to the Thames Head Inn.

Bus

There is no bus route to the source itself; you need to take a taxi or walk from Kemble or Cirencester. Andy James Coaches runs two-hourly buses between Cirencester and Chippenham (on the main London-Bristol railway line) via Kemble. Alex Cars Bus runs hourly between Kemble and Cirencester. Further details available from Gloucester

Public Transport Information (☎ 0452 425543).

At the end of the route, many local buses pass near the Thames Barrier on the south side of the river, through Charlton and Woolwich. Contact London Transport Travel Service (☎ 0171 2221234).

Train

There are regular train services to Kemble from London and Birmingham, via Cheltenham. To get away from the Barrier, it's a 15 minute walk west to Charlton Station from where trains run to Charing Cross.

Riverbus

A riverbus (☎ 0171 9303373) runs between the Thames Barrier and Westminster five times a day, costing £4.30 for a single journey and £6 return. Boat services (☎ 0181 3050300) also run between Greenwich and the Thames Barrier.

Car

The nearest parking place to the source is the Thames Head Inn, on the A443 one mile south-east of the junction with the A429. Cars should not be left here for more than a few hours.

The trail ends at the Thames Barrier (☎ 0181 8541373), Eastmoor St, off the A206 one mile west of Woolwich or one mile east of the junction with the A102(M). There is parking at the visitors centre, but again long-term parking is not available.

THE ROUTE

The Thames Path is evolving. The whole length has not been officially designated a national trail and some sections of the route have yet to be resolved. All Thames Path guides have inaccuracies and by the time this book is published there will be further changes. At times you have to weigh up all the available information and make a personal choice of route. An OS map is essential in helping you make a suitable decision and this guide will lead you through some sections that could possibly cause confusion.

The Start: Kemble or Cirencester

There are two towns near the source: Kemble (two miles away) is small with convenient train access; and Cirencester (four miles away) is larger and a more interesting place to stay.

B&Bs in Kemble include *The Willows* (☎ 01285 770667), near the station, charging from £18, and the decent *Smerrill Barns* (☎ 01285 770907), one mile north of Kemble, charging £25. *The Thames Head Inn* (☎ 01285 770259) is near the source with B&B from £25 and camping at £3 a night.

At the junction of three Roman roads,

SOUTHERN ENGLAND

Weirs & Locks

Evidence exists of weirs being built on the Thames before Roman times. Weirs ensure sufficient depth of water for navigation or for powering a mill. They provide a more consistent source of water for irrigation in dry summers as well as controlling minor flooding in the winter.

But there is a conflict. A weir presents an obstruction for boat traffic and, in the past, mill owners simply refused to let boats pass their stretch of the river. This conflict surfaces in the Magna Carta signed by King John in 1215 where the right of free movement along the river is enshrined. The only solution was to open a gate in the weir and drag a boat upstream, or let it surge down stream. These 'flash' locks could be hard work, and sometimes dangerous. 'Pound' locks, with gates and a system of raising and lowering the water level, were developed near Oxford in the 1630s and have evolved to the type we see today. At some locks there are separate dry ramps with rollers (boatslides) over which light boats can be dragged.

The locks on the Thames are a pleasure to pass. Most are very well kept with beautiful gardens. From Lechlade to Teddington there are 44 locks on the Thames and each of them has a unique postcard which you can buy from the lock keeper. Collecting all the cards is an unusual souvenir but will require some lengthy diversions as not all the locks are on the route of the Thames Path. ∎

including the Fosse Way, Cirencester was the second largest city in Roman Britain. Today the town has a fascinating museum plus several fine historical buildings, many dating from medieval times when Cirencester was a wealthy wool-trade centre.

The church of St John the Baptist is particularly magnificent. The TIC (☎ 01285 654180) in the marketplace can provide accommodation details. The 18th-century *Golden Cross Inn* (☎ 01285 652137) provides B&B close to the town centre from £18. Nearer the start of the walk, the *Royal Agricultural College* (☎ 01285 640644) provides comfortable rooms at £20 to £40. At the top end, *The Jarvis Fleece Hotel* (☎ 01285 658507) is central and provides good rooms from £65 for a single, with special offers at weekends.

Reaching the Source Leave Kemble on the minor road to Tarlton until it meets the A433. Turn right to reach the *Thames Head Inn*. From the inn carry on along the A433 towards the railway bridge. After about 50m, just before the bridge, there are gates on your left. Take this track through the abandoned goods yard, parallel to the railway line, until you reach a stile which takes the path across the railway line. Beware, this is a busy line. On the other side of the line, follow the path to a gate. Cross this and make your way diagonally across the meadow to a copse of trees where you will find the official source of the Thames marked by an engraved stone.

It is a longer, more pleasant walk from Cirencester. Leave the town, taking the A429 after the junction with the A419. At the first houses you reach, opposite Woodhouse Haulage Co, take the footpath running just beyond them and follow it through the Agricultural College grounds to a grey gate. This leads you past some houses on your left, then through another grey gate on to a bridleway. Stay on the bridleway as it passes through a copse of trees to some farm buildings. The path turns off the bridleway here to the left, passing in front of the barns through a gate. Follow the path through fields to reach a road. You will see a large estate on your right.

Cross the road and climb over the steps in the wall opposite. There will be a copse of trees to your left; keep it on your left and follow it round, crossing stiles, until you reach the source of the Thames.

Day 1: Thames Head to Cricklade
10 miles (16 km), 4 hours

This is a day of anticipation as the minor dip in a field develops into a real river. By the time you reach Cricklade it can be defined a river, and you will have walked through cultivated fields and fallow meadows as well as some picturesque Cotswold villages. A substantial part of the walk passes through the Cotswold Water Park; former gravel pits which now provide leisure amenities.

There are a few places where the official path, as described in the guidebooks, has been changed or could be confusing. The first is between Upper Mill Farm (2½ miles from the source) and Neigh Bridge (4½ miles), where there has been extensive redesignation of the footpaths. There are plans to signpost these paths. The path now stays by the Thames for all this section, instead of diverting to Somerford Keynes.

After leaving Upper Mill Farm you continue with the stream on your right until you reach a brand new bridge. Do not cross this; follow the side of the fields, skirting round an old millpond opposite a farmhouse, keeping the stream on your right. By following a public footpath sign to 'Neigh Bridge, ½ mile' you reach a second new footbridge. Cross this to follow a path sandwiched between the Thames and the first Cotswold Water Park lake. Keeping the stream on your left you reach Neigh Bridge and return to the original route.

Ashton Keynes, an old and pretty village, is a suitable halfway point. At *The Plough Inn* the welcome is friendly and the food reasonable.

There may be confusion after you leave Ashton Keynes, taking the path signposted to Waterhay. The route described in the guidebooks crosses a road on the southeastern side of the village into a sports field. The fields beyond this have been replaced by gravel pits and the path is being redirected.

If you cannot find the new path, from the point where the trench has been built, walk parallel to the line of trees and you will eventually join a path marked by posts on either side. After about half a mile this joins an unmade track. Turn left here and then right at the first footpath which is signposted 'Cricklade 3 miles' and marked as the Thames Path. You are now back on the official route.

About a mile before Cricklade, just as you reach North Meadow, there is a bridge over the river. The official route is planned to cross the river and lead you down the south bank into Cricklade. This is not yet signposted and it is easier, more straightforward and more picturesque to take the path through the Meadow by the north bank.

Cricklade Cricklade is a sleepy old Roman town. Its churches and buildings contain fine examples of architecture from Norman times to the present. Accommodation is available in two old coaching inns which are both in the high street: *The White Hart Hotel* (☎ 01793 750206) from £30, or *The Bear Inn* (☎ 01793 750005) from £18.50.

Day 2: Cricklade to Lechlade
11 miles (17.5 km), 4½ hours
The river is now well established, but not yet navigable. Accordingly there is no continuous path alongside the river, and two lengthy sections of today's walk are by road. There are great promises about how this section will be improved, but it is unlikely before the next edition of this book. A map is essential as the paths through rural farmland are not well signposted.

The route is particularly confusing after you cross Water Eaton Footbridge. If in doubt make for the farm buildings of Water Eaton House to the south-west and join the road which takes you to Castle Eaton. Although alternative routes are marked on your OS map many rights of way are impassable.

Castle Eaton is the largest settlement you will pass today. *The Red Lion* has a good

garden overlooking the river and serves filling pub food.

Lechlade Lechlade is a quintessential Cotswold town. The church spire is visible from afar and the town itself, although slightly back from the river, owes its wealth to the trade on the Thames. There is a wide choice of accommodation. B&Bs include *Westcott Cottage* (☎ 01367 253158) with double rooms at £35. In the market square the *Red Lion* (☎ 01367 252373) provides B&B from £18 or *The New Inn* (☎ 01367 252296) is £45 a double. If you want to extend this section you can add five miles and stay in Radcot.

Day 3: Lechlade to Newbridge
16 miles (25.5 km), 6½ hours
The remote and rural feel to the walk is retained, although the river is now a substantial waterway, crossed by historic bridges. 'Pill boxes' line the bank: built in WWII as a defence against invasion. You pass locks (look out for Old Father Thames at St Johns Lock, relocated from the source in 1974) and at times will have to scramble along overgrown paths.

Five miles from Lechlade, *The Swan* (☎ 01367 810220) at Radcot – the scene of Civil War clashes – does B&B from £25.50. Another five miles and you reach Tadpole Bridge where *The Trout Inn* provides a welcome drink and a wide-ranging menu.

About two miles after leaving Tadpole Bridge you reach Ten Foot Bridge. Most route descriptions take the path across this bridge and then through fields to Duxford, rejoining the river round to Shifford lock. The new footbridge at Shifford lock allows you to take a more interesting alternative route. Continue along the north bank, passing through gates at the end of the Chimney Nature Reserve, and along the bank until you reach a wooden bridge. Cross this and take a footpath to your left to reach Shifford Lock. Cross the wooden footbridge to join the south bank.

Newbridge Newbridge is a small village,

SOUTHERN ENGLAND

notable for its river crossing and two busy hostelries. *The Rose Revived* (☎ 01865 300221) is the only accommodation in the village, charging £50 a double for B&B. About 3½ miles further at Bablock Hythe the *Ferryman Inn* (☎ 01865 880028) provides functional rooms, charging £40 a double for B&B.

Day 4: Newbridge to Oxford
14 miles (22.5 km), 5½ hours

Throughout today's walk there is a perceptible growth in human activities. From Newbridge, you pass the Ferryman Inn then leave the river for 2½ miles. As an alternative route, you can try contacting the landlord of the Ferryman Inn who runs an irregular ferry service across the river. The path on the other side stays by the river until it rejoins the official path at Pinkhill Lock.

You may wish to break your journey at Swinford Bridge, one of the last two remaining toll bridges. Refreshments are available at the *Talbot Inn* on the northern bank.

The path is better defined and as you approach Oxford you will notice the hum of traffic, a shock after four days of quiet. More leisure craft are moving on the river and before you realise it the Thames has brought you into the heart of Oxford.

Oxford Much of the fascinating history and architecture in Oxford is based around the university, but the city is a regional centre for trade and industry. Wool from the Cotswolds in medieval times often passed through Oxford and, in this century, heavy industry (notably car manufacture) was also established here. Being a working city, rather than just a university town, means that Oxford isn't as quaint as Cambridge or as compact as Durham, but with 650 buildings officially designated as being of historical or architectural merit, most within easy reach of the centre, this is a city to discover.

The TIC (☎ 01865 726871; after-hours prerecorded tourist information) is in The Old School, Gloucester Green. *The Oxford Town Trail* walks leaflet can be obtained here, and tours start from here daily. Bus information is available from Oxford Bus Company (☎ 01865 785400).

Accommodation is plentiful and the TIC will help with lists and reservations. Some central possibilities include *Oxford Backpackers* (☎ 01865 721761), at 9A Hythe Bridge St, charging £9, and the *YHA Hostel* (☎ 01865 62997) £9.10. Another cheap option during vacation periods is college-owned accommodation such as the *Canterbury Road Houses* (☎ 01865 554642) with rooms from £15. For B&B try *The Falcon Hotel* (☎ 01865 722995), Abingdon Rd, charging £26/45 for singles/doubles, or the smarter *River Hotel* (☎ 01865 243475), Botley Rd, with doubles for £64.

Day 5: Oxford to Dorchester
16 miles (25.5 km), 6½ miles

This stage could be described as the heart of the walk. It is good walking and there is a fascinating mix of riverside views and historical buildings, especially ecclesiastical remains; the river is active, and depending on the weather, you will see many punters, rowing eights and hired cruisers out and about.

The *Isis Inn* at Iffley Lock and the *Kings Arms* at Sandford Lock, although close to Oxford, are pleasant refreshment spots. Abingdon is an attractive and well-established market town and is a good alternative stop. The TIC (☎ 01235 522711) can help find accommodation. A good B&B is *Helensbourne* (☎ 01235 530200) in East St Helens St from £20.

Dorchester Sometimes called Dorchester-on-Thames, to distinguish it from its namesake in Dorset, this was a Roman garrison town and a Saxon bishopric. It still has an historical atmosphere, sustained in part by the large number of antique shops. The abbey church of St Peter and St Paul dominates the town. For B&B try the old *Fleur De Lys Inn* (☎ 01865 340502) on the high street with double rooms at £45, or *Willowmour* (☎ 01865 340444) in Martins Lane, which costs from £20 for a single room. For

DAVID ELSE

CHARLOTTE HINDLE

DAVID ELSE

Top Left: Stile, Weaver's Way, Norfolk Broads
Top Right: North Downs Way waymarker
Bottom: Avebury stone circle, The Ridgeway

DAVID ELSE

DAVID ELSE

DAVID ELSE

DAVID ELSE

Top: Holkham Bay, Norfolk Coast Path
Middle Left: Church ruins near Thurne, Norfolk Broads
Middle Right: Potter Heigham road sign, Norfolk Broads
Bottom: Walkers strolling through fields of summer flowers on Pedders Way

details of other accommodation in the area call Wallingford TIC (☎ 01491 826972).

Day 6: Dorchester to Pangbourne
16 miles (26 km), 6½ hours

Passing the pleasant towns of Benson and Wallingford, today the river is forced through its equivalent of the highlands, the Chiltern Hills, to create the Thames Valley. The path occasionally strays onto the foothills.

If you are feeling literary, you could stay at *The Beetle & Wedge Riverside Hotel* (☎ 01491 651381) at Moulsford, characterised in *The History of Mr Polly* by HG Wells. Single rooms start at £80.

Pangbourne Goring is worth aiming for at lunch time, or possibly overnight. For details see the section on The Ridgeway Path which crosses the river here.

Pangbourne and Whitchurch are towns on opposite sides of the Thames, connected by a toll bridge. In Whitchurch the *Ferry Boat Inn* (☎ 01734 842161) has twin rooms at £41. In Pangbourne, *The George Hotel* (☎ 01734 842237) – once home of Kenneth Grahame, author of *Wind in the Willows* – has single rooms from £40, doubles from £55. B&Bs include *The Cross Keys* (☎ 01734 843268) from £18, and the homely *Weir View House* (☎ 01734 842120) from £25. *The Swan*, opposite, no longer provides accommodation, but serves good pub food. The town itself has a number of places where you can eat.

Day 7: Pangbourne to Henley-on-Thames
15 miles (24 km), 6 hours

There are two distinct stages in today's walk. In the first half (before Reading) you pass through countryside and settlements where people mostly live *and* work. After Reading, you feel the influence of London: a high proportion of residents are commuters and an air of affluence descends on the towns and villages.

Just beyond Mapledurham Lock the route takes you through a housing estate. This is well signposted and the guidebooks are

fairly descriptive. Along the main A329 be warned – the Roebuck has now changed its name to Beethoven's and the path down to the river is easy to miss.

Reading itself is a dull city but it does have some historical sites and a TIC (☎ 01734 566226) which can help find accommodation if required. Signs of industry line the river and you pass the important junction with the River Kennet that once provided a route through to the port of Bristol. (A walk along the Kennet & Avon canal is described elsewhere in the Southern England – Short Walks chapter).

Henley-on-Thames Henley-on-Thames is an old town with plenty of character, best known for its rowing regatta in the first week of July (when accommodation is very hard to find). It has a TIC (☎ 01491 578034) in the town hall. B&B is available at *The Wheatsheaf* (☎ 01491 573234) from £20 or *Mervyn House* (☎ 01491 575331) for £18. *The Red Lion* (☎ 01491 572161), an upmarket hotel by Henley Bridge, has double rooms at £99.

There are plenty of restaurants in town. *The Villa Marina* (☎ 01491 575262) serves Italian food, while pubs such as the *Anchor* and the *Row Barge* are friendly and serve good food. Information on buses is available from the Thames Transit 24-hour Information Hotline (☎ 01865 772250).

Day 8: Henley-on-Thames to Maidenhead
15 miles (24 km), 6 hours

This section of the walk passes through some prosperous and well-kept countryside. The nation's privileged elites have had their entertainment, and their scandals, at places such as Medmenham and Clivenden. Towns and villages such as Marlow and Cookham are obviously still thriving, certainly if the number of restaurants is any measure of success.

Leaving Henley in regatta week, a short diversion will be necessary, avoiding sections of the river here. Three miles on, in Aston, *The Flower Pot Hotel* (☎ 01491

574721) has single/double ensuite rooms at £39/49. The historic and beautiful village of Hurley is worth a short diversion, and if you time it for lunch try *The Rising Sun*.

Marlow is a busy town with plenty of shops and places to eat. If you want to stay overnight contact the TIC (☎ 01628 483597). After Marlow, where you rejoin the Thames, the guidebooks take you over the A404. This has now changed and the path continues under the main road, towards Bourne End. As you enter Bourne End you pass a marina and then the path weaves behind some private gardens to reach the railway bridge. There is a footbridge parallel to the railway bridge, which you cross. On the other side, join the right bank to walk down to Cookham, and then on to Maidenhead.

Maidenhead The town of Maidenhead has an air of faded glory, like a run-down seaside town, and little to commend it. By the river, however, there is a sense of the golden age, before WWI, when this part of the Thames was a playground for the upper and middle classes. Some of the hotels, such as the infamous *Skindle's*, scene of many an illicit affair, are closed, while others have a faded glory. *Boulters* (☎ 01628 21291), by the lock itself, retains its style with double rooms starting at £85. By Maidenhead Bridge, comfortable B&B is available at *Bridge Cottage Guest House* (☎ 01628 26805) or the nearby *Ray Corner Guest House* (☎ 01628 32784), both charging from £25.

Day 9: Maidenhead to Staines (via Windsor)
14 miles (22.5 km), 5½ hours

Beyond Maidenhead the river now weaves under the transport infrastructure of roads and railways that lead towards London. Despite that it retains a surprisingly rural feel and there is a sense of grandeur as you wander along the meadows which open out into a stunning view of Windsor Castle.

Windsor Royalty have lived in Windsor

since 850. Standing on chalk bluffs overlooking the river, Windsor Castle is one of the greatest surviving medieval castles. It is well worth a visit, but very busy at weekends and holiday periods. Elsewhere in the town, the Guildhall is a fine sight, and plenty of other old buildings create a unique atmosphere. Nearby attractions include Eton and Windsor Great Park.

The TIC (☎ 01753 852010) is at the top of the high street. The staff will help make accommodation bookings, but charge a fee of £2.50. Central B&Bs are *Mrs Hughes* (☎ 01753 866036), at 62 Queens Rd, from £20, *Langton House* (☎ 01753 858299), at 46 Alma Rd, from £39 double, and *Alma House* (☎ 01753 862983), at No 56, from £26. There are plenty of restaurants and pub. *Francescoes*, in Peascod St, is popular for pizza and pasta, and *The Merry Wives of Windsor*, on St Leonards St, provides good food.

If you are heading for the *YHA Hostel* (☎ 01753 861710), as you approach Windsor cross the bridge at the A332 into Clewer village. The hostel is in Mill Lane, a mile west of the centre of Windsor. It costs £9.10.

Windsor to Staines Beyond Windsor, the route of the towpath was closed by Queen Victoria, so now walkers have to divert along a boring and busy main road. The republican feeling this engenders can be given full vent as you reach Runnymead – democratic history was made here by the 12th-century bishops and barons who forced King John to sign the Magna Carta, ending the powers of absolute monarchy. Also in Runnymead is the Commonwealth Air Forces Memorial.

Staines Outwardly, Staines is a modern commuter town, but it has been an important river crossing for centuries. Its lengthy history is not very evident and it serves as a stopping point rather than as a place to explore. There are a number of places to stay in Staines: two worth a try are *The Penton Guest House* (☎ 01784 458787), at 39 Penton Road, with B&B from £25, and *Rose*

Villa (☎ 01784 458855), at 146 Commercial Road, with B&B from £20. A short walk from the river before reaching Staines is the quiet village of Englefield Green where you can stay at *Bulkeley House* (☎ 01784 431287) on Middle Hill, a good B&B charging £48 for a twin.

Day 10: Staines to Kingston-upon-Thames
15 miles (24 km), 6 hours

For the first time there is much more variety in the type of housing lining the river. Flats, bungalows and even houseboats line the riverside path creating a sense of tidy suburbia. But it's not totally built up and there are long stretches of meadows and fields.

About eight miles from Staines, and just beyond Shepperton Lock, a company called Nauticalia (☎ 01932 254844) runs a ferry across the river, hourly in the winter until 5.30 pm, or half hourly in the summer until 7.30 pm, and costs 60p. This is an attractive little diversion from the official route, and provides you with an opportunity to walk around Desborough Island and then take the road to Walton-on-Thames where you then rejoin the official path at Walton Bridge.

The route goes through the grounds of Hampton Court (☎ 0181 7819500), a royal palace which was given to King Henry VIII by Cardinal Wolsey. It is a beautiful building, with superb gardens and a 300 year old maze. It's open daily.

Kingston-upon-Thames Kingston-upon-Thames is on the fringe of Greater London, but is a distinct town in its own right. On a range of social measurements it was recently pronounced the most liveable borough in England: some may say that this is a very debatable accolade, but there you have it.

The TIC (☎ 01815 475592) can guide you to the few tourist attractions and help you to find accommodation. On the river is *The Hermes Hotel* with single rooms from £30 (☎ 01815 465322). In the town itself you could try *The Avalon* in Milner Rd (☎ 01812 553992) from £22 for B&B or *281 Richmond Road* (☎ 01815 467389), from £12.50 for B&B

Day 11: Kingston-upon-Thames to Battersea
15 miles (24 km), 6 hours

On this penultimate day, despite being in Greater London, the Thames retains a semi-rural air. On one side of the river, and often both, there is parkland, open common or ornamental gardens. But at Putney the buildings finally drag themselves up to dominate both sides of the river and from now on you are well and truly in the city.

From Kingston, the Thames Path runs simultaneously along both banks of the river. Choose what's best for you – there are several sites of interest along the river. You can, of course, cross and recross on the many bridges which link the two banks. These are

---

The House of Lords – Appointed at Random?
As you walk the final stages of the Thames Way through London, you pass the Houses of Parliament and may like to consider the following.

The Parliament of the United Kingdom consists of two chambers: the House of Commons and the House of Lords. Members of Parliament are elected to the House of Commons in General Elections, held roughly every four to five years. Members of the House of Lords are either appointed, or get there on the basis of sheer luck. In fact, Britain must be one of very few modern industrial democracies which chooses some of its senior politicians completely at random.

Of the 1,030 members of the House of Lords, 613 are 'hereditary peers'. Their sole qualification to sit in the 'Upper Chamber' is that they are the eldest sons of people who previously had a seat there. As Lloyd George said in 1909, 'There are no credentials. They do not even need a medical certificate. They need not be sound either in body or in mind. They only require a certificate of birth – to prove they are the first of the litter. You would not choose a spaniel on these principles.' ∎

SOUTHERN ENGLAND

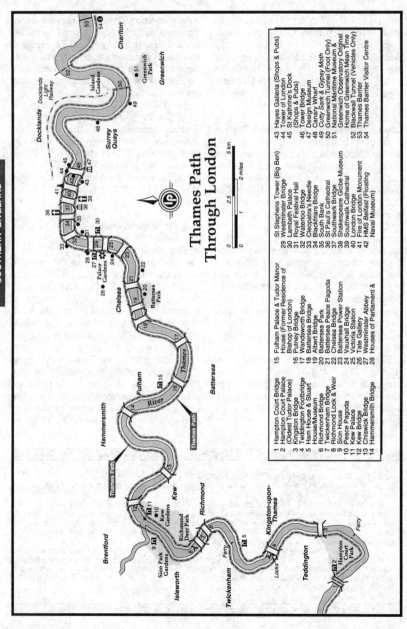

Thames Path
Through London

1 Hampton Court Bridge
2 Hampton Court Palace (Oldest Tudor Palace)
3 Kingston Bridge
4 Teddington Footbridge
5 Ham House & Stuart House/Museum
6 Richmond Bridge
7 Twickenham Bridge
8 Richmond Lock & Weir
9 Sion House
10 Peace Pagoda
11 Kew Palace
12 Kew Bridge
13 Chiswick Bridge
14 Hammersmith Bridge

15 Fulham Palace & Tudor Manor House (Former Residence of Bishop of London)
16 Putney Bridge
17 Wandsworth Bridge
18 Battersea Bridge
19 Albert Bridge
20 Battersea Park
21 Battersea Peace Pagoda
22 Chelsea Bridge
23 Battersea Power Station
24 Vauxhall Bridge
25 Victoria Station
26 Tate Gallery
27 Westminster Abbey
28 Houses of Parliament &

29 St Stephens Tower (Big Ben)
30 Westminster Bridge
31 Lambeth Palace
32 Royal Festival Hall
33 Waterloo Bridge
34 Cleopatra's Needle
35 Blackfriars Bridge
36 South Bank
37 St Paul's Cathedral
38 Southwark Bridge
39 Shakespeare Globe Museum
40 Southwalk Cathedral
41 London Bridge
42 Fire of London Monument
43 HMS Belfast (Floating Naval Museum)

44 Hayes Galleria (Shops & Pubs)
45 Tower of London
46 St Kathrine's Dock (Shops & Pubs)
47 Tower Bridge
48 Design Museum
49 Canary Wharf
50 Cutty Sark & Gypsy Moth
51 Greenwich Tunnel (Foot Only)
52 National Maritime Museum & Greenwich Observatory Original Home of Greenwich Mean Time
53 Blackwall Tunnel (Vehicles Only)
54 Thames Barrier
55 Thames Barrier Visitor Centre

shown on the Thames Path Through London map.

Battersea Once you reach Battersea, the rest of London is easily accessible by bus or on foot. North of the river is Chelsea, Sloane Square or, a little further, Earls Court. To the south is Clapham. All have plenty of accommodation options – too numerous to mention here. Refer to a general guidebook (such as Lonely Planet's *Britain* or the *London city guide* or phone the London TIC accommodation information line (☎ 0891 505487). Once you've found a place, you're better off staying for two nights, returning by public transport when you've finished the route tomorrow.

Day 12: Battersea to the Thames Barrier
16 miles (25.5 km), 6½ hours

This day's walk takes you through the heart of London – past buildings, bridges and historical sites which feature prominently on London's standard tourist trail. You will also pass curious nooks and crannies, places you might not have otherwise visited. Once again, the Thames Path route runs along both sides of the river, so you'll have to choose the side which seems most interesting to you.

Some walkers finish at Tower Bridge; this famous landmark makes a fitting end to the trip. Beyond Tower Bridge, the final sections of the route remains cluttered with the detritus of the old London docks and industry, although this can be interesting in itself and there are places which are being regenerated, symbolised by Canary Wharf – the glass-clad, pyramid-peaked tower which dominates the skyline. Some sections of the route follow pleasant riverside embankments, go past yacht marinas, renovated houses, and restored remnants of London's industrial heritage; other sections follow dirty roads through unattractive areas where you can't even see the river. You have to take the rough with the smooth.

At Greenwich, the two routes rejoin and there's plenty to see: the *Cutty Sark* and *Gypsy Moth* sailing ships; the Maritime

Museum; and of course the Meridian which gave its name to Greenwich Mean Time. There are also a couple of nice pubs for lunch.

Beyond Greenwich, the last few miles take in some parkland, old wharfs, busy roads, scrap-metal yards and forgotten backstreets. In other words, the real London which tourists rarely see. Ahead you see the great silver shells of the Thames Barrier (the gates are raised in high-water conditions to prevent the capital from flooding), and pass under the control tower to finish at the *Barrier Cafeteria*, with a terrace overlooking the river. Time for a cake and cup of tea to celebrate!

The South Downs Way

Official Name South Downs Way National Trail
Distance 100 miles (160 km)
Duration 6 to 8 days
Start Winchester
Finish Eastbourne
Regional Centres Winchester, Petersfield, Chichester, Worthing, Brighton, Eastbourne
Counties Hampshire, West Sussex, East Sussex
Areas East Hampshire and Sussex Downs Areas of Outstanding Natural Beauty
Summary Mostly undemanding walking along well-maintained paths and tracks. Steep sections are brief and the SDW never rises above 270m. Walkers share the Way with bikes and the occasional horse.

The South Downs Way (SDW) mostly follows the chalk ridgeline which divides the lowland Weald from the Channel coast. Since the land is generally well drained and the climate of Southern England is mild, it can be done at any time of year.

This ancient route was first followed by nomadic tribes, keen to avoid the marsh and dense forest below the Downs. Later settlers all left their mark: Bronze Age cross-dykes, burial barrows, and the sparse remains of Iron Age hillforts.

The countryside has two distinct faces. From Winchester to Butser Hill and the county boundary between Hampshire and Sussex, the route threads from hilltop to hilltop through mostly open pastureland. From Butser Hill until the final exhilarating clifftop section between Alfriston and Eastbourne, it follows the pronounced saddle of the Downs, dipping to cross the five river valleys which slice through them. At first, plantations and natural woods restrict views. But from the River Arun eastward, only cloud can mask the sweeping panoramas northward over woods and chessboard Weald farmland, and southward to the Channel coast.

Agriculture and livestock rearing have co-existed for centuries on and around the Downs. Shepherds would drive their sheep off the sweet upland grasses to graze the harvested fields below. In return, those sheep would fertilise the fields for the next year's crop. This balance between arable land and pasture has always been subtly shifting, but the advent of mega-agriculture has caused more dramatic change: where ancient hedges and fences have disappeared, the land now resembles an Ohio cornfield. But most of the Downs still retain their gentle, small-scale charm, although walkers a generation from now may not be able to say the same thing.

Even though London is under two hours away and the coastal resorts seethe with holidaymakers in summer, the SDW is no major highway. Apart from summer weekends and away from the car parks, which punctuate the Downs at nearly every point of road access, you often have only those sheep and cows for company.

Sheep, so often an environmental menace, are the good guys on the South Downs. Look down at your feet to see why. Where they graze, the turf is as smooth as a golf fairway. Elsewhere, coarse grasses and scrub invade. These days, there are probably as many cattle as sheep grazing the uplands.

The Downs are classified as an Area of Outstanding Natural Beauty. This ringing title doesn't give the same degree of protection against man's ravages as, say, National Park status. Even so, they haven't suffered too much and the brick-and-flint villages below them are mostly unspoilt and well worth meandering through.

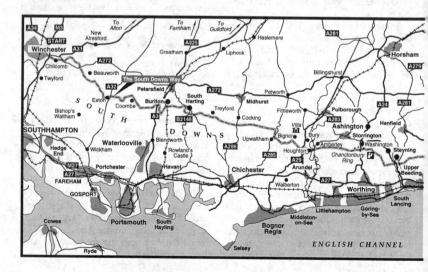

DIRECTION, DISTANCE & DURATION

The route begins in the historic town of Winchester and runs south-eastward to the seaside resort of Eastbourne. Going this way, the prevailing westerly winds propel you forward, and you move from the less dramatic, more enclosed part of the Way to celebrate its final stage by walking the sheer clifftops of the Seven Sisters, undoubtedly the highlight of the walk. Waymarking is, in general, excellent, although there are a few points in Hampshire where you will need to be vigilant.

The SDW is 100 miles long. However, since there is little accommodation directly on the route, plan for a total extra 10 to 15 miles to/from overnight stops. If you're pushed for time, you can omit the first two days by joining the route at Buriton. The day-by-day breakdown that we suggest is a gentle one which anybody, however wheezy, can manage. Many more challenging combinations are possible, such as amalgamating days three and four, or four and five and making Steyning your overnight stop. Hours given for each stage are walking times only; add extra for lunch, rests, visits to museums etc.

STAGES

For an eight day walk, as described here, the best places to begin and end each day are:

Day	From	To	Distance
1	Winchester	Exton	12 miles (19 km)
2	Exton	Buriton	13 miles (21 km)
3	Buriton	Cocking	11 miles (17 km)
4	Cocking	Amberley	11½ miles (18.5 km)
5	Amberley	Upper Beeding	13 miles (21 km)
6	Upper Beeding	Lewes	15 miles (24 km)
7	Lewes	Alfriston	13½ miles (22.5 km)
8	Alfriston	Eastbourne	11 miles (17.5 km)

INFORMATION

At Winchester's TIC (☎ 01962 840500) in the Guildhall, the friendly staff can reserve accommodation for you all the way to Eastbourne through their 'Book A Bed Ahead' service. There are also TICs in Petersfield (☎ 01730 268829), Arundel (☎ 01903 882268), Worthing (☎ 01903 210022), Brighton (☎ 01273 323755), Lewes (☎ 01273 483448) and Eastbourne (☎ 01323 411400).

Books

You *can* follow the route with only a map and a keen eye for acorn signs. But if you do, you'll miss a lot. Useful books include the 'official' *South Downs Way National Trail Guide* by Paul Millmore (CC & OS), which is clear and informative, and includes colour sections from all relevant OS 1:25,000 maps, which saves having to buy separate sheets. *A Guide to The South Downs Way* by Miles Jebb (Constable) is more discursive, but still packed with practical, step-by-step information.

The South Downs Way and the Downs Link by Kev Reynolds (Cicerone) contains useful information, but the text rarely rises above literal description, which can be better assimilated from a map – not his, however, as they are unhelpful pen squiggles! *The*

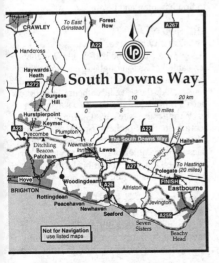

SOUTHERN ENGLAND

South Downs Way Accommodation Guide (Sussex Downs Conservation Board) includes campsites as well as selected accommodation, costs only £1.25 and is invaluable.

Maps
The SDW is covered by OS Landranger (1:50,000) sheets 185 and 197 to 199. It also features on Pathfinder (1:25,000) sheets 1264 and 1265, 1285 to 1288, 1306 to 1308 and 1324. If you have trouble interpreting maps, pack *The South Downs Way* by John Godfrey – a series of large scale (1:10,000) aerial photographs with the route superimposed.

Warnings
Some parts of the SDW in Hampshire are still not formally ratified. Grudgingly signed 'temporary route for South Downs Way walkers only', they could change if the CC succeeds in pushing its way through the territory of 'nimby' locals. Make no mistake, you are striding through metaphorical minefields here, where designated paths get ploughed over and where the talk in pubs can turn to uprooted waymarks. Keep your map handy.

Despite the lush green all around you, there's little groundwater on the Downs since rain quickly percolates through the chalky soil. Carry at least one waterbottle and purifying tablets in case you need to top up at a dubious trough or stream.

PLACES TO STAY & EAT
There's plenty of accommodation in villages within easy reach of the route, but not a lot directly on it, so build in the extra time and distance when planning. Although YHA hostels are adequately spaced in the eastern section of the route, there are none in the first 60 miles between Winchester and Truleigh Hill. We provide some hostel and B&B suggestions in the route description. For a wider choice, use the *RA Yearbook* and the *National Trail Companion* (details in the Books section of the Facts for the Walker chapter), or the *The South Downs Way Accommodation Guide* mentioned in the books section. Most villages

have a general store and a pub at the very least. Nearly all pubs serve bar snacks and often full-scale meals.

GETTING THERE & AWAY
Bus
National Express coaches link Winchester with London (via Heathrow airport), and various other parts of the country. From Eastbourne, frequent buses run to both Brighton and London.

Train
Fast trains run at least hourly between London's Waterloo Station and Winchester. An hourly service from Eastbourne to London's Victoria Station calls at Gatwick Airport. There's also a coastal line which runs from west to east, serving towns such as Chichester, Worthing, Shoreham, Brighton, Lewes and Eastbourne – all accessible by bus from points along the Way.

Car
The route begins in Winchester, just off the M3 motorway, which links Southampton with London. It finishes in Eastbourne, from where the A22 leads to London. The A27 runs along the south coast from Eastbourne to Southampton and beyond.

THE ROUTE
The Start: Winchester
Allow yourself a good half-day in Winchester, capital of Saxon England, and nowadays the county town of Hampshire. Principal sites include the splendid cathedral (for more details on this and on places to stay and eat in Winchester, see the Clarendon Way section in the Southern England – Short Walks chapter). At the tomb of St Swithin, pause to say a quick prayer for good weather up on the Downs. Rain on his birthday, tradition says, means rain for the next 40 days.

Day 1: Winchester to Exton
12 miles (19 km), 4 to 6 hours
This is not a physically challenging first day through fields and some woodland. Leave Winchester by the bridge at the end

St Catherine's Hill & Twyford Down

If you have a spare afternoon before starting the route, consider this walk through history (ancient and modern) on the south side of the city.

From the YHA Hostel, follow the fast-flowing river downstream to the Itchen Navigation Canal, in its time a vital waterway up which came marble from Normandy for the cathedral, and other imports from Europe, bartered for cloth spun from the wool of the Downs sheep. At Tun Bridge, a footpath from the car park winds its way to the summit of St Catherine's Hill, from where you can enjoy fine views of Winchester and the Itchen Valley and hear the drone of traffic speeding through the notorious M3 Twyford Down cutting.

There, the Department of Transport forced a cleft 150m wide and 30m deep through two Sites of Special Scientific Interest, an Area of Outstanding Natural Beauty and a significant wildlife habitat. Popular opposition was headed by the self-styled Donga tribe, which took its name from the ancient tracks which once crisscrossed the Down. The battle was lost to the bulldozers, but the campaign and the massive media coverage it received caused the department to rethink and even desist from a number of equally brutal proposed rapes of the countryside.

If you really want to see the scar, just follow your ears and traverse the valley to the south-east. The sight is grotesque, but will make you appreciate the tranquillity of the South Downs all the more. ■

SOUTHERN ENGLAND

of Broadway and turn right into Chesil St. After 200m turn left up East Hill, then bear right along Petersfield Rd. Where Chalk Ridge bears left after half a mile, take the footpath which goes straight ahead to an SDW plaque marking the official start of the Way and the first of several hundred acorn waymarkers. Once you've crossed the footbridge over the busy bypass, there are no navigational problems for several miles.

After 7½ miles, *Milbury's* pub does meals and B&B and makes a pleasant rest stop. Look out for the 18th-century treadmill in the back bar above a 100m-deep well.

From here, despite lengthy negotiations and an expensive public enquiry, the Way follows a narrow, potentially dangerous lane from the summit of Beacon Hill to Exton and the Meon Valley, rather than taking a more scenic route to Old Winchester Hill.

Exton In Exton, *The Shoe* serves meals and bar snacks. Nearby *Corhampton Lane Farm* (☎ 01489 877506) does B&B. Alternatively, try *Harvestgate Farm* (☎ 01489 877675) or *Rectory Court* (☎ 01489 878618) in Meonstoke, some 15 minutes walk off the route. J-Line Taxis of Swanmore (☎ 01489 892299) runs a taxi service from The Shoe to West Meon (where there are more B&Bs) for £6.

Day 2: Exton to Buriton

13 miles (21 km), 4 to 6 hours

This is a day of varied walking, mainly through pasture and arable land. Beginning and ending in woodland, it also includes the first steep, but brief, ascents of the route – and the first of many spectacular vistas to come.

Nobody knows how on earth Old Winchester Hill – a good 11 miles from Winchester, as the crow flies – got its name. Standing on the bumps and ridges of its Iron Age fort, you can look back over the Meon Valley to the darker green of the New Forest and trace the line of silver water to the south, splitting the Isle of Wight from the coast.

It's odd to find HMS *Mercury* some nine miles inland. The outbuildings of this land-locked naval station are now as trashed as any derelict inner-city tenement. Much more agreeable is Butser Hill. At a mere 270m, it's the highest point on the SDW and marks the beginning of the Downs proper. Savour a rolling descent to the reconstruction of a Celtic farm – well worth an hour's lingering – followed by a gentle ascent through Queen Elizabeth Country Park and Forest (ignore the multi-coloured signs which guide weekend walkers, and follow the gravel path which leads constantly north-east) to Buriton and bed.

SOUTHERN ENGLAND

Weald & Downland Open Air Museum

The Weald & Downland Open Air Museum at Singleton is three miles south of Cocking along the A286. Over 30 buildings, dating from medieval times to the 19th century (including a village school, a Tudor market hall and a watermill) have been saved from destruction and transported to this 40-acre site. In season, you can see thatching, charcoal burning, sheep-shearing, corn-grinding and other traditional rural crafts. Hourly buses run between Haslemere and Chichester via Buriton and Singleton. ■

Buriton Pronounced 'Berryton', this village makes a great overnight stop, with pubs, a fine Norman church, cottages of sandstone and flint and a duckpond. B&Bs include *Pilmead House* (☎ 01730 266795), *Mrs Bray* (☎ 01730 264278), *Mrs Beeson* (☎ 01730 266822), *Mrs Bushel* (☎ 01730 263880) and *Manor Lodge*, (☎ 01730 266171), all of which do packed lunches and dinners on request.

The Master Robert (☎ 01730 267275) does B&B, and 'the hotel boasts two conference rooms, one of which can be used as a skittle alley'. Now there's a detail to boggle the mind. The friendly *Five Bells* (☎ 01730 263584) does self-catering and, if you ask, lets you camp for free in their garden. Both pubs provide food.

The general store is open daily (until 12.30 pm on Wednesday and Sunday) and there are eight buses a day to nearby Petersfield. Walker-friendly B&Bs here include *Mrs Bewes* (☎ 01730 264744) at £16 per person.

Day 3: Buriton to Cocking
11 miles (17 km), 4 to 5 hours

Today the Way rollercoasters over a succession of steep, rounded grassy domes including Tower Hill, Harting Downs and Beacon Hill (there are more beacons to come, each marking a high point where fires were lit four centuries ago to warn of the approaching Spanish Armada). Each has superb views, particularly southwards to Chichester and the Channel.

Cocking It's prudent to reserve accommodation in Cocking since the choice is limited. The *Blue Bell Inn* (☎ 01730 813449) is friendly ('Please remove your muddy boots.

Socks welcome'), serves meals and does B&B. The *Village Tea Rooms* (☎ 01730 813336) provides B&B and packed lunches on request. *Manor Farm* (☎ 01730 812784) offers B&B and camping facilities. Hourly buses run north to Haslemere – with regular trains to London.

Day 4: Cocking to Amberley
11½ miles (18.5 km), 4 to 5 hours

The Way takes you through forest and farmland of the Cowdrey Estate. In the middle of a field stands what looks like a fire watchtower. Not so. It was erected by the estate so that visiting deerhunters – who paid handsomely for their thrills – could just stand and shoot. Not only the deer were gratified by the venture's financial failure. More profitable nowadays are pheasants, reared for the gun, which cackle and scatter into the undergrowth at your approach.

You then cross Slindon Estate, which is owned and managed by the NT, which is encouraging the reintroduction of sheep, ousted from much downland by intensive arable farming. Through it slices Stane Street, a Roman road which ran between the port of Noviomagus – nowadays, Chichester – and Londinium.

The NT has restored the wondrously named *Gumber Bothy* camping barn (☎ 01243 814484) where you can either camp or sleep in the barn (sleeping bags for hire), self-cater and take a hot shower, all for £4. The bothy is badly signposted where the SDW intersects Stane Street. If you overnight there, you're well poised to make a detour next morning to Bignor Roman Villa (see aside).

Onwards from here, pause smugly just

before you negotiate the snorting traffic of the A29; you are now exactly halfway between Winchester and Eastbourne. Beyond here, the SDW avoids an unpavemented section of the B2139. Acorns lead you across a new footbridge over the River Arun to meet the B2139 west of Houghton Bridge.

Amberley With trim gardens and houses of flint, stone, brick and half-timber, Amberley lies less than half a mile off the revised route. The village shop opens daily (mornings only on Wednesday and weekends). You can eat at the *Black Horse*, the *Bridge Inn* and adjacent *Boathouse Brasserie*, both beside the station (which has hourly trains to London). Opposite, *Houghton Bridge Tearooms* serves food until 5 pm. For accommodation, unless something is set up in the village (check by phoning Arundel TIC) you must go to nearby Bury, where B&Bs include *Mrs Clarke* (☎ 01798 831843) and *Mrs Hare* (☎ 01798 831438). Arundel is four miles off route, but is linked to Amberley by hourly train, and has a *YHA Hostel* (☎ 01903 882204, £7.45) and several B&Bs, including *Mrs Jollands* (☎ 01798 831234) and *Mrs Hardy* (☎ 01798 831295).

Amberley Museum, 'the museum that works', is based in an old chalk pit beside the station. From March to October you can meet a clay-pipe maker, blacksmith, wheelwright, broom maker, boatbuilder and other traditional artisans.

Day 5: Amberley to Upper Beeding
13 miles (21 km), 4 to 6 hours
Once you've puffed your way up from the Arun valley, this is a day of easy walking

along the spine of the Downs following chalk and flint track. You only need to change your stride for a steepish drop to the village of Washington and the ascent to the crests again. If the ascent doesn't take away your breath, the wrap-around views will.

Chanctonbury Ring, with superb views to the south and east towards Worthing, Shoreham and, for the first time, Brighton, makes an ideal rest stop. The coppice of beech trees was originally planted in 1760 by a local landowner who, according to legend, would climb up the hill with bottles of water to nurture his young saplings. He must have turned in his grave when the 1987 storm took out the heart of his plantation, but it did reveal Iron Age and Roman remains which are still being excavated.

Upper Beeding Steyning, just one mile off route, is designated an Outstanding Conservation Area, has a choice of B&Bs and deserves a detour. You can camp at *White House* (☎ 01903 813737).

Just before the River Adur, you cross the Downs Link, another LDP, connecting the South and North Downs Ways. From the A2037, just beyond the river, buses go to Shoreham, where accommodation is plentiful. Alternatively, you can push on for two miles to *Truleigh Hill YHA Hostel* (☎ 01903 813419, £8.25), still indicated as 'Tottington Barn' on OS maps.

Day 6: Upper Beeding to Lewes
15 miles (24 km), 5 to 7 hours
After climbing from the Adur valley the Way sticks close to the ridge. Brief rollercoaster ups and downs are succeeded by long flat

SOUTHERN ENGLAND

Bignor Roman Villa
In Bignor Roman Villa (open March to October) about two miles north of the Way, you can still see parts of the original walls and underfloor heating system, plus a collection of tools, coins and domestic items. Best of all are the mosaics: winter snug in a warm cloak, a rasta-haired Medusa, Venus eyeing up a pair of gladiators, and Ganymede, the androgynous Greek shepherd boy. ∎

stretches through arable land and lush, sheep-cropped grassland.

At Devil's Dyke lookout and *hotel* you can enjoy a meal or a drink on the terrace and savour the scenery. The route is signed both SDW and 'West Sussex Border Path 1989' from here until the top of a lane which rises steeply from Saddlescombe. At this point the ways diverge, the SDW going straight ahead. Watch out. Someone has made off with the relevant digit of the fingerpost.

Watch out too for another welcome change to the original SDW; a footbridge takes the route over the new four-lane A23 and into Pyecombe, where *Mrs Reeve* (☎ 01273 843766) on Church Lane does fine B&B. You can camp at nearby *Pangdean Farm* (☎ 01273 843302). From the stop behind the BP garage, buses run near-hourly to Brighton, stopping right outside *Brighton YHA Hostel* (☎ 01273 556196).

Passing just south of Jack & Jill, a pair of restored 19th-century windmills, you gradually regain height until Ditchling Beacon, where you see for the first time, beyond the sprawl of Brighton, a pair of white cliffs: the westernmost of the Seven Sisters and a treat in store for the final day.

The Way is less well signed and less trodden as it drops towards *Newmarket Inn*, which offers bar and restaurant meals, but not B&B – although they'll let you camp in the rear garden. From here, buses run every half hour to both Brighton and Lewes.

Alternatively, you can bypass Newmarket Inn and divert to the charming country town of Lewes (pronounced 'Lewis') by continuing straight ahead along a clear track where a waymark points the SDW sharp south-west and away from the crest. At nearby Kingston, *Castelmer Fruit Farm* (☎ 01273 472524) offers camping. You might alternatively head for the bright lights of Brighton.

Lewes Lewes has plenty of accommodation for all budgets. After hours, a board in the window of the TIC at 187 High St (☎ 01273 483448) indicates what's still available. And there's no lack of fancy restaurants. Alternatively, try a takeaway from *Mr Chips*, at 38 Western Rd, or from the Charcoal Grill, at 61 High St.

The streets and alleys are well documented with plaques and signs. Tom Paine, a major intellectual inspiration for the American Revolution, lived at Bull House, 92 High St, and expounded his ideas to the Headstrong Club at the *White Hart Hotel*, where you can see a copy of the Declaration of Independence. John Harvard, founder of the university of the same name, also lived in Lewes.

Follow your nose and the aroma of malt and hops to 6 Cliffe High St and browse around the timewarped shop attached to Harveys Brewery, whose 1859 Porter was Runner-Up Champion Beer of Britain at the 1995 Great British Beer Festival.

Brighton

Holiday resort, university town and home to Europe's largest marina, Brighton can add a touch of metropolitan spice to your journey. Nicknamed 'London-by-the-Sea', it has a host of bars, night-spots, B&Bs and places to eat.

It differs from other resorts on the South coast in its unique blend of faded elegance and downright seediness, inherited when George IV came down here on the original dirty weekend. The Royal Pavilion, built for that same George when he was Prince Regent, is well worth visiting for its would-be oriental architecture and sumptuous furnishings.

There's a YHA hostel here and endless B&Bs. The TIC (☎ 01273 3337755) will advise.

Explore the traffic-free Lanes and North Lanes for antique shops and pubs. *Food for Friends* on Market St does cheap, tasty vegetarian food in a relaxed atmosphere. If you've the energy, check out *The Zap* club under one of the arches on the seafront, which offers all the flavour of a London West End night-club without the pretension. ■

Day 7: Lewes to Alfriston
13½ miles (22.5 km), 5 to 7 hours

Today the route finally leaves the spine of the Downs. It's a spectacular farewell. Apart from a few short, sharp dips and rises, you can stride along the gently undulating route, enjoying your last extensive views northwards over the Weald.

At Rodmell, which has several B&Bs, be careful where the Way meets a busy road. Although there's no SDW sign, the official route goes right to follow the highway for half a disagreeable mile, then turns sharp left towards the River Ouse. A right turn here

takes you to *Telscombe YHA Hostel* (☎ 01273 301357, £7.45), after two miles. Trains to and from Lewes and Brighton stop hourly at Southease Station.

Alfriston Alfriston sits at the foot of the Downs, flaunting its flint and timber-framed cottages at the tourists, who arrive by the coachload in high season. There's a *YHA Hostel* (☎ 01323 870423, £8.25), several B&Bs and hotels and one general store. You can camp at *The Tanneries* (☎ 01323 870449).

This ex-smuggling town is rich in pubs

Cycling the South Downs Way

The SDW is unique among long-distance trails in Britain since its whole length is designated as a bridleway. This means that cyclists – and horses – can share the route with walkers. The only exception is the final stage between Alfriston and Eastbourne where cyclists take the 7½ mile bridleway alternative which begins at Plonk Barn and crosses Windover Hill. This final stage may not be as spectacular as the walkers' trail which hugs the coastal cliffs, but it still offers vistas as dramatic as anything you've seen so far. Cycling's only disadvantage is the number of bar-handle gates – 83 of them, actually – where you have to leave the saddle briefly.

Time Cycling the SDW takes as long or as short as you like, since you can easily cut out the off-route, off-Downs villages or even head to the holiday resorts on the coast. Consider, for example, swooping downhill from Devil's Dyke to spend the night at Brighton Youth Hostel. One of the team at Peter Hargreaves Cycles in Winchester (see Bike Shops) has ridden the entire Way in a single day: you could always call here for information and spare parts. We suggest, however, a more leisurely progress of some 25 miles a day which will allow you plenty of time to enjoy a few off-track detours. Using the route description above, by joining two walker's days into one, you can complete the SDW in four days of cycling with three overnight stops.

Bike & Equipment It's quite possible to bounce your way along the route on a touring bike, but you'll be more comfortable on a mountain bike, which is ideal for the varied terrain.

The tracks, particularly up on the ridgeline, are often strewn with flints and sharp stones and your tyres will take a pounding. Also, your brakes will work overtime on the steep descents, and anything that can rattle loose will rattle loose. So be prepared and pack spare inner tubes (so that you can fix a flat at your leisure at the end of the day), a puncture repair kit and tyre levers, spare brake and gear cables, spare brake blocks, Allen keys, a small adjustable spanner/wrench, and a screwdriver (if needed for your bike).

You can wear anything on a bike, from standard tracksuit and T-shirts to full lycra body suit, although proper cycling shorts avoid chafing. Spare clothing should protect you from bad weather just as if you were walking. The only essentials are 'mits' – fingerless gloves with padding at the palm to cushion the inevitable shocks – and, of course, a helmet.

Bike Shops In Winchester, *Peter Hargreaves Cycles* (☎ 01962 860005), at 26 Jewry St, gives friendly, helpful service. Once you leave town, however, any fault that you can't fix yourself will mean a diversion southwards to, for example, *Arundel Cycle Hire & Repair* (☎ 01903 883712), at 4 School Lane, Arundel, open daily except Thursday, or to Worthing, Shoreham or Brighton on the coast.

Joe and Paul at *Lewes Cycles* (☎ 01273 483399), 28 Western Rd, Lewes, close on Sunday and Monday. During their lunch break they can always be found in the Black Horse Inn opposite the shop.

Getting There & Away Bikes are allowed on trains, the only exceptions being rush hour arrivals in London before 10 am and departures between 3.30 and 6.30 pm. ∎

with character. The *George Inn*, licensed since 1397, offers food and good beer. The *Star*, only a few years younger and once frequented by pilgrims, also functions as a hotel behind its fine medieval facade. When we passed the *Market Inn*, it had a handwritten sign on its door which read (in capitals; their exclamation marks, not ours): 'Downland walkers you are really welcome, but would you please take off those boots!!! Thanks.'

Despite appearances, Alfriston hasn't completely sold out to the tourist; a note on the town noticeboard read 'Ferret found on Wilmington Long Man. Ring to identify as yours'. All the same, a little fresh mud from your boots will do the town a power of good.

Day 8: Alfriston to Eastbourne
11 miles (17.5 km), 4 to 6 hours

You have, in principle, a choice for this final stage since there are two official SDW routes between Alfriston and Eastbourne. You *could* take the bridleway which curls inland, but this is best left to cyclists and horse-riders. Instead, head due south and enjoy an exhilarating finale along the clifftops.

The two ways part almost immediately at Plonk Barn (not, alas, a rustic wine bar), just after you've crossed the Cuckmere River. Here, where the inland bridleway turns left, the coastal route heads right. You rejoin the meandering Cuckmere at Exceat, where it's well worth pausing at the excellent Interpretation Centre. *Foxhole Bottom Camping Barn* (☎ 01323 870280) is nearby.

Route and river meet the open sea at Cuckmere Haven, where the home stretch lies before you. Turning east to follow the coast, the Way soon climbs steeply to the crest of Haven Brow, the first of the Seven Sisters cliffs (there are, in fact, eight but this doesn't alliterate so neatly). With staggering views over the Channel, and the exhilaration of being so close to the sea, the Sisters can't fail to thrill.

At Beachy Head, the Downs finally tumble into the sea. Here, the candystriped lighthouse below makes a fine landmark for the end of the route. Savour it because the official end of the SDW, a couple of miles

further on beside an undistinguished refreshment kiosk, is nondescript. Better still, continue along the promenade and enjoy an alternative finish at the end of Eastbourne's fine 19th-century pier.

Eastbourne A haven for the retired, and well past its heyday, Eastbourne is an unexciting return to civilisation. Hotels and B&Bs border the seafront and most of the roads leading off it. Supply exceeds demand, and it's worth shopping around. The TIC on Cornfield Rd (☎ 01323 411400) is well signposted. There's a *YHA Hostel* (☎ 01323 721081, £7.45), and you can camp at *Rookery Caravan Site* (☎ 01323 762146).

Local attractions include the pier, the Victorian bandstand, the small lifeboat museum and the Eastbourne Heritage Centre. The town has a multitude of fish & chips shops and tearooms. If these aren't your personal cup of tea, try the *Pizzeria Sanremo* on Grove Rd for authentic Italian food, or *Maxims* on South St, which serves food until 1 am.

The South West Coast Path

Official Name The South West Coast Path National Trail, or South West Way (SWW)
Distance Officially 594 miles (950 km); unofficially 613 miles (987 km)
Duration 7 weeks
Start Minehead
Finish Poole
Regional Centres Minehead, Ilfracombe, Barnstaple, Bideford, Bude, Wadebridge, Newquay, Penzance, Falmouth, St Austell, Plymouth, Torbay, Exmouth, Weymouth, Poole
Counties Somerset, Devon, Cornwall, Dorset
Areas Exmoor National Park, the North Devon, South Cornwall, East Devon and Dorset Areas of Outstanding Natural Beauty, plus 20 sections of Heritage Coast
Summary Britain's longest national trail follows the undulating coastline of the south-west peninsula which, while often beautiful, can be very exposed to wind and coastal fog. The ups and downs of the coves also make some stretches particularly demanding.

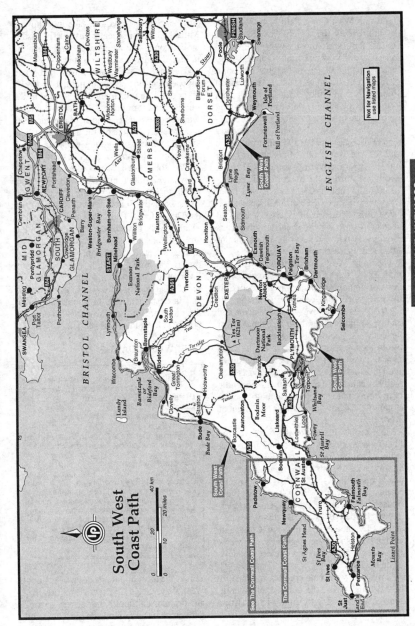

South West Coast Path

SOUTHERN ENGLAND

Not for Navigation
use listed maps

The South West Coast Path National Trail, also known as the South-West Peninsula Coastal Path and (most neatly) the South West Way or SWW, is Britain's longest long-distance path (LDP). It follows the coast through four counties: from Minehead in Somerset, along the north Devon coast, around Cornwall, via Lands End, then along the south Devon coast to Poole in Dorset.

The Path's official length has recently been revised upwards to 594 miles but if you walk all the way from Minehead to Poole you'll end up covering some 613 miles. About one-third of the exceptionally beautiful coastline belongs to the NT, and other areas form part of Exmoor National Park. Two-thirds of the Path is also designated Heritage Coast, but its sheer length means you must also transit several large and uninviting seaside resorts and towns.

The South West Coast Path is partly based on trails created by coastguards to patrol the area for smugglers, and was used for this purpose until last century. Coastguards needed to examine every coastal nook and cranny, so the path tends to hug the edge of the coast very closely. The nature of the terrain means that you need to be prepared for a fair amount of walking up and down steep hillsides. The South West Way Association has calculated that if you did the whole route from end to end, you'd actually ascend a total of 27,300m – three times the height of Everest.

Most people undertake this walk for the stunning scenery and the flora and fauna that comes with it, but there are specific sights along the way too. The path passes right through the picturesque villages and towns of Clovelly, Boscastle, Tintagel, Port Isaac, St Ives, Mousehole, Helford, Portloe, Charlestown, Fowey, Polperro, Looe, Bantham, Branscombe, Lyme Regis, Lulworth Cove and Studland. It also transits England's most westerly point at Land's End and its most southerly at The Lizard.

Along the way you could also make a short detour to visit the old market town of Dunster, take a ferry to Lundy Island from Ilfracombe, ride the surf on Britain's best surf beaches at Newquay, take in a show at Minack Open Air Theatre, inspect the castles at Falmouth and St Mawes, and visit the unique Swannery at Abbotsbury.

The Path is well served with YHA and independent hostels, camping barns, B&Bs and pubs, many of them well attuned to the needs (and appetites) of long-distance walkers. Note that some of these facilities require short detours off the actual path. You should avoid busy summer weekends when accommodation can be fully booked.

The South West Way is often divided for convenience into four sections: the Somerset & North Devon Coast Path; the Cornwall Coast Path; the South Devon Coast Path and the Dorset Coast Path. Only five per cent of visitors walk the whole path in one go, but anyone reasonably fit should be able to manage at least one section. Most popular is the 162.5 miles through Cornwall, from Padstow to Falmouth via Land's End. This section can easily be walked in two weeks, and is described here in detail. The other three sections of the SWW are also outlined briefly at the end of this section.

CORNWALL COAST PATH

> **Official Name** The South West Coast Path National Trail – Cornwall Section
> **Distance** 162.5 miles (262 km)
> **Duration** 2 weeks
> **Start** Padstow
> **Finish** Falmouth
> **Regional Centres** Bude, Wadebridge, Newquay, Penzance, Falmouth, St Austell, Plymouth
> **Counties** Cornwall
> **Areas** Cornwall Area of Outstanding Natural Beauty, the Trevose Head, St Agnes, Portreath, Penwith and Lizard Heritage Coasts
> **Summary** A moderately strenuous coastal walk, with some tough bits thrown in, including clifftops, beaches and resort towns, plus some rural inland sections. Continual ups and downs are tiring, but the fascinating contrasts of the route make up for this.

This is the most popular section of the South West Way. Generally, the views are rocky and dramatic, although the scenery becomes gentler the further round you get from Land's

End. There's plenty to see – secret coves, wrecks, the remains of cliff castles, tumuli, settlements, disused mines and quarries, a wide range of birdlife, seals etc – and it's well worth carrying a pair of binoculars.

In places the route follows beaches and, if the tide is high, you'll be walking through the soft sand of the dunes. Although some parts of the walk cut inland, most of it hugs the coastline. Landslides and erosion (natural and human) can result in unexpected changes to the route.

Cornwall's main tourist season is from Easter to the end of September. Some B&Bs and places to eat close during winter. Over the Easter holiday and during July and August it may be difficult to find accommodation, particularly near the main tourist towns, so it's best to book in advance; if you want to stay in the hostels it makes sense to book ahead at any time.

Be warned, too, that coastal fog can be a problem, blotting out the path ahead very suddenly. Driving wind can be another hazard, especially when the Path is following the clifftop, and your rucksack acts like a sail.

Direction, Distance & Duration
Although the SWW can be walked in either direction, it seems traditional to go anticlockwise; ie doing the northern coast of the peninsula first. The published guides all assume you walk this way, and it's confusing trying to follow their detailed directions in reverse. However, the South West Way Association (SWWA) does publish a reverse route guide (see Books below).

In most places the Path is clearly waymarked with the national trail acorn symbol, although these have an irritating habit of vanishing just at the very points when the route is least clear. In theory, you can't go far wrong except when transiting towns and villages because you're following the coast with the sea to your right (assuming you go anticlockwise), but the number of other paths crisscrossing the coastline can certainly lead you astray if you don't keep a good eye on the map.

From Padstow to Falmouth is just under 163 miles. There are several short cuts and some of the more boring bits (through town outskirts) can be skipped by taking a bus. These options are outlined in the route description.

Anyone reasonably fit should be able to walk this stretch in 12 to 14 days, although you might want to add in a few more for sightseeing. Remember that high winds and sea mists can make clifftop walking slow and dangerous at times. When the mist is down, it's better to hole up somewhere for the day, rather than risk ending your walk prematurely on a path leading over a cliff edge. If time is tight, the stretch from St Ives to The Lizard lets you take in some of Britain's best known beauty spots in just five days. If you'd prefer to take your time, St Ives would be a good place to spend a couple of days, with pleasant beaches and the new Tate Gallery.

Stages
For a 14 day walk, as described here, the most convenient places to begin and end each day are:

Day	From	To	Distance
1	Padstow	Treyarnon Bay	
			(17 km)
2	Treyarnon Bay	Newquay	12½ miles
			(20 km)
3	Newquay	Perranporth	11 miles
			(18 km)
4	Perranporth	Portreath	12.5 miles
			(20 km)
5	Portreath	St Ives	17 miles
			(27 km)
6	St Ives	Pendeen Watch	
			(21 km)
7	Pendeen Watch	Sennen Cove	9 miles
			(15 km)
8	Sennen Cove	Porthcurno	6 miles
			(9.5 km)
9	Porthcurno	Penzance	11 miles
			(17.5 km)
10	Penzance	Porthleven	13 miles
			(21 km)
11	Porthleven	The Lizard	13 miles
			(21 km)
12	The Lizard	Coverack	11 miles
			(18 km)
13	Coverack	Helford	13 miles
			(21 km)
14	Helford	Falmouth1	10 miles
			(16 km)

SOUTHERN ENGLAND

SOUTHERN ENGLAND

Information

Along the Cornwall section of the route, there are TICs in Padstow (☎ 01841 533449), Newquay (☎ 01637 871345), Penzance (☎ 01736 62207), St Ives (☎ 01736 796297) and Falmouth (☎ 01326 312300). They can help with bookings and general enquiries, but the most detailed information about the route is available from the South West Way Association (SWWA).

Books The SWWA (☎ 01752 896237) publishes a detailed description of the whole route in 37 leaflets, each covering a short section (75p plus 20p postage each). They are available from the secretary, Mrs M Macleod (SWWA), 1 Orchard Dve, Kingkerswell, Devon TQ12 5DG. The ones most relevant to the walk described below are:

Padstow to Porthcothan
Porthcothan to Newquay
Perranporth to Portreath
Portreath to Hayle
Hayle to Zennor
Zennor to Sennen Cove
Sennen Cove to Porthcurno
Porthcurno to Penzance
Penzance to Porthleven
Porthleven to The Lizard
The Lizard to Helford
Helford to Falmouth

The SWWA also publishes the invaluable *South West Way Complete Guide* (£3.99) which complements the leaflets with information on accommodation, transport, planning tips, the latest state of path conditions, and even tidetables.

If you want to do the walk the reverse way round, the SWWA also publishes a supplement called *The Other Way Round* for £2.30. It only details the actual walk, so you'd still need the main guide for accommodation lists etc.

The official Aurum Press/CC guides cover the South West Coast Path in four sections: *Minehead to Padstow* by Roland Tarr, *Padstow to Falmouth* by John Macadam, *Falmouth to Exmouth* by Brian Le Messurier and *Exmouth to Poole* by Roland Tarr; £10.99 each.

Bartholomew publishes *Walk the Cornish Coastal Path* (£4.99) by John Mason, and *Walk South Devon Coastal Path & Dartmoor* (£5.99) by John Mason & Eric Hemery. These are handy ring-bound combined guides and maps with some background information.

There's also *South West Way – Minehead to Penzance* and *South West Way – Penzance to Poole* by Martin Collins (published by Cicerone, £8.95 each).

The NT publishes a series of *Coast of Cornwall* leaflets, available from NT shops in the area. These give fascinating details about what you can see on the parts of the walk owned by the NT. The ones of particular relevance to the walk described are:

No 8: St Agnes & Chapel Porth (50p)
No 9: Godrevy to Portreath (60p)
No 10: West Penwith: St Ives to Pendeen (80p)
No 11: West Penwith: Cape Cornwall to Logan Rock (70p)
No 12: Loe Pool & Gunwalloe (70p)
No 13: The Lizard, West Coast (70p)
No 14: Kynance Cove (60p)
No 15: The Lizard, East Coast (70p)
No 16: The Helford River (70p)

If you have trouble getting hold of them, write to the National Trust, Cornwall Regional Office, Lanhydrock, Bodmin, Cornwall, PL30 4DE, enclosing the price of the leaflets and a donation towards the postage costs.

For a light-hearted look at the realities of walking the path with a dog in tow, look out for Mark Wallington's *500 Mile Walkies* (Arrow, £4.99) in which hapless mutt Boogie is tricked into taking the longest walk of his life.

Maps The OS Landranger (1:50,000) maps needed for the Cornwall Coast Path are Nos 200 (*Newquay & Bodmin*), 203 (*Land's End & The Lizard*) and 204 (*Truro & Famouth*).

If you're only going to do a short stretch of the path a good alternative might be the Altos Explorer *Penwith-Land's End* map-guide (£3.95), showing the path from St Ives

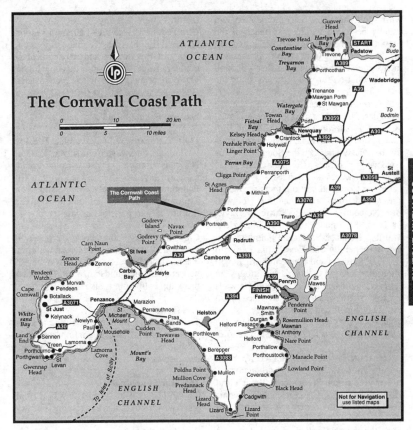

The Cornwall Coast Path

SOUTHERN ENGLAND

to Penzance. It's available from the South West Way Association (see Books) and from some shops in the area.

Warnings Since much of the walking is on clifftops and headlands, you are often exposed to the wind – listen for gale and rain forecasts. The weather, tides and ferry services across river mouths can all greatly affect the timing of your walk, so it's worth getting information about these before you set off (see the earlier Books and Information sections). A tidetable (readily available in local shops and reproduced in the SWWA

handbook) would also be useful – wading across rivers at low tide can save a lot of mileage – but only when conditions are right, otherwise it can be fatal. If you want to swim (for relaxation, *not* to cross river mouths), note that many of the beaches have strong currents. Flags mark safe places for swimming and lifeguards are sometimes on duty; if in doubt, ask the locals.

Places to Stay & Eat

As prime tourist destinations, Somerset, Dorset, Devon and Cornwall all offer a wide range of facilities for all budgets. Villages with food, beer and accommodation can usually be found within easy reach of the footpath. Some B&Bs also offer evening meals. If you don't want to make the arrangements yourself there are TICs that will book accommodation for you in towns along the way, albeit at a price.

A selection of places to stay is listed in the route description. For a wider choice, as well as the *RA Yearbook* and the *National Trail Companion* (see the Books section in the Facts for the Walker chapter), the South West Way Association publishes a *Complete Guide* which includes an accommodation list.

On the Cornwall section, there are campsites at Padstow, Porthcothan Bay, Holywell Bay (Newquay), St Agnes, Portreath, Hayle, St Ives, St Just, Penzance, Marazion, Mullion, Kennack Sands and Falmouth, but they're generally only open from Easter to October. Farmers and other landowners will often allow individuals (but not groups) to camp on their land, but you should always ask first and make sure you leave the field in the state you found it. TICs have lists of official camping grounds, as does the *South West Way Complete Guide* (see Books earlier in this section).

The route is quite well served by YHA hostels. The ones on the Cornwall section are at Treyarnon Bay, Perranporth, Land's End (St Just), Penzance, Coverack and Pendennis Castle (Falmouth). There are independent hostels at Newquay, Sennen and Kelynack along the route described, as well as several more on other sections of the SWW.

Villages generally have a pub, a Monday to Saturday bus service and a small store. Most have one early closing day a week (either Wednesday, Thursday or Saturday) when shops, post offices etc all close. This may or may not be abandoned in peak season. Some cafes which claim to stay open all year actually turn out to be closed when you troll up on a wet and blustery day; conversely some places that are technically closed may suddenly open again to take advantage of unseasonal good weather. Even pubs that serve meals during the week sometimes shut up kitchen on Sunday.

Getting There & Away

Bus For the Padstow to Falmouth section, National Express has regular services to Falmouth from London and other parts of the country. To get to the start, this coach goes via Wadebridge, from where you catch a Western National bus (☎ 01209 719988) to Padstow. There are two-hourly buses between Falmouth and Penzance.

Train The nearest railway station to Padstow is Bodmin Parkway, from where Western National buses go to Padstow from Monday to Saturday. At the end of this walk, Falmouth is at the end of the branch line from Truro, where you can get mainline connections to various parts of the country.

Car The Coast Path section described in detail here starts in Padstow, which is reached from Wadebridge, a town on the A39 between Barstaple and Penzance. The end of the walk, Falmouth, is also on the A39.

The Route

The following is a suggested itinerary, but there are almost endless variations available. Additional stops are mentioned in the route description.

The Start: Padstow

On the Camel estuary, Padstow is a small place which still clings to a fishing industry, making its harbour a pleasant part of town. Back from the harbour, there are a few twisty old streets of attractive houses, although the outskirts are dreary.

The TIC (☎ 01841 533449) is on New Quay, and you could use it to line up accommodation along the SWW. There are no hostels but B&B is available from *Mrs McGregor* (☎ 01841 532767), at 2 Dennis Rd, *Mrs Champion* (☎ 01841 532551), at 8 Treverbyn Rd or *Mrs Gidlow* (☎ 01841 532391), at the Cross House Hotel in Church St. Beds cost from £14 a head. The nearest *campsite* is at Dennis Cove (☎ 01841 532349).

In recent years the *Fish Restaurant* (☎ 01841 532485), at Padstow, has leapt to national prominence as its owner-chef, Rick

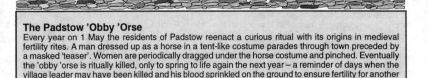

The Padstow 'Obby 'Orse
Every year on 1 May the residents of Padstow reenact a curious ritual with its origins in medieval fertility rites. A man dressed up as a horse in a tent-like costume parades through town preceded by a masked 'teaser'. Women are periodically dragged under the horse costume and pinched. Eventually the 'obby 'orse is ritually killed, only to spring to life again the next year – a reminder of days when the village leader may have been killed and his blood sprinkled on the ground to ensure fertility for another year. ■

Stein, hosted a fish cookery show on TV. You'll need to book ahead to be sure of a table, and the restaurant is closed on Sunday night when its partner-eatery *St Petroc's Bistro* in New St is almost equally popular. There are a few lovely rooms to let above the Fish Restaurant and many more at St Petroc's. The Steins also run a delicatessen and the Middle St cafe, with yet more rooms for B&B; prices start at £48 for a small double with breakfast. To reserve a room in any of their properties phone ☎ 01841 532700.

Day 1: Padstow to Treyarnon Bay
10½ miles (17 km), 4 to 6 hours
This stage makes a relatively easy introduction to the SWW. The route leaves Padstow harbour beside the toilets on North Quay Pde and passes a granite war memorial. Just after St George's Cove you can cross the beach from Gun Point to Hawker's Cove if the tide is out, and then follow the path again. At high tide stick to the main path as it winds round the coastguard station. The path then climbs up behind the Coastguard Station to Stepper Point, marked by the Daymark Tower. If it's a clear day you might just be able to make out Bodmin Moor on the horizon.

The SWW continues along the coast to Butter Hole Cove and Gunver Head, before dipping down to a valley and up the other side again, with distant views of the Merope Islands. Ahead, you'll see the limestone and slate Porthmissen Bridge, a multi-sided arch carved by the sea, where razorbills and guillemots nest in summer. Take care while walking around the collapsed Round Hole cave, then follow the path downhill to

Trevone car park. *Trevone Bay Hotel* (☎ 01841 520243) does B&B for £18.50 per person and there's a seasonal cafe.

From Trevone the Path follows the coastline round to the beach at Harlyn Bay. Under the *Harlyn Inn* an Iron Age cemetery was excavated in 1900, but the finds have been removed to Truro Museum, which also houses two 3000 year old Celtic gold lunulae (necklets) found nearby. (At high tide it may be necessary to detour inland from this point to reach Constantine Bay.)

From Harlyn, if you can cross the beach, you will come to The Cellars, once storage places for the pilchard harvest (see aside), with a Latin inscription reading 'Lucri Dulcis Odor' (Sweet is the scent of riches). The SWW continues round Cataclews Point, skirting Mother Ivey's Bay and Merope Rocks, where ravens nest. A caravan park mars the scenery at this point and a sewage works discharges effluent into the Bay.

At Trevose Head you can visit the lighthouse (usually open only in the afternoons).

Treyarnon Bay The SWW then turns south and bypasses Constantine Bay to reach Treyarnon Bay. Here you'll find a *YHA Hostel* (☎ 01841 520322, £7.45), a pub and the *Treyarnon Bay Hotel* (☎ 01841 520235), with rooms from £10 per person. Note that swimming in the Bay is dangerous.

Day 2: Treyarnon Bay to Newquay
12½ miles (20 km), 5 to 7 hours
This day's walk is a little tougher than yesterday's 'warm up', and close to Newquay it's blighted by development – two

Farewell to the Pilchard

The days are long gone when shoals of pilchard 16 million strong were sighted off the Cornish coast. Once upon a time these shoals would appear like clockwork each July. 'Huers' would take up position along the headlands to watch through telescopes for the tell-tale signs: a red tinge to the water and circles of screeching gulls. The huers would alert the fisherfolk by shouting 'hevva' (shoal) down a tin trumpet and sending semaphore signals, which enabled them to ring the fish with their nets. The fish were then pulled into shore to be salted and stored before export to France, Spain and particularly Italy.

In 1870 there were 379 registered 'seines' (pilchard businesses consisting of three boats, two nets and fish storage cellars). However, by 1920 the industry was effectively dead, probably killed off by uncontrolled and excessive fishing.

In Newlyn, Britain's last salt pilchard factory now houses The Great Pilchard Story (☎ 01736 332112), a working museum whose theme is the history of the pilchard trade, a more interesting tale than you might imagine. It's open from Easter to October, Monday to Saturday from 10 am to 6 pm, and costs £2.95. ∎

reasons why you might want to do the last few miles by bus.

South of Treyarnon Bay you can see Trethias Island, a nature reserve. The Path follows the headland, bypassing an Iron Age fort chopped into three parts by erosion. You'll also pass a shop and a bus stop. B&B is available in Porthcothan, should you need it.

From Porthcothan the SWW dips steeply down to Porth Mear valley, then up again on the other side. It's worth making a detour to Park Head where you get a wonderful view of Bedruthan Steps, a series of rock stacks on the beach which have been a popular tourist attraction since the railway reached Newquay in 1875.

A story, probably dreamt up to please 19th-century tourists, suggests that the stacks are a giant's stepping stones for crossing the sands, but Bedruthan Steps probably took its name more prosaically from the original staircase down to the beach or even from the ladders used to descend nearby Carnewas Mine. Crowds can be dense here in summer.

The NT owns the surrounding land and has built a viewing platform from which you can also inspect local rock formations, including the Queen Bess Rock (now minus its head) and Samaritan Island, named after the *Samaritan*, shipwrecked while en route to Turkey and Russia with a cargo of satin. The beach has recently been reopened to

visitors, although swimming can be dangerous and the cliffs continue to crumble. There's a shop, toilets and a seasonal cafe. (Inland from Park Head is the NT-owned *bunkhouse barn* at Pentire where basic dormitory accommodation is available for groups of up to 12 people for £50 a night. For more details contact Simon Ford on ☎ 01208 63046. The barn is rarely available in July or August.)

The SWW continues along the clifftop to the village of Mawgan Porth, which is on a bus route and has numerous places to stay including *Tanzarra Villa* (☎ 01637 860628) with B&B year-round from £12.50 per person, and *Sea Vista Hotel* (☎ 01637 860276) from £15.

From the *Mermaid* pub by the bridge, the route heads inland, and continues for two miles along the clifftop above Watergate Bay and its fine beach. The peace is likely to be shattered by the ear-shattering sound of RAF jets flying into the nearby base at St Mawgan.

Approaching Newquay, you reach Trevelgue Head, which boasts remains of the most extensive Iron Age fort in Cornwall. The SWW then continues around St Columb Porth Beach, past *Porth Bay Hotel*, down steps beside a bus shelter and under a road bridge before continuing along the cliff until it joins Lusty Glaze Rd and Newquay proper.

Unless you're a stickler for walking every inch you might well prefer to hop on the first bus you see rather than slog through the outskirts of town.

Newquay Britain's sprawling surfing capital is likely to come as a nasty shock after the relative quiet of the countryside, but it does at least have an interesting history as a former pilchard port (note the Huer's House above the harbour) and a silver and lead mining centre. The railway station, bus station and TIC (☎ 01637 871345) are all conveniently close to each other. Cheap B&Bs are plentiful and there are two independent hostels: *Newquay Cornwall Backpackers* (☎ 01637 874668), at Beachfield Ave, from £4 to £6.50, depending on the season; and *Fistral Backpackers* (☎ 01637 873146), at 18 Headland Rd, £5 in a six-bed dormitory. There are also several large caravan parks/camping grounds nearby. *Trenance Caravan & Chalet Park* (☎ 01637 873447), at the southern end of Edgcumbe Ave, charges £4.75 per person.

Day 3: Newquay to Perranporth
11 miles (18 km), 4 to 6 hours

The SWW passes through Newquay on the main road and is then signposted up the steps from the north side of the quay to Towan Head. It then proceeds above Fistral Beach, round Pentire Point East, above Crantock Beach and round Pentire Point West. Today's main problem is crossing the Gannel River between Pentire Point East and Crantock Beach; although there are two ferries and four bridges it will depend on the time of year and the state of the tide how far upstream you will have to go before you can cross. The official crossing is from Pentire to Crantock Beach via Fern Pit ferry. However, the ferry service only operates from the end of May to mid-September (daily from 9 am to 7 pm); phone ☎ 01637 871021 for more details. When the tide is at its lowest it's possible to wade across, avoiding an eight mile detour.

Once you have crossed the river, you pass through Crantock village and then through Porth Joke with a pretty, generally deserted

beach. Holywell village can be bypassed if the tide is low, but a visit is a chance to have a drink in the ancient *Treguth* pub, and to view the well with reputed healing powers which gave it its name.

Penhale Camp, the area around Penhale Sands, is Ministry of Defence (MOD) property, so keep seaward of the white signposts. Hidden amid the sands is the 8th-century St Piran's Oratory, believed to be the oldest church in Cornwall, but sadly reburied to protect it from erosion. The ruins of the 12th-century St Piran's Church are still visitable, however.

If the tide is out you can approach Perranporth along Perran Beach. At other times, however, you'll need to pick your way along the path between the cliff and the Perran Sands Holiday Centre.

Perranporth Perranporth itself is a smallish, not especially inspiring resort with a tourist information point (☎ 01872 573368) in the *Beiners Arms Hotel*. At Droskyn Point, west of the village, the *YHA Hostel* (☎ 01872 573812), costing £7.45, is housed in a former coastguard station. Alternatively, *Mr & Mrs Wells* (☎ 01872 572380) offer B&B from £11 a head at 44 Tywarnhayle Rd.

Day 4: Perranporth to Portreath
12½ miles (20 km), 5 to 7 hours

This stretch of the SWW is fairly easy to walk as it follows well-used paths along the clifftop with occasional dips into valleys.

From Perranporth hostel follow the cliff path, looking out for old mineshafts which now provide homes for greater horseshoe bats. There are particularly spectacular views from Cligga Head. The SWW drops into Trevellas Porth and then again into Trevaunance Cove, which has a waterside pub and a surfing beach. The effort of going up from the cove is rewarded by the pleasure to be gained from the walk to St Agnes Head. Look out for nesting kittiwakes, guillemots and razorbills as you go. Grey seals and basking sharks may also be visible. The SWW then passes through attractive St Agnes, which boasts terraces of old miners'

SOUTHERN ENGLAND

cottages and a museum in an old chapel. *The Frying Dutchman* (☎ 01872 552664), Quay Rd, on the cliff path nearby, offers B&B from £19. A detour inland leads to St Agnes Beacon (188m) and even better views.

Beyond St Agnes Head you pass the ruins of Wheal Coates. At low tide it's possible to cross from Chapel Porth to Porthtowan via the beach, keeping a wary eye out for the incoming tide. At Porthtowan you'll find two pubs, a cafe and a shop, but an inadequately shielded sewage outfall means that the beach has to be cleared twice a day.

Unfortunately, between Porthtowan and Portreath, you must follow the fence of the Nancekuke Defence Area for two miles. At the gate of the Defence Establishment you can either take the road into town or follow the cliff round past the Daymark Tower instead.

Portreath Portreath has shops and two decent pubs – the *Basset Arms* and *The Portreath*. For B&B try *Suhaili* (☎ 01209 842110) from £16, and *Glenfeadon House Hotel* (☎ 01209 842650) from £17. From Portreath, buses run along the coast and cut inland to Camborne and Redruth to connect with trains.

Day 5: Portreath to St Ives
17 miles (27 km), 8 to 10 hours
The walk from Portreath is strenuous at first but gets easier. However, the stretch from Gwithian to Hayle is hard going and unscenic. You may prefer to take a bus direct to St Ives instead of walking it.

Leaving Portreath, you need to look for a narrow country road leading past houses at the south end of the harbour. The SWW then climbs up to Tregea Hill and six miles of NT clifftop property. The path crosses Carvannel Downs and Reskajeage Downs, with fine views out to sea. Unfortunately, the B3301 runs close to the cliff here, but a path has been cut on the seaward side to keep walkers clear of the road.

Eventually you reach Hell's Mouth, a striking cleft in the rocks. Look for grey seals as you walk towards Navax Point. The SWW

then continues around Godrevy Point where a lighthouse visible on Godrevy Island probably inspired Virginia Woolf's *To The Lighthouse*. A small cafe is open in summer.

After crossing the Red River (named for the colour given to the water by tin ore washed down from Camborne), the SWW skirts the picturesque village of Gwithian, with many thatched cottages. The *Pendarves Arms* pub is worth a stop, and there's B&B accommodation at *Mrs Eddy's* (☎ 01736 753077), at 3 Churchtown Rd, from £13. You then need to follow marker-posts for three exhausting miles through the Towans sand dunes to Black Cliff – a stretch so tough that it drove the author of the SWWA pamphlet to question whether the Sahara could be worse!

From Black Cliff the official SWW unfortunately diverts inland and follows the B3301 and A3074 from Hayle to Lelant. Birdwatchers will want to divert along the loop marked 'The Weir' for the chance to spot some estuarine waders. Should you want to stop in Hayle, *Mrs Cooper* (☎ 01736 752855), at 54 Penpol Terrace, charges from £15 for B&B, or there's hotel accommodation at *The White Hart* (☎ 01736 752322) for £25 a head. There's also a bus link to St Ives and a rail link to St Erth and the main line. But most people will want to press on round Porthkidney Sands and Carbis Bay, following the railway line to St Ives, an altogether better place to stay.

St Ives St Ives is a delightful seaside resort with narrow streets lined with fishermen's and miner's cottages. Inevitably it gets packed out in July and August when booking accommodation in advance is essential. The TIC (☎ 01736 796297) is in The Guildhall in Street-an-Pol. The railway station is by Porthminster Beach, with the bus station nearby, up Station Hill.

It's well worth taking time out from the walking to visit the Tate Gallery, a subsidiary of the London one, which displays paintings of the St Ives' school of modern art. The impressive building, by local architects Eldred Evans and David Shalev, replaced an old gasworks, and has wide central windows framing the surfing scene on Porthmeor Beach below. Inside, the collection is small and exclusive, with works by Ben Nicholson, Barbara Hepworth, Naum Gabo, Terry Frost, Patrick Heron and other local artists. It's open April to September, Monday to Saturday, from 11 am to 7 pm (to 9 pm on Tuesday and Thursday); October to March, Tuesday to Sunday, 11 am to 5 pm. Entry is £3; a £3.50 ticket includes admission to the Barbara Hepworth Museum. The cafe on the roof is almost as popular as the gallery itself and does crab salads and sandwiches.

The Barbara Hepworth Museum, on Ayr Lane across town from the Tate, is open the same hours. The beautiful garden forms a perfect backdrop for some of the sculptor's larger works.

You might also want to visit the Bernard Leach pottery showroom, on the road to Zennor. It's open from 10 am to 5 pm on weekdays.

For a place to stay, *Ayr Holiday Park* (☎ 01736 795855), half a mile from town, charges from £8.50 for a tent. For noncampers,

the main road into St Ives from Penzance, above Carbis Bay, is lined with B&Bs and guesthouses in the £14 to £16 bracket. The north-facing section of the town, overlooking Porthmeor Beach, also has many options. The *Toby Jug Guesthouse* (☎ 01736 794250), at 1 Park Ave, is good value with B&B from £13 per person.

Across the other side of town, *Palm Trees Guesthouse* (☎ 01736 796109), at 2 Clodgy View, is a friendly place above Porthmeor Beach, charging from £15 per person. At 1 Sea View Place, *Penclawdd* (☎ 01736 796869) charges £13 to £16 per person; *Gowerton* (☎ 01736 796805), at No 6, charges around £14 per person.

The *Sloop Inn* (☎ 01736 796584), beside the harbour, charges from £20 a head. You can also try good seafood meals here. *The Grey Mullet* (☎ 01736 796635), at 2 Bunkers Hill, is an excellent guesthouse in the old part of town close to the harbour. Rooms cost from £17 to £21 per person. Opposite is an attractive cottage called the *Anchorage* (☎ 01736 797135) with slightly lower prices. *Kandahar* (☎ 01736 796183), at 11 The Warren, is right on the rocks by the

SOUTHERN ENGLAND

The St Ives School of Art

In 1811 Turner visited Cornwall and sketched the scenery of the West Penwith area. Shortly after the Great Western Railway was extended to St Ives in 1877, Walter Sickert and James McNeill Whistler also arrived in Cornwall to discover its wonderful light. Whistler's sketches from this period show both Porthmeor Beach and Clodgy Point.

By 1885 some artists had already set up base in St Ives and by 1902 the artists' colony was well enough established to be mentioned in a catalogue of the Whitechapel Art Gallery in London. Like Newlyn, St Ives attracted a steady flow of artists from overseas who came to take advantage of the readily available studio space. Amongst the many British artists who came to St Ives to work at this time were Charles Ginner and Matthew Smith; amongst the foreign artists were Canadian Emily Carr and New Zealander Frances Hodgkins. These first-wave artists mainly produced landscape paintings, but rendered in a simpler style than was customary elsewhere.

On a day trip to St Ives in 1928 Ben Nicholson and Christopher Wood encountered the naive paintings of local artist Alfred Wallis, which provided the inspiration for a second wave of St Ives' artists. At around the same time Bernard Leach established a local pottery and started to turn out pots influenced by his Japanese travels. With war looming in the 1930s, Ben Nicholson finally moved to St Ives with his partner, sculptor Barbara Hepworth, as did Naum and Miriam Gabo. These new-wave artists quickly evolved a distinctive style of abstract painting, which was taken up and developed by Peter Lanyon, Terry Frost and Patrick Heron. St Ives was at the height of its artistic influence during the late 1940s and 1950s.

Nicholson left St Ives for good in 1958 but Hepworth and Leach remained until their deaths in 1975 and 1979 respectively. Although the town continues to harbour a thriving artistic community, its days of real influence are probably behind it. ■

water. It charges £24 per person for a room with bath, £17.50 without.

Fore St, the main shopping street, is crammed with eating places. There are several other places to eat along the Wharf, including *Hoi Tin Chinese Restaurant* and the *Bay View Cafe*. *Hunters* (☎ 01736 797074), on St Andrews St, is a bring-your-own-bottle seafood and game restaurant. Nearby, *Wilbur's Cafe* (☎ 01736 796663) features US cooking. The pricey *Pig'n'Fish* (☎ 01736 794204) in Norway Lane is renowned for its seafood.

Day 6: St Ives to Pendeen Watch
13 miles (21 km), 7 to 9 hours

This is one of the hardest stretches of the walk, and the going is particularly tough because the route is not only up and down but also uneven and boggy in places, especially after rain. However, these difficulties are more than compensated for by the superb views out to sea and by the interesting flora which includes orchids and royal fern. Note that although the SWW follows the road quite closely the few villages are inland so you need to take food and water with you; a couple of B&Bs near Pendeen offer seasonal cream teas, but that really is it. However, Zennor has a wonderful old church, a small museum and a good pub; with time on your hands you might like to split the day by spending the night here.

To find the SWW from St Ives, walk along Fore St and follow the signs for Porthmeor Beach. For a little way out of St Ives it's likely to be busy in season with casual walkers, but they quickly drop away as the going gets tougher. The SWW keeps close to the cliff, with the steep dips down into the coves keeping the pace slow. Shortly after River Cove the path drops down to rocks where you can sometimes watch grey seals basking off The Carracks, twin off-shore islets. It then climbs steeply to 90m at Zennor Head where you can follow a path inland for half a mile to visit Zennor village.

If you don't think you're going to be able to make it all the way to Pendeen, Zennor makes a pleasant place to spend the night, with several farms offering simple B&B; try *Treen Farm* (☎ 01736 796932) or *Pennance Farm* (☎ 01736 796972) both from £12.50. *The Tinners Arms* does excellent fisherman's pie, while from 4 to 6 pm in summer you can get a delicious cream tea at *Hillside Farm*, about half a mile west of the village centre.

The 60 year old Wayside Museum in an old mill is open from Easter to September; in summer doors stay open till 7 pm, allowing walkers plenty of time to take it in at the end of a day's trekking. Admission is £1.85. The 15th-century church contains a curious benchend depicting a mermaid with a comb and mirror. Legend relates that the mermaid lured the local squire's son, Matthew Trewhella, into the sea at Pendour Cove. On the wall outside, look for a memorial stone to John Davey of Boswednack (died 1891), 'the last to possess any considerable traditional knowledge of the Cornish language'. Assuming you're in for the long haul to

---

The Lawrences in Zennor
Rejected from the army as unfit, the writer DH Lawrence arrived in Zennor with his wife, Frieda, in 1916 and they stayed at the *Tinners Arms* before moving into Higher Tregerthen cottage, just north of the village. Here Lawrence worked on *Women in Love* and nurtured plans for what he called 'a tiny settlement' to be shared with his friend, the New Zealand writer Katherine Mansfield, and her partner John Middleton Murry. Unfortunately, like many later visitors, Mansfield found the crying of the seagulls disturbing and the community soon split up.

Zennor was (and still is) a conservative place which didn't take kindly to having a bearded writer and his German wife settled nearby. Accusations of spying were soon flying around and the police regularly visited the cottage by the 'savage Atlantic'. Finally, the Lawrences were officially ordered to leave – a 'nightmare' he later described in his partly autobiographical novel *Kangaroo*. ∎

Pendeen, the SWW from Zennor Head continues along the clifftop and round assorted coves to Gurnard's Head, which is topped by remnants of an Iron Age fort. From here on there are plentiful traces of the old Cornish mining industry and you should beware of open shafts. Look out, also, for climbers on dramatic Bosigran Cliff. If you're tiring, a footpath detours half a mile inland to Morvah, from where you can catch a bus to St Just or Penzance.

Just before Pendeen you'll pass close to Geevor Tin Mine, which is open to the public from March to October, Sunday to Friday from 10.30 am to 4 pm; in winter the museum stays open, but you can't tour the mine workings.

Pendeen Watch At Pendeen Watch the lighthouse can be visited in the afternoon. Several places in Pendeen offer B&B. Try the *Radjel Inn* (☎ 01736 788446), a friendly pub with rooms from £12.50 per person, or *The Old Smugglers' Haunt Tea Rooms* (☎ 01736 788310), from £14.

Day 7: Pendeen Watch to Sennen Cove
9 miles (15 km), 4 to 5 hours
The first part of today's walk, as far as Cape Cornwall, is fairly easy, and the area is worth exploring for its disused quarries and mines, religious and historic ruins, and subtropical plants, although some people find the detritus of past mining activities unattractive.

From Pendeen Watch the SWW once again follows the clifftop, bypassing a series of old tin and lead mines; it actually passes through the grounds of Levant Mine, which closed down in 1919 after an accident led to

the death of 31 miners. Cornwall's oldest beam engine can now be inspected by visitors from July through September, Sunday to Friday from 11 am to 5.30 pm (for other opening times call ☎ 01736 786156).

Shortly after this, look out for the Crowns Mine at Botallack, perched picturesquely right on the rocks. Apparently when the Prince and Princess of Wales visited in 1865, she was wearing a white flannel cloak and a white straw hat trimmed in blue. She, however, was not walking the entire coast path!

Just past the ruins of Crowns Mine, the footpath skirts Botallack village where there's food and accommodation; try *Manor Farm* (☎ 01736 788525) with B&B for £16. Just before Cape Cornwall the SWW cuts slightly inland. *Boswedden House Hotel* (☎ 01736 788733) is nearby, with B&B from £18.

Cape Cornwall was originally thought to be England's most westerly point, before that title passed to Land's End. The SWW doesn't actually go out as far as the Cape, but it's worth diverting to for its chimney and views.

From Cape Cornwall the SWW follows an unmetalled road inland to Carn Gloose where a mysterious walled pit could be a Neolithic shrine. You need to continue inland towards St Just for a mile to reach *Land's End YHA Hostel* (☎ 01736 788437, £8.25) in the Cot Valley. Bunk beds are also available for £5 in *Kelynack Bunkbarn* (☎ 01736 787633), also in the Cot Valley. Buses run from St Just to Penzance Station.

The village of St Just makes an excellent place to spend the night, despite the short detour inland. In the heart of the village is a

Cornish Hedges
Hedges are normally thought of as plants and bushes, but in Cornwall they're just as likely to be made of stones, either large block stones or rounded ones ('grounders') on top of which smaller stones are piled up. These 'hedges' are held together with a soil mortar, which quickly sprouts grass, hawthorn and other plants and can look particularly pretty in spring. In these exposed parts, stone hedges can offer farm animals much-needed shelter from the wind and rain. ■

square, part of which was used in medieval times to perform miracle plays. It's ringed with pubs, all of them offering food: the *Wellington* possibly has the edge for meals but the smaller *Star* is the most atmospheric drinking hole. There's also a fish & chips shop in the main square. A comfortable bed with excellent breakfast is available for £15 a head from Paul and Wendy Michelmore at *2 Fore St* (☎ 01736 787784), immediately beside The Star. In St Just, being a fairly alternative sort of place, you can stock up on healthy picnic ingredients in the few shops. Note that the week-long music festival in mid-July offers everything from ceilidhs in the main square to organ recitals in the church (which, incidentally, contains two medieval frescos showing St George and Christ of All the Trades).

From St Just, the SWW continues along the cliff to the mile-long Whitesand Bay, which is good for swimming and surfing. At high tide you'll have to skirt round the top of the Bay where it's surprisingly easy to lose the SWW altogether. Immediately afterwards you come to the village of Sennen Cove.

Sennen Cove Sennen Cove has a pub, cafes and B&Bs; try *Myrtle Cottage* (☎ 01736 871698), by the path, which charges from £13.50 and serves cream teas. Alternatively there's *Whitesands Lodge* (☎ 01736 871776), an independent hostel with dorm beds (£8) and a few guesthouse rooms (£12.50 a head); breakfast costs another £2.50. While you're in Sennen Cove look out for the round house by the car park. This was an old capstan created in 1876 from the winding gear of a disused mine and used to be used to winch boats up from the beach. These days it houses the predictable craft shop.

Day 8: Sennen Cove to Porthcurno
6 miles (9.5 km), 3 hours

It's under two miles from Sennen Cove to Land's End, completely dominated by Peter de Savary's tacky theme park dumped down on the headland without regard for its iconic status. In summer, it's extremely crowded,

with stands selling everything from burgers to strawberry-and-clotted-cream crêpes. That said, the Spirit of Cornwall exhibit is mildly interesting, and the complex does provide 250 jobs in an unemployment black spot. You save on the £4 entrance fee by walking in. To have your picture taken by the signboard listing your home town and its distance from this famous point costs £5.

The comfortable *Land's End Hotel* (☎ 01736 871844), the 'first and last hotel in England', is part of the Land's End complex and is the only place to stay right at Land's End. Staying the night does at least give you the chance to stroll around the headland in the evening after the crowds have gone. B&B costs from £32.50 to £55. You can eat here too, in the *Atlantic Restaurant* or in the *Trenwith Arms*, which is also the Land's End base for the Land's End-John o'Groats Association, all of whose members have made the 886⅓ mile end-to-end journey under their own steam.

Continuing along the well-marked but unsheltered path, you soon leave the day trippers behind and pass through the hamlets of Porthgwarra (with a small, seasonal cafe) and St Levan.

The open-air theatre at Minack Point (above Porthcurno) has one of the world's most spectacular settings and it's certainly worth taking in a play if the weather's good. It was built by indomitable local woman, Rowena Cade, who did much of the construction with her own hands, continuing until her death in 1983. She got the idea in 1935 after her family provided the local theatre group with an open-air venue for a production of *The Tempest*, which proved so successful that annual performances were instituted. There are shows at the theatre (☎ 01736 810181) from late May to late September; tickets cost £6/2.50. Seats are hard, so bring a cushion or hire one here. Steep steps lead down to the beach and to a house once used by Rowena Cade.

Porthcurno There are several B&Bs around Porthcurno, including *Corniche* (☎ 01736 871685), at Trebehor, from £15. Call from the phone box in the car park and they will pick you up. They serve evening meals too, or there's the *Cable Station* pub behind the beach. The beach *cafe* does tea and coffee but closes around 6.30 pm. Should you be interested, Cornwall's secret wartime communications centre in underground tunnels at Porthcurno is now open to the public as a small museum of submarine telegraphy. From April to October there are tours on the hour from 11 am to 3 pm (Friday only; Wednesday too from July to September). Swimming from Porthcurno beach (the eastern end of which is used by naturists) is not advisable as there are often dangerous currents.

Day 9: Porthcurno to Penzance
11 miles (17.5 km), 6 to 8 hours

This day's walk is generally fairly easy, although the path is occasionally overgrown with stinging nettles, making long trousers a wise precaution. Nearing Penzance, you may prefer to catch a bus from Paul or Newlyn rather than trek through the outskirts.

From Porthcurno, following the SWW along the clifftop you'll find an offshoot path leading to Logan Rock, an 80-ton, once-rockable rock owned by the NT. In 1824 one Lieutenant Hugh Goldsmith pushed the rock clean off its perch, an exploit which was greeted with local outrage. The *Logan Rock Inn* in nearby Treen village displays a poster detailing how the cost of replacing the stone finally came to £130 8s 6d, a sum which the Lieutenant was forced to bear.

From Logan Rock, the walk up to Penzer Point (near the village of Mousehole) is superb, though occasionally tough. Tiny Penberth Cove and Porthguarnon are inviting places to pause a while, while Lamorna Cove boasts an excellent cafe serving delicious crab sandwiches on granary bread and mouthwatering desserts. The *Tremeneth Hotel* (☎ 01736 731367) has rooms from £15 a head. Further inland, *The Wink* pub was originally an illegal beer house.

After Penzer Point you reach Mousehole (pronounced 'Mowzl'), a picture-postcard fishing village with several pubs, hotels and restaurants. It takes its curious name either from a cave-mouth in the cliff south of the village or from the narrow gap between its harbour walls. Mousehole was once a pilchard-fishing port, and tiny cottages cluster round the edge of the harbour. Like St Ives, it attracts artists, and there are several interesting craft shops. Expect crowds in summer. The excellent *Ship* (☎ 01736 731234) does good seafood and fresh fish; B&B costs £20 per person. The more up-market *Lobster Pot* (☎ 01736 731251) charges £23.50 for lobster; rooms overlooking the harbour cost £40 per person. *Annie's Eating House* serves cream tea for £2.75. There are infrequent buses to Penzance.

The SWW from Mousehole to Newlyn mostly follows the road, although you can cut inland before Mousehole and walk to Newlyn via the village of Paul, where a monument commemorates Dolly Pentreath who died in 1778 and is regarded as the last person to have spoken only Cornish.

Newlyn, on the southern side of Penzance, was the centre of a community of artists in the late 19th century, among them Dame Laura Knight; some of their handiwork can be inspected in Newlyn Museum and Art Gallery, New Rd, which is open Monday to Saturday from 10 am to 5 pm. It's not a particularly attractive walk from Newlyn Harbour to Penzance, so you might prefer to catch one of the regular buses instead.

Penzance Penzance harbour spreads along Mount's Bay, with the Scilly Isles ferry terminal to the east, the train and bus stations just to the north and the main beach to the south. The town itself spreads uphill towards the domed Lloyds Bank building with a statue of local man, Humphrey Davy, inventor of the miner's lamp, in front. There are some attractive Georgian and Regency houses in the older part of town around Chapel St where you'll find the exuberant early 19th-century Egyptian House. Further down towards the harbour is the Maritime Museum.

The National Lighthouse Centre in Wharf Rd relates the history of the lighthouses that have helped keep ships off this dangerous coast. It's open daily from March to October, 11 am to 5 pm; entry is £2.50/1. Some examples of the Newlyn school of painting are exhibited in Penzance Museum & Art Gallery on Morrab Rd, which is open daily except Sunday from 10.30 am to 4.30 pm for £1/50p (Saturday 10.30 am to 12.30 pm; free). Walkers may also want to take a look at the Cornwall Geological Museum in Alverton St, which is open Monday to Saturday from 10 am to 4.30 pm (Sunday from 10.30 am to 4 pm from July through September).

The TIC (☎ 01736 62207) is in the car park by the railway and bus stations. There are direct trains and buses to London and many other destinations if you're ending the walk here.

Penzance YHA Hostel (☎ 01736 62666, £9.10) is in an 18th-century mansion at Castle Horneck, Alverton, on the outskirts of town. To get there take bus Nos 5B, 6B or 10B from the railway station to the nearby *Pirate Inn*.

Penzance has lots of B&Bs and hotels, especially along the Promenade, Alexandra Rd and Morrab Rd. Try *Pendennis Hotel* (☎ 01736 63823), on Alexandra Rd, charging around £13 per person, or *Kimberley House* (☎ 01736 62727), at 10 Morrab Rd, around £15. In the older part of Penzance, the *Georgian House Hotel* (☎ 01736 65664), at 20 Chapel St, charges £17 or £25 ensuite.

For eats, *Dandelions*, at 39A Causeway Head, is a vegetarian cafe and takeaway with daily specials like vegetable and cheese ratatouille for £2.50. The *Chocolate House*,

at 44 Chapel St, serves delicious food, including crab sandwiches. Two nearby pubs are well worth frequenting and both serve good food: the kitschy *Admiral Benbow*, on the corner of Chapel St and Abbey St, is crowded with figureheads and other nautical décor (don't miss the seafarer crawling along its roof); the *Turk's Head* is more sedate and cosy.

Day 10: Penzance to Porthleven
13 miles (21 km), 5 to 7 hours

Leave Penzance along the main A30, take the footbridge over the railway line and join the SWW by the heliport. The path then trundles along Mount's Bay beach to Marazion, opposite picturesque St Michael's Mount. (If you prefer to skip the Penzance outskirts, there's a bus to Marazion – but the walk as far as the St Michael's Mount causeway is actually fairly easy.)

Follow the busy main road through Marazion (which has several pubs and numerous shops) and then take the path along the clifftop to Prussia Cove (to skip the Marazion outskirts, hop on a bus and ask for Henfor Terrace).

Prussia Cove is named after the King of Prussia Inn which was run by John Carter, a notorious 18th-century smuggler. In 1947 the cove was the site of the worst shipwreck recorded in Cornwall when the *Warspite* battleship ran aground.

The SWW follows the lovely beach at Praa Sands (worth stopping for a dip and something to eat, but packed out in summer) and then climbs up onto the spectacular cliffs

St Michael's Mount
In 1070 St Michael's Mount was granted to the same monks who built Mont St Michel off Normandy. Though not as dramatically sited as its French counterpart, St Michael's Mount is still impressive. High tide cuts the island off from the mainland, and the NT-run priory buildings (☎ 01736 710507) rise loftily above the rocks. During the Middle Ages it was an important place of pilgrimage, but since 1659 the St Aubyn family have lived here.

At low tide, you can walk across the causeway to the Mount from Marazion, but at high tide in summer a ferry (☎ 01736 710265) lets you save your legs for the stiff climb up to the house which is open from April to October, Monday to Friday, 10.30 am to 5.30 pm; entry is £3.70. ∎

and past the remains of Wheal Prosper and Wheal Trewavas. The cliff edge here is dangerously crumbly, so the SWW runs slightly inland to Tregear Point just before Porthleven. You'll know you're getting there when you pass a memorial cross set up by a vicar who decided shipwreck victims should be buried in consecrated ground (until then they'd always been buried outside the churchyard).

Porthleven Porthleven is a fishing village with a pleasant dockside, a long jetty and the *Ship Inn* pub. On Peverell Terrace, there's B&B at *Seefar* (☎ 01326 573778) from £12 per person, and at the *An Mordros Hotel* (☎ 01326 562236) from £14.50.

Day 11: Porthleven to The Lizard
13 miles (21 km), 5 to 7 hours

The first part of today's walk is generally easy-going, but the last section can be tiring. Leaving Porthleven you follow Loe Bar Rd and Mounts Rd from the far end of the harbour, passing the old coastguard station. Very soon you pass the Loe Pool, Cornwall's largest natural body of freshwater and owned by the NT. Some people believe this was where King Arthur abandoned his sword Excalibur. In winter the Pool is an excellent place to watch migratory wildfowl like widgeon and teal.

Loe Bar is extremely dangerous for swimmers. Watch your footing on the cliffs all the way to Poldhu Cove; the rock can be slippery when wet. At low tide you can walk along the beach to Gunwalloe Fishing Cove; at high tide you'll need to follow the official SWW which passes a monument to Henry Trengrouse who invented rocket life-saving equipment in 1807.

The SWW continues round Halzephron Cliff to Dollar Cove, before cutting across the headland and continuing beside the Towans golf course towards Poldhu Cove. It's well worth diverting onto the headland to examine Gunwalloe church, which has an unusual detached bell tower cut into the cliff-face. In the 11th century when the Domesday Book was compiled, Gunwalloe seems to

have had a large population, despite which the church now stands in splendid isolation, with the sea threatening to cut it off from the mainland altogether.

South of Poldhu Point, the SWW passes the Marconi memorial, set up to commemorate the first transatlantic telegraphic communication in 1901. The SWW then drops to Polurrian Cove, climbs up again and then drops back to pretty Mullion Cove, just over a mile north of Mullion itself. *Trematon* (☎ 01326 240344), on the path near Mullion, charges from £12.50 per person for B&B; evening meals are also available. Look out for nesting sea birds on Mullion Island, a few hundred metres off shore.

The walk from here to The Lizard via Kynance Cove is superb, although it can be tough going. Kynance Cove has been attracting tourists since the 18th century. Expect crowds in summer. The off-shore islands – Asparagus Island, Sugarloaf Rock, The Bellows and The Bishop – can be reached on foot at low tide, but be careful not to be cut off by the incoming tide.

To return to the SWW cross a footbridge over a stream and walk past a cafe to reach the top of the cliff. The route then wanders past old serpentine workings to reach Lizard Point, Britain's most southerly point and called Lizard Head on old maps. The lighthouse here can usually be visited during the afternoon and the cafes are open year-round.

The Lizard The Lizard is distinguished by its unusual serpentine rock and mild climate. B&B accommodation for around £13 a head is available at *Green Cottage* (☎ 01326 290099) and at *The Most Southerly House* (☎ 01326 290300) on Lizard Point. A short detour inland to Landewednack leads to a church with serpentine pillars in its porch. The last Cornish sermon was read here in 1674.

Day 12: The Lizard to Coverack
11 miles (18 km), 4 to 6 hours

The first part of today's walk via some old serpentine workings is fairly easy, but after Cadgwith it gets tougher.

Just before Cadgwith you'll pass the Devil's Frying Pan, a vast crater probably caused by the collapse of a cave. Cadgwith is a particularly attractive Cornish fishing village with pretty thatched cottages. Stop for a pint and a crab sandwich at the *Cadgwith Cove*.

North of Cadgwith, electric fencing indicates an area where efforts are being made to return the clifftop to grazing, which might result in the return of plants which have lost ground to gorse and blackthorn. Should it be successful it is even possible that Cornish choughs might reestablish themselves in what was once a favoured habitat.

Past Caerleon Cove and the ruins of old serpentine works, Kennack Sands is popular with families in summer and there are several beach cafes. You then need to climb steeply up to Beagles Point and Pedn Boar, both owned by the NT.

Coverack Bungaloid development heralds Coverack, a harbour village with the *Paris Inn* for drinks and a YHA Hostel (☎ 01326 280687, £7.45) or *Bakery Cottage B&B* (☎ 01326 280474), from £13 per person.

Day 13: Coverack to Helford
13 miles (21 km), 5 to 7 hours
This is a moderately easy stretch of coast: the SWW follows the coast to Godrevy Cove, and then heads inland to avoid disused quarries.

From Coverack take the road past the beach and keep straight on past the houses to the fields, keeping to the path closest to the sea; this runs to Lowland Point, a raised beach. From there you pick your way through quarry workings to Godrevy Cove, before turning inland to Porthoustock – popular with divers, so the cafe by the beach may be open all year round. Porthallow (pronounced 'Pralla') has a bus service and an excellent pub, the *Five Pilchards*, right on the beach, which is, unfortunately, another pollution black spot. Pictures on the wall tell the story of the many shipwrecks which took place on the Manacles, a mile out to sea.

The SWW then continues to Nare Head

and Nare Point, with fine views over the Helford River.

Pretty Gillan Creek can be crossed (over slippery stones) up to an hour before and after low water. Alternatively, you can walk round the creek through tiny St Anthony or head inland through Flushing and cross over on the road. If pressed for time, you could stay on the road through Manaccan (with food, drink and places to stay) to Helford.

Helford Helford is a delightful village: the country retreat of such luminaries as Tim Rice, Pete Townsend and Peter de Savary. There's a popular thatched pub, the *Shipwright's Arms* and B&B accommodation at *Heronsway* (☎ 01326 231424), Orchard Lane, from £15 per person.

Day 14: Helford to Falmouth
10 miles (16 km), 4 to 5 hours
The official SWW uses the ferry (☎ 01326 250116) from Helford Point to Helford Passage, but this only operates from Easter to the end of October and is subject to weather and tidal conditions. If you can't use the ferry, you're faced with an 8½ mile detour. It's wise to phone ahead, preferably from Coverack, and check. If there's no ferry and you don't want to make the detour, there are weekdays buses from Coverack to Falmouth and journey's end. Assuming the ferry is available, the walk from Helford Passage round Rosemullion Head and Pennance Point to Falmouth is fairly easy.

From the north shore of the Helford river the SWW proceeds through tiny Durgan where a half-mile inland detour leads to Glendurgan, a tree-filled NT garden (with teashop) which is open Tuesday to Saturday from March through October, admission £2.90.

You then continue through Mawnan Shear and Parson's Beach. With time to spare you can divert a mile inland to Mawnan Smith for a drink at *The Red Lion* pub. After that the SWW continues via Rosemullion Head, Maen Porth and Pennance Point to reach Falmouth – this section's journey's end.

Falmouth This is not Cornwall's most exciting town, but it is nonetheless a tourist centre with plenty of accommodation and services. As a port it came to prominence in the 17th century as the terminal for the Post Office packet boats which took mail to America. The dockyard is still important for ship repairs and building. There's a TIC (☎ 01326 312300), at 28 Killigrew St, by the bus station in the town centre. From the Prince of Wales pier below, there are ferries to St Mawes.

For a place to stay, *Pendennis Castle YHA Hostel* (☎ 01326 311435), costing £8.25, is right inside the 16th-century castle, in a converted Victorian barracks; follow the English Heritage (EH) castle signs to find it. It's open daily from mid-February through September, and daily except Sunday and Monday in October and November. Alternatively, Melvill Rd, near the railway station, is lined with B&Bs. *Wayside Lodge* (☎ 01326 317260), at No 5, has a range of rooms and charges from £14 per person. In attractively cobbled Church St, *Bon Ton Roulet* (☎ 01326 319290) is a good place for a celebratory meal, or there's beer and pub food in the *Kings Head*.

OTHER WALKS ON THE SOUTH WEST COAST PATH

If you want to do more than the Cornwall section of the SWW described in this book, the basic outlines of the other three sections will be useful. Books on the whole route have already been discussed, and most of the other general information applies. Other maps you will need are the OS Landranger (1:50,000) sheets 180 *Barnstaple & Ilfracombe*, 181 *Minehead & Brendon Hills*, 190 *Bude & Clovelly*, 192 *Exeter & Sidmouth*, 193 *Taunton & Lyme Regis*, 194 *Dorchester & Weymouth*, 195 *Bournemouth & Purbeck*, 201 *Plymouth & Launceston* and 202 *Torbay & South Dartmoor*.

Getting There & Away

The start of the route is Minehead, on the main A39 between Taunton and Barnstaple, served by National Express coaches in the summer. The route ends at Poole, on the A350 near Bournemouth, with daily National Express services. Local bus services along the coast are limited, and often dry up at weekends. The county phone lines for timetable information are invaluable: Somerset ☎ 01823 255696, Dorset ☎ 01305 224535, Devon ☎ 01392 382800 and Cornwall ☎ 01872 322142.

For train access, there's no British Rail station at Minehead, although it's at the end of the private West Somerset Railway from Bishops Lydeard, accessible by bus from Taunton Station. Phone ☎ 01643 707650 for 24-hour recorded timetables. Poole is on the main line between Southampton and Weymouth.

Somerset & North Devon Coast Path

159 miles (256 km), two weeks

With all its Butlins paraphernalia, Minehead is not necessarily the best introduction to the Coast Path. However, you're very quickly free of the tack, and walking through Exmoor National Park, with the chance to see wild red deer. The cliffs here are extremely high, which makes for some strenuous climbing up and down; the highest point of the entire Coast Path is at the Great Hangman (318m), near Combe Martin.

Lynton and Lynmouth are delightful settlements linked to each other by a Victorian Cliff Railway, but expect hordes in summer. The scenery gets less dramatic as you head south for Ilfracombe and Mortehoe and some fine sandy beaches, once again phenomenally popular in summer. Further south again, and there's fine cliff walking between tacky Westward Ho! (the only town in Britain – and possibly the world – with a ! in its name) and tiny Clovelly, which is so chocolate-boxy that it has had to build a Visitor Centre and start charging for admission.

There's another popular beach resort at Bude, but from then on the coast gets rockier and the villages smaller. Tintagel has been ruined by its dubious connections with King Arthur, but nearby Boscastle is still very pretty, as are tiny Port Gaverne and Port Isaac.

South Devon Coast Path

172 miles (277 km), 15 days

The western reaches of this stretch of the Coast Path continue to pass along rocky coastline, liberally sprinkled with picturesque small villages. However, you will eventually have to circumnavigate the conurbation of Plymouth, and from Dartmouth onwards much of the coastline becomes one solid seaside resort, often with a railway line shadowing it.

From Falmouth you can cross the Carrick Roads by ferry to St Mawes, after which the Path pushes through the delightful Roseland Peninsula and the villages of Portloe and Mevagissey. St Austell is worth skipping round by bus although the old port of Charlestown can be a picture on a sunny day when the tall ships are in dock.

After St Austell, the Path transits some immensely popular small Cornish resorts: Fowey, Polperro and Looe. It then crosses into Devon and follows Whitsand Bay to Rame Head. Plymouth then looms, but you can pick up the Path on its far side and continue to Bigbury-on-Sea where Burgh Island boasts a wonderfully restored Art-Deco hotel, famous for the days when Noel Coward and Agatha Christie frequented it.

The Path then skirts the South Devon Heritage Coast, through pretty Bantham, to Salcombe, a medium-sized resort, and then on to delightful Dartmouth with a wide choice of gourmet restaurants and places to stay. A ferry crosses the Dart to Kingswear where you can pick up the Path to Brixham. From there on, however, you'd be walking through the solidly built-up resort of Torbay, with Teignmouth and Dawlish hot on its trail. You may prefer to take a bus into Exeter instead.

Dorset Coast Path

99 miles (159 km), 8 days

From Exmouth eastwards the Coast Path once again escapes into the countryside, although Budleigh Salterton, Sidmouth and Seaton are all fair-sized resorts, overrun with families throughout July and August.

Crossing into Dorset, the Path runs through Lyme Regis, famous for its fossils and for the scene in *The French Lieutenant's Women* where Meryl Streep stands on The Cobb and stares out to sea. East again and the Path passes through pretty thatched Abbotsbury with its unique swannery, best visited in May or June to see the nests and the cygnets.

Shortly afterwards the Path starts to follow Chesil Beach, a curving bank of stones enclosing the Fleet Lagoon. Eventually it fetches up at Portland Harbour and Weymouth, which has a couple of museums worth stopping for and a wide choice of pubs and fish restaurants.

East of Weymouth the Path passes some stunning coastal scenery at Lulworth Cove, Kimmeridge Bay and Chapman's Pool, before swooping round Durlston Head into Swanage, a so-so seaside resort. North from here is Studland, then Studland Point – official end of the SWW. A short ferry ride brings you to Poole, and this, for most walkers, is journey's end.

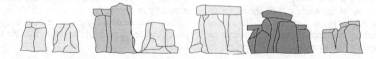

Wales – Short Walks

Brecon Beacons National Park

The Brecon Beacons National Park (which is known as Parc Cenedlaethol Bannau Brycheiniog in Welsh) contains a large group of mountains, in a line running from west to east, forming the natural border between South and Mid Wales. There are four separate ranges within the group and a wide variety of terrain, which understandably makes the Beacons one of Wales' most appealing, and hence most popular walking areas.

In the far west of the park is the Black Mountain, which is wild and relatively remote. East of here is Fforest Fawr, which is lower and less austere. In the centre are the Brecon Beacons, giving their title to the whole park; this is the highest range and the most favoured by walkers.

In the east are the rather confusingly named Black Mountains (plural), where the eastern escarpment is followed by Offa's Dyke, the ancient frontier between Wales and England. (Offa's Dyke Path, a long-distance path (LDP), covered elsewhere in this book, follows much of this historical frontier.)

Although the Beacons cannot compare on the drama scale with Snowdonia, these are still the highest mountains in southern Britain: a range of gigantic rolling whale-backs, with broad ridges and table-top summits, cut by deep valleys, where sides fall so steeply the grass has given up the ghost and exposed large areas of bare rock and scree.

Within this area there's a fantastic choice of day-walks. The route we describe is along one of the most frequented sections, but it's justifiably popular, and gives you an excellent introduction to the Beacons' potential and beauty.

BRECON BEACONS RIDGE WALK

Distance 13 miles (21 km)
Duration 6½ to 8 hours
Start Storey Arms
Finish Brecon
Regional Centres Merthyr Tydfil, Brecon
County Powys
Area Brecon Beacons National Park
Summary A full day's walk, mostly through high, open country where weather conditions can be demanding, with some steep ascents and descents. There are some flat sections of tame farmland towards the end of the walk. The paths are clear throughout, with several shorter versions of the walk possible.

This route follows the most impressive section of the Brecon Beacons' central ridge, taking in four of the park's highest summits and crossing the heads of several large valleys. These vast bowl-like corries were formed by glaciers some 10,000 years ago, which then went on to carve the U-shaped valleys beyond. It's classic textbook geography, and you may see

WALES

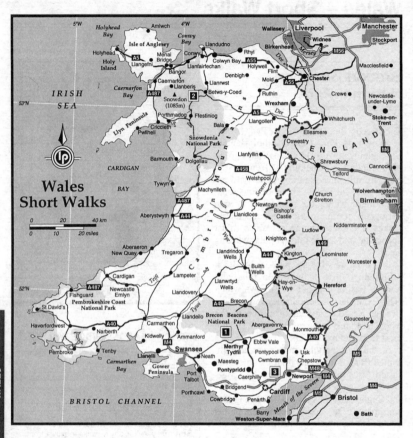

Wales
Short Walks

WALES

groups of bored schoolkids struggling along the ridge, pens and soggy notebooks in hand, gamely attempting to take it all in.

The highest point on this route is the summit of Pen y Fan (pronounced 'Pen er Van', which literally translated means Peak of the Top), which measures in at 886m (2907 ft). Other major summits are Corn Du (873m), Cribyn (795m) and Fan y Big (719m). This route also passes through tranquil farms and woodland, and along the banks of the meandering River Usk, providing an interesting contrast to the peaks and ridges on the high ground.

The rounded nature of the Beacons, when viewed from below, belies their seriousness. It can get wet and cold up here, with winds strong enough to blow you over. Take appropriate clothing, plus map and compass. You see day trippers with none of these, but you also hear horror stories of people who get lost, sometimes fatally. Don't be one of them.

Direction, Distance & Duration

This walk starts at Storey Arms, a high point on the main road, about 7½ miles south of Brecon. It ends at Brecon. It can be done in reverse, but this involves a lot more ascent. The total distance is 13 miles.

There are a lot of ups and downs on this route, so it requires about 6½ to eight hours of walking, but with stops you should allow seven to nine hours in total. The route is not waymarked, and there are no signposts on the high ground. In the farmland towards the end of this route the paths are signposted.

Shorter Alternatives You could do parts of the ridge as an out-and-back route from Storey Arms. It's so spectacular that retracing your steps doesn't really matter. From Storey Arms to Pen y Fan and back is six miles, three to four hours walking. If you don't want to backtrack, you can shorten the route by dropping off the main ridge earlier, and aiming north to Brecon. The ridges that extend from Pen y Fan, Cribyn and Fay y Big all have paths, but the easiest route to follow is the old road that leaves the ridge at Bwlch ar y Fan, between the two final peaks, making the total distance between 8½ and 10 miles. Another option to reduce the day's mileage is catching the bus (or staying overnight) at Llanfrynach. (More details in Stage 3 of the route description.)

Information
Brecon TIC (☎ 01874 622485) is in the Cattle Market car park, open daily. The PIC (☎ 01874 623156) shares the same office and is open daily from April to the end of September. At other times, the TIC can help with information. The National Park Visitor Centre (☎ 01874 623366) is near the village of Libanus, five miles south-west of Brecon, but it's hard to reach without wheels. They all stock a good range of books, maps and information leaflets, including a free accommodation list, and a series of walking booklets (£1.25 or less) covering the main areas in enough detail for most people spending a few days here.

Books Guidebooks covering walking in the Brecon Beacons include *Best Walks in Southern Wales*, by Richard Sale (Constable), which has a section on the Brecon Beacons ridge route. The *Visitor Guide* leaflets in the Harveys maps (see below) are also a very good source of route information.

Maps Most of the park is covered by Ordnance Survey (OS) Landranger (1:50,000) sheets 160 and 161, and OS Outdoor Leisure (1:25,000) sheets 11, 12 and 13. The route described here is all on sheet 11. Harveys has a 1:40,000 map covering most of the park, and two 1:25,000 Superwalkers; the route described here is on *Brecon Beacons East*.

Guided Walks & Local Services
The national park organises a series of guided walks throughout the summer, varying from gentle to strenuous. There's no charge, but a donation is appreciated. For details contact PICs above.

For a longer walk, with everything taken care of, you could consider doing the 'Black to Black', a 50 mile, five day, organised 'self-guided' route across the whole Brecon Beacons park including the central ridge described in this section. For an all-in price you get accommodation, meals, food, maps, guidebooks, pickups and drop offs. For details contact the Cambrian Way Walkers Association, listed in the Other Walks in Wales section below.

Places to Stay & Eat
The town of Brecon, on the northern edge of the park, makes a good base. Its Welsh name is Aberhonddu (pronounced 'Aber Honthee'), and you'll see this on road signs. As a tourist centre it is very busy during the summer months, and Friday and Saturday nights are always lively, with pubs full of

WALES

Warning – Jazz Festival
Some years ago, a few musicians got together for a bit of jamming. This developed into Brecon Jazz – now one of Europe's leading music festivals, held in mid-August and attracting crowds of literally thousands. If you're into jazz, or just into good times, it's great – but note that accommodation (apart from camping) is almost impossible to find. ■

local good-time boys and girls, plus reinforcements from the nearby barracks.

The *YHA Hostel* (☎ 01874 665270, £6.75) is at Ty'n-y-Caeau (pronounced 'Tin-er-Kiy'), a large country house about 2½ miles from Brecon. There's another hostel at *Llwyn-y-Celyn* (☎ 01874 624261; £7.45), on the A470 between Merthyr Tydfil and Brecon, which is nearer the start of this walk, but further from the finish. Three miles south-east of Brecon, in Cantref, is the *Held Bunkhouse* (☎ 01874 624646), which charges £7.50 per person. There's a simple campsite at *Neuadd Farm* (☎ 01874 86247), 2½ miles south of Brecon near the small village of Cantref, charging backpackers from £1 per night. A bit nearer, with more facilities, is *Brynich Caravan Park* (☎ 01874 623325), about two miles east of Brecon centre, where backpackers pay around £3.

For pricier accommodation, the central and comfortable *Wellington Hotel* (☎ 01874 625225) charges around £49 for a double, with attached pub, coffee shop and wine bar. The nearby *George Hotel* (☎ 01874 623422) is £35/55 for singles/doubles, including breakfast, with a good-value restaurant.

Most B&Bs are a few minutes walk outside the centre. Along a street called The Watton (towards Abergavenny) are the *Paris Guesthouse* (☎ 01874 624205), from £15, and the smarter *Lansdowne Hotel* (☎ 01874 623321), with single/double ensuite rooms from £26/45. On Bridge St, west of the river, *The Walker's Rest* (☎ 01874 625993) charges £13.50, and *Beacons Guest House* (☎ 01874 623339) from £16.50, or £19.50 ensuite. The restaurant is also open to nonresidents and the food is highly recommended (main dishes from £5.50). On nearby St David's

St, *Cambridge House* (☎ 01874 624699) has jovial owners and good rooms from £14 per person.

Brecon has several cafes, teashops and a surprising number of takeaways, including Chinese, Indian and fish & chips. On Bridge St is the smart bistro *Welcome Stranger* (☎ 01874 622188), open for evening meals, with main courses between £7 and £12. The town also has a good selection of pubs, most doing bar food, including *The Three Horseshoes* and *The Sarah Siddons*.

On the route itself, there's no cafe or pub ideally placed for lunch, so take all you need with you from Brecon (which has several shops). Near the end of the walk in Llanfrynach, there is a pub and also a couple of B&Bs, where you might want to stay if you'd prefer to be outside the town (see the route description for details).

Getting There & Away
Bus Buses leave and arrive at the Bulwark in the centre, near the TIC. Brecon can be reached from other parts of Britain by National Express, although most routes go via Cardiff, where you may have to change. Brecon can also be reached by Stagecoach Red & White (☎ 01633 266336) buses from Newport and Abergavenny, or from Hay-on-Wye and Hereford. Both routes have services every two hours in each direction every day except Sunday. If you're travelling to/from West Wales, Silverline (☎ 01685 382406) has a service between Swansea and Brecon. If you're coming from Cardiff, you can also get a Red & White bus to Merthyr Tydfil (running every half hour daily except Sunday) and change there.

Between Merthyr and Brecon there's a

Silverline bus every two hours. This is also the route from Brecon to the start of the walk (the first goes at around 9 am, and two hourly after that, Monday to Saturday, and afternoons only on Sunday). Ask the driver to shout when the bus reaches Storey Arms, as it's easy to miss.

Train Brecon has no railway station. The nearest are at Abergavenny (via Newport) and Merthyr Tydfil (via Cardiff), from where you can get one of the buses mentioned above.

Car Brecon is on the A470 (between Cardiff and Conwy) and on the A40 (between Gloucester and West Wales). To reach the start of the walk at Storey Arms by car is easy, and there are two car parks nearby. However, if you park here and do the whole route, you have to get back afterwards. You can catch a bus, but they don't run after late afternoon, so you might be better leaving the car in Brecon and catching a bus to Storey Arms before starting the walk.

Taxi Brecon to Storey Arms costs about £7.50. Try Captains Cabs (☎ 01874 625108).

The Route
Stage 1: Storey Arms to Pen y Fan
3 miles (5 km), 1½ to 2 hours

Near the phone box, on the east side of the road, a gate leads onto a footpath which goes steeply uphill onto the moorland. After about 20 minutes, at the crest of a broad ridge, the paths divide: the main path leads down into Baen Taf Fawr valley and then up again onto the ridge, heading for the peak of Corn Du (which fittingly translates as the Black

Horn). To save losing height, take the other path, aiming north then east, round the head of the valley to meet the ridge just below the obelisk overlooking Llyn Cwm Llwch.

The obelisk is dedicated to the memory of a young boy called Tommy Jones, who died here in 1900. He was lost in the valley while walking with his father, but somehow made his way up to this exposed spot, where his body was found some weeks after he went missing. A newspaper had offered a reward, but the money instead paid for this memorial.

From the obelisk, the route is clear: straight up the path (pitched with stones to prevent further erosion) south-easterly to the summit of Corn Du (about 1¼ hours from Storey Arms), with fine views north down to Brecon, west over Fforest Fawr and – most spectacularly – eastwards along the ridge, with Pen y Fan and the other table-top summits seemingly lined up for inspection.

Once again the route is clear: down the ridge and steeply up again, with Cwm Llwch to your left (north) and the Taf Fechan valley to your right (south), with the Upper Neuadd reservoir on the valley floor. A few steep rock steps at the top of the path bring you to Pen y Fan summit (886m), marked by a large cairn and trig point. Here, the views are even better: eastwards, beyond Cribyn and Fan y Big, you can see the Black Mountains.

Stage 2: Pen y Fan to Fan y Big
2 miles (3 km), 1¼ to 1½ hours

Take care leaving the summit of Pen y Fan, especially in mist. The path does not aim straight for Cribyn, but goes south, 'off the back' of the table top, before curving round on the ridge-crest once again. The Taf Fechan valley is still to the right (south), but

Storey Arms
The route starts at Storey Arms, about 7½ miles south of Brecon. There was once a pub with this name here, on the highest point of an ancient drove route, and later the turnpike road (now the A470), that crosses the mountains between South and Mid Wales. Today it's an outdoor centre and there's not a beer in sight. ■

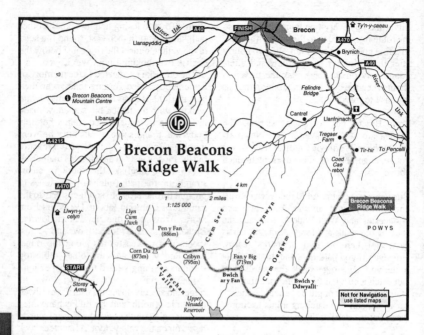

Brecon Beacons Ridge Walk

1:125 000

Not for Navigation use listed maps

to your left a new valley, Cwm Sere, opens out, overlooked by steep cliffs on the north-east face of Pen y Fan. Cribyn's summit (795m) is reached about 20 to 30 minutes from Pen y Fan.

The path continues east, dropping over grassy slopes, with yet another spectacular corrie (the head of Cwm Cynwyn) to your left. From here it's a steep slog up to the final summit: Fan y Big (719m).

At Bwlch ar y Fan, between Cribyn and Fan y Big, an old road crosses the ridge. It's popular with mountain-bikers, and you may also see 4WD enthusiasts churning it up. It's also a shorter route towards Brecon.

Stage 3: Fan y Big to Llanfrynach
5 miles (8 km), 2½ to 3 hours

A broad grassy ridge leads south from Fan y Big, curving east then north round the head of the Cwm Oergwm valley. The path becomes boggy around the right-angled

bend at Bwlch y Ddwyallt, but the going is not too bad.

Several other paths join from the right, coming up from the Talybont valley. Ignore these, and continue north-east, down the grassy ridge, with Cwm Oergwm on the left, and great views back up the valley to Fan y Big and the other summits dominating the skyline. The path drops off the ridge and enters an area of scattered bushes and small trees, and a few walls, although you don't cross any of them yet. Pay close attention to the map, dropping down a steep section to reach a gate and stile (with a yellow footpath marker) in the corner formed by two walls. Cross the stile and continue downhill, aiming north-west through woodland marked on the map as Coed Cae rebol.

More yellow footpath markers lead you near to the ruined farm of Tir-hir, along the edge of a field, over a stream and then along a track, to a tar lane near Tregaer Farm. Turn right and follow the lane into Llanfrynach village.

This is your first brush with civilisation, so a pint in the *White Swan* may be called for. If you need B&B, try *Ty Fry Farm* (☎ 01874 665232, £13), or *Llanbrynean Farm* (☎ 01874 665222, £15.50 to £17 per person). There's also a bus to Brecon every two hours Monday to Saturday. The last one leaves at around 7 pm.

Stage 4: Llanfrynach to Brecon
3 miles (5 km), 1¼ to 1½ hours

Leave Llanfrynach on the 'main' road northwards, passing the church to your right. At a children's playground on the left, there's a signpost indicating Felindre Bridge. Follow this path across several fields, over stiles (more yellow footpath markers), over a lane, past Cynrig fish farm, along a track, and through the garden of Abercynrig Mill (past the remains of an old bridge).

Go over the new footbridge (signposted to Brecon) and follow the stiles and markers through more fields and a patch of woodland.

The busy A40 Brecon bypass gets increasingly close. Just before you meet it, the path drops to a field, crosses a stile and then goes under the A40 through a tunnel frequented by local graffiti artists. This brings you into fields beside the River Usk. The path keeps close to the bank (with the river on your right-hand side). Where it divides, keep right, nearer the river, all the way back to Usk Bridge in Brecon, which marks the end of this route.

Snowdonia

Snowdonia is the mountainous region of North Wales, taking its name from Mt Snowdon – the highest mountain in England and Wales – which dominates the area. Several other significant peaks surround Snowdon: to the east are the Glyderau and Carneddau ranges, while to the west are the Nantlle Hills and Moel Hebog. To the south lie the Moelwyns, the Rhinogs, the Arans and Cadair Idris.

The area is contained within the Snowdonia National Park which covers an area of over 800 sq miles (approximately 2000 sq km). Its name is Parc Cenedlaethol Eryri in Welsh; Eryri means 'home of the eagles', although these days you're more likely to see falcons and buzzards flying around the mountainsides.

The mountains in the north-west of the park are the remains of eroded volcanoes, with sharp ridges and steep cliffs. Beneath the summits are quiet cwms that were carved by glaciers long since melted. What remains is a postglacial landscape of a striking nature. Further south towards Cadair Idris and east over the Carneddau, the hills become more rounded, although still retaining a ruggedness that differs from the uplands of England. Snowdonia is varied not only visually, but culturally. In the west are mainly Welsh-speaking people, from farming and slate-mining backgrounds. In the east the communities are closer to the Anglicised flatlands of Clwyd and mainly English speaking. This contrast has an historical thread: where the cultures divide are the remains of frustrated English attempts to occupy Wales in the 1200s and 1300s, where Roman colonial ambitions had similarly failed several centuries earlier. (Imagine groups of young Roman conscripts being chased around these hills by a bunch of hairy Welshmen on magic mushrooms and I think you'll get the general idea!)

The survival of the Welsh language is a testament to Welsh spirit and determination, and as you pass along the Nantlle Ridge and read, scratched on a rock, 'You English can visit Wales, but please don't come and live here', you can see that for some the division is alive and kicking. However, Welsh people are generally hospitable (especially if you're not English!) and Snowdonia offers some of the best walking in Britain, so a visit here is highly recommended. If you don't have the time to travel to Scotland for the big mountains, then North Wales goes some way towards supplying the goods.

In this section we describe five day-walks over four different mountain groups in the

WALES

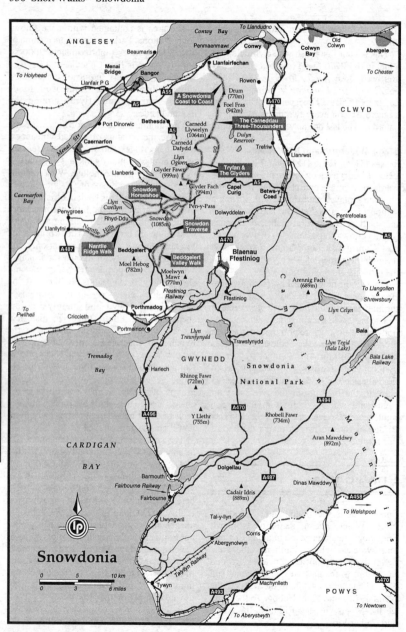

ANGLESEY

Conwy Bay

To Llandudno

Beaumaris

Penmaenmawr

Conwy

Colwyn
Bay

Old
Colwyn

Abergele

To Holyhead

Menai
Bridge

Bangor

Llanfairfechan

To Chester

Llanfair P G

Rowen

Drum
(770m)

A470

CLWYD

Port Dinorwic

Bethesda

A5

A5

Foel Fras
(942m)

A Snowdonia
Coast to Coast

Caernarfon

Carnedd
Llywelyn
(1064m)

The Carneddau
Three-Thousanders

Dulyn
Reservoir

Trefriw

Llanrwst

Caernarfon
Bay

Llanberis

Carnedd
Dafydd

Llyn
Ogwen

Glyder Fawr
(999m)

Tryfan &
The Glyders

A5

Snowdon
Horseshoe

Glyder Fach
(994m)

Capel
Curig

Betws-y-
Coed

Pentrefoelas

A5

Penygroes

Llyn
Cwellyn

Rhyd-Ddu

Pen-y-Pass

Snowdon
(1085m)

Snowdon
Traverse

Dolwyddelan

A470

Llanllyfni

Nantle Hills

Nantle
Ridge Walk

Beddgelert

Moel Hebog
(782m)

Beddgelert
Valley Walk

Blaenau
Ffestiniog

A487

Moelwyn
Mawr
(770m)

Arennig Fach
(689m)

To Llangollen
&
Shrewsbury

Ffestiniog
Railway

Ffestiniog

To
Pwllheli

Criccieth

Porthmadog

Llyn Celyn

Bala

Portmeirion

Llyn
Trawsfynydd

Trawsfynydd

Llyn Tegid
(Bala Lake)

Bala Lake
Railway

Tremadog
Bay

Harlech

GWYNEDD

Rhinog Fawr
(720m)

Snowdonia

National Park

CARDIGAN

BAY

Y Llethr
(755m)

A470

Rhobell Fawr
(734m)

A494

Aran Mawddwy
(892m)

Barmouth

Dolgellau

A487

Dinas Mawddwy

A458

Fairbourne Railway

Fairbourne

Cadair Idris
(889m)

To Welshpool

Llwyngwril

Tal-y-llyn

Corris

Snowdonia

Abergynolwyn

0   5   10 km
0   3   6 miles

Talyllyn Railway

Tywyn

A493

Machynlleth

POWYS

A470

To Aberystwyth

To Newtown

WALES

> **Warning**
> Unless you have the appropriate mountain skills, the high-level routes described in this section are not recommended in the winter as they are often covered by snow or ice and become a very different proposition. The walking season is longer than in Scotland and good conditions (ie the hills are free of snow) can be expected from April to November. Even in summer though, don't underestimate the weather conditions on the summit, as they are always very different from conditions lower down. ■

northern part of Snowdonia to give you an idea of what the area has to offer. These are:

The Snowdon Horseshoe – a classic hand-out-of-pockets trip for experienced walkers with a head for heights

A Snowdon Traverse – another classic, but this time with your hands safely in your pockets!

Tryfan & The Glyders – yet another classic, over three major peaks to the west of Snowdon

The Carneddau Three-Thousanders – fine, open mountain-walking in the quieter north-eastern part of the park

The Nantlle Ridge Walk – a good ridge walk in the 'forgotten' area west of Snowdon

Some of these routes are popular, and are likely to be crowded in high season, while others are visited less frequently and you can enjoy remote and spectacular ridges virtually undisturbed. At the end of this section, we outline how some of the above routes can be linked together to form a three day or four day linear route across Snowdonia, a North Wales Coast to Coast. We also describe a low valley walk, in the area between Snowdon and the Moelwyns, ideal if the weather is bad, you feel lazy or don't have a head for heights.

THE SNOWDON HORSESHOE

> **Distance** 9½ miles (15 km)
> **Duration** 5 to 7 hours
> **Start & Finish** Pen-y-Pass
> **Regional Centres** Llanberis, Caernarfon, Porthmadog, Bangor, Llandudno
> **County** Gwynedd
> **Area** Snowdonia
> **Summary** A classic route. It includes a very exciting and exposed mountain scramble requiring the use of the hands! It should be treated with caution, especially in wet conditions, and not attempted in heavy rain, high wind, ice or snow. For experienced walkers only. (Less serious options are outlined later in this section.)

Snowdon, at 1085m (3558 ft) above sea level (ASL), is the highest mountain in England and Wales and arguably the most spectacular. Its Welsh name, Yr Wyddfa, refers to the 'burial place' of a giant slain by King Arthur. The beauty of the peak lies along its fine ridges, which drop away in great swooping lines from the summit. Beneath these ridges are cliffs of sweeping corners that lead to airy pinnacles, falling to deep lakes and green sheltered cwms, which are home to birds of prey and rare alpine plants.

But Snowdon also has great ugliness. The mountain railway chugs its way noisily from Llanberis to the summit complex of station, cafe and giftshop, and on the southern slopes the hydroelectric pipeline from Cwm Dyli cuts a stark angular scar into the surrounding greenery. Even the paths stand out like veins, suffering from the impact of over half a million visitors each year.

Despite all this, Snowdon is still a wonderful mountain, and we thoroughly recommend a walk on its ridges and slopes. The Snowdon Horseshoe route described here takes in the main summit, plus the Crib Goch ridge and three other major peaks of the ancient crater rim.

This is the most famous route on the mountain, and we've included it because it's such a classic, universally reckoned to offer one of the best mountain days in Britain. But it's also one of the most serious bits of walking included in this book: only for those who enjoy balancing on very sharp ridges with steep drops on either side.

Direction, Distance & Duration

This circular route starts at Pen-y-Pass, six miles from Llanberis. By beginning with the Crib Goch ridge and going anticlockwise

WALES

you tackle the scrambling when you are fresh. The total distance is seven miles on the map, but with the ascent and scrambling involved this route will seem longer: allow a minimum of four hours. In bad conditions it could take twice that! If the weather deteriorates when you're halfway through, a possible escape is the Miners Track (described below). Another is to take the train from the summit (if you can bear the shame!), or simply to follow the path beside the railway back to Llanberis. Any one of these descents will take about two hours.

Alternatives If all this sounds a bit too airy, Snowdon can be sampled on a circular walk from Pen-y-Pass by going up the Pyg Track (described in the section on the Snowdon Traverse) and down the Miners Track (described as an escape route in this section). This is an even more popular circuit than the Horseshoe, as it avoids all the scrambling. Although it's easier than the Snowdon Horseshoe, it should still be treated with respect in the event of less than perfect weather.

Information

There are TICs in Betws-y-Coed (☎ 01690 710426), Llanberis (☎ 01286 870765), Caernarfon (☎ 01286 672232), Llandudno (☎ 01492 876413) and Porthmadog (☎ 01766 512981). They have travel information and copies of the Gwynedd Public Transport Guide, an essential booklet covering all bus, train and coach timetables in the area.

Weather bulletins are displayed at the Outside shop in Llanberis, and Cotswold Camping and Climber & Rambler shops in Betws-y-Coed. Plas-y-Brenin mountain centre in Capel Curig has weather information on display in reception. Snowdonia has a Mountaincall service (☎ 0839 500449) for up-to-the-minute weather information.

Books Snowdonia is very well covered by a range of practical walking guidebooks. *Hill Walking in Snowdonia* and *Scrambles in Snowdonia* by Steve Ashton (Cicerone), are both very popular (but beware – some of the

'scrambles' are rock climbs!). *A Guide to Wales' 3000-foot Mountains* by H Mulholland (Mulholland-Wirral, £3.90) covers the main summits with the help of text, maps and photo-diagrams. *Snowdonia Walks Pathfinder Guide* (published by the OS) describes a range of routes, including some good low-level walks in the area. A picture book that also has good route information is *On Foot in Snowdonia* by Bob Allen (£14.99).

Maps The OS Outdoor Leisure (1:25,000) sheet 17 covers all the walks described in this Snowdonia chapter. You can also use the Landranger (1:50,000) sheet 115, or Harveys Walker (1:40,000) or Superwalker (1:25,000) maps which cover the whole area in three sheets.

Guided Walks & Local Services

Snowdonia is a rock-climbing centre, and several experienced mountaineering guides are available for rock-climbing, scrambling and hill-walking. Try Snowdonia Mountain Guides (☎ 01690 750554), High Trek Snowdonia (☎ 01286 871232) or Nick Banks (☎ 01690 710288) in Betws-y-Coed, who also does B&B. The Climber & Rambler shop in Betws-y-Coed arranges guiding and multi-activity days. Plas-y-Brenin National Mountain Centre (☎ 01690 720214) has a comprehensive range of courses from hill-walking to dryslope-skiing for a few hours to a few days. Many of the YHA hostels in the area also offer activity courses.

Places to Stay & Eat

A good place to base yourself for any Snowdon walk is the village of Llanberis, the capital of walking and climbing in North Wales. It was once a slate-mining centre and now thrives on tourism, which has created a vast range of hotels, B&Bs, pubs, cafes and gear shops, plus several visitor attractions.

Llanberis YHA Hostel (☎ 01286 870280, £8.25) is on the edge of the village. Also recommended is the *Heights Hotel* (☎ 01286 871179), on the main street, which offers B&B for £10.50 and a bed for £7.50, and has cheap bar food. There's an artificial climbing wall in the back room for the energetic. For luxury try the *Royal Victoria Hotel* (☎ 01286 870253) at the southern end of the village. DB&B is £46.50 and B&B is £43, but it does have cheap offers of £30 sometimes.

For food, top of the list is *Pete's Eats* on the high street, the area's classic cafe where tea comes in pint mugs and you can top up your cholesterol level for under a fiver (open to 8 pm in the summer). Places for an evening meal include *Y Bistro* (top of the range), *The Padarn Lake Hotel* (mid-range) and numerous fish & chips shops along the high street (cheap).

East of Llanberis is *Nant Peris Campsite*, cheap at £2 a night plus 50p for showers. Opposite, the *Vaynol Arms* has bar food and is popular with walkers and climbers. A little further up Llanberis Pass is *Gwastadnant Bunkhouse* (☎ 01286 870356). Weekend prices are £4 a night in the bunkhouse, £2 to camp or B&B for £13. Prices drop to £2.50, £1.50 and £12.50 during the week.

At Pen-y-Pass (meaning 'Top of the Pass'), the start of the route, there is a *YHA Hostel* (☎ 01286 870428, £9.10) on the site of the old coaching station. The cafe next to the car park has some wonderful B&B photographs of Snowdon in the early 20th century and is well worth the visit, especially if you combine it with a hot drink and a sausage butty!

Nearby, the *Pen-y-Gwryd Hotel* (☎ 01286 870211) has B&B for £20 to £25 and dinner for £15. The bar ceiling was signed by all the members of the successful 1953 Everest Expedition. (Another place to consider staying is the small town of Capel Curig, which is described in the Tryfan & The Glyders section.)

Getting There & Away

Bus The daily National Express (No 390) route from Manchester and London to Pwllheli stops in Llandudno, Bangor and Caernarfon. From Bangor, Williams Buses (☎ 01286 870484) operate six times per day to Llanberis (no buses on Sunday). KMP (☎ 01286 870880) operate a half-hourly bus between Caernarfon and Nant Peris (every hour on Sunday).

The excellent Snowdon Sherpa buses run all over the area. There are routes between Llandudno and Betws-y-Coed, between Betws and Bangor via Capel Curig, and between Betws and Llanberis via Capel Curig and the Pen-y-Grwyd Hotel. Another service runs between Llanberis and Caernarfon via Pen-y-Pass, Pen-y-Grwyd, Beddgelert and Rhyd-Ddu, and yet another between Porthmadog and Beddgelert via Llanberis. So it's easy to get back to Llanberis wherever you end your walk. Get a timetable, and it all falls into place. Note, however, that the service is very limited in winter (November to March).

For information about the Snowdon Sherpa and other bus or train routes telephone the Transport Co-ordination office for Gwynedd (☎ 01286 679535) or pick up the Public Transport Guide from any TIC.

WALES

Slate Mining in Llanberis

Slate mining in the Llanberis area ended in 1969, but it is difficult to ignore the slag piles that dominate the valley opposite the village. Llyn Padarn lies between the village and the quarries and the lake railway, along which slate was once transported to the coast, and now functions as a tourist attraction. Beneath the open-cast slate mines there is now a pump storage station that was installed during the 1970s. During times of low demand, water is pumped up through the mountain from Llyn Peris to Marchlyn reservoir. When electricity is needed quickly it can be made available by releasing water from the top lake to power enormous turbines inside the mountain on its way down to Llyn Peris.

Guided tours into the power station are run daily from the Power of Wales visitor centre, situated on the small bypass road around the village centre, for about £5. You can wander around the spectacular and extensive quarry workings for free, but at your own risk. If you are unlucky with the weather both of these are good alternatives to walking on the tops. ■

Train The nearest mainline stations to Llanberis are Llandudno Junction and Bangor, with regular services to/from Crewe, where you can connect with trains to the rest of the country. In the summer you can take the train between Llandudno Junction and Blaenau Ffestiniog via Betws-y-Coed. A narrow-gauge tourist railway runs through from Blaenau to Porthmadog. There are regular trains between Porthmadog and Birmingham via Machynlleth.

Car Pen-y-Pass can be approached from Llanberis (on the A4086 six miles south of Caernarfon) or from Capel Curig and Betws-y-Coed on the A5. The car park at Pen-y-Pass costs £4 per day, less after 1 pm, but often fills in summer, when a 'park & ride' system operates between the Vaynol Arms in Nant Peris and Pen-y-Pass. It's also possible to hitch between Llanberis and Pen-y-Pass, as most people in cars are walkers too (but you should always take the usual precautions).

The Route
Stage 1: Pen-y-Pass to Crib Goch Summit
3½ miles (5.5 km), 1 to 2 hours

Take the Pyg Track from the car park behind the cafe and follow the paved path to Bwlch-y-Moch. ('Pyg' is sometimes written 'PyG', because it's named after the Pen-y-Gwryd Hotel at the foot of the pass, although Bwlch-y-Moch means Pass of the Pig – so it's sometimes spelt 'Pig Track'.)

At this pass turn right (east) to follow a good path along the ridge. The best route keeps to the east ridge. The path zigzags a little and there are some short rock steps to climb, but there are some cairns along the way. If the rock doesn't look as though thousands of boots have scuffed it smooth then you're off route! The last part of the ridge near the summit is quite exposed. The view from the summit of Crib Goch (921m) across the narrow ridge ahead to Snowdon is tremendous.

Stage 2: Crib Goch to Crib-y-Ddysgl
1 mile (1.5 km), 1 to 2 hours

This is the airy bit! If you didn't like the ascent to Crib Goch then crawl back down the way you came up. The ridge is less than a metre wide in places. The best technique is to keep to the left side of the crest and use your hands to hold onto the top while ignoring the drop! It is also possible to follow a narrow path which is about three metres down on the left (south) side of the ridge. After about 200m of this you have to negotiate the pinnacles. Each one has a small gangway leading around it. After the last pinnacle the path descends steeply to a wide col of red scree (Bwlch Coch). In an emergency it is possible to descend steeply north from here into Cwm Uchaf to escape.

From Bwlch Coch continue along the ridge. There are one or two short rock steps, and eventually the ridge widens and you arrive at the delightfully flat and broad summit of Crib-y-Ddysgl (1065m), where there is a trig point.

Stage 3: Crib-y-Ddysgl to Snowdon Summit
½ mile (1 km), 30 minutes

This is the middle section of the horseshoe and the least interesting bit, despite the fact that you will stand on the highest point in England and Wales. Follow the broad ridge from Crib-y-Ddysgl down its west side to the Fingerstone (a standing stone, about two metres high, that marks the point where the Miners Track and the Pyg Track join the summit ridge). In bad weather you can descend directly from here – see the end of this section.

A few metres beyond the Fingerstone is the railway. Try not to be run over by steam trains and follow the tracks (not forgetting to wave at passengers) to the summit station, where there is a cafe, bar and shop where you can buy anything from a pint of beer to a 'Snowdon the Hard Way' T-shirt. You can even post your mail from the highest post-box in Britain so that it will arrive postmarked 'Snowdon Summit'. The actual summit is about 100m to the east of the cafe complex where there is a cairn.

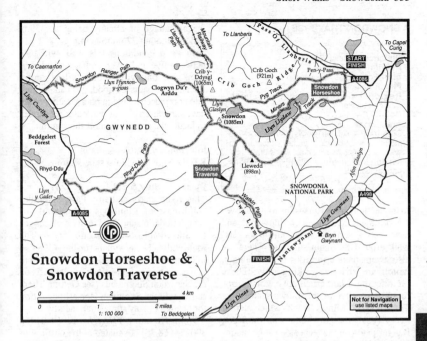

Snowdon Horseshoe &
Snowdon Traverse

0   2   4 km
0   1   2 miles
1: 100 000
To Beddgelert

Not for Navigation
use listed maps

WALES

Stage 4: Snowdon Summit to Llewedd West Summit

1½ miles (2.5 km), 1½ hours

To find the path to Llewedd go down the ridge by the back of the cafe and turn left, after about 150m, by a cairn and standing stone, to descend to Bwlch-y-Saethau. Follow the ridge path to the west (highest and first) summit of Llewedd (898m).

If you look over the left side of the ridge you will see the huge, sweeping cliffs of Llewedd. There is a chilling atmosphere here, common to most north-facing cliffs, that attracts climbers in winter and summer. Although the face was first climbed in 1883, the major rock climbs on Llewedd were made in the early 20th century by climbers such as George Mallory, who later disappeared at 28,000 ft on Everest in 1924.

Stage 5: Llewedd Summit to Pen-y-Pass

3 miles (5 km), 1 to 2 hours

From the west summit the path drops down to a tiny col where a steep gully emerges from the north face. Nip up onto the east summit and follow a good path down to where the ridge flattens and the path starts to descend steeply to Llyn Llydaw (about half a mile from the west summit). At the outflow of Llyn Llydaw join the Miners Track to Pen-y-Pass.

Alternative Descent: The Pyg Track & Miners Track

If, after completing Stage 3, you need to escape in the case of bad weather, or have just run out of time, you can descend quickly back to the start. From the Fingerstone (at the point where the path from Crib-y-Dysgyl to the Snowdon summit meets the railway track) a clear zigzag path descends south towards Llyn Glaslyn. This is the Pyg Track. Keep descending to meet the Miners Track near the lake shore. From here the Miners Track is wide and clear all the way to Pen-y-Pass.

A SNOWDON TRAVERSE

Distance 8 miles (13 km)
Duration 5 to 7 hours
Start Pen-y-Pass
Finish Nantgwynant
Regional Centres Llanberis, Bangor,
Caernarfon, Porthmadog, Llandudno
County Gwynedd
Area Snowdonia
Summary A high but relatively straightforward
mountain-walk on clear paths, although with
few signposts or waymarks there is the poten-
tial for bad weather to make conditions
dangerous.

In the section on the Horseshoe route (above)
we outlined the nature of Snowdon, and
described a serious 'hand-out-of-pockets'
walk around the main summits. There are
also several paths up and down the mountain,
which are strictly walking only. These
include the Llanberis Path (which runs
roughly parallel to the railway), the Pyg
Track and the Miners Track (which start at
Pen-y-Pass), the Rhyd-Ddu and Snowdon
Ranger paths on the west side of the mountain, and Watkin Path to Nantgwynant, south
of the summit. Any two of these can be
joined to form a traverse of the mountain; we
recommend combining the Pyg Track and
the Watkin Path to give a varied and spectacular day on the mountain.

The Pyg Track starts at Pen-y-Pass, on the
east side of Snowdon, and takes the most
efficient route to the summit. From here the
Watkin Path descends the south side of the
massif into the beautiful valley above the
village of Beddgelert. An alternative descent
from the summit, if you are heading for the
Nantlle Ridge, is the Snowdon Ranger Path.

If you want to do a circular walk and return
to Pen-y-Pass, then the best option after
going up the Pyg Track is to come down the
Miners Track, as described at the end of the
section above.

Direction, Distance & Duration

The traverse is a linear walk and can be done
in either direction. We recommend going
east to west. Starting at Pen-y-Pass you have
the advantage of already being at 359m,
leaving another 726m to gain.

In good conditions this walk will take
between five and seven hours, but if conditions are bad you should allow more.
Because the paths are good, you can be lured
into complacency and in poor weather make
navigational errors. In particular be careful
to locate the correct path off the summit.

Information, Books & Maps

See the Snowdon Horseshoe section.

Places to Stay & Eat

This route starts at Pen-y-Pass, six miles
south-east of Llanberis. For details of
accommodation and food in these places see
the Snowdon Horseshoe section above. The
route ends at Nantgwynant (on the A498 two
miles north-east of Beddgelert). From here
you can return to Pen-y-Pass or Llanberis on
the Snowdon Sherpa bus (see Getting There
& Away in the Snowdon Horseshoe section
for details) or stay somewhere nearby.

Bryn Gwynant YHA Hostel (☎ 01766
890251, £8.25) is situated at the outflow of
Llyn Gwynant, about a mile north-east of
where the Watkin Path meets the main road.
Bryn Dinas Bunkhouse (☎ 01766 890234)
provides cheap overnight accommodation in
timber cabins at £5.95 and in the farmhouse
at £7.50 a head. This place has the advantage
of being a mere step from the end of the
Watkin Path. (From the main road turn left,
and it's 150m along on your right.)

Accommodation near Beddgelert includes the *Forest Campsite*, half a mile or so
north of the village on the A4085, which has
showers and hot water for £3.50 (adults) and
£1.50 (children). There are also two straightforward campsites signposted just off the
A498, north-east of Beddgelert. In the middle
of the village is the independent hostel *Plas
Tan-y-Graig* (☎ 01766 890329) at £15 a
night.

In Beddgelert itself, B&Bs include the
friendly *Ael-y-Bryn* (☎ 01766 890310), charging from £15 (£17 ensuite), and *Glanafon*
(☎ 01766 890231, £15 to £18). *Plas Colwyn
Guesthouse* (☎ 01766 890458) offers B&B

WALES

from £15 (£19 ensuite); it also has a good restaurant (open to nonresidents) where three-course meals start at £12. The owners are local organisers for the Cambrian Way, so they know what walkers want; they can also assist with local weather forecasts and recommend local guides.

There are three pubs in the heart of the village, all with accommodation and evening meals, including the *Prince Llewelyn Hotel* (☎ 01766 890242), with singles/doubles for £21/44. Despite its name *Beddgelert Antiques & Tearooms* (☎ 01766 890543) also does B&B from £17. In the evenings the tearoom becomes a smart little bistro.

Top of the range in Beddgelert is the *Royal Goat Hotel* (☎ 01766 890224), charging £34 per person for a double. Apart from the places already listed, Beddgelert has *Lyn's Cafe* for meals, snacks and local specialities like 'Set Tea with Welsh Bread' for £2.50. There's also a more internationally flavoured ice-cream and pizza place on the main street, plus a couple of small stores and giftshops.

Getting There & Away

Bus To reach Pen-y-Pass by bus see the Snowdon Horseshoe section. To get either to or from Beddgelert, the Snowdon Sherpa which passes through regularly provides a good connection with Llandudno, Llanberis, Porthmadog and Caernarfon. Express Bus Co (☎ 01286 674570) runs a service to and from Porthmadog.

Train The nearest station to Beddgelert is Porthmadog. This, and the nearest stations to Llanberis, are described in the Snowdon Horseshoe section.

Car To reach the start of this route see the earlier Snowdon Horseshoe section. You can either approach Beddgelert from Caernarfon on the A4085, or from Porthmadog on the A498.

From the A5 and Capel Curig take the A4086 to reach Pen-y-Pass, branching onto the A498 for Beddgelert.

The Route
Stage 1: Pen-y-Pass to Snowdon Summit
4½ miles (7 km), 3 to 5 hours
From Pen-y-Pass car park follow the Pyg Track west from the cafe. The path is well made with large slabs laid like paving stones. It takes 40 minutes to reach Bwlch-y-Moch.

Rhododendrons – Invasion in Pink
Walking in Snowdonia in May, you can hardly fail to notice the profusion of beautiful pink flowers all over the hillsides. You, like us, will probably stop to wonder at this amazing floral display, take a few photos and marvel at the joys of nature. Don't be deceived: these are rhododendrons, the scourge of these hills.

Rhododendrons were introduced into Britain about 200 years ago as an ornamental shrub planted mainly in the estates of large houses. They thrived in British weather conditions, but it wasn't until this century, with the break-up of many of these estates, that they started to spread unchecked. Their environmental impact is devastating, and they are now threatening not only the existence of many of the indigenous plant and animal species in Snowdonia, but also the very nature of the landscape. Their dense foliage and poisonous roots mean that no other plants can grow beneath them, with the result that mosses, ferns and tree seedlings start to disappear. This, in turn, deprives the plant-eating animals, birds and insects of a vital food supply. Rhododendron leaves themselves are poisonous to most animals, and so do not provide an alternative source of nutrition. The disappearance of herbivorous animals inevitably leads to the decline of the carnivorous animals and birds which feed on them.

So why don't the locals just get rid of them? Good idea, but apparently easier said than done. One of the main problems with rhododendrons is their apparent indestructibility. They can tolerate all extremes of weather; they require minimal daylight for survival, so will grow happily in dense woodland; they grow back very rapidly after cutting, and each bush produces several million seeds every year. Their natural lifespan currently seems to be endless, and herbicides, to be effective, need to cover every branch of a shrub. They are a conservationist's nightmare. Their single redeeming feature is the spectacular flowers, but if it wasn't for those flowers, no-one would have imported them into Britain in the first place. ■

From here you can see down to Llyn Llydaw inside the old volcano crater which makes up the famous 'horseshoe'.

The path crosses inside the crater and traverses for another hour. The Miners Track comes up from the left, before a steep set of switchbacks lead to the ridge. At the Fingerstone (a standing obelisk) on the crest of the ridge turn left and follow the final 500m along the railway track to the summit. (See summit description in Snowdon Horseshoe section.)

Stage 2A: Snowdon Summit to Nantgwynant

3½ miles (5.5 km), 2 to 3 hours

Follow the south-west ridge (behind the cafe) and turn sharply left after 100m to descend to Bwlch-y-Saethau (pass of the arrows). Before the ascent towards the peak of Llewedd, the Watkin Path descends to the right (west) and swings south-west into Cwm Llan, and then follows the stream past the old quarry buildings and along the overgrown tramway to Nantgwynant. The path is large and obvious all the way.

Nantgwynant is in a beautifully green valley thick with rhododendron bushes. The rhododendrons were introduced from the Himalayas, but now they grow so readily that the park authorities are actively destroying them in order to protect other species (see aside). The valley has two lakes, Llyn Gwynant and Llyn Dinas, below which nestles the picturesque village of Beddgelert.

Stage 2B: Snowdon Summit to Snowdon Ranger

3½ miles (5.5 km), 2 hours

This is an alternative descent to the west from the top of Snowdon. It is ideal if you plan on going onto the Nantlle hills.

Return down the Llanberis Path, beside the railway track, to a fork after 500m, near the Fingerstone. Take the left fork, follow the railway for another 300m and then fork left again (north-west) along a ridge above the cliffs of Clogwyn Du'r Arddu. The path swings west past Llyn Ffynnon-y-gwas and continues clearly all the way to the Snowdon Ranger YHA Hostel.

TRYFAN & THE GLYDERS

Distance 5 miles (8 km)
Duration 5 to 6½ hours
Start & Finish Llyn Ogwen
Regional Centres Bangor, Llandudno
County Gwynedd
Summary A classic mountain-walk including three popular summits over 914m (3000 ft). Boulder-hopping high up can make it slow going, especially in the wet, but there are good paths lower down. It is difficult to navigate in cloud on the Glyder plateau, so map and compass skills are required. There is terrain requiring some scrambling on Tryfan, but it can be avoided.

The peak of Tryfan (914m, 3000 ft) looks a bit like a huge dinosaur when seen in profile from the road to Capel Curig, as its prickly back curves over in a huge arc. The long pillars of the east face rise from a platform of heather to a dramatic rocky summit. South of Tryfan (pronounced 'Tre-van', not 'Triffan') are the more rounded peaks of Glyder Fawr (999m) and Glyder Fach (994m), which form a long ridge bordered on the northern and eastern sides by steep cwms and cliffs. Linking Tryfan to The Glyders (Glyderau in Welsh) is a steep line of rocky needles affectionately known by walkers all over Britain as Bristly Ridge (although you won't see the name marked on maps). The Glyderau summit plateau is strewn with shattered boulders that have been moved by ice to form strange shapes and eerie towers.

At the foot of Glyder Fawr lies Cwm Idwal, a national nature reserve that attracts over 400,000 visitors each year. Central to this cwm is the Devil's Kitchen, a dark and austere gorge that cuts deeply into the surrounding cliffs. It's a place of Celtic aura and fantasy that befits a landscape reminiscent of the legends of King Arthur. The Countryside Commission for Wales and the National Trust (NT) try to protect the delicate and valuable environment of Idwal and help visitors enjoy the existing beauty. In contrast to this the RAF continue to use the area as a fighter-jet training alley, so on weekdays prepare to be dive bombed!

The route we describe here starts with an ascent of Tryfan, then joins the main Glyder ridge and descends via the Devil's Kitchen. The walking on this range is distinctly rocky, and walking on Tryfan involves some easy scrambling, but for those who are inexperienced or like to keep their hands in their pockets there is an alternative route. For the adventurous and experienced, there are many possibilities for more tricky scrambling routes.

Many people have problems navigating on the summits in bad weather, and this route is not recommend unless the visibility is good or you have some skill at using a compass and map to navigate.

Direction, Distance & Duration

This is a circular walk which can be done in either direction. We recommend starting with the ascent of Tryfan and going clockwise because the terrain is rough and rocky in this early section. The walk measures only five miles on the map, but it often takes longer than you'd think because the ground is rough. The round trip can be done in four hours if you push it, but five to 6½ hours walking time is more likely.

Longer Alternative If you reach Llyn y Cwn, at the top of the Devil's Kitchen path, in good time and want to bag another summit over 3000 ft, you can go on to Y Garn and descend the north-east ridge back to Idwal. This is quite straightforward although you need to make sure you descend the correct ridge (once on it, however, the descent is less steep than the Devil's Kitchen). This extention adds an extra 45 minutes to an hour onto the overall time.

Information

See the earlier Snowdon Horseshoe section.

Places to Stay & Eat

Idwal Cottage YHA Hostel (☎ 01248 600225, £6.75), at the west end of Llyn Ogwen, is ideally situated for this route. There is a small snack bar in the nearby car park that is well placed for when you come down, even if you are not staying at the hostel.

Along the A5 towards Capel Curig are two campsites. The nearest one to Tryfan is *Gwern Gof Uchaf*, with cold water and toilets for £1.50 a night. Further east is *Gwern Gof Isaf*, which has camping for £2, a camping barn for £3 and a bunkhouse for £4 per person, plus 50p for showers.

The village of Capel Curig, about five miles south-east of Llyn Ogwen, has several good options. The *Bryn Tyrch* (☎ 01690 720223) has B&B accommodation from £20, though the bar food is expensive. *Cobdens Hotel* (☎ 01690 720243) and the *Tyn-y-Coed Hotel* (☎ 01690 720331) are more pricey, both offering B&B for around £28. The *Bron Eryri Guest House* (☎ 01690 720240) next to the Tyn-y-Coed boasts B&B for £17 with ensuite bedrooms, TV and a cosy lounge. There is a large campsite just outside the village towards Betws-y-Coed (£1.50 a night). Also in Capel Curig is *Plas-y-Brenin Mountain Centre* (☎ 01690 720214), with B&B for £18. There are bar meals available and free general interest lectures or guest speakers each evening. You can also get a weather forecast here.

Betws-y-Coed is 10 miles south-east of Llyn Ogwen and has a wide range of places to stay and eat (plus two large outdoor equipment shops). *Henre Farm* has a campsite, and *Greenbank* (☎ 01690 710 288), just up the small road behind Cotswold Camping, is a recommended B&B run by New Zealanders Nick and Lindsay Banks, charging £14.50. Dave and Sue Walsh run the nonsmoking *Maelgwyn House* (☎ 01690 710252), which has B&B with ensuite bathrooms for £16.50. Top of the range is *Ty Gwyn* (☎ 01690 710383), a pub-restaurant just over the Waterloo Bridge at the southern end of the village with accommodation from £27.

For self-catering provisions, there's a *Spar* grocery store, and the *Tan Lan Bakery* has great cream cakes for the indulgent. *Dil's Diner*, next to the station, does fry-up breakfasts that are good value. There is also a *Little Chef* for fast food and *The Stables Bar* in the *Royal Oak Hotel* has really good-value bar meals (usually between £4 and £6) and a busy atmosphere (Thursday night jazz), plus

WALES

good pints of *Speckled Hen* beer that comes in long tall glasses. The *Waterloo Hotel* also serves bar food. If you prefer a pub with a 'front room' type atmosphere then try *The Pont-y-Pair*, opposite the bridge in the centre of the village, or the back room at the *Glan Aber Hotel* (☎ 01690 710325), which also has good mid-range accommodation.

Bethesda, five miles north of Llyn Ogwen, is less geared for visitors than other towns in the area, and as a result there is a dearth of accommodation. *Ogwen Bank* (☎ 01248 600486) is just out of town towards Ogwen and has caravans to rent. There are a number of pubs but the only one that is welcoming to walkers is the *Douglas Arms*. The interior is very old fashioned and transactions are conducted in pounds, shillings and pence (which Britain stopped using in 1971). They put your new money in the till though! Bethesda is quite close to Bangor, and many people go to *The Fat Cat* or *O'Shea's Irish Pub*, which has good music on a Saturday, both on the high street near the cathedral, or the *Bellevue* in Upper Bangor (lots of students).

Getting There & Away
Bus The nearest towns to Llyn Ogwen are Bangor and Betws-y-Coed. See the Snowdon Horseshoe section for details of how to get there. D&G (☎ 01248 600787) operates one bus daily from Bangor or Betws-y-Coed.

Train See Snowdon Horseshoe section for rail links to Bangor, Betws y Coed and Porthmadog.

Car Llyn Ogwen is beside the main A5 road about halfway between Bethesda and Capel Curig. There is a daily charge for car parking at Idwal Cottage at the start of the route.

The Route
Stage 1A: Llyn Ogwen to Tryfan Summit, via the North Ridge
½ mile (1 km), 1½ to 2 hours
Start from the lay-by nearest the eastern end of Llyn Ogwen, at the foot of the north ridge of Tryfan, where a wall runs down to meet the road. Go through the kissing gate and

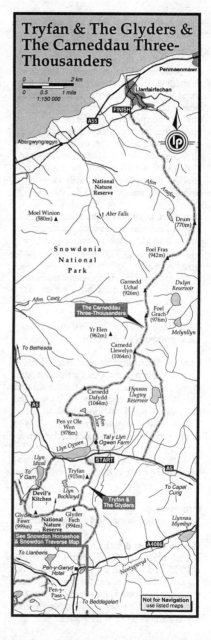

Tryfan & The Glyders & The Carneddau Three-Thousanders

follow the wall south up to where it meets a large cliff. This is Milestone Buttress, so called (surprise!) because there used to be a milestone on the London to Holyhead road here. From the foot of this buttress ascend leftwards (east) over loose rocks. A maze of paths weaves through heather and scree, east at first and then round to the south near the base of steep broken cliffs. There isn't a single well-defined route; you have to make your own way up onto and along the ridge. You'll have to use your hands a bit, but if it gets serious you're off route. (If you can't see an obvious way onto the ridge or don't like scrambling, a precipitous path called Heather Terrace runs along the east side of the ridge, missing the summit.)

After one to 1½ hours of steady ascent you reach the foot of an imposing rock buttress. Follow the path around its left (east) side, to reach a small col below a fine amphitheatre after another 15 minutes. Descend a little from the col into the amphitheatre, then go up the first deep and obvious gully (west), under a boulder at the top and back onto the ridge. The summit is about 100m further along the ridge. The standing stones of Adam and Eve mark the spot. Daredevils can leap from one stone to another, to get 'the freedom of Tryfan', but remember that help is a long way away if you break a leg trying. Better enjoy a rest and sandwich instead. (One walker we know reports having his lunch disturbed by a rescue helicopter practising here by balancing its wheels on the stones – so be prepared.)

If you haven't already noticed, the lake in Cwm Bochlwyd down to your west looks like a map of Australia. Further away, to the south-west, the summits of the Snowdon Horseshoe appear as distant giants, while to the north the view of the classic U-shaped Nant Ffrancon valley leads the eye out to the Anglesey coast.

Stage 2A: Tryfan Summit to Bwlch Tryfan

⅓ mile (500m), 30 minutes

Descend southwards from the summit. There are a few cairns along the way. Keep to the right (west) side of the ridge, especially in the lower part, until you arrive at Bwlch Tryfan, the wide pass underneath Glyder Fach, crossed by a large drystone wall.

Stage 1B & 2B: Alternative route from Llyn Ogwen to Bwlch Tryfan

1¼ miles (2 km), 1 to 2 hours

This is a good way to miss out the really steep bits described in Stages 1A and 2A above – getting onto the tops with your hands in your pockets!

From the outflow at the west end of Llyn Ogwen at the road bridge on the A5 near the YHA hostel, follow the well-defined path south-east for 300m. Don't follow the main path round to Llyn Idwal, but carry straight on at the first right-hand bend past the lake in Cwm Bochlwyd. The path leaves the lake and climbs gradually, heading south-east, to Bwlch Tryfan.

Stage 3: Bwlch Tryfan to Glyder Fawr Summit

1¼ miles (2 km), 1½ to 2½ hours

Above the bwlch a steep ridge rises to the south in a series of rocky needles. This is Bristly Ridge (and for happy rock scramblers it provides a wonderful outing). The steep and stoney walkers' path goes to the left of the ridge. It is a bit loose underfoot but it brings you out at the top of the ridge, where it flattens into a plateau of huge blocks, and the summit of Glyder Fach is visible to the south-west. (About 100m before you reach the summit you will pass the Cantilever Stone, a huge monolith suspended on its side over a drop, a bit like a huge rock diving board – with a very bad landing.)

From this summit, the path descends slightly, passing a particularly spiky outcrop called Castell-y-Gwynt (castle of the wind) on its left (south) side (you can go over the top if you're a peak-bagger), and then drops to a col overlooking Cwm Bochlwyd. The path continues, clearly at first and then over rocks (if there is mist, pay close attention to your navigating) south-west to the summit of Glyder Fawr, one of several small 'castles' and rock towers standing on the broad summit plateau.

WALES

Stage 4: Glyder Fawr Summit to Llyn Ogwen

2½ miles (4 km), 1½ hours

The path leaves the summit heading south-west then curves and descends over steep scree north-west to Llyn-y-Cwn. The way here is quite eroded and fairly loose under-foot, but it takes you down onto the flat col very quickly. From the lake turn right (north-east) to follow the Devil's Kitchen path, which swings back left after 200m to follow a rocky path down through the cliffs to reach the base of the Devil's Kitchen – a steep gorge with a waterfall. (The spray and mist from the waterfall look like smoke from a cooking fire in certain conditions – hence the name.) This path offers a surprisingly easy way through some otherwise steep terrain. From here the paved path takes you either east or west of Llyn Idwal to the YHA hostel, car park and snackbar at the west end of Llyn Ogwen.

THE CARNEDDAU THREE-THOUSANDERS

Distance 11½ miles (18 km) for the linear route, 7 miles (11 km) for the circuit
Duration 6 to 7 hours (4½ to 6 hours, circuit)
Start Llyn Ogwen
Finish Llanfairfechan
Regional Centres Bangor, Llandudno, Conwy
County Gwynedd
Area Snowdonia
Summary A classic linear route, taking in six summits over 914m (3000 ft), with straightfor-ward walking on mostly good paths. Also a circular option taking in three '3000-ers'. In the winter the Carneddau generally attracts more snow than other areas, and even in summer the weather can be atrocious on the tops.

The Carneddau mountains lie in the north-eastern section of the national park. The group takes its name from Carnedd Dafydd and Carnedd Llewelyn (*carnedd* actually means mountain, plural *carneddau*), and has a more isolated atmosphere than many other peaks in Snowdonia because its mountains are broad and open, although hidden amongst the grassy slopes are cliffs of a scale more often seen in the highlands of Scotland than in Wales. (Strangely, although Carnedd Dafydd and Carnedd Llewelyn are known by the Welsh plural name, the Carneddau, the nearby mountains of Glyder Fawr and Glyder Fach are nearly always called The Glyders, rather than the Glyderau.)

We describe two possible routes to the main summits: one is a traverse, the other a circular walk. Both start at Llyn Ogwen, on the A5 between Bethesda and Capel Curig, and ascend steeply to the summit plateau. The traverse continues across the tops to finish by the sea at Llanfairfechan. The circuit returns from Carnedd Llewelyn to the A5, one mile east of the starting point.

Direction, Distance & Duration

The linear walk starts at Llyn Ogwen and ends at Llanfairfechan. It can be walked in either direction but if you start from Ogwen you have the advantage of being already at 300m (1000 ft). Llanfairfechan is at sea level. The circular walk can be walked in either direction, but an ascent of Pen yr Ole Wen is better early in the day. On the top of the Carneddau you can cover quite a lot of ground fairly quickly, and so the 12 mile traverse can be covered in six or seven hours

The Welsh Threes

The Carneddau summits make up six of the peaks over 3000 ft in Wales. The whole round of the fourteen 3000-footers, known as The Welsh 3000-ers or more simply The Welsh Threes, can be completed in a long day starting from the summit of Snowdon. The route follows the northern half of the horseshoe and then descends to Llanberis Pass, before climbing to Elidir Fawr, Y Garn, The Glyders and Tryfan. That's all before you nip across the six Carneddau peaks described here. The record is about five hours. Doesn't it make you sick? For more casual walkers, the 14 peaks can be split over a few days and enjoyed at leisure. See the Snowdonia Coast to Coast section. ∎

of walking. The circuit option is a good four hour walk.

Information

See the Snowdon Horseshoe section.

Places to Stay & Eat

For details on accommodation, food and information in the Ogwen Valley see the Tryfan & The Glyders section. In Llanfairfechan a good place to stay is *The Towers* (☎ 01248 680012), run by Colin & Sue Goodey, who offer B&B for £15. It's easy to find on the seafront (turn seaward from the traffic lights in the middle of the village). *The Split Willow* (01248 680647) has B&B for £30 (single) and £40 (double) with bar meals or à la carte meals available. There are a number of pubs, a bistro, Chinese restaurant and fish & chips shops for evening food.

Getting There & Away

Bus To reach the start of the walk in the Ogwen Valley see the Tryfan & The Glyders section. Once you're in Llanfairfechan, National Express runs two daily coach services between Pwllheli – pronounced 'Puchlwelly' – (No 390) and Holyhead (No 545) and London and Manchester, which both stop here. Llanfairfechan is also on the Crossville Cymru (☎ 01492 596969) route between Llandudno and Caernarfon.

Train The nearest stations to the Ogwen Valley are Bangor and Betws-y-Coed, and Llanfairfechan is close to Llandudno Junction (all details in the Snowdon Horseshoe section). Regional Railways has a regular service (almost every hour) between Llanfairfechan and Llandudno junction.

Car The route starts at the eastern end of Llyn Ogwen, two miles south of Bethesda on the A5. The approaches are described in the previous Tryfan & The Glyders section. Parking at Ogwen Cottage costs £4 daily. There is car access to Llanfairfechan from the main A55 North Wales Coast Rd.

The Route

Stage 1: Llyn Ogwen to Pen yr Ole Wen Summit

2 miles (3 km), 1½ to 2 hours

From the eastern end of Llyn Ogwen take the track towards Tal y Llyn Ogwen farm. Just before the farm gate, the path follows a stream, Afon Lloer, north and uphill. Before reaching Cwm Lloer, turn left (west) along the ridge to the summit of Pen yr Ole Wen (978m). This is the first of the Carneddau summits. There are great views over to The Glyders, with Snowdon behind, and down to Bangor and Anglesey.

Stage 2: Pen yr Ole Wen to Carnedd Llewelyn Summit

3 miles (5 km), 1 to 2 hours

Follow the ridge north then north-east to Carnedd Dafydd (1044m). From here the path turns right (east) for about one mile along the ridgetop to Carnedd Llewelyn (1064m). The cliffs of Ysgolion Duon (the black ladders) drop away steeply to the north. From the summit of Carnedd Llewelyn the view of Tryfan is magnificent.

Yr Elen detour (1½ miles (3 km), 1 hour, there and back) If you want to bag all the Carneddau tops over 3000 ft you will need to take an out-and-back detour to the summit of Yr Elen (962m). The walk is worthwhile if you have the time and the energy. There is a dramatic drop down into Cwm Caseg from the summit.

Stage 3A: Carnedd Llewelyn to Llanfairfechan (via Drum)

6½ miles (10 km), 3 to 4 hours

On the linear route from Carnedd Llewelyn, the high ground can be followed north to Foel Grach (976m). About 50m north of the summit is a stone shelter with a couple of small benches inside. It's a great place to retreat from the weather if the winds are strong, but sleeping there should be reserved for emergency situations only.

From Foel Grach the broad, flat and grassy ridge continues northwards, with gentle rises

WALES

to Carnedd Uchaf (926m) and Foel Fras (942m), and eventually to Drum (770m), the final top. From the summit of Drum descend a broad ridge on a vehicle track in a north-westerly direction to Llanfairfechan.

Stage 3B: Carnedd Llewelyn to the A5
3 miles (5 km), 1½ to 2 hours

This is the circular route (back to Ogwen) and the easiest escape from Carnedd Llewelyn in bad weather. The path leads south-east from the summit of Carnedd Llewelyn down a steep, narrow ridge, with some near-sheer drops on either side which could be tricky in mist, to the steep-sided bwlch at Eryl Farchog (about 45 minutes from Carnedd Llewelyn).

Turning right (south) here, a steep zigzag path takes you down to the Ffynnon Llugwy reservoir. Follow the path along its east bank to join the tarred service road leading to the A5, about one mile east of your starting point. It's an eyesore but at least you can't lose the way!

THE NANTLLE RIDGE

> **Distance** 8 miles (13 km)
> **Duration** 5 to 7 hours
> **Start** Rhyd-Ddu
> **Finish** Llanllyfni, near Penygroes
> **Regional Centres** Porthmadog, Caernarfon
> **County** Gwynedd
> **Area** Snowdonia
> **Summary** A fine ridge walk, quieter than the other routes described in this area, with some exposed sections. Paths are clear but not waymarked. Suitable for reasonably fit walkers.

The Nantlle Ridge is not as well known as some other walking routes in Snowdonia. This part of the park is a bit more wild and woolly than some of the more popular places and there is less in the way of tourist amenities. It has the stark character of a place that is depressed, and the mountains around it can appear grey and foreboding on a typical autumn afternoon when the rain splatters on the slates in the fading light. But in summer, when the grass shines and the clouds throw bright shadows across the slopes, it looks alive and awake, vibrant with colour.

From the crest of the narrow ridge that is the backbone of this area, the views of the mountains and out into the Irish sea are quite stunning in clear weather. If bad weather comes from the south-west then these hills receive the worst of it, but in winter the warmer air coming over the sea will sometimes keep these hills free of snow, when the slightly higher inland areas are covered.

Direction, Distance & Duration
The ridge can be walked in either direction. Starting at Rhyd-Ddu is preferable, as the ascent of Y Garn this way is easier than from the west, but if you start at Llanllyfni the Cwellyn Arms in Rhyd-Ddu is a great place to finish!

The walk described is eight miles from Rhyd-Ddu to Llanllyfni, but the number of passes along the ridge mean quite a few ups and downs, which slows progress a bit so you should allow five to seven hours. If you are coming from the west and can get a lift to the end of the track at Cwm Silyn you can do the ridge in about four to five hours.

Places to Stay & Eat
There is a *YHA Hostel* (☎ 01286 650391) at the foot of the Snowdon Ranger path, about one mile from Rhyd-Ddu towards Caernarfon. Rhyd-Ddu is only two miles from Beddgelert, where there are plenty of places to stay (see the Snowdon Traverse section). One of the best features of this walk is the *Cwellyn Arms* pub at Rhyd-Ddu, which serves good food and has an open fire to welcome the most disheartened of weary walkers.

At the Llanllyfni end of the ridge there is B&B for £19 at *Tyn Llwyn Cottage* (☎ 01286 881526), just after you reach the lane that leads to Llanllyfni. It is only open April through October. A little further towards the village is the *Oznam Holiday Centre* (☎ 01286 881568) which has B&B, packed lunch plus evening meal for £19.50, but you should telephone beforehand.

Getting There & Away
Bus Rhyd-Ddu is on the Snowdon Sherpa

route between Caernarfon and Beddgelert (see the Snowdon Horseshoe section for more information). The National Express daily coach from Manchester and London stops at Caernarfon en route to Pwllheli. Express Bus Co (☎ 01286 674570) runs an hourly service between Porthmadog and Caernarfon stopping at Llanllyfni (with three buses in each direction on Sunday and public holidays). The Crossville Cymru (☎ 01492 596969) Trawscambria daily coach service runs from Cardiff through central Wales to Holyhead. It stops in Machynlleth, Porthmadog and Penygroes, among a lot of other places on its 12 hour journey.

Train There is a regular train service from Birmingham New Street to Porthmadog, from where you can reach Llanllyfni by bus. Trains run from Crewe to Llandudno Junction and Bangor (see the Snowdon Horseshoe section).

Car Rhyd-Ddu is about two miles north of Beddgelert on the A4085 to Caernarfon. Llanllyfni is on the A487 Caernarfon to Porthmadog road, about a kilometre south of Penygroes. It is possible to drive up to the

start of the track to Cwm Silyn, where there is a field for parking, but there have been many cases of car theft here. It is more advisable to leave your vehicle at Rhyd-Ddu and persuade someone to give you a lift down to the start. The B4418 connects Penygroes and Rhyd-Ddu and is not serviced by public transport.

The Route
Stage 1: Rhyd-Ddu to Y Garn Summit
1½ miles (2.5 km), 1 to 1½ hours

From the junction by the pub at Rhyd-Ddu take the B4418 west (signpost to Nantlle and Penygroes) for 300m. On a bend there is a stile and two gates; take the narrower gate and follow the track onto open grassy slopes. A path leads steadily but steeply to the summit of Y Garn (633m).

Stage 2: Y Garn to Bwlch Dros Bern
2 miles (3 km), 1 to 2 hours

From Y Garn follow the south ridge, ending with a steep and sometimes greasy scramble to the summit of Mynydd Drws y Coed (695m). This ridge is exposed in places – you can avoid the hardest bits on their left (east) side. The ridge continues over the summit of

WALES

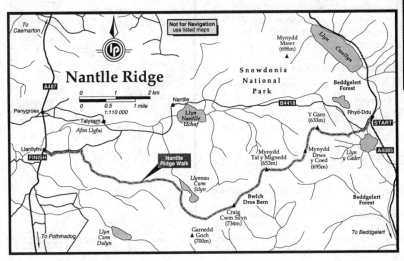

Mynydd Tal y Mignedd (653m), where there is a huge summit cairn marked as an obelisk on the OS map. From here the ridge swings south-west and descends to the obvious col, Bwlch Dros Bern.

Stage 3: Bwlch Dros Bern to Llanllyfni
4½ miles (7 km), 2 to 3 hours

From the bwlch you have a choice: you can continue over the top of Craig Cwm Silyn (734m) – best approached by initially following the path skirting rocky outcrops on the right, then a path to the left that zigzags up to the summit – and Garnedd Goch (700m) before descending grassy slopes to the north-west. Or you can descend the north side of the bwlch, and then traverse west to Llynnau (lakes) Cwm Silyn once the ground becomes flatter (no path). Both options take you to the track which leads from the lakes to the farm at Maen-llwyd, and the lane which leads into Llanllyfni. Turn left at the junction passing Tyn Llwyn Cottage (B&B) to reach the village.

Other Direction If you do this route the other way, starting in Llanllyfni, take the lane going east just north of the chapel (signposted Tan yr allt). When you reach Tyn Lwyn Cottage (after about half a mile) turn right past a quarry and a scrap yard. The lane eventually becomes a track which leads you to the lakes in Cwm Silyn.

BEDDGELERT VALLEY WALK

> **Distance** 5½ miles (9 km)
> **Duration** 3 to 4 hours
> **Start & Finish** Beddgelert
> **Regional Centres** Porthmadog, Caernarfon
> **County** Gwynedd
> **Area** Snowdonia
> **Summary** A straightforward valley and low hill-walk, past several interesting features, on good paths.

Beddgelert (pronounced 'Beth-gelert') is a village on the south-west side of Snowdon, where the main roads from Caernarfon and Capel Curig meet and head south towards Porthmadog. It's quite easy to reach, and there's a good choice of places to stay and eat, so it makes a good base for exploring. This walk starts and finishes in Beddgelert and keeps mainly to low valleys, so it's ideal if the weather is too bad to go up on the higher peaks. There is a nice lookout about halfway round, so you're not completely enclosed, and there are several interesting features from North Wales' early industrial era, including an old railway track (complete with tunnels) and some copper mines (some disused, one reopened). Signposting is good, paths are clear, and it's almost impossible to get lost on this route.

Direction, Distance & Duration
This circular walk can be done in either direction, but a start with Gelert's Grave and the railway line is better. Also the ascent this way is more gentle. The total distance is 5½ miles, which will take about three to four hours walking time, although you should

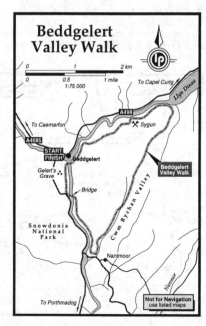

The Beddgelert Legend

Beddgelert is Welsh for 'Grave of Gelert'. The National Trust (NT) leaflet available in the village reports that a saint from Ireland, called Celert, is thought to have founded a small church and community here during the early years of Christianity in Britain. When he died and was buried here, the settlement took its name from his grave. By medieval times the site was covered by a large Augustinian monastery, although there is very little remaining today, except some windows which have been reused in the church.

Another story goes back to the 13th century, when Prince Llewelyn had a hunting lodge here (the NT shop by the bridge is built on the site). Apparently, the prince went hunting one day without his faithful dog called Gelert. Returning some time later he found the dog covered in blood and the bed of his baby son empty. Llewelyn thought Gelert had killed the baby, so he killed the dog. As it was dying, the prince heard a baby's cry. Llewelyn's son was unharmed and nearby was the body of a wolf which the faithful hound had killed to protect the baby. Naturally, Llewelyn was rather upset about this misunderstanding and buried his dog in a fine grave not far from the hunting lodge, which can still be visited today. (Follow the signposts.)

A third story involves one Mr David Pritchard, the landlord of the Royal Goat Hotel in the early 19th century. Business was apparently a bit slack, so he resurrected the old legend about the dog, with its catchy 'look before you leap' moral, and built the 'grave' near the town, where it could easily be reached by visiting gentry. The ploy worked and a steady stream of romantic visitors came to Beddgelert. They've been arriving ever since and the Royal Goat has never looked back. ■

allow extra for visiting Gelert's Grave, having lunch etc, and at least another hour if you want to visit the working copper mine at Sygun. For general information and information on places to stay and eat etc, see Beddgelert in the Snowdon Traverse section.

The Route
Stage 1: Beddgelert to Bwlch-y-Sygun
3 miles (5 km), 1½ to 2 hours

Leave Beddgelert village by walking down the lane westwards, along the south bank of the river, following a clear signposted path to Gelert's Grave. Follow this path and branch off to the grave (a few hundred metres from the river) when you see the sign. After looking (it won't take long) retrace to the main path and continue following the river downstream.

After 500m the riverside path meets the track of the disused railway. Go left across a brown girder bridge, now converted to carry walkers instead of trains, and follow the old track (the river is now on your right). This was once the Welsh Highland Railway, which hugged the steep river-valley side as it wound through the Pass of Aberglaslyn, running between Porthmadog and Caernarfon. It opened in 1922 but closed in 1937, leaving the pleasant (and flat) footpath for

walkers to enjoy. The old railway goes through three fine old tunnels carved out of the rock. The third is long and the complete darkness in the middle disorientating, although there is a way round the outside if you don't like the dark.

At the end of the third tunnel you reach Nantmoor, at the foot of the Cwm Bychan Valley. Turn left (north) off the railway and up a footpath through trees. There are remains of an old copper-processing works down to your right. The path leaves the trees and enters open moorland, climbing steadily past old mine workings and the remains of pylons of an aerial runway which once carried copper ore down to the works at Nantmoor. (Don't be tempted to enter any of the old mine shafts – they haven't been maintained for decades and are very unsafe.)

Continue up the valley, to reach the col of Bwlch-y-Sygyn at the top. Cross a fence by a ladder stile and go left for 100m to reach a junction. There are fine views down to Llyn Dinas, up the Nantgwynant valley, with the bulk of Snowdon behind.

Stage 2: Bwlch-y-Sygyn to Beddgelert
2½ miles (4 km), 1½ to 2 hours

From Bwlch-y-Sygyn junction, take the

right turn, northwards downhill on a clear path of grey slate chippings, through a splendid section of open rocky moorland (although a few rhododendron saplings are beginning to sprout here) and then steeply down to the lake of Llyn Dinas (reached about 20 to 30 minutes from the junction).

Go over the stile here and follow the path alongside the river flowing out of the lake downstream (the river on your right). This leads to a track, which soon brings you out in the car park of Sygun Copper Mine, which has been reopened as an award-winning visitor attraction. (If being unable to explore at Cwm Bychan was disappointing, now's your chance to go underground in safety.)

From the mine rejoin the track, which leads through fields and past a couple of campsites to become a tar lane which eventually brings you out by a bridge and the main A498. Do not cross the bridge, but go left over a stile and follow another path down beside the river, past a splendid row of cottages, over one more bridge and into the centre of Beddgelert.

A SNOWDONIA COAST TO COAST

Distance 38½ miles (62.5 km)
Duration 4 days
Start Llanfairfechan
Finish Llanllyfni
Regional Centres Llandudno, Bangor, Caernarfon, Porthmadog
County Gwynnedd
Area Snowdonia
Summary A long-distance route, combining four of the day-walks described in this Snowdonia chapter into a continuous trek, including a traverse of all the 3000 ft peaks. Mostly on good paths, but in poor weather you may need to use navigational skills. Some sections are steep and rocky, but can be avoided.

This route is an ideal way of linking four of the day-walks described in this Snowdonia section into a continuous trek. Combined with ascents of Elidir Fawr and Y Garn, you can complete the full round of the Welsh summits over 3000 ft. Because most of the routes in this section have already been described above, the general description

here is short. The northern stages of this route are also followed by the long-distance Cambrian Way and Snowdonia to the Gower routes outlined in the Other Walks in Wales section below.

Direction, Distance & Duration
This route can be walked in either direction, but by starting in Llanfairfechan and walking north-east to south-west you ascend the steep north ridge of Tryfan (better than descending it) and avoid the long drag out of Llanllyfni. The itinerary looks like this:

Day	From	To	Distance
1	Llanfairfechan	Llyn Ogwen	11½ miles (18 km)
2	Llyn Ogwen	Nant Peris	10 miles (17 km)
3	Pen-y-Pass	Snowdon Ranger	8 miles (13 km)
4	Rhyd-Ddu	Llanllyfni	9 miles (14.5 km)

Books
Apart from those mentioned in the Snowdon Horseshoe section above, a specific book which might be useful for this route is *The Welsh Three Thousands* by Roy Clayton (Grey Stone Books, £4.50), which covers the classic linear route (27 miles), with suggestions on accommodation and some historical background.

Places to Stay & Eat
It is possible to complete the walk and either camp, stay in hostels or use B&Bs each night according to your budget. There are plenty of other places to eat, too. For more details see the individual route sections.

The Route
Day 1: Llanfairfechan to Ogwen
11½ miles (18 km), 5 to 7 hours
This is identical to the linear walk described in the Carneddau section. The only difference is the direction, which should be reversed. Leaving Llanfairfechan, take the road opposite the main bus stop in the middle of the village (signposted to the golf course) and then take the first left up the hill to a stile

WALES

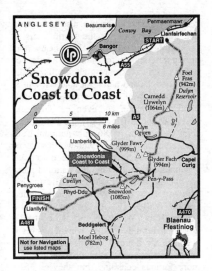

by a farm. This leads to the path skirting Garreg Fawr and crosses the old Roman road on its way to the summit of Drum.

Day 2A: Ogwen to Nant Peris (or Pen-y-Pass) via Elidir Fawr
10 miles (17 km), 5 hours

Follow the route described in the Tryfan & The Glyders section until you reach Llyn y Cwn, at the top of the Devil's Kitchen path. From here, ascend broad slopes north-east to the summit of Y Garn (947m). From Y Garn the path continues along the ridge northwards. The next summit is Foel Goch (831m), after which the ridge descends to Bwlch y Brecan (just before the summit of Mynydd Perfedd). Here the path swings west to cross the hillside as it continues to the summit of Elidir Fawr (923m) – the only 3000 ft peak that is not included in any of the day-walk sections. From the summit the easiest descent is to retrace your steps to Bwlch y Brecan and follow the path beside the Afon Dudodyn directly to Nant Peris. Stay in Nant Peris or take a bus or hitch to Pen-y-Pass (see the Snowdon Horseshoe section for details on accommodation etc).

Day 2B: Ogwen to Nant Peris (or Pen-y-Pass) via The Glyders
3 miles (5 km), 2½ to 3 hours

The above description follows the Fourteen Peaks route (via Elidir Fawr), but is not the most direct route to Pen-y-Pass. As an alternative, from Ogwen there are two good paths leading over The Glyders. The easiest is the Miners Track (not to be confused with the track on Snowdon) which follows Nant Gwern y Gof on the east side of Tryfan into Cwm Tryfan. It then goes over the top of the ridge (near to Llyn Caseg Fraith – Lake of the Speckled Mare) and continues in a southerly direction down the other side to the Pen-y-Gwryd Hotel and Pen-y-Pass. This is a good option in poor weather as you spend very little time high up. Even if you don't want to bag Elidir Fawr, this descent would combine well with ascending via the Devil's Kitchen, and crossing the two Glyder summits.

Day 3: Pen-y-Pass to Snowdon Ranger
8 miles (13 km), 4 to 5 hours

From Pen-y-Pass take the Pyg Track to the summit of Snowdon (as described in Stage 1 of the Snowdon Traverse section). From the summit of Snowdon take the path to the Snowdon Ranger youth hostel (see Stage 2B of Snowdon Traverse section). You can stay in the *Snowdon Ranger Hostel* or near Beddgelert (see the Snowdon Horseshoe section for details).

Another possibility is to descend the Rhyd-Ddu path from the top of Snowdon along the south-west ridge and above the cliffs of Llechog. This path brings you to the start of the Nantlle Ridge.

Day 4: Snowdon Ranger to Llanllyfni
9 miles (14.5 km), 5 hours

From Snowdon Ranger take a bus, hitch or hike the one mile to Rhyd-Ddu. From there follow the route over the Nantlle ridge to Llanllyfni (see the Nantlle Ridge section for details of route, places to stay and information).

WALES

Pembrokeshire

Pembrokeshire is a former county in West Wales. Officially it's part of Dyfed, but the old name is still widely used. The area is well known for its relatively mild climate, which means you can generally enjoy Pembrokeshire year-round, although it does get hammered by some spectacular gales, especially in winter.

Pembrokeshire is also known as Little England Beyond Wales due to the strong influence of English 'incomers' (the first lot arrived in the 11th century and they're still pouring over the border today, usually as holidaymakers). Despite this, the Welsh language is still alive and kicking in Pembrokeshire, especially in the north of the county. An ancient division called the 'Landsker Line' divides the more Anglicised south from the traditionally Celtic north of the county.

The Celts were the original inhabitants of Pembrokeshire, and left their mark on the landscape in the form of ancient standing stones and the remains of settlements which date back well over 2000 years. The 'bluestones' of Stonehenge were quarried here, although no-one is quite sure why, or how they were transported all the way to their present resting place in Southern England.

Pembrokeshire's later residents left a rich architectural and cultural legacy which can be readily seen in the castles such as Pembroke and Carew, or the fascinating cathedral and bishop's palace in St David's, Britain's smallest city, which was a stronghold of early Christianity.

However, for many visitors, Pembrokeshire's dramatic coastal scenery is the main attraction, along with an equally impressive array of wildlife. The varied beaches, cliffs, coves and harbours of the area are contained within Pembrokeshire Coast National Park – Britain's only coastal national park. The offshore islands of Skomer, Skokholm, Grassholm and Ramsey (named by 10th

century Viking invaders) are also in the park, and home to some of the world's largest populations of sea birds such as shearwaters and gannets, not to mention hordes of puffins, kittiwakes, cormorants, gulls and the rarer choughs and peregrine falcons. Out at sea Atlantic grey seals, porpoises and dolphins are common, and even the odd shark. The coastline is fringed by the Pembrokeshire Coast Path, a 186 mile national trail, covered in this book and well worth a day or two even if you haven't got time to do it all.

Inland, and still within the national park, are the little-known Preseli Hills (called Mynydd Preseli in Welsh), the secluded Gwaun Valley (Cwm Gwaun) and the Milford Haven Waterway, one of the world's largest natural harbours, which upstream becomes the tranquil Daugleddau Estuary. These areas have just as much to offer as the more famous coastline, but they're often overlooked by visitors, so if you're after solitude they could well be the place for you – particularly the Preselis, where this section's day-walk is based.

A PRESELI HILLS CIRCUIT

Distance 14½ miles (24.5 km)
Duration 5½ to 6 hours
Start & Finish Newport
Reginal Centres Haverfordwest, Fishguard, Cardigan
County Dyfed (formerly Pembrokeshire)
Area Pembrokeshire Coast National Park
Summary A circular walk over open moorland, through woods and forests and along a deep wooded valley. Paths are generally well marked. There are some steepish ascents and descents, but nothing beyond the capabilities of any reasonably fit and experienced walker.

The Preseli Hills (also spelt Presely or Preselly) are the highest landmass in West Wales, rising to 536m at Foel Cymcerwyn. They are bisected by the steep-sided and heavily wooded Gwaun Valley. The views from the summits of the Preselis on a clear day are exceptional – you can see as far as the Gower Peninsula to the south-east, and to the Llyn Peninsula and the mountains of

Snowdonia in North Wales. In extremely clear conditions you may even see Ireland's Wicklow Hills.

Apart from the views, another notable feature of the Preselis is the abundance of Neolithic monuments. These vary from the impressive burial chamber of Pentre Ifan to the remains of Iron Age hillforts, like Carn Ingli, and numerous standing stones such as Bedd Morris. This route takes in some of these prehistoric highlights.

The scenery on this route is also varied. From the small coastal town of Newport (between Fishguard and Cardigan – not to be confused with Newport, Gwent, which is near Cardiff), it goes across Carn Ingli and the hills south of the town, dips into the tranquil, wooded Gwaun Valley at Llanerch, then rises again to wilder moorland, passing Tafarn-y-bwlch and Bwlch-gwynt before looping back to the start via Sychbant and Bedd Morris.

Although the hills are not particularly high they can be exposed, and they occasionally get a covering of snow in winter, so take appropriate clothing.

Direction, Distance & Duration

This circular route starts and ends at Newport. It can be done in either direction, but an ascent of Carn Ingli is better done near the beginning when you're fresh and so you get a preview of the land the route passes through. Another possible start/finish point, if you have wheels, is Sychbant Picnic Site in the Gwaun Valley.

This route is not specifically waymarked, although there are some signposts which point you to the next village, hill or whatever, but a map should definitely be carried.

The total distance is 14½ miles. There's a reasonable amount of ascent and descent, but nothing very serious, so you should allow around 5½ hours of walking, plus an hour for lunch or looking at ancient monuments (longer if you're an historian or big eater).

Shorter & Longer Alternatives
A number of short cuts are possible. By going straight from Carn Ingli to Mynydd Caregog, you

can turn it into a five mile stroll. It's also possible to cut across from Llanerch to Sychbant, straight down the Gwaun Valley, and miss out the southern part of the route, making a total of around eight miles.

A small extension (two miles extra) can be made to the Duffryn Arms in the Gwaun Valley (see Places to Stay & Eat). If you really wanted to get the miles in, you could extend the route southwards to the small village of Rosebush, which has a pub, small store and cafe, although they don't always seem to keep regular hours.

Information
There's a PIC in Newport (☎ 01239 820912) and TICs in Fishguard (☎ 01348 873484), Cardigan (☎ 01239 613230) and Haverfordwest (☎ 01437 763310). Most of these are seasonal – call the National Park Headquarters in Haverfordwest (☎ 01437 764636) if visiting in winter.

Books & Maps Guidebooks specifically covering the Preseli Hills include *Walking in the Presely Hills* by Brian John (published by the national park, £2.45), which describes seven circular walks, many of which can be linked. The same author and publisher has also produced the *Upper Gwaun Valley Walks Pack* (£1.95).

The Carningli Walks (edited by Brian John and published by Carningli Rural Initiative, £4.95) features several walks around the Newport area.

OS Landranger (1:50,000) sheet 145 covers this area. For more detail use the OS Outdoor Leisure (1:25,000) sheet 36.

Guided Walks & Local Services
The Pembrokeshire Coast National Park runs guided walks in the Preseli Hills. You'll find details at the information centres listed above or in the free visitor newspaper *Coast to Coast*.

Places to Stay & Eat
In Newport, the modern *YHA Hostel* (☎ 01239 820080, £7.45) is on Lower St Mary St. *Morawelon Caravan & Camping*

WALES

Park (☎ 01239-820565), west of Newport at Parrog Beach, charges £2 and is open from April to September. There's an *independent hostel/bunkhouse* at Brithdir Mawr, two miles from Newport, charging £4; their blurb says they live on permaculture principles and practise daily meditation (phone in advance, ☎ 01239 820164).

B&Bs include *2 Springhill* (☎ 01239 820626), Parrog Rd, with good sea views, open year-round and charging £15; and *Hafan Deg* (☎ 01239 820301), off Long St, from £14 per person. *Llysmeddyg Guesthouse* (☎ 01239 8200080) on East St charges £18.50 for a bed or £21 B&B. It also hires out mountain bikes. On the outskirts of Newport, the excellent *Grove Park Guesthouse* (☎ 01239 820122), Pen-y-Bont, charges from £18 per person for B&B – an evening meal is £12.50. The staff will pick you up from Fishguard Station.

There are several places you could try for accommodation and also for a meal in East St. The *Golden Lion Hotel* (☎ 01239 820321) does B&B from £18. It also has a bar, and a restaurant with a takeaway section. *Cnapan Country House* (☎ 01239 820575) charges from £24 per person, and is open from March to December. It has a restaurant (closed Tuesday), which also serves good vegetarian dishes.

The *Llwyngwair Arms* (☎ 01239 820267), East St, has a restaurant specialising in Indian food and takeaways, and a bar serving real ales. *Fronlas Cafe* (☎ 01239 802351), Market St, does lunches, cream teas and evening meals. Bring your own wine.

If you'd rather not be on the coast, *Tregynon Country Farmhouse Hotel* (☎ 01239 820531) in the Gwaun Valley is a nonsmoking place, charging £20 to £35 per night for B&B.

On the route we describe, there's nowhere to get refreshments so you should be self-sufficient with food and drink, unless you walk one mile west of the main route near Sychbant, down the Gwaun Valley to Pontfaen, where you'll find the *Duffryn Arms*, a friendly Welsh pub which hasn't changed for about fifty years. It's a single room in the landlady's rather tumbledown house, with beer served in jugs through a hatch. Food is limited to chocolate, crisps and pickled eggs.

Getting There & Away
Bus Richards Brothers Bus (☎ 01239 820751) operates hourly to Cardigan and Haverfordwest via Fishguard. Call 'Bws Dyfed' (☎ 01267 231817) for more details of other local services.

Train The nearest railway station is Fishguard, which has two trains a day from London, via South Wales.

Car Newport is on the A487 between Fishguard and Cardigan. There is a car park on Long Street, opposite the PIC.

Taxi If you miss your bus connection, local companies in Fishguard include Marshall's (☎ 01348 874093). Fares to Newport from Fishguard are about £10.

The Route
Stage 1: Newport to Carn Ingli
1½ miles (2.5 km), 1 hour
From the centre of Newport, take Market St uphill, signposted 'Cwm Gwaun', past the castle on your right. Keep on this road for about half a mile to reach a phone box, where you take a track on the right uphill. After 300m you fork left to join a path running alongside a wall. Go right (west) at the next path junction up to the peak of Carn Llwyd.

On the flanks of Carn Llwyd pick up another path heading south across the moor which climbs up to Carn Ingli summit. It's a bit of a scramble to the top, so take time here to catch your breath and admire the marvellous views.

Stage 2: Carn Ingli to Llanerch
1½ miles (2 km), 45 minutes
From Carn Ingli take the path down the south-east side of the hill to the lane. Turn right and follow the road, which becomes a dirt track, past the farms of Dolrannog Isaf, Dolrannog Uchaf and Pen-rhiw (watch out for farm dogs!), and into the woods. You

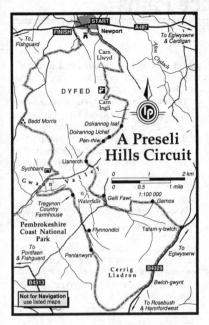

emerge from the woods at Llanerch Farm. Follow the farm track out onto the quiet road which runs down the Gwaun Valley.

If you are taking the short cut to Sychbant, turn right along the valley road, then follow the directions in Stage 4 to get back to Newport.

Stage 3: Llanerch to Sychbant
7½ miles (13 km), 3 hours

If you are going for the southern part of this route, follow the road straight on (south-east) for 200m then turn right into the woods on the opposite side of the valley. Follow the path alongside pools and waterfalls up through the woods to a tarred road at Gelli Fawr. Turn right, and go along this road for 300m then turn left onto a signposted bridleway. Follow this up past a pretty

secluded cottage and onto open moorland at Gernos (farm dogs again!). Go through the farm and take the dirt track across the moor to Tafarn-y-bwlch.

At Tafarn-y-bwlch you meet the B4329 road. Turn right and follow it for about one mile to Bwlch-gwynt, where a bridleway on the right winds around the lower slopes of Cerrig Lladron (although it's not far to the summit, which has great views). Stay on the bridleway, going down past Penlanwynt and Ffynnondici, eventually coming to a tar lane. Cross this and continue down to Tregynon Country Farmhouse. Here, fork left (west) down into the densely wooded Gwaun Valley once again, heading for a signposted footpath which crosses a wooden footbridge across the boggy valley floor. The path meets the road which runs down the valley. Turn right along this to Sychbant Picnic Site. (Or go left for about a mile to reach the Duffryn Arms.)

Stage 4: Sychbant to Newport
4¼ miles (7 km), 1½ hours

From Sychbant Picnic Site, follow the track up through the woodland into the forestry plantation. You finally emerge on the west side of the plantation from where a path leads to Bedd Morris standing stone, next to the lane which runs down towards Newport.

Turn right onto this lane. You can follow it all the way to Newport, or leave it for a short while by turning left onto a track about 100m before the first small conifer windbreak. Follow this downhill, keeping straight on until you reach a new farm track, where you turn right to rejoin the Newport road.

After 100m on the road, turn left onto a bridleway and follow this for about half a mile, traversing the hills above Newport. At the second footpath turn left (downhill) to the A487, where you turn right for the final few steps into town.

WALES

Wales – Long-Distance Paths

Owain Glyndwr's Way

Alternative Name Ffordd Owain Glyndwr
Distance 120 miles (215 km)
Duration 7 to 10 days
Start Knighton
Finish Welshpool
Regional Centres Shrewsbury, Birmingham, Machynlleth
County Powys
Area Central Wales
Summary An undulating walk mainly on good paths, farm tracks and minor roads through the quiet rolling hills and pretty valleys of mid-Wales. A few sections pass through bleak moorland where conditions are more difficult. Map and compass are essential.

The walk is named after Owain Glyndwr, the Welsh warrior-statesman who led an ill-fated rebellion against English rule in the early 15th century. It passes many sites connected with the rebellion, including the town of Machynlleth where Glyndwr held parliament as Prince of Wales.

The route follows 120 miles of path and lane through mid-Wales, the area between Snowdonia and the Brecon Beacons – a much quieter and less visited part of Wales, especially when compared to these busy national parks to the north and south. The walk is predominantly lowland moor or farmland, and takes in lakes, gentle hills and beautiful valleys.

From Knighton (which is close to the English border), the route heads west to Machynlleth (about 12 miles from the west coast) before heading north-east to Welshpool. (Both Knighton and Welshpool are on the Offa's Dyke Path. It would be easy to make this walk circular by returning to Knighton southwards down the Offa's Dyke Path.)

Although quite undulating, the route never rises above about 500m (and rarely drops below 200m). If you want peace, tran-

quillity and solitude then this walk is for you; it is not unusual to walk all day without meeting a soul.

The one downside to this walk is the rather high proportion of road-walking, perhaps as much as 25 miles in total. Fortunately, most of this is minor lanes and so the problem is not so much one of traffic, but the discomfort of having tar underfoot. Having said that, there is a three mile stretch leaving Machynlleth which is positively hazardous!

Powys County Council currently has a full-time project manager assigned to Glyndwr's Way, whose main aims are to improve the waymarking and reduce the amount of road-walking, so hopefully the situation will improve in due course. The council's intention is that the walk should be given national trail status.

DIRECTION, DISTANCE & DURATION

The route can be followed in either direction, but we describe it from Knighton to Welshpool simply because the available guidebooks go this way.

There is a variety of waymarking along the route; it can be erratic at times and often nonexistent. The most common waymark is a yellow arrow on a green aluminium plate but wooden posts with yellow or blue signs are also used. New signs being installed are on yellow, blue or white plastic discs.

The walk is 120 miles long. Poor waymarking, hilly conditions (and the fact that the same path never seems to be followed for long!) all add up to fairly slow going. If you normally average 2½ miles per hour walking, then don't be surprised to cover this walk at a rate of two miles per hour, or less. Getting lost is virtually inevitable!

Most people tackle the walk in eight to 10 days. We have described it in nine, although

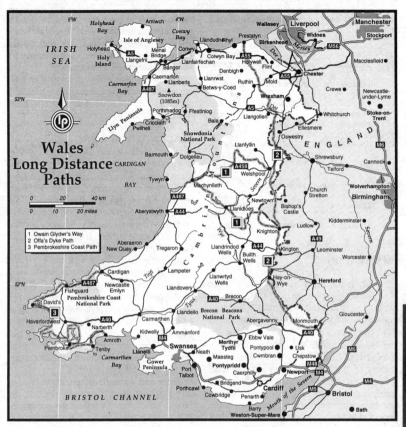

Wales
Long Distance Paths

Map key:
1 Owain Glydwr's Way
2 Offa's Dyke Path
3 Pembrokeshire Coast Path

Day 4 is long, and could be split into two, and Days 5 and 6 could be combined if you didn't want to stop in Machynlleth. Energetic walkers may feel the last two days can be combined by taking a short cut just prior to reaching Dolanog. Hours given in the route descriptions are approximate walking times only. You need to add more for lunch stops, map-reading (a lot on this route) and sightseeing. If you don't intend to camp, you need to plan your time around accommodation availability; it's sometimes scarce on this route, and this limits flexibility.

The town of Machynlleth is the halfway point of this walk and, if you don't wish to tackle the walk in one go, it has a train service to Shrewsbury (via Welshpool) from where you can get to most other parts of Britain.

Machynlleth would also be a good place to break for a day, possibly to the Centre for Alternative Technology or get the train to Aberystwyth.

STAGES
For a nine day walk, as described here, the

most convenient places to start and end each day are:

Day	From	To	Distance
1	Knighton	Felindre	13½ miles (21.5 km)
2	Felindre	Abbey Cwmhir	15 miles (24 km)
3	Abbey Cwmhir	Llanidloes	15 miles (24 km)
4	Llanidloes	Aberhosan	17 miles (27 km)
5	Aberhosan	Machynlleth	6 miles (9.5 km)
6	Machynlleth	Llanbrynmair	13 miles (21 km)
7	Llanbrynmair	Llanwddyn	17 miles (27 km)
8	Llanwddyn	Meifod	16 miles (25.5 km)
9	Meifod	Welshpool	8 miles (13 km)

INFORMATION

There are TICs at Knighton (☎ 01547 528753; it's known as the Offa's Dyke Centre), Machynlleth (☎ 01654 702401) and Welshpool (☎ 01938 552043). All can supply the *Glyndwr's Way Accommodation List* (10p), plus a series of 16 leaflets describing the route published by Powys County Council (£1.60). These describe some history of the route and surrounding area, and contain wildlife notes. The leaflets were published in 1977/8, and unfortunately have not been updated to take account of more recent changes to the route. It is important you also get a separate sheet called *Supplementary Information for Walkers*, which outlines changes and fills the gaps. If the TICs are out of stock, or you need more specific information, contact the Owain Glyndwr's Way Project Manager (☎ 01654 703376).

Books & Maps

Owain Glyndwr's Way by Richard Sale (Constable) is the route's only dedicated guidebook. This is as much a guide to the history of the area as to the actual route itself. Comprehensive at times, there are bits where you are left to find your own way. The hand-drawn maps are probably more useful than

the text, which sometimes 'wanders'. This is not a comprehensive guide (like those covering the more popular LDPs such as the Pennine Way or Coast to Coast in England); you definitely need a map as well.

Owain Glyndwr's Way is covered by Ordnance Survey (OS) Landranger (1:50,000) sheets 148, 136, 135, 125 and 126 (south to north).

PLACES TO STAY & EAT

You can cover the entire Glyndwr's Way without a tent, staying in B&Bs, pubs and guesthouses. We provide some suggestions in the route description. For a wider choice, use the *RA Yearbook* or the *National Trail Companion* (for details see the Books section of the Facts for the Walker chapter), or the *Glyndwr's Way Accommodation List* (see the above Information section).

Knighton and Welshpool have a good range of services, with several B&Bs, pubs and cafes. Elsewhere on the route, accommodation is fairly scarce and you need to plan around what is available. Booking in advance is essential on remote sections. Llanidloes and Machynlleth are the only two places of any size on the route, and both offer several pubs, hotels, shops, takeaways and restaurants. Make the most of them.

There are a couple of points to bear in mind when booking accommodation. Firstly, check exactly where the accommodation is in relation to the route. Just because the postal address is Machynlleth does not mean that the place is physically close to the town itself! Although this is true for any walk, it seems particularly so in Wales. Make it clear when you book that you are walking Glyndwr's Way; often you can arrange to get picked up from the route if the accommodation is some distance from it. The accommodation guide gives grid references for each place listed, so do use it. The second point is to make sure your accommodation offers (and you book) an evening meal when staying at a remote B&B.

If you wish to camp, several of the B&Bs in the *Accommodation List* offer camping facilities. As the route is generally very remote you can easily pitch a tent almost anywhere, although you must get permission when on private land. Although there are sufficient shops on the route for stocking up, they are far from plentiful so do plan ahead.

There are several pubs along the way for lunch-time stops, but on some days you will need to be self-sufficient. Note that in this part of Wales, some pubs keep traditional hours: open lunch times and evenings only.

GETTING THERE & AWAY
Bus
There is no bus service to Knighton, but the town can be reached by train. Midland Red operates several services a day between Shrewsbury and Welshpool. Contact Shrewsbury TIC (☎ 01743 350761) for more information.

Train
The easiest way to get to/from the walk is by train. Knighton is on the *Heart of Wales* line between Shrewsbury and Swansea, with four trains a day (three on Sunday). Welshpool is served by the *Cambrian Coaster* between Birmingham and Pwllheli – via Shrewsbury and Machynlleth – several trains a day.

Car
The route starts in Knighton, which can be reached from the A49 between Shrewsbury and Hereford by the A4113. From Welshpool, where the route finishes, the A458 leads to Shrewsbury.

THE ROUTE
The Start: Knighton
The border market town of Knighton sits on a hill set around a clocktower, with a good selection of pubs and shops, and a couple of banks. As well as being the start of our walk, Knighton is the halfway stage of the Offa's Dyke Path, which explains why Knighton's TIC (☎ 01547 528753) is in the Offa's Dyke Centre.

Knighton has neither the charm of Machy-

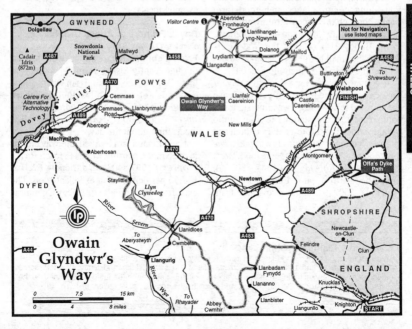

nlleth nor the appeal of Welshpool, so if you arrive early enough in the day it may be worth considering an immediate start to the walk. There are accommodation possibilities around Llancoch (six miles) and this makes a nice late-afternoon or early-evening walk.

Places doing B&B in Knighton include *The Red Lion* (☎ 01547 528231) with twin rooms for £30, *The Knighton Hotel* (☎ 01547 520530) at £64 for two people sharing, and *The Fleece House* (☎ 01547 520168), from £17 per person.

Day 1: Knighton to Felindre

13½ miles (21.5 km), 5 to 6 hours

The official start of the route is the clocktower in the centre of town. From here go up the picturesque 'narrows' (a narrow street of old houses dating from Tudor times) out onto the Llandrindod road. After a mile or so of road-walking, you'll come across a sign pointing right onto a track which follows the Wilcombe brook up its valley – a testing little climb!

Beyond here the terrain is easier, taking you along country lanes and good farm tracks, through this sheep-farming area with its green rolling hills and pretty valleys. From Bailey Hill (400m) the Way leads down to the small hamlet of Llancoch, about half a mile north of Llangunllo Station.

If you are looking for a short first day, or fancy a lunch-time pint, then you can leave the path and follow the railway line 1½ miles south (passing the station) to Llangunllo village, which has a 13th-century church and slightly younger but run-down pub, *The Greyhound*, which does not serve food. B&B is available at *Rhiwlas* (☎ 01547 550256), near the station, and *Cefnsuran Farm* (☎ 01547 550219), about two miles from

Llangunllo (pickup service available). Both provide evening meals on request and Cefnsuran Farm can provide transport to the *Hundred House Inn* in nearby Bleddfe where meals are available.

From Llancoch the route continues west to Ferley. The name comes from the Welsh 'fferllyd' meaning cold, and this is an indication of what is to come. After a couple of miles of hill-farming country, the Way leads onto open moorland, through heather and bracken round Pool Hill and on towards Beacon Hill. Routefinding is not easy on this stretch, which is in the process of being properly signed. It's easy to be seduced into following the main track which goes off to the west, but this makes regaining the route quite a trek – try to avoid it!

At Felindre, *The Wharf Inn* (☎ 01547 510209) does bar snacks, and the *village shop* (half-day closing on Thursday and Sunday) also offers B&B and camping, but no evening meal. *Trevland* (☎ 01547 510211) offers B&B from £15, and/or evening meals.

Day 2: Felindre to Abbey Cwmhir

15 miles (24 km), 6 to 7 hours

From Felindre the route is well signed through gently rising farming country to three Bronze Age tumuli, from where a lane descends for three miles to Llanbadarn Fynydd (7½ miles from Felindre). *The New Inn* (☎ 01597 840378) offers B&B as well as meals throughout the day.

From Llanbadarn Fynydd, the Way climbs to open moor, skirting woods to reach *Bwlch Farm* (☎ 01597 840366), a friendly B&B at £17.50 per person with excellent food. The walk from Bwlch Farm to Abbey Cwmhir is

Llananno & Llanbister Churches
The villages of Llananno and Llanbister can be easily reached from today's route. Although off the path, they have splendid churches which may be worth a visit. Llananno Church boasts some magnificent oak carving dating from the 15th century. Llanbister Church (beautifully positioned on the River Ithon) dates back to the 6th century and contains the original music gallery of 1716. ■

WALES

a delight. It begins with a fine ridge walk rising to a 450m summit, before dropping through Neuadd Fach wood into the lovely valley of Bachell Brook.

Abbey Cwmhir Abbey Cwmhir has a pub, *The Happy Union* (☎ 01597 851203), doing B&B and evening meals, and a shop. If both are closed then knock on either of the doors and the owners will open up for you. Other B&Bs include *Home Farm* (☎ 01597 851666), from £13, which also has camping facilities.

Little remains of the Cistercian abbey from which the village gets its name. It was founded in 1143 but never completed, although its plans would have made it one of the largest in Britain after York, Durham and Winchester. Owain Glyndwr destroyed the Abbey in 1401 after finding most of the monks to be English. This halted construction and the damage was never repaired. The abbey was finally closed in 1536 during Henry VIII's Dissolution of the Monasteries.

Day 3: Abbey Cwmhir to Llanidloes
15 miles (24 km), 6 to 7 hours
Be sure to stock up at Abbey Cwmhir as there are no shops or amenities until Llanidloes. The walk leaves Abbey Cwmhir opposite *The Happy Union* and follows a track up through the forest opposite, to join an ancient track known as The Monks Way; it's believed to have been used to connect Abbey Cwmhir with its sister house of Strata Flora. The track climbs through forest to the bleak Upper Esgair Hill (450m) before descending through open moor to the village of Bwlch-y-Sarnau. Good tracks lead from here to Blaentrinant, from where on a clear day you can see the peak of Cadair Idris, far to the north-west.

Beyond Blaentrinant a map is essential to follow the route which seems to zigzag its way to Newchapel (12 miles from Abbey Cwmhir). Don't let routefinding problems overshadow this glorious stretch of the walk, which has splendid views of the Dethenydd mountains. From Newchapel you cross a pretty wooded valley then join a lane leading down to Llanidloes.

Llanidloes Beautifully positioned on the River Severn (10 miles from its source), Llanidloes has a TIC (☎ 01686 412605) and much to offer visitors. Its main feature is the 16th-century market hall, a black and white timber-frame building in the centre of town. It is now a museum of local industry, after serving a variety of functions including Quaker meeting house and town prison. The church of St Idloes has magnificent arches thought to have come from Abbey Cwmhir. On a more practical side, Llanidloes has banks, a supermarket, a chemist, pubs, restaurants and takeaway food. There is also public transport if you need an escape route. The daily National Express coach between Aberystwyth and London's Victoria stops here. Midland Red also has a service to Shrewsbury; ask at the TIC for details.

Places to stay include *Lloyds' Hotel* (☎ 01686 412284), one of the first buildings you come to after you walk over the footbridge on the way into town, with B&B from £15, and the more lively *Red Lion* (☎ 01686 412270) where B&B starts at £28. The *Severn View Guesthouse* (☎ 01686 412207) is over the river (but on the route) with twin rooms for £30.

Day 4: Llanidloes to Aberhosan
17 miles (27 km), 7 to 8 hours
Once again, be sure to take advantage of the amenities in Llanidloes as there are no shops now until Machynlleth. Accommodation is also fairly sparse.

Leave Llanidloes north along Long Bridge St and turn left at the roundabout to cross the River Severn on Long Bridge. Then turn left onto the B4518, and follow this road for about three miles before taking a left sign at a cattle grid down to Bryntail Farm. The track now descends into the Clywedog Valley and you suddenly find yourself at the foot of the rather intimidating 65m (212ft) concrete wall of Clywedog Dam. A steep climb takes you back up the other side of the dam (along the road) to impressive views of the 6½ mile long Clywedog Reservoir and its forest-sloped surrounds.

You follow the edge of the water for

several miles, rejoining a tar lane before entering the daunting Hafren forest, which contains about 17 sq miles of conifer plantation. Luckily our route only cuts through the north-east corner! Leaving the forest, follow the road down to the B4518 just north of Staylittle.

Go left on the B4518 then almost immediately take a track left up to open moor. The *Star Inn* (☎ 01650 521345) at Dylife, about a mile further along the B4518, does meals and B&B from £17. Routefinding is easy as you follow an exposed track to the summit of Penycrocbren, then drop to a mountain road where B&B is available at *Rhydy Porthmyn* (☎ 01650 521433), an 18th-century drovers' inn, halfway between Llanidloes and Machynlleth.

Glyndwr's Way now climbs over the Plynlimon range through moorland that can be bleak in bad weather. Leave the road on a track towards Glaslyn lake, then take a less distinct track off to the right, which descends down a beautiful, partially wooded valley to Aberhosan.

Aberhosan B&B is available at *Caeheulon* (☎ 01654 703243) from £16.50; it is slightly off the track but a lift service is available. Alternatively, if you have the energy, follow Glyndwr's Way up the steep hill of Cefn Modfedd out of Aberhosan and instead of turning right as you approach the summit, go straight on to *Talbontdrain* (☎ 01654 702192) with twin rooms at £30. This remote farm has an idyllic setting and the food is superb. From here you can follow the minor road straight down to Machynlleth, rejoining Glyndwr's Way as you do so the next morning. It is about an hour's walk from Talbontdrain to Machynlleth.

Day 5: Aberhosan to Machynlleth
6 miles (9.5 km), 2 to 3 hours
This is an easy day, although the climb out of Aberhosan up Cefn Modfedd is quite demanding, but it's not long before the Way is signed off right to drop down to Blaen-y-pant. The path leads to the village of Forge

before following the road into Machynlleth. Take the rest of the day off – you've earnt it.

Machynlleth Machynlleth is a good place for a rest-day. If you don't wish to tackle the whole walk, or if your feet are giving up on you, then this is a good place to escape, with several trains per day to Shrewsbury and Birmingham. If you want a change of scene, to the south-west lie the coastal resorts of Borth and Aberystwyth, and just a few miles north are the mountains of Snowdonia. The Centre for Alternative Technology is four miles north of Machynlleth and can be easily reached by bus. For information on this and other attractions in the area contact the TIC (☎ 01654 702401).

Places to stay in Machynlleth include the appropriately named *Glyndwr Hotel* (☎ 01654 703989), the lively *Dyfi Forester Inn* (☎ 01654 702004) and the quieter *Pendre Guesthouse* (☎ 01654 702088), all with B&B for around £15 and evening meals available.

Day 6: Machynlleth to Llanbrynmair
13 miles (21 km), 5 to 6 hours
The route begins with a treacherous three mile stretch of road-walking, which you thankfully leave by a track to the right soon after Penegloes. The track climbs to open country before descending to the quiet village of Abercegir. Routefinding on this stretch, and indeed for the rest of the day, is easy, with good waymarking.

From Abercegir the route once again climbs onto open moor. Along these hilltops are lovely views of Cadair Idris as you follow a distinct track before descending to Cemmaes Rd. At the junction of three major roads, it is not a particularly pleasant place to delay, but there is a very welcome shop at the petrol station.

The five mile walk from Cemmaes to Llanbrynmair is truly a delight, through rolling hills and pleasant scenic valleys. Although the initial climb out of Cemmaes is quite steep the going is easy. After climbing to a derelict farm, Rhyd-yr-aderyn, the route descends towards Llanbrynmair passing beautiful rowan trees. It's a shame

WALES

the day finishes with a couple more miles of more road-walking.

Llanbrynmair has a shop (open to 8 pm) and a pub, *The Wynnstay Arms* (☎ 01650 521431), which offers double rooms at £26 for B&B, and evening meals.

Day 7: Llanbrynmair to Llanwddyn
17 miles (27 km), 8 to 9 hours

If you have managed to get this far without a compass then expect to use it today. This stage includes the most inhospitable stretches of the walk. It is, however, possible to split this day, breaking at Llangadfan (10 miles), the only place where shelter and refreshment can be found – although beyond here you can rest easy knowing that the worst is over.

Soon after leaving Llanbrynmair the route climbs past Hen Chapel to a stretch of bleak open moor before dropping down through a forestry plantation to join a lane which follows the River Gam to Dolwen Farm. Waymarking on the moor is not too bad but it is easy to get lost in the plantation. However, your compass should ensure you meet the lane at some point (even if not the correct one!).

East of Dolwen Farm you cross a particularly lonely stretch of moor. A compass is needed for this stretch, but following the line of the bottom of the bracken is a reasonable indication of the direction required. If in doubt, you can drop east to a road and then follow that into Llangadfan; bad weather makes this hard to avoid!

Llangadfan has a shop at the petrol station, and the *Cann Office Hotel* (☎ 01938 820202) serves meals at lunch time and in the evenings and also offers B&B from around £18.

The final seven mile forested walk from Llangadfan to Llanwddyn is well signed and easy under the feet. The Dyfnant forest is a huge plantation with a maze of forestry tracks but blue or yellow arrows will keep you on course for this pleasant walk to Lake Vyrnwy and its impressive dam with 33 arches. This is also a Royal Society for the Protection of Birds (RSPB) reserve. The route passes the Lake Vyrnwy Visitor Centre & TIC (☎ 01691 870346) and RSPB shop (☎ 01691 870278).

Places to stay in the area include the *Lake Vyrnwy Hotel*, which is rather expensive with twin rooms starting at £80. More affordable is the *Froheulog Caravan Park* (☎ 01691 870662) offering B&B from £15 with an exceptionally friendly welcome for walkers – more than adequate compensation for being at the top of a rather steep hill!

Day 8: Llanwddyn to Meifod
16 miles (25.5 km), 6 to 7 hours

The going is quite easy from now to the end of the route, as bleak moorland is replaced by pretty valleys, pleasant riverside walks and gentle farmland. Waymarking is also good on this section.

From Llanwddyn the route follows forest tracks and minor roads to the village of Llwydiarth where there is a shop. Briefly follow the B4395 from Llwydiarth, then go left just before Pont Llogel Bridge to follow the River Vyrnwy for a mile or so before leaving it to go left, back up to the higher ground. (It is possible to follow the pleasant riverside walk all the way to Dolanog, joining the Ann Griffiths Walk – named after the famous composer of Welsh hymns and rejoining Glyndwr's Way at Dolanog. As this also shortens the walk by three or four miles it makes it quite possible to reach Welshpool today if you are feeling reasonably energetic.)

Dolanog has a shop with limited supplies, and from here the route is never far from the Vyrnwy, starting with a lovely stretch through woods before climbing slightly away from the river to follow a minor lane into the village of Pontrobert. There is a shop here and also a pub, the *Royal Oak Inn* (☎ 01938 500243), offering B&B and food.

The path continues to follow the river through gentle farmland before climbing Gallt yr Ancr (Hill of the Anchorite) and descending through Duffryn Hall wood to Meifod. *Glascoed* (☎ 01938 500365) does B&B with excellent food. Nearby *The King's*

WALES

Owain Glyndwr

Owain Glyndwr is a Welsh hero, but suprisingly little is known about him. Some of the most detailed, but often highly embellished, stories of his life emerge from the writings of the Welsh bards (poets), especially the work of one Iolo Goch.

From these writings we know that Owain Glyndwr was the son of a wealthy landowner, descended from the royal houses of Powys and Gwynedd, and lived in Wales in the second half of the 14th century. As was common in those times, he became a squire to the English nobility, in particular to Henry of Bolingbroke, later King Henry IV. (Wales had been ruled by the English since the campaigns of Edward I, between 1272 and 1307.) Glyndwr fought for the English army in mainland Europe and in Scotland, and then settled in mid-Wales with his wife and children. He was a cultured man, speaking English, Welsh, Latin and French. Little may have ever been heard of him had not his neighbour Reginald Grey, Lord of Ruthin, stolen some land from him.

Glyndwr decided to fight Grey in court, but the Welsh people were regarded as barbarians by most of the English and the case was dismissed, apparently with the words 'What care we for barefoot Welsh dogs?' At around the same time Henry IV was engaged in a military campaign in Scotland. Glyndwr refused to take part, and was labelled a traitor by the king. He was forced to flee his home for some time, but it is recorded that on 16 September 1400, Glyndwr met his brothers and a few close associates at Glyndyfrdwy, on the banks of the River Dee. A flag showing the red dragon of Wales was raised, and he was proclaimed the Prince of Wales – a deliberate stand against English rule. So began a long, drawn-out fight for Welsh independence.

No single event seems to have provoked the Welsh rebellion, but the persistent demeaning of the Welsh by their neighbours was brought to a head by Glyndwr's humiliation. Carried along on this tide of hatred, and doubtless bearing his own grievances, Glyndwr became a beacon of hope. He was glorified by the Welsh bards, who created the image of a hero with magical powers in contact with the spirits.

Glyndwr's first move against the English was disastrous; his army was routed in Ruthin and in Anglesey. Royal pardons followed, and that would have been the end of it, if the English parliament had not passed draconian laws preventing a Welshman from living in England, holding official office or marrying an English woman. The Welsh rose again, occupying Conwy Castle in 1401, while Glyndwr moved into mid-Wales with a small army. He defeated the English in heroic fashion at Hyddgen, but lacking military strength, he sued for peace with Henry. Under pressure from his barons, Henry would not agree to a treaty, so in early 1402 Glyndwr's army devastated North Wales. They laid seige to Harlech and Caernarfon castles before moving south again, where they had a decisive victory against the English at Pilleth near Knighton. Continuing south, they ransacked Abergavenny and Cardiff. Henry, in retaliation, invaded Wales with 100,000 troops but, after a fortnight of storms and no sign of the enemy, they retreated, many confirmed in their belief that Glyndwr was in league with the spirits and could command the elements.

By the end of 1403 Glyndwr controlled most of Wales, and in early 1404 he captured Harlech Castle, moving in there with his family. Secure in his position as the Prince of Wales he called the first Welsh parliament at Machynlleth. French and Spanish representatives attended the parliament, and a treaty was signed between Wales and France. The French failed in their promise to send military support, and events began to turn sour as a new protagonist appeared on the English scene: Prince Henry, son of Henry IV, and hero of the Battle of Agincourt. Warlike in temperament, and far more determined than his father to trounce the Welsh, he delivered shattering blows to the Welsh army at Grosmont and Usk. The people of South Wales began to renounce the rebellion, and Glyndwr's position started to look shaky, particularly when Beaumaris Castle on Anglesey was recaptured by the English.

Help for Glyndwr arrived in two forms. The Archbishop of York led the people of Northumbria in revolt against the king, so distracting his attention from the Welsh renegades, and the French finally sent troops to support the Welsh. Greatly encouraged, Owain Glyndwr led the last invasion of England in August 1405. It was a huge anticlimax, and the Welsh retreated without a serious battle being fought.

Welsh fortunes declined further in 1406, with Prince Henry wreacking havoc in the south, and Glyndwr was forced to retreat to the north. His hopes and plans for a Wales free of its English oppressors were shattered, and gradually the English regained control. There was no last glorious stand, and around 1406 Glyndwr simply disappeared. Theories have him dying anonymously in battle, or spending his last years wandering in the mountains, living quietly among friends. The Welsh bards paint a more romantic picture of him sleeping in a hidden cave with his followers, waiting for the right moment to rise again against the English. The only sure thing is that nobody knows. ■

Head (☎ 01938-500256) also does B&B and meals.

Day 9: Meifod to Welshpool
8 miles (13 km), 3 to 4 hours

The day starts with a steep climb through woods out of the vale of Meifod, the views behind just about compensating for the sweat! The walking to Welshpool is easy-going on minor roads, through farmland and small copses. The last four miles (after the caravan park at Pant) are entirely on tar, which is rather hard on the feet at this late stage, but brings you into the centre of Welshpool. There doesn't seem to be an official end to the walk, but a visit to Powis Castle on the edge of town will more than suffice if you want a fitting finale. The castle dates from the 11th century, and is thought to have been the site of one of the Glyndwr rebellion's last battles. (For more details, see the aside on Powis Castle in the Offa's Dyke Path section of this chapter.)

If you are still in the mood for more, or just need a pleasant way back to Knighton, two miles east of Welshpool is Hope village where you can join the Offa's Dyke Path and head south.

Welshpool Welshpool, known as the 'Gateway to Wales' (although many border towns claim this title), is situated in the valley of the River Severn, separated from England˙ by Long Mountain and the Breidden Hills. Of English Georgian character, rather than Welsh, it attracts many tourists and has *cafes, pubs* and *hotels* galore. There are several trains a day to Shrewsbury and Birmingham.

For a place to stay, Welshpool has several possibilities catering for all budgets. If you want to celebrate the end of the walk in style, *The Royal Oak* (☎ 01938 552217), in the centre of town, has double rooms at £70 and also does good food. Other B&B options include *Hafren Guesthouse* (☎ 01938 554112) on Salop Road, *Tresi-Aur* (☎ 01938 552430) on Brookfield Road, and *Severn Farm* (☎ 01938 553098), all around £14.

The TIC can provide other alternatives.

Offa's Dyke Path

Official Name Offa's Dyke Path National Trail (Llwybr Clawdd Offa)
Distance 177 miles (285 km)
Duration 9 to 12 days
Start Sedbury Cliffs
Finish Prestatyn Beach
Regional Centres Newport, Welshpool, Hereford and Chester
Counties Gloucestershire, Gwent, Hereford & Worcester, Powys, Clwyd
Areas England/Wales border (Welsh Marches)
Summary A well-trodden route through varied and historically potent terrain, usually easy to follow but some sections strenuous with continual ascents and descents. This route is suitable for fit, well-equipped and prepared walkers competent with a map and compass. There are over 700 stiles to climb, so don't carry too much in your pack.

Offa's Dyke was a grand linear earthwork pivotal in the history of the Welsh Marches (the border of Mercia and Wales). It was conceived and executed in the 8th century by the Mercian king Offa, to keep back the Welsh to the west. Today, at least 80 miles of the ditches and banks remain, and the border between England and Wales continues to be defined roughly by the dyke.

Offa's Dyke Path (ODP) runs from the Severn Estuary at Chepstow in the south through the beautiful Wye Valley and Shropshire Hills to end on the coast at Prestatyn in North Wales. The Path, rather than sticking religiously to the dyke, which is overgrown in some places and built over in others, detours along quiet valleys and ridges offering the walker a tremendous range of scenery.

You walk from river flatland to hill country, through oak forests, heathland and bracken. You'll see dense and dark conifer forest and the patchwork of green fields bound by hedges. The track also comprises high moors and the more exacting mountainous conditions of the Clwydian range in the north. The Welsh Marches are dotted with ruined castles and abbeys, ancient hillforts,

WALES

and even some sections of Roman roads. You'll also go along canal towpaths and past other monuments to the Industrial Revolution.

You'll walk through some remote country, but sometimes are near places serviced (if infrequently) by public transport. Offa's Dyke Path links villages offering a good range of accommodation options.

DIRECTION, DISTANCE & DURATION

Offa's Dyke Path is best done from the south to the north coast: from the Severn Estuary near Chepstow to the Dee Estuary at Prestatyn. The sun and wind will be mostly on your back, and the popular guidebooks describe the walk this way. Offa's Dyke Path is generally well waymarked, but routefinding will be easier if you are conscientious about following the white acorn markers; don't be fooled by the numerous other footpath and bridleway markers.

The total length of Offa's Dyke Path is 177 miles. Walking about 12 miles a day is a comfortable average in this terrain. You will meet people racing to cover the distance in nine days, but to really take in what this walk has to offer, we recommend two weeks. It's a good idea to allow for a rest-day around Hay-on-Wye, and more time for sightseeing off the path, for example visiting Tintern Abbey or Powis Castle in Welshpool.

Short cuts, for those with less time or energy, include parts of the Wye Valley Walk, including the valley floor north of Redbrook to Monmouth, rather than ascending to rejoin Offa's Dyke Path.

If you aren't fond of very strenuous walking, the days between Knighton and Brompton Crossroads and the second last day from Llandegla to Bodfari are the most demanding physically. You could divide each of these sections into two walking days (stopping at Newcastle and at the Druid Inn in Llanferres near Mold).

STAGES

For a 12 day walk, the most convenient stages are:

Day	From	To	Distance
1	Sedbury Cliffs	Monmouth	17½ miles (28 km)
2	Monmouth	Pandy	17 miles (27 km)
3	Pandy	Hay-on-Wye	17½ miles (28 km)
4	Hay-on-Wye	Kington	15 miles (24 km)
5	Kington	Knighton	13½ miles (22 km)
6	Knighton	Brompton Crossroads	15 miles (24 km)
7	Brompton Crossroads	Buttington Bridge	12½ miles (20 km)
8	Buttington Bridge	Llanymynech	10½ miles (17 km)
9	Llanymynech	Chirk Mill	14 miles (22.5 km
10	Chirk Mill	Llandegla	16 miles (25 km)
11	Llandegla	Bodfari	17 miles (27 km)
12	Bodfari	Prestatyn	12 miles (20 km)

INFORMATION

There are Offa's Dyke information offices at Chepstow and Prestatyn. TICs at various places along the way, including Tintern and Hay-on-Wye, stock Offa's Dyke Path material. The Offa's Dyke Association (ODA) Information Office and Heritage Centre (☎ 01547 528753), West St, Knighton, Powys LD7 1EW, aims to conserve the Welsh border region along Offa's Dyke Path and educate people about it. Membership costs £14 and student concession rates are available.

Books

The ODA publishes various good-value booklets: *Offa's Dyke Path – Where to Stay, How to Get There & Other Useful Information* (£1.40); *Backpackers' & Camping List*; *Accommodation & Transport* (£1.70); *Offa's Dyke South to North Route Notes* (and a similar publication for the north-to-south route) (£ 1.20) and a not-so-clear set of strip maps (£2.50). All are available from the ODA Information Office and Heritage Centre, or from TICs along the route.

The *Offa's Dyke Path National Trail Guide* covers the walk in two books:

WALES

Chepstow to Knighton by Ernie & Kathy Kay and *Knighton to Prestatyn* by Mark Richards (published by Arum Press, £9.99). *Langton's Guide to Offa's Dyke Path* (published by Langton, £12.99) covers the route in one book, with much practical information (such as accommodation and transport) also crammed in.

Walking Offa's Dyke Path – A journey through the border country of England and Wales by David Hunter (Cicerone, £8.99) is recommended for its extensive background information and much practical information in a handy format. The sketch maps are adequate together with the route descriptions provided.

Aerofilms Guide: Offa's Dyke Path (South) and Wye River Valley (Ian Allen Publishing, £9.99) covers the walk with an interesting collection of aerial photographs with the trail superimposed.

Maps

Take a compass and a good set of maps, as there will be times when you need them. The route is covered by OS Landranger (1:50,000) sheets 162, 161, 148, 137, 126, 117 and 116. Outdoor Leisure (1:25,000) sheets 14 and 13 cover the southern part of the walk. Many people seem to rely on the two-volume Aurum Press publications which contain the relevant sections of OS 1:25,000 maps, but these are limiting if you have to leave the route.

LOCAL SERVICES

Offa's Dyke Baggage Carriers (☎ 01497 821266), Hay-on-Wye, collects and transports luggage along the route. Some B&Bs and hotels also provide a luggage-transporting service.

PLACES TO STAY & EAT

You can cover the entire Offa's Dyke Path using hotels, B&Bs or youth hostels. We provide some suggestions in the route description. For a wider choice, use the *RA Yearbook* and the *National Trail Companion* (details in the Books section of the Facts for the Walker chapter), or the *Offa's Dyke Path – Where to Stay, How to Get There & Other Useful Information* booklet, published annu-

ally by ODA, which also lists helpful extras like places doing packed lunches, and luggage/people transport services. (For these extras ask the price in advance.)

It's also possible to camp the whole way; there are several campsites on or near the route plus many other places where you could pitch a tent. The ODA has a *Backpackers' & Camping List*, although sites are listed north to south.

The Path is well served by a range of pubs, cafes, restaurants and shops where you can buy food and drink. Note that many pubs in this part of the world keep traditional hours and so will be closed from 3 to 7 pm, and possibly all day Sunday.

GETTING THERE & AWAY
Bus

You can reach Chepstow and Prestatyn by National Express coaches from most parts of Britain. Local bus services to points on or near Offa's Dyke Path are listed in the ODA's *Where to Stay* booklet.

Train

You can go by train to Chepstow (usually via Newport) and Prestatyn (on the Chester to Holyhead line), which both have regular services to other parts of the country.

Car

The route starts at Chepstow, reached by leaving the motorway immediately after you've crossed the Severn Bridge coming from England. Parking cars for the duration of the walk is offered by arrangement by some of the places to stay (see the ODA's *Where to Stay* handbook for details).

At the end of the walk, Prestatyn is on the A548 between Llandudno and Chester.

THE ROUTE

This is one possible itinerary: alternative overnight stops are suggested in the route description, as are several short cuts or escape routes.

The Start: Chepstow

Near the confluence of the Wye and Severn

WALES

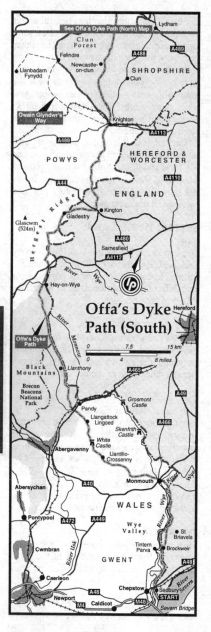

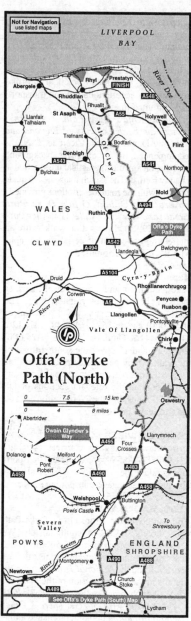

rivers, Chepstow was first developed as a base for the Norman conquest of south-east Wales. It later prospered as a port for the timber and wine trades, but as river-borne commerce declined, so Chepstow's importance diminished to that of a typical market town.

The main attraction in town is the fairly well-preserved Chepstow Castle on the towering cliffs of the River Wye. Construction began in 1067, making it the first stone castle in Wales, perhaps in Britain. The castle (☎ 01291 624065) is open daily from 9.30 am to 6.30 pm in summer, and until 4 pm in winter; entry is £2.90. The helpful TIC (☎ 01291 623772) is nearby.

There is a good range of places to stay and eat including several along Bridge St. Near the start of the walk, there's *Upper Sedbury House* (☎ 01291 627173) on Sedbury Lane, where B&B costs £15 per person and camping costs £2.50. *Langcroft* (☎ 01291 625569), 71 St Kingsmark Ave, a short walk from the centre, charges £15. On Bridge St, the *Afon Gwy* (☎ 01291 620158) has ensuite B&B overlooking the river for £32, a good

restaurant and bar meals for around £5. The friendly *Bridge Inn* offers large sandwiches for £3.25, and good bar snacks for around £5.

Day 1: Sedbury Cliffs to Monmouth

17½ miles (28 km), 9 hours

The official start of Offa's Dyke Path is Sedbury Cliffs, with views over the estuary and mudflats of the River Severn, from where the route makes its way through a housing estate and through Chepstow town. Many walkers avoid this relatively boring patch by starting at Chepstow Castle, crossing the nearby old bridge and going up a footpath to join Offa's Dyke Path on the north side of the river. Offa's Dyke Path then leads through a maze of small farms and past some grand old houses, over a range of wooded hills providing some scenic lookouts and steep ascents.

This is one of the longest walking days on Offa's Dyke Path and is physically demanding if you're not in peak condition. You could consider combining parts of the Wye Valley Walk with Offa's Dyke Path between Tintern

Tintern & Tintern Abbey

The tall walls and empty, arched windows of Tintern Abbey, a 14th-century Cistercian abbey on the banks of the River Wye, have been painted by Turner and lauded by Wordsworth. It's one of the most beautiful ruins in Britain. As a result, the village of Tintern swarms with visitors in summer. The abbey ruins are awe-inspiring, though best visited towards the end of the day, after the crowds have dispersed.

This Cistercian house was founded in 1131 by Walter de Clare, but the present building dates largely from the 14th century. It lasted until the Dissolution, and, when compared with other religious sites that were laid to waste at this time, a remarkable amount remains.

The abbey (☎ 01291 689251) is open from late March to late October, daily 9.30 am to 6.30 pm, and from November to March, Monday to Saturday, from 9.30 am to 4 pm, and from 2 to 4 pm on Sunday. Entry is £2.

Tintern village extends along the course of the River Wye – the abbey ruins are on the west bank. The TIC (☎ 01291 689566) is north of the town at the old railway station, quite a way from the abbey. Snacks are available.

If you decide to stay in the area, there's a good selection of B&Bs and hotels in Tintern village, especially near the river. Recommended is the comfortable *Valley House* (☎ 01291 689652) on Raglan Rd. B&B costs £17.50 per person with ensuite. The up-market *Parva Farmhouse Hotel* (☎ 0129 689411; fax 689557) charges £24 per person or £29 for a room with a river view. A four-course evening meal costs £16.50.

The *Royal George Hotel*, on the corner of Raglan Rd, prides itself on its chef and serves a full meal for £17 in its restaurant. You can ask to see the bar meals menu and sample the excellent food for considerably less. Try the tasty cheese-and-leek Welsh pie for £5.50.

The *Abbey Mill*, on your left as you approach the main road after crossing the footbridge over the Wye River (after you've descending from Offa's Dyke Path), closes early at around 5.30 pm but has pleasant outdoor tables where you can enjoy a drink. ■

and Monmouth, especially north of Redbrook. Alternatively, if you arrive at Chepstow around midday, visit the impressive castle, then walk to Tintern for the night. See famous Tintern Abbey and go on to Monmouth the next day. (If time is really short, there's a regular Red & White bus service between Chepstow and Monmouth, via Tintern.)

The scenic ruins of Tintern Abbey (see aside), which inspired Wordsworth to compose his 'lines', are visible from the path at two main lookouts in Tintern Woods. To reach the Abbey you drop downhill from Offa's Dyke Path. To save you slogging all the way back up again, a footpath runs from Tintern to rejoin Offa's Dyke Path at Brockweir.

At Brockweir, Offa's Dyke Path divides into upper and lower (flatter but a mile longer) alternatives. Nearby, the *Country Inn* (☎ 02191 689548) might be suitable for lunch or overnight (B&B costs £17.50). The upper and lower routes rejoin at Bigsweir Bridge. From here, you could head east to St Briavels (1½ miles off Offa's Dyke Path) where the *YHA Hostel* (☎ 01594 530272, £8.25) is in the 800 year old castle. The nearby *Crown Inn* (☎ 01594 530205) serves meals until 9.30 pm.

Beyond here, the next settlement is Redbrook, which has shop, and a *Little Chef* roadside restaurant further along the Wye Valley. B&Bs include the *Old Brewery House* (☎ 01600 712569), by the river, from £12.50, and *Tresco* (☎ 01600 712325) which costs £13.50.

After Redbrook you won't see the original Offa's Dyke again until near Knighton, another 54 miles on. From Redbrook you could opt to follow part of the Wye Valley Walk – an easy stroll on flat ground all the way, with the odd stinging nettle or bramble the only hardships – along the river to Monmouth.

Monmouth This small town, on the Welsh west bank, is at the confluence of the rivers Wye and Monnow. The beautiful and unique

13th-century stone-gated Monnow Bridge was built as part of the city defences.

The TIC (☎ 01600 713899) is at Shire Hall on Agincourt Square – the centre of town. The Nelson Museum & Local History Centre (☎ 01600 713519), on Priory St, is open all year and worth a visit.

Places to stay include the *YHA Hostel* (☎ 01600 715116, £6.75, camping £3.50). *Monnow Bridge Caravan & Camping* (☎ 01600 714004), near the bridge, charges from £2 per tent. Friendly *Steeples B&B* (☎ 01600 712600), over the cafe on Church St, charges £20 for rooms with ensuite. The *Riverside Hotel* (☎ 01600 715577), Cinderhill St, is the smartest place in town, charging from £34 per person for rooms with ensuite. The food and drink at the *Green Dragon* are highly recommended. There are several other eating places around or near Agincourt Square including the *Punch House* and the *Bull Inn*. Self-caterers will find *supermarkets* and *bakeries*.

There are regular buses between Monmouth and Chepstow, Lydney and Coleford, and Hereford and Newport (the nearest railway stations). Taxi services include Whiteways (☎ 01600 716274).

Day 2: Monmouth to Pandy
17 miles (27 km), 9 hours

This is one of the longer days, featuring leisurely walking with many pleasant views over the rolling countryside. The area is largely devoted to sheep farming. Walkers can lose their way around the Hendre Farm, so it helps to have a good map handy.

One of the highlights of the day is White Castle (about 11 miles from Monmouth), a 13th-century Norman castle complete with moat. (You could consider taking the castle's alternative route (31 miles) which follows higher ground than Offa's Dyke Path past Pembridge, Skenfrith, Grosmont and Longtown castles to rejoin Offa's Dyke Path near Pen-y-Beacon on the Black Mountains.)

At Llantilio Crossenny is an *inn* and *B&B* in the 16th-century farmhouse, *Little Treadham Farm* (☎ 01600 85326). At Llangattock Lingoed there's another *inn*, plus

WALES

Crossways Farm and *Old Court* where B&B costs around £14.

Towards the end of the day's walk, a steep mountain to the west (the Skirrid) dominates the landscape. A few miles on, a long flat mountain comes into view with the small town of Pandy just below it – this is Hatterall Ridge, part of the Black Mountains and the easternmost part of Brecon Beacons National Park, which you'll cross the next day.

In Pandy, the *Lancaster Arms* on Offa's Dyke Path at the foot of the Black Mountains caters well for walkers. B&B costs £17.50 with ensuite, and you can order a packed lunch or enjoy an evening bar meal for around £5. Pandy is on the A465, on the bus route between Abergavenny and Hereford. There is also the *Park Hotel* (☎ 01873 890271) with B&B from £18 to £24.

Day 3: Pandy to Hay-on-Wye

17½ miles (28 km), 9½ hours

This day takes you to the highest section of the walk and some of its most exposed country at the top of the Black Mountains. The walk is long and tiring and calls for stamina.

Extremes of weather may also be encountered, so be well prepared. You can get anything from snow to strong winds and sunshine up here. (Many walkers elect to have a rest in Hay-on-Wye the next day.)

Offa's Dyke Path begins with a long, steady climb to the first summit at 464m, then continues with an easy, gradual climb to the highest point at 703m over the next seven miles. The views, particularly over the patchwork of farmlands to the east, are spectacular on a clear day.

The ground cover on the ridge is bracken or peat which can turn into dust in dry summer conditions, but when it rains it becomes very boggy. The high country is fairly bleak – various cairns dot the landscape. There are no trees, almost no shelter and limited escape routes. The temperature will be a few degrees cooler than in the valleys below and winds will be stronger up here. There is often fog or low cloud on the

mountain. In places the ridge becomes fairly wide and there are several paths – a map and compass are essential. In short, be prepared for adverse weather, as you can expect to spend six hours crossing the mountain.

From Hay Bluff (Pen-y-Beacon), the northern end of Hatterall Ridge at 677m (2221 ft), there are extensive views to the east, north and west; there's also one of the steepest descents of the whole walk – down to the tarred road and car park below. Hay-on-Wye, from the ridgetop, seems near but is still four miles or 2½ hours away, mostly downhill through farmland.

(An alternative to staying on Hatterall Ridge all day is to descend into the Vale of Ewyas to the west after only three miles on the mountain. The scenery here is less bleak, with Llanthony Abbey – only a mile from Offa's Dyke Path – a highlight. From here it is possible to walk along the lane northwards to Hay-on-Wye. Allow two hours for a side trip to the abbey.)

Off the mountain there's accommodation at Longtown. *Olchon Cottage Farm* (☎ 01873 860233), half a mile from Offa's Dyke Path on Turnant Rd, offers B&B for £14 in an old, converted barn-farmhouse.

If you want to break this stage, at Llanthony there's the small and friendly *Half Moon Hotel* (☎ 01873 890611) where B&B costs £17 to £20. Capel-y-Ffin *YHA Hostel* (☎ 01873 890650, £6.75, camping £3.50) is 2½ miles from Offa's Dyke Path, eight miles south of Hay-on-Wye.

Hay-on-Wye If you have time, spend a well-earned rest-day here. There's an excellent range of places to stay and eat in town plus the almost 30 second-hand bookshops for which the town is world famous.

The friendly *Rest for the Tired* (☎ 01497 820550), a 16th-century building at 6 Broad St, does B&B for £16 with ensuite. The recommended *Cwm Dulais House* (☎ 01497 820640), Heol y Dwr, costs £15 per person; while *Hendre*, on Bear St, charges £14 per person in winter and £16 in summer. The more up-market *Old Black Lion* (☎ 01497 820841), on Lion St, charges £22 for ensuite

WALES

B&B, and serves excellent meals in its restaurant if you want to splurge. The bar meals are cheaper but of the same high standard. *The Granary* offers a good selection of delicious food. You can have a main course with cake and coffee for under £7. The *Blue Boar* serves authentic Thai food.

Day 4: Hay-on-Wye to Kington
15 miles (24 km), 7½ hours
This day is full of contrasts. Beginning with a pleasant stroll along the River Wye, the path turns left up a valley of dense conifer forest, climbing to a succession of country lanes and fields. After three miles of undulating tracks you arrive at Newchurch, a minor cluster of houses, a cemetery and post office. (One little stretch to take care on is at Bronydd Farm, about half an hour out of Hay-on-Wye. Someone has replaced the official waymarks with blue plastic markers, which may be less obvious from a distance.)

Leaving Newchurch, the path climbs again to moors, through Hill Farm with one of the few water taps on the route. Another two miles takes you to Gladestry which has a post office, pub, and infrequent bus services.

From Gladestry go up steeply onto the moorlands of Hergest Ridge, with extensive views in all directions including south-west to the Black Mountains, and a popular strolling destination for Kington's residents.

As you approach Kington, descending through the bracken, stay alert and make sure you follow the national trail and Offa's Dyke markers – there are several walking tracks and bridleways up here. The special Hergest Croft Gardens on Offa's Dyke Path into town are open from late March until October from 1.30 to 6.30 pm.

In Kington (a former Saxon town which has seen better days), the faded *Burton Hotel* (☎ 01544 230323) on Mill St is expensive (£27.50). Other more welcoming places to stay include *Church House* (☎ 01544 230534), on Church Rd, with B&B from £17.50 and *Cambridge Cottage* (☎ 01544 231300), at 19 Church St, with B&B from £12.

Day 5: Kington to Knighton
13½ miles (22 km), 8 hours
This stretch is quite short, but other than that it's an average day for Offa's Dyke Path: through hill country, with moderate ascents, some shelter and no supplies en route. It's fairly easy to have your packs sent on to Knighton from Kington because of the direct road linking the two towns. Carrying less on your back is highly recommended from here on as the increasing gradients and frequency of the hills make the walking much tougher.

Head out of town by crossing a dangerously busy road to begin your ascent through the fields to the highest golf course in England – watch out for flying golf balls as you cross the fairway. You'll soon rejoin the dyke (which often reaches five to seven metres high on this day) near Three Yews and stay on it most of the day. You'll cross heathland and walk through conifer forest. Enjoy the views down pretty green valleys as the dyke and Offa's Dyke Path again takes to the ridges. You'll pass historic Burfa Farm, a restored medieval farmhouse and nearby Burfa hillfort, before descending steeply into Knighton.

Knighton There is an austerity about Knighton (Trefyclawdd in Welsh – 'town on the dyke') that makes it, at best, begrudgingly inviting. The old heart of town is attractive in a practical way but the modern houses give the place an air of bleakness. You'll find several B&Bs, including *The Fleece House* (☎ 01547 520168) on Market St in an 18th-century former coaching inn. *King Offa's Restaurant* in the *Knighton Hotel* (☎ 01547 520530) serves good traditional meals. Bar meals cost around £6. It's expensive to stay at this hotel (B&B starts at £29) but there are discount rates (£22.50) for ODA members. There are several pubs in town including the *George & Dragon* and the *Horse & Jockey* which has a beer garden – all serve bar meals. Stock up on food for the demanding next day at the supermarket and bakery. Call in at the Offa's Dyke Centre to look at the displays.

WALES

Day 6: Knighton to Brompton Crossroads

15 miles (24 km), 10 hours

'It looks easier on the map' is a valid comment for this section of the walk. Until you walk it, the various guidebooks seem to exaggerate when they say this is the toughest section of the whole route. The pattern for the day is a steep climb, then a relatively level section of ridgetop walking, then a steep drop, followed immediately by another steep climb and so on. If not jarring on the knees, the switchbacks will certainly help to tire you out and slow your rate of progress. A taxi service for your backpack may be a godsend here, though the cost is around £15.

Offa's Dyke Path is at its most impressive from Llanfair Hill, the dyke's highest point at 429m, to Clun forest with fine views to Clun castle then on to Edenhope Hill before a steep descent to the Unk valley. Over the next few miles you'll tread in the footsteps of many others along the 15 mile Kerry Ridgeway, Wales' oldest road, in use for over 4000 years.

You could split this demanding stage by staying at the village of Newcastle-on-Clun, one mile west of Offa's Dyke Path, where *The Quarry House* (☎ 01588 640 774) has B&B for £17. The nearby *pub* also has accommodation. If you have a schedule to keep to, the local M&J taxi service (☎ 01588 640273) could take you to your prebooked accommodation (eg to Brompton Hall or Churchstoke) for about £8. Another option around here is the *YHA Hostel* (☎ 01588 640582, £6.75, camping £3.50) at Clun, about three miles east of Offa's Dyke Path.

Brompton Hall at Churchstoke (near the Blue Bell Inn and the crossroads of the A489 and the B4385), right on the dyke, offers fine hospitality and food for around £20 per person. Nearby *Drewin Farm* (☎ 01588 620325) at Cwm offers B&B for £14.

Day 7: Brompton Crossroads to Buttington Bridge (Welshpool)

12½ miles (20 km), 6½ hours

Offa's Dyke Path today starts with a long, straight, flat stretch, over the Plain of Montgomery passing near to the historic town of Montgomery, which is worth a visit (add an hour's walking time). Both the Aurum Press' National Trail guide and David Hunter's Cicerone guidebook detail the diversion to Montgomery and how to get back onto Offa's Dyke Path without retracing your steps.

The route continues, rising gradually and steadily. It leads to one moderate climb over Long Mountain (with its good views) and a moderate descent directly from historic Beacon Ring with its hillfort to Buttington.

At the end of the day, Buttington doesn't offer much except the *Green Dragon* pub. B&B costs £13 at *Mona Broxton's home* (☎ 01938 570225), at 1 Plas Cefn. Nearby Welshpool is a much better prospect with many facilities including a good range of places to stay and eat as well as things to do. When you're almost in Buttington on the B4388 keep going straight ahead to the phone box and ring the B&B of your choice in Welshpool. (Most places charge around £14 per person.) Suggestions include *Severn Farm* (☎ 01938 553098), *Hafren* (☎ 01938 554112), and *Tresi-Aur* (☎ 01938 552430).

WALES

Powis Castle

While you're in Welshpool don't miss visiting Powis Castle, half a mile south-west of town. Built in around 1200, this is one of the National Trust's finest properties in Wales. More of a regal country house than a castle, it is fully furnished and has impressive terraced gardens established in the 17th century. The castle houses the Clive of India Museum – a collection of artefacts and treasures from the subcontinent, amassed over 200 years ago by Robert Clive. The grounds are open to the public until 6 pm but last admissions to the castle and the Clive of India Museum are at 4.30 pm. Admission costs £5.80. ■

Day 8: Buttington Bridge (Welshpool) to Llanymynech

10½ miles (17 km), 6 hours

If you stayed in Welshpool for the night, head back to Buttington and to the Shropshire Canal which you'll be walking alongside for the first part of this stage. Here's your chance for a relatively relaxing day of easier walking – enjoy the scenic canals with water weeds and flowers, old stone bridges, maybe a narrow boat, and swans, sometimes with fluffy cygnets. Offa's Dyke Path follows virtually flat terrain for all this day – in this regard it is the easiest part of walking Offa's Dyke Path.

The first hour along the six metre wide canal may put you into a meditative frame of mind. This is followed by about three hours on fairly flat ground or levee banks mostly along the River Severn, past the Breiddens – a few hills in line with Long Mountain.

Around lunch time you'll reach the *Golden Lion Hotel* (☎ 01691 830295) at Four Crosses which is a good place to stop for refreshments (B&B costs £17). From here, Offa's Dyke Path follows the Montgomery Canal all the way to Llanymynech. An hour past Four Crosses, the canal crosses the River Vyrnwy via a stone aqueduct – a curious sight, but only a taste of greater things to come two days hence.

(An alternative to walking this stage – if you're short of time – is to visit Powis Castle in Welshpool, allowing from two to four hours, and then catch a bus or take a taxi direct to Llanymynech.)

In hospitable Llanymynech you can stay at *Cae Bryn* (☎ 01691 830234), on North Rd. Excellent B&B here is £15 and camping costs £2 per person. There's good food at the *Bradford Arms* restaurant. The *Dolphin Hotel* with friendly service is good for an evening meal and drink. There's also a good Indian restaurant, the *Raj Doot* (☎ 01691 831661).

Day 9: Llanymynech to Chirk Mill

14 miles (22.5 km), 8 hours

North of Llanymynech Offa's Dyke Path, in sharp contrast with the flat terrain of the previous day, goes through a Robin Hood's delight with winding tracks, a series of smaller hills with fine vantage points, and dense green forests.

A highlight of this day could be a visit to Chirk Castle if you can get there during opening hours (April to September, Tuesday to Friday and Sunday from noon to 5 pm).

If you miss the castle visit it's worth continuing on another 1½ to two hours to Pentre or Pontcysyllte for the night as there are more places to see and things to do. You'll be able to take in the views along the Dee Valley, which is famous for kayaking and canoeing. You could eat at the golf club overlooking Chirk Marina with its narrow canal boats.

There's a *YHA Hostel* (☎ 01978 860330, £8.25) at Twndwr Hall, Llangollen, three miles from Offa's Dyke Path. Other places to stay, which are closer to Offa's Dyke Path, include *Sun Cottage* (☎ 01691 773760) at Pentre where B&B costs £13 or *Cefn y Fedw Farm* (☎ 01978 823403) near Panorama at the top of Garth, Trevor, with B&B for £16 and camping for £3.

Day 10: Chirk Mill to Llandegla

16 miles (25 km), 9 hours

This day offers the most varied scenery. Offa's Dyke Path north leaves the actual dyke for good. Early on (if you start from Chirk) Offa's Dyke Path arrives at the River Dee and the famous Pontcysyllte aqueduct, one of the highlights along Offa's Dyke Path. In 1805 engineer Thomas Telford completed the construction of the 302m long aqueduct, which stands 38m above the River Dee allowing barges and pedestrians to cross the valley.

Next, you ascend through Trevor Wood, avoiding the older lower path through the forest. The Panorama Walk and the short, steep ascent to the hilltop fort of Castell Dinas Bran (in ruins but offering magnificent views) is well worth the half hour detour.

An alternative is to continue over the other side from Castell Dinas Bran down into Langollen for the night. Do more sightseeing in the afternoon and take an alternative track the next morning past the ruins of Vale Crucis Abbey, which compares favourably with Tintern Abbey. If you take this option, rejoin Offa's Dyke Path at the Rock Farm.

Either way, you'll end up on a narrow path traversing a scree slope below the otherworldly Eglwyseg Crags looming large on your right while on your left is more familiar, picturesque scenery. Following the narrow official path on the scree could be risky on a wet and windy day: there is often little protection from the elements, the drop is often steep, and finding your footing can be more precarious than usual. Instead, stay down on the road or follow the fence just above the treeline below the scree. The route can be confusing around here. The waymarking is fairly clear but Offa's Dyke Path doesn't follow the exact line of the rights of way on the OS maps south of World's End.

After the scree, it is pleasant to reach a wood and soon after, World's End – more hospitable than its name suggests – with a refreshing stream attracting lots of day trippers on weekends.

From here you walk uphill on a tarred road until you reach signposts marking the way across the bracken-covered moor. The path could be very boggy here or even quite dusty during a dry summer. Much conservation work has been done to prevent erosion including boards over the peat bogs. After two miles you come down through the pine forest to a reservoir and head towards Llandegla, which you reach after one mile. The village offers a good range of accommodation including *The Hand* (☎ 019878 790337) and *2 The Village* (☎ 019878 790266). The *Willows Restaurant* has a three-course set menu for £17, but check out what bar meals the village pubs are offering.

Day 11: Llandegla to Bodfari
17 miles (27 km), 10 hours
This is one of the longest and most strenuous stages of the walk, and includes a traverse of the open, rugged and heather-covered Clwydian Range – comparable to the stage from Knighton to Brompton Crossroads – with several steep climbs and descents. Up

here it can be very windy and cool but the views on a fine day include the mountains of Snowdonia, the sea and, to the north-east, Liverpool. You could opt to walk it in two days and stay overnight at the *Druid Inn* (☎ 01352 810225) on Ruthin Rd in Llanferres near Mold, two miles off Offa's Dyke Path. B&B costs £17.75.

You'll arrive very tired in Bodfari and will welcome a home-cooked meal like those provided (from £5) at *Fron Haul* (☎ 01745 710301) where B&B costs £15.50 and camping £2.

Day 12: Bodfari to Prestatyn
12 miles (20 km), 7 hours
After the 'downhill all the way' expectations built up on the previous day, once you see the coastline in the distance and know that you are only 12 miles from finishing the long-distance path, you may quicken your pace. Be patient! The last day takes you over the foothills of the Clwydian Range and is just as demanding as any other 'average' day on the trail. You'll still be crossing hills with only two miles to go and the beach in full view. On the whole, however, this day's terrain is relatively easy and the scenery pleasant with good views up to the final steep descent into Prestatyn.

Along the way, Rhuallt has *The Smithy's Arms* and the *White House Hotel* (☎ 01745 582155), with B&B for £15 and camping at £3.50 per tent, and places to eat as well as a large *caravan park*. Near this town Offa's Dyke Path follows a temporary route to avoid the A55. This section has special waymarkings but vandals may have removed some of the national trails signs.

Prepare for the shock of Prestatyn's busy high street, especially in summer, as this is a popular seaside resort. Continue to the sea to finish the walk officially and sign the walker's register at the Offa's Dyke Centre (open daily from 10 am to 4.30 pm).

There are many places to stay and eat in Prestatyn including *Sophie's* (☎ 01745 852442), at 17 Gronant Rd, and *Traeth Ganol Guest House* (☎ 01745 853594), at 41 Beach Rd West. Camping at *Nant Mill*

WALES

Caravan & Tenting Park, by the junction of the A547 and A54, costs from £7 to £9 per tent. There are lots of pubs including *Offa's Tavern* on High St, which offers bar meals for £4 to £7, or you could celebrate the end of your walk with a Tandoori at *The Suhai* (☎ 01745 856829), at 12 Bastion Rd, on the high street corner.

Pembrokeshire Coast Path

Official Name The Pembrokeshire Coast Path National Trail
Distance 189 miles (304 km)
Start Amroth, near Tenby
Finish St Dogmaels, near Cardigan
Duration 13 to 16 days
Regional Centres Tenby, Pembroke, Fishguard, Cardigan
County Dyfed (formerly Pembrokeshire and Cardiganshire)
Area Pembrokeshire Coast National Park
Summary This clifftop trail includes some of the finest beaches in Britain and offers the best coastal scenery in Wales. There's some strenuous walking as the path rises and falls between the beach and the cliffs but overall the walk is not difficult.

Lying entirely within the Pembrokeshire Coast National Park in south-western Wales, the Pembrokeshire Coast Path (PCP) passes through tiny fishing villages, skirts secluded coves and crosses some sparsely populated regions.

The rocks here are amongst the world's oldest, some formed almost 3000 million years ago, but you don't have to be a geologist to appreciate the spectacular patterns and colours of the rock formations in the cliffs. As well as being renowned for its superb coastal scenery, the area is of particular interest to birdwatchers – only parts of the Scottish coast attract more varied sea bird life. The best months for good weather and lack of crowds are said to be May and September. Since the climate in this part of the country is mild it's possible to walk this path at any time of the year, but from November through February all of the YHA hostels and some of the B&Bs are closed.

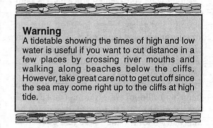

Warning
A tidetable showing the times of high and low water is useful if you want to cut distance in a few places by crossing river mouths and walking along beaches below the cliffs. However, take great care not to get cut off since the sea may come right up to the cliffs at high tide.

DIRECTION, DISTANCE & DURATION

Although the path may be walked in either direction, there are several advantages in walking from south to north (starting at Amroth). First, some of the wildest walking is in the north so it makes sense to start in the tamer south. Second, it's more interesting from a cultural point of view; you'll be walking from the English part of Pembrokeshire into the more Welsh part. (For more details on this cultural division see the Preseli Hills Circuit in the Pembrokeshire section of the Wales – Short Walks chapter.) Third, you'll spend less time walking towards the sun, and the wind will also usually be behind you.

The official length of the path is 186 miles, but the actual distance walked will be over 200 miles to include detours when the tide is high or to visit places of interest such as St David's.

Although the path is rated medium to strenuous owing to the number of steep climbs and descents along its route, it's not hard going, particularly if you take it slowly. And there are numerous worthwhile distractions along the way, including Tenby (an attractive seaside town), St David's (the smallest city in Britain, with its fine cathedral), several ruined castles, Iron Age forts, superb beaches and nature reserves – not to mention the pubs, many of which are conveniently situated right by the path.

You need to allow 13 to 16 days for this

WALES

walk, plus extra time for side trips to some of the nearby islands (Skomer, Skokholm etc) and for St David's. Note that the hours given for each stage in the main route description are walking times only; you should allow an extra hour or two for rests, lunch stops, and so on.

If you're a fast walker some of these days can be doubled. You can walk from Amroth to Manorbier in a day, and from Trefin to Fishguard in one long day. There are several possibilities for short cuts – across the Angle peninsula, for example – and, if time is really tight, there's a good bus service along the northern section.

STAGES

For a 15 day walk, as described here, the most convenient places to start and end each day are:

Day	From	To	Distance
1	Amroth	Tenby	7 miles (11.5 km)
2	Tenby	Manorbier	8½ miles (13.5 km)
3	Manorbier	Bosherston	15 miles (24 km)
4	Bosherston	Angle	15 miles (24 km)
5	Angle	Pembroke	13½ miles (22 km)
6	Pembroke	Sandy Haven	6 miles (26 km)
7	Sandy Haven	Marloes Sands	14 miles (22.5 km)
8	Marloes Sands	Broad Haven	13 miles (21 km)
9	Broad Haven	Solva	11 miles (18 km)
10	Solva	St David's*	15 miles (24 km)
11	St David's*	Trefin	13 miles (21 km)
12	Trefin	Pwll Deri	10 miles (16 km)
13	Pwll Deri	Fishguard	10 miles (16 km)
14	Fishguard	Newport	12½ miles (20 km)
15	Newport	St Dogmaels	15½ miles (25 km)

* via Whitesands Bay, but short cuts are possible allowing more time to see St David's.

INFORMATION

There are Park Information Centres (PICs) at Saundersfoot (☎ 01834 811411), Pembroke (☎ 01646 682148), Broad Haven (☎ 01437 781412), St David's (☎ 01437 720392), Newport (☎ 01239 820912) and Haverfordwest (☎ 01437 760136), all of which are open from April through September and for a week over the school holiday in mid to late October. (Some PICs double as TICs.) There are also TICs (open all year) at Narberth (☎ 01834 860061), Tenby (☎ 01834 842402), Pembroke (☎ 01646 622388), Haverfordwest (☎ 01437 763110) and Fishguard (☎ 01348 873484). There are TICs at Cardigan, Fishguard harbour, Pembroke Dock, Kilgetty and Milford Haven, but they close over the winter.

The national park publishes *Coast Path Accommodation*. It's stocked by all the visitor centres but since it includes some accommodation not verified by the tourist board, TICs may keep their stocks behind the counter. Phone the Pembrokeshire Coast National Park (☎ 01437 764636) for further information. The national park's annual newspaper, *Coast to Coast*, is also useful (it contains a tidetable – see the Warning aside), as is the *Coast Path Mileage* leaflet (20p). If you want to qualify for a certificate proving you've done the walk, pick up a form before you start and get it stamped by hostels and B&Bs along the way.

Books & Maps

Although 10 years old, CJ Wright's *Guide to the Pembrokeshire Coast Path* (Constable, £9.95) is comprehensive and interesting, with detailed, hand-drawn maps. The *Pembrokeshire Coast Path National Trail Guide* by Brian John (Aurum Press, £9.99) includes OS maps (1:25,000) and colour photos. Both these guides describe the route from north to south.

The *Pembrokeshire Coastal Path* by Dennis Kelsall (Cicerone, £9.99) describes the route in the preferred south to north direction, and includes background information, line maps and an accommodation list.

The route is covered by OS Outdoor

WALES

Leisure (1:25,000) sheets 35 and 36. While the detail is excellent the sheet size is enormous.

GUIDED WALKS

Park wardens lead walks along parts of the path in a series of 29 'Coast Path Snippets' of five to seven miles, from April through August. In May/June, they lead a 14 day walk of the entire path (£55). Phone ☎ 01437 781412 for details.

The Old Court House Walking Holidays (☎ 01348 837095) organises self-guided walks with pickups provided and accommodation at its vegetarian guesthouse in Trefin.

PLACES TO STAY & EAT

There's a wide range of places to stay and eat since this is a popular holiday area. B&Bs and hotels are listed in the route description; you must book in advance for some places, particularly in the summer. For a wider choice, as well as the *RA Yearbook* and the *National Trail Companion* (see the Books section in the Facts for the Walker chapter), see the leaflets listed under Information earlier. Some B&Bs arrange transport to meet you, taking you back to the path the next day. There are nine YHA hostels on or near the path. They can be booked through the West Wales Booking Bureau at *St David's YHA Hostel* (☎ 01437 720345). The service costs £2.50 and bookings must be made two weeks in advance.

There are also campsites near most beaches, and with permission from the farmer you can camp in any field. Camping on beaches is not officially allowed.

GETTING THERE & AWAY
Bus

The National Express daily coach between London and West Wales goes via Kilgetty, three miles from Amroth. There's a local bus link, but it's often quicker to walk.

The same National Express service also stops at Carmarthen, 30 miles south-east of Cardigan. Frequent bus services link these two towns. Between St Dogmael's and Cardigan there are hourly buses from Monday to Saturday.

Train

There are trains from Swansea to Kilgetty (three miles from Amroth); continue on to the next station, Saundersfoot, for the Pentlepoir YHA Hostel.

The nearest railway station to Cardigan is 18 miles away at Fishguard. There is a bus, but it's better to take the bus between Cardigan and Camarthen and join the railway there.

Car

Amroth is south of the A477, six miles from Tenby. St Dogmael's is north of the A487 two miles from Cardigan.

THE ROUTE

This is a suggested itinerary, but there are any number of variations possible with longer days or additional stops. Some of these are detailed in the route description.

The Start: Amroth

Amroth is a busy little seaside resort beside a long sandy beach. The path begins right outside the *New Inn* at its far eastern end. On the bridge a plaque commemorates the opening of the path in 1970.

If you're spending the night in Amroth, *New Inn House* (☎ 01834 813815) couldn't be better located. It's a small B&B that charges from £11 per person. The *Ashdale Guest House* (☎ 01834 813853) charges £13.50.

The *Pentlepoir YHA Hostel* (☎ 01834 812333, £6.75) is 1½ miles inland from Saundersfoot, about four miles from the start of the path.

Day 1: Amroth to Tenby

7 miles (11.5 km), 3½ to 4 hours

Although this easy section can be walked in a half day it's a good limber-up and Tenby is an attractive town with accommodation for all budgets. There are several places for food along the way.

Follow the road from the New Inn through Amroth. As the road turns inland you'll see a sign for the PCP to the left. It climbs steeply up onto the cliffs, with good views back

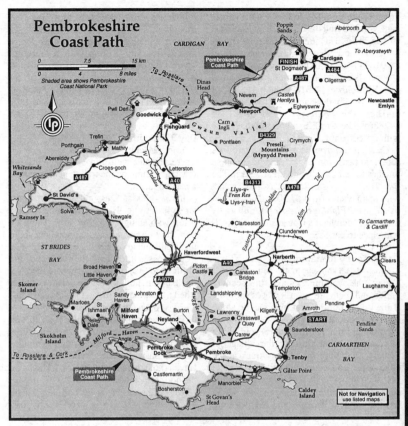

Pembrokeshire Coast Path

CARDIGAN BAY

ST BRIDES BAY

CARMARTHEN BAY

WALES

Not for Navigation use listed maps

along the beach. After two miles you reach *Wiseman's Bridge Inn* (☎ 01834 813236), right by the beach, with B&B from £15.

In the jolly seaside village of Saundersfoot, the PIC (☎ 01834 811411) has information about the numerous B&Bs in the area. These include *Harbour Light* (☎ 01834 813496), with B&B from £15.50.

From Saundersfoot the PCP runs along the edge of Rhode Wood. At *Trevayne Farm* (☎ 01834 813402), near Monkstone Beach, there's camping for £2 per person. The path rises and falls crossing small valleys, then follows Waterwynch Lane into Tenby.

Tenby The Welsh name for this genteel seaside town, Dinbych y Pysgod (Little Fort of the Fishes), is as charming as Tenby itself. Elegant Georgian houses, most of them now hotels, rise above the harbour. The most interesting building to look round is the late 15th-century Tudor Merchant's House. There are also boat trips to the Cistercian monastery on nearby Caldey Island. The path goes right past the TIC (☎ 01834 842402).

There's no shortage of places to stay along the Esplanade, and on Victoria St, Picton Terrace and Sutton St, which lead off it.

Prices range from £15 to £30. On the Esplanade you will find the *Clarence House Hotel* (☎ 01834 844371), *Bellini's Hotel* (☎ 01834 843333) and also the *Panorama Hotel* (☎ 01834 844976). There's a good choice of cheaper B&Bs along Harding and Warren Sts. *Weybourne* (☎ 01834 843641), at 14 Warren St, charges around £13. More up market, the *Fourcroft Hotel* (☎ 01834 842886), The Croft, is a comfortable place with B&B from £37.

Candy Restaurant near Tudor Square does set breakfasts for £3.95, and two-course lunches for £5.25 (all with great views). The *Bay Tree*, on Tudor Square, is good value, with main dishes from £7.50 and occasional live music. *Plantagenate Restaurant* is by the Tudor Merchant's House and is an excellent place to eat.

Day 2: Tenby to Manorbier
8½ miles (13.5 km), 3½ to 4½ hours
Today, the walking is easy, the scenery varied and there are several places for food. If the tide is out the first mile can be along the sands of South Beach. When the red flags fly at Giltar Point (a firing range) you'll have to make a detour through the village of Penally, following the railway track at the edge of the golf course. Penally has a good pub, the *Crown Inn*, a post office, B&Bs and campsites. *Brambles Lodge* (☎ 01834 842393) is near the path and charges from £12.

Beyond Giltar Point are some great views, and the cliffs are dotted with caves and blowholes. Just above the sandy beach at attractive Lydstep Haven is the tiny village of Lydstep. The *Lydstep Tavern* is a good place for a drink. The high limestone cliffs at nearby Lydstep Point (owned by the National Trust) are popular with day trippers and rock-climbers.

One mile beyond and 200m from the beach at Skrinkle Haven is *Manorbier YHA Hostel* (☎ 01834 871803, £8.25), in futuristic grey and yellow, and looking more like a motorway service station than a hostel.

The path heads inland from Skrinkle Haven, around the army camp, and then follows the cliffs to Manorbier Bay. Ivy-clad Manorbier Castle is well worth a visit. In Manorbier village there's the *Castle Inn*, a post office and a shop with a tearoom. There's B&B at *The Old Vicarage* (☎ 01834 871452), from £19, and *The Dak* (☎ 01834 871209), for £15. There's camping at *West Moor Farm* (☎ 01834 871204), on the PCP two miles west of Manorbier, for £1.

Day 3: Manorbier to Bosherston
15 miles (24 km), 5½ to 7 hours
There's excellent clifftop walking today, but few places right on the trail to get food; take a packed lunch.

It's 3½ pleasant, easy miles from Manorbier to Freshwater East, a busy little seaside resort with an ugly *caravan park*. There's a pub, the *Freshwater Inn*, but you have to go up the hill and into the village to reach it. The PCP crosses the sand then follows the clifftops to Stackpole Quay, where there's a tiny harbour, built to service the now demolished Stackpole Court, and a National Trust *tearoom* open during the season.

There are some spectacular rock formations along this stretch of the coastline, including Stackpole Head. About two miles beyond Stackpole Head you reach Broad Haven (note there's another Broad Haven on the northern section of the walk).

West of here is the army's artillery range. The western section is permanently off-limits to hikers apart from those on occasional national park guided walks. The eastern section is open when not in use by the army. Signs and flags indicate that the area is closed. Phone ☎ 01646 661321 ext 4336 for advance information.

To reach Bosherston from Broad Haven either take the short cut through the nature reserve or follow the PCP around St Govan's Head, the most southerly point in Pembrokeshire, to visit the tiny St Govan's Chapel, set into the cliffs. It dates from the 6th century and was once a place of pilgrimage.

In Bosherston, there's B&B at *St Govan's Inn* (☎ 01646 661311) from £15, and good pub grub. The other place to eat is *Ye Olde Worlde Cafe*. Less than a mile north of

Bosherston, *Home Farm* (☎ 01646 661244) does B&B for £16.

Day 4: Bosherston to Angle
15 miles (24 km), 5½ to 7 hours

There's some wonderful coastal scenery on this section but if the range is closed it's a tedious nine mile walk along roads. Castlemartin is the only place to get food.

If the range is not closed the PCP continues along the coast from the car park above St Govan's Chapel. This is a beautiful stretch with numerous caves, blowholes and natural arches. In about 3½ miles of easy walking you reach Stack Rocks and a car park; below is the natural arch known as the Green Bridge of Wales.

Here you must turn inland and follow the road to join the B4319 from Bosherston to Castlemartin. With the rumble of tanks and sudden ear-splitting detonations from the range, this is not a peaceful section of the path.

There are two routes to Castlemartin, both along roads – either the B4319 or the lanes through Warren. Note that the latest OS map shows a pub just outside Warren but it's closed. There's B&B at *Warren Farm* (☎ 01646 661250) for £14.

There's no shop in Castlemartin but the *Welcome Inn* does food. *Court Farm* (☎ 01646 661228) offers B&B from £14. At *The Old Vicarage* (☎ 01646 661227), West Farm, you can camp for £2 and there's B&B for £14.

From Castlemartin the route continues along the B4139. There's B&B at *Chapel Farm* (☎ 01646 661312) for £16, and *Gupton Farm* (☎ 01646 661268) for £13. You reach the coast again at the wide beach of Freshwater West. The undertow is strong here; it's a dangerous place to swim.

If you're short of time you could cut nine miles off the PCP by taking a short cut to the north side of the peninsula from here. The main route continues along the coast, another beautiful section with caves, tiny islands and little bays.

At West Angle Bay there's the *Wavecrest Cafe* above the sandy beach. Across the

water is St Anne's Head, where, in February 1996, the *Sea Empress* ran aground and released its cargo of oil, swamping West Angle beach among many others in Pembrokeshire. The clean-up operation has removed most visual traces of the oil but it will be years before the full damage to the ecosystem becomes clear.

The path continues round the headland past Thorn Island, where there's a large hotel. Soon after Angle Point there's the quirky *Old Point House* pub, definitely worth stopping at.

Angle is not a pretty village. There's camping for £2 at *Castle Farm* (☎ 01646 641220). For B&B try *Timothy Lodge* (☎ 01646 641342), on the edge of the village. It costs £13. There's good food at the *Hibernia Inn*.

Day 5: Angle to Pembroke
13½ miles (22 km), 5 to 6 hours

Today's walk is easy, but the scenery is not what you might expect in a national park – oil refineries and a power station. There's nowhere to get food and water on the path.

The route runs right around the edge of Angle Bay, a three mile walk past the pebbly beach in the shadow of the vast oil refinery. You pass Fort Popton, dating from 1860, now a Field Studies Council research centre, then continue round Bullwell Bay, past (or even under) several oil-tanker jetties.

The tall chimney straight ahead is part of Pembroke Power Station. Plans to burn orimulsion emulsified hydrocarbon fuel, with increased health and environmental risks for the area, are being vigorously opposed by the local community. The PCP turns inland crossing fields to bypass the power station.

For the next five miles from here to Pembroke the route follows a combination of lanes and paths across fields. Hundleton is just off the path but there's a shop here and you can get food at the *Hundleton Inn*. At Quoits Mill the route joins the B4320 which it follows into Pembroke.

Pembroke The main attraction in this market town is the 900 year old castle, birth-

WALES

place of the Henry Tudor, the future King Henry VII. Just across the road, the Museum of the Home is also well worth seeing. There's a PIC (☎ 01646 682148) by the castle entrance; the TIC (☎ 01646 622388) is south of the castle on Commons Rd.

For B&B, try wisteria-clad *Beech House* (☎ 01646 683740, £12.50), at 78 Main St; *Merton Place House* (☎ 01646 684796, £14), at 3 East Back (by Main St), with rather more character; or the *Kings Arms Hotel* (☎ 01646 683611), Main St, from £22.50, also with a good restaurant and the best bar food in Pembroke. Faggots, peas and potatoes are £3.75.

Henry's Gift & Coffee Shop is the unmissable pink building near the Kings Arms, and a great place for a snack or light lunch. The *Watermans Arms*, on the PCP just over the bridge, has lovely views of the castle.

Day 6: Pembroke to Sandy Haven
16 miles (26 km), 6 to 8 hours

This is the one of the least attractive sections of the whole walk, with several miles along roads and through towns. There are, however, numerous places to get food along the way.

From Pembroke, cross the bridge and continue along the road past the Watermans Arms. Soon turn off left and follow the PCP through woods and farmland into the suburbs of Pembroke Dock. It's easy to get lost in the backstreets – ask directions for the Martello (or Guntower). Recently restored, this harbourfront guntower now houses a TIC (☎ 01646 622246). Opposite is the *King's Arms*, a friendly pub.

Continue along the main road past the shopping centre and supermarket for just under a mile to the roundabout. There's a pub here, the *First & Last*. Follow the A477 for almost two miles, crossing the large Cleddau Bridge which provides some interest on an otherwise tedious section of the walk. (Upstream from here is the 'Secret Waterway' – discussed later in this chapter.)

Just after the bridge, turn off and go through the woods to join the road in the run-down village of Neyland. Continue

along sideroads through Llanstadwell, which has a picturesque church, to Hazelbeach where the *Ferry Inn* (☎ 01646 600270) is an excellent place for a drink or lunch. The mixed grill costs £7.95, while B&B is from £15.

The PCP now skirts another oil refinery, following the perimeter fence, and leads you into Milford Haven – not a place to linger long, though there's an interesting local museum on Milford Marina and several B&Bs and restaurants. The TIC (☎ 01646 690866) is on Charles St, which is one block back from Hamilton Terrace. The first B&B you reach is *Pebbles Guest House* (☎ 01646 698155), east of here on Pill Fold, and has B&B from £13.50. *Belhaven House Hotel* (☎ 01646 695983), on Hamilton Terrace, charges from £15 per person. There's an excellent cheap place to eat, near the TIC, called the *Welcome Cafe*.

Continue past the docks and over the bridge, straight ahead into the suburb of Hakin, then around the remains of yet another refinery, now dismantled. Sandy Haven estuary can be crossed only during the two hours either side of low tide. At other times it's a four mile detour via Herbrandston and Rickeston Bridge. If you're waiting for the tide, the closest pub is the *Sir Benfro* (☎ 01646 694242), just under a mile from Sandy Haven in Herbrandston. They also have B&B for £30. Across Sandy Haven, *Skerryback Farmhouse* (☎ 01646 636598) has B&B for £15. *Bicton Farm* (☎ 01646 636215) is an excellent place, similarly priced.

Day 7: Sandy Haven to Marloes Sands
14 miles (22.5 km), 5 to 6½ hours

The beautiful scenery today seems all the more attractive after two days of industrial landscapes. Even more pleasing is that most of the walk is on level ground, and the pub at Dale makes a good lunch stop.

From Sandy Haven, there's four miles of excellent clifftop to the Gann, another inlet that can be crossed only during the two hours either side of low tide (at other times it's a 2½ miles detour via Mullock), then a lane

WALES

into the holiday village of Dale. The *Griffin Inn* is an excellent place for lunch. Salmon shantie costs £4.25. There's also the *Beachhouse Bistro*. Up-market B&B costs £20 at the *Post House Hotel* (☎ 01646 636201).

From Dale there's a short cut across to Westdale Bay, saving about five miles. The coastal route continues around St Anne's Head, an exhilarating section of the path that can be windy. If the foghorn is operating it can be quite deafening.

From Westdale Bay it's two miles along the cliffs to Marloes Sands; the *YHA Hostel* (☎ 01646 636667, £6.75) is 400m from the beach. A mile east at Marloes, there's B&B at *Greenacre* (☎ 01646 636400) and *Foxdale* (☎ 01646 636243), Glebe Lane, from £14 per person; both are open year-round. For a drink and a meal there's the *Lobster Pot Inn* and the *Foxes Inn*.

Day 8: Marloes Sands to Broad Haven
13 miles (21 km), 4½ to 6 hours
There's nowhere for food along this scenic stretch of the path, a mix of beach and woodland, but tap water is available at St Bride's Cross. You may see grey seals on this stretch.

From Marloes Sands the PCP continues along the cliffs to Martin's Haven, from where you can reach the nature reserve islands of Skomer and Skokholm. Taking the day off to visit one of them is highly recommended. There's camping for £1.50 at *West Hook Farm* (☎ 01646 636424). It takes just over an hour to walk from Musselwick Sands to St Bride's Cross, where there's an interesting 13th-century church.

From St Bride's Cross it's a reasonably easy five mile stretch to Little Haven, a pretty village with an excellent pub, the *Swan Inn*. Crab sandwiches are £2.95, and they also have cawl (thick soup with bread and cheese) for £3. For B&B try the *Little Haven Hotel* (☎ 01437 781285), from £16, or *Mount Pleasant*, £13.

Broad Haven, half a mile north over the hill, is a popular holiday centre with pubs, shops and B&Bs. The *YHA Hostel* (☎ 01437 781688, £9.10) is beside the TIC (☎ 01437 781412) and car park. B&Bs include *Mrs*

Hopkins (☎ 01437 781502), from £13, and *Lion Rock* (☎ 01437 781645, £14).

Day 9: Broad Haven to Solva
11 miles (18 km), 4 to 5½ hours
There's varied walking – cliff paths and sandy beaches – on this pleasant section, and some stiff climbs.

For two miles north of Broad Haven the path follows the coast, joining the road near Druidstone. *Druidstone Hotel/Villa* (☎ 01437 781221) is an interesting place right by the road, with B&B for £25. Non-residents can eat here, but the licence doesn't allow you to have a drink without a meal.

From Druidstone Haven the path runs along the cliffs again. Nolton Haven is an attractive little beach and the *Mariners Inn* (☎ 01437 710469) has B&B for £19.50 and good bar food. Nearby *Nolton Haven Farm* (☎ 01437 710263) does B&B for £14.

The path climbs onto the cliffs again and there are good views north along Newgale Sands, one of the best beaches in Wales. Although the official path follows the road most people walk down to the beach, a popular place for surfers. Should you feel the urge, Newsurf (☎ 01437 721398), at the filling station, rents boards (from £2) and wetsuits. There's also a pub, shop and cafe here. *Newgale Campsite* (☎ 01437 710253) charges from £2 per person.

Solva YHA Hostel (☎ 01437 720959, £7.45) is not at Solva but 1½ miles north of Newgale at Whitehouse.

From the beach the path climbs again onto the cliffs and the five mile walk to Solva village is along a gloriously rugged section with impressive rock formations.

Solva lies half a mile inland on an inlet, and is a popular mooring spot for visiting yachts. The *Harbour House* pub is right by the slipway. On Main St the *Ship Inn* has more atmosphere. Nearby are several cafes, and the *Papillon Rouge* restaurant where main dishes are around £8.95. There's B&B at *Llys Aber* (☎ 01437 721657, £15) and *Pendinas* (☎ 01437 721283, £14). In Lower Solva try *Gamlyn* (☎ 01437 721542).

WALES

Day 10: Solva to St David's
15 miles (24 km), 5 to 7 hours

Much of this section of the coast is owned by the National Trust and it's a beautiful area. There's nowhere for food actually on the path, but there are several places where you could detour into St David's.

The route climbs out of Solva onto the cliffs and the superb coastal scenery continues – interesting rock formations, natural arches, caves and small islands.

It's 4½ miles from Solva to busy Caerfai Bay where there's a nice sandy beach, and two campsites; *Caerfai Farm* (☎ 01437 720548) charges from £2.50.

The path continues on the cliffs, a pleasant 20 minute walk to St Non's Bay. St Non was the mother of St David, the patron saint of Wales. He is said to have been born on the site of the ruined chapel here, in AD 462. The holy well has long been a pilgrimage site. There's a modern chapel and a retreat nearby.

A half hour's walk brings you to Porthclais, where there's a landing-stage, a disused quarry and lime kilns. Continuing round the headland there are good views across to Ramsey Island, now a nature reserve that can be visited from St Justinian's. This section is an easy walk, but can be busy with day trippers in summer. In just over two miles you reach Whitesands Bay. There's pub grub at the *Whitesands Bay Hotel* (marked 'Hotel' on OS maps). The *St David's YHA Hostel* (☎ 01437 720345, £7.45) is half a mile north-east of Whitesands Bay.

St David's There's something very special about St David's that even the crowds of holiday-makers in summer fail to extinguish. The magic must have worked for Dewi Sant (St David), who chose to found the first monastic community here in the 6th century. His relics are kept in a casket in the magnificent cathedral.

The cathedral makes St David's a city, the smallest in Britain – in reality the size of a small town. The PIC and TIC (☎ 01437 720392), at the town hall, are open daily. In the first half of August, usually excellent open-air Shakespeare plays are staged in the atmospheric ruins of the Bishop's Palace.

There's B&B at *Alandale* (☎ 01437 720333), at 43 Nun St, for £14.50 (£16.50 with ensuite) and *Ty Olaf* (☎ 01437 720885), Mount Gardens, for £13.50 to £15.50. The *Old Cross Hotel* (☎ 01437 720387), Cross Square, charges from £31.

There are several teashops to choose from, but the best is the *Gossip Column*, the Italian-run place above the Londis supermarket on the square. *Cartref Restaurant* does more substantial meals. There's also the *Dyfed Cafe* for fish & chips, and at the other end of the culinary spectrum, *Morgan's Brasserie* (☎ 01437 720508) with main dishes for around £12. The *Farmer's Arms*, Goat St, is the place to drink.

Day 11: St David's to Trefin (Trevine)
13 miles (21 km), 4½ to 6 hours

Most of this section is easy walking with superb views; Porthgain would be a good place for a long lunch.

From St David's, there's a wonderfully wild heather-covered section of the path around St David's Head, with an Iron Age fort at the end of the promontory, and then an excellent clifftop hike to Abereiddy, which has a small beach and the ruins of the slate quarry. Inland, there's B&B accommodation for £17 at *Trevaccoon Farm* (☎ 01348 831438).

A further two miles brings you to Porthgain, a former brick works and slate centre. In an age of theme-pubs, the *Sloop Inn* is famous for its old fashioned ordinariness. It's an excellent place for a pint and there are pub meals from £3. The nearby *Harbour Lights Restaurant* (☎ 01348 831549) does two-course dinners for £19.50.

Just inland from the path, Trefin is a small village with a post office, B&Bs and a *YHA Hostel* (☎ 01348 831414, £7.45). B&Bs include the comfortable vegetarian *Old Court House* (☎ 01348 837095) for around £18, and *Park Court Farm* (☎ 01348 831217) from £12.50, with camping from £2.50.

Day 12: Trefin (Trevine) to Pwll Deri
10 miles (16 km), 3½ to 4½ hours

From Trefin, it's an easy three miles to Abercastle where there's a slipway and small beach. The same distance again brings you to the beach at Aber Mawr. There's B&B inland at *Tregwynt Mansion* (☎ 01348 891685) for £18.

In under an hour you reach Penbwchdy, the western end of one of the most impressive stretches of cliffs on the path. It's a wild 40 minute walk to join the road at Pwll Deri. There's a stunning view from here back along the cliffs. *Pwll Deri YHA Hostel* (☎ 01348 891233, £7.45) must have one of the finest locations of any hostel in Britain.

Day 13: Pwll Deri to Fishguard
10 miles (16 km), 3½ to 4½ hours

There's excellent cliff scenery and reasonably easy walking on this 10 mile section but nowhere to get food or water.

The PCP takes you past Strumble Head lighthouse. Inland at *Fferm Treinwen* (☎ 01348 891238) there's camping for £1. About 2½ miles beyond Strumble Head, a memorial marks the spot at Carregwastad Point where the last invasion of Britain occurred. In February 1797, a band of French mercenaries and convicts landed here and raided houses in the Pen Caer area.

Rounding the headland in an hour, you see Fishguard Bay ahead.

Fishguard This is a pleasant little town, surprisingly attractive for a ferry port. The lower part, with a railway station, a beach and ferries for Ireland, is known as Goodwick. Fishguard town is 20 minutes beyond, up the hill. Throughout 1997, the town commemorates the bicentenary of the aforementioned invasion. The TIC (☎ 01348 873484) is at 4 Hamilton St.

In Goodwick, *The Beach House* (☎ 01348 872085) has B&B from around £13. In Fishguard town, *Hamilton Guest House & Backpackers Lodge* (☎ 01348 874797), at 21 Hamilton St, is a friendly independent hostel (£9) near the TIC. There's comfortable B&B at *Cri'r Wylan* (☎ 873398), Penwallis, from

£14 to £16, a short walk from the TIC. The nicest place to stay is at *Three Main Street* (☎ 01348 874275), from £25, which also has a superb restaurant. The *Royal Oak Inn* is on the square, and is full of invasion memorabilia. There's a *fish & chips shop* opposite.

Day 14: Fishguard to Newport
12½ miles (20 km), 5 to 6 hours

There are superb views from the cliffs on this section, and several places for food and drink.

Leaving Fishguard you follow the PCP around picturesque Lower Fishguard, the old part of town that was the location for the 1971 film version of *Under Milk Wood*, starring Richard Burton and Elizabeth Taylor.

In just under three miles you go through *Fishguard Bay Caravan Park* (☎ 01348 811415), where you can camp for £3. There's a cafe here. An excellent place for lunch is *Aux Pavots* (☎ 01348 811491) at Pwllgwaelod. Formerly a pub, it's now a restaurant (open 11 am to 5 pm). Half-a-lobster salad is £6.

Although it's possible to take a short cut through the valley that almost divides Dinas Head from the mainland, don't be tempted – it's a wonderful walk around the headland.

At Cwm-yr-Eglwys there's the ruins of a church and graveyard in a picturesque site overlooking the water. At Brynhenllan, *Mrs James* (☎ 01348 811234) has B&B from £12.50.

After the climb following the road out of Cwm-yr-Eglwys, it's an easy walk to Newport, although the path may be overgrown in places.

Newport This small town (not to be confused with the much larger town of the same name in Gwent) grew up round the Norman castle, and the rocky outcrop of Carn Ingli, which dominates the town and beach. The PIC (☎ 01239 820912) is on Long St. If you wanted a day away from the coast, or even an evening stroll, Carn Ingli and some other routes in the area are described in the Preseli Hills Circuit section under Pembrokeshire in

WALES

the Wales – Short Walks chapter, which also covers places to stay and eat in Newport.

Day 15: Newport to St Dogmaels
15½ miles (25 km), 6 to 7½ hours

This day finishes the PCP with a flourish – some of the best walking of the whole route, although there's nowhere to get food and drink.

East of Newport Sands, the coast along the first half of this section is wild and uninhabited with numerous rock formations and caves. Pwll-y-Wrach, the Witches' Cauldron, is the remains of a collapsed blowhole. You may see seals on the rocks in this area.

Just before Ceibwr Bay, the route joins the road for a short distance. From here the route is quite tough, but it's a wonderful rollercoaster through stunning cliff scenery to Caemaes Head, which has superb views across Cardigan Bay. (There's camping (£2) at *Allt-y-goed* (☎ 01239 612673).) Take a rest here, and take stock; the end of the PCP is near, and the last four miles, all along the road from here, are something of an anticlimax after the excellent scenery earlier in the day.

You reach the *Poppit Sands YHA Hostel* (☎ 01239 612936, £7.45) in less than a mile. There's B&B from £12.50 at *Briar Bank* (☎ 01239 612339).

The official end of the coast path is three miles beyond Poppit Sands at St Dogmael's. The *Ferry Inn* is a popular place for a postwalk celebration but service can be abrupt. Cheaper and more friendly is the *Teifi Netpool Inn*, where fish & chips cost £3.50. It's just under two miles from St Dogmael's to Cardigan.

Cardigan The former county town of Cardiganshire was an important seafaring and trading centre until the harbour silted up. The TIC (☎ 01239 613230) is in the same building as the theatre, on Bath House Rd.

There are several good places to stay on Gwbert Rd, in the north of the town. Nonsmoking *Maes-a-Môr* (☎ 01239 614929), Park Place, Gwbert Rd, charges from £16. A few doors down is *Brynhyfryd Guest House*

(☎ 01239 612861), from £15. For a light meal, the *Theatr Mwldan Café*, in the theatre building, is excellent (a five-grain vegieburger costs £2.10), and the *Black Lion Hotel* might be another place for a celebratory pint.

Other Long-Distance Paths in Wales

In the chapters on Wales we have covered the Pembrokeshire Coast, Offa's Dyke and Glyndwr's Way long-distance paths, and a selection of day-walks in Pembrokeshire, the Brecon Beacons and Snowdonia, plus another multi-day possibility in Snowdonia, linking four of the day-walks together.

Of course, Wales has much more than this to offer, and we hope the samples we have provided encourage you to travel further and explore some of the quieter corners of Wales for yourself. In this section are a few more pointers. A very useful leaflet called *Walking Wales* is available from the Welsh Tourist Board, from TICs all over Wales, and from the Wales Information Bureau in London (☎ 0171 409 0969).

THE WYE VALLEY
You may reach Wales by crossing the Severn Bridge from England to arrive in Chepstow. This town is the start of the Offa's Dyke Path, described in this chapter, which follows the Wye Valley (the border between England and Wales) to Monmouth before aiming north-west along the edge of the Black Mountains. Between Chepstow and Monmouth, Offa's Dyke Path runs parallel to another long-distance path called the Wye Valley Walk. If you base yourself at Chepstow, Monmouth or somewhere midway such as St Briavels YHA Hostel, you can do day-walks using sections of both these routes. This is an Area of Outstanding Natural Beauty, and well worth a visit on foot.

Also within easy reach of Monmouth is Symonds Yat, the most spectacular section

BRYN THOMAS

BRYN THOMAS

DAVID ELSE

Top: The Church of St Brynach, Pembrokeshire Coast Path
Bottom Left: 13th-century St Govan's Chapel, Pembrokeshire Coast Path
Bottom Right: Main ridge, near Pen y Fan, Brecon Beacons

BRYN THOMAS

BRYN THOMAS

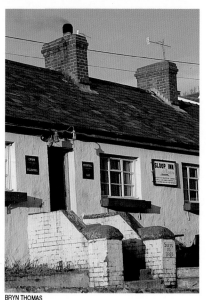

BRYN THOMAS

Top: Danger sign on cliff edge, Pembrokeshire Coast National Park
Bottom Left: Strumble Head lighthouse, Pembrokeshire Coast National Park
Bottom Right: Sloop Inn, Porthgain, Pembrokeshire Coast Path

of the River Wye, where it flows through a winding, deep-sided valley edged with woodland, which was much admired by fanciful Victorian 'tourers' as a place of great beauty. Although Monmouth is in Wales, most of the woodland is part of the Forest of Dean, which is in England (as it's on the east bank of the Wye).

The Forest of Dean has much in common with both countries, and is rich in remains from prehistory – the area is dotted with ancient stones – and from the more recent past when this was a small-scale coal-mining and charcoal-burning centre. Forest Enterprise produce an *Out & About in the Forest of Dean* leaflet which outlines waymarked walking trails, campsites and places of interest all over the forest and is available from local TICs.

To reach Symonds Yat from Monmouth you simply follow the Wye Valley Walk along the west bank of the river, past King Arthur's Cave and Merlins' Cave (one of many sites in Wales supposedly visited by these legendary figures – the first Arthurian legends were written by one Geoffrey of Monmouth) to a place called Biblins, where an intriguing wood and wire suspension bridge carries walkers across to the east bank.

From the east bank you follow level paths through an area called The Slaughter (supposedly the site of a battle between Romans and ancient Britons) to the small settlement of Symonds Yat, where there are a couple of pubs – ideal for lunch – and some B&Bs.

Up a steep path from here is Symonds Yat Rock, which is an excellent lookout. To get back to Monmouth you can retrace your steps, or catch a ferry across the river from near the pub and walk back down the other side to Biblins. There you cross the river again and then either follow the east bank or go up through the hills of Highmeadow Woods – reckoned to be one of the most scenic and interesting parts of the forest – returning to Monmouth via the 'Naval Temple' at Kymin, a monument to commemorate the Battle of the Nile.

Another option is to start at the small village of Christchurch, north of the main road between Monmouth and Coleford, the Forest of Dean's 'capital' (access by bus). From here, a circular route, designed and waymarked by a local group of the Ramblers' Association, goes through Highmeadow Woods past a good lookout at the Beck Stone near Staunton, and several ancient sites, before reaching the Wye near Biblins once again. The route can also be joined at Staunton. The local RA group produces a leaflet with a route description and background information on this area, and many other parts of the Forest of Dean, which are available in local TICs. All these walks are shown in detail on the OS Outdoor Leisure (1:25,000) sheet 14, and it's highly advised you use it if you plan to wander in the woods, as the network of paths and tracks can be confusing.

If you don't want to retrace your steps back to Monmouth, you can continue further along the Wye Valley Walk as far as Welsh Bicknor (on the opposite bank to English Bicknor, naturally), where there's a YHA hostel.

From here, the route goes through England via Goodrich, Ross-on-Wye, Hereford and then west again to cross the border back into Wales at Hay-on-Wye (where it also joins Offa's Dyke Path once again). Beyond here the upper Wye is followed through mid-Wales to the market town of Rhayader. A pack of maps and information sheets has been jointly produced by the county councils of Gwent, Powys and Hereford & Worcester; a single guidebook is planned. Another which covers the route is *Wye Valley Walk* by Heather and Jon Hurley (Thornhill Press). All should be available at local TICs.

THE TAFF TRAIL

Your journey through Wales may start in Cardiff, the capital, which has several interesting things to see and a good choice of places to stay and eat. From here you could consider taking the Taff Trail, a 77 mile waymarked route between Cardiff and Brecon, using canal towpaths, disused railway lines and paths, specifically designed for walkers and cyclists. The route starts in Cardiff Dock, the original Tiger Bay, although recently much smartened up with new buildings and a controversial barrage scheme. It then follows the River Taff north from the capital via the fantastical Castell Coch (Red Castle) and the market town of Pontypridd, through the former heartland of the South Wales coal-mining industry, to the rather grim town of Merthyr Tydfil (Pontypridd to Merthyr could be done on the train).

From Merthyr the scenery improves as you go east of the Brecon Beacons, through Pontsticill to Talybont-on-Usk then along the Monmouthshire & Brecon Canal to Pencelli and Brecon. A handy series of leaflets has been produced by the Taff Trail Project in Aberdare (☎ 01685 883880), and is available from TICs along the route.

ABERGAVENNY & THE USK VALLEY

Another way of heading north from Cardiff would be by train or bus to Pontypool or Abergavenny, from where you could walk though some of the less mountainous bits of the Brecon Beacons National Park along the towpath of the Monmouthshire & Brecon Canal, which follows the valley of the River Usk. From 'Ponty' to Brecon is 33 miles, and Abergavenny to Brecon is 20 miles, but you could break the walk at Crickhowell, which has a *YHA Hostel* and several *B&Bs*, or just start your walk from there. There are numerous other villages along the route, offering accommodation in *B&Bs* or *pubs*, including Talybont-on-Usk and Pencelli mentioned above, and Llanfrynach, mentioned in the Brecon Beacons section of the Wales – Short Walks chapter.

The route just described is the northern half of the Usk Valley Walk. The southern part goes between Pontypool and Caerleon (site of a Roman amphitheatre and possibly one of the sites of the court of King Arthur – and his famous round table), near the large town of Newport (Gwent).

Around Abergavenny

Before you head up the canal for Brecon, you

might consider a day or two in Abergavenny, visiting any of the three hills which are within striking distance of the town. Three miles to the north is the cone-shaped Sugar Loaf, with a steep climb to the top. A couple of miles south of the town is Blorenge, also popular as a launching pad for hang-gliders. Three miles north-east of Abergavenny is Skirrid-fawr: from the top are good views of Sugar Loaf, the Usk Valley and the Black Mountains. The routes are described in detail in *Thirty Walks in the South Black Mountains & the Abergavenny Area* (80p), available from the TIC.

BLACK MOUNTAINS

The Black Mountains are the easternmost section of the Brecon Beacons National Park. Offa's Dyke Path (described in full in this chapter) runs through the Black Mountains from Pandy to Hay-on-Wye, and this section could be followed as a day-walk. The views are spectacular but the route is along a high, exposed grassy ridge that can be very windy. Pandy is on the A465, on the bus route between Abergavenny and Hereford.

It's definitely worth dropping down to visit the ruins of Llanthony Priory, where the remaining buildings now house a *pub* and a delightfully atmospheric *hotel*. Further north up this valley is the *Capel-y-Ffin YHA Hostel*. As a less strenuous alternative to walking along the ridge, you could follow the River Honddu from Llanfihangel, lower down in the valley. TICs stock the two leaflets that cover walks in the northern and southern parts of this area.

The highest point in the Black Mountains is Waun Fach (798m; 2660 ft). Reaching this on foot is a serious proposition. If you've got a car, it's best to drive via Patrishow (an interesting 13th-century church in an idyllic location) to the end of the track in the Mynydd Du Forest. Follow the old railway track up to Grwyne Fawr Reservoir, where a path runs up Waun Fach. Alternatively, the peak can be reached from Llanbedr up to the ridge that runs north via Pen-y-Gadair Fawr.

FFOREST FAWR & THE BLACK MOUNTAIN

This area lies to the west of the Brecon Beacons range, in the western part of the Brecon Beacons National Park. It is not visited often as the main Beacons range, but there is a great variety of scenery and several good walking opportunities.

To explore Fforest Fawr, the *youth hostel* at Ystradfellte makes a good base, and along the rivers and streams to the south there are a number of attractive waterfalls in this wooded area. The most attractive is Sgwd-yr-eira (the spout of snow), where you can actually view the falls from behind the water. It's an easy two mile walk south of Ystrad-fellte, on the River Hepste. There are other falls at Ponteddfechan and Coelbren. Look out for the leaflet on *Waterfall Walks* at local TICs.

The Black Mountain is the westernmost part of the park (not to be confused with the Black Mountains in the east). The name repetition is not surprising – when the weather is bad, any bare piece of high ground in the Brecon Beacons National Park deserves the name. This western section of the park contains the wildest, least visited walking country. The highest point, Fan Brycheiniog (or Camarthen Van), can be reached from the YHA hostel at Llanddeusant or along a path that leads off the sideroad just north of the Dan-yr-ogof Showcaves. The caves themselves are worth a visit, and are on the main A4067 between Sennybridge and Ystradgynlais (once known as 'Why Strangle Us' by US serviceman based here in WWII).

WEST WALES

Walks in this area which are fully described in this book are the PCP, and a day-walk that takes you into the Preseli Hills. For other day-walks in this part of Wales, you can follow sections of the PCP for a few hours, then return to your start by following paths inland. Or you can walk for a whole day and catch a bus back to your starting point. For example, if you based yourself in the village of Newport for a few days, you could go up Carn Ingli and the surrounding hills on one day, and on the next day walk along the coast path to Fishguard or Cardigan and then catch a bus back. Details of places to stay in Newport and transport in the area are fully described in the Pembrokeshire section of the Wales – Short Walks chapter.

Another part of the Pembrokeshire Coast National Park which is often overlooked is Daugleddau Estuary, a broad tranquil wetland area where four large rivers meet. So few people visit this area it's been dubbed 'The Secret Waterway' by the local tourist organisation. For walkers, there are several short routes called Secret Waterway Trails, and a 50 mile circular route, the Landsker Borderlands Trail, which pass through the area.

The villages of Landshipping and Law-renny can both be reached by public transport from Haverfordwest, Pembroke or Tenby, and from there you can wander along the riverbanks, and through quiet villages and farmland. Carew Castle is worth a visit, there are some historic shipbuilding sites, and several of the villages have pleasant *pubs* and *teashops* which make good lunch stops. The birdwatching here is also excellent.

To tie in a lot of these options, you could take the bus between Pembroke and Tenby, get off at Carew, visit the castle, then walk north on one of the Secret Waterway Trails to Cresswell Quay, pick up the Landsker Borderlands Trail, and follow this through Lawrenny and Landshipping to Canaston Bridge, on the bus route between Haver-fordwest, Narberth and Tenby. This is over 20 miles, so it would be a long day, but you could always shorten it by getting the bus out of Lawrenny or Landshipping, or splitting it in two by staying overnight in the area. Lawrenny and Cresswell Quay both have *B&Bs*. More information is available from Narberth TIC (☎ 01834 860061).

For details on shorter circular walking routes all over Pembrokeshire, local TICs sell a very good range of booklets produced by the national park, including *The Daug-leddau Estuary* and *Around Newport*. More information on the longer trails is also avail-able from local TICs, or the main TIC at

Haverfordwest (☎ 01437 763110). For more information on the area, including routes, guided and self-guided walking holidays of varying lengths, accommodation, transport, and so on, contact Preseli Pembrokeshire Walking Holidays at Menter Preseli (☎ 01437 767655) or Landsker Countryside Holidays (☎ 01834 860965).

MID-WALES

Mid-Wales is often overlooked by visitors to Britain. It just seems to be a fairly empty space on the map between the Brecon Beacons and the southern part of Snowdonia, near Machynlleth. However, the lack of features such as main roads and towns, and the presence of several large mountains, indicate that this area is of great interest to walkers. In the early 1970s this area narrowly missed being declared a national park, which has kept it out of the limelight ever since.

The mountains of mid-Wales, although not quite as high as those in Snowdonia, are just as wild, and the high ground is no place for novices. There are also lower walks through valleys, woods and farmland which are more suitable for everyone. Good bases from which to explore mid-Wales include Llandovery, from where you can also reach the Black Mountain section of the Brecon Beacons National Park, or Builth Wells or Rhayader, from where you can head west into the high ground or explore sections of the less imposing River Wye on the Wye Valley Walk, described more fully earlier in this section.

Other good bases include Llangurig, Llanidloes or Machynlleth. The waymarked Owain Glyndwr's Way (see earlier in this chapter) goes though several of these towns, and is an excellent introduction to mid-Wales; even if you haven't got time to do it all, following a few stages would be a great way of seeing the area. Two other long-distance paths pass through mid-Wales, on their way between the northern and southern extremities of the country; see Trans-Wales Routes. Mid-Wales walking holidays are offered by Dinefwr Treks

(☎ 01591 610638), based near Llandovery. Prices start at £90 for weekend breaks and rise to £315 for a week, including accommodation, food and guide.

TRANS-WALES ROUTES

Winding through Wales between Cardiff and Conwy, traversing just about every bit of high, wild landscape it can find of the way, is the Cambrian Way. It bills itself as a 'mountain connoisseur's walk' – and that's certainly true. It includes the Black Mountains, an east-west traverse of the Brecon Beacons National Park, the heart of remote mid-Wales including the summit of Plynlimon (Pumlumon), plus the high peaks of Cadair Idris, the Rhinog Mountains, Snowdon and the Carneddau.

For experienced walkers and backpackers this would be an excellent trip, although the 274 miles make it longer, and much harder, than the Pennine Way, and it would probably take between three and four weeks to complete. However, help is at hand.

An enterprising group of hoteliers along the Cambrian Way have divided the route into five stages and offer self-guided or guided one-week walking holidays along 'their bit'. Aimed at both British walkers and walkers from abroad, the packages include accommodation, food, luggage transfer, transport to drop-off points, maps and route cards. There are even plans for mobile phones in case of emergency. Full details are available from Nick Bointon (☎ 01550 750274), Cambrian Way Walkers Association, Llanerchindda Farm, Llandovery SA20 0NB, or Alan Thomas (☎ 01873 810362) at the Dragon Hotel, Crickhowell. The route is described in *The Cambrian Way* by A Drake (available through Cordee, £4.50).

The other main trans-Wales route is Snowdonia to the Gower. This was designed and written about by Tony Gillham in his book of the same name. The route can be covered in between 11 and 14 days, as it is more direct than the Cambrian Way, although they overlap in many places, particularly the northern section between Cadair Idris and the North Wales coast. The southern parts of the two walks are quite different: the Cambrian Way goes from Cardiff and across the whole width of the Brecon Beacons, while (as its name suggests) the other route ends on the Gower Peninsula – an Area of Outstanding Natural Beauty and Heritage Coast – visiting only the western side of the Brecon Beacons Park.

The concept of Snowdonia to the Gower is rather different to many other long-distance paths too; rather than being encouraged to follow a single line, walkers on Snowdonia to the Gower are encouraged to take alternative routes, either high or low according to taste, passing areas of particular interest or as dictated by convenient places to stay. The author states in his introduction that he wants the route to remain like this, hopefully to avoid the 'ghastly scars of erosion' seen on other, waymarked, more publicised routes. *Snowdonia to the Gower* (available through Cordee, £14.95) is a hardback book, with route description, glossy photos, beautifully drawn aerial views and maps and good background information.

Also available is *The Snowdonia to the Gower Companion*, a slim booklet with a condensed version of the text and accommodation details, designed to be carried on the route.

THE NORTH SNOWDONIA AREA

Apart from the selection of routes we describe in full in the Snowdonia section of Wales – Short Walks chapter, the North Snowdonia area has a lot more to offer. In this book we have chosen well-known and well-trodden routes for two reasons: firstly, to show you the most spectacular walks in the area, and secondly, to protect some of the quieter mountain walks from becoming overcrowded.

If you wish to visit the quieter places, a small amount of research and careful perusal of an OS or Harveys map will unveil their locations and thus enable you to enjoy them, but without the company of many other people. Places to start include the mountain groups just south of Snowdon – Moel Hebog, the Moelwyns, the Rhinogs, the Arans and Cadair Idris. But the list of possible walks is almost endless.

If the weather is bad on Snowdon and the other high peaks, you could consider some coastal walking, particularly around the north and west of the Isle of Anglesey where there are huge sea cliffs and sweeping sandy beaches. Have a look at the OS Landranger (1:50,000) sheet 114 and you're sure to find some inspiration. You can choose between short day-walks (South Stacks is a good place to start) or something longer (see *The Isle of Anglesea Coast Path* published by Footprint Press). Similarly the Llyn Peninsula west of Abersoch offers great coastal scenery, and the weather here is often good when it's bad on the high ground.

WALES

Llanfairpwllgwyngllgogerychwyrndrobwllllantysiliogogogoch

(St Mary's church in the hollow of the white hazel near a rapid whirlpool and the church of St Tysilio near the red cave)

Scotland – Short Walks

WALKING IN SCOTLAND
Walking Conditions & When to Go

Scotland is not only further north than England and Wales, the terrain is higher and less populated. These factors have a number of implications for walkers: walking, in general, is mostly in remote areas; mountain-walking, in particular, is a more serious affair; and climate is of greater concern, especially during winter.

Unless otherwise stated, all the routes described in both this chapter and the Scotland – Long-Distance Paths chapter are described as for summer only. This is usually May to September for mountains, although walking the West Highland Way or Southern Upland Way is normally OK between April and October. (Winter walking in the higher areas of Scotland is 'technical' – requiring, at the very least, an ice-axe, crampons and mountaineering experience.)

Note that July and August is holiday time in Britain, so everywhere is likely to be busier than normal – although only a few parts of Scotland ever get *really* crowded. Midges (see Pests) can also be a problem at this time. The most pleasant time to be in Scotland is May to mid-June – before the midges come out. September (and sometimes October) is also good, although days are colder and shorter.

Access

The situation regarding right of access to open country in Scotland is different to that in England and Wales. This is partly the result of legislation and partly the result of the Scottish tradition of 'freedom to roam'. Providing you do not cause damage or intentionally disrupt a lawful activity, such as deer 'stalking' (hunting), and that you leave land if (in the very unlikely event) you are asked to do so by the owner, you should not have any trouble. There is much cooperation between organisations such as the Scottish Landowners' Federation, the Mountaineer-

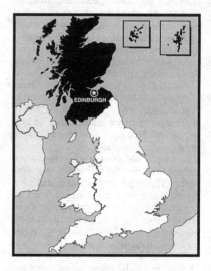

ing Council of Scotland and the Ramblers' Association to promote responsible access to the countryside. In 1996 a Concordat on Access was agreed to by such bodies in an Access Forum convened by Scottish Natural Heritage, a government body.

Most of the routes described in this book cross land with no access restrictions. You should, however, be prepared to avoid certain areas where you might disrupt or disturb wildlife, deer stalking and grouse shooting (which mainly take place between 12 August and the third week in October), and lambing (generally between mid-April and the end of May). This is particularly important if you want to go beyond the routes in this book to explore the hills of Scotland further.

Rights of Way Rights of Way do exist in Scotland, but local authorities are not required to list and map them, as in England and Wales. As a result, they are not shown on Ordnance Survey (OS) maps. There is,

SCOTLAND

however, a Scottish Rights of Way Society which does much to publicise those routes which have or deserve to have legal status and to defend those which are under threat. (Their guide, *Scottish Hill Tracks*, costs £10.95.) These routes include ancient drove roads used for cattle and sheep being taken to distant markets (often in England) military roads constructed mainly in the 18th century for the use of English troops stationed in Scotland, and kirk and coffin tracks generally associated with a particular clan.

Books

There's a huge number of books on walking in Scotland. As a starter try *Great Walks*

Munros & Munro-Bagging

In 1891 Sir Hugh T Munro, a member of the recently founded Scottish Mountaineering Club, published a list of over 500 Scottish mountains over 3000 ft – a height at which they were regarded as gaining particular significance. (This old 'imperial' measurement's metric equivalent is 914m, although it rather loses some of the original mystique when translated.) Sir Hugh differentiated between 283 'Separate Mountains' or 'mountains in their own right' (usually those with a significant drop on all sides or some other distinguishing feature, such as distance from the next peak or 'peculiarity of formation'), and those surrounding peaks which were merely satellites of the Separate Mountains. At the same time, he inadvertently gave his name to all main mountains on the list. It is now the aspiration of many walkers to reach the summit (or 'bag') of as many 'Munros' as possible. The satellite peaks have become known as 'tops'.

The practice of Munro-bagging must have started soon after the list was first published, because by 1901 one Reverend AE Robertson had climbed the lot. These days, Munro-bagging has become a national passion: keen walkers and climbers keep their own Munro tick-list, and attempt to add to it in the same way golfers try to get their handicap down. Well over a thousand walkers have managed to bag them all, earning themselves the title 'Munroist'. These days there are all sorts of records: oldest person to have bagged all Munros; first person to bag them all at one go; fastest person to bag them all at one go (66 days); first person to do them all on a mountain bike... There have been people who bagged them strictly in order of south to north, strictly in order of height, and there are even rumours of someone doing them in alphabetical order. Madness it may be, but for normal mortals Munros do offer some wonderful walking and some great views; there's no reason why any reasonably fit visitor shouldn't bag a few during a Scottish visit.

Note, however, that the final tally of Munros is not fixed. Most commentators have it standing at 277, while one respected almanac lists 281. It's recorded that Sir Hugh himself was working on a revision before he died in 1919. In the following years, some mountains absent from his original list have been measured at over 3000 ft by more accurate surveys, while others have been demoted. Other mountains' claims to Munro status are often disputed (even though they're over 3000 ft, and on the list) because they're considered not to have the requisite drop on all sides (making them a 'top' as opposed to a mountain in its own right).

Some people say that arguments are pointless, and that Munros should be those on Sir Hugh's original list (whatever his errors) with no additions or removals, while 'revisionists' passionately believe in keeping the list 'up to date', adding 'new' Munros when appropriate or mercilessly scrubbing any pretenders that don't quite make the grade. Other people wryly note that the continuing debate does little more than provide material for bearded men to rant on about in pubs and bothies.

The bible for all aspiring Munro-baggers is *The Munros*, edited by Donald Bennet (published by the Scottish Mountaineering Club), revised and reprinted several times over the years, but always with good general descriptions, maps and photos to whet your appetite. For more detail on Munro route descriptions, and advice on how to bag them all most efficiently or enjoyably, *The High Mountains of Britain & Ireland* by Irvine Butterfield is an absolute must. This book also covers the 'Furth Munros' – in Wales (Snowdonia), England (The Lake District) and various places in the Republic of Ireland.

Once you've bagged all your Munros and Tops, there are other groups of summits to aim for. Consider the Corbetts – Scottish Hills over 700m (2500 ft), with a drop of at least 150m (500ft) on all sides – or the Donalds – those over 610m (2000 ft). Some English Lake District mountains over 610m (2000 ft) have recently been dubbed the Wainwrights. Most curious are the Marilyns: hills and mountains which rise 150m (500 ft) above their surroundings, regardless of absolute height, distance or topographical merit. These are listed in *The Relative Hills of Britain* by Alan Dawson (Cicerone) and do include many Munros. In case you're wondering, the total is 1542. Currently. ∎

SCOTLAND

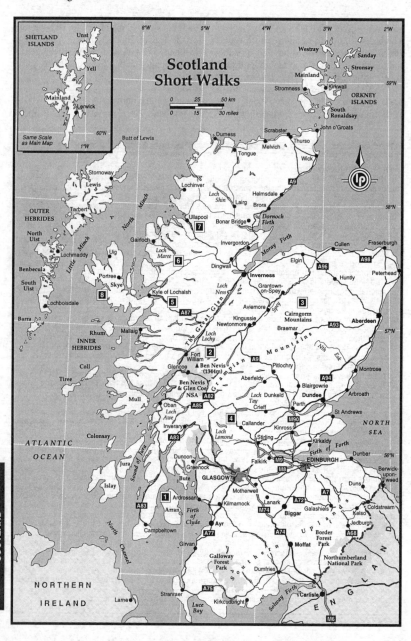

Scotland by Hamish Brown et al (published by Printwise Publications) which describes a good range of routes of varying difficulty all over the country. Or try *100 Best Routes on Scottish Mountains* by Ralph Storer (published by Sphere).

If you're a peak-bagger, the Scottish Mountaineering Club publishes *The Munros Hillwalkers Guide* and another to *The Corbetts* (see aside), and several *District Guides* listing mainly high-level walks, plus other more serious routes in glens and rock-climbing opportunities for those with experience, including *The Southern Highlands*, *The Cairngorms* and *The Islands of Scotland*. These books are between £15 and £18 each, and are all published by Cordee.

The High Mountains Companion is a condensed text of Irvine Butterfield's *The High Mountains of Britain & Ireland*. Both books cover the British Isles, but concentrate on the mountains of Scotland, and are described in more detail in the Books section of the Facts for the Walker chapter. *200 Challenging Walks in Britain & Ireland*, also described in the Facts for the Walker chapter, has a good Scotland selection.

And just in case you thought all walks in Scotland were up the biggest mountains, there's *Exploring Scottish Hill Tracks* by Ralph Storer (David & Charles), with a marvellous range of circular routes and longer expeditions for walkers and mountain bikers

along ancient drove roads, whisky roads and even coffin roads.

Also recommended if you don't always want to attack high peaks are the *Pathfinder Guides* (published by OS & Jarrold) to *Loch Lomond & The Trossachs*, *Fort William & Glen Coe* and *Skye*. These books each cover about 30 routes, from low and easy to high and hard, with OS map excerpts, colour photos and background information.

Highly recommended if you like mountains but can't stand the intensity of Munro-bagging for its own sake is *The First Fifty* by Muriel Gray. This 'antidote to every walking book you've ever read' is by a hip and popular TV personality who just happens to like mountain-walking, and likes even more to de-bunk the mystique and fastidiousness that can sometimes envelope other writers and books on walking in Scotland.

Maps

There are well-established routes up the more popular Scottish mountains, such as Ben Lomond and Ben Nevis. On other routes however, paths, where they exist, may be discontinuous and not generally well marked by cairns or signs, such as routes south of the border. The walker in Scotland should be competent in the use of map and compass, and be prepared to navigate difficult terrain if cloud descends (as it often does). Maps should always be carried; possibly OS Landrangers (1:50,000), although in many areas Harveys (1:40,000 or 1:25,000) or the OS Outdoor Leisure (1:25,000) maps will be helpful in giving more detail.

Pests

You might encounter the infamous biting Highland Midge while walking in Scotland, particularly in the high rainfall areas of the West Highlands from the end of May until September. They are most troublesome in the early morning, in the evening and in the shade. Defences include full body cover (including nets worn over the head!), creams and sprays, and (fortunately for the walker) constant movement. Less common, but

SCOTLAND

potentially more serious, are ticks from sheep and deer which you may pick up by brushing against vegetation such as bracken; ticks can transmit Lyme disease.

Places to Stay

See the Accommodation section of the Facts for the Walker chapter for details on Scottish hostels and bothies.

Isle of Arran

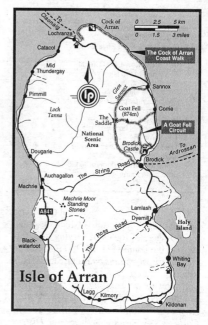

Arran is called 'Scotland in miniature'; the steep mountains and deep valleys in the north of the island are reminiscent of the Highlands, while the rolling heath and moorland of the south is similar to southern Scotland. There's even a long straight valley dividing the north from the south, a minor version of the mainland's great Highland Boundary Fault.

Arran is only an hour's ferry ride from the mainland and is easily accessible from most parts of Strathclyde (Glasgow's hinterland). Consequently, it is very popular; families come for a week on the beach at the southern 'resorts', golfers for a round on one of numerous courses on the island, and anglers to try their luck at sea-fishing. Sailors, cyclists, windsurfers and pony trekkers also come here to do their stuff. On bank holidays the throng is joined by hordes of Glasgow bikers. They are peaceful enough, but some people may want to avoid the constant parade of gleaming motorcycles up and down the seafront. At other times this island seems to be big enough to absorb everyone, especially walkers, who can leave the hullabaloo behind and head into Arran's marvellous mountains and glens.

There's enough here to keep any walker happy for quite a few days. The island's highest mountain is Goat Fell (874m, 2866 ft), near Brodick (Arran's main town), and one of the most popular points on the island. We describe some walks involving Goat Fell itself, and outline several other options in the area.

In the north-west of Arran are the Pirnmill Hills. Although not quite as high as Goat Fell, and less rugged in appearance, they are far less frequently visited. Finally, there are some lovely coastal walks, worthwhile at any time, but particularly when the hills are shrouded in cloud. Possibly the best of these is the walk from Lochranza to Sannox, which is briefly described at the end of this section.

A GOAT FELL CIRCUIT

> **Distance** 11¼ miles (18 km)
> **Duration** 6 to 7½ hours
> **Start & Finish** Brodick
> **Regional Centre** Brodick
> **Region** Strathclyde
> **Area** Isle of Arran National Scenic Area
> **Summary** A quite demanding walk, over some steep ridges, to the highest point on the island. Paths are mostly clear, but high sections are potentially confusing and dangerous in bad weather.

SCOTLAND

There are several routes up to the summit of Goat Fell. The most popular are from Brodick Castle and from Corrie on the east side of the mountain. A quieter and more pleasing approach goes from The Saddle, at the heads of Glen Rosa and Glen Sannox, on the west side of the mountain. The route we describe goes from Glen Rosa to The Saddle, then up the steep and narrow West Ridge to North Goat Fell, continuing along Stacach Ridge to the summit, from where you can descend to either Brodick Castle or Corrie.

Paths are generally good and easy to follow, except up the West Ridge, and between North Goat Fell and Goat Fell, where great care should be taken in bad weather, as there are very steep cliffs on either side of the ridge. When the sun shines, Arran masquerades as an island in the Mediterranean, but it can get very cold, wet and windy up here, so come well prepared. Map and compass knowledge are essential.

Brodick Castle & Country Park, Goat Fell and Glen Rosa are National Trust for Scotland (NTS) owned, and there are no access restrictions.

Direction, Distance & Duration

This route can be done in either direction, but clockwise is recommend as the overall ascent is more gentle (although some sections are very steep), and the high peak comes towards the end of the route. There are signposts where paths leave the road, but not on the mountain. The distance on the map is 11¼ miles, but there's at least 800m of ascent on this route, and some tricky bits of routefinding if the mist comes down, so allow six to 7½ hours walking time, plus extra for lunch, photos and admiring the view; around seven to nine hours in total.

Information

Brodick's tourist information centre (TIC) (☎ 01770 302140) is on the pier, and has a sub-office on the ferry itself. Both have plenty of leaflets, including *Walks on Arran* (which provides several useful pointers), and accommodation lists. Brodick also has banks and a post office.

Books & Maps The only book dedicated to Arran is *44 Walks on Arran* by Mary Welsh (£5.95). Forest Enterprise have produced a useful little booklet on *Forest Walks in Arran*, available from TICs (50p).

Arran is covered by OS Landranger (1:50,000) sheet 69. Pathfinder (1:25,000) sheets 441 and 454 have more detail. Harveys have 1:25,000 maps of *South Arran* and *North Arran*. The latter covers routes in this section, with a very good information booklet detailing several walking and scrambling routes, plus background on geology and wildlife.

Guided Walks

The Rangers at Brodick Castle & Country Park (☎ 01770 302462) lead walks throughout the summer, ranging from afternoon wildlife strolls through the low forests to full days out (weekly) on Goat Fell and other peaks.

Places to Stay & Eat

The best base is Brodick, which is where the ferry from the mainland arrives. It is also the centre of the island's public transport system (although Lamlash, to the south, is actually the capital). The nearest *SYHA hostels* are at Lochranza (☎ 01770 830631) in the north of the island, and Whiting Bay (☎ 01770 700339, £5.25) in the south. Neither are ideal for this route, but the island's excellent bus service means that you can get to/from most places fairly easily. The most popular campsite for walkers is the beautifully situated *Glen Rosa Farm* (☎ 01770 302380), about 1½ miles from Brodick Pier; it is well placed for the start of the route. Facilities are limited (water taps and basic toilet block), but the price is only £2. Wild camping is not allowed anywhere on Arran without permission.

For B&B, Brodick has a wide choice. Opposite the ferry pier, the *Douglas Hotel* (☎ 01770 302155) charges from £15 (room only) per person. Shore Rd runs along the seafront and is lined with other options. Most display their prices and facilities, so you can cruise the strip looking for something to fit your specifications. Some do evening meals as well, and these are also open to non-residents. Worth trying are *Tigh Na Mara* (☎ 01770 302538), from £16.50 per person, and the recommended *Dunvegan House* (☎ 01770 302811) from £52. On Alma Rd, further back from the sea, are more choices including *Belvedere* (☎ 01770 302397), from £15. On the north side of town, near the golf course, is *The Orwin* (☎ 01770 302009), with ensuite rooms for £20.

If you'd prefer to stay in Corrie, near the start/finish of some of the optional routes we describe here, try the *Corrie Hotel* (☎ 01770 810273) with B&B from £20 (£25 ensuite), or the *Blackrock Guest House* (☎ 01770 810282), from £19.

For places to eat in Brodick, *Stalkers Eating House* (☎ 01770 302579), on Shore Rd, does good-value meals for between £4 and £6. Pubs doing bar meals include *Duncan's Bar* on Shore Rd and the *Ormidale Hotel* (near the golf club). More up market is the award-winning *Creelers Seafood Restaurant* (☎ 01770 302810), 1½ miles north of Brodick. It's a bistro-style place with some outside seating, and main dishes from around £10 to £15. For self-catering, or stocking up on hill food, Brodick has two supermarkets and several smaller shops.

Getting There & Away

Bus Ardrossan (on the mainland) can be reached from most parts of Britain by National Express, sometimes via Glasgow. Local buses run regularly between Glasgow and Ardrossan. On Arran, Stagecoach buses (☎ 01770 302000) circle the coast road, several times per day in each direction and along the String Road across the centre of the island. This makes linear walking routes out from Brodick easy: you can always catch a bus back. Bus and postbus services are listed in the very handy *Arran Transport Guide* leaflet, available from the TIC.

Train ScotRail trains run several times a day between Glasgow and Largs, via Ardrossan. Some services go all the way to the harbour, to connect with ferry sailings. Otherwise,

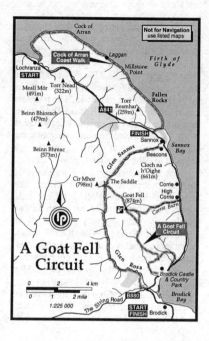

A Goat Fell Circuit

you'll have to get off at Ardrossan South Beach, and walk or taxi to the harbour.

Boat The ferry between Ardrossan and Brodick is operated by Caledonian MacBrayne (CalMac) (Brodick ☎ 01770 302166 or Ardrossan ☎ 01294 463470), with four or five sailings per day in each direction (three in winter). The return fare is £6.

If you're travelling to/from north-west Scotland, there is a summer-only ferry between Claonaig on the Kintyre peninsula and Lochranza in north Arran. From Claonaig you can head south to Campbeltown and the famous Mull of Kintyre, or north to Oban and the coast road to Fort William.

Car Arran is linked to the mainland by ferry. The most popular goes from Ardrossan, about 25 miles south-west of Glasgow, charging about £50 return for cars. Much cheaper, and kinder to Arran, is to leave vehicles in the guarded harbour car park (about £3 per day), take the ferry as a passenger, and to make use of Arran's excellent bus service.

The Route
Stage 1: Brodick to The Saddle
5½ miles (9 km), 2½ to 3 hours

From Brodick, head northwards along the coast road. At a junction, take the String Road left towards Blackwaterfoot, and after 50m turn right (signposted Glen Rosa). Follow this past the campsite, where the tar ends, and continue along a clear track west and then north into the glen itself. Up to your right (north-east) is the bulk of Goat Fell. To your left are Beinn a Chliabhain and A'Chir, leading to the dramatic peak of Cir Mhor (798m) overlooking the head of the glen.

The Saddle is the low point between Cir Mhor and Goat Fell, and the track, which becomes a path about halfway up the glen, heads straight for it. From the campsite to The Saddle takes about 1½ to two hours. At The Saddle, to the north you will see Glen Sannox dropping away towards the sea. To your immediate left are the slopes of Cir Mhor, with the high castellated ridge of Caisteal Abhail (Arran's second-highest summit) visible to the north-west, across the deep and intimidating Coire nan Uamh. To the immediate right (south-east) is the West Ridge, leading steeply up to North Goat Fell. The Stacach Ridge between here and Goat Fell itself, topped by four smaller peaks, can be clearly seen.

Shorter Alternative If the weather is inclement, or you lack the desire to tackle the West Ridge up to Goat Fell, you can either retrace your steps to Brodick, or continue down Glen Sannox. The first section of descent is very steep and great care must be taken, especially in the wet. An eroded path leads down to the valley floor and then follows the north side of the burn along the glen (boggy in places), crossing the burn just before reaching the coast road at Sannox. From The Saddle to Sannox takes about two to 2½ hours. You can catch a bus back to

Brodick, or refresh yourself at the nearby *Ingledean Hotel* bar and restaurant. (Don't miss the much photographed metal sheep at the end of Sannox jetty.) Just north over the bridge, the unpretentious *Golf Club* serves teas, snacks, meals, and home-made cakes.

Stage 2: The Saddle to Goat Fell Summit
1¼ miles (2 km), 1½ to 2 hours

From The Saddle, aim west to south-west, up the fairly clear ridge-crest path towards North Goat Fell. There are some narrow, exposed sections, and a few near-vertical 'steps' where you'll need to use your hands. Fortunately, the vertical bits and the exposed bits do not coincide. After one to 1½ hours you near the summit of North Goat Fell (810m). The final section is a scramble, but the summit can be reached more easily by passing below the top (keep it on your left) to reach the ridge, and then turn back to approach from the east across large slabs and boulders.

From North Goat Fell, a path leads along the Stacach Ridge south-east and then south to Goat Fell. The ridge is topped with four smaller peaks. These are passed mostly on the left (east) side, as the path takes the easiest route, but some can also be passed on the right. The summits of the minor peaks should not be attempted unless you are a confident rock-climber.

The final section requires some hopping and leaping over piles of giant boulders, to reach Goat Fell summit (874m) about 30 minutes from North Goat Fell. The summit is marked by a trig point and view indicator. On a clear day the views are amazing, and knowing what you're looking at helps put it all into perspective. You might glimpse Skiddaw in the Lake District (see the Cumbria Way section of this book) over 100 miles away, or Ben Lomond (also mentioned in this book), practically a neighbour at 44¾ miles. Closer to hand you can, of course, see over the whole of Arran. Particularly dramatic is the conical mass of Holy Island, jutting out from the sea in Lamlash Bay.

Stage 3A: Goat Fell Summit to Brodick

4½ miles (7 km), 2 to 2½ hours

You have two choices for the descent: this stage describes the straightforward, but often busy, Castle Path, back to Brodick; Stage 3B is a more peaceful descent, and takes the shorter, but steeper, Corrie Path, from where you can catch a bus back to Brodick.

From the summit, a path leads directly due east across boulders, then down steep scree before easing slightly to follow a ridge, with the deep valley of Coire Lan to the left (north). At a junction of paths, keep right, and head south-east and then south on a clear path, badly eroded in places, down a valley and into the woodland around Brodick Castle (about 1½ to two hours from the summit). There are several short waymarked walks through the forest, and you can follow the signs to the castle itself, or keep more to the west on a track which brings you out near the junction of the String Road and the coast road, on the north edge of Brodick town.

From Brodick Castle back to the town is 1½ miles. If you're camping at Glen Rosa, it is tempting to cut across the fields and head straight for your tent. There is no right of way here, and the short cut is much harder than it seems. You must negotiate several fences and the river (too wide to be jumped), and avoid some areas of bog, not to mention various farmers and country park rangers.

Stage 3B: Goat Fell to Corrie

2½ miles (4 km), 1½ to 2 hours

Follow the directions in Stage 3A as far as the junction, where you keep left (right goes to Brodick Castle) and continue heading east. The path is marked by cairns, but in bad weather take care, as cliffs on the north side of the path drop straight into Coire Lan. The path swings north, crossing a burn and heads east again down the valley, over a high fence, through a patch of woodland, to meet a track which leads down to the coast road, at the southern end of Corrie village. Here you can wait for the bus. If you've got some time to spare, the bar at the *Corrie Hotel* is pleasant. If you miss the last bus, through too much time on the hill or in the pub, you can get a taxi back to Brodick (☎ 01770 600725).

Other Options in the Goat Fell Area

If you don't want to tackle the steep ridges described in the route above, you can go up and down Goat Fell on the more straightforward Castle Path. The total distance from/to Brodick is nine miles, and you should allow about five to six hours walking time. To go up and down the Corrie Path from/to Corrie is a distance of five miles and takes about four to five hours walking. You could, of course, combine the two routes into a traverse.

If the ridge route gives you a taste for more, Goat Fell is surrounded by a number

---

Other Things to do on Arran

If the cloud is on the high peaks, and you've already done the Cock of Arran Coast Walk we recommend, there are a few other interesting ways to pass the time on Arran. North of Brodick is the small Heritage Museum open Monday to Saturday, covering the history of the island. Beyond here (2½ miles north of town) is Brodick Castle & Country Park. The castle is the ancient stronghold of the dukes of Hamilton, now in the hands of the National Trust for Scotland (NTS), but still with more of a lived-in feel than some NTS properties. The kitchens and scullery, complete with displays of peculiar kitchen devices, are well worth a look. The Country Park has several short walking trails and the walled garden is particularly attractive.

On the west side of the island, reached by the String Road across the centre, are the Machrie Moor Standing Stones. This is an eerie place, and these are the most impressive of the six stone circles on the island. There's another group at nearby Auchagallon.

Blackwaterfoot is the largest village on the west coast, and it has a large resort hotel. From here, you can walk down to the King's Cave, Drumadoon – Arran is one of several islands that lays claim to a cave where Robert the Bruce had his famous arachnid encounter. This walk could be combined with a visit to the Machrie standing stones. ■

SCOTLAND

of other peaks including Cir Mhor, Ciogh na h'Oighe, Castheal Abhail and Beinn Tarsuinn – some of the peaks on the superb ridges running down either side of Glen Rosa and Glen Sannox. There are numerous possibilities for linking them up to form excellent day-walks. For example, a circuit from Glen Rosa over Beinn a Chliabhain, Beinn Tarsuinn and Beinn Nuis; or, from Sannox, over Suidhe Fhearghas, Caisteal Abhail and Cir Mhor finishing down Glen Sannox. As with all Scottish mountains, treat these with great respect. A map and compass are essential; the weather can change frighteningly quickly, the paths are not always clear and there are precipitous drops from some of the ridges.

THE COCK OF ARRAN COAST WALK

If you want a change of scenery, or the cloud is too low for any walk in the hills, there is a very fine route along the coast in the far north of the island, between Lochranza and Sannox. You can get to/from both villages easily by bus. Even in miserable weather, this route is atmospheric and interesting, as it passes Lochranza Castle, some impressive cliffs, the site of a landslip at Fallen Rocks, the isolated fishing cottages at Fairy Dell and Laggan, Ossian's Cave, and of course the Cock of Arran itself, a prominent block of sandstone (not named after a rooster). There is also a very good chance of seeing seals and a variety of sea birds. This eight mile walk takes about four to five hours.

Ben Nevis & Glen Coe

Two of Scotland's most famous place-names, Ben Nevis and Glen Coe, lie in the Western Highlands, near Fort William, the region's capital. From Glasgow and Loch Lomond, the A82 – today also dubbed the 'Road to the Isles' – snakes across remote Rannoch Moor, winds through magnificent Glen Coe to follow the long finger of Loch Linnhe, the start of the Great Glen, all the way to Fort William. Ben Nevis, the highest

mountain in Scotland and Britain, is just over three miles from Fort William and overlooks the town.

The complex geology of this part of Scotland has bequeathed scenery par excellence and many great walking opportunities – most beyond the scope of this book. In this section we describe three 'taster' day-walks to show you something of the area, hopefully inspiring you to explore further on your own.

As well as the Road to the Isles, Fort William can be reached from Glasgow on the fabulous West Highland Railway, which also provides access to some more remote parts of this fine mountain area (see aside).

GLEN COE & GLEN ETIVE CIRCUIT

> **Distance** 10 miles (16 km)
> **Duration** 5 hours
> **Start & Finish** Altnafeadh
> **Regional Centre** Fort William
> **Region** Highland
> **Area** Ben Nevis & Glen Coe National Scenic Area
> **Summary** A rough and quite demanding walk over two high mountain passes. As several streams need crossing, don't attempt this walk during or after heavy rains.
>
> **Note** Throughout this section, we have differentiated between Glen Coe – the glen, and Glencoe – the village.

Glen Coe is known as the 'glen of weeping', not, allegedly, because of the rainfall levels (although this is one of the wetter areas of Scotland), but because it was the scene of the infamous massacre of the MacDonalds by the Campbells in 1692. Charles Dickens felt it 'bleak and wild and mighty in its loneliness' but these days it is a magnet for tourists, walkers and mountaineers alike. At the head of the glen are the two splendid peaks of Buachaille Etive Mor and Buachaille Etive Beag (the shepherds of Etive), which can also be seen from the West Highland Way (described in the Scotland – Long-Distance Paths chapter) which also passes this way.

The impressive glen is the product not only of glacial processes but also of its own-

SCOTLAND

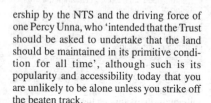

The West Highland Railway

The West Highland Railway (WHR) runs between Glasgow and Fort William, through some of Scotland's most wild and spectacular mountain scenery, which is also some of Britain's finest walking country. Stations such as Arrochar & Tarbet, Crainlarich, Bridge of Orchy and Spean Bridge allow you to set off on a seemingly endless range of wonderful mountain walks direct from the platform. There are several opportunities for circular walks, or you can get off at one station, have a good walk, then catch the train again from another station up or down the line. From Fort William Station, it's only a few miles walk to Scotland's highest peak, Ben Nevis.

Possibly the most intriguing place to get off the train is at Corrour, which at 400m ASL, is the highest station in Britain. Corrour Station lies in the middle of Rannoch Moor, so soft and boggy that the line here had to be laid on a platform of earth, ashes and brushwood. It's a tribute to the railway's Victorian engineers that it has remained in place for over a century, and nobody has ever managed (or wanted) to build a road up here.

From Corrour you can reach lonely peaks, or wind your way through remote valleys out of reach to mere motorists. (A classic walking route from Corrour to Glen Nevis is described in detail in this section.)

As you go north on the West Highland Railway, the magic continues. Beyond Fort William the train runs to Mallaig, from where it's a short ferry ride to the Isle of Skye, with a branch line to Oban, gateway port for the Outer Hebrides.

For a walker, this railway is an absolute gift, and for any visitor to Britain a ride on the WHR is a must. In summer (May to September) there are three trains per day (two on some Sundays) in each direction. There's also a standard passenger coach attached to the sleeper train which travels between London and Fort William (see the main Getting Around chapter for details), which is very handy for getting to walks as it comes through Glasgow heading north early in the morning.

For more details phone the national timetable service (☎ 0345 484950) or ScotRail reservations (☎ 0345 550033). For more ideas on where to go, get a copy of *Walks from the West Highland Railway* by Chris & John Harvey (published by Cicerone Press). It covers some 40 walking routes ranging from fairly gentle strolls to serious mountain expeditions attaining the dizzy heights of some 18 Munros, and is well worth buying if you're in the area for more than a few days. ■

---

ership by the NTS and the driving force of one Percy Unna, who 'intended that the Trust should be asked to undertake that the land should be maintained in its primitive condition for all time', although such is its popularity and accessibility today that you are unlikely to be alone unless you strike off the beaten track.

The lofty peaks and ridges which flank the glen should be left to the mountaineer, but in this section we describe a good rough walk circumnavigating Buachaille Etive Beag which serves up a flavour of 'primitive' Glen Coe. The appeal of this route is the remote and rugged landscape you pass through; the walk itself is quite a challenge and you might be glad of a stick for balance when negotiating stream crossings.

Direction, Distance & Duration

The route is described in an anticlockwise direction because the most difficult stream crossing is encountered at the start. The views down Glen Coe as you walk west are superb too. The nine miles includes ascents totalling over 600m. Five hours should see the route completed, but allow longer for stops, or if you know you're slow over rough paths. The route follows rights of way.

Information

The Fort William TIC (☎ 01397 703781) is open all year, and there's a seasonal TIC (☎ 01855 811296) at Ballachullish near Glencoe village. The NTS Visitor Centre (☎ 01855 811307) near Clachaig (but due to move to the NT Campsite at Invercoe) is open April to October with exhibitions and an audiovisual presentation. Glencoe Ski Centre (see below) has a museum of Scottish Skiing and Mountaineering and there's a Folk Museum in Glencoe village open from May to September.

SCOTLAND

Books & Maps Useful for walkers in the area is *Fort William & Glen Coe Walks* (published by Jarrold) which includes 1:25,000 OS maps, covers several routes in the area, including another account of the walk we describe here. *Glencoe: the Changing Moods* by Alan Thomas (Lochar) offers a largely photographic interpretation of the area and the NTS annually produces their own guide: *Glencoe*.

This walk is on OS Landranger (1:50,000) sheet 41, Outdoor Leisure (1:25,000) sheet 38 and Harveys (1:25,000) Superwalker map of Glen Coe (with a useful little visitor guide).

Guided Walks & Local Services
The Glencoe Ranger Service takes guided walks, from June to August (☎ 01463 232034) and the Glencoe Outdoor Centre (☎ 01855 811350) provides activity holidays and courses. The Ski Centre (☎ 01855 811303) operates a mountain chairlift which will take you to 650m (2133 ft) for a bird's eye view of the glen.

Places to Stay & Eat
If you're into historic ambience then *Kings House Hotel* (☎ & fax 01855 851259), at the head of Glen Coe and arguably the oldest licensed inn in Scotland, is worth considering. (You'll find better service than the Wordsworths did in 1803 when William's sister Dorothy wrote in her journal of poor food and damp rooms; the place 'as dirty as a house after a sale on a rainy day'!) Rooms start at around £20 per person (above the noisy bar!) with breakfast extra. This hotel is also on the West Highland Way, and popular with walkers. The *Clachaig Inn* (☎ 01855 811252) at the lower end of the glen has a rustic appeal, and was voted Scottish Pub of 1994: prices for B&B start from £26 . Both these hotels offer bar and restaurant meals.

Glencoe village has a *SYHA Hostel* (£6.95) and a few of eating places. *Dunire Guesthouse*

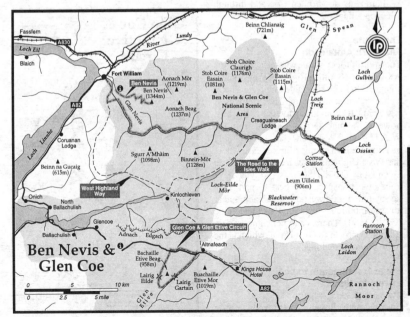

(☎ 01855 811305) and *Strathlachan* (☎ 01855 811244) both do B&B from around £12, and there's also *Leacantium Farm Bunkhouses* from £6 and *Red Squirrel Campsites* £3 (both ☎ 018552 811256). The *NTS Campsite* (☎ 01855 811397) at Invercoe, open April to October, is also £3. Other places to eat in the area include *Glen Coe Ski Centre* (at the head of Glen Coe opposite Kings House Hotel), with a log cabin restaurant open in the summer, and the NT Visitors Centre snack bar.

Getting There & Away
Bus Citylink buses (☎ 0990 505050) between Glasgow and Fort William use the A82, via Bridge of Orchy and Rannoch Moor, with around four services a day.

Train The nearest stations to Glen Coe are at Bridge of Orchy and Fort William (both on the West Highland Line) from where you'll have to take the bus as above.

Car The A82 between Glasgow and Fort William runs down Glen Coe and through Glencoe village.

The Route
The Start: Altnafeadh
The route proper starts where it leaves the A82 road at a Scottish Rights of Way Society signpost 'to Loch Etiveside' opposite a large 'igloo' cairn just east of The Study (GR 187563). If you are travelling by bus, however, or making this a detour from the West Highland Way, your start will probably be Altnafeadh, a couple of miles east, where the West Highland Way leaves the A82 to ascend the Devil's Staircase. If you have your own transport it is best to park in a lay-by half a mile west of Altnafeadh – near an Automobile Association (AA) telephone (GR 213560). There's another signpost here 'Public Footpath to Glen Etive' which is the route you return along.

Stage 1: Altnafeadh to Loch Etiveside Sign
2¼ miles (3.5 km), 1 hour
From Altnafeadh you have to walk west on

the A82, almost to the AA telephone, before escaping right on a path along the old road, which provides some relief from the traffic, but not from the noise, as it leads you west below the steep north end of Buachaille Etive Beag. Ahead can be seen The Three Sisters on the south side of Glen Coe with the high peak Bidean nam Bian just peeping over. The old road rejoins the A82 about a mile west of the AA telephone, and the traffic must now be endured for another half a mile or so to the real starting point of this walk.

Stage 2: Loch Etiveside Sign to Lairig Eilde Pass
2¼ miles (3.5 km), 1 hour
The stony track leads south-west from the signpost to Loch Etiveside with excellent views across Glen Coe to the spiky, precipitous ridge of Aonach Eagach. The path leads to the stream of Allt Lairig Eilde, the 'moment of truth'; if it's in spate it is dangerous to cross, but even in average conditions

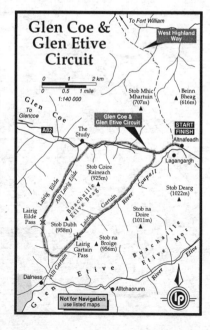

Glen Coe & Glen Etive Circuit

0   1   2 km
0   0.5   1 mile
1:140 000

To Fort William
West Highland Way

Glen Coe
To Glencoe

A82
The Study

Stob Mhic Mhartuin (707m)
Beinn Bheag (616m)

Glen Coe & Glen Etive Circuit

START FINISH
Altnafeadh
Lagangarbh

Stob Coire Raineach (925m)
Stob Dearg (1022m)

Lairig Eilde
Allt Lairig Eilde
Buachaille Etive Beag
River Coupall
Gartain

Lairig Eilde Pass
Stob Dubh (958m)
Lairig
Stob na Doire (1011m)

Stob na Broige (956m)
Lairig Gartain Pass
Buachaille Etive Mor
River Etive

Dalness
Allt Gartain

Glen Etive
Alltchaorunn

Not for Navigation use listed maps

it can be difficult, so if in doubt – retreat. If you make it (perhaps with the aid of a stick for balance, or with wet feet) you should be able to make all of the remaining burn crossings on this walk.

The well-defined path continues along the north-west side of this burn for around a mile before crossing back more easily. (There is evidence of a faint path on the south-east side of the burn, avoiding the crossings, but the going would be much more difficult on this.) The way, marked by a few cairns, now leads upwards, bending round to the south, with views of increasingly wild country – the jagged ridges of Stob Coire Sgreanahach with rocky gorges below. You might be lucky to see red deer here, and when you eventually reach the top of the pass (490m, 1600 ft) the views now open up across Glen Etive to the Stob Dubh beyond.

Stage 3: Lairig Eilde Pass to Lairig Gartain Pass

2½ miles (4 km), 1½ hours

Continue down the path on the other side of the pass, crossing a burn. The steeper descent continues down to Dalness in Glen Etive. You can avoid about 100m of this descent (and the subsequent 100m ascent) by taking a path which leads to the left when a fenced enclosure is reached just to the right of the path, about a mile from the top of the pass. This path traverses round the slope and crosses the burn you have been following just above a waterfall. Continue the traverse to the next burn, the Allt Gartain, where you join a small path coming up from the right.

Now heading north-east, go up the steep and fairly narrow valley, with the Allt Gartain tumbling down it in a series of small waterfalls. The route up involves some easy scrambling in places and on a fine day there are many opportunities to stop beside the waterfalls and enjoy the views back down to Loch Etive. (An alternative, but less interesting route, keeping up to the left, avoids this trickier section.)

Stage 4: Lairig Gartain Pass to Altnafeadh

3 miles (5 km), 1½ hours

Eventually you reach the col with extensive views ahead to the mountains around Loch Treig and a final opportunity to look back to Loch Etive. The remainder of the walk back to Altnafeadh can now be seen. This classic U-shape valley (resulting from glacial erosion) slopes less than Lairig Eilde and is very marshy! There are some cairns at first, but the problem is not so much in finding the route as in avoiding the muddiest places on it. The only useful tip we can offer is to keep on the north-west side of the burn, and to enjoy the fine situation between Buachaille Etive Beag on the left and Buachaille Etive Mor on the right, as you return to the A82 to finish.

BEN NEVIS

> **Distance** 9 miles (14 km)
> **Duration** 6 to 8 hours
> **Start & Finish** Glen Nevis, near SYHA hostel
> **Regional Centre** Fort William
> **Region** Highland
> **Area** Ben Nevis & Glen Coe National Scenic Area
> **Summary** A steep, stony path and a long day; only to be attempted in summer and in good weather, unless you are an experienced mountaineer – cloud can make navigation very difficult on the summit plateau. Severe weather (always likely) can be dangerous, and when snow is lying (typically until May) ice-axes are essential.

There's something irresistible about an attempt on the highest peak in a country and hence many are drawn to Ben Nevis. The mountain measures in at 1344m (4406 ft), and any walk involves this full ascent, as the start is virtually at sea level! Despite its popularity, a walk up 'The Ben' should not be undertaken lightly and you should be well prepared with mountain equipment, adequate food and drink, and well warned that this mountain can be a dangerous place. 'Nevis' has been traced back to Gaelic and Irish words meaning 'dread' and 'terrible'.

The mountain has a colourful history: the

SCOTLAND

path from Glen Nevis was an old pony track constructed at the time of the summit observatory (now in ruins), which was opened in 1883. During the previous two summers, one Clement Wragge, soon nicknamed 'the inclement rag', made a daily ascent up here to take weather observations. The observatory closed in 1904, but a small 'hotel' annex continued to open in summer until about 1918. In 1911 a Model T Ford was 'driven' to the summit in a publicity stunt – a feat which took five days!

Contestants in the Ben Nevis race (1st Saturday in September) run up to the top in less than an hour, and back down in half an hour!

The old pony track is now the so-called 'tourist path', but it is absolutely not a jaunt and the local Mountain Rescue Team have described it as 'a very arduous rock-strewn track, with sheer or steep edges in several places and often shrouded in mist and slippery with rain'. On a good day, however, you are rewarded for this long haul by the views and the sense of achievement. If you don't strike it lucky with the weather, we describe a lower alternative route below.

Direction, Distance & Duration
This route is essentially up and down by the same path, but some variation is possible at the start/finish. The new Ionad Nibheis Visitor Centre with informative displays makes a good starting point; from here you cross the River Nevis by suspension bridge on a path signed 'Achintee and Ben Path'. Alternatively, the start can be from the SYHA hostel – these two paths meet at a small plantation above the hostel. The route then goes via Halfway Lochan to the summit.

The route is about 4½ miles each way, but the ascent (and descent) of over 1300m and inevitable stops along the way means that up to eight hours should be allowed for the round trip.

Shorter Alternative
If you don't want to go all the way to the summit, or if there is snow, ice or cloud on the upper part of the mountain, a path from just above Halfway Lochan

allows splendid views of the intimidating cliffs of the Ben's north-east face. Return by the same route, or by the Ben Nevis Low-Level Circuit described at the end of this section.

Information
Fort William TIC (☎ 01397 703781) is on the high street (open all year). Nevis Sport displays up-to-date weather info and there's a weathercall service for the Western Highlands on ☎ 0891 654669. Ionad Nibheis Visitor Centre (☎ 01397 705922), 1½ miles up Glen Nevis, is open during the summer season. There are information boards here, and at the SYHA hostel.

Books & Maps Many books carry descriptions of the route up Ben Nevis, but the neatest guide to this and other nearby routes is the *Fort William and Glen Coe Walks* (published by Jarrold) incorporating the relevant large-scale OS map. *Walks from the West Highland Railway* (Cicerone Press) also has walks from Fort William. Leaflets covering this route include *Ben Nevis – walking the path from June to September* produced by the Ranger Service, and *Great Walks No 2* by Fort William and Lochaber Tourism. Maps are listed in the Glen Coe & Glen Etive section above.

Guided Walks & Local Services
Highland Ranger Service offers guided walks from Ionad Nibheis (see above). Mountain Craft (☎ 01397 722213) can provide a professional mountain guide. The Glen Nevis Centre (next to the SYHA hostel) hires out boots and rucksacks.

Places to Stay & Eat
In Glen Nevis, one of the best and most convenient places to stay is *Achintee Farm* (☎ 01397 702240), with B&B from £14, with the option of an evening meal, and bunkhouse accommodation for £6: there's self-catering too. Other possibilities include the *SYHA Hostel* (☎ 01397 702336, £7.80) and *Glen Nevis Caravan & Camping Park* (☎ 01397 702191), from around £6 per pitch

SCOTLAND

(also holiday cottages and caravans). *Glenlochy Guesthouse* (☎ 01397 702909) is quite convenient at Nevis Bridge, from £15 for B&B. In Fort William itself there's bags of choice: wall-to-wall B&Bs/hotels with bargains to be had, so you're best off asking in the TIC or looking round, especially along the A82 approach from Glasgow where there's cut-throat competition.

For food in Glen Nevis the Glen Nevis Caravan & Camping Park has *Cafe Beag* with main courses from £5 and *Glen Nevis Restaurant & Bar* with bar meals (including 'haggis wi' neeps') plus a small shop – all open during summer months.

For more details on places to stay and eat in Fort William, see the end of the West Highland Way section in the Scotland – Long-Distance Paths chapter.

Getting There & Away
Bus Citylink (☎ 0990 505050) has regular coaches between Fort William and Glasgow. Gaelic Bus runs buses four times a day from Fort William up the Glen as far as the SYHA hostel.

Train The splendid West Highland Railway (☎ 0345 484950) takes you to Fort William from Glasgow, or even from London on the overnight sleeper (see the main Getting Around chapter for details).

Car Fort William is on the A82. To reach Glen Nevis take the A82 east out of Fort William (towards Inverness) keeping ahead at the small roundabout on the minor road signed 'Glen Nevis'. Apart from Ionad Nibheis Visitor Centre or just beyond the youth hostel, the Glen has limited parking.

The Route
Stage 1: Achintee to Halfway Lochan
1½ miles (2.5 km), 1½ to 2 hours
From the car park at the Ionad Nibheis Visitor Centre take the path across the suspension bridge. Follow the riverbank upstream, below Achintee Farm, then turn up alongside a stone wall to reach the Ben Nevis Path, going up across the slopes of Meall an

t-Suidhe ('hill of rest' and pronounced 'Melan-Tee'). There's a small plantation where a path comes up steeply from the SYHA hostel. Continue on up, over a couple of footbridges, to follow a gully which the Red Burn flows down on your right. As the ground begins to level off a little, the path turns sharp left. Keep along the path and don't take the short cut. Your route will soon turn right again then level out as Halfway Lochan (correct name: Lochan Meall an-t-Suidhe) comes into view.

Stage 2: Halfway Lochan to Ben Nevis Summit
3 miles (5 km), 2 to 3 hours
Just east of Halfway Lochan the path turns right to reach Red Burn Ford. The ruins of 'Halfway House', used in association with the summit observatory, are nearby. (In days gone by, walkers were charged one shilling (5p) for walking to the summit, the proceeds being used for path maintenance.) This is the midpoint of the ascent and a good place to take stock. Is the weather fit to continue? Are you? From here to the top and back is a good three to five hours. If in any doubt, enjoy the view and go back down or take the route to

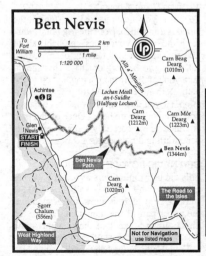

SCOTLAND

the Allt a Mhuillin described in the following Ben Nevis Low-Level Circuit section.

If you decide to continue, start zigzagging steeply up Ben Nevis proper. Keep to the path as short cuts are loose and slippery. The angle of ascent eases at around 1200m and the path forks beside a large circular stone shelter. The right-hand path is easier, but either will take you across the plateau to the summit cairn and trig point. Take care on this final section as the last bit of the path goes very close to the edge of the cliffs and gullies on the north face of the mountain. Keep particularly well clear of any patches of snow. In poor visibility, once you've reached the summit cairn, don't lose sight of it until you are ready to descend.

The summit is a bit of a wasteland with the remains of the substantial walls of the observatory, several cairns and an emergency shelter as well as the trig point – all set in a boulder-strewn 'moonscape'. However, the views are exceptional with the islands of Mull, Rum and Skye seawards to the west, and all around, myriads of mountain peaks as far as the eye can see.

Stage 3: Ben Nevis Summit to Glen Nevis

4½ miles (7 km), 3 hours

To return, you must retrace your steps. If the cloud is down then, from the trig point, walk for 150m (count your paces – probably about 200 paces) on a grid bearing of 231°, then follow a grid bearing of 281°. This should take you safely off the plateau and on to the path. Remember to allow for magnetic variation. (If you don't know what this means – you shouldn't be up here.) Once on the path continue to go carefully – most accidents occur during the descent.

BEN NEVIS LOW-LEVEL CIRCUIT

This circular route offers a pleasant alternative if you don't want to go all the way to the summit, or if there is snow, ice or cloud on the upper part of the mountain. Follow the directions in Stage 1 of the previous route description as far as Halfway Lochan.

From Halfway Lochan take the path which leads north then east, beneath the intimidating cliffs of the Ben's north-east face. The path continues traversing below Carn Dearg before climbing alongside the Allt a Mhuillin ('whisky burn') to a crossing point about 100m before a private Scottish Mountaineering Club (SMC) hut. From the crossing point take the path heading down on the north-east side of the burn. It gets boggy lower down before meeting a rough driveable track.

Head left at the first track junction (where the track to the right enters the forest), crossing the Allt a Mhuillin at a water intake point. After half a mile or so the track divides: head downhill on the right-hand fork to a further junction, where again you head downhill. Turn left at a T-junction; you'll shortly pass under some pylon lines and then cross a small burn. A small sign indicates 'footpath to main road' and you turn right immediately after the bridge to head down alongside the burn, emerging at the whisky distillery which gives the burn its nickname. The distillery offers conducted tours with a wee dram, after which you can walk pleasantly back to Fort William.

THE ROAD TO THE ISLES

> **Alternative Name** The Road to the Isles – Corrour Station to Glen Nevis road-head
> **Distance** 14½ miles (23 km) to Glen Nevis road-head; plus 6½ miles (10 km) to Fort William
> **Duration** 8 to 10 hours to Glen Nevis road-head
> **Start** Corrour Station
> **Finish** Glen Nevis road-head or Fort William
> **Regional Centre** Fort William
> **Region** Highland
> **Area** Ben Nevis & Glen Coe National Scenic Area
> **Summary** A long and remote route with stony, rough and boggy sections and several river crossings to negotiate. It is best avoided in wet weather. A very satisfying route for experienced walkers.

The Road to (or, indeed, from) the Isles is an ancient route which traverses the Western Highlands of Scotland, between central Scotland and Skye and other Hebridean Islands, via Fort William. It was much used by cattle drovers (and cattle thieves) heading for the cattle fairs at Crieff and Falkirk. Armies, their quarries and refugees would march and flee along the route. (The 'Road to the Isles' handle is also used today by the modern A82, which runs to the south of its original namesake.)

An old Scottish song about the Road to the Isles runs 'By Loch Tummel, and Loch Rannoch and Lochaber I will go'; the walk described in this section goes through the heart of Lochaber. It starts at Corrour Station on the West Highland Railway line (see aside), which at 408m above sea level (ASL) makes it the highest point on the British Rail network. It is 11 miles from the nearest public road. The route heads to Fort William, where it meets up with the railway again.

The route follows rights of way, passing between major mountain ranges – Ben Nevis and the Aonachs on one side, the Mamores on the other – before descending through a dramatic rock gorge (mini-Himalayan in character) down to the road-head in Glen Nevis. The route goes through wild and remote country – though there is a bothy about halfway along the route – and should only be attempted by experienced hill-walkers and in suitable weather conditions.

Direction, Distance & Duration
This route is best done from east to west. Following the route in this direction means that the majority of your progress will be downhill. It also means that your accommodation options will be greater. The total distance from Corrour Station to the Glen Nevis road-head is 14½ miles. This takes about eight hours of walking, but you should allow at least 10. It's another 6½ miles from the Glen Nevis road-head to Fort William.

Information
The main TIC serving this area is in Fort William (☎ 01397 703781), so if you're getting the train from Fort William to Corrour Station call in to check on the weather.

Books & Maps *Exploring Scottish Hilltracks* by Ralph Storer covers this walk as well as

many other fine routes with helpful plans and background info. *Walks from the West Highland Railway* (Cicerone), details several routes from Corrour Station.

The whole route is covered by OS Landranger (1:50,000) sheet 41 *Ben Nevis*.

Places to Stay & Eat
The options at Corrour are limited, so don't turn up on spec or you might be unlucky. Your choice is the simple, but popular, *Loch Ossian SYHA Hostel* (☎ 01397 732207, £4.10), a couple of miles from Corrour Station, or *Morgan's Den* bunkhouse (☎ 01397 732236), the old station building, charging around £4. There's absolutely NO food or meals to be had anywhere here, so you need to be completely self-sufficient. (The nearest shop is 20 miles away!)

If you've got suitable gear there's a *bothy* at Staoineag, about halfway along the walk, which would let you split the walk into two days. You can end the walk at *Glen Nevis SYHA Hostel*, two miles before Fort William. For details on this and other accommodation in Fort William see the section on Ben Nevis above.

Getting There & Away
There are no roads leading to the start of this walk, so the only way to Corrour is by train on the West Highland Railway (☎ 0345 484950 for timetable information), either from Glasgow or Fort William, or one of the intermediate stations. The first train south from Fort William running on Monday to Saturday would allow you to make an early start on the walk from Corrour, as would the sleeper service from London (see the aside in the Getting Around chapter) with a request stop at Corrour. It's too late on Sunday to be feasible.

If you haven't left a car at the Glen Nevis road-head or haven't arranged to be picked up from there at the end of the route, you might be able to hitch down to Fort William as the Glen is a popular day-trip destination. For details on public transport at the Fort William end, see the Ben Nevis section. For details on walking options from Glen Nevis

SCOTLAND

road-head to Fort William see the end of this section.

The Route
Stage 1: Corrour Station to Creaguaineach Lodge
4 miles (6.5 km), 1½ hours

From Corrour Station on a clear day you get a preview of Ben Nevis and nearby mountains. Once you've savoured the view, cross to the west of the railway line and follow the track to the north-west, alongside the line. The track is used by all-terrain vehicles, which are better designed for crossing boggy patches than your booted feet. But when we went through there were good bridges where the track crossed and recrossed a burn. (You can glimpse Loch Ossian to the right beneath Beinn na Lap, one of the easiest Munros to climb.)

After about a mile you get to a point where the Allt Luib Ruairidh stream runs through an underpass below the railway line; the track from the Loch Ossian SYHA Hostel also comes under here and you join it after crossing the bridge over this stream. Continue ahead on the much better track below the railway line down to a bridge across the Allt a' Chamabhread, just before it empties into Loch Treig. There are excellent views ahead; to the left are the Mamores with the shapely Binnein Beag on their right – you'll pass below this peak about three-quarters of the way along this route, and it acts as a marker against which you can measure your progress.

Walking round Loch Treig you may well

be feeling it lives up to its name, which means 'Forsaken', so it's something of a surprise to see Creaguaineach Lodge ahead. It just survived the raising of the water level in the 1930s, when the loch was dammed as part of the hydroelectric scheme for the aluminium works at Fort William; it is still in use. Immediately before the Lodge there is a major bridge over the Abhainn Rath (flowing down a small gorge into Loch Treig). At the south end of this is a junction marked by a Scottish Rights of Way Society signpost.

Stage 2: Creaguaineach Lodge to Luibeilt
3½ miles (6 km), 2 hours

Although the original right of way to Glen Nevis, and the path shown on the OS map, follow the north side of the Abhainn Rath, the preferred route (and that indicated by the signpost) keeps to the south side; this is to avoid the river crossing which is otherwise necessary at Luibeilt, and which can prove a major difficulty after wet weather. The signposted route follows a rough path alongside the river, swinging left to cross two small tributaries and then right where it climbs a narrow section of the valley to a wide level area near Staoineag Bothy.

The path continues along the valley floor, crossing a substantial tributary, to another step in the valley, down which the river tumbles. Above this the valley becomes wide and flat again and would feel very remote if it were not for the group of conifer trees around Luibeilt, and the nearby Meanach Bothy, now visible ahead. The river meanders

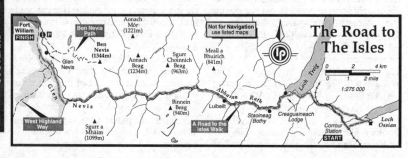

here and the optimum route is not always obvious, particularly as another major tributary is reached, but there are stepping stones if you can find them. The marshy ground between here and Luibeilt is clearly subject to regular flooding, but the ground is firm immediately alongside the river. Luibeilt itself is a ruin, though much of the roof is still in place, and adjacent to it it is a locked barn; if you need shelter there's Meanach Bothy, but to reach this you must cross the river – the very crossing you have avoided by following the south side of the river! A rough, yet driveable, track leads south from Luibeilt to Kinlochleven, about seven miles away; an escape route if required.

Stage 3: Luibeilt to Glen Nevis Road-Head

7 miles (11 km), 4 hours

Continuing north-west, follow a track which winds between stony knolls, some quarried for road stone, and then head along a grassy track, back again into wild country. You are now getting near to Binnein Beag which comes into view again on the left. Ahead is the massive Aonach Beag and its outlier Sgurr a' Bhuic, which you'll pass to your right.

About a mile after Luibeilt and shortly before a major confluence in the river, the path ascends a stony slope on the left and then traverses along the side of glacial deposits towards a small metal hut (known as 'The Water Shed') on the far side of the Allt Coire a' Bhinnein. A small dam diverts this burn from its natural course down Glen Nevis towards Loch Treig. Its bed is strewn with boulders, and a stick helps your balance when crossing it. The hut is in a poor state, but offers limited shelter.

From the hut follow the usually dry river bed to the north for about 200m to join the path on the north side of the infant River Nevis – at this point it's called Water of Nevis – (below the hillock of Tom an Eite), then the path turns west.

The ground ahead is often peaty. Where the peat is exposed, the remains of ancient trees are sometimes apparent – relics of the

very different vegetation that was once present. As a result there are many boggy stretches making the going slow. Alternative paths do exist, but it's tricky finding the best option; the highest usually turned out to be a good choice for us.

As you eventually leave Binnein Beag behind, many more fine peaks in the Mamores come into sight and there's a dramatic view of Ben Nevis' north-east profile.

Ahead is what appears to be an enclosed basin, and you may begin to wonder how the river finds its way out. On the way down to it there is a substantial bridge over the burn which drains the coire between Ben Nevis and Aonach Beag alongside the ruins of the old Steall cottage. Steall means waterfall, and you'll soon see the reason for the cottage's name: a fall which cascades down more than 100m of rock slabs. Steall Hut, on the other side of the river, is private and reached by a bridge comprising just three wire ropes – try it if you dare, and imagine negotiating it in high winds with a rucksack filled for a week's stay!

The way out of this sanctuary now becomes apparent – the river takes an abrupt turn to the right and tumbles down a steep rocky gorge, the bed of which is filled with massive boulders. Fortunately there is a well-constructed path clinging to the valley side. After a sharp turn back to the left (and an excellent view back up this dramatic gorge to An Steall), you'll soon reach the Glen Nevis road-head. The last few miles before the road-head will probably be quite crowded, as this is a popular strolling zone.

Glen Nevis Road-Head to Fort William

From here it is still some 3½ miles to the SYHA hostel or six miles to Fort William (two to three hours). If you don't want to try and get a lift and prefer to avoid the traffic and tar, there is a track through the forest starting at Achriabhach, about 250m after the road crosses to the other side of the river. Alternatively, you can leave the road in parts to follow the riverbank along informal paths.

The Cairngorms

With Aviemore (the nearest thing Britain has to a 'mountain resort') on their doorstep, the Cairngorms may be better known to visitors as a winter ski area. But this extensive mountains range is very popular with climbers and hill-walkers all year round. The Cairngorms is a vast plateau, some 1200m (4000 ft) high, interrupted by round summits such as Ben Macdui (1309m, 4293 ft), Britain's second highest mountain, and, of course, Cairn Gorm itself at 1245m (4083 ft).

Cairn Gorm is the most accessible summit in the range and has given its name to the entire range. However, the mountain range's real name is Am Monadh Ruadh, meaning the red hills, a reference to the often exposed red granite rock, whilst the name Cairn Gorm means blue hill!

Whatever you call this area, the high plateau is undoubtedly serious terrain and not the place for a casual stroll. You are only about 650 miles from the Arctic Circle here, and at altitudes of 1000m or more you are certainly in an arctic environment. Weather conditions in the Cairngorms are notoriously bad, with low cloud, snow, high winds and freezing conditions possible at any time of the year. In winter (which generally stretches from November to May), conditions require ice-axe, crampons and mountaineering skills. Combine bad weather with a lack of easily recognisable features and you could find yourself in a navigational nightmare. Hence, unless you are a mountaineer the routes we describe in this section should only be attempted in summer. Even then, walkers should be prepared for the worst.

You may be wondering after this gloomy preamble why anyone would bother with the Cairngorms at all. The answer is simple – these are the wildest uplands anywhere in

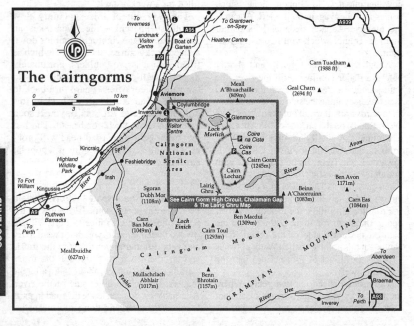

Crofting & The Clearances

Many Highland settlements are described as 'crofting communities': what does it mean? The word croft comes from the Gaelic *coirtean*, meaning a small enclosed field. Until the early 19th century, the land of the Highlands was generally owned by clan chiefs, and their tenants farmed land on the 'run-rig' system. The land was divided into strips which were shared among the tenants. The strips were periodically shuffled around so no tenant was either stuck with bad land or always enjoyed the good land. Unfortunately, it also meant the tenants might end up with several widely scattered strips and they had no incentive to improve those strips because they knew they would soon lose them. Accordingly, the system was changed and the land rented out to the tenants as small 'crofts', averaging about three acres. Each tenant then built their own house on their croft and the former tight cluster of homes was scattered. They could additionally graze their animals on common land which was jointly held by all the local crofters.

Despite these changes, crofting remained a precarious life. Rents were extortionate, and the small patch of land barely provided a living. Each year the tenancy could be terminated and the crofter lose not only the croft but the house they had built on it.

This is exactly what happened in the 1840s. The landowners realised that the land could be more profitably used for large-scale sheep or deer farming, and the crofters were simply forced off. The guidebook to Dunrobin Castle, seat of the Sutherland family, blithely notes that this family 'proceeded to make large-scale improvements to Sutherland's communications, land and townships which involved the clearance of some 5000 people from their ancestral dwellings'.

Many people moved to the towns and cities of lowland Scotland, while others emigrated to Canada, America and Australia, leaving the landscape pretty much as it looks today. Crofting tenancies still exist but complex regulations now protect the crofters. ■

Britain, with arctic tundra, superb high corries and awesome rock formations carved out of the range by glacial activity. The wildlife is pretty good too, especially the birds. Golden plover, ptarmigan and dotterel are found on higher ground and lower down are the smaller birds, such as the siskin, redpoll and crested tit. You may even come across a capercaillie, a large turkey-like bird which flies. There are loads of red deer and imported reindeer in the area, as well as mountain hares, foxes and pine marten.

And don't be put off if you're not a hardy peak-bagger. On the north side of the range (within easy reach of Aviemore) are two large forest areas: Rothiemurchus Estate and Glenmore Forest Park, which includes Loch Morlich. Rothiemurchus is privately owned (by the Grant family of whisky fame), but both are open to the public. Happily, there are many walking opportunities in these forest areas which are suitable for all walkers, and which can be undertaken at times of year when the plateau should only be left to those with skis, crampons and X-ray vision.

In this section we describe both a high-level circuit (including the summit of Cairn Gorm) and a medium-level route which will take you some way into the Cairngorm range and give you a taste of its scale and wildness, without exposing you to any great danger.

CAIRN GORM HIGH CIRCUIT

Distance 7 miles (11 km)
Duration 5 to 6 hours
Start & Finish Cairngorm Ski Area – Coire Cas car park
Regional Centre Aviemore
Region Scottish Highlands
Area Cairngorm National Scenic Area
Summary A serious expedition onto an exposed and often hostile plateau; needs mountain skills, experience and caution. No known restrictions on access at the time of writing.

This is one of the most popular routes for walkers in the Cairngorms, not only because of its easy access, but because of the chairlift (used by skiers in winter, but open all year – subject to the weather) which allows walkers to take the soft option and ascend Cairn Gorm without raising a sweat. Hence, a taste of the high peaks with their fantastic views can be readily achieved on a single day-walk. The main features of this walk, apart from the ski paraphernalia and the (dubious) attraction of dining in the highest cafe in Britain, is the summit of Cairn Gorm itself and the dramatic summits of Coire an t-Sneachda and Cairn Lochan. The route concludes with a fine descent of Lurcher's Ridge.

It can't be stressed too much that walking in this area is no doddle. The plateau is vast, with precipitous edges and steep rock, and severe weather conditions are possible, even in 'summer'. Although the weather down below may appear settled, the weather on the tops may be a different matter and inexperienced walkers should only proceed to the tops with a competent guide.

Direction, Distance & Duration

This route can be done in either direction, but we describe it clockwise, going up to Cairn Gorm summit (by path or by chairlift), and then around the top rim of Coire an t-Sneachda and Cairn Lochan with the descent down the ridge alongside Lurcher's Gully. You might prefer to do it the other way round if you've got the sort of weak knees that find going up easier than coming down – the chairlift at the end of the day will be a welcome sight. However, if this is your intention, don't rely on getting a lift down – you could miss the last ride, or it could stop running because of bad weather (not uncommon).

From the car park to the top of Cairn Gorm the ascent is about 620m – allow two hours (or half an hour from the upper chairlift station, from which the climb is only about 160m). It's about 2½ miles around the rim of the corries and the same again down Lurcher's Ridge and back to the car park. There's not really any escape route (though you can make it a shorter circuit by descending Fiacaill a' Choire Chais) – if you find conditions bad on Cairn Gorm, or don't like all that wide open space, go back down the way you came.

Information

The busy TIC (☎ 01479 810363) on Grampian Rd in Aviemore is open all year. They have accommodation guides, a *bureau de change*, weather information and a good range of books and maps. There's a neat Rothiemurchus Visitor Centre (☎ 01479 810858) at Inverdruie with displays and audiovisual presentation and Glenmore Visitor Centre (☎ 01479 861220) has more specific stuff about forests with details of a wayfaring (orienteering) course and trails and treks varying in length from one to 11 miles – there's a Guide Map available. There's also a small info desk at the Ski Complex near the top car park and the start of the High Circuit, but they will probably try to persuade you that you shouldn't go onto the plateau unless you join one of their ranger-led parties (see Guided Walks below).

Books The most comprehensive guidebook is *The Cairngorms* by Adam Watson in the SMC District Guide series (£17.95), available through Cordee. *Walks in the Cairngorms near Aviemore* and *Short Walks in the Cairngorms*, both by Ernest Cross (published by Luath Press, £3.25 each), describe the main routes for walkers.

Great Walks Scotland by Hamish Brown et al (Printwise Publications, 1992) and *Exploring Scottish Hill Tracks* by Ralph Storer (David & Charles), both include the Lairig Ghru. The Cairngorms also feature in *The Munros Hillwalkers Guide*, *The High Mountains of Britain & Ireland* and *The High Mountains Companion* detailed in the general Scotland introduction.

Maps Apart from the OS Landranger (1:50,000) sheet 36, other more suitable maps for the walker are the OS Outdoor Leisure (1:25,000) map of *Aviemore & the Cairngorms*, and the Harveys (1:40,000) Walker's Map and (1:25,000) Superwalker *Cairn Gorm*.

Guided Walks

There are lots of walks arranged in the area by Rothiemurchus Visitor Centre (see

SCOTLAND

Information), who also hire out mountain bikes. Cairngorm Ranger Service has guided walks upon the plateau using the chairlift for access. Walks meet at the chairlift office (☎ 01479 861261).

Places to Stay & Eat

The nearest settlement to the start of this walk is Glenmore village, located on the Ski Road, an incongruous 11 mile strip of highway through the forest, linking Aviemore with the ski slopes. (Glenmore is about seven miles from Aviemore.) Forest Enterprise runs the large and well-maintained *Glenmore Camping & Caravan Park* (☎ 01479 861271) here, charging £2.50 per person. Just opposite the campsite is the *Loch Morlich SYHA Hostel* (☎ 01479 861238, £6.95) – an old country house in a great location. There are also two B&Bs in Glenmore (near the Visitor Centre), both charging £13 per person: *Mrs O'Donnell* (☎ 01479 861255), at 3 Queens Houses, and *Mrs Ferguson* (☎ 01479 861223), at Cairn Eilrig. For food supplies, hot meals, teas and outdoor gear there is the *Shop & Cafe* near the campsite.

Your other accommodation options are in the small settlements of Coylumbridge and Inverdruie (also on the Ski Road) or in Aviemore. Coylumbridge has the *Campgrounds of Scotland* (☎ 01479 810120), on a site charging £3.50 per person. It also has the best of the large resort hotels with pools and sauna: the *Coylumbridge Hotel* (☎ 01479 810661) charges from £39 including B&B and evening meal. Inverdruie has an array of accommodation; have a look at *Mrs Maclean's* at Bendruie (☎ 01479 810621) or *Mrs Harris* at Junipers (☎ 01479 810405), both from around £14.

In Aviemore, the smart *SYHA Hostel* (☎ 01479 810345, £7.80) is near the TIC. This resort has a huge choice of B&Bs and hotels and we could only scratch the surface here; the TIC has lots of information.

For something to eat in Aviemore, just stroll along the main street. There's a small supermarket, shops, and a wide choice of restaurants for most tastes and budgets.

Starting at the southern end of town, next to the TIC is *Harkai's Fish & Steak Restaurant* (with good breakfast specials) then *Asha Indian Restaurant*, *Pizzaland* next to the station, and *Smiffy's Fish & Chip Restaurant* – all eat in or take away. Pubs include the *Winking Owl*, towards the northern end of town, and the *Old Bridge Inn*, which is rather out of the way on Dalfaber Rd, reached by a railway underpass from the TIC.

Getting There & Away

Bus Aviemore is well served by bus and easily reached from Kingussie, Perth, Inverness, Glasgow, Edinburgh (even from London) by direct National Express. Most buses go to/from the railway station or the TIC (where you can also make bus bookings and enquiries). Operators include Scottish Citylink (☎ 0990 505050) and Highland Bus & Coach (☎ 01463 233371).

From Aviemore to Glenmore and the Ski Complex (£2.20 one way), there's a bus operated by the Cairngorm Chairlift Co (☎ 01479 861261) with regular services.

Train Aviemore Station is on Grampian Rd and there are direct ScotRail services from London, Glasgow, Edinburgh and Inverness.

Car The A9 provides a fast route to Aviemore from the south or from Inverness. You then take the B970 to Coylumbridge and continue up the Ski Road to the Coire Cas car park.

The Route
Stage 1: Coire Cas Car Park to Cairn Gorm Summit
2 miles (3 km), 2 hours

Purists start walking from the Coire Cas car park, but you may want to miss the slog up and take the chairlift to the Top Station, and the Ptarmigan Restaurant (guess what – the highest in Britain!). For details see Chairlift Alternative below.

To avoid the ski paraphernalia as far as possible (which you may as well do if you are not going to avail yourself of the lift), your best way up to the Ptarmigan Restaurant is by the ridge of Sron an Aonaich. To get onto this ridge, walk alongside the tow on the north-east side of the car park. This ascent is mainly through heather, and reaches a path which crosses the tow just below the crest of the ridge; turn right along this path which leads onto stony ground. Further ski-tows and fences come up from the left, and on a clear day there are excellent views behind you across Loch Morlich and ahead to the right of the corries which you will be traversing later. Keep to the path near the crest of the ridge to reach the restaurant alongside the chairlift's Top Station.

Behind the buildings a paved path leads upwards between poles; it becomes a little less formal the higher you go, but you are left in no doubt as to your route to the summit of Cairn Gorm. (The Summit Weather Station and Radio Station was established in 1965 to assist in Search and Rescue operations.)

Chairlift Alternative The chairlift travels up to 1100m ASL from the car park (which is at 650m). Although it dispenses with a good deal of effort, it'll hurt the pocket – to the tune of around £4.20 return in summer. The chairlift doesn't operate when there are

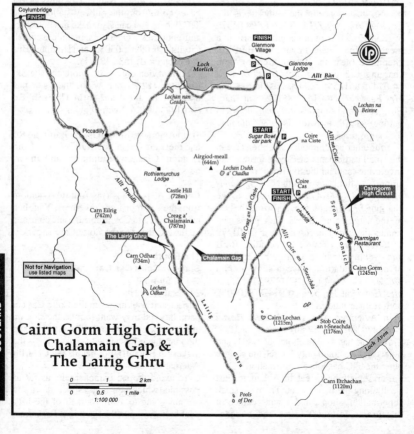

Cairn Gorm High Circuit, Chalamain Gap & The Lairig Ghru

strong winds, but you probably wouldn't want to be on the mountain on such days anyway. In 1996, proposals to replace the chairlift with a funicular railway (which could operate regardless of winds) were put forward. These proposals are being opposed by environmental organisations. If they get approval, the funicular railway might be completed by 1999.

Stage 2: Cairn Gorm Summit to Cairn Lochan

2 miles (3 km), 1½ hours

If it is clear you should be able to see a path about 100m below you to the west-south-west; you must pick your own route down the bouldery slope to reach it. If you can't see the path, only proceed if you are confident of finding your way down with a compass bearing; otherwise return to the Ptarmigan Restaurant.

You are now on the high Cairngorm plateau, with glimpses of massive crags and tucked-away lochs. The path leads onwards, just a little to the west of south, across a broad col, and then upwards, again over boulders, to reach the summit of Stob Coire an t-Sneachda. The route down from here to the west-south-west is marked by cairns, leading to another col. (Don't be tempted by the path which leads south from here – unless you are bound for Ben Macdui.)

There is a small path up Cairn Lochan, but it forks a number of times and your choice should always be upwards; there is a substantial cairn above the cliffs of Cairn Lochan at a good lookout before the top is reached. Beware of straying too far to the right – the cliffs are sheer – as you continue to the summit.

Stage 3: Cairn Lochan to Coire Cas Car Park

3 miles (5 km), 1½ hours

Descend to the west from the summit, but still keep a safe distance from the cliffs on the right – there are some cairns, but soon you must find your own route, descending across the boulder-strewn slope to a wide

valley. A path leads down this valley into Coire an Lochain. Cross this and continue slightly uphill swinging round to the right to gain a broad ridge. Head north to a large cairn on a knoll, and enjoy the views back from here to the cliffs which you traversed in the last stage.

From this cairn a path goes down the easy-angled, broad ridge which separates Coire an Lochain from Lurcher's Gully. (This is the site of a major controversy between the ski company, who wants to extend their infrastructure to here, and environmentalists who have (so far) successfully resisted this.) From the foot of the ridge the path swings a little to the right to pass below the major corries, crossing burns and being joined by other paths, as it leads to the car park. Sections here pass over peaty ground and are very boggy, leading to the path getting wider as walkers seek to avoid the worst of the bog. (Perhaps path improvements such as those near the car park will be made. But this will require funding – perhaps walkers should be making a contribution.)

CHALAMAIN GAP & THE LAIRIG GHRU

Distance 13 miles (21 km), but can be cut short – see Shorter Alternatives
Duration 6 to 7 hours for the full route
Start Sugar Bowl car park on Cairngorm Ski Road
Finish Coylumbridge or Glenmore
Regional Centre Aviemore
Region Scottish Highlands
Area Cairngorm National Scenic Area
Summary Generally good mountain paths, but crosses some boulder fields and boggy areas, and there are a number of streams to be forded. The walk reaches a height of 840m ASL and uses rights of way.

The Lairig Ghru is generally regarded as the finest mountain pass in Britain – accessible only to those on foot. It follows a great glacial trough cut through the Cairngorm plateau providing a natural route from Aviemore to Braemar. The full route, however, is 28 miles, which can be reduced to 20 miles if transport is available to Coylumbridge and

SCOTLAND

from Linn of Dee to Braemar. It is a very strenuous walk and without any escape route if conditions turn bad. Further, unless you have a cooperative driver, the route back from Braemar to Aviemore (some 55 miles by road) is tricky by public transport, involving three separate and infrequent services.

Here we describe a route which takes you to the top of the Lairig Ghru from the northern end, returning towards Aviemore through Rothiemurchus Forest. It can be cut short by not proceeding to the summit of the pass – a useful option if conditions are bad.

Direction, Distance & Duration

The route is best undertaken in the direction described below, as the starting point is higher than the finishing point. It is five miles to the top of the pass from the Sugar Bowl car park. This includes two ascents: about 240m to the Chalamain Gap, and a further 240m up the Lairig Ghru – allow three hours. The return to Coylumbridge or Glenmore is eight miles downhill.

Details on information services, places to stay and eat etc are covered in the previous Cairn Gorm High Circuit section.

Shorter Alternatives By omitting the ascent of the Lairig Ghru and heading straight for Rothiemurchus Forest (after descending from the Chalamain Gap) the route is reduced to 9½ miles, and a further saving of more than a mile can be made if you catch the bus from the west end of Loch Morlich to Glenmore.

The Route
Stage 1: Sugar Bowl Car Park to Allt Druidh

3 miles (5 km), 1¾ hours

The Sugar Bowl car park is on the north-east side of the Ski Road on a sharp bend about two miles beyond Glenmore village. From here, cross the road and take the path down to a footbridge over the river. Continue up the other side of the valley to the right, but then swing sharply left to follow the path above the river with a reindeer enclosure on

your right. The views from this path are excellent – the ski area is to the left and above this is the summit of Cairn Gorm.

After a slight descent you ford a burn on giant stepping stones, and then continue up to the Chalamain Gap, a rocky gorge with a jumble of boulders on its floor, which you must pick your way across. From the south-western end there are magnificent views across the Lairig Ghru to Sgor Gaoith, above Loch Einich, and views of Braeriach. The descent from here to join the Lairig Ghru path is fairly easy and straightforward. (Maps and books published before about 1992 show the Sinclair Hut here, but it has been removed and there is no longer a shelter of any sort.)

Stage 2: Up Allt Druidh to Lairig Ghru Summit

2 miles (3 km), 1¼ hours

You are now on the main Lairig Ghru path, which almost at once crosses over to the west side of Allt Druidh stream (difficult if it is swollen by heavy rain or snow melt). Follow the stony path south-east, over heather littered with boulders, between the steep valley sides with their great cliffs sculpted by the glaciers which once passed this way. Moraines left by the melting ice partly block the valley floor in places, and the stream disappears underground.

The path is marked by occasional cairns. As the summit is approached there is a small shelter built of rocks and from here it is important to keep left for the last 200m to the highest point of the pass. Ahead you will now see Cairn Toul and the prominent peak of Bod an Deamhain (also known as the Devil's Point, but more correctly translated from the Gaelic as 'the Devil's penis').

If you still have any energy it is worth continuing for another 500m or so to the delightful Pools of Dee, an ideal place on a good day for a picnic. The Pools of Dee are said never to freeze, but this is probably because they are hidden from view by a thick layer of snow during that part of year when they could be frozen.

SCOTLAND

JOHN HARVEY

JOHN HARVEY

DAVID ELSE

Top: Loch Treig, the Road to the Isles Walk
Middle: 14th-century castle ruins, Sanquhar, Southern Upland Way
Bottom: Sgurr na Moraich summit, Five Sisters of Kintail, Glen Shiel

DAVID ELSE

JOHN HARVEY

JOHN HARVEY

JOHN HARVEY

JOHN HARVEY

Top Left: North Goat Fell, Isle of Arran
Top Right: Inversnaid, West Highland Way
Middle: Ettrick Head, Southern Upland Way
Bottom Left: Ptarmigan peak path, Ben Lomond

Bottom Right: Black Rock Cottage & Buachaille
Etive Mor, West Highland Way

Stage 3: Lairig Ghru Summit to Piccadilly Path Junction

5 miles (8 km), 2 hours

Retrace your steps back to the point where you joined the Lairig Ghru path. After fording the Allt Druidh keep to the left, alongside the stream. The path is across heather-covered glacial moraine into which the streams have cut quite deep valleys. As the first trees are reached, bringing new interest to the landscape, a path goes off to the right to Rothiemurchus Lodge, which is used by the army. Our route keeps straight ahead through the native Caledonian pines – remnants of the great forest which once covered much of the Scottish Highlands. The path junction known as Piccadilly is marked by a large cairn and direction signposts.

Stage 4A: Piccadilly Path Junction to Coylumbridge

3 miles (5 km), 1 hour

Turn left at Piccadilly to take the track to Aviemore along a wide valley to a river confluence. Cross the river by the Iron Bridge, erected in 1912 by the Cairngorm Club. Turn right and then fork right (signed Coylumbridge) along a narrow path flanked by pines. This leads on to more open and mature woodland and finally into rough parkland, reaching Coylumbridge alongside the Campgrounds of Scotland site by the river.

Stage 4B: Piccadilly Path Junction to Glenmore

3 miles (5 km), 1 hour

Turn right at Piccadilly and follow the substantial track towards Loch Morlich. Just after crossing a high deer fence, you join the dirt road from Rothiemurchus Lodge, and you can follow this to the Ski Road. You can catch a bus here or walk 1¼ miles along the road to Glenmore.

Alternatively, as you approach Loch Morlich there is a track to the right, and you can take this round the south side of the loch to join the Ski Road beyond Glenmore – the best option if you are walking back to Sugar Bowl car park.

Ben Lomond

Distance 6½ miles (11 km)
Duration 5 to 6 hours
Start & Finish Rowardennan
Regional Centres Glasgow and Stirling
Area Loch Lomond National Scenic Area
Summary This is a pretty strenuous walk rising nearly 1000m from almost sea level. The main 'tourist' path may be used both ways, in which case you are unlikely to get lost on this stony, well-tramped highway. Here we also describe the Ptarmigan Route, a different ascent which we recommend for the more intrepid and map-wise walker.

Loch Lomond, famous for its 'bonny, bonny banks', lies in the southern part of the Western Highlands, just north of the Highland Boundary Fault, which geologically separates the highlands from the central valley of Scotland. On its eastern side is Ben Lomond (974m, 3194 ft) Scotland's most southerly Munro (see aside) and the first 'proper' mountain you see as you travel north from Glasgow. The West Highland Way, which is described later in this book, passes between Loch Lomond and Ben Lomond, and many walkers take a day off this long-distance route to detour up the mountain. Nearly all agree it's worth it.

Most people use the 'tourist route', which starts at Rowardennan, about halfway up the eastern shore of the loch. On a fine day in summer it is little more than a strenuous uphill walk on a clear path (mountain runners make the ascent and descent in just over an hour!), but don't expect to be alone.

If you are competent with a map and compass, properly equipped, and conditions are clear and settled, then go for the scenic and less crowded Ptarmigan Route, which we also describe here, following a minor unmarked path on open moorland overlooking Loch Lomond. You can then descend via the tourist route, turning the walk into a circuit.

Sometimes in this area you can see the Ptarmigan, a bird species which gives the route its name. The Ptarmigan is a cousin of the red grouse. It has a speckled appearance, but in winter turns white in harmony with the snow.

The lower slopes of the mountain are planted with spruce and larch, but above this the open land is owned by the NTS and used for grazing, which eliminates tree growth. It's thought that the name Lomond comes from the old word 'llumnan' meaning 'beacon'. This is appropriate as the peak can be seen from all around. In good weather you'll be able to see for miles around from its summit.

Note that this is a summer only route. In winter even the 'tourist' route can become a serious expedition with ice-axe and crampons required. Strong winds and a marked temperature drop may assault you as you near the summit at any time of the year.

Direction, Distance & Duration

The distance for either route is about seven miles, requiring a walking time of five to six hours, not allowing for stops to gasp for breath (optional) or to look at the views (compulsory), or to refuel (highly desirable). Allow about six to seven hours in total and take plenty of rations and liquid replacement.

If you want a shorter route, your only option is retracing your steps. There are no easy alternative ways down; the sides of Ben Lomond fall steeply down to the loch and the forest is pretty inhospitable too.

Information

The nearest (seasonal) TIC is at Drymen (☎ 01360 660068). Stirling TIC (☎ 01786 475019) is open all year. There is a PIC at Balloch Country Park at the south end of the loch.

Books & Maps *Loch Lomond & Trossachs Walks* (published by Jarrold) covers several routes of various lengths in this area, including Ben Lomond, and incorporates the relevant sections of the OS 1:25,000 map for each walk. For shorter wanders in the area, *Walk Lock Lomond & the Trossachs* (pub-

lished by Bartholemew) describes over 30 routes with brief background information.

OS Landranger (1:50,000) sheet 56 is adequate; but OS Pathfinders (1:25,000) sheets 380 (NS 29/39) and 368 (NN 20/30) show more detail.

Guided Walks

NTS rangers (☎ 01360 870224) lead guided walks on Ben Lomond, and the Loch Lomond Park Rangers (☎ 01389 758216) also do occasional guided walks in the area with themes such as 'Bog Day' or 'Ptarmigan Teaser'.

Places to Stay & Eat

At Rowardennan, the *SYHA Hostel* (☎ 01360 870259) is idyllic and convenient, but you'll be competing with the 50,000 or so who walk the West Highland Way each year, so don't rely on last-minute arrangements. Nearby is the *Rowardennan Hotel* (☎ 01360 870273) with B&B from £25 between April and October, a bar, which is open from 11 am to midnight, and meals midday to 9 pm. Mrs Maxwell at *Blairvockie Farm* (☎ 01360 870242), one mile from Rowardennan, offers B&B during college vacation periods for around £15. She makes walkers very welcome, but doesn't take bookings for singles. The *Forestry Commission campsite* (☎ 01360 870234) at Cashel is open from April to October, but check first if you're planning a low-season visit (around £4 per adult).

If you are coming up the west side of Loch Lomond and crossing over to Rowardennan on the ferry (see below) then there is accommodation at the smart *Inverbeg Inn* (☎ 01436 860678) and camping at *Inverbeg Holiday Park* (☎ 01436 860267) at £8 for two people.

Getting There & Away

Bus/Ferry Bus services operated by Midland Bluebird (☎ 01324 613777) run between Glasgow and Balmaha via Drymen and Balloch. From Balmaha it's another six miles to Rowardennan, along the West Highland Way, although you may be able to hitch.

SCOTLAND

Alternatively, in summer, use the regular Scottish Citylink (☎ 0990 505050) between Glasgow and Fort William, as far as Inverbeg and then take the (summer only) passenger ferry (☎ 01360 870273), leaving at 10.30 am, 2.30 and 6.30 pm to Rowardennan (returns 10.00 am, 2.00 and 6.00 pm).

Car The start and finish of this circular route is at Rowardennan car park at the end of the lane from Drymen, which can be reached from Glasgow via the A809, or from Stirling (to the east) via the A811. The lane goes through Balmaha, but is a dead-end, so after your walk you must return the same way.

The Tourist Route
Rowardennan to Ben Lomond Summit
3½ miles (5.5 km), 3 to 4 hours
From the car park take the path directly behind the public toilets signed 'Ben Lomond Path'. It goes up through forest plantation and then across open hillside. The path is unmistakably marked by the passage of many thousands of boots (and less suitable footwear). Work by professional path builders goes on to repair and improve it: foundations provided by matting or rock, gradients eased by zigzagging, but most significantly, drainage to reduce erosion by water. Even so, you'll still have to beware of boggy bits if you are to gain the summit!

The Ptarmigan Route
Stage 1: Rowardennan to Ptarmigan Summit
2½ miles (4 km), 2 to 3 hours
From the car park continue north along the unpaved road past the hostel. The road soon crosses over a burn; take the left fork, following the West Highland Way and, just after a sign for a Ranger's Cottage (on the right), cross over another burn and then immediately turn right on a small path leading up through the trees and past a small waterfall. The new fence you will shortly see to the right has been put up to foster the regeneration of native woodland. Loch Lomond oakwoods are pretty special!

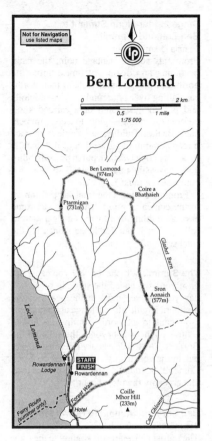

Follow the path left of the fence and on through a kissing gate. It's quite steep and you'll soon leave the trees behind. Continue north, following the fence which eventually bends away to the right. The gradient eases and the path climbs more gently up the shoulder of the hill under some craggy outcrops. At another kissing gate Ben Lomond summit comes into view. As you near the crest of the ridge don't forget to take in the views, especially across the loch to the Arrochar Alps. Continue up the path, which is steep and zigzagging in places, and up onto Ptarmigan summit.

SCOTLAND

Stage 2: Ptarmigan Summit to Ben Lomond Summit

½ mile (1 km), 1 hour

From this superb vantage point the path, becoming less distinct at times, turns first north and past a small lochan, then north-east, going over or around a series of knolls and passing just south of a cairned knoll before descending slightly to a col with peat hags, Bealach Buidhe, half a mile from Ptarmigan summit. (This section of the route is pleasant in fine weather, but in poor visibility you can easily miss the way, so use of a compass is a must.)

From here begins the final steep climb up to the conical summit. This involves some easy scrambling, but there is a clear path to follow. Watch out for loose stones on the final section.

The Summit Whichever way you came up, once you've reached the summit, on a clear day you can see most of the peaks of the Southern Highlands and range upon range of mountains to the north. Southwards lie the central plain and, beyond, the hills of the Borders. The Clyde estuary is unmistakable, but the jewel in this crown must be Loch Lomond, Scotland's largest freshwater loch and arguably the most beautiful.

Ben Lomond Summit to Rowardennan

3½ miles (5.5 km), 2 hours

The tourist path starts off slightly to the right of the crest of the summit ridge; don't stray to the left in bad visibility – there are sheer drops! Lower down, this main highway is well marked and unmistakable, the kind of path which, while common in mountain areas of England and Wales, is comparatively rare in Scotland where the hill-walker is expected to be able to find the way by map-reading and navigation!

Until the final forested section, the route traverses open land with wide-open views. Descending, you can see Inverbeg on the other side of the Loch with the sizeable delta at the mouth of Douglas Water and the wild Luss hills rising beyond. The

many islands (Inches) of Loch Lomond are concentrated in the southern part of the loch. You can even see Conic Hill on the east side of the loch, marking The Highland Boundary Fault.

North-West Scotland

For serious walkers, North-West Scotland (also called Wester Ross and Sutherland) is heaven. This is a remote and starkly beautiful highland area, sparsely populated, with beautiful glens and lochs, a fine coastline of rocky headlands and white sand beaches, and some of the finest mountains in Britain – some say Europe. The sheer number of peaks and their infinite variety attracts walkers from all over the country (and further afield) year after year. The small and crowded islands are as close as it gets to real wilderness, but the emptiness that is integral to this area's charms naturally makes things difficult for walkers from abroad on a short visit. But for those who have the time and inclination, the effort will be well rewarded.

In summer the clear air provides rich colours and great views from the ridges and summits. In winter the views can be clear, but the weather conditions often make walking a much more serious enterprise. At any time of year the walking can be hard, so this is no place to begin learning hill techniques. But if you are a fit, competent walker, with the necessary gear and skills required for survival in the mountains, then North-West Scotland will never disappoint.

The routes we describe in this section are nontechnical (ie no ropes), have relatively easy access (by car or public transport), and good accommodation options nearby. These routes are but a mere taster of the fine opportunities available.

The Isle of Skye is often classed as North-West Scotland too, but in this book it gets its own section.

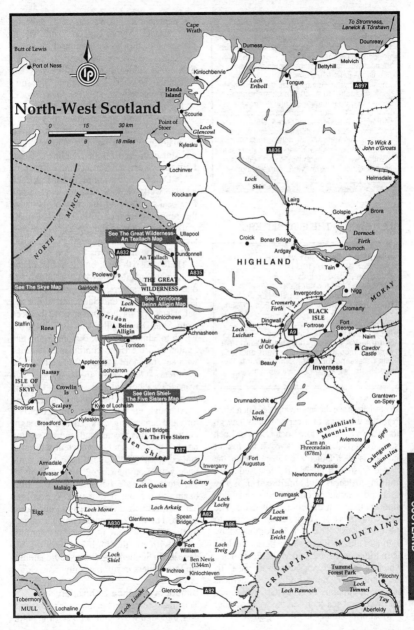

North-West Scotland

0   15   30 km
0   9   18 miles

Warning
One final reminder: all the routes here are described as for summer. In Scotland that means May to September, although weather conditions can be bad, and potentially lethal, at any time of year. Scottish mountain-walking in winter (October to April) is a different game – more like mountaineering – and not covered in this book. The routes can be undertaken in winter, and some experienced walkers and mountaineers revel in it, but this requires crampons, ice-axe, rope and the right attitude. To deal with mountains covered in snow and ice, not to mention low cloud, high winds and short days, you really need to know what you're doing.

GLEN SHIEL – THE FIVE SISTERS

Alternative Name The Five Sisters (of Kintail)
Distance 6½ miles (10.5 km)
Duration 7 to 10 hours
Start Glen Shiel top car park
Finish Ault a chruinn, Glen Shiel
Regional Centres Inverness, Fort William, Kyle of Lochalsh
Region Highland
Area Kintail National Scenic Area
Summary A top quality ridge walk taking in five separate mountain summits. Hard and long with no escape route or room for error in bad conditions. Navigational skills are a must.

Most visitors see the large valley of Glen Shiel from the windows of a car or bus as they go down the main road from Loch Lochy or Loch Ness, towards the Isle of Skye. At the foot of the glen is Loch Duich and Eileen Donan, the classic 'castle on an island': featured on a million postcards and shortbread tins. The hills and mountains on either side of Glen Shiel are the main attraction for walkers. The vast wilderness of Glen Affric stretches to the north-west. The glen is dominated by high and almost inaccessible peaks, such as Carn Eige, and Monar and Mullardoch lochs, which drain into Loch Ness in the east. To the south is yet more highland wilderness and the mountains of Knoydart, which are cut by several sea-lochs on the western side.

Most of the routes in this area are reserved for experienced hill-walkers and dedicated long-distance Munro-baggers, and beyond the scope of this book. Fortunately, some of the finest mountains are close to the Glen Shiel road, allowing relatively easy access. When the weather is kind there are some excellent views.

These mountains are known as the Five Sisters of Kintail, and together they form a ridge on the north-west side of Glen Shiel. From north to south the mountains are Sgurr na Moraich, Sgurr nan Saighead, Sgurr Fhuaran, Sgurr na Carnach and Sgurr na Ciste Duibhe. Sgurr simply means 'peak', and the walk we describe here, crossing all five peaks, following the crest of the ridge that runs between them, is reckoned by many walkers to be one of the great Scottish classics. (For the peak-baggers, Fhuaran and Ciste Duibhe are Munros.)

There's a sixth peak on our route, called Sgurr nan Spainteach, which although not one of the five sisters, is still sizeable (higher than both Moraich and Saighead). It doesn't get 'sister' rating because it can't be seen from Shiel Bridge, the best lookout from which to admire the five. Beyond Sgurr nan Spainteach, the ridge continues eastwards, with several more peaks, often called 'The Brothers'. Only very strong walkers can manage the whole ridge in a day. Most content themselves with just the female siblings.

Although incredibly rewarding, this is a long and demanding walk. There are no signposts, and only occasional cairns, so you need to be completely competent with map and compass. There's also no escape route once you're on the ridge; the slopes are all too steep for safe descents. If your time begins to run out before you've even got halfway, retracing your steps is your safest option. The whole mountain range is owned by the NTS; there are no access restrictions.

As with all the high-level routes we describe in Scotland, walkers should attempt the Five Sisters in summer only.

Direction, Distance & Duration
This linear route can be done in either direction, although we recommend starting at the

SCOTLAND

south-eastern end, as the walk up to the ridge from the road at this point (although steep and long) is less arduous. Measured on the map, the distance is 6½ miles, but with all the ups and downs the total distance is longer. It takes most people seven to 10 hours walking time – so allow extra for lunch and map-reading stops. (If you stay at Shiel Bridge add an extra hour to walk there from the end of the route.)

Information

Shiel Bridge TIC (☎ 01599 511264) is near the petrol station. Local tourist news is covered in *The Visitor*, a free paper for Skye and Wester Ross. There's a NTS visitor centre (☎ 01599 511354) at Morvich (see Places to Stay). (For information on guided walks see the following Torridons section.)

Books If you want more detail and background information on Glen Shiel, or suggestions for alternative routes, the area is described in several books, including *The Munros* by Donald Bennett, *The High Mountains of Britain & Ireland* by Irvine Butterfield and *200 Challenging Walks in Britain & Ireland* by Richard Gilbert, all detailed in the Books section of the Facts for the Walker chapter.

Books on this particular area include: *The North West Highlands – SMC District Guidebook* by Bennett & Strang (published by Scottish Mountaineering Trust, available from Cordee), which covers mountain routes in detail; and *Exploring the Far North West of Scotland* by Richard Gilbert, also published by Cordee, which paints a broader picture of the area, covering low-level and coastal walks as well as hills and mountains. Gilbert is a true aficionado of this area, although an Englishman by birth, and this book has some fine pictures, in case the cloud is down when you climb the hill! The locally produced leaflet *Where to Walk in the Lochalsh District* has several short walks in the area, including one in Glen Shiel.

Maps The Five Sisters Ridge, Glen Shiel, plus parts of the wilderness south of the glen and eastern Skye, are on OS Landranger (1:50,000) sheet 33. If you want more detail get (1:25,000) Pathfinder sheet 205.

Places to Stay & Eat

The best place to base yourself is Shiel Bridge village, at the western end of the glen. There's a *campsite* (☎ 01599 511221), charging £2.50 per person and £1 per car, plus a petrol station and shop selling groceries. About two miles west of Shiel Bridge in the small village of Ratagan is a *SYHA Hostel* (☎ 01599 511243, £5.40), in a spectacular position overlooking the Five Sisters. About 2½ miles north-east of Shiel Bridge, at Morvich, just past Ault a chruinn (where this route finishes) is another *campsite* owned by the NTS (☎ 01599 511354). Prices range from £4.60 for a tent and one person to £8.70 for a tent, a car and two people.

B&Bs in Shiel Bridge include *Shiel House* (☎ 01599 511282) charging £15. For an evening meal, your only close choice is the reasonable *Five Sisters Restaurant*, which also does takeaways. About one mile north of Shiel Bridge, on the main road, is the smart *Kintail Lodge* (☎ 01599 511275), with B&B from £37 and DB&B from £59 per person, with discounts if you stay three nights or more.

Ault a chruinn (where this route ends) has a shop, post office and cafe, open to 9 pm in the summer. There's also the good-quality *Glomach House* (☎ 01599 511222) with B&B from £15 to £25 per person, dependant on the season. They will also do your washing and can drop you off at the start of your walk and/or collect you from the finish point.

Another option at the eastern end of the glen is the *Cluannie Inn* (☎ 01320 340238), about five miles from the start of the route. This old coaching inn is now a smart hotel, with a good restaurant and fine rooms (some with four-poster beds) charging between £35 and £40 per person for B&B. They welcome walkers, and offer a drop-off-pickup service. There's even a gym, in case you still have energy to spare after a day on the mountains.

Getting There & Away

Bus The bus between Inverness and Kyle of Lochalsh (via Invergarry) runs four times per day in each direction (twice on Sunday), stopping at Shiel Bridge. There's also a bus

SCOTLAND

between Glasgow and Kyle (via Fort William) three times per day in each direction (one on Sunday). Operators are Skyeways (☎ 01599 534328) and Highland Bus & Coach (☎ 01463 233371). There's also a daily postbus between Kyle and Letterfearn (at the north-western end of Loch Duish), via Ault a chruinn, Shiel Bridge and Rattagan.

Train Fort William, Inverness and Kyle are all served by trains to/from Glasgow, but from these three places to Glen Shiel you'll have to catch the bus.

Car Glen Shiel is on A87 which branches off the A82 (between Fort William and Inverness) at Invergarry, and runs to Kyle of Lochalsh (often shortened to Kyle).

The Route

The route we describe starts at a car park (usually called 'the top car park') near the top of Glen Shiel, about halfway between Shiel Bridge and the Cluanie Inn, about 1½ miles east of the Bridge of the Spaniards battle site (see aside). From Shiel Bridge you can catch a bus on its way to Inverness or Fort William, or hitch. Lifts are fairly easy to get, as most people don't mind helping walkers (just because we say hitching is possible, it doesn't mean we recommend it).

Stage 1: Glen Shiel Top Car Park to Sgurr na Ciste Duibhe

1½ miles (2.5 km), 2½ to 3½ hours

From the car park go north, through the gap in the plantation and straight up the slope, aiming towards Bealach an Lapain, the lowest point on the ridge, between Sgurr nan

Spainteach and Saileag. There's no clear path. The ridge looks tantalisingly close, but it takes about one to 1½ hours to get there.

At Bealach an Lapain, turn left (west) and keep to the ridge crest, over several minor peaks to reach the rocky summit of Sgurr nan Spainteach, the 'sixth sister'. From here you get a great view to the north-west of Sgurr Fhuaran, across the head of the huge Choire Dhomdhain valley.

Descend into a rocky col, then go steeply up again to reach the summit of Sgurr na Ciste Duibhe (1027m) the first of the Five Sisters. From this summit, the views are now tremendous: north-east across to Glen Affric, north-west to Skye and the jagged edge of the Cuillin Hills, south-west to the Glen Shiel Ridge and the wilderness beyond. In the distance, if the skies are clear, you can see the Western Isles, dark against the sea, from Barra in the south to the large lump of Lewis in the north.

Stage 2: Sgurr na Ciste Duibhe to Sgurr Fhuaran

1½ miles (2.5 km), 2 to 3 hours

Continue west, away from the summit (avoid the apparently easier route leading off to the north), and head steeply down to a col. Then turn to the north and head up again, to Sgurr na Carnach (1002m). Sgurr na Carnach is about one hour from Sgurr na Ciste Duibhe. Keep going north along the ridge, down and then steeply up, to reach the summit of Sgurr Fhuaran (1067m), one to 1½ hours from Carnach. This is the highest point on this walk, marked by a cairn and the tear-jerking memorial plaque to a dog called Tetley who died here in 1994 whilst undertaking his 194th Munro.

SCOTLAND

The Bridge of the Spaniards

The 'Bridge of the Spaniards' in Glen Shiel is the site of a battle fought in 1719 between English soldiers loyal to King George and Jacobite rebels, supporters of the Stuart 'pretenders', in a now largely forgotten uprising between the more famous campaigns of 1715 and 1745. History relates that Spanish mercenaries were involved in the battle, fighting for the Scottish side, and landing by boat at Eilean Donan Castle in Loch Shiel, although the bridge itself was built by Telford some 100 years later. ■

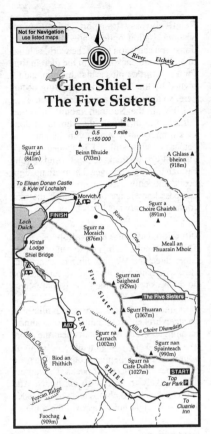

Not for Navigation
use listed maps

River Elchaig

Glen Shiel –
The Five Sisters

0   1   2 km
0   0.5   1 mile
1:150 000

Sgurr an Airgid (841m)

Beinn Bhuide (703m)

A Ghlass bheinn (918m)

To Eilean Donan Castle & Kyle of Lochalsh

Morvich

Sgurr a Choire Ghairbh (891m)

FINISH

River Croe

Loch Duich

Sgurr na Moraich (876m)

Kintail Lodge
Shiel Bridge

Meall an Fhuarain Mhoir

Sgurr nan Saighead (929m)

Five Sisters

The Five Sisters

A87

Sgurr Fhuaran (1067m)

GLEN

Allt a Choire Dhomdain

Sgurr na Carnach (1002m)

Sgurr nan Spainteach (990m)

Allt a Choire Chuil

Biod an Fhithich

Sgurr na Ciste Duibhe (1027m)

SHIEL

START
Top Car Park

Forcan Ridge

To Cluanie Inn

Faochag (909m)

descent is much harder than it appears, with steep cliffs on the west side, and it's no quicker than keeping to the 'proper' route.) Continue on to the summit of Sgurr na Moraich (876m), which is the last of the five sisters. It has a rounded and grassy summit, which is a pleasant relief at this stage after the steep rock on the rest of the ridge.

Stage 4: Sgurr na Moraich to Ault a chruinn

1½ miles (2.5 km), 1½ to 2 hours

From this last summit, head north-west over broad grassy slopes and down towards the new bridge over the loch, visible far below. Keep left (west) as you come down to the river (but do not enter the gully) and you'll meet a path. Once you're on the path it's not too hard to follow, but picking it up needs great care, especially in mist or darkness. Too far left and you're in the gully, too far right and you're on top of some steep (and unpassable) cliffs. The path brings you out near the cafe, which serves exceedingly welcome teas, cakes and meals, before the last couple of miles along the (unavoidable) verge of the main road back to Shiel Bridge.

THE TORRIDONS – BEINN ALLIGIN

The celebrated Torridon peaks provide every delectation the rambler could desire: deep corries, imposing buttresses, airy pinnacles and magnificent views. Nowhere in Britain do mountains so proclaim their individuality.

Irvine Butterfield in
The High Mountains of Britain & Ireland

Stage 3: Sgurr Fhuaran to Sgurr na Moraich

2 miles (3 km), 1 to 1½ hours

From the summit, make sure you follow the ridge north-west and then north (don't be confused by the other ridge that leads east). There is a long descent to a col, then up (not so far this time) over the summit of Sgurr nan Saighead (929m) and on to a north-western outlier (869m). (From here, if you're heading for Shiel Bridge, it is possible to aim west, then north-west, over or round a smaller peak called Sgurr an t-Searraich, and descend to the road this way. However, this

Alternative Name The Beinn Alligin Ridge
Distance 6½ miles (10.5 km)
Duration 5 to 6 hours
Start & Finish Torridon House Bridge
Regional Centres Kyle of Lochalsh, Inverness
Region Highland
Areas Wester Ross National Scenic Area
Summary A hard, immensely rewarding, circular walk along a horseshoe ridge, over two major summits and three optional minor peaks. Several steep and exposed sections, and some scrambling, which can be avoided. Navigational skills required, especially in bad weather.

SCOTLAND

The Torridon Mountains mark the southern edge of the Flowerdale Forest – a wild and complex area of lochans, moors and peaks. The quote above is just one of many, reflecting the wonder that this area holds for walkers.

Within the Torridon group are three major mountains: Liathach (pronounced 'Lee Attack' by English people, and 'Lee Agagh' by the locals) is a massive wall of a mountain, with several peaks along its central ridge, including Mullach an Rathain (1023m) and Spidean a Choire Léith (1054m); next is Beinn Alligin, again with several peaks, the highest being Sgurr Mhor (986m); east of here is Beinn Eighe (972m), not quite as high as Liathach, but with several outliers, making it bigger 'on the ground'. The fourth mountain in this area is Beinn Dearg (914m), wedged between Alligin and Liathach. At first it seems insignificant, but its full glory only becomes apparent when seen from one of the neighbouring peaks.

Many Torridon routes are serious undertakings, often with technical manoeuvres, and beyond the scope of this book, but Beinn Alligin's summit can be reached without technicalities, although it is still a serious mountain and not suitable for the unfit or inexperienced. As Scottish peaks go, this mountain is relatively easy to 'do', and is a splendid introduction to the walking potential in this area. At 986m, Sgurr Mhor gets Munro status, while neighbouring Tom na Gruagaich (922m) is a 'top'. The three subsidiary peaks, the 'Horns of Alligan', also stand out. These are linked by a curving ridge that contains a huge corrie called Toll a Mhadaidh ('the fox hole').

Even more dramatic is the great gash of Eag Dhuibh ('the black cleft') in the back wall of the corrie, running from the summit ridge to the base, seemingly splitting the mountain in two.

According to the commentators, Beinn Alligin means 'the beautiful mountain' or 'the mountain of jewels'. Either way, it's definitely a gem – a mountain which allows walkers to get a feel for the high and wild Scottish peaks, without having to be a mountaineer or cover long approach routes.

Relatively easy transport and numerous accommodation options are further attractions; you can be on top of the world at lunch time, but safe back down in the glen in time for tea. A further plus is that this mountain is owned by the NTS, and no stalking occurs here, so there are no access restrictions.

Like all the Scottish mountain routes described in this book, this should be done in summer only. And even in summer, patches of snow still lurk in shaded corners, the mist can be thick, and the winds strong enough to blow you over. There are no signposts, and only a few cairns, so map and compass knowledge is essential if the mist comes down (always likely).

Direction, Distance & Duration

This is a circular walk, and so can be done in either direction. We recommend going anticlockwise. This way, if you're a scrambler you do the peaks early in the route before fatigue strikes.

On the map, the distance is 6½ miles, but on steep broken ground this figure is almost meaningless. The route starts near the shore of a sea-loch and you gain almost 1000m on your way to the top, plus another 300m or so going between the main peaks, so walking time is likely to be five to six hours. Add extra for lunch and photos and you'll need at least six to eight hours to cover the route.

Information

There's a very useful NTS visitors centre (☎ 01445 791221) in Torridon village, opposite the youth hostel. Before heading for the high peaks you can check the weather forecast here. Other TICs in the area are at Gairloch (☎ 01445 712130), North Kessock (☎ 01463 731505) and Lochcarron (☎ 01520 722357).

Books & Maps The Torridons are described in the Books section of the Glen Shiel walk above. The OS Landranger (1:50,000) sheets 19 and 24 overlap on Beinn Alligin. The OS Outdoor Leisure (1:25,000) sheet 8, which neatly covers the area, is much more useful (and the Cuillin of Skye).

Guided Walks

NTS rangers based at the visitors centre (see above) organise day-walks on Alligin and other peaks in the area. Guided walks are run twice a week during July and August costing £5 per person, leaving the visitors centre at 10 am. One walk is a high-level walk, but does not climb any mountains, while the other is a Torridan ridge walk. Check with the visitors centre for more information. Mountain guides based in this area (at Strathcarron) include Martin Moran (☎ 01520 722361), who also has several books to his credit. Daily rates for walks and climbs on the Torridan mountains start at £110 per day, reasonable if shared between a small group.

Martin also organises a series of courses. Most are for technical rock and ice climbers, but the spring/autumn Munros course is designed for walkers, allowing the less experienced to appreciate harder mountains in the company of a guide. No technical rock-climbing is required. Instruction is given in map-reading and other 'hill skills'. Mountains include Beinn Alligin, An Teallach, the Five Sisters (all described in this book) and some peaks on Skye. The week-long course costs £320, and includes all food and very comfortable accommodation.

Island Horizons (☎ 01520 722232) runs a series of week-long holidays in many parts of Scotland, including Skye and the Torridons, starting from £300 all inclusive. Some weeks are women only, or exclusively for over-60s.

Places to Stay & Eat

The best place to base yourself is Torridon village or nearby Inveralligin. Most walkers head for the splendid *SYHA Hostel* (☎ 01445 791284, £6.75), at the junction of the A869 and the minor road alongside the loch. There is a simple *campsite* nearby.

For B&B, *Mrs MacDonald* (☎ 01445 791229) charges £14 per person. Or try *Mrs Rose* (☎ 01445 791256) who also charges £14.50, plus £8.50 for dinner. Popular and very comfortable is the *Loch Torridon Hotel* (☎ 01445 791242) on the south side of the loch, with summer prices from £50 to £120 B&B,

but this is only worth considering if you have your own wheels.

For supplies, the village has a well-stocked post office shop.

Getting There & Away

Bus & Train First, get to Inverness or Kyle of Lochalsh. Inverness has good National Express, Scottish Citylink and rail connections to/from the rest of Britain. Kyle can be reached by bus from Fort William or by train from Inverness.

There are three trains a day (except Sunday) in each direction between Inverness and Kyle, stopping at Strathcarron Station. The first train from Inverness gets in at 9.45 am, and connects with the postbus, which leaves Strathcarron at 9.50 am and goes to Torridon via Lochcarron and Shieldaig. The next train from Inverness gets into Strathcarron at about 12.30 pm. A train from Kyle gets in at just about the same time. A local bus runs daily (except Sunday) in summer, and Monday, Wednesday and Friday in winter. It meets these trains and then goes to Torridon, via Lochcarron and Shieldaig. Going the other way, this bus leaves Torridon about 10 am arriving back at Strathcarron in time for the 12.30 pm trains to Kyle and Inverness. Of course, the rail timetables may change, so the bus will probably alter too, to keep in line with the trains. To check the latest situation, phone the local bus company (☎ 01520 755239), or a local TIC.

There's also a twice-daily postbus service (except Sunday) from Achnasheen (on the railway between Inverness and Kyle) through Kinlochewe, to Torridon village, along the loch (past the start of this walk) to Inveralligin and Diabaig. It then turns around and returns to Achnasheen. For details, ask at the post office in Torridon or at any of the villages along the route.

Car Torridon village lies at the eastern end of Loch Torridon, on the main A890/896 between Kyle of Lochalsh and Kinlochewe, which itself is on the road between Gairloch and Inverness.

The Route
Stage 1: Torridon House Bridge to Sgurr Mhor Summit
3½ miles (5.5 km), 3 to 4 hours

The route starts about two miles west of Torridon village, on the road towards Inveralligan, near Torridon House, where the lane crosses the Coire Mhic Nobuil river. To get here from the village you can walk or tie in with the morning postbus (see the above Getting There & Away section). Near the bridge is a car park, frequented by walkers with wheels. After the walk, you might be lucky and find a lift.

From the bridge, a path leads up the east bank of the Coire Mhic Nobuil river through a small wood, and then into moorland. The path leads you into a triangular sloping bowl, between the three main Torridon mountains. Straight ahead is the blunt western wall of Beinn Dearg. To the right (east) is the western end of Liathach Ridge, and to the left (west) is Beinn Alligin. The path crosses a bridge and aims roughly northwards, towards the eastern end of the Alligin horseshoe ridge.

As you get higher, the path becomes indistinct, but continue up the crest of the broad and increasingly steep ridge, aiming for the three Horns of Alligin. You reach the base of the first horn about 1½ to two hours after leaving the bridge. You can scramble over this and the next two rocky peaks, or keep your hands in your pockets and take the path which tends left, avoiding the peaks on their southern side.

After the third horn, drop to a small col, and then go up again, swinging round to the left (north-west), to keep the steep drop down into the corrie on your left. To your right (north-east) the view really begins to open out: a beautifully jumbled mosaic of lochans, moors and smaller peaks, with Loch Maree beyond and the coast town of Gairloch visible on the bay. Behind, too, the view keeps on getting better: down the corrie and over Loch Torridon, then up again to the mountains around Bienn Damph.

With all this to look at, time flies, and you soon reach the summit of Sgurr Mhor (three to four hours from the bridge). With the extra height your view is almost 360°, with range upon range of wonderful peaks, too numerous

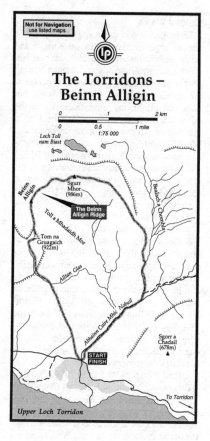

to mention, spread out in all directions. Most notable to the south-west are the Cuillin Hills on the Isle of Skye, and to the east, the summits of Beinn Eighe, where exposed quartz makes them appear eternally snow-capped.

Stage 2: Sgurr Mhor Summit to Torridon House Bridge
3 miles (5 km), 3 to 4 hours

From the summit, head north-west, down a grassy slope keeping the corrie edge to the left. We've been expounding on the views, but there's more than half a chance of bad weather and limited visibility up here. If this

SCOTLAND

Beinn Eighe Mountain Trail

If all this high Scottish mountain stuff is just too daunting, but you'd still like to do something on foot in this wonderful area, you might consider the Beinn Eighe Mountain Trail, which starts and finishes on the banks of Loch Maree, a few miles west of Kinlochewe (on the main road to Gairloch) about 18 miles from Torridon. This waymarked route is only four miles long, but you should still allow two hours, and take the usual precautions with footwear, waterproofs and food. A booklet produced by Scottish Natural Heritage is available in local TICs, which has a map of the route and plenty of info about local wildlife. ∎

is the case, take particular care on this section, as the top of Eag Dhuibh, the giant gash which dominates the view from below, is hereabouts, just waiting to trap the unwary walker in mist. If, however, the day is clear, the cliffs on either side of the gully nicely frame the view of the glen far below, and this is one of Scottish walking's many classic vistas. (Don't try to descend this way.)

After Eag Dhuibh, go steeply up again over large boulders, to reach the summit of Tom na Gruagaich, about one to 1½ hours from the summit of Sgurr Mhor. There's a nice trig point to lean against as you have a last look at the view before starting to descend. It is possible to follow the ridge all the way down, but most people take the smaller corrie between the main western ridge and the one that extends from Tom na Gruagaich, going steeply down over scree and boulders, to cross the lower shoulder of the main ridge once again and over easier ground back to the bridge.

THE GREAT WILDERNESS – AN TEALLACH

Alternative Name The An Teallach Ridge
Distance 14 miles (22.5 km)
Duration 8 to 9 hours
Start Corrie Hallie, near Dundonnell
Finish Dundonnell,
Regional Centre Inverness
Region Highland (Ross-shire)
Area Wester Ross National Scenic Area
Summary A long, tough mountain-walk in a remote area. Paths are faint or nonexistent, with some exposure and scrambling. Bad weather is always possible. Aptitude with a map and compass is essential and the walk is for experienced walkers only.

The Great Wilderness is a particularly remote area of North-West Scotland, stretching from Little Loch Broom in the north to Loch Maree in the south, and from the Fannich Hills in the east to the west coast village of Poolewe; an area of about 180 sq miles. For visitors from countries where wilderness areas are a bit larger, this title may seem exaggerated, but within these boundaries there are no roads or houses, and no cafes, pubs or shops selling tartan walking sticks – by British standards, wilderness indeed. The landscape is mountainous, with some fine, austere peaks. There are lochs and lochans of all shapes and sizes, rivers and waterfalls, peat bogs and grassy valleys, but very few trees. It may seem strange when you see Fisherfield Forest, Letterewe Forest and Dundonnell Forest on the map, but 'forest' here means hunting ground; this is prime deer-stalking country, and must be avoided at certain times of year (see Stalking Information below).

An Teallach is one of Scotland's finest mountains, standing proudly on the edge of The Great Wilderness, and a classic in anyone's book. An Teallach (pronounced 'An Chelluck') means The Forge, a name which bears no relation to its shape (The Castle might be better), but comes instead from the mountain's red Torridonian sandstone, which glows like a smithy's fire when lit by the setting sun. However suspect the nomenclature, there is no denying the drama of the effect, especially when seen from the coast. The shadows of a summer evening throw into greater relief the fortifications of An Teallach's renowned and rocky ridge, which forms the highlight of the route described here.

SCOTLAND

Like the mountain, the route is a classic – one of Britain's best high mountain traverses. For Munro-baggers, Sgurr Fiona (1060m) and Bidein a' Ghlas Thuill (1062m) can be ticked off, and eight 'tops' are thrown in for good measure. In fine weather the ridge crest is an exciting scramble on good rock, although there are parts which are difficult, with a fair degree of exposure. These can all be avoided, however, as a path which runs below the ridge, avoids the trickiest bits. In bad weather, particularly outside the summer months, it becomes a major mountaineering challenge. Whatever the conditions, it is not a route to be undertaken lightly, and should be avoided by those who lack the experience or the skills. Once on the mountain itself, there are no paths marked on the map. Escape routes are limited, but detailed in the following description.

An Teallach, then, is for connoisseurs, and for experienced hill-walkers – well prepared, well equipped and adept with map and compass. Its ascent and traverse make for a long, demanding and immensely satisfying mountain-walk. From the ridge and summits you have unrivalled views across The Great Wilderness and its less accessible mountain peaks. On clear days you can see to the Torridons in the south, the far-off hills of the distant north, the beautiful coastline of Wester Ross, and the islands of the Outer Hebrides. If the cloud is down, you will have to imagine it all, and buy a nice picture book later.

Direction, Distance & Duration

This route is almost circular, starting at Corrie Hallie (two miles south-east of Dundonnell), and ending at Dundonnell. By following the direction described you start on an easy path leading directly to the foot of the ridge, which is best traversed south to north.

The distance is 14 miles, but the nature of the route, which involves at least 1300m of ascent, plus tortuous descents, not to mention tricky navigation, takes a minimum seven to 8½ hours of walking. Add to this time for rests, lunch, navigation and admir-

ing the view and you should allow between eight and 10 hours. The nearest accommodation (see below) is two or three miles from the start, along the main road. If you don't tie in with the bus, allow extra time to walk this.

Information

The nearest TICs are to the north and south of Dundonnell, at Ullapool (☎ 01854 612135) and Gairloch (☎ 01445 712130), but they can advise on local transport and accommodation options. For weather forecasts, phone one of the information lines listed in the Dangers & Annoyances section of the Facts for the Walker chapter, but remember – on a hill this size, so close to the sea, conditions are always changeable. (For information on guided walks see the Torridon section.)

Books & Maps An Teallach is included in *The Munros, The High Mountains, 200 Challenging Walks, The North West Highlands SMC Guidebook* and *Exploring the Far North West of Scotland* – all detailed in the Facts for the Walker chapter.

An Teallach and The Great Wilderness are on OS Landranger (1:50,000) sheet 19, which also covers the north Torridons. For more detail get OS Pathfinder (1:25,000) sheet 120.

Stalking Information The estates around An Teallach are privately owned, and 'stalking' (hunting) takes place at certain times of the year. There is a tradition of mutual tolerance between walkers and stalkers in Scotland, which boils down to this: if there's no stalking in the area (often just one glen within the estate) walkers can usually go there, and if there *is* stalking in the area, then walkers are asked to avoid it.

The stalking season for game birds (including grouse and pheasant) is 12 August to 1 February. Deer are hunted at any time of year, but mostly in September and October. In practice, stalking rarely takes place near popular paths, but before setting out for a walk on An Teallach, check at your accommodation when stalking takes place; local people know what's happening and who to contact.

Places to Stay & Eat
In Dundonnell village, the smart *Dundonnell Hotel* (☎ 01854 633204), charging £45 to £50 per person ensuite, with a full Scottish breakfast (haggis and oatcakes with your toast, eggs and bacon). About 1½ miles west, in Camusnagaul, is an independent hostel, *Sail Mhor Croft* (☎ 01854 633224), open all year with good self-catering facilities for £7.50 per night or £10.25 B&B. Also in Camusnagaul is *Mrs Ross* (☎ 01854 633237), who charges £14 for B&B. She also has self-catering chalets and caravans to let. At Badrallach, about 10 miles from Dundonnell, there's a *campsite & bothy* (☎ 01854 633281) both for £2.50 per person.

The Dundonnell Hotel is the only place nearby for eating out, with evening bar meals and a smarter restaurant. The hotel is open all day, serves teas, home-made shortbread and, of course, beer, making it conveniently placed for a reviving drink at the end of the walk. The petrol station opposite has ice-creams as an alternative reward for your efforts, plus chocolate and snacks for hill-fuel. For more than this, the nearest store is at Badcaul, three miles beyond Camusnagaul.

Getting There & Away
Bus The daily Westerbus (☎ 01445 712255) service between Inverness and Gairloch, goes via Dundonnell on Monday, Wednesday and Saturday, so you can get from Inverness to Dundonnell, do the walk the next day, then return to Inverness the day after that. On Tuesday, Thursday and Friday, this bus between Inverness and Gairloch goes via Achnasheen and Kinlochlewe, and every morning there's a postbus (☎ 01463 256200) from Achnasheen to Dundonnell. To get back to Achnasheen by postbus, you must go via Gairloch (and possibly spend a night there).

Train Achnasheen is on the railway line between Inverness and Kyle of Lochalsh with three trains a day in each direction. The postbus (see above) from Achnasheen to Dundonnell meets the first train (only) from Inverness, and you could also connect by catching the first train from Kyle.

Car Dundonnell is at the eastern end of Little Loch Broom about 100 miles from Inverness on the A832, between Gairloch and Braemore Junction, which is on the A835 between Inverness and Ullapool.

The Route
The route starts at Corrie Hallie, two miles along the A832, south-east of Dundonnell. There is a lay-by (the starting point for many walks in the area). Without a car, you can walk, or tie in with a bus.

Stage 1: Corrie Hallie to Sail Liath Summit
6 miles (9.5 km), 2½ to 3 hours
From the lay-by, go through a gate onto a well-defined track, running south, climbing gradually through silver birch and bracken (plus bluebells in spring), and with a burn on your right, mostly hidden, but refreshingly audible. After crossing some stepping stones, the path gets steeper, then reaches a rocky plateau (about 45 minutes from the start), with fine views beginning to open out. To the right (west) is the formidable ridge of An Teallach itself. To the left are the hills around Ben Dearg and the Fannichs, and ahead the peaks of The Great Wilderness begin to appear.

At this point you leave the track (the junction is marked by two cairns), taking a smaller, but well-trodden path on your right which leads towards Shenavall. Continue along this path as it gradually rises towards the broad shoulder of Sail Liath, the first of An Teallach's tops to be tackled. After about 30 minutes from the junction you must leave the path (at about its highest point), and strike right (north-west), up the shoulder of Sail Liath. From now until almost the end of the walk there is no path marked on the map, although you will pick up occasional paths

SCOTLAND

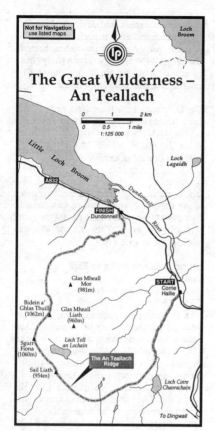

Not for Navigation
use listed maps

Loch
Broom

The Great Wilderness – An Teallach

0   1   2 km
0   0.5   1 mile
1:125 000

Little Loch Broom

A832

Loch
Lagaidh

Dundonnell

FINISH
Dundonnell

River

Glas Mheall
Mor
(981m)

START
Corrie
Hallie

Bidein a'
Ghlas Thuill
(1062m)

Glas Mheall
Liath
(960m)

Sgurr
Fiona
(1060m)

Loch Toll
an Lochain

The An Teallach
Ridge

Sail Liath
(954m)

Loch Coire
Chaorachain

To Dingwall

SCOTLAND

on the ground. Not here though, as you make your own route, first up a steep slope of shattered boulders, studded with bilberry, juniper, and occasional clumps of wild thyme. There is a bit of a scramble to the top of the first steep rise, and then it becomes easier as you pass over a grassy slope to the small, rocky plateau of Sail Liath's summit (954m). There is a cairn, wind-shelters and the most wonderful view. Ahead, you now get a much closer view of the ridge to come, the buttresses of Corrag Bhuidhe leading on to the two summits of Sgurr Fiona, and Bidein a' Ghlas Thuill.

Stage 2: Sail Liath Summit to Bidein a' Ghlas Thuill

3 miles (5 km), 3 to 3½ hours

From Sail Liath go westwards, down a slippery drop to a narrow gap, then straight back up a steep, rocky path to a minor top (unnamed on the OS map) above Cadha Gobhlach – the forked pass. Descend again, northwards, to the pass. (If the weather is bad, this is a possible escape route down to Loch Toll an Lochain). From the pass take a steep path up to the ridge proper, across a rocky outcrop to the foot of Corrag Bhuidhe Buttress, and the rocky pinnacles beyond.

The next section, from Corrag Bhuidhe Buttress to Sgurr Fiona, is the steepest and most difficult part of the route, and includes an exposed 10m 'bad step' (hard scramble). These difficulties can be avoided by taking a narrow path running left of the buttress wall, south-west of the ridge crest. Even when taking this 'easier' option, you should take care, as sheep and previous walkers have created a confusing selection of tracks. So that you don't miss the views, there are several points from which you can scramble up the path, back to the ridge crest itself, which should of course be approached with care. In order to savour at least some of the ridge's delights, you should perhaps aim to regain its crest before the lofty heights of Lord Berkeley's Seat.

For those who decide the conditions are good enough, and the spirit and flesh are both willing and able, keep to the ridge crest. The rocky pinnacles of Corrag Bhuidhe provide a dramatic challenge, and some good scrambling on sound rock. The experience is heightened by the sheer cliff faces dropping down to the loch below. The pinnacles lead up to the narrow top of Corrag Bhuidhe (1036m). Continue to clamber along the line of the ridge to reach the bulky form of Lord Berkeley's Seat (1047m). Ahead is the magnificent pointed peak of Sgurr Fiona.

Leaving Lord Berkeley's Seat, continue along the ridge. Care must still be taken as the scrambling continues. You know the worst is over when you reach a pleasant sandstone stairway leading up to the sharp and stony summit of Sgurr Fiona (1060m). This is another wonderful lookout, and a fine place for lunch. After all the excitements of the ridge, this peak feels like the summit, but that honour belongs to Fiona's sister, Bidein a' Ghlas Thuill, which is higher by a massive three metres. Still, stay here awhile to admire the peaks, from Suilven and Coigach to the Fannichs, through the peaks of The Great Wilderness like Ruadh Stac Mhor and Slioch and on to the Torridons. Perhaps the coast is bathed in sunshine, and the Summer Isles are living up to their name.

From Fiona, Bidein seems distant, with a lengthy descent and ascent, but it's not as far as it looks. It is, however, unpleasantly loose underfoot as you go steeply down to the curved gap between the two summits (in emergencies you can descend very steeply from here to Loch Toll an Lochain) and then up again to the summit trig point. Take a break and, yes, admire the views once more. Alternatively, of course, you can sit and curse the clouds, and mutter about the unfair lack of view after all that effort you put in.

Descent As is often the case in Scotland, getting off the mountain is sometimes harder than getting up it. From this point there's a choice of routes; which route you take depends on where you need to end up (Dundonnell or Corrie Hallie). Whichever way you go, navigation is particularly important to avoid dropping into the wrong valley.

Stage 3A: Bidein a' Ghlas Thuill to Dundonnell

5 miles (8 km), 2 to 2½ hours

From Bidein a' Ghlas Thuill the most direct way back to Dundonnell goes northwards, by the minor peak and bealach south-west of Glas Mheall Mor, and then down the ridge to the west and north of Coir a Mhuillinn. About halfway down you meet a path which eventually takes you down to the main road, only 300m east of the Dundonnell Hotel.

Alternatively, from the bealach you can drop into the Coir a Mhuillinn valley itself, and follow the stream north-easterly, con-

touring north after two miles or so to pick up the path mentioned above, which leads to Dundonnell.

Stage 3B: Bidein a' Ghlas Thuill to Corrie Hallie via Glas Mheall Mor

4 miles (6.5 km), 2 to 2½ hours

To reach Corrie Hallie, the most straightforward way (which also bags you another peak) is to head north from the summit, and then go east to Glas Mheall Mor. This is gained by a pleasant walk along a gentle north-easterly ridge to the cairn marking the final top of An Teallach. Then it is a steep scramble down loose scree towards the stream that drains this narrow corrie between Ghlas Mheall Mor and Ghlas Mheall Liath. Follow this stream down on its north side, passing a little lochan on your right, and you will meet up with a more distinct path which is designed to allow less ambitious folk to visit the very pleasant waterfalls, where you might like to loiter awhile. Or, with the end so near, you may want to push on, eventually reaching the main road opposite Dundonnell House, about 500m north of Corrie Hallie lay-by.

Stage 3C: Bidein a' Ghlas Thuill to Corrie Hallie, via Glas Mheall Liath

3½ miles (5.5 km), 2 to 2½ hours

This more challenging way to return to Corrie Hallie includes the summit of Glas Mheall Liath, and may appeal if you want a bit more scrambling and like the completeness of a mountain horseshoe. This route seems to follow more closely the natural sweep of the mountain, although it involves a rather unpleasant bit of descent at the end.

From Bidein you will see Glas Mheall Liath south of west, at the end of a narrow and rocky ridge. A path runs along the southern side of this ridge: on your left are some interesting pinnacles of rock, with scrambling options, and good lookouts. On your right you get good views of the ridge you traversed earlier in the day.

The character of the rock changes as you approach Glas Mheall Liath; the Torridonian sandstone is capped with big boulders of

SCOTLAND

grey cambrian quartzite, which take some concentration as you step across them towards the summit cairn. From here, you continue roughly south of west, down these unpleasantly steep boulders to reach a heathery terrace and the great stone slabs of the valley side. Finally you meet the stream which drains the loch. Follow this downstream to pick up a rather indistinct path, marked by decidedly erratic cairns. You pass a small lochan, then pick up the good path past the waterfalls mentioned above.

Skye

Speed bonny boat, like a bird on the wing, over the sea to Skye.
Carry the lad, that's born to be King,
over the sea to Skye.

The Skye Boat Song is quite possibly the world's best known song about Scotland, but it's not only the tales of Prince Charlie and his Flora MacDonald which attract visitors to the Isle of Skye. For walkers and climbers there's the attraction of some of the most impressive mountains in the British Isles; the spectacular Black Cuillin and Red Cuillin hills.

The name 'Cuillin' is derived from the Norse 'Kjollen', meaning keel-shaped. Both the Red and the Black Cuillin are igneous formations, but their mineral compositions are very different. The Black Cuillin rocks are mainly gabbro, a coarse crystalline rock, which is rich in iron and magnesium, giving it a dark colour, with sections of smooth basalt on the surface. The basalt has eroded more readily, leaving gullies and chimneys, whilst glacial action has carved out corries and sculpted the sharp spectacular ridges. A peculiar property of the rocks is localised magnetic influences – a rather important consideration if you're intending to navigate by compass! The Red Cuillin, a product of later igneous activity, are comprised of

granite, which incorporates quartz and which is more rounded in character.

Most visitors to Skye will, if the weather is kind (and that is not always the case) merely admire the Black Cuillin's jagged ridges, towers and pinnacles from a safe distance. Most of these airy peaks are the domain of mountaineers and rock-climbers, and way beyond the scope of this book, but happily there are a few places where walkers with some mountain experience can get 'Skye-high' for a closer Cuillin encounter. And should the cloud be down, there are also some rewarding low-level walks along the island's glens and coast.

In this section we describe a long low-level route. We also describe a challenging route up Bruach na Frithe onto the Cuillin ridge itself, one of few peaks on Skye accessible to experienced mountain-walkers without hands-on scrambling.

The hamlet of Sligachan, at the head of a sea-loch on the east side of the central part of the island, is the transport hub for the routes we describe here. It is fairly easy to reach by public transport and has good accommodation options. Along with Glenbrittle (further west), it has been a base for walkers and climbers on Skye for about a century.

COAST & CUILLIN – ELGOL TO SLIGACHAN

Distance 11 miles (17.5 km)
Duration 6 hours
Start Elgol
Finish Sligachan
Regional Centres Broadford, Portree, Kyle of Lochalsh
Region Highland
Area Isle of Skye National Scenic Area
Summary A long, linear route along coastal cliff path and through remote glens, flanked by rugged Cuillin mountains. Pathfinding is pretty straightforward, but the going is rough and stony. Map and compass knowledge is required.

This low-level route follows in the steps of Bonnie Prince Charlie's post-Culloden wanderings through the heart of the Black Cuillins. It is a good alternative if cloudy

SCOTLAND

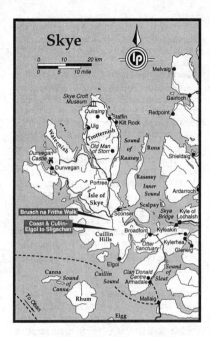

weather prevents a high ascent. Whereas most Scottish routes in this book are for summer only, this route has a longer season and could generally be undertaken at any time between April and October/November.

The first leg of the route – as far as Camasunary – follows a clifftop, which requires some care in the wet (see Shorter Alternatives). The second leg passes below the towering Cuillins and follows the awesome splendour of Glen Sligachan to arrive at Sligachan.

Direction, Distance & Duration

There are two reasons for doing this 11 mile walk from south to north: firstly, transport logistics (see Getting There & Away) are easier; secondly, the views in this direction are really stunning. You will need around six hours to cover the 11 miles; it may sound like a lot but the going is quite tough. If you reach Elgol by the midday postbus (see Getting There & Away) you need to be sure you have

plenty of daylight hours ahead of you. The route is a right of way.

Shorter Alternatives It is possible to avoid the initial airy clifftop section of this walk by starting at Kirkibost, three miles north-east of Elgol, and following a rough but driveable track to Camasunary. (This track also provides an escape route if you decide not to continue with Stage 2.) You could convert the full linear walk into a shorter circuit by walking from Elgol to Camasunary and then following the above-mentioned track back to Kirkibost. You could then walk to Elgol or – if you are in time – catch the afternoon postbus.

Information

The TIC in Portree (☎ 01478 612137) is open all year and has a fax weather forecasting service (when it's working). Broadford TIC (☎ 01471 822361) is open from April to October. The award-winning Aros Experience, in Portree, provides a tour through the history of Skye from 1700 to the present (in six languages) and there are adjacent forest walks. There's a neat little folk museum at Luib (between Broadford and Sligachan), and an environmental centre in Broadford (☎ 01471 822487) which specialises in otters as well as running guided walks and wildlife tours.

Books & Maps Skye has inspired many scribes, and for the transient visitor/walker there's an excellent little series of guidebooks written and published by Charles Rhodes: *Selected Walks – Southern Skye* covers the area we describe. There's also *Selected Walks – Northern Skye* and *Walks from Glen Brittle* (English & German). Longer 'classics' include *The Magic of Skye* by W A Poucher. The Scottish Mountaineering Club's *Guide to Skye* is very useful for the serious and experienced walker wanting to spend some time on the island.

The Cuillins and both of the walks described here are covered by OS Landranger (1:50,000) sheet 32 and OS Outdoor Leisure (1:25,000) sheet 8.

SCOTLAND

Guided Walks & Local Services

Shorter guided walks are mentioned above. Ted Badger (☎ 01471 866228) in Elgol also offers 'Nice and Easy Walks'. For something more serious, Skye Mountain Guides (☎ 01478 612682) and Skye High (☎ 01471 822116) provide mountaineering guides.

If you want to adapt the route, Bella Jane Boat Trips (☎ 01471 866244) will take you from Elgol across Loch Scavaig to landing steps near Loch Coruisk from where you can walk to Sligachan via Loch Coruisk.

Sutherland's (☎ 01478 640400) provides a summer bus service between Sligachan and Glenbrittle, sometimes with commentary and photography stops and the option to walk the return trip by footpath through the hills.

Places to Stay & Eat

There are a limited number of places to stay in Elgol, but they really only operate during summer months. Walkers are welcome at *Strathaird House* (☎ 01471 866269) near Kirkibost, some 10 miles from Broadford and five miles from Elgol; B&B starts from around £16, evening meals at £12.50, and self-catering from £130 per week. Mrs Mary MacIntosh at *Cnoc Ban* (☎ 01471 866294) is very friendly and offers B&B at £14 in a traditional house with family and single rooms. She burns peat on the fire and will dry wet gear on a pulley airer; she'll also do an evening snack if you're stuck, or arrange a meal locally. There's also *Blaven Bunkhouse* (☎ 01471 822397), nine miles from Broadford on the Elgol road, at £6 per night with duvets, heating and drying. Elgol has a small tearoom, but it closes quite early.

If you can be self-sufficient with overnight gear you could stay in the superbly situated bothy near Camasunary (between Stage 1 and Stage 2 of the walk); this involves a detour of less than 500m off the route.

At Sligachan, the *Coghills* (☎ 01478 650303) have a campsite and bunkhouse (both at £6 per person) or self-catering cottages (£300 per week), all seasonal. Otherwise, you can live it up at the traditional *Sligachan Hotel*, (☎ & fax 01478 650204), open all year, from £25 to £35 for B&B. The hotel offers the only food

in Sligachan with a smart dining room and the more reasonably priced *Seumas's Bar* which serves food all day, starting with walkers' breakfasts.

Portree, the island's capital, is another possible place to stay as transport is good from here and there's a wider range of facilities. Try *Craiglockhart Guest House* (☎ 01478 612233), with B&B for £16 to £20, the *Pier Hotel* (☎ 01478 612094) from £14 to £18, or just walk around the quayside and take your pick. The A850 (Viewfield Rd) has plenty of choices for B&B too, eg *Mrs McPhie* (☎ 01478 612093), and *Mrs MacFarlane* (☎ & fax 01478 612870), both from £18. There are plenty of places to eat too.

The *SYHA hostels* at Broadford (☎ 01471 822442, £7.80) and Kyleakin (☎ 01599 534585, £7.80) are both of a good standard; Glenbrittle (☎ 01478 640278, £5.40) is more modest.

Getting There & Away

Bus & Train You can use train or bus to reach the mainland jumping-off points for Skye. The ScotRail (☎ 0345 484950) train services from Glasgow tie in with the Mallaig ferry to Armadale, from where buses go to Portree and Kyleakin via Broadford. Alternatively, you can reach Kyle of Lochalsh by train from Inverness. (This opens up the possibility of a great scenic round trip combining the two highland rail services with a bus across Skye.) Citylink buses (☎ 0990 505050) also travel from Glasgow and Inverness and will take you to Broadford, Sligachan (or Portree).

There are no trains on Skye. Highland Buses (☎ 01463 233371) operates services connecting Portree, Sligachan, Broadford and Kyleakin.

To reach the start of this route you could take a morning bus (daily except Sunday) from Sligachan (or Portree) to Broadford, connecting with the 10.45 am postbus from Broadford Post Office to Elgol, arriving at 12.45 pm. On weekdays there's also an afternoon postbus from Broadford to Elgol.

Car In 1995 the controversial Skye Bridge was opened (with a hefty toll of over £4 each

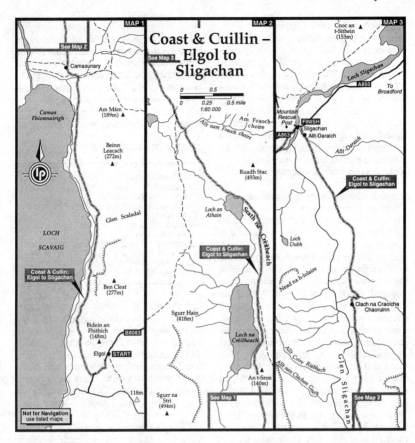

Coast & Cuillin – Elgol to Sligachan

MAP 1 / MAP 2 / MAP 3

0   0.5
0   0.25   0.5 mile
1:60 000

Not for Navigation
use listed maps

way), so the ferry from Kyle of Lochalsh to Kyleakin is no more. If you prefer to speed by bonny boat to Skye, you can opt for the five minute ferry crossing from Glenelg to Kylerhea (☎ 01599 511302), which runs from April to October, or the 30 minute ferry trip from Mallaig to Armadale (Caledonian MacBrayne ☎ 01471 844248), which takes cars only during the summer months.

The Route
Stage 1: Elgol to Camasunary
3.5 miles (5.5 km), 2 hours
From Elgol Post Office head downhill

towards the pier and take the second lane on the right (signed as a right of way). There are splendid views south from here of the 'Small Isles': Soay, Eigg, Rhum and Canna. The lane leads past some houses and a plaque commemorating a USAF pilot who crashed his F111 nearby. The path diverts round a house through a gate (signed 'Footpath to Coruisk'). A well-trodden path continues across a grassy slope, with super views across Loch Scavaig, before gradually descending to cross the first burn. The ground below Ben Cleat then becomes steeper with rocky sections and the narrow

SCOTLAND

path needs full attention and sure feet. If you want to look at the views – and you must – then stop!

You then drop down to Glen Scaladel to ford the burn. The path continues up the other side through bracken and stunted trees and above a steep, rocky cliff. Cross a boggy patch and carry on above one further rocky cliff and then over more level ground to reach Camasunary. There's a bridge over the burn here and a substantial house reached by a rough driveable track that comes in from Kirkibost (see Shorter Alternatives).

Stage 2: Camasunary to Sligachan
7½ miles (12 km), 4 hours

The route to Sligachan forks right from the track just before the house is reached and in front of a ruin – there is a sign on the wall. Follow a stony path through boggy heather between the main Black Cuillin massif on the left and the bulk of Bla Bheinn (pronounced 'Bla Ven') on the right. After about half a mile and a gentle rise, Loch na Crèitheach comes into sight. The loch occupies a glaciated rock basin overlooked by the intimidating black cliffs at the southern end of Sgurr Hain to the left. The way ahead looks as if it will be blocked by Ruadh Stac, but the path continues round the loch and across alternating wet and dry ground. It then bends round to the left past Loch an Athain. You'll notice a change in the geology here; the path now follows the valley separating the gabbro of the Black Cuillins on the left from the red granite of the Red Cuillins on the right.

Soon after, two lochans come into view. There's a cairn marking the point where a path from Loch Coruisk joins this route. You reach the watershed about half a mile further on, but this not-so-great divide is less than 100m ASL. The path keeps well up on the right side of the valley, and the going is fairly good over dryish ground beneath Marsco, with views into the great Harta Corrie opposite, and Sgurr nan Gillean and its outliers above. As you proceed, the Sligachan Hotel comes into view, although it is still about three miles

away. Boggy stretches become more frequent and there is a series of burns to be crossed – the most significant is the Allt na Measarroch. Immediately after this it is well worth taking the 100m detour to the right to avoid the worst of the boggy ground hereabouts. You can look forward to the final improved half mile of the path, and maybe some liquid refreshment at the hotel.

BRUACH NA FRITHE

> **Distance** 8½ miles (13.5 km)
> **Duration** 6 to 8 hours
> **Start & Finish** Sligachan
> **Regional Centres** Broadford, Portree, Kyle of Lochalsh
> **Region** Highland
> **Area** Isle of Skye
> **Summary** This ascent involves rough going and scrambling, and needs clear, settled weather for routefinding. Mountain experience plus map and compass knowledge is essential.

The summit of Bruach na Frithe (pronounced 'Bruack na Free'), is a turning point on the main Cuillin Ridge, and provides magnificent views along the ridge. At 958m (3142 ft), this peak is a Munro and has been described as the least difficult of the Black Cuillin peaks to ascend, being the only one not defended by cliffs. The easiest route is up (and down) Fionn Choire, a steep-sided 'bowl' whose head-wall leads up to Bruach na Frithe. An attractive alternative for those willing to tackle an easy scramble, which is airy in places, is the ascent by the North-West Ridge followed by the descent of Fionn Choire.

> **Warning**
> Due to the magnetic properties of the gabbro rock, compasses give distorted readings on the summit ridge. Also, the route up and down the choire would be far from straightforward in poor visibility. Hence this summit should only be attempted in good weather when the way can be clearly seen.

SCOTLAND

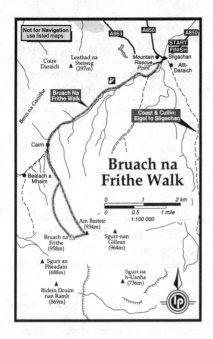

Not for Navigation
use listed maps

Coire
Daraich

Leathad na
Steiseig
▲ (297m)

Mountain
Rescue
Point

A863   A850   A850

START
FINISH
Sligachan

Allt-
Daraich

P

Bruach Na
Frithe Walk

Beinn na Caoidhe

Coast & Cullin:
Elgol to Sligachan

**Bruach na
Frithe Walk**

Cairn

Bealach a
Mhaim

0   1   2 km
0   0.5   1 mile
1:100 000

Am Basteir
(934m)

Bruach na
Frithe
(958m)

▲ Sgurr-nan
Gillean
(964m)

▲ Sgurr an
Fheadain
(688m)

Sgurr na
h-Uanha
▲ (736m)

▲ Bidein Druim
nan Ramh
(869m)

Direction, Distance & Duration

The approach is along a footpath following a right of way from Sligachan to Glenbrittle over the Bealach a Mhaim (continuing along here would provide another option on a poor day). The total distance covered is 8½ miles, and involves almost 1000m of ascent, so you need between six and eight hours to cover the route.

The choice between two alternative ascents can be left until the foot of Fionn Choire, about 1½ hours into the route.

Places to stay, information, maps and books are covered in the Elgol to Sligachan section above.

The Route
Stage 1: Sligachan to the Base of Fionn Choire

2½ miles (4 km), 1½ to 2 hours
From Sligachan Bridge turn west along the A863 towards Dunvegan for a little over 500m. Just after the road passes through a cutting near

a lay-by take the track signed 'Footpath to Glenbrittle' towards Alltdearg House. Just as you approach the house a signed footpath diverts around the grounds to the north, across a stretch of boggy ground; the firmest route keeps near to the fence on the left.

You'll soon pick up a stony path which runs alongside the Allt Dearg Mor, a burn which tumbles down a series of rock ledges. After some two miles the path begins to level out in Coire na Circe, and the going becomes soft under foot. Continue on, fording a sizeable tributary, to reach a large cairn. Here the path for Bruach na Frithe forks left across boggy ground with another burn to cross (more easily) some 200m after the cairn. Follow the ascending path for about 20 minutes, with Allt an Fionn Choire (a burn with small waterfalls pouring from the corrie above) on your left (east), until you reach a substantial cairn on top of a rock slab.

This is a good place for a rest, while you decide which route to take to the summit.

Stage 2A: Base of Fionn Choire to Bruach na Frithe Summit (easier route via corrie)

1½ miles (2.5 km), 2 to 2½ hours
From the large cairn keep ahead on the small cairned path to the right (west) of the burn. After ascending a short way the path reaches the sill at the edge of the corrie. You need to cross the burn to gain a large cairn on the opposite side; this may be easier above a burn junction. From the cairn there is no discernible path, but you can pick out a line of small cairns swinging slightly left across the corrie floor towards some slabs of rock in the scree ahead.

After crossing this level stretch a small path ascends to the left of a dry stream bed in a small gorge, where the burn has disappeared below bouldery ground. There are no cairns, but a pretty obvious path roughly follows the left-hand side of the burn, which disappears in places. Where the angle steepens the route zigzags up the scree and boulders to reach the ridge at Bealach nan Lice where you turn right on a small path under the rock outcrop of Fionn Choire. This

SCOTLAND

takes you to the east ridge of Bruach na Frithe, which you follow to the distinctive cylindrical trig point on the summit.

Stage 2B: Foot of Fionn Choire to Bruach na Frithe Summit (scramble via North-West Ridge)

2 miles (3 km), 2 to 2½ hours

From the cairn on top of the rock slab head up the steep slope of grass, boulders and scree on the right – there are occasional cairns and the direction is south-south-west. Cross a marshy depression and then, higher again, you'll reach a small pool. The steep slope up to the left is tackled to join a more obvious path (which has come up from Bealach a Mhaim). This zigzags up steep scree and then grass to a narrowing of the ridge and a brief easing of the angle.

There is a short, steep section before an almost horizontal narrow section about 150m in length – a superb situation for those with a head for heights. At the end of this the main ridge scramble lies ahead. Difficulties encountered near the ridge-crest can be avoided by going to the right, but don't take the path which traverses round to the right at the start of the rocks. There is plenty of evidence of the routes which have been taken by those who have gone before, and with the occasional use of hands for balance and to help with upward progress you should reach the cylindrical trig point with a great feeling of exhilaration and achievement (or perhaps just relief!). Either way, enjoy the superb views, and perhaps check out your compass to see for yourself how the gabbro affects the needle!

Stage 3: Descent from Bruach na Frithe Summit to Sligachan

4½ miles (7 km), 2½ hours

The descent retraces Stage 2A. From the summit take the east ridge, keeping close to the crest but avoiding obstacles on their left and then passing below Fionn Choire to reach Bealach nan Lice, about 400m from (and 60m lower than) the summit. Turn left down a stony path into Fionn Choire. There is a burn on the left (west), but this disappears in places. In mist the route can be confusing. The standard advice is that by following any of the watercourses leading north, the Allt Dearg Mor flowing down to Sligachan will eventually be reached, but BEWARE: some of the watercourses are cut into ravines and there are steep sections with small waterfalls. So, you're best off retracing Stage 2A which will lead you back to the path on the north-west side of the Allt Dearg Mor, down to Sligachan.

Other Short Walks in Scotland

In this book we have described a very small selection of day-walks in Scotland. There are, of course, many more options, in fact the choice is almost limitless. Places we haven't even touched on, which are great for walking, include the Arrochar Alps west of Loch Lomond, the Pentland Hills near Edinburgh, the Great Glen between Fort William and Inverness (mentioned briefly below), and the mountains around Lochnagar south-east of the Cairngorms, not to mention the islands such as Harris, Orkney and Shetland.

People who have been coming to Scotland for 50 years or more are still finding new places to explore and new peaks to bag. If you are hooked on this part of Britain, further guidebook suggestions are mentioned in the Facts for the Walker chapter. For general advice, the Scottish Tourist Board (☎ 0131 332 2433) produces a *Walking in Scotland* booklet, describing 80 routes in various parts of the country, plus safety tips and other information. (You can order this direct from their Brochure Enquiry Service ☎ 0345 511511.)

Scotland – Long-Distance Paths

Southern Upland Way

Distance 212 miles (341 km)
Duration 12 to 20 days
Start Portpatrick, near Stranraer
Finish Cockburnspath, North Sea coast
Regional Centres Ayr, Dumfries, Galashiels, Berwick-upon-Tweed
Region Dumfries & Galloway, the Borders
Area Southern Uplands
Summary This very long route passes mostly through remote country and reaches heights over 700m (2300 ft), with paths generally good, although muddy farm tracks will also be encountered.

The Southern Upland Way, opened in 1984, was Britain's first official coast-to-coast footpath, traversing the mainland of Scotland at one of its widest points. The route goes 'across the grain' of the land, like a rollercoaster over mountains, moorland and extensive conifer plantations, descending to cross major rivers before rising again. It also passes through agricultural land and sections of broadleaf forest.

Along with the scenic variety, you can expect a wide range of weather conditions during a complete crossing. It's important not to be too rigid with your timetable; if bad weather is encountered during mountain or remote sections it may well be sensible (if not essential) to alter your plans for the day. Bad weather is especially likely during the winter but, although April to September is the best time, the Southern Upland Way can still be attempted at any time of year.

The route is not especially well served with accommodation choices, so you may have to consider camping or long days to get from one roof to another. These factors, combined with the route's length and the remote nature of the landscape, make it a far more serious proposition than the West Highland Way or most other national trails in England and Wales.

DIRECTION, DISTANCE & DURATION

This route is usually followed from southwest to north-east. The prevailing wind is then behind you, and you can hope for drier weather as you proceed. The route is well waymarked with 'thistle hexagons' and signposts, but you should still have maps and a compass for navigating. In general, however, if you go 500m or so past an unsigned junction without seeing a marker, you should consult your map and be prepared to retrace a little. The waymarks take precedence over the route shown on maps, and changes are being made all the time.

The full walk of 212 miles may take you as few as 12 days or as many as 20 days, depending on what you regard as a comfortable pace. (See the notes on Distances & Times in the Terms & Definitions Used in This Book section of the Facts for the Walker chapter.) A reasonable daily average for this route might be 15 miles with an ascent of 600m, which should be covered in about eight hours including a few reasonable stops. We provide information on distance and ascent in the route descriptions to help you plan your own itinerary.

STAGES

While planning, it is important to take account of the main roads intersecting the route on which there are bus services, and the one railway line with a convenient station. These enable you to reach the Southern Upland Way from places such as Ayr, Glasgow and Edinburgh to the north, or Dumfries, Carlisle and Berwick-upon-Tweed to the south, and also enable you to walk parts of the Way using public transport to and from it.

We have therefore divided the route description into nine stages based on the availability of public transport, and have left it to you to decide the actual itinerary, based on the accommodation you will be using and the distance you want to walk each day. *It is not intended that you cover one stage per day.* The stages we have used are:

Stage	From	To	Distance
1	Portpatrick	Castle Kennedy	13 miles (21 km)
2	Castle Kennedy	Bargrennan	27 miles (43 km)
3	Bargrennan	Dalry	24 miles (38.5 km)
4	Dalry	Sanquhar	27 miles (43 km)
5	Sanquhar	Beattock	28 miles (45 km)
6	Beattock	Traquair	33 miles (53 km)
7	Traquair	Melrose	18 miles (29 km)
8	Melrose	Lauder	10 miles (16 km)
9	Lauder	Cockburns path	32 miles (52 km)

INFORMATION

Your best starting point is the small colour *Southern Upland Way* leaflet available from local Tourist Information Centres (TICs), which has several useful addresses. For information on where to stay, the *Accommodation List* is available from the Ranger Services based at Dumfries (☎ 01387 261234) and Jedburgh (☎ 01835 830281). They also have leaflets on the wildlife, history and archaeology of the area, and short circular walks based on the Southern Upland Way.

The free *Southern Upland Wayfarer* newspaper gives handy hints and carries useful ads. *A Guide to Public Transport across the Southern Upland Way* is available from the Department of Roads and Transportation, Borders Regional Council (☎ 01835 823301), Newtown St, Boswells, Melrose TD6 0SA. For more general information the relevant tourist boards are Borders (☎ 01835 863435/863688) and Dumfries & Galloway (☎ 01387 253862).

Books & Maps

If you're seriously thinking of tackling a substantial amount of the Way we highly commend *The Official Guide to the Southern Upland Way* by Roger Smith, published by Her Majesty's Stationery Office (HMSO), which comes in a pack including the relevant parts of the seven Ordnance Survey (OS) Landranger (1:50,000) maps for the entire length. It's a bit pricey at £17.50 but about half what it would cost to buy all the maps individually.

Serious students of the mountain areas around the Southern Upland Way might want the Scottish Mountaineering Club (SMC) guide to *The Southern Uplands*. By contrast a really enjoyable read is Ronald Turnbull's *Across Scotland on Foot* (Greystone Books) which has an illuminating chapter: 'The Southern Upland Way or not?'.

GUIDED WALKS & LOCAL SERVICES

This is really self-guiding country but some accommodation providers offer a vehicle back-up service for you or your pack (details in the *Accommodation List*) over sections of the Southern Upland Way. You'll need to plan your provisioning carefully as shops are few and far between in some areas; again, the leaflet helps.

PLACES TO STAY & EAT

Over much of the route, opportunities for overnight stops at hotels, B&Bs and hostels are very limited, and you will have to walk 20 miles or more on some days. If you camp or use bothies this will give you more flexibility, but of course you have to carry more weight. We give brief details of where accommodation is available in the route description which should enable you to plan your walk and divide it into daily stages. More detail, including addresses and telephone numbers, is available in the invaluable *Accommodation List* (see Information earlier) and in the *National Trail Companion* (see the Books section in the Facts for the Walker chapter).

GETTING THERE & AWAY
Bus, Train & Ferry

Stranraer may be reached by bus or train from Glasgow and Carlisle, and ferry from Northern Ireland, and there is a bus service about six times a day from there to

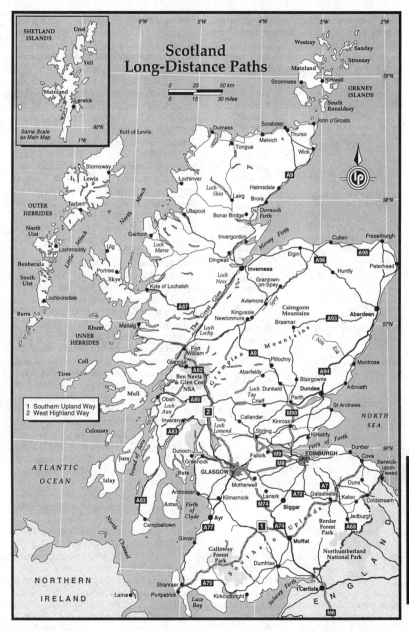

Scotland
Long-Distance Paths

1 Southern Upland Way
2 West Highland Way

route has bus services to Edinburgh and Berwick-upon-Tweed (on the main East Coast railway line).

An indication of bus and train services along the Way are given below for each stage:

Stage	Road	Transport	To/From
1	A75	bus	Stranraer, Dumfries
2	A714	bus	Girvan
3	A713	bus	Ayr, Castle Douglas, Dumfries
4	A76	bus	Glasgow, Dumfries
		train	Glasgow, Dumfries, Carlisle
5	A74, M74 (A701, A708)	bus	Glasgow, Edinburgh, Dumfries, Lockerbie/ Carlisle, Dumfries, Lockerbie/ Carlisle
6	B709 (A72)	bus	Peeblesirk, Selkirk
7	A6091, A7	bus	Galashiels, Edinburgh, Carlisle Edinburgh, Carlisle
8	A68	bus	Galashiels, Edinburgh
9	A1	bus	Edinburgh, Berwick-upon-Tweed

Car

The route starts in Portpatrick, six miles from Stranraer on the A77. The route ends at Cockburnspath, just off the A1 between Edinburgh and Berwick-upon-Tweed.

THE ROUTE
The Start: Portpatrick

The neat picture-postcard harbour and community of Portpatrick once had aspirations as a ferry terminal, but it's settled for the more modest role of servicing anglers, sailors and walkers and there's a good choice of accommodation here, and in Stranraer about one mile north of the Way. The TIC at

Stranraer (☎ 01776 702595) can help with bookings.

Stage 1: Portpatrick to Castle Kennedy
13 miles (21 km), 250m ascent

A delightful coastal stretch of about two miles makes this first stage of the Southern Upland Way worthwhile. The rest of this stage is mainly along minor roads and tracks, and has little to recommend it.

From Portpatrick to Killantringan Lighthouse at Black Head the Southern Upland Way goes above impressive cliffs (take care, especially in poor visibility) and around scenic coves. It passes a golf course, a coastguard station, and a little double-hexagonal building at the landfall of a submarine telephone cable to/from Ireland. The route ahead is not always obvious, but trust the thistle signs which show the way amongst rocks back to the clifftop. The lighthouse comes dramatically into view, and the Southern Upland Way joins the small road leading inland from it. Enjoy the view north across Killantringan Bay, as it will be more than 200 miles before you come to the sea again!

After some roads and tracks the route reaches a cairn on top of a hillock, which has fine views on a clear day. Descend south-east onto a grassy path then a series of minor roads, paths and muddy tracks to Castle Kennedy, which has a *hotel* and *B&Bs*.

Stage 2: Castle Kennedy to Bargrennan
27 miles (43 km), 500m ascent

On this stage, the Southern Upland Way has its first feeling of remoteness, passing over moorland and through extensive forest plantations.

From Castle Kennedy, a tar drive takes you through the pleasant wooded grounds of the castle to reach a small road, only to forsake it shortly, in favour of a wooded glen. The Southern Upland Way goes to the right of the minor road again, through a conifer plantation, before descending to cross a railway line on a footbridge and the Water of Luce by a suspension bridge. New Luce, about one mile off the Southern Upland Way, has a *hotel*, a *B&B* and *camping*.

SCOTLAND

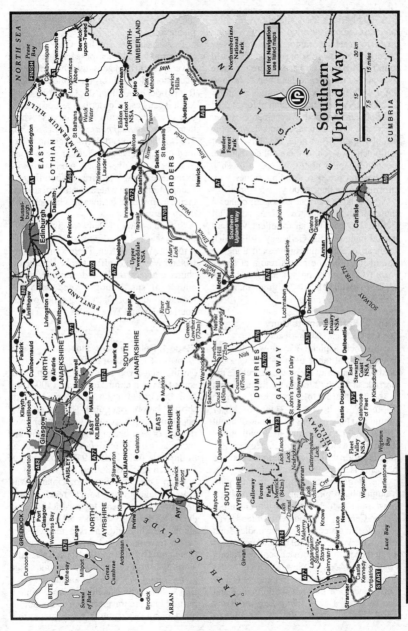

A muddy track leads straight over moorland past remote, deserted Kilhern, winding down to meet the minor road from New Luce. After passing some waterfalls you'll soon reach Balmurrie Farm where the route rises across rough moorland before following a wide heathery ride through a conifer plantation. After a short stretch of forest road the Southern Upland Way emerges in an open area with old ruins and a welcome 'beehive' *bothy* (but note, the only item of equipment we found there other than the wooden sleeping platforms was a brush!). Just beyond are two standing stones with information on their 4000 year history.

After a large cairn at a lookout comes a choice of routes: either over Craig Airie Fell (320m; 1050 ft) for an excellent view all around including the Galloway Hills which lie ahead, or continuing on the path along the side of the fell. The routes rejoin at *Derry Farm* (B&B and camping), and you follow tracks, roads and paths to Bargrennan, which has a *hotel* and a *campsite*.

Stage 3: Bargrennan to Dalry
24 miles (38.5 km), 500m ascent

The Southern Upland Way now enters the first significant range of hills to be encountered, the Galloway Hills, which include the Merrick, at 842m (2764 ft) the highest point in the Southern Uplands. The Southern Upland Way, however, keeps to lower ground and only reaches an altitude of about 310m (1000 ft), contenting itself with views of the hills which overlook it. Most of this stage is within the Galloway Forest Park, and the going is good underfoot.

The stage starts along a mossy path through a larch plantation. After crossing a forest road (which leads to the Glentrool Visitor Centre), the Southern Upland Way goes into some nice deciduous woodland and follows the Water of Trool to *Caldons Campsite*. It then traverses above Loch Trool along a path with excellent views, then continues alongside Glenhead Burn to join and follow a dirt road, first through wild country and then by Loch Dee – *White Laggan Bothy* (GR 466775) is about 350m off the route to

the south – and onwards through conifer plantations.

Past Loch Dee Angling Club's hut the Southern Upland Way forks left to cross the River Dee and then goes right. From here the plantation closes in on the route and apart from a brief break alongside Clatteringshaws Loch it can best be described as boring until you reach the road to Mid Garrary, where there's a scout *bunkhouse* (GR NX531790). The Southern Upland Way leaves this minor road on a path between further plantations. You then rise over open moorland with extensive views before descending to Clenrie farm from where a vehicle track and then a narrow road follows the Garroch Burn down the valley.

St John's Town of Dalry (to give it its full title) is reached by a fine suspension bridge across the Water of Ken. There's a Southern Upland Way ranger office (tucked beside the church), *hotels*, *B&Bs* and *camping*, plus a couple of small shops. *Kendoon SYHA Hostel* is north of Dalry, 1½ mile) off the Southern Upland Way.

Stage 4: Dalry to Sanquhar
27 miles (43 km), 900m ascent

On this stage you really get to grips with some hills as it climbs to 580m (1900 ft) on Ben Brack and again to 440m (1445 ft) shortly before Sanquhar. There are few opportunities for escape if the weather deteriorates or you become tired, but there are two usefully placed *bothies* – one at Manquhill (GR NX671945) and one at Polskeoch (GR NS686019).

From Dalry, the Southern Upland Way crosses rough grazing land to reach Butterhole Bridge and then Stroanpatrick. Across the B729, the more serious stuff begins, as it climbs steadily and enters a planted area before traversing just below the summit of Manquhill Hill (421m; 1380 ft). It isn't really worth the short detour to the summit as the going is hard over tussocks and there is Ben Brack ahead with excellent views all round. Further tops are traversed before the Southern Upland Way enters more plantation,

SCOTLAND

passes Allan's Cairn and joins a forest road down to Polskeoch.

After some two miles along a minor tarred road, the Southern Upland Way sets off again uphill to cross the ridge to the north before a long but easy descent on grassy paths to Sanquhar.

Sanquhar boasts a castle and the oldest post office in Britain. It also offers you a wide choice of *hotels* and *B&Bs* (vehicle back-up can be provided by *Drumbringan Guesthouse* (☎ 01659 50409)), plus *camping* and shops.

Stage 5: Sanquhar to Beattock
28 miles (45 km), 1550m ascent

This stage includes three 'highlights': the halfway point of the Southern Upland Way; the highest point of the Southern Upland Way, at 710m (2335 ft), on Lowther Hill; and the highest village in Scotland, Wanlockhead at 425m (1395 ft). In spring, and from 12 August to 1 November, walkers are requested to take a deviation from the route between Cogshead and Wanlockhead to avoid disturbing shooters and their grouse, so adding about two miles.

From Sanquhar to Wanlockhead there are two humps to cross, with Cogshead set steeply down between them. Wanlockhead, with its industrial heritage comes as a bit of a contrast to the grouse moors which overlook it. There's an *SYHA Hostel* and many *B&Bs*. Take time if possible to visit the Mining Museum.

From here the Southern Upland Way climbs up to Lowther Hill, crossing and recrossing the tarred road to the radar station's 'golf ball' domes. Lowther Hill and Green Lowther offer excellent views in fine weather but four separate communication stations have got there before you, and you'll have to stay outside their fenced enclosures and make do with the views from just below the summit.

The change in character of the hills is maintained, with the norm now being high ground dissected by valleys rather than hills rising from generally lower ground as in the

Galloways. The Southern Upland Way responds to this by keeping to the highest ground it can over Cold Moss, and eschewing the apparently easier option of going round Laght Hill to go straight up it by a very steep though short ascent. It then drops down to the A702 at Over Fingland in a wide valley which is draining north to the River Clyde.

Just beyond the A702 in Watermeetings Forest, lo and behold, you are at the halfway point of the Southern Upland Way. Let the spirit soar despite the earth-to-sky thick-pile conifers flanking the forest road, then continue upwards again over Sweetshaw Brae, Hods Hill and Beld Knowe above the Daer Reservoir, before descending through forest plantation to the Cloffin Burn. The *bothy* at Brattleburn (GR NT016070) is out of sight about 400m west of the Southern Upland Way; do not confuse it with Mosshope Cottage to the left of the Southern Upland Way.

Continue through forest and across meadows to a minor road down to Beattock, which has a *hotel*, *B&Bs* and *camping*. There's a wider range of accommodation, shops and so on in Moffat, just over a mile away.

Stage 6: Beattock to Traquair
33 miles (53 km), 1200m ascent

This stage takes you over the watershed, at 520m, between drainage to the Irish Sea and to the North Sea.

From Beattock, you cross the River Annan and follow Moffat Water for about a mile. Then the Southern Upland Way turns up to the right and winds through plantation on a forest road, before taking a path up a deeply incised valley. This leads to some dramatic scenery; the Selcloth Burn has created a deep gorge which the path traverses above before climbing to the watershed.

Beyond, a forest road is soon joined, leading down to Over Phawhope (*bothy* at GR NT182082), and a minor road alongside the delightful Ettrick Water is then followed for over six miles (past *Ettrick Valley campsite*).

SCOTLAND

over six miles (past *Ettrick Valley campsite*). This is left at Scabcleugh, the path ascending beside little waterfalls, before crossing the flank of Pikestone Rig. The Southern Upland Way doesn't take the obvious route down from the Rig but instead dips and turns around Earl's Hill, picking up a forest track for the descent to *Tibbie Shiel's Inn* (and *campsite*) at St Mary's Loch (scene of the Southern Upland Way official opening in 1984). From the inn the Southern Upland Way goes in front of the Sailing Club House, following a small path along the lochside before joining a service road to meet the A708.

Crossing the A708, the Southern Upland Way returns to wild and open country, following generally good paths and tracks. There is an easy ascent up a forested valley to traverse heather-covered hills, before descending to Traquair and the River Tweed over grassy fields and a short stretch of the B709 road.

There's a couple of B&Bs at Traquair, including *Traquair Mill* (☎ 01896 830515) offering vehicle back-up, but there's more scope for accommodation and facilities in Innerleithen just over a mile north. Historic Traquair House is open to the public between Easter and October.

Stage 7: Traquair to Melrose
18 miles (29 km), 800m ascent
This is a varied stage with forest, heather covered moor, fields and a somewhat suburban stretch (partly riverside) around Galashiels and into Melrose.

Turning your back on Traquair and the Tweed Valley, follow a lane (which can be muddy) climbing steadily into forest. Minch Moor rises on the right and a signed footpath leads to its summit, said to be a fine lookout, but it was in cloud when we passed by.

The Southern Upland Way continues along a wide cutting between plantations and then keeps left onto the heathery crest of Brown Knowe (523m), which does provide good views. The next tops are skirted on the right and left but a short ascent is then made

to a summit with three massive stone cairns known as the Three Brethren. (*Broad-meadows SYHA Hostel* is a mile or so off to the south.) Then descend alongside and through forest to the River Tweed, crossed at Yair Bridge.

Beyond the bridge you cross fields and numerous stiles to reach the outskirts of Galashiels. From Galashiels to Melrose the Southern Upland Way goes alongside on a rather unkempt old railway (now cycle) track.

Both Galashiels and Melrose have a wide choice of accommodation.

Stage 8: Melrose to Lauder
10 miles (16 km), 300m ascent
This is essentially an agricultural stage, along farm tracks and over fields, and it can be very muddy in parts.

From Melrose the Tweed is crossed yet again, this time by the Chain Suspension Bridge, dating from 1826 and limited to pedestrians and 'light carriages'. The Southern Upland Way heads north, following in part the line of an old road which may be Roman in origin (there was a Roman fort east of Melrose with a signal station above on North Eildon Hill) and is straightforward all the way to Lauder. The Southern Upland Way diverts over steep open land approaching the town; watch out for stray golf balls!

Lauder seems a sleepy little town; however not only is it a fox-hunting centre with horses in abundance, but it proffers several *hotels* and *B&Bs* and *camping* in the grounds of splendid Thirlestane Castle.

Stage 9: Lauder to Cockburnspath
32 miles (52 km), 900m ascent
This final stage starts with a traverse of the southern part of the Lammermuir Hills' extensive grouse moors, and then passes mainly through farmland, though there are some mainly wooded valleys, and the final couple of miles include a fine clifftop walk.

From Lauder the Southern Upland Way weaves through the grounds of Thirlestane Castle (open occasionally to visitors) and into woodland, emerging onto the A697.

SCOTLAND

Cross and head uphill on a lane, through the end of a wood, and then across improved pasture land. The Southern Upland Way leaves the main track to Braidshawrig, crossing Blythe Water to remain a while longer on grassy pasture. It then joins a track at Scoured Rig which leads down past Braidshawrig and across the heather moor with numerous butts for grouse shooting. Beware that you are not mistaken for a grouse during the shooting season, which starts on 12 August! When the track attains a ridge crest, the Southern Upland Way turns to the right on a path to its final significant summit, Twin Laws, topped by two cylindrical towers each with a stone seat in a recess facing south. A Southern Upland Wayfarer will however be looking to the north-east for a glimpse of the North Sea, visible on a clear day. The descent to Watch Water Reservoir is easy, and then a minor road leads to Longformacus, which has a *B&B*.

A short distance along a further minor road out of the village, the Southern Upland Way branches off over moorland to descend through a small plantation to the B6355. From here the route follows the steep-sided Whiteadder Valley to the interesting settlement of Abbey St Bathans (*SYHA Hostel*), where the Whiteadder, joined by the Monynut Water, is crossed. The Southern Upland Way, now leaving the river, heads east across fields and along country lanes to reach the A1, passing between this road and the railway line, before crossing into Penmanshiel Wood on a pleasant green track. It seems a cruel climb at this point up through the wood but you're rewarded with clear views of the sea at last, and the descent some 150 or so steps through Pease Dean Reserve towards Pease Bay may be enlivened by sightings of butterflies and birds. The Bay signals the fact that you have indeed walked coast-to-coast.

The final clifftop walk lies ahead with impressive coastal scenery (if you can ignore the serried ranks of caravans) and the memorable Cove Harbour tucked below, where you can dip your toes in the water. You'll have to wrench yourself away and head inland, beneath the A1 and the railway line, to reach the mercat cross in the village square at Cockburnspath, the official end of the Southern Upland Way. Well done!

There are *B&Bs* here and in nearby Grantshouse. To extricate yourself see the earlier Getting There & Away section.

OTHER WALKS IN THE BORDERS

The Southern Upland Way passes through the administrative regions of Dumries & Galloway and the Borders, and both are worth visiting for shorter walking trips, especially if you consider the Southern Upland Way's entire length too much of a challenge, or impossible due to time constraints.

The Borders, especially, is making a real effort to attract walkers and has a whole range of useful leaflets and information sheets covering day-walks in the area ranging from a few miles up to 10 miles or more. The landscape here consists of green hills, river valleys, woodland, farms and villages, with a network of paths, tracks and drove roads (once used for the movement of cattle). One writer described the Borders as 'rolling not rocking, spacious rather than overly spectacular' and regular walkers here point out that you can enjoy fresh air and wide open views while still being within a fairly easy walk of a village with a B&B, a pub or a fish & chips shop.

Places to base yourself include the pleasant historical towns of Galashiels and Melrose, both easy to reach with a good selection of places to stay and eat. From here you can follow short sections of the Southern Upland Way along the River Tweed, or explore its tributary Gala Water or go up into the nearby Eildon Hills, a National Scenic Area (NSA). Another place to visit on foot (or tying in with local buses) is Abbotsford, the birthplace of Sir Walter Scott, author of *Rob Roy* and *Ivanhoe* and other Scottish classics.

Further west is Peebles and further east is Kelso; both are also good bases for day-walks around the area. From Kelso you can reach Kirk Yetholm (end of the Pennine Way, described elsewhere in this book) and explore the high Cheviot Hills, a natural frontier between England and Scotland. Jedburgh is another place from where you can sample the Cheviots. Also nearby is Dere Street, an old Roman road which linked the hills to the town of St Boswells, north of the River Teviot.

The Borders also has a coastline, between Cove (near the end of the Southern Upland Way) and the England-Scotland border just north of Berwick-upon-Tweed. A 40 mile waymarked trail running the whole length of the coast between Berwick and Cockburnspath (the end of the Southern Upland Way) is planned and would be a very interesting route. If you had two or three days, a section of this could be combined with an inland section of the Southern Upland Way, providing an excellent Borders taster. Also planned is a 60 mile circular route, called the Border Abbeys Way, linking many of the historical Borders towns listed above, such as Kelso, Jedburgh, St Boswells, Melrose, Selkirk and Galashiels.

Another new route is the St Cuthbert's Way, linking Melrose to the island of Lindisfarne (mentioned in the Northumberland section of this book).

Books on this area include *The Border Country* by Alan Hall (Cicerone, £7.99). A series of guided walks, led by members of the Countyside Ranger Service (☎ 01835 830281), runs throughout the year. Local TICs will have details. Walking holiday companies operating in the Borders include Make Tracks (☎ 0131 447 9847) in Edinburgh. There's also the week-long Scottish Borders Festival of Walking, held every year, with a whole series of guided and self-guided walks, plus a programme of talks and evening events.

For more information about walking in the Borders, accommodation (including places which specifically welcome walkers), transport, the festival, and so on, the region's main TIC is at Jedburgh (☎ 01835 863688 or 863435). Other TICs in the region (open Easter through October) are Melrose (☎ 01896 822555), Galashiels (☎ 01896 755551) and Kelso (☎ 01573 223464).

West Highland Way

Distance 95 miles (153 km)
Duration 6 to 8 days
Start Milngavie, near Glasgow
Finish Fort William
Regional Centres Glasgow, Fort William
Area Highland
Summary Scotland's most popular footpath through a tremendous range of landscape is easy to follow but hard going in many places, especially in the northern sections.

This superb 95 mile hike through the Scottish Highlands begins in Milngavie (which is pronounced 'Mullguy'), seven miles north of the centre of Glasgow. The route passes through some of the most spectacular scenery in Britain. It starts in the Lowlands, but the greater part of this trail is amongst the mountains, lochs and fast-flowing rivers of the Highlands. It runs along Loch Lomond, and in the far north the route crosses wild Rannoch Moor to reach Fort William via magical Glen Nevis, in the shadow of Ben Nevis. The trail is well signposted and uses a combination of ancient ways: the old drove roads along which cattle were herded in the past, the old military road (built by troops to help control the Jacobites in the 18th century) and disued railway lines.

The first section of the walk is fairly easy-going as far as the northern shore of Loch Lomond. After that, particularly north of Bridge of Orchy, it's quite strenuous and remote; you need to be properly equipped with good boots, maps, a compass, and food and drink. There's no shelter on Rannoch Moor if the weather turns bad, which it's quite likely to do. The area has a very high rainfall and the wind in the narrow mountain valleys and on the more exposed areas can reach gale force.

DIRECTION, DISTANCE & DURATION

Since the northern section is more challenging, it is generally advised that walkers planning to do the whole route start at

Milngavie. This also gives the advantage of having the wind and sun behind you.

The official route length is 95 miles, although you will need to add extra for any diversions off the route, such as ascents of Ben Lomond. Most people do the walk in six or seven days. The location of accommodation centres in the north of the walk means that you will either have some very long days or rather short days in this section.

STAGES

Note that times given here are walking times only; allow an extra hour or two for rest stops. For a seven day walk, as described here, the most convenient places to start and end each day are:

Day	From	To	Distance
1	Milngavie	Drymen	12 miles (19 km)
2	Drymen	Rowardennan	14 miles (22.5 km)
3	Rowardennan	Inverarnan	14 miles (22.5 km)
4	Inverarnan	Tyndrum	13 miles (21 km)
5	Tyndrum	Kings House Hotel	19 miles (30.5 km)
6	Kings House Hotel	Kinlochleven	9 miles (14.5 km)
7	Kinlochleven	Fort William	14 miles (22.5 km)

To do the walk in six days spend the third night in Crianlarich, the fourth night in Bridge of Orchy, and reach Kinlochleven on the fifth night, stopping for lunch at Kings House Hotel.

Most people will want to add an extra day in order to go up Ben Nevis (1344m; 4408 ft). Ben Lomond and Beinn Dorain are other mountains beside the trail that are worth attention. Add another day if you want to walk from Glasgow to Milngavie along the Clyde, Allander or Kelvin walkways.

INFORMATION

For a free leaflet listing accommodation on the West Highland Way contact the Loch Lomond Park Ranger Service (☎ 01389 758216), Balloch Castle, Balloch; the Coun-tryside Ranger Service (☎ 01397 705922), Ionad Nibheis, Glen Nevis, Fort William; or the Scottish Tourist Board (☎ 0131 332 2433). Pick up a copy of the free *West Highland Wayfarer* newspaper at Milngavie Station or at TICs.

There are TICs in Glasgow (☎ 0141 204 4400); Drymen (☎ 01360 660068), open from late May to the end of September; Tyndrum (☎ 01838 400246), open from April to October; and Fort William (☎ 01397 703781).

The trail is marked with signposts and the Scottish waymarker (a thistle within a hexagon), with yellow arrows to show route changes.

Books & Maps

The best guidebook is the expensive *West Highland Way* by Bob Aitken & Roger Smith (HMSO, £14.95). The guide comes with its own 1:50,000 OS route map, compiled from the four OS maps (Nos 41, 50, 56 and 64) that cover the whole area.

Most people find that the best option is just to take the excellent Harveys *West Highland Way Map* (£6.95). Drawn at a scale of 1:40,000 from recent air surveys it also includes lots of additional information for walkers, such as TICs etc.

The OS guidebook *West Highland Way* (£10.99) has good route descriptions and detailed, but dated, mapping at 1:25,000. There are some serious flaws – it's missed the Drymen bypass even though it was built about 10 years ago! There's also *A Guide to the West Highland Way* by Tom Hunter (Constable), and the cheap and cheerful Footprint *West Highland Way* map guide (£3.95).

GUIDED WALKS & LOCAL SERVICES

C-N-Do (☎ 01786 445703), at 77 Stirling Enterprise Park, Springbank Rd, Stirling FK7 7RP, organises walking holidays on the West Highland Way with vehicle support.

Rather than taking a full tour, you can make the going easier for yourself by using a pack-carrying service. Travel-Lite (☎ 0141 956 6810) charges £25 to pick up your bag each morning and deliver it to your next

SCOTLAND

B&B or hostel (a total of up to eight collections and deliveries).

PLACES TO STAY & EAT

Accommodation should not be too difficult to find, though between Bridge of Orchy and Kinlochleven it's quite limited. In May, which is the most popular month to walk the West Highland Way, you must book all accommodation in advance. July and August are also busy.

There are three SYHA hostels on the walk at Rowardennan, Crianlarich and Glen Nevis as well as in Glasgow and Fort William. There are bunkhouses at Drymen, Inverarnan, Tyndrum, Bridge of Orchy, Kinlochleven and Glen Nevis. Even more basic are the free bothies and camping barns at Rowchoish and Doune.

In some areas on the West Highland Way camping is not permitted. However, some hotels and B&Bs allow camping in their grounds, and there are several official sites.

Most B&Bs provide evening meals if requested in advance, and also packed lunches if you ask on arrival. Some B&Bs, particularly those not directly on the route, will send someone to meet you and drive you back next morning.

GETTING THERE & AWAY
Bus

National Express/Scottish Citylink (☎ 0990 808080) runs coaches between Glasgow, Fort William and most parts of the country. There are frequent buses from the bus station to Milngavie, but they take twice as long as the train.

Train

Glasgow has excellent rail links with the rest of the country – 20 trains a day taking five hours from London's Euston to Glasgow Central. It's then a 10 minute walk to Glasgow's Queen St for trains to Milngavie (every half hour, 20 minutes). If you only want to do part of the walk, Crianlarich, Upper Tyndrum (on the Fort William line) and Lower Tyndrum (on the Oban line), and Bridge of Orchy are all served by trains.

Fort William is on the West Highland Line and the most scenic way to end your walk is by taking this famous line back over Rannoch Moor to Glasgow, or on to Mallaig. The train costs £21.50, which is more than twice the price of the bus.

Car

Milngavie is seven miles north of Glasgow on the A82/A809 (exit 17 off the M8).

Ferry

In summer there are ferry services across Loch Lomond between Rowardennan and Inverbeg (☎ 01360 870273), Inversnaid and Inveruglas (☎ 01877 386223), and Ardleish and Ardlui (☎ 01301 704243). It's not necessary to use a ferry on the actual walk.

THE ROUTE
The Start: Glasgow & Milngavie

Glasgow Many walkers will be coming up to Milngavie through Glasgow. The TIC (☎ 0141 204 4400) is on George Square. See the Getting There & Away section above for rail and bus information.

The best-value, centrally located guesthouse accommodation is at *McLay's Guesthouse* (☎ 0141 332 4796), at 264 Renfrew St, behind Sauchiehall St. B&B is from £16.50. The excellent *SYHA Hostel* (☎ 0141 332 3004, £10.45) is about half a mile beyond, at 7 Park Terrace. Nearby, the *Glasgow Backpackers Hostel* (☎ 0141 332 5412), Kelvin Lodge, at 8 Park Circus, is only open from July through September. Beds are from £8.90. Just south of here, *Berkeley Globetrotters* (☎ 0141 221 7880), at 63 Berkeley St, has beds from £8 (£6.50 if you have your own bedding).

Milngavie There are plenty of shops, eating places and B&Bs in Milngavie. For B&B, *Barloch Guest House* (☎ 0141 956 1432), Strathblane Rd, or *West View Guest House* (☎ 0141 956 5973), at 1 Douglaston Gardens, cost around £15. The pick of the places to eat is *Toscana*, Italian-run and good for just a coffee or a full-meal pasta from £3.95.

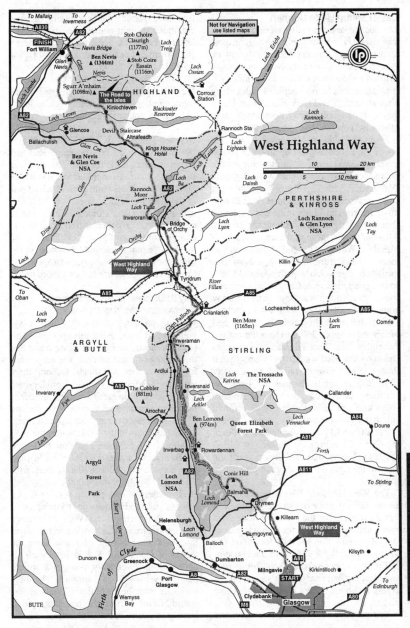

Day 1: Milngavie to Drymen
12 miles (19 km), 4½ to 5½ hours

The first day is easy-going through unspectacular rolling countryside and farmland. About three miles of the walk is along a disused railway track that can be muddy if it's wet; there's then a couple of miles along a quiet road. The *Beech Tree Inn* at Dumgoyne is the only convenient lunch stop; otherwise you'll need to bring a picnic.

From the start at Milngavie Station go down the underpass and up into the pedestrianised town centre. An unmissable granite obelisk commemorates the West Highland Way and is virtually the only point on it where walkers usually get lost! A small sign on a nearby building indicates that you should turn right here. Follow the stream, Allander Water, through the trees, and up to Mugdock Wood. At the end of the wood you meet a road; turn left then almost immediately right onto a path again. There's soon a good view over Craigallian Loch and soon after you pass some little holiday homes that look rather like Russian dachas.

Turn left onto the road, the B821, and follow it for about 300m to join the path to the right. The West Highland Way skirts Dumgoyach Hill and after Dumgoyach Bridge joins a disused railway track. After about 800m you pass the path to Glengoyne Distillery, which can be visited. Another 800m and you reach the *Beech Tree Inn*, a pub that serves food all day.

B&B from £17 is available near Killearn at *Croy Cunningham Farm* (☎ 01360 550329). The village of Killearn is off the route to the right – it has shops, a post office and a *pub*.

The West Highland Way continues along the old railway track to Gartness where you join the road. Cross the attractive bridge and weir and follow the road for a mile to *Easter Drumquhassle Farm* (☎ 01360 660893), which has B&B for £16.50 in the house or £10 in the wigwams (£6 if you bring your own sleeping bag and food). It's a good place to stay and there's even a washing machine (£1).

You get your first view of Loch Lomond

from here. Passing the ugly quarry, the road continues straight ahead, then turns sharp left. Just before the bend, on the right there's B&B from £14 at *Gateside Lodge* (☎ 01360 660215) and from £16 at *Knopogue* (☎ 01306 660735). Just after the bend, the West Highland Way follows the path to the right. Continue on the road if you're going to Drymen, and cross the A811.

Drymen There's a TIC (☎ 01360 660068) in the library. At 8 Old Gartmore Rd, *Mrs Bolzicco* offers B&B for £16. The top place to stay is the *Winnock Hotel* (☎ 01360 660245) with B&B from £36. The best pub is the *Clachan* which dates back to 1734, making it Scotland's oldest pub. If you're hungry it has a dozen different steaks to choose from, from £11 to £13. There's also the only Indian restaurant/takeaway on the route, the *Drymen Tandoori*, and a *Spar* shop for self-caterers, a *cafe* and two more *pubs*.

Day 2: Drymen to Rowardennan
14 miles (22.5 km), 5 to 6½ hours

Walking on the second day is still easy-going, apart from the climb up Conic Hill (358m), mostly along undulating paths and the banks of Loch Lomond. The only place for food supplies is Balmaha (around three hours from Drymen). The path from Drymen goes gradually upwards through the dense woods to Garadh Ban Forest. Near the end of the trees, just over an hour from Drymen, a side path runs to the left down to the road to Milton of Buchanan. There are two good B&Bs here: *Dunleen* (☎ 01360 870274), and *Mar Achlais* (☎ 01360 870300) from £16. There are no pubs or shops in the village, but B&B owners offer a pickup service if you want to go in to Balmaha or Drymen.

The West Highland Way continues through the trees, over a stile and into open moorland. Crossing the burn you begin the ascent of Conic Hill, a gain in altitude of about 200m. Eventually you get a superb panorama over Loch Lomond. The best views are from the top of the hill, only a short detour. Conic Hill is the boundary point, from here you're in the Highlands.

SCOTLAND

The path descends through a pine wood to lochside Balmaha. There's comfortable B&B from £18 per person at *Bay Cottage* (☎ 01360 870346). There's also a *pub*, shop and *cafe* here.

The route now hugs the shore, passing a marker, commemorating the opening of the West Highland Way in 1980, at the lookout. In under an hour you reach Milarrochy where there's a *campsite*, charging £5.85 if you're not a member of the Camping & Caravan Club (CCC). There's a shop here. About 800m beyond, to the left, is *Critreoch* (☎ 01360 870309) with B&B from £16. The path now dives into a dark forest before emerging to follow the road. Opposite, *Cashel Farm* (☎ 01360 870229) offers B&B from £17.

About 300m beyond Cashel Farm is another *campsite* (£3.50 for a tent and one person), where there's a good shop and takeaway. The route continues along the road until just after Sallochy House, where it dives into the trees and climbs through Ross Wood to Rowardennan. Rowardennan is really just the *Rowardennan Hotel* (☎ 01306 870273), with B&B from £36 per person and bar food served between noon and 9 pm. From the hotel a side path leads up to the summit of Ben Lomond (974m), a seven mile return trip.

The *SYHA Hostel* (☎ 01360 870259, £6.95) is 20 minutes beyond Rowardennan Hotel; booking is required from May to mid-June. Continue for 10 minutes to the *National Trust Campsite*.

Day 3: Rowardennan to Inverarnan
14 miles (22.5 km), 6 to 7½ hours
This day's walk begins with four miles of Forestry Commission track, followed by a six mile section (often muddy) down by the loch. After that it gets easier. The only place for food along the way is the large *Inversnaid Hotel*, seven miles beyond Rowardennan.

From Rowardennan follow the Forestry track parallel to the loch-shore. After Ptarmigan Lodge you can leave the Forestry Commission track to follow an alternative, lower trail through the trees. The high route is easier but less interesting. From both

routes you can reach *Rowchoish Bothy*, with a fireplace and sleeping platform with space for eight people, plus about 10 on the dirt floor. It's free and always open.

About 400m after the bothy, the low route joins the high route, and soon after, the forestry track becomes a path again. It dives down to the loch and there's some difficult walking along a sometimes muddy trail to Inversnaid. *Inversnaid Hotel* (☎ 01877 386223) has 109 rooms at £28 per person, and runs a small ferry across to Inveruglas.

From Inversnaid to the foot of Glen Falloch is one of the most difficult parts of the route, especially in wet weather. The path goes up and down through wooded slopes (oak and birchwood) and can involve some scrambling. The loch is now much narrower and the valley deeper. The path passes the outlaw Rob Roy's cave, though there's little to see. There's basic accommodation at *Doune Bothy* (with the same facilities as Rowchoish Bothy). Half a mile beyond there's a landing-stage used by the ferry (☎ 01301 704244) across to Ardlui (summer only).

At this point you leave the loch for a pleasant walk through Glen Falloch. Below Beinglas Falls, *Beinglas Farm* (☎ 01301 704281) offers B&B from £16, or wigwam accommodation from £7. Leave the route and cross the river to reach the wonderful *Inverarnan Drover's Inn* (☎ 01301 704234), in Inverarnan. It has smoke-blackened walls, bare wooden floors, a grand hall filled with moth-eaten stuffed animals, and wee drams served by barmen in kilts. It's a great place for atmosphere or a serious drinking binge. You can even stay here (B&B for £17), but rooms are nothing special and service is reported to be very slow in the morning, which is not ideal if you want an early start. Opposite is the *Stagger Inn*, more of a restaurant than an inn, where the traditional Scottish food is excellent. Nearby there's B&B at the delightful *Rose Cottage* (☎ 01301 704255) for £15.

Day 4: Inverarnan to Tyndrum
13 miles (21 km), 4½ to 5½ hours
This day is much easier than the previous

SCOTLAND

day, and in open countryside following the river. Unfortunately you're also following the busy road and railway line. Unless you make a detour down to Crianlarich (20 minutes each way) there's nowhere to get food until Tyndrum.

From Inverarnan the route follows the River Falloch most of the way to Crianlarich. At the beginning the valley is narrow but it gradually opens out; some of the walk is through woodland.

About 1¼ hours beyond Inverarnan you cross under the railway line through a small tunnel and over the A82 to join the old military road. The road climbs out of Glen Falloch towards the trees.

At the stile into the forest there's a side path down to Crianlarich; this is the approximate halfway point on the West Highland Way. There's no need to go down to Crianlarich but the village does have a railway station, post office, shops (the *Mace* store is open on Sunday), and places to stay and eat, but no bank. The *SYHA Hostel* (☎ 0183 8300260) costs £6.95; there's B&B at *Glenardran Guest House* (☎ 01838 300236) for £17.50, *Craigbank Guest House* (☎ 01838 300279) for £15, and *Northumbria* (☎ 01838 300253) for £16. The *Rod & Reel* is the place to drink; there's also a good *restaurant* here.

Back on the West Highland Way, from the stile the route climbs to the left, with good views across to Ben More, and continues through the trees for about two miles to cross under the railway line and over the road again.

Just across the river you reach the remains of St Fillan's chapel. Turn left and follow the track reaching *Auchtertyre Farm* (☎ 01838 400251) in 20 minutes. There's B&B here for £15 and wigwam accommodation for £7.

The trail crosses the road once more and in under an hour reaches Tyndrum, formerly a lead-mining settlement.

Tyndrum The village is strung out along the A82. There's a TIC (☎ 01838 400246) in the car park of the *Invervey Hotel* (☎ 01838 400219). The hotel has a good pub and offers

B&B from £20. Other places to stay in Tyndrum include *Glengarry Guest House* (☎ 01838 400224) from £15, and *Dalkjell* (☎ 01838 400285) for £16. The *Royal Hotel* (☎ 01838 400272) charges from £20. There's a *campsite* by the river, an outdoor equipment shop and self-service restaurant (the *Clifton Coffee Shop*) by the petrol station and a taxi/pack-carrying service available on ☎ 01838 400279.

Day 5: Tyndrum to Kings House Hotel
19 miles (30.5 km), 6½ to 8 hours

An early start is necessary for this, the longest day on the walk. Mainly on good surfaces, the walk is not difficult but it does cross the wildest section of the West Highland Way, Rannoch Moor. The only places for food are the pub at the Bridge of Orchy Hotel and, an hour beyond, the Inveroran Hotel.

From Tyndrum the path runs parallel to the A82 and the railway line for a while and then rejoins the old military road. This is easy, clear walking with lovely views. The path climbs gradually to pass the entrance to Glen Orchy and the beginning of the really mountainous scenery.

There's B&B at *Auch Farm* (☎ 01838 400233) for £14 per person. It's three miles from Tyndrum, just before you cross the river at the foot of Beinn Dorain.

It's just under three miles on to Bridge of Orchy which is nothing more than a railway station, post office, church and *Bridge of Orchy Hotel* (☎ 01838 400208). B&B costs from £25, there's bunkhouse accommodation for £7 and camping for £2.50. Breakfast is £5.50 and there are excellent bar meals from around £6 served between noon and 3 pm, 6 and 8.30 pm, and also from 3 to 6 pm at weekends.

Cross the old bridge (built in 1750) and climb through the trees up to the moorland from where there are superb views across to Rannoch Moor. The path winds down to the secluded *Inveroran Hotel* (☎ 01838 400200) where there's B&B for £25. Bar food is served daily from noon to 6.30 pm; dinner from 6.30 to 8.30 pm.

The West Highland Way follows the road which soon becomes a track and climbs gently past three tree plantations and onto the wild moor. There's no shelter for about seven miles and it can be very wild and windy up here. The summit is marked by a cairn at 445m and from here there's a wonderful view down into Glencoe.

As the path descends towards the road you can see the chairlift of the Glen Coe Ski Centre to the left. There's a *cafe* and skiing museum at the base station, about 500m off the West Highland Way. *Kings House Hotel* (☎ 01855 851259) is just over a mile ahead. Dating from the 17th century, the building was used after the Battle of Culloden as barracks for the troops of George III (hence the name). There's accommodation from £20 per person, but breakfast costs an extra £6.50. There's a restaurant and popular climbers' bar at the back, where a filling plate of haggis, neeps and tatties costs £4.50. Food is served all day at weekends but only from noon to 2 pm and 5 to 8 pm during the week.

If you can't get a bed here you may want to consider taking the bus to Glencoe (11 miles west) where there's a wider selection of accommodation, including the *SYHA Hostel* (☎ 01855 811219).

Day 6: Kings House Hotel to Kinlochleven
9 miles (14.5 km), 3 to 4 hours

The superb mountain scenery continues. This day is not long but includes the climb up the Devil's Staircase (a 330m gain in altitude) and a long knee-cracking descent to Kinlochleven. There's nowhere to get food en route, and no shelter.

From Kings House Hotel the route goes along the old military road, soon joined by the A82. There's a car park on the bend at Altnafeadh. From here it's a fairly steep climb, zigzagging in places, up the Devil's Staircase. From the cairn at 548m the views are stunning, especially on a clear day, and you should be able to see Ben Nevis.

The path winds slowly down towards Kinlochleven, hidden below in the glen. As you descend you meet the pipes of the Black-water Reservoir built to supply water to the town's hydroelectric power station. Crossing the river you reach Kinlochleven, an unusual place for these parts because it was built as a factory town, smelting aluminium. It's an ugly place but offers a return to 'civilisation': shops, restaurants, and plenty of accommodation.

Kinlochleven The first B&B you reach is *Quirang* (☎ 01855 831580), at 43 Lovat Rd, with comfortable accommodation for £14. *Edencoille* (☎ 01855 831358), Garbhein Rd, offers B&B from £15. About 100m from the centre of Kinlochleven is the popular *West Highland Bunkhouse* (☎ 01855 831471), charging £6, with showers and a drying room. *Kinlochleven Campsite* (☎ 01855 831666) has wigwams as well as space for tents.

At the *Tailrace Inn* (☎ 01855 831777), Riverside Rd, there's B&B for £16 and good pub grub served from 11 am to 10 pm. There's cheap food at the *Harlequin Bakery & Restaurant*, a Co-op shop, *fish & chips* shop, and laundrette. The *Antler Bar* is another good place to drink.

The best place to stay is a 20 minute hike continuing along the West Highland Way. Set up on the hillside, *Mamore Lodge Hotel* (☎ 01855 831213) has B&B from £18, great views over Loch Leven and a pleasant bar.

Day 7: Kinlochleven to Fort William
14 miles (22.5 km), 5½ to 7 hours

The final day is one of the hardest but most enjoyable, through varied terrain and with spectacular views that include Ben Nevis. You need to be prepared for bad weather as there's little shelter. There's nowhere to buy food until almost the end of the West High-land Way, so you need to carry food and drink.

From Kinlochleven follow the road out of town to the wigwams where the West High-land Way becomes a path that climbs through the woods and past the side track to the Mamore Lodge. At about 250m above the loch you can see far down the next wide glen, with the old military road running through it.

SCOTLAND

The highest point is at 335m; shortly beyond you reach a ruined farmhouse, and another just under a mile further on. The trail continues gently downhill to enter the trees in just under two miles.

Walk through the woods for a mile to emerge at Blar a'Chaorainn, which is nothing more than a bench but the information panel with Fort William bus and train timetables could be useful. This is a good place for a picnic with a view.

After Blar a'Chaorainn the path goes through some more forestry plantations (with views of Ben Nevis), with some steep sections down to cross streams. You can make a short detour to see Dun Deardail, an Iron Age fort with walls that have been partly vitrified (turned to glass) by fires beside them.

Shortly after the fort, cross another stile and descend into Glen Nevis following the Forestry Commission track. Across the valley the huge bulk of Ben Nevis fills your vision. A side track leads down to the *SYHA Hostel* (☎ 01397 702336, £7.80). The *Glen Nevis Caravan & Camping Park* (☎ 01397 702191) is nearby. These would be good bases if you wanted to polish off your walk with an ascent of 'The Ben' (for details see the Ben Nevis & Glen Coe section in the Scotland – Short Walks chapter).

You pass an interesting little graveyard, just before you meet the road that runs up the glen. Turn left here and, soon after, there's a large visitor centre on the right. Across the river is *Achintee House* (☎ 01397 702240) with bunkhouse accommodation (£6) and B&B for £15.

If you're pushing on to the bitter end, continue along the roadside down into Fort William. The West Highland Way ends, like so many other British LDPs, with a bit of an anticlimax, just a sign by the busy but rather anonymous road junction on the edge of town. If you want something more typically Scottish to celebrate your arrival, the nearby giftshop can provide anything from shortbread to tartan walking sticks.

Fort William Separated from Loch Linnhe

by a bypass, Fort William has lost any charm it may once have had to modern development. However, it has good bus and train connections (buses leave from near the railway station).

The TIC (☎ 01397 703781) is in the centre of town in Cameron Square. There are good outdoor shops, including Nevisport (☎ 01397 704921), near the railway station, and West Coast Outdoor Leisure (☎ 01397 705777) at the other end of the high street. You can get a shower and store luggage at Marco's An Aird Community Centre (☎ 01397 700707), near the railway station.

There's an *SYHA Hostel*, a *campsite*, a *bunkhouse* and a few *B&Bs* in Glen Nevis, a few miles away (see the Ben Nevis & Glen Coe section of the Scotland – Short Walks chapter).

The cheapest place in town, and a short walk from the railway station, is *Fort William Backpackers' Guesthouse* (☎ 01397 700711), Alma Rd, charging £8.50 per night and very popular. In the same area, there are numerous B&Bs in and around Fassifern Rd. *Mrs MacLeod* (☎ 01397 702533), at 2 Caberfeidh, Fassifern Rd, charges £14.50 per person.

Achintore Rd, which runs south along the loch, is almost solidly B&Bs and hotels, most of them large and characterless. More interesting is the B&B-cum-art gallery at *The Lime House* (☎ 01397 701806) which has beds for £12. Comfortable *Ashburn House* (☎ 01397 706000) has rooms with bath for around £32 per person.

The *Alexandra Hotel* (☎ 01397 702241), The Parade, is a large, traditional hotel with comfortable doubles with bath for £38. The *Grand Hotel* (☎ 01397 702928), in the high street, is the other large, central hotel, with rooms from £28 per person.

For a big meal to celebrate finishing the West Highland Way, the best place in town is also the best located: *Crannog Seafood Restaurant* is on the pier, with an uninterrupted view over the loch and excellent food; it has half a dozen oysters for £7 and main courses for between £6 and £10. Not in the same culinary league but with an entertaining touristy floorshow there's *McTavish's Kitchen* on the high street. There's a self-service cafe downstairs.

For cheaper meals, the *Nevisport Cafe*, in the gear shop, caters for the outdoor crowd but doesn't stay open late. Most other places to eat line the high street. Try the *McTavish's Garrison Restaurant* or *Grog & Gruel*, a traditional ale house with restaurant. *Café Chardon*, upstairs in Maclennan's store, has soup for £1.75 and sandwiches for £2.50. If you're self-catering, there's a good choice of shops and supermarkets.

If the celebrations are to continue, the Jacobite Bar in the *Ben Nevis*, on the high street, is a popular music venue and a good place for a drink. The *Nevisport Bar*, in the Nevisport gear shop, is also popular.

Other Long-Distance Paths in Scotland

If you are a long-distance walk fanatic, you may be interested in some of Scotland's other LDPs, especially if the West Highland Way sounds too busy, and the Southern Upland Way too long and serious. There are not many LDPs in Scotland, official or otherwise (even the official ones aren't called national trails), reflecting the right to roam in the wilderness tradition of Scottish walking.

FIFE COASTAL WALK

The Fife Coastal Walk is described in the *National Trail Companion* as 'a little-known path which deserves greater recognition'. This is true. It's easy to reach (the start at North Queensferry is just across the Firth of Forth, famous for its railway bridge from Edinburgh), and at 94 miles can be done in a week and are mostly over flat and undulating country, with a few steep bits thrown in. It isn't fully waymarked, and you're very unlikely to meet other walkers, so you'll need to keep a close eye on the map, but the sea is always on your right (or left if you go the other way) so you won't get disastrously

lost. Highlights, apart from the stunning scenery and quiet fishing villages, include the Royal and Ancient Golf Club at St Andrews. The route ends at Newburgh, from where Perth is easy to reach, or you can head back to Edinburgh. As far as we know, there's no specific guidebook yet, but one is bound to come out soon. Ask for details at Edinburgh or local TICs. The Automobile Association (AA) book *Exploring Britain's Long Distance Paths* describes the route, and the above-mentioned *National Trail Companion* (covered in the Boooks section of the Facts for the Walker chapter) covers accommodation.

THE SPEYSIDE WAY

The Speyside Way is Scotland's second-oldest official LDP (opened in 1981, just a few months after the West Highland Way). This is another lowland route, running alongside the 'silvery' Spey, one of Scotland's famous salmon-fishing rivers. It starts on the coast at Spey Bay, just east of the town of Elgin, and runs inland to Tomintoul, on the northern edge of the Cairngorm Mountains. At only 45 miles, this route can be done in three or four days.

If you had a week in the area it could possibly be combined with some high-level walking in the Cairngorms (also described in the Scotland – Short Walks chapter). It was originally planned to follow the River Spey all the way to Glenmore, near Aviemore (the Cairngorms jumping-off point), but this has been postponed. If it is revived, it would be a wonderful route between the mountains and the sea. This route has also been called the 'Whisky Trail' as it passes near several distilleries, including the famous Glenlivet and Glenfiddich, many of which are open to the public.

If you stop at them all, the walk may take longer than three or four days! Once again, information is thin on the ground, but *Exploring Britain's Long Distance Paths* and the *National Trail Companion*, mentioned above, cover just about everything, and there's also the *Speyside Way* leaflet produced by

SCOTLAND

Moray District Council Ranger Service (☎ 01340 881266).

THE GREAT GLEN

Another long route (about 50 miles, 80 km) has been proposed along the Great Glen, from Inverness south beside Loch Lochy and Loch Ness to Fort William, where walkers could connect with the West Highland Way. If this comes about it will be another good route. In the meantime, there are plenty of good day-walks here; Forest Enterprise has produced a *Great Glen Forest Walks* leaflet, available from local TICs, describing a range of waymarked paths in the area. You can look for the fabled Loch Ness Monster as you go!

Appendix – Specialist Walking Publishers in Britain

Cicerone Press
  2 Police Square, Milnthorpe, Cumbria LA7 7PY
  (☎ 015395 62069)

Cordee
  3A De Montfort St, Leicester, LE1 7HD
  (☎ 01162 543579) (Cordee are also distributors
  for many other specialist British walking publishers, and should be able to locate most titles)

Countryside Books
  Highfield House, 2 Highfield Ave, Newbury,
  Berkshire, RG14 5DS (☎ 01635 43816)

Dalesman Publishing Co
  Clapham, Lancaster, LA2 8EB
  (☎ 015242 51225)

Footprint Press
  19 Moseley St, Ripley, Derbyshire DE5 3DA
  (☎ 01773 512143)

GEOprojects
  9-10 Southern Court, South St, Reading, RG1
  4QS (☎ 01734 393567)

Harveys
  12-16 Main St, Doune, Perthshire, FK16 6BJ
  (☎ 01786 841202)

John Merrill Guides (see Footprint)

JNM Guides (see Footprint)

Leading Edge
  Old Chapel, Buttersett, Hawes, North Yorkshire,
  DL8 3PB (☎ 01969 667566)

Ramblers' Association
  1-5 Wandsworth Rd, London SW8 2XX
  (☎ 0171 5826878)

Readon Publishing, 56 Upper Norwood St,
  Leckhampton, Glostershire, GL53 0DU
  (☎ 01242 231800)

Scarthin Books
  The Promenade, Cromford, Derbyshire, DE4
  3QF (☎ 01629 823272)

Sigma Press
  1 South Oak Lane, Wilmslow, Cheshire, SK9
  6AR (☎ 01625 531035)

Stile Publications
  24 Lisker Drive, Leeds Rd, Otley, LS21 1DQ
  (☎ 01943 466326)

The Backpackers Press
  2 Rockview Cottages, Temple Walk, Matlock
  Bath, Derbyshire, DE4 3PG (☎ 01629 580427)

Glossary of British Terms & Abbreviations

Some English words and phrases commonly used in Britain will be unrecognisable to visitors from abroad, even if they regard English as their own first language, so we have attempted to translate some of these. In this section we have also included particular British walking terms, and several Welsh, Scottish or regional English words, mainly to do with landscape, that you are likely to come across during your travels.

4x4 – four-wheel drive car
AA – Automobile Association
aber – river mouth (Wales)
afon – river (Wales)
a bhainn river (Scotland)
ASL – above sea level
ABTA – Association of British Travel Agents
aye – yes/always (Scotland & Northern England)

BABA – book-a-bed-ahead scheme
bach – small (Wales)
bag – reach the top of (as in 'to bag a couple of extra peaks' or 'Munro-bagging')
bailey – outermost wall of a castle
bairn – baby (Scotland & Northern England)
banger – old, cheap car
bangers – sausages
bank holiday – public holiday (ie when the banks are closed)
bap – bread roll (Northern England)
bar – gate (York)
beck – stream (Northern England)
ben – mountain (Scotland)
bent – not altogether legal
berk – idiot, fool
bevvy – a drink (originally Northern England)
bevvying – drinking
billion – a million million, not a thousand million
bimble – *see* ramble (bimbler – someone who bimbles)

biscuit – cookie
bitter – a type of beer (ale)
black pudding – a type of sausage made from dried blood
bloke – man
bodge job – poor-quality repair
bothy – hut or mountain shelter (Scotland)
BR – British Rail
brae – hill (Scotland)
brambles – berry-cane
bridleway – path that can be used by walkers, horse riders and cyclists
broad – lake (East Anglia)
broch – defensive tower (Scotland)
bryn – hill (Wales)
BT – British Telecom
BTA – British Tourist Authority
bun – bread roll, usually sweet
burgh – town (Scotland)
burn – stream (Scotland)
bus – local bus; *see also* coach
butty – sandwich, usually filled with something hot, ie bacon butty, or (a British speciality) chip butty
B&B – bed and breakfast

cadair – stronghold/chair (Wales)
caer – fort (Wales)
cairn – pile of stones to mark path or junction, also (in Scotland) peak
canny – good, great (Northern England)
capel – chapel (Wales)
car bonnet – hood
car boot – trunk
carreg – stone (Wales)
carry-out – takeaway
cash point – automatic teller machine (ATM)
CC – Countryside Commission
CCC – Camping & Caravanning Club
ceilidh – pronounced kaylee, informal evening entertainment and dance (Scotland)
CHA – Co-operative Holidays Association

chine – valleylike fissure leading to the sea (south, especially Isle of Wight)

chips – hot, deep fried potato pieces (aka French fries), traditionally eaten with fish or in a butty (*see* butty)

clint – the bit of rock sticking up between two grikes (*see* grikes)

close – entrance

clough – small valley

clun – meadow (Wales)

coach – long-distance bus; *see also* bus

coaching inn – originally an inn along a stage-coach route at which horses were changed

cob – bread roll (Northern England)

coch – red (Wales)

coed – forest/wood (Wales)

common – a piece of land which may be private, but on which people have traditional rights of access, formerly for grazing animals, more often these days for recreation

coombe – valley (Southern England)

corrie – bowl-shaped cliffs, at the end of a steep sided valley, usually formed by glacial erosion

couchette – sleeping berth in a train or ferry

courts – courtyards

crack – good conversation, good times (originally Ireland, also Northern England), now used to mean 'happening', as in 'what's the crack?', ie 'what's going on?'

crag – exposed rock (craig in Scotland)

crannogh – artificial island settlement

crisps – salty flakes of fried potato, in a packet (what the rest of the world calls chips)

croft – plot of land with adjoining house worked by the occupiers (Scotland)

cromlech – burial chamber (Wales)

CTC – Cyclists' Touring Club

cut – a canal or artificial stretch of water

cwm – valley (Wales) or corrie

DB&B – dinner, bed and breakfast

de – south (Wales)

dead-end road – no through road

dear – expensive

din (dinas) – fort (Wales)

dinner – usually evening meal, except in some northern regions where it's the midday meal

DIY – do-it-yourself

dosh – money

downs – rolling upland, usually grassy, characterised by lack of trees

drove road – ancient route, once used for bringing cattle and sheep from farm to market

du – black (Wales)

duvet – thick padded bed cover

duvet jacket – thick padded coat, as used by mountaineers and walkers

East Anglia – Eastern England, usually the counties of Norfolk and Suffolk

EH – English Heritage

EN – English Nature

eisteddfod – festival in which competitions are held in music, poetry, drama and the fine arts (Wales)

ESA – Environmentally Sensitive Areas

Essex – derogatory adjective, as in Essex girl, meaning tarty, and identified with '80s consumerism

evensong – daily evening service (Church of England)

fag – cigarette; *also* a boring task

fagged – exhausted

fanny – female genitals, not backside (which is why inane people giggle when Fan y Big, a mountain in Wales, is pronounced in the English way, rather than the correct Welsh way: 'Van er Big')

fawr – big (Wales)

fell – large hill or mountain (Northern England), also hill or mountain side

fen – drained or marshy low-lying flat land (south-east England)

ffordd – road (Wales)

firth – estuary (Scotland)

fiver – five-pound note

FIYTO – Federation of Youth Travel Organisations

flip-flops – thongs

folly – eccentric, decorative (often useless) building

fret – worry; *also* mist from the sea (Northumberland)

gaffer – boss or foreman

gate – street (York)

gill – also spelt gyhll, small steep-sided valley (Northern England)

ginnel – alleyway (mostly northern England)

glan – shore (Wales)

glas – blue (Wales)

glen – valley (Scotland)

glyn – valley (Wales)

GR – grid reference (on maps)

grand – (slang) one thousand pounds

greasy spoon – cheap basic cafe

grike – narrow fissure, usually in limestone 'pavement' areas.

gully – small steep-sided valley

gutted – very disappointed

guv, guvner – from governor, a respectful term of address for owner or boss, can be used ironically

gwyn – white (Wales)

gwrydd – green (Wales)

haar – fog off the North Sea (Scotland)

hag – bog (Northern England)

half (as in 'half a bitter') – half a pint (of beer)

hamlet – small settlement

hammered – drunk (Northern England), or tired

haus – col (Northern England)

HF – Holiday Fellowship

HMSO – Her Majesty's Stationary Office (official government publisher)

Hogmanay – New Year's Eve (Scotland)

honeypot – crowded place

horseshoe route – curved or circular, ie up one ridge and down another, round a valley

hotel – accommodation with food and bar, not always open to passing trade

hows – *see* haus

HS – Historic Scotland

IDP – International Driving Permit

inn – pub, usually with accommodation

jam – jelly

jelly – jello

jumper – sweater

ken – know (Scotland)

kipper – smoked herring (fish)

kirk – church (Scotland)

kissing gate – swinging gate and fence built to allow people through, but not animals

knoll – small hill

kyle – narrow strait of water (Scotland)

ladder stile – two small ladders, back to back, so walkers can cross walls and fences

lager lout – *see* yob

laird – estate owner (Scotland)

lass – young woman (Northern England)

lay-by – parking space at side of road

LDP – long-distance path

ley – clearing

lift – elevator

linn – waterfall (Scotland)

llan – enclosed place or church (Wales)

llyn – lake (Wales)

lock – part of a canal or river that can be closed off and the water levels changed to raise or lower boats

lolly – money; *also* candy on a stick (possibly iced)

lorry – truck

love – term of address, not necessarily to someone likeable

lunch – midday meal, either light or large

mad – insane, not angry

manky – low quality (Southern England)

Martello tower – small, circular tower used for coastal defence

mate – a friend of any sex, or term of address for males

mawr – big (Wales)

MBA – Mountain Bothies Association

metalled – surfaced (road), usually with tar (bitumen)

MOD – Ministry of Defence

moor – high, rolling, open, treeless area

motorway – freeway

motte – mound on which a castle was built

muggy – 'close' or humid weather

Munro – mountain of 3000 ft or higher (Scotland)

mynydd – mountain (Wales)

nant – valley/stream (Wales)

nappies – diapers

navvy – labourer who built canals and railways in the 19th century (short for navigator)
NDW – North Downs Way
newydd – new (Wales)
nimby (from 'not in my back yard') – protectionist, territorial
NNR – National Nature Reserve
NT – National Trust
NTS – National Trust for Scotland
NYMR – North York Moors Railway

oast house – building containing a kiln for drying hops (SE)
ODP – Offa's Dyke Path
offie – *see* off-license
off-license – shop selling alcoholic drinks to take away
ogof – cave (Wales)
OS – Ordnance Survey (mapping agency)

p (pronounced 'pee') – pence
pasty – eg Cornish Pasty, hot pastry roll with savoury filling
pavement – sidewalk
pavement – (landscape) any flat area of exposed rock, especially limestone
PCP – Pembrokeshire Coast Path
pen – headland or peak (Wales)
pend – arched gateway (Scotland)
pete – fortified houses
PIC – Park Information Centre
Pict – early Celtic inhabitants (from the Latin pictus, meaning painted) after their painted body decorations
pike – peak (Northern England)
pint – about 0.75 litres
pint glass – what British beer gets served in
pissed – drunk (not angry)
pissed off – annoyed (really pissed off – angry)
pistyll – waterfall (Wales)
pitch – playing field
pitched – laid with flat stones, ie to improve a path
plas – hall/mansion (Wales)
pont – bridge (Wales)
pop – fizzy drink (Northern England, Wales)
postbuses – minibuses that follow postal delivery routes, carrying passengers too

pub – short for public house, a bar usually with food, sometimes with accommodation
pull-in – *see* lay-by
punter (literal) – somebody punting (ie poling) a boat
punter (slang) – customer, or somebody placing a bet
pwll – pool (Wales)

quid (money) – pound – always singular, ie 'here's that six quid I owe you' or '25 quid will do me fine'

RA – Ramblers' Association
ramble – a relatively short or non-strenuous walk (rambler – someone who rambles)
reiver – notoriously cruel warrior, bandit (an archaic word from Northern England)
reservoir – artificial lake, usually formed by damming a river
rhiw – slope (Wales)
rhos – moor/marsh (Wales)
roll-up – roll-your-own cigarette
RSPB – Royal Society for the Protection of Birds
rubber – eraser
rubbish bin – garbage can
rugger – rugby
RUPP – Road Used as a Public Path

sack – rucksack, pack, backpack
sacked – fired
SAE – stamped addressed envelope
Sassenach – an English person or a lowland Scot (Scotland)
sett – tartan pattern
shout (as in 'my shout') – to buy a group of people drinks, usually reciprocated
shut – partially covered passage
SIC – Student Identity Card
SMC – Scottish Mountaineering Club
snicket – alleyway (York)
SDW – South Downs Way
sporran – purse (Scotland)
SRWS – Scottish Rights of Way Society
SSSI – Site of Special Scientific Interest
strath – valley (Scotland)
squeeze gate – narrow gap in wall to let people through, but not animals
subway – underpass for pedestrians

SUW – Southern Upland Way
sweet – candy
SYHA – Scottish Youth Hostels Association

ta – thanks
tarn – small mountain lake (Northern England)
tea – the British national drink, but also a meal, usually light, eaten at the end of the afternoon, except in the parts of the country where 'dinner' is eaten only at midday, in which case 'tea' is a cooked evening meal.
teashop – a smart cafe, in country areas
thwaite – clearing in a forest
TIC – Tourist Information Centre
tor – Celtic word describing a hill shaped like a triangular wedge of cheese
torch – flashlight
traveller – nomadic, new-age hippy
tre – town (Wales)
trig point – a pillar, usually concrete, but sometimes stone or brick, about one metre high used for the making of Ordnance Survey maps (trig is short from trigometric). These pillars are marked on maps, and a real life-saver if you're walking in the mist and need a bit of navigational confirmation. The OS actually does not use trig points any more (as most maps are made by aerial surveys and other means) so some trig points have been removed. In popular walking areas, local rambling groups and other interested parties have 'adopted' trig points, promising to keep them in good repair for the benefit of other walkers
tube (slang) – *see* underground
tumulus – ancient burial mound (plural tumuli)
twitchers – keen birdwatchers
twitten – passage, small lane
twr – tower (Wales)
ty – house (Wales)

underground (as in trains) – subway
UNESCO – United Nations Educational, Scientific & Cultural Organisation
uisge-bha – the water of life: whisky (Scotland)

VAT – value-added tax, levied on most goods and services
verderer – officer upholding law and order in the royal forests

way – usually a long-distance path or trail, as in Pennine Way, Southern Upland Way
WHW – West Highland Way
wold – open, rolling country
WTB – Wales Tourist Board
wynd – lane (Scotland)

YHA – Youth Hostels Association
ynys – island (Wales)
yob – hooligan
ystwyth – winding (Wales)

Index

LONELY PLANET JOURNEYS

JOURNEYS is a unique collection of travel writing – published by the company that understands travel better than anyone else. It is a series for anyone who has ever experienced – or dreamed of – the magical moment when they encountered a strange culture or saw a place for the first time. They are tales to read while you're planning a trip, while you're on the road or while you're in an armchair, in front of a fire.

JOURNEYS books catch the spirit of a place, illuminate a culture, recount a crazy adventure, or introduce a fascinating way of life. They always entertain, and always enrich the experience of travel.

THE GATES OF DAMASCUS
Lieve Joris
Translated by Sam Garrett

This best-selling book is a beautifully drawn portrait of day-to-day life in modern Syria. Through her intimate contact with local people, Lieve Joris draws us into the fascinating world that lies behind the gates of Damascus. Hala's husband is a political prisoner, jailed for his opposition to the Assad regime; through the author's friendship with Hala we see how Syrian politics impacts on the lives of ordinary people.

Lieve Joris, who was born in Belgium, is one of Europe's leading travel writers. In addition to an award-winning book on Hungary, she has published widely acclaimed accounts of her journeys to the Middle East and Africa. *The Gates of Damascus* is her fifth book.

'Expands the boundaries of travel writing' – Times Literary Supplement

KINGDOM OF THE FILM STARS
Journey into Jordan
Annie Caulfield

Kingdom of the Film Stars is a travel book and a love story. With honesty and humour, Annie Caulfield writes of travelling in Jordan and falling in love with a Bedouin. Her book offers fascinating insights into the country – from the traditional tent life of nomadic tribes to the first woman MP's battle with fundamentalist colleagues. *Kingdom of the Film Stars* unpicks some of the tight-woven Western myths about the Arab world, presenting cultural and political issues within the intimate framework of a compelling love story.

Annie Caulfield, who was born in Ireland and currently lives in London, is an award-winning playwright and journalist. She has travelled widely in the Middle East.

'Annie Caulfield is a remarkable traveller. Her story is fresh, courageous, moving, witty and sexy!' – Dawn French

LONELY PLANET PHRASEBOOKS

Building bridges,
Breaking barriers,
Beyond babble-on

Nepali phrasebook — Listen for the gems

Ethiopian Amharic phrasebook — Speak your own words

Latin American Spanish phrasebook — Ask your own questions

Ukrainian phrasebook — Master of your own image

Greek phrasebook

Vietnamese phrasebook

- handy pocket-sized books
- easy to understand Pronunciation chapter
- clear and comprehensive Grammar chapter
- romanisation alongside script to allow ease of pronunciation
- script throughout so users can point to phrases
- extensive vocabulary sections, words and phrases for every situations
- full of cultural information and tips for the traveller

'...vital for a real DIY spirit and attitude in language learning' – Backpacker

'the phrasebooks have good cultural backgrounders and offer solid advice for challenging situations in remote locations' – San Francisco Examiner

'...they are unbeatable for their coverage of the world's more obscure languages' – The Geographical Magazine

---

Arabic (Egyptian)
Arabic (Moroccan)
Australia
   Australian English, Aboriginal and Torres Strait languages
Baltic States
   Estonian, Latvian, Lithuanian
Bengali
Burmese
Brazilian
Cantonese
Central Europe
   Czech, French, German, Hungarian, Italian and Slovak
Eastern Europe
   Bulgarian, Czech, Hungarian, Polish, Romanian and Slovak
Egyptian Arabic
Ethiopian (Amharic)
Fijian
French
German
Greek

Hindi/Urdu
Indonesian
Italian
Japanese
Korean
Lao
Latin American Spanish
Malay
Mandarin
Mediterranean Europe
   Albanian, Croatian, Greek, Italian, Macedonian, Maltese, Serbian, Slovene
Mongolian
Moroccan Arabic
Nepali
Papua New Guinea
Pilipino (Tagalog)
Quechua
Russian
Scandinavian Europe
   Danish, Finnish, Icelandic, Norwegian and Swedish

South-East Asia
   Burmese, Indonesian, Khmer, Lao, Malay, Tagalog (Pilipino), Thai and Vietnamese
Spanish
Sri Lanka
Swahili
Thai
Thai Hill Tribes
Tibetan
Turkish
Ukrainian
USA
   US English, Vernacular Talk, Native American languages and Hawaiian
Vietnamese
Western Europe
   Basque, Catalan, Dutch, French, German, Irish, Italian, Portuguese, Scottish Gaelic, Spanish (Castilian) and Welsh

LONELY PLANET TRAVEL ATLASES

Lonely Planet has long been famous for the number and quality of its guidebook maps. Now we've gone one step further and in conjunction with Steinhart Katzir Publishers produced a handy companion series: Lonely Planet travel atlases – maps of a country produced in book form.

Unlike other maps, which look good but lead travellers astray, our travel atlases have been researched on the road by Lonely Planet's experienced team of writers. All details are carefully checked to ensure the atlas corresponds with the equivalent Lonely Planet guidebook.

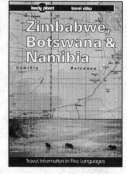

The handy atlas format means no holes, wrinkles, torn sections or constant folding and unfolding. These atlases can survive long periods on the road, unlike cumbersome fold-out maps. The comprehensive index ensures easy reference.

- full-colour throughout
- maps researched and checked by Lonely Planet authors
- place names correspond with Lonely Planet guidebooks
  – no confusing spelling differences
- legend and travelling information in English, French, German, Japanese and Spanish
- size: 230 x 160 mm

Available now:
Chile & Easter Island • Egypt • India & Bangladesh • Israel & the Palestinian Territories •Jordan, Syria & Lebanon • Kenya • Laos • Portugal • South Africa, Lesotho & Swaziland • Thailand • Turkey • Vietnam • Zimbabwe, Botswana & Namibia

---

LONELY PLANET TV SERIES & VIDEOS

Lonely Planet travel guides have been brought to life on television screens around the world. Like our guides, the programmes are based on the joy of independent travel, and look honestly at some of the most exciting, picturesque and frustrating places in the world. Each show is presented by one of three travellers from Australia, England or the USA and combines an innovative mixture of video, Super-8 film, atmospheric soundscapes and original music.

Videos of each episode – containing additional footage not shown on television – are available from good book and video shops, but the availability of individual videos varies with regional screening schedules.

Video destinations include: Alaska • American Rockies • Australia – The South-East • Baja California & the Copper Canyon • Brazil • Central Asia • Chile & Easter Island • Corsica, Sicily & Sardinia – The Mediterranean Islands • East Africa (Tanzania & Zanzibar) • Ecuador & the Galapagos Islands • Greenland & Iceland • Indonesia • Israel & the Sinai Desert • Jamaica • Japan • La Ruta Maya • Morocco • New York • North India • Pacific Islands (Fiji, Solomon Islands & Vanuatu) • South India • South West China • Turkey • Vietnam • West Africa • Zimbabwe, Botswana & Namibia

The Lonely Planet TV series is produced by:
Pilot Productions
The Old Studio
18 Middle Row
London W10 5AT UK

For video availability and ordering information contact your nearest Lonely Planet office.

Music from the TV series is available on CD & cassette.

PLANET TALK

Lonely Planet's FREE quarterly newsletter

We love hearing from you and think you'd like to hear from us.

When...is the right time to see reindeer in Finland?
Where...can you hear the best palm-wine music in Ghana?
How...do you get from Asunción to Areguá by steam train?
What...is the best way to see India?

For the answer to these and many other questions read PLANET TALK.

Every issue is packed with up-to-date travel news and advice including:

- a letter from Lonely Planet co-founders Tony and Maureen Wheeler
- go behind the scenes on the road with a Lonely Planet author
- feature article on an important and topical travel issue
- a selection of recent letters from travellers
- details on forthcoming Lonely Planet promotions
- complete list of Lonely Planet products

To join our mailing list contact any Lonely Planet office.

Also available: Lonely Planet T-shirts. 100% heavyweight cotton.

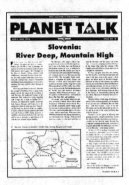

LONELY PLANET ONLINE

Get the latest travel information before you leave or while you're on the road

Whether you've just begun planning your next trip, or you're chasing down specific info on currency regulations or visa requirements, check out Lonely Planet Online for up-to-the minute travel information.

As well as travel profiles of your favourite destinations (including maps and photos), you'll find current reports from our researchers and other travellers, updates on health and visas, travel advisories, and discussion of the ecological and political issues you need to be aware of as you travel.

There's also an online travellers' forum where you can share your experience of life on the road, meet travel companions and ask other travellers for their recommendations and advice. We also have plenty of links to other online sites useful to independent travellers.

And of course we have a complete and up-to-date list of all Lonely Planet travel products including guides, phrasebooks, atlases, Journeys and videos and a simple online ordering facility if you can't find the book you want elsewhere.

*www.lonelyplanet.com
or
AOL keyword: lp*

LONELY PLANET PRODUCTS

Lonely Planet is known worldwide for publishing practical, reliable and no-nonsense travel information in our guides and on our web site. The Lonely Planet list covers just about every accessible part of the world. Currently there are eight series: *travel guides, shoestring guides, walking guides, city guides, phrasebooks, audio packs, travel atlases* and *Journeys* – a unique collection of travel writing.

EUROPE

Amsterdam • Austria • Baltic States phrasebook • Britain • Central Europe on a shoestring • Central Europe phrasebook • Czech & Slovak Republics • Denmark • Dublin • Eastern Europe on a shoestring • Eastern Europe phrasebook • Estonia, Latvia & Lithuania • Finland • France • French phrasebook • Germany • German phrasebook • Greece • Greek phrasebook • Hungary • Iceland, Greenland & the Faroe Islands • Ireland • Italian phrasebook • Italy • Lisbon • Mediterranean Europe on a shoestring • Mediterranean Europe phrasebook • Paris • Poland • Portugal • Portugal travel atlas • Prague • Russia, Ukraine & Belarus • Russian phrasebook • Scandinavian & Baltic Europe on a shoestring • Scandinavian Europe phrasebook • Slovenia • Spain • Spanish phrasebook • St Petersburg • Switzerland • Trekking in Spain • Ukrainian phrasebook • Vienna • Walking in Britain • Walking in Switzerland • Western Europe on a shoestring • Western Europe phrasebook

Travel Literature: The Olive Grove: Travels in Greece

NORTH AMERICA

Alaska • Backpacking in Alaska • Baja California • California & Nevada • Canada • Florida • Hawaii • Honolulu • Los Angeles • Mexico • Miami • New England • New Orleans • New York City • New York, New Jersey & Pennsylvania • Pacific Northwest USA • Rocky Mountain States • San Francisco • Southwest USA • USA phrasebook • Washington, DC & the Capital Region

CENTRAL AMERICA & THE CARIBBEAN

Bermuda • Central America on a shoestring • Costa Rica • Cuba • Eastern Caribbean • Guatemala, Belize & Yucatán: La Ruta Maya • Jamaica

SOUTH AMERICA

Argentina, Uruguay & Paraguay • Bolivia • Brazil • Brazilian phrasebook • Buenos Aires • Chile & Easter Island • Chile & Easter Island travel atlas • Colombia • Deep South • Ecuador & the Galápagos Islands • Latin American Spanish phrasebook • Peru • Quechua phrasebook • Rio de Janeiro • South America on a shoestring • Trekking in the Patagonian Andes • Venezuela

Travel Literature: Full Circle: A South American Journey

ANTARCTICA

Antarctica

ISLANDS OF THE INDIAN OCEAN

Madagascar & Comoros • Maldives • Mauritius, Réunion & Seychelles

AFRICA

Africa - the South • Africa on a shoestring • Arabic (Moroccan) phrasebook • Cape Town • Central Africa • East Africa • Egypt • Egypt travel atlas • Ethiopian (Amharic) phrasebook • Kenya • Kenya travel atlas • Malawi, Mozambique & Zambia • Morocco • North Africa • South Africa, Lesotho & Swaziland • South Africa, Lesotho & Swaziland travel atlas • Swahili phrasebook • Trekking in East Africa • West Africa • Zimbabwe, Botswana & Namibia • Zimbabwe, Botswana & Namibia travel atlas

Travel Literature: The Rainbird: A Central African Journey • Songs to an African Sunset: A Zimbabwean Story

MAIL ORDER

Lonely Planet products are distributed worldwide.They are also available by mail order from Lonely Planet, so if you have difficulty finding a title please write to us. North American and South American residents should write to Embarcadero West, 155 Filbert St, Suite 251, Oakland CA 94607, USA; European and African residents should write to 10a Spring Place, London NW5 3BH; and residents of other countries to PO Box 617, Hawthorn, Victoria 3122, Australia.

NORTH-EAST ASIA

Beijing • Cantonese phrasebook • China • Hong Kong • Hong Kong, Macau & Guangzhou • Japan • Japanese phrasebook • Japanese audio pack • Korea • Korean phrasebook • Mandarin phrasebook • Mongolia • Mongolian phrasebook • North-East Asia on a shoestring • Seoul • Taiwan • Tibet • Tibet phrasebook • Tokyo

Travel Literature: Lost Japan

MIDDLE EAST & CENTRAL ASIA

Arab Gulf States • Arabic (Egyptian) phrasebook • Central Asia • Central Asia phrasebook • Iran • Israel & the Palestinian Territories • Israel & the Palestinian Territories travel atlas • Istanbul • Jerusalem • Jordan & Syria • Jordan, Syria & Lebanon travel atlas • Lebanon • Middle East • Turkey • Turkish phrasebook • Turkey travel atlas • Yemen

Travel Literature: The Gates of Damascus • Kingdom of the Film Stars: Journey into Jordan

ALSO AVAILABLE:

Travel with Children • Traveller's Tales

INDIAN SUBCONTINENT

Bangladesh • Bengali phrasebook • Delhi • Hindi/Urdu phrasebook • India • India & Bangladesh travel atlas • Indian Himalaya • Karakoram Highway • Nepal • Nepali phrasebook • Pakistan • Rajasthan • Sri Lanka • Sri Lanka phrasebook • Trekking in the Indian Himalaya • Trekking in the Karakoram & Hindukush • Trekking in the Nepal Himalaya

Travel Literature: In Rajasthan • Shopping for Buddhas

SOUTH-EAST ASIA

Bali & Lombok • Bangkok • Burmese phrasebook • Cambodia • Ho Chi Minh City • Indonesia • Indonesian phrasebook • Indonesian audio pack • Jakarta • Java • Laos • Lao phrasebook • Laos travel atlas • Malay phrasebook • Malaysia, Singapore & Brunei • Myanmar (Burma) • Philippines • Pilipino phrasebook • Singapore • South-East Asia on a shoestring • South-East Asia phrasebook • Thailand • Thailand's Islands & Beaches • Thailand travel atlas • Thai phrasebook • Thai audio pack • Thai Hill Tribes phrasebook • Vietnam • Vietnamese phrasebook • Vietnam travel atlas

AUSTRALIA & THE PACIFIC

Australia • Australian phrasebook • Bushwalking in Australia • Bushwalking in Papua New Guinea • Fiji • Fijian phrasebook • Islands of Australia's Great Barrier Reef • Melbourne • Micronesia • New Caledonia • New South Wales • New Zealand • Northern Territory • Outback Australia • Papua New Guinea • Papua New Guinea phrasebook • Queensland • Rarotonga & the Cook Islands • Samoa • Solomon Islands • South Australia • Sydney • Tahiti & French Polynesia • Tasmania • Tonga • Tramping in New Zealand • Vanuatu • Victoria • Western Australia

Travel Literature: Islands in the Clouds • Sean & David's Long Drive

THE LONELY PLANET STORY

Lonely Planet published its first book in 1973 in response to the numerous 'How did you do it?' questions Maureen and Tony Wheeler were asked after driving, bussing, hitching, sailing and railing their way from England to Australia.

Written at a kitchen table and hand collated, trimmed and stapled, *Across Asia on the Cheap* became an instant local bestseller, inspiring thoughts of another book.

Eighteen months in South-East Asia resulted in their second guide, *South-East Asia on a shoestring*, which they put together in a backstreet Chinese hotel in Singapore in 1975. The 'yellow bible', as it quickly became known to backpackers around the world, soon became *the* guide to the region. It has sold well over half a million copies and is now in its 9th edition, still retaining its familiar yellow cover.

Today there are over 240 titles, including travel guides, walking guides, language kits & phrasebooks, travel atlases and travel literature. The company is the largest independent travel publisher in the world. Although Lonely Planet initially specialised in guides to Asia, today there are few corners of the globe that have not been covered.

The emphasis continues to be on travel for independent travellers. Tony and Maureen still travel for several months of each year and play an active part in the writing, updating and quality control of Lonely Planet's guides.

They have been joined by over 70 authors and 170 staff at our offices in Melbourne (Australia), Oakland (USA), London (UK) and Paris (France). Travellers themselves also make a valuable contribution to the guides through the feedback we receive in thousands of letters each year and on our web site.

The people at Lonely Planet strongly believe that travellers can make a positive contribution to the countries they visit, both through their appreciation of the countries' culture, wildlife and natural features, and through the money they spend. In addition, the company makes a direct contribution to the countries and regions it covers. Since 1986 a percentage of the income from each book has been donated to ventures such as famine relief in Africa; aid projects in India; agricultural projects in Central America; Greenpeace's efforts to halt French nuclear testing in the Pacific; and Amnesty International.

'I hope we send people out with the right attitude about travel. You realise when you travel that there are so many different perspectives about the world, so we hope these books will make people more interested in what they see. Guidebooks can't really guide people. All you can do is point them in the right direction.'

– Tony Wheeler

LONELY PLANET PUBLICATIONS

Australia
PO Box 617, Hawthorn 3122, Victoria
tel: (03) 9819 1877 fax: (03) 9819 6459
e-mail: talk2us@lonelyplanet.com.au

USA
Embarcadero West, 155 Filbert St, Suite 251,
Oakland, CA 94607
tel: (510) 893 8555 TOLL FREE: 800 275-8555
fax: (510) 893 8563
e-mail: info@lonelyplanet.com

UK
10a Spring Place,
London NW5 3BH
tel: (0171) 428 4800 fax: (0171) 428 4828
e-mail: go@lonelyplanet.co.uk

France:
71 bis rue du Cardinal Lemoine, 75005 Paris
tel: 1 44 32 06 20 fax: 1 46 34 72 55
e-mail: 100560.415@compuserve.com

World Wide Web: http://www.lonelyplanet.com
or *AOL keyword: lp*